NEW ZEALAND WARS

VOLUME II : 1864-72

Officers of the New Zealand Armed Constabulary Field Force
(Parihaka, Taranaki, November, 1881.)

Front Row: Captain Baker, Captain Anderson, Lieut.-Colonel J. M. Roberts, Captain G. Mair, Captain H. W. Northcroft, Captain W. B. Messenger, Major F. Y. Goring.

Back Row: Captain W. E. Gudgeon, Captain H. Morrison, Captain Gordon, Captain Taylor, Captain Powell, Captain Fortescue, Captain Stuart Newall, Captain Tuke.

THE

NEW ZEALAND WARS

A History of the

MAORI CAMPAIGNS AND THE PIONEERING PERIOD

by

JAMES COWAN

Volume II: The Hauhau Wars, 1864–72

AMS PRESS
NEW YORK

Reprinted from the edition of 1922, Wellington
First AMS EDITION published 1969
Manufactured in the United States of America

Library of Congress Catalog Card Number: 76-100514
SBN: complete set: 404-00600-0
volume 2: 404-00602-7

AMS PRESS, INC.
New York, N.Y. 10003

Preface to Volume II

THIS VOLUME of the New Zealand Wars History carries on the narrative of the Maori campaigns from the commencement of the Hauhau War in Taranaki in 1864 to the final expeditions against Te Kooti in 1872. The period covered is the most critical and the most adventurous in New Zealand's history, and the story here given is the first complete account written of the numerous campaigns conducted under the colony's self-reliant military policy which dispensed with the aid of Imperial troops.

The description of the Pai-marire, or Hauhau religion, under whose impulse the war against the *pakeha* was waged with a desperation unknown in the earlier years, contains much that has not previously been recorded. For this and for many other word-of-mouth contributions to a better knowledge of the Maori side of the long racial conflict my thanks go forth to my old warrior friends, both Kawanatanga and Hauhau. Many a day was spent, frequently on the fern-grown site of some fortification or on some battle-ground, in gathering from the veteran bush fighters of two races the stories of the past—stories, in the case of the Maori, often given a high dramatic value by the graphic manner of the narrator. The stirring tales of the past have been drilled into the memory of the native of the old type by unvarying repetition in the tribal home, until every incident of a day's action has been indelibly impressed, to be released like a phonograph record when the time comes. This remark applies in particular to the generation of men now fast passing away; the young Maori's mind has been transformed by books and colleges, and he has lost the marvellous memorizing powers of his forefathers.

For documentary evidence of special value I am indebted to Captain G. A. Preece, N.Z.C., of Palmerston North, one of the very few colonial soldiers who kept a diary throughout the war. His private journal of the period 1869–72 is of particular importance for its narrative of the last expeditions against Te Kooti in the Urewera Country. These expeditions in the final period of guerrilla warfare, carried out under most arduous conditions in a savage and roadless territory, are now described in detail, through the co-operation of Captain Preece and the hearty assistance of his comrade Captain Gilbert Mair, N.Z.C.

Death has claimed many of the veterans, *pakeha* and Maori, who were among my authorities and helpers—chief among them that good soldier Colonel Porter. I regard it as fortunate that so much material enabling us to picture accurately the life and incidents of a vanished day was gathered while there was yet time.

Wellington, New Zealand,
March, 1923.

J. COWAN.

Contents

PAGE

CHAPTER 1: PAI-MARIRE 1

A new phase of Maori warfare—The Pai-marire or Hauhau religion—Tribes united in a holy war against the *pakeha*—The confiscation of Taranaki territory—Prophets of the *Niu*—Mixture of Christian and pagan faiths—Powerful appeal of Pai-marire to the Maori temperament—Magic spells to avert the bullets—Great political value of the religion—The Hauhau chants—Marvellous Powers attributed to the priests—Hypnotic influence of the Pai-marire—A singular night seance—White renegades share in the Hauhau ceremonies—The surprise at Te Ahuahu (1864)—British soldiers decapitated—The heads sent from tribe to tribe—Te Ua's apostles.

CHAPTER 2: THE ATTACK ON SENTRY HILL REDOUBT .. 21

A story of fanatic courage—Hauhau war-party attempts to storm Sentry Hill Redoubt, Taranaki—The fortified mound of Te Morere—Te Kahu-pukoro's narrative of the assault—Hepanaia the prophet and his warriors—Daylight attack on the redoubt—Maori incantations to avert the soldiers' bullets—"*Hapa, hapa, Pai-marire*"—The storming-party repulsed with heavy loss—Tamati Hone's dirge for the fallen: "My brave canoes lie broken on the shore."

CHAPTER 3: THE BATTLE OF MOUTOA 30

"The Isle of Heroes"—War between Upper and Lower Wanganui tribes—Hauhau propaganda on the river—Captain Lloyd's head at Pipiriki—Savage ceremonies round the *niu* pole—Pai-marire converts plan attack on Wanganui Town—Down-river natives oppose their passage—Challenge to fight on Moutoa Island—Scenes in the rival camps—The children's Hauhau war-game—The battle on the island—An eye-witness's story—The friendly tribes hard pressed at first—Tamehana te Aewa's heroic stand—Complete defeat of the Hauhaus—Death of Matene the prophet.

CHAPTER 4: THE SIEGE OF PIPIRIKI 37

Military post established at Pipiriki, Wanganui River—Major Brassey's force builds redoubts—Formidable gathering of Hauhau tribes—Attack on the redoubts—A twelve days' siege—Sniping and guerrilla tactics—Ammunition and food run low—Messages for relief sent to Wanganui Town—A truce with the Hauhaus—Lieutenant Newland's plucky mission to the Maori camp—A force from Wanganui raises the siege.

PAGE

CHAPTER 5: CAMERON'S WEST COAST CAMPAIGN 46

Operations against the West Coast tribes—General Cameron takes the field—Hauhau war-parties concentrated on the Waitotara—British army attacked at Nukumaru—Hauhau warriors charge into the camp—Two days' heavy skirmishing—Tu-Patea's narrative of the fighting—The death of Assistant Adjutant-General Johnston—Cameron declines to attack Weraroa *pa*—Acrimonious correspondence with the Governor—Sir George Grey's successful strategy—Weraroa outflanked by colonial forces—Capture of Hauhau party at Arei-ahi—The General's slow march up the coast—Engagement at Te Ngaio, Kakaramea—Heavy losses of the Maoris—British headquarters fixed at the Wai-ngongoro—Lieut.-Colonel Colvile's operations near Warea, Taranaki—Several villages attacked and destroyed—General Cameron's departure—The Government's self-reliant war policy—Gradual withdrawal of the Imperial troops.

CHAPTER 6: CHUTE'S TARANAKI CAMPAIGN 61

General Cameron's energetic successor—General Chute enters on a bush campaign—Operations against the South Taranaki tribes—Capture of Te Putahi *pa*—The storming of Otapawa—Death of Lieut.-Colonel Hassard—" Die-hards " rush the *pa*—Kimble Bent at Otapawa—Swift movements against Ngati-Ruanui and Nga-Ruahine Tribes—Numerous villages destroyed—Work of the native contingent under Kepa—Chute's march through the forest—The Whakaahurangi track—The troops short of provisions—Nine days in the bush—Arrival at New Plymouth and return march down the coast—Skirmishing in the Warea district—Lieut.-Colonel Butler's operations from the Wai-ngongoro.

CHAPTER 7: PAI-MARIRE ON THE EAST COAST: KEREOPA, AND THE MURDER OF MR. VOLKNER 72

Pai-marire propaganda on the Bay of Plenty coast—Kereopa te Rau and Patara Raukatauri Te Ua's prophets—Arrival at Opotiki and conversion of the Whakatohea Tribe—The Rev. C. S. Volkner and the Rev. Thomas Grace taken prisoners—Mr. Volkner hanged near his mission station—Kereopa's atrocities in the church—He eats the missionary's eyes—Narrow escape of Mr. Grace—H.M.S. " Eclipse " to the rescue—Seizure of the cutter " Kate " at Whakatane, and murder of Mr. James Fulloon—Pai-marire influence at Tauranga—The chief Hori Tupaea attempts to join the Hauhaus—His capture at Lake Rotoiti by Ngati-Pikiao—A curious scene in the bush—The story of Tomika te Mutu's song and its sequel.

CHAPTER 8: A MOUNTAIN WAR: THE FIGHTING AT TE TAPIRI .. 84

A battle-ground on the Urewera border—Ngati-Manawa and Arawa bar Kereopa's progress to the plains—Redoubts built at Te Tapiri—Whakatohea and Urewera Hauhaus lay siege to the Queenite forts—Gallant work of the small garrisons—Maori heroines—Kereopa's redoubt at Hinamoki—The ceremonies at the *niu* pole—Skirmishing between the forts—Kereopa the Eye-eater—Daring attack by the Queenites on a hill *pa*—The storming of the fort, and the fight at the *niu*—Many deeds of bravery—Desperate plight of the Tapiri garrisons—Decision to retreat to the plains—The crossing of the Rangitaiki—Raharuhi destroys the log bridge—Major Mair and his Arawa to the rescue.

PAGE

CHAPTER 9: OPERATIONS AT MATATA AND TE TEKO .. 96

The Hauhaus on the Lower Rangitaiki—Operations by Major Mair and the Arawa—A campaign in the great swamp—Two months' difficult work around Matata—The forts in the morass—Capture of several positions—The Hauhaus retreat to Te Teko, on the Rangitaiki—Mair lays siege to the *pa*—Skilful sapping operations—The five trenches of the Arawa—Intense rivalry in the sap-digging—Incidents of the siege—Capture of Pa-harakeke—The surrender of the Hauhaus in Te Teko—Capture of some of Volkner's and Fulloon's murderers—Five executed in Auckland.

CHAPTER 10: THE EXPEDITION TO OPOTIKI 106

Punitive force despatched to Opotiki—Difficulties of the landing—Skirmishing on the sandhills—Opotiki villages occupied—Operations against the Whakatohea—The fort at Te Puia—The Wanganui mounted men in action—A cavalry charge at Kiore-kino—Sharp work with sword and revolver—The capture of Te Tarata *pa*—Hauhaus evacuate Te Puia and retreat on the Waioeka—Intermittent skirmishing—The pursuit of Kereopa—Expeditions up the Waimana and Waioeka valleys.

CHAPTER 11: EAST COAST OPERATIONS: FIGHTING AMONG THE NGATI-POROU 117

The Pai-marire mission to the East Coast—Visit of Patara and Kereopa—Rongowhakaata and other tribes become Hauhaus—Part of Ngati-Porou converted—Hauhau outbreak in the Waiapu Valley—Aowera sub-tribe takes the field against the rebels—A skirmish at Mangaone—Ropata Wahawaha first distinguishes himself—Ngati-Porou loyalists armed by the Government—Force of colonial troops despatched to Waiapu in H.M.S. "Eclipse"—Skirmishes in the Waiapu Valley—Storming of Pa-kairomiromi—Gallant defence of Te Mawhai *pa*—Attacks on Pukemaire fortress—Capture of the Hauhau mountain strong-hold Hungahunga-toroa—Surrender of rebel Ngati-Porou, and restoration of peace at the East Cape.

CHAPTER 12: THE SIEGE OF WAERENGA-A-HIKA 125

Hauhauism in the Poverty Bay district—Enemy fortification near the mission station at Waerenga-a-Hika—Ngati-Porou co-operate with Government forces against the Hauhaus—Description of the *pa*—A seven days' siege—Military settlers lose several men—Hauhaus charge out from the stockade and are heavily repulsed—Hand-to-hand encounters—Major Fraser's makeshift artillery—The Hauhaus surrender; losses over a hundred killed—Arrest of Te Kooti Rikirangi and transportation with the Hauhaus to the Chatham Islands.

CHAPTER 13: THE FIRST WAIROA CAMPAIGN 129

Pai-marire emissaries at the Wairoa (Hawke's Bay)—Many of the Ngati-Kahungunu become Hauhaus—The Queenite faction armed by the Government—A military force despatched to Wairoa—Ngati-Porou, under Ropata Wahawaha, go to the assistance of the loyalists—Engagement at Omaru-hakeke—Captain Hussey Killed—Dr. Scott's narrative of the fight—Skirmish near the Waihau lakes (Tiniroto)—Engagement at Te Kopane, near Wai-kare-moana.

PAGE

CHAPTER 14: THE FIGHT AT OAMARUNUI (HAWKE'S BAY) .. 137

Hawke's Bay in 1866—Town of Napier threatened by Ngati-Hineuru Hauhaus—Panapa the prophet and his war-party—Mr. Donald McLean (Superintendent of Hawke's Bay) takes action against the Hauhaus—Napier Militia called out and drilled—Colonel Whitmore attacks Ngati-Hineuru at Omarunui—Defeat of the Maoris with heavy loss—Peita Kotuku's narrative—Major Fraser cuts off Te Rangihiroa's war-party at Petane—Prisoners deported to the Chatham Islands.

CHAPTER 15: MCDONNELL'S TARANAKI CAMPAIGN 143

The position in South Taranaki—Settlement of the confiscated lands begun—Survey work on the plains—Major McDonnell takes command of the field force—Redoubts garrisoned at Manawapou and Waihi—Ngati-Ruanui begin a campaign of ambuscades—Attack on a convoy near Waihi—A trooper tomahawked—An ambush near Hawera; narrow escape of surveyors—Night attack on Pokaikai village—McDonnell attacks Pungarehu—A sharp battle in the bush—Gallant rearguard action—Skirmishes at Popoia, Tirotiro-moana, and other bush settlements—How the Maoris guarded the tracks; the device of the *tawhiti*—First expedition to Te Ngutu-o-te-manu—A fortified log-hut settlement.

CHAPTER 16: THE TAURANGA BUSH CAMPAIGN 153

Campaign against the Piri-Rakau Hauhaus—Survey-parties obstructed—Bush skirmishes inland of Tauranga—Forces attack Te Irihanga and Whakamarama villages—Fighting in the fringe of the great forest—Gilbert Mair's narrow escape at Whakamarama—Work of the Arawa, under Major Mair—Skirmishes and destruction of Hauhau settlements at Oropi, Te Puke, Te Akeake, Paengaroa, and elsewhere—Second attack on Whakamarama—Encounters in the bush—Fight at Te Umu-o-Korongaehe—Whakamarama settlement and crops destroyed—Skirmish at Te Kaki—Hazardous scouting operations.

CHAPTER 17: HAUHAU INVASION OF THE ROTORUA DISTRICT .. 161

Waikato and Ngati-Raukawa menace Rotorua—Invasion via Patetere and Mamaku—Arawa out-villages attacked, and Ohinemutu threatened—Return of the Arawa from the Piri-Rakau campaign, and encounters with the invaders—The fight at Te Koutu—Lieutenant Mair's sharp skirmish in the old *pa*—Defeat of the Hauhaus—Mair's thirty-nine warriors.

CHAPTER 18: CAPTURE OF PURAKU PA, TARUKENGA .. 166

Hauhaus fortify a position at Puraku, Tarukenga, overlooking Rotorua—Gilbert Mair's lone-hand scouting-work—The *pa* attacked by 1st Waikato Militia and the Arawa—Mair despatched to outflank the stronghold—A difficult bush march—A dramatic episode—Mair's interview with a Hauhau warrior—The entrenchment attacked and captured—Pursuit of the Hauhaus—Description of the *pa*—Maori skill in military engineering.

PAGE

CHAPTER 19: SKIRMISHING IN THE OPOTIKI DISTRICT .. 174

Hauhau raiding-parties troublesome in the Opotiki Valley—Ambuscades, forays, and murders—Tamaikowha's savage warfare—Two settlers killed; two others narrowly escape—Military settlers form the Opotiki Volunteer Rangers—Expeditions in pursuit of Ngai-tama and Urewera raiders—Skirmishes in the Waimana forests and gorges—Expeditions up the Whakatane.

CHAPTER 20: THE OPENING OF TITO KOWARU'S CAMPAIGN (TARANAKI, 1868) 179

Titokowaru, of Nga-Ruahine, becomes the war-leader of South Taranaki tribes—A new plan of campaign—Ambuscades and surprise attacks on redoubts—Titokowaru's picked war-party, the "Tekau-ma-rua"—Horse-stealing on the plains—Armed visits to Te Ngutu-o-te-manu — Action by Mr. Booth and Colonel McDonnell—Three military settlers killed at Te Rauna, near the Wai-ngongoro—Reinforcements for the new operations—A trooper ambushed near Waihi and cut to pieces—Revival of cannibalism by the Hauhaus—Eating of human flesh at Te Ngutu-o-te-manu—Titokowaru's boastful letter—The Hauhau headquarters in the forest—Pagan ceremonies in "Wharekura" —The deserter, Kimble Bent, at Te Ngutu-o-te-manu—His strange life of bush adventure.

CHAPTER 21: THE DEFENCE OF TURUTURU-MOKAI 187

The "Rorke's Drift" of Taranaki—Story of the Turuturu-mokai Redoubt—Garrisoned by Armed Constabulary and Military Settlers, under Captain Ross—Tardy repair of the redoubt—Titokowaru's spies watch the work—An early-morning attack —Twenty defenders against sixty Hauhaus—Two hours' desperate fighting—Narratives of survivors: Cosslett, Johnston, John Beamish, and George Tuffin—Half the defenders killed and several wounded—Death of Captain Ross—The pagan rite of the *Whangai-hau*—A human heart offered in burnt sacrifice to the gods of battle—Heroic resistance of the survivors—Help at last from Waihi—Colonel McDonnell's dramatic vow.

CHAPTER 22: TE NGUTU-O-TE-MANU: THE FIRST ATTACK .. 202

McDonnell avenges Turuturu-mokai—Expedition against Te Ngutu-o-te-manu *pa*—Skirmish in the clearing—Destruction of the village and Titokowaru's sacred house "Wharekura"—Fighting a rearguard action—Difficult work of carrying out the wounded —A brave padre.

CHAPTER 23: THE REPULSE AT TE NGUTU-O-TE-MANU .. 206

McDonnell's second attack on Titokowaru's forest stronghold—A long bush march to the rear of Te Ngutu-o-te-manu—The column heavily fired on—Hauhaus skirmish out from the *pa*—A destructive cross-fire—Uselessness of untrained men in bush fighting—McDonnell's decision to retreat—Officers vainly wait for orders —Death of Major Von Tempsky, Captain Buck, and other officers and men—McDonnell's retirement with the wounded—War-rite of the *Whangai-hau*—Captain Roberts collects the remnant and fights a rearguard action—A night in the forest—Roberts's narrative of the battle—The killing of Von Tempsky

PAGE

—McDonnell's report—The day after the fight—Scenes of savagery in "The Bird's Beak" *pa*—Funeral pyre of the slain whites—The cannibal feast; a soldier's body cooked and eaten—The battlefield to-day—Von Tempsky's sword.

CHAPTER 24: TE KOOTI'S ESCAPE FROM CHATHAM ISLANDS .. 222

The exiles at Wharekauri—Te Kooti becomes their prophet and leader—Founder of a new religious cult—His magnetic influence over the Maori prisoners—Singular scenes in the meeting-house—Te Kooti's ritual—Mismanagement of the military guard—A fatal reduction—Te Kooti's plans for escape—Seizure of the schooner "Rifleman"—The voyage to New Zealand—Peita Kotuku's narrative—A human sacrifice: Te Kooti casts Te Warihi overboard—Arrival at Whareongaonga, East Coast—The escapees and their equipment—The march inland.

CHAPTER 25: THE FIRST ENGAGEMENTS WITH TE KOOTI .. 235

European force pursues Te Kooti—Captain Westrup badly defeated at Paparatu—Te Kooti's victory greatly enhances his prestige—Colonel Whitmore assumes the direction of operations—Captain Richardson's engagement at Waihau—Another success for Te Kooti—Whitmore takes up the pursuit—An arduous winter march inland—Engagement on the Ruakituri River—Captain Carr and Mr. Canning killed—An indecisive fight—Te Kooti retreats to Puketapu, and Whitmore withdraws to Poverty Bay.

CHAPTER 26: WHITMORE'S DEFEAT AT MOTUROA .. 244

The position on the West Coast—Disorganization of the Taranaki field force—A state of semi-mutiny—Colonel McDonnell resigns and is succeeded by Colonel Whitmore—Territory north of the Patea abandoned to the Hauhaus—A convoy skirmish at Turangarere—Patea and Wairoa the advanced posts—Titokowaru's triumphant progress southward—Whitmore plans to surprise him at Moturoa—Armed Constabulary reinforcements—A night march from Wairoa camp—Moturoa *pa* attacked in the early morning—Hauhaus on the alert—An unfinished stockade—Whitmore's failure to scout the position—The storming-party—Attackers meet a heavy fire and are beaten off—Death of Major Hunter—Roberts's "Young Division" (No. 6 A.C.) comes up in support—Whitmore orders a retreat—A gallant rearguard action—Desperate fighting at close quarters—Maori battle-rite of the *Whangai-hau:* an omen of success—Plucky work of No. 2 Division—Close-quarters skirmishing in the bush—Heavy losses of Whitmore's force—Withdrawal to the Kai-iwi River—The battlefield to-day—Tu-Patea's narrative—The Wairoa Redoubt.

CHAPTER 27: THE POVERTY BAY MASSACRE 263

Te Kooti's raid on the Poverty Bay settlements—Warnings disregarded—Major Biggs's fatal confidence—Hauhau war-parties surprise the Matawhero settlers—Major Biggs and Captain Wilson and their families slaughtered—Thirty-three Europeans and thirty-seven friendly Maoris killed—A Hauhau's narrative of the raid—Fugitives gather at the Turanganui Redoubt—Women and children sent to Napier and Auckland—Te Kooti fortifies himself at Makaretu.

PAGE

CHAPTER 28: MAKARETU, AND THE SIEGE OF NGATAPA .. 270

Te Kooti driven from Makaretu—His fortress on Ngatapa Mountain—European and Maori force attacks the position—Gallant work by Ropata and Captain Preece—Failure of the first attack—Arrival of Colonel Whitmore—Second attack on Ngatapa—A Ngati-Porou storming-party—The inner defences reached—Hauhaus abandon the fort at night—The pursuit by Ngati-Porou—Summary execution of more than a hundred prisoners—Te Kooti takes refuge on the Upper Waioeka.

CHAPTER 29: THE FINAL CAMPAIGN AGAINST TITOKOWARU .. 285

Colonel Whitmore returns to the West Coast—Armed Constabulary operations against Titokowaru renewed—Corps of Guides formed—A scouting adventure at the Okehu Gorge—Attack on Taurangaika *pa*—A skilfully designed stronghold—Titokowaru evacuates the *pa* and is driven across the Waitotara—The peach-grove ambuscade at Papatupu—Last instance of cannibalism in New Zealand—The engagement at Otautu—Titokowaru takes refuge in the forest—The attack at Whakamara—A chase through the bush—Ruthless methods of warfare—Decapitation of captured Hauhaus—Rewards paid for the heads—The bush column reaches Taiporohenui—Titokowaru at Te Ngaere—Whitmore crosses the great swamp—Escape of the Hauhaus to the Upper Waitara—The massacre at Pukearuhe—Shells fired at Mokau Heads—Expeditions up the Waitotara, Whenuakura, and Patea Rivers—End of the Taranaki War—Field force transferred to the Bay of Plenty.

CHAPTER 30: TE KOOTI'S RAID ON WHAKATANE 314

Attack on Bay of Plenty settlements planned by Te Kooti—The Lower Whakatane Valley invaded—Attack on the Ngati-Pukeko in Rauporoa *pa*—Defence of the mill and redoubt at Te Poronu—The French miller's gallant stand—His death in the redoubt—The siege of Rauporoa—Its capture by the Hauhaus—Lieutenant Gilbert Mair and his Maoris to the rescue—A forced march from Matata—Hauhaus plunder the Whakatane settlement—Te Kooti's withdrawal to the Rangitaiki—Pursuit by Major Mair—Te Kooti in Tauaroa *pa*—Escape to the Urewera Mountains.

CHAPTER 31: TE KOOTI'S ATTACK ON MOHAKA 327

The guerrilla leader's swift movements—A dash across the Urewera Country—Sudden descent on Mohaka, Hawke's Bay—Massacre of European settlers and Ngati-Pahauwera Tribe—Te Huke and Hiruharama stockades besieged—Capture of Te Huke—Gallant defence of Hiruharama by the Maoris and Trooper George Hill—Withdrawal of Te Kooti to Waikare-moana—Colonel Lambert's futile pursuit.

PAGE

CHAPTER 32: WHITMORE'S INVASION OF THE UREWERA COUNTRY (1869) 337

Colonel Whitmore organizes an expedition to the Urewera Country—Two columns used in the attack—Whitmore's advance from Fort Galatea—Capture of Te Harema *pa* and Ahi-kereru—Whitmore's Guides ambuscaded in the gorge at Manawa-hiwi—A veteran scout's story—Difficult mountain and forest march to Ruatahuna—The bugle in the mountains—The "Officers' Call"—The advance of the left wing—Lieut.-Colonel St. John's march up the Whakatane—Capture of Whataponga—Death of Lieutenant White at Te Paripari—Burial under fire—Heavy bush skirmishing—Fighting at Hukanui and Tahora—Arrival at Ruatahuna—Attack on Orangikawa *pa* at Tatahoata—Captain Travers killed—Capture of the *pa*—Arrival of Colonel Whitmore—United operations against the Urewera—Intermittent skirmishing—Fights at Orona and Wai-iti—Captain Mair's narrative—Peka Makarini and Te Kooti's advance-guard—Ambuscade on the Waikare-moana track—Arawa auxiliaries decapitate Urewera slain—Proposed march to Waikare-moana abandoned—Whitmore's return to Fort Galatea—Carrying out the wounded—Major Mair's hazardous march via the Horomanga—Colonel Herrick's expedition to Lake Waikare-moana—Futile operations.

CHAPTER 33: THE SURPRISE AT OPEPE 362

An expedition to Lake Taupo—Lieut.-Colonel St. John's cavalry escort—The camp at Opepe—Fatal carelessness of St. John and the cavalry subaltern—Te Kooti's advance-body surprises the camp—Nine troopers slaughtered—A survivor's thrilling story—George Crosswell's marvellous escape—His flight naked across the Kaingaroa Plain—A despatch-rider killed near Heruiwi—Peita Kotuku's narrative of the encounter.

CHAPTER 34: THE TAUPO CAMPAIGN (1869) 371

Te Kooti's arrival at Taupo—Horonuku te Heuheu joins his forces—A visit to King Tawiao at Tokangamutu—Skirmishing on the east side of Lake Taupo—Te Kooti defeated on the Pononga ridge—His last redoubt, the Mahaukura *pa* at Te Porere—Attack by Armed Constabulary and Kupapa Maoris—Capture of the *pa*, with heavy loss to the Hauhaus—Death of Captain St. George—Peita Kotuku's narrative—Te Kooti's flight to the bush—Friendly Maoris' brave scouting expedition to Taumarunui—Te Kooti retreats to the Patetere forest—The fighting at Tapapa.

CHAPTER 35: DEFEAT OF TE KOOTI AT ROTORUA 387

Te Kooti's dash on Ohinemutu, Rotorua—Lieutenant Gilbert Mair intercepts him and saves Ohinemutu—Pursuit of Te Kooti by Mair and a small force of Arawa—A gallant running fight—Hauhaus chased for twelve miles—Skirmishing at Wai-korowhiti and Kapenga—Peka Makarini, Te Kooti's bugler, shot by Mair at Tumunui—Te Kooti's flight to the Urewera Mountains—Mair receives his captaincy and the New Zealand Cross—New policy in Government military operations—Only native forces used in the bush campaigns—Pursuit of Te Kooti and Kereopa—Ngati-Porou, Arawa, and Wanganui contingents.

PAGE

CHAPTER 36: OPERATIONS AT WAIKARE-MOANA 401

Native expedition to Waikare-moana under Mr. Hamlin and Lieutenant Witty—Skirmishing on and around the lake—Mr. Large's scouting enterprise—Successful operations against the Hauhaus—Occupation of Matuahu *pa*—Retreat of the Urewera—Surrender of some of the hostiles.

CHAPTER 37: THE CHASE OF TE KOOTI: EXPEDITIONS TO THE UREWERA COUNTRY (1870) 409

Ngati-Porou expedition to the Urewera Country—Ropata and Porter march on Maunga-pohatu—Porter captures the Ngati-Kowhatu Tribe at Horoeka *pa*—Complete surprise of the Hauhaus—Ropata engaged at Te Kakari—Fighting with the Ngati-Huri mountaineers—The first Government expedition reaches Maunga-pohatu—Ngati-Porou march out to the Bay of Plenty—Junction with Kepa and the Wanganui contingent at Ohiwa—Expedition to the Waioeka Gorge—Defeat of the Hauhaus at Maraetahi—Escape of Te Kooti and Kereopa—Te Kooti's raid on Tolago Bay—A fruitless pursuit—Further search expeditions by Ngati-Porou, under Ropata and Porter.

CHAPTER 38: THE UREWERA COUNTRY: EXPEDITIONS OF THE ARAWA CONTINGENT (1870–71) 419

A special corps of Arawa Maoris enlisted for service—Captains Mair and Preece in command, Nos. 1 and 2 Companies, Arawa Flying Column—Patrol-work on the border of the Urewera Country—Surrender of the Ngati-Whare Tribe at Fort Galatea—Tamaikowha makes peace with the Government—Paerau and other Urewera chiefs break away from Te Kooti—Mair and Preece march in search of Te Kooti (1871)—Arrival at Ruatahuna—March over the Huiarau Mountains to Waikare-moana—Scouring the Urewera Ranges—March to Maunga-pohatu—Te Kakari *pa* surrounded and occupied—Narrow escape of the murderer Kereopa—Meeting with Tamaikowha at Tauaki—Return of the column to Te Teko via Waimana and Opotiki—A month's rough campaigning.

CHAPTER 39: NGATI-POROU'S SEARCH FOR TE KOOTI .. 427

Further expeditions of Ngati-Porou, under Ropata and Porter—Te Kooti reported to be in Te Wera forest—Ngati-Porou search that country—Visit to Waimana Valley and Maunga-pohatu—Return to the Upper Wairoa—Te Houpapa and other places searched—Description of campaigning conditions—Living on bush foods—Primitive customs among the Urewera mountaineers—Masters of bushcraft—Picking up the fugitives' trails—Fourth expedition of Ngati-Porou—Te Wera forest searched—The column divides.

CHAPTER 40: TE KOOTI DEFEATED AT WAIPAOA 432

Captains Mair and Preece renew the search for Te Kooti—March through the Urewera Country—Snow on the Huiarau Mountains—Stormy weather at Waikare-moana—Scouting around Lake Waikare-iti—Severe wintry conditions on the ranges—Letter from Te Kooti found in a camp—Smoke seen in the Waipaoa Valley—Capture of a woman—Te Kooti's forest camp surprised

PAGE

—Mair and Preece rush the *pa*—Three Hauhaus killed in the encounter—Te Kooti's narrow escape—Execution of a prisoner, Wi Heretaunga—Preece reports the engagement to Porter—Ngati-Porou follow up the trail—The Arawa column returns by sea—Another Urewera expedition—Scouting, marching, and counter-marching in the bush.

CHAPTER 41: PORTER DEFEATS TE KOOTI AT TE HAPUA .. 447

Smoke-signs in the ranges—Captain Porter's Ngati-Porou on the trail—Te Kooti's retreat discovered—A bush camp at Te Hapua—Porter attacks at dawn—A premature gunshot saves Te Kooti—Eleven Hauhaus killed—The leader once more evades his pursuers—Porter and his men snowed in at Opokere, Maunga-pohatu—The fugitives retreat to Ruatahuna and the Waiau country—Ropata builds redoubts at Maunga-pohatu and Ruatahuna—Capture of Kereopa at Te Roau—His execution at Napier—Ngati-Porou return to the East Coast.

CHAPTER 42: THE LAST UREWERA EXPEDITIONS (1872) .. 458

Captains Mair and Preece again search the Urewera Ranges—March to the Waiau region, west of Waikare-moana—The fugitives' trail found—Preece's Arawa encounter Te Kooti's party on the Mangaone—Firing across a gorge—Last engagement in the Maori wars (14th February, 1872)—Government men's defective ammunition—Te Kooti's final escape—Arawa column returns to Fort Galatea—Preece's last search—The Urewera Country traversed once more, from Ahi-Kereru to Waikare-moana—Scouting the western border of the ranges—No further sign of Te Kooti—He crosses the Kaingaroa Plain to the King Country Captain Ferris's search expeditions—Captain Rushton scours Te Wera forest—End of the Maori wars.

CHAPTER 43: FRONTIER PERILS AND THE FINAL PEACE .. 468

The Upper Waikato border in the "seventies"—Hauhau raids threatened—Murders on the *Aukati* line—Purukutu and party kill Timothy Sullivan—Alarm among the out-settlements—The frontier farmers' cavalry corps—Patrolling the King Country border—Blockhouses and redoubts garrisoned—Moffat killed at Taumarunui—Towhiao and his followers make peace—March through the frontier settlements—Armed Constabulary sent to Kawhia—Trouble on the Taranaki frontier—Te Whiti, the prophet of Parihaka—Ngati-Ruanui's ploughing campaign on the plains—Redoubts built and garrisoned by Armed Constabulary—John Bryce's march on Parihaka—Constabulary and Volunteers take possession—The prophets arrested and Maoris dispersed—Te Whiti, a man of peace and a restraining force—His character and teachings much misunderstood—Te Kooti pardoned—His last years—King Country fanatics make trouble—Mahuki's raid on Alexandra Township—Constabulary and Te Awamutu Cavalry arrest Mahuki and his band—Later military expeditions—The Urewera oppose surveys and roads—Armed forces despatched to Ruatoki and Te Whaiti—A peaceful ending—Honi Toia's outbreak at Hokianga—H.M.S. "Torch" sent to Rawene—March of Colonel Newall's column to Waima—The shots in the bush—Surrender of Hone Toia and his men—Good work of the Maoris in the Great War.

APPENDICES

PAGE

Supplementary Notes to Chapters 503
The Fanatic Faith 523
Maori Field Fortifications: Description of a *pa* at Manutahi (Taranaki) 523
Surveying under Fire: Pioneer Work on the Taranaki Frontier .. 528
The New Zealand Cross 536
The Poverty Bay Massacre 538
The Pukearuhe Massacre 540
The Defeat of Te Kooti at Rotorua 543
Sikhs against the Maoris 546
The Waikare-moana Expedition (1870) 547
Turuturu-mokai Redoubt, Taranaki 548
Rua Kenana, the Prophet 548
" Lest We Forget " 549
List of Engagements and Casualties 550

INDEX 555

LIST OF ILLUSTRATIONS

	PAGE
Officers of the N.Z. Armed Constabulary	*Frontispiece*
Te Ua, the Founder of Pai-marire	5
Patara Raukatauri	18
Sentry Hill Redoubt	22
Mataitawa Stockade	28
Moutoa Island, Wanganui River	34
The Last *Niu*, Upper Wanganui	44
General Sir H. J. Warre	56
General Chute's Column on the March	67
Seizure of the Schooner " Eclipse " at Opotiki	75
Matata *Pa*, 1865	99
H.M.S. " Brisk "	107
Volkner's Church, Opotiki	108
Attack on Omaru-hakeke Stockade	130
Scene of the Omarunui Engagement, Hawke's Bay	136
Mr. S. Percy Smith	144
Eru Tamaikowha	175
Waihi Redoubt, Taranaki	183
Turuturu-mokai Redoubt, Taranaki	186
George Tuffin	197
Lieut.-Colonel T. McDonnell, N.Z.C.	212
Waitangi, Chatham Island	227
The Schooner " Rifleman "	228
Peita Kotuku	230
Te Rangi-tahau	232
Sketch of the Moturoa Battlefield	250
Major Kepa te Rangihiwinui, N.Z.C.	252
Mr. William Wallace	255
Major R. Biggs	267
Ngatapa Hill Fortress	272
Major Ropata Wahawaha, N.Z.C.	278
Detail of Fortification, Tauranga-ika	289
The *Niu* Mast at Whakamara	297
Captain H. W. Northcroft, N.Z.C.	299
Pukearuhe Redoubt, from the North	305
The Original Redoubt, Pukearuhe	306
The Gascoignes' Home, Pukearuhe	308
The Blockhouse, Pukearuhe Redoubt	309
Later Blockhouse, Pukearuhe	310
Major M. Noake	312
Captain H. A. Mair	323
George Hill, N.Z.C.	331
Major-General Sir George Whitmore	339
" Big Jim," the Maori Scout	342

	PAGE
The Lower Gorge of the Whakatane	346
Te Paripari, Urewera Country	348
Junction of the Whakatane and Mahakirua, Urewera Country	350
After Fifty Years: Captain Mair at Captain Travers's Grave, Tatahoata	353
The Steamer " Stormbird "	361
G. Crosswell, Survivor of the Opepe Surprise	366
Te Heuheu Horonuku	374
Captain J. St. George	379
Topia Turoa	383
Captain Gilbert Mair, N.Z.C.	390
Captain Mair and his Arawa Soldiers	394
Tohe te Matehaere	395
Lake Waikare-moana, from Onepoto	400
Major J. T. Large	402
Sir James Carroll	406
Maunga-pohatu Range, Urewera Country	410
Colonel T. W. Porter, C.B.	412
Solomon Black, N.Z.C.	415
Thomas Adamson, N.Z.C.	416
Captain Porter and Ngaitai Maoris	417
Captain Preece, N.Z.C.	423
The Urewera Mountains	430
Netana Whakaari	445
Te Whiu Maraki	455
Kereopa Kai-whatu	456
Onepoto Redoubt, Waikare-moana	459
Colonel Lyon	469
Wahanui	471
Orakau Blockhouse	472
The Maori King's Flag	475
Parihaka	476
Colonel J. M. Roberts, N.Z.C.	479
Armed Constabulary Camp at Waikino, Taranaki	481
Normanby Redoubt, Taranaki	482
Watch-tower, Manaia Redoubt	483
Pungarehu Redoubt	484
Rahotu Stockade and Camp	484
Taranaki Rifle Volunteers at Parihaka	485
Armed Constabulary Field Force, Parihaka	486
Te Whiti surrendering at Parihaka	487
Tohu Kakahi after Arrest at Parihaka	489
Colonel Goring	491
Major Gascoyne	492
Te Kooti's House at Te Awahou, Rotorua	493
Opunake Redoubt	495
Armed Constabulary Force	495
No. 3 Division Armed Constabulary	495
Urenui Redoubt, North Taranaki	497
Taranaki Bush Rangers' Redoubt, Wai-iti	498
Pukearuhe Redoubt	499
The Mahurehure Leaders, Waima, Hokianga	500
Te Kooti's War-flag, " Te Wepu "	545

PLANS AND SKETCH-MAPS

	PAGE
Weraroa *Pa*, Waitotara	50
Otapawa *Pa*, South Taranaki	64
Entrenchment, Opotiki Church Redoubt	109
Waerenga-a-Hika *Pa* and Battlefield	124
Puraku *Pa*, Tarukenga, Rotorua	169
Manutahi Redoubt, South Taranaki	181
The Battlefield of Moturoa	245
Ngatapa Hill Fortress	274
Cross-sections of Ngatapa	280
Tauranga-ika *Pa*	286
Sections of Tauranga-ika *Pa*	288
Rauporoa *Pa*, Whakatane	318
Mohaka (H.B.), 1869	326
Urewera Country, with Routes of Whitmore's Expedition, 1869	336
Scene of the Surprise at Opepe	363
Scene of Waipaoa Engagement, 1871	434
Scene of Te Hapua Engagement, 1871	448
Kohitau Redoubt, Maunga-pohatu	453
The Urewera Country	460
Hawera Blockhouses	478
Redoubts at Pipiriki	519
Te Teko *Pa* and Major Mair's Saps	519
Orona and Te Wai-iti, Urewera Country	520
Scene of Captain Mair's Defeat of Te Kooti, Rotorua	521
Waikare-moana and the Urewera Country (showing scenes of last fights in the Maori wars)	522
Manutahi *Pa*, North Taranaki	524

Chapter 1

PAI-MARIRE

THE DEFEAT OF the Kingite tribes and the settlement of the confiscated lands with large bodies of drilled men assured peace, albeit a sullen one, in the Waikato, but Cameron's successful campaign, 1863–64, by no means secured the general pacification of the Maoris. While British cannon were battering to dust the last defences of the Kingite warriors, a new and infinitely more desperate and formidable plan of campaign was formulating itself in Taranaki. Less than a week after the fall of Orakau the colony was startled by the reports of a new phase of warfare in Taranaki, accompanied by a fanatic ferocity unknown in the previous campaigns. This hardening-up of the Maori fighting-spirit in a kind of holy war imparted to the racial struggle a savagery and a bitter persistence that carried the war up to the young "seventies." If it developed to the utmost the Maori *amor patriae* and the peculiar military tactics in which the natives excelled, it produced also a determination on the part of the British colonists to see the fight through in their own way. The beginning of the Hauhau campaign saw the beginning of New Zealand's policy of self-reliance in matters military. After 1865–66 the numerous campaigns and bush operations were conducted by the colonial forces; and, although there were very critical hours when it seemed as if the aid of Imperial troops would again have to be called for the heavily strained resources of the settlements met the demands, with the assistance of those native tribes which for a variety of reasons, political and otherwise—expediently accepted by the *pakeha* as loyalty to the Queen—decided to throw the weight of their arms against the Hauhaus. It was in fact only the help of these loyalist or Kupapa tribes, under the leadership of colonial officers, that turned the scale and brought lasting peace to the old frontier.

The confiscation of land, the territory of the so-called rebels, was a prime factor in the renewal of the war. The Native Land Settlement Act, framed by the Whitaker-Fox Ministry, and passed by the Legislature in 1863, entrusted enormous powers of confiscation to a Government which ignored the just protests of such men as Sir William Martin and Bishop Selwyn. Arbitrary appropriation of the land which for centuries had been the property of large tribes — appropriation without adequate consideration for the rights of non-resisters and for the innocent children of the native belligerents — was inevitably a source of bitter and undying hatred. The confiscation of huge areas of Waikato and Taranaki territory enabled the Government to reward its forces with land-grants, but the crude and unjust manner of the seizure, the unconcealed wish of many colonists and even some politicians for a war of extermination of the Maori, went to give strong colour to the native belief that the white man's desire for land was the all-controlling factor. Some thoughtful people perceived the great tactical danger of a confiscation policy, quite apart from any question of ethics. It would stiffen the martial fibre of the race; it would debase a chivalrous kind of warfare into guerrilla campaigns of utter savagery. The Waitara seizure was ever in the Maori mind. The injustice done to Ngati-Awa by that act of spoliation had never been atoned for. The politicians and officials persisted in regarding the Maoris as rebels because they had rightfully defended their home-land. A more reasonable, more just view was that taken by a writer in an English magazine (the "Cornhill") in 1865. "The Maori revolt," he declared, "is the more excusable that it is instinctive. The chiefs probably cannot prevent it. They cannot check their intense attachment to their land—their 'mother' as the Maori calls it—which belongs to races that have not yet become commercial."

Early Governments imperfectly appreciated the peculiar depth and strength of the Maori's regard for his ancestral land; they could not understand why a race should fight to the death for a country which for the most part lay in a waste condition. Patience, conciliation, and an honest endeavour to understand the native point of view and to remove mutual misunderstandings were counselled by a few, but in truth the interests operating for strong-handed action were all-powerful. The wrong perpetrated at the Waitara should have been righted generously, but nothing was done, apart from the grudging renunciation of the purchase, to compensate Wiremu Kingi te Rangitaake for the wholly illegal acts which had sent him into an unwilling rebellion. The Taranaki and Ngati-Ruanui Tribes who had come to Ngati-Awa's assistance were punished for their rebellion by measures of potential confiscation which affected more or less the whole West Coast from Waitotara to the White Cliffs. It is true that provision and promises were made for the restoration of land to those who had not rebelled, but these promises were not properly kept. Military settlers were placed on the territory of some *hapus* that had remained peaceful, and of such complications hostility was the inevitable fruit. Both races were strong and stubborn, and the Maori blood was prone to fire up into savagery at threatened intrusion. The Maori, too, had come to realize that now or never was the time to assert himself to the utmost, and throw off a rule whose character and effects he had not realized to the full when he accepted the British overlordship in 1840. To-day the two races are so indissolubly blended in social intercourse, in national ideals, in a common pride of country, that they can afford to look back without passion on the conflict of race interests in the "sixties," finding but a pathetic lesson in the spectacle of the two headstrong, independent peoples of our earlier cruder years challenging each other to a death struggle for the prize of the land—in a bounteous country where there was room for twenty times their number. The intense devotion with which the Maori held to his land is difficult, perhaps, for the present generation to realize. Only when one discusses the subject with a native of the olden time, a venerable man or woman who has fought the *pakeha* and marched chanting around the sacred *niu* mast, is the power of this land-love made manifest.

The land—always the land, from the days of Wakefield onward—that was the *putake o te riri,* the grand root of all trouble. But when the white fire of a fanatic religion fused the people in a federation of hate against the *pakeha* all problems merged into one, that of race-mastery. So, when Pai-marire captured the impressionable and essentially religious Maori nature it spread like a fire in dry fern, and we find tribes who had no grievance whatever against the white man united in casting off semi-civilization, and throwing themselves into the battle for Maori independence.

The Pai-marire or Hauhau religious cult, which welded so many tribes in a bond of passionate hate against the *pakeha,* was partly a reaction from the teachings of the Christian missionaries, and partly a recrudescence of the long-discredited but unextinguished influence of the Maori *tohunga* or priest. It was a blend of the ancient faith in spells and incantations and magic ceremonies with smatterings of English knowledge and English phrases and perverted fragments of church services. Ridiculous as they were when analysed, the sum of the teachings had a most powerful effect upon the impressionable Maori. Pai-marire appeared just at the hour when the hostile tribes, embittered by heavy losses in men and property, were in a mood to welcome a new battle-cry and new hope of turning the tide of war against the *pakeha.* By its appeal to the imagination and the strong religious sentiment of the Maori it took the place of the missionary faith which the people had once embraced with fervour, but stronger still was the appeal which it made to their love of country and kin. It supplied the necessary links of a common aspiration between tribe and tribe, and this chain was the stronger because it was forged in the heat of a great religious revival. That this revival was in the nature of a return to barbarism and superstition did not lessen its irresistible call to the Maori; it was all the more welcome because it enabled him to throw off the last restraints of the now unpopular churches. The old *tohunga Maori,* schooled in the ancient religion, were the first to accept Pai-marire; they were astute enough to recognize that by adopting it they would secure the ancient ascendancy of their class over the people which the Rongo-Pai had impaired though not destroyed. These priests became so many Mad Mullahs advocating the doctrine of fire and tomahawk so strangely at variance with the title of the religion. No Mohammedan leader preaching a jehad against the infidels was more fiercely passionate in his denunciation of the aliens than were the chief apostles of Hauhauism; and no fighting race was ever more receptive to the gospel of a crusade than the tribes from coast to coast of the Island when Kereopa brandished the smoke-dried head of a slain white soldier before his excited congregations and initiated them in the ceremonies of the *niu.* The old fanatic fire has burned to ashes, but the haunting, heart-stirring chants remain; and many there remain, too, of the disciples who marched round the sacred mast painted red for war, intoning the song of Te Ua; for Pai-marire, with its variations of Tariao and Wairua-Tapu, endured long after the war. Even to-day the Ringa-tu or Wairua-Tapu ritual, the offshoot of Pai-marire, is a regularly established Church, numbering several thousands of adherents, and the sign and token of this Maori sect to-day is the magic gesture of Te Ua to turn aside the *pakeha's* bullets, the sign of the upraised hand, the *ringa-tu,* palm outwards, on a level with the head, as if in the act of warding off the enemy's projectiles. So persists the fanatic sign of old, long after the fiery faith that inspired it has gone.

The Pai-marire faith had its origin in the half-crazed brain of a Maori of the Taranaki Tribe named Te Ua Haumene, whose home was near Cape Egmont. He had taken a Scriptual name, Zerubbabel (maorified into Horopapera). He had imbibed the teachings of the missionaries, and was a close student of the Bible, particularly of the Book of Revelations. The ecstatic visions of the Dreamer he interpreted in his own peculiar fashion. Strange visions appeared to him in the semi-delirium of his night seances with the spirits. Curious stories are related by the Maoris of the first coming to Te Ua of the *anahera,* or angels, from

From a photo, about 1866]
Te Ua Horopapera Haumene, the founder of the Pai-marire Religion
(Te Ua made his submission to the Government in 1865)

whom he received inspiration. The angel Gabriel ("Kaperiere" in the Maori version) appeared to him, and revealed to him a new religion which was to give the Maori dominion over all the hosts of the *pakeha*. Te Ua promulgated this miraculously revealed faith, and, although little regarded at first, he gradually drew around him a band of believers. There was not much of the ancient Maori religion in his system of incantations and spells. For the *atua Maori* of old there were substituted troops of angels, headed by Gabriel, and these supernatural visitants were to give the faithful the gift of tongues, and confer upon them many strange and wonderful powers. Te Ua's guiding spirit or supreme deity was the Atua Pai-marire, meaning "Good and peaceful God," a phase that came to be applied to the religion which he founded. The term "Hauhau," by which the disciples of the new faith came to be known, had its origin in the exclamation "Hau!" used at the end of the chorus chanted by the disciples. Literally it means "wind"; but it has another and more esoteric significance, for it was the term applied to the life-principle of man, the vital spark. "*Anahera hau,*" or "wind angels," one of the curious phrases originating with Te Ua, was a reference to the fancy that the angels came to the Maoris on the winds of heaven, and that they ascended and descended by the ropes which were left dangling from the yardarms of the sacred mast, called the *niu*. "Hau," "hauhau," or "whakahau," is also a battle-cry meaning "Strike! Attack!"

This *niu* was the central symbol of worship under Te Ua's dispensation. The term was the olden Maori word for the short sticks used by the *tohunga* in his mystic arts of divination, particularly before a battle. Te Ua's *niu* was a tall pole or flag-mast, round which the faithful were to march in procession chanting their hymns. The first *niu* erected in Taranaki is said to have been part of one of the masts of the steamer "Lord Worsley," wrecked near Cape Egmont in 1862. Crossed with a yard, rigged with stays and halliards, and adorned with flags of curious design, it was the first visible emblem of the fantastic religion. Te Ua stood at the foot leading the chants, while his band of believers went round him chanting the responses in the "angel"-inspired ritual. Each tribe as it fell convert to the magic of Pai-marire set up its *niu* under the direction of Te Ua or his sub-priests. By the end of 1865 a *niu* stood in nearly every large village from Taranaki to the Bay of Plenty (excepting the Arawa country), and from the north of the Wellington district to the Waikato frontier. Some of these masts of worship were of great size, and very decorative they were when the war-flags of many colours and many devices were displayed upon them from truck to yardarm, while below the earnest worshippers marched around the sacred pole. A remarkably lofty *niu* was that which stood at Whakamara, in the Ngati-Ruanui and Pakakohi country, inland from Patea; it was 70 feet or 80 feet in height, and was crossed with three yards; the blocks through which the flag-halliards were rove had been taken from a vessel wrecked on the coast. This *niu* was destroyed by the Government forces under Colonel Whitmore in 1869. Another celebrated *niu* stood on the village square at Taiporohenui, the headquarters of Te Ua and the Ngati-Ruanui in 1865–66. Often a wood-carving of a bird was placed on the truck of the pole; this represented a *rupe,* or dove. Carved knobs sometimes decorated the ends of the yard or the crosstrees; one of these knobs was called Rura and the other Riki, the names of two of Te Ua's gods. Riki was war-god; when the red flag called by that name was hoisted to the masthead it was a signal that fighting was about to begin. On the Whakamara *niu* there were carved *rupe* at some of the yardarms, from which also dangled ropes for the convenience of the spirits in descending on the people.

Some of the ancestral beliefs were mingled with Te Ua's perversion of Biblical teaching. The incarnation of his personal *atua,* or guardian diety, was the owl, or *ruru,* a bird which is regarded with veneration by the Taranaki Maoris; they say it is a god and has a hundred eyes. Sometimes, the old natives say, when Te Ua was in a village distant from his home a *ruru* would appear and fly about him or perch near him: this the prophet would regard as a warning to return to his home. Kimble Bent, the *pakeha-Maori,* related to me that when Te Ua was in Otapawa *pa,* on the Tangahoe River, early in 1866, a *ruru* flew from the forest at dusk and perched on the ridge-pole of the house in the front of which the prophet was sitting. Te Ua called to it and recited an incantation, and the bird flew back to the bush. Te Ua thereupon announced to the people that his owl-god had appeared to him and warned him to return to his home on the coast. He left Otapawa next morning. A few days later the *pa* was stormed and taken by the British troops under General Chute. Such incidents went to confirm the popular belief in the Pai-marire high priest's great personal *mana* and his supernatural attributes.

The peculiar appeal of Pai-marire to the popular imagination made it a most powerful instrument for Maori nationalist propaganda. With the assumption of supernatural virtues by the priests was blended a kind of mesmeric influence over the devotees which made them oblivious to danger and swept them into desperate efforts to regain the ancient supremacy of the race. Te Ua and his apostles impressed their disciples with the belief that implicit faith in Pai-marire and the observance of the rules laid down by the founder would ensure success in war. A cardinal principle in the religion as first practised was the belief that the *pakeha's* bullets could be averted by certain magic spells. Thus the faithful marched to battle chanting their hymns and holding the right hand up on a level with the face, palm toward the enemy, while they cried in quick sharp tones, "*Hapa, hapa! Pai-marire, hau!*" "*Hapa*" means to pass over or ward off; the act and the formula were supposed to avert the bullets from the true believer. In exactly the same spirit the Arabs of the Sudan charged upon the British squares, and the wild tribes of the north-west frontier of India came rushing down against rifle and machine-gun. Even repeated defeats and the deaths of their first war-prophets did not demolish the faith in the incantations and the magic sign of the upraised hand; and not only were the hostile tribes completely carried away by the spell of the ceremonial and chants, but the people friendly to the British were attracted by the new religion. Veteran Kupapa, or friendly natives, who served on the Government side in the Hauhau campaigns describe the curious blending of fear and fascination which came over them when they watched from their entrenchments the Pai-marire devotees marching round their poles, and listened to the wild music of their rhythmic chantings.

This belief in the efficacy of spells for securing protection from the enemy's weapons has been a feature of many a racial war or crusade. Among the North American Indians and the Mohammedan peoples of Africa and Asia there have been many instances of the same fanatic faith.* Even among the Scottish Highlanders of a past generation we hear of curious examples of a confidence in the power of wise men to avert hurt in battle. An old Western Highlander who lived at Broadford, in the Isle of Skye, used to tell how it came to pass that so many soldiers had returned safe to the Isles after the French and Spanish campaigns. It was because there was a blind man in Broadford who was able to put the charm upon them. "On each in turn he laid his hands," Miss Gordon Cumming wrote in her book "In the Hebrides," "and they went away looking straight before them. One man half turned his head and saw his own shoulder—an evil omen—and sure enough he lost that arm; but though the balls fell around the others as thick as peas they were nowise hurt, but returned as living proofs of the blind man's power." In the Boxer War in China the rebel leaders pretended to be invulnerable to bullets. A cable message from Constantinople in 1914 described a Kurdish rising under the Vali of Betliz in which the sheikhs who led the outbreak convinced the peasants that they could turn the bullets of the enemy into dust before they struck them. The superstition was revived in the recent Maplah rebellion in India. A cable message from Delhi, 11th January, 1922, states that a notorious chief named

---

* "The Suffi and Hadda Mullahs exerted the whole of their influence upon their credulous followers. The former appealed to the hopes of future happiness. Every Ghazi who fell fighting should sit above the Caaba at the very footstool of the throne, and in that exalted situation and august presence should be solaced for his sufferings by the charms of a double allowance of celestial beauty. Mullah Hadda used even more concrete inducements. The muzzles of the guns should be stopped for those who charged home. No bullets should harm them. They should be invulnerable. They should not go to Paradise yet: they should continue to live honoured and respected on earth."—"The Story of the Malakand Field Force" (Winston Churchill), page 257.

Also see note on the North American Indian Messianic craze in 1890, at the end of this chapter.

Chembrasseri Thangal, one of the leaders of the rising, who, with five others, had been sentenced to death by a military court, had deluded his followers into the belief that he possessed mystic powers and was invulnerable to bullets. A few years ago, in the revolt of a section of the Boers against British rule, a fanatic prophet named Van Rensburg assured Beyers's men that he would make them invisible to their foes in battle. To this day some of the survivors of the Hauhau wars tell how they uttered a spell called *huna,* the purpose of which was to conceal them from their pursuers. No cover was supposed to be necessary: the *huna* was sufficient, they believed; it raised a friendly mist which befogged the foe. We read of very much the same kind of supernatural mist in the " Iliad."

The political value of such faith was enormous. Pai-marire attracted even many of those who had no faith in Te Ua, but who joined with their fellow-Maoris in lamenting the deaths in the Kingite wars and the losses of land, and in putting forth an effort to sweep the land clear of the *pakeha.* Spreading out fanwise from the foot of Taranaki Mountain to the heart of the Island, to the north and to the south and to the eastern seaboard, it united in a common body of hostility to the Government all those tribes who had grievances against the British. It was fortunate for the European population that no military genius showed himself in the early stages of Pai-marire, and that no Maori statesman with a brain like Wiremu Tamehana's threw himself into the task of making the most skilful use of the common bond established by the new religion. Te Kooti came on the scene three years too late to turn the Hauhau cult to the fullest account, and by that time he had evolved a system of worship of his own which closely resembled a Christian church service. The missioners chosen by Te Ua to promulgate the faith were not men of high capacity intellectually, and such savage apostles as Kereopa made the tactical mistake of committing murders and precipitating war before the union of the tribes was completed. It is clear that Te Ua charged his messengers to the East Coast and other tribes to carry out their mission peacefully, and to refrain from acts which would involve premature war.

Several times a day the Hauhaus in every settlement gathered at the foot of the *niu* pole of worship and marched in procession round and round the mast, chanting in chorus the Pai-marire incantations taught by the prophet. Many of these chants, sounding very musical as they rang through the forest that walled in the rebel villages, were simply meaningless strings of English words rounded into the softer Maori; others were either transliterations or mispronunciations of parts of the Church of England services, with a sprinkling of Latin from the Roman Catholic ritual. Some phrases were military orders, picked up at the soldiers' camps. Some others showed a nautical origin; Te Ua boxed the compass like any *pakeha* sailor.

"Porini, hoia!" ("Fall in, soldiers!") was the call when the Pai-marire prophet marched to the *niu* and took his stand at its foot, within a kind of altar-rail painted blood-red. The people fell in, in military order, and round and round the sacred mast they went, and as they marched they recited in a high chant this curious medley, believing it a most potent incantation given to the sons of men by the angels:—

Kira, wana, tu, tiri, wha—Teihana!
Rewa, piki rewa, rongo rewa, tone, piki tone—Teihana!
Rori, piki rori, rongo rori, puihi, piki puihi—Teihana!
Rongo puihi, rongo tone, hira, piki hira, rongo hira—Teihana!
Mauteni, piki mauteni, rongo mauteni, piki niu, rongo niu—Teihana!
Nota, no te pihi, no te hihi, noriti mino, noriti, koroni—Teihana!
Hai, kamu, te ti, oro te mene, rauna te niu—Teihana!
Hema, rura wini, tu mate wini, kamu te ti—Teihana!

[TRANSLATION]

Kill, one, two, three, four—Attention!
River, big river, long river, stone, big stone—Attention!
Road, big road, long road, bush, big bush—Attention!
Long bush, long stone, hill, big hill, long hill—Attention!
Mountain, big mountain, long mountain, big staff, long staff—Attention!
North, north-by-east, nor'-nor'-east, nor'-east-by-north, north-east, colony—Attention!
Come to tea, all the men, round the *niu*—Attention!
Shem, rule the wind, too much wind, come to tea—Attention!

Then the measure of the incantation changed and took a less staccato and more musical note. "*E te Matua, pai-marire*" ("O Father, good and gracious") the leader began, and all the people responded, "*Rire, rire, hau!*" Then they chanted in a wild cadence, sometimes falling softly away, then rising and swelling into a volume that throbbed with a fervour intense, the ritual of "*Waiata mo te ata,*" or "Morning Song," beginning with this *karakia*—

To mai Niu kororia, mai merire!
To mai Niu kororia, mai merire!
To mai Niu kororia, mai merire!
To rire, rire!

[TRANSLATION]

My glorious Niu, have mercy on me !
[or pity me !]
My glorious Niu, have mercy on me !
My glorious Niu, have mercy on me !
Have mercy, mercy !

The words "*mai merire*" were a transliteration of the Latin "*miserere mei*" in the Roman Catholic prayers. Another burst of "Morning Song" followed:—

Atua pai-marire,
Atua pai-marire,
Atua pai-marire,
Rire, rire !

Atua Tamaiti, pai-marire,
Atua Tamaiti, pai-marire,
Atua Tamaiti, pai-marire,
Rire, rire !

Atua Wairua-Tapu, pai-merire,
Atua Wairua-Tapu, pai-merire.
Atua Wairua-Tapu, pai-merire,
Rire, rire !

This chant, rhythmic and haunting in its frequent repetitions, was inspired by the Church of England prayer-book. It called upon God the Father, God the Son, and God the Holy Ghost to "have mercy upon us—mercy, mercy."

In the evening assemblies in the meeting-house there was much chanting of hymns and prayers. This was one of the evening hymns:—

To tangikere Pata, mai merire,
To tangikere Pata, mai merire,
To tangikere Pata, mai merire.

To tangikere Titekoti, mai merire,
To tangikere Titekoti, mai merire,
To tangikere Titekoti, mai merire.

To tangikere Orikoti, mai merire,
To tangikere Orikoti, mai merire,
To tangikere Orikoti, mai merire.
To rire, rire !

Translated, and avoiding the repetitions of the Maori, these lines were—

O Father, have mercy on me !
Holy Ghost, have mercy on me !
Mercy, mercy !

A maorified version of the Benediction was chanted with one voice, all the people holding up the right hand on a level with the head as they intoned in solemn music these words:—

Kororia me te Pata,
Ranei tu,
Ranei to,
Riiko—e !
Te wai te pikine,
Huoro Pata
Hema ta pi
Wai wi rau te,
Rire, rire, hau !

["Glory to the Father and to the Son and to the Holy Ghost, as it was in the beginning and ever shall be, world without end"—and, instead of "Amen," "*Rire, rire, hau !*"]

The words in a Maori dress were simply "pidgin," imitating the sounds of the English. An aged half-caste woman who saw much of Hauhauism in the "sixties" says that it was a long time after she first heard the "*Kororia,*" as it was termed, before she discovered what it meant. "The Hauhaus used to come to me," she narrates, "and say, 'Our gods taught us this; it is English and you ought to know it.' The people believed that when they had learned all these incantations well their gods Rura and Riki would give them power to walk upon the water and perform many other miracles".

Goodness and mercy were the distinguishing attributes of the Hauhau faith, if one judged it by the hymns and prayers; but these chants all formed part of a scheme designed to exalt the Maori and obtain for him spiritual and material advantage over the hated white man, and the "good and peaceful" refrains soon became war-cries in the most desperate racial struggle yet waged in the Island.

Curious stories are told of the hypnotic power which the chants of Te Ua, combined with personal magnetic influence of the wizard-like *tohunga Maori,* exercised over many of the people. A half-caste member of the Ngati-Rangiwewehi section of the Arawa Tribe (the woman already mentioned) described some of the scenes which she witnessed when the *niu* of Pai-marire stood at Puhirua, on the north-west side of Lake Rotorua, 1865–67. Ngati-Rangiwewehi and one or two allied *hapus* were the only people of the Arawa who accepted the Hauhau faith; they were predisposed towards it because of their heavy losses in 1864 in the rifle-pits of Te Ranga. Moreover, the prophet Kereopa was a member of the tribe. The prophet of the *niu* at Puhirua in 1865 was a *tohunga* named Tiu Tamehana, and when he led his disciples in the rites they seemed perfectly oblivious to all outside things. Said Heni te Kiri-karamu, narrating the strange scenes in Puhirua,—

I never would have anything to do with Pai-marire myself, but my mother, two of my young daughters, and my brother Neri were living with the Hauhaus at Puhirua, and they became converts. The Pai-marire believers seemed to be possessed of a spirit; they would keep on circling round and round the *niu* pole perhaps for an hour, half-dazed, holding their hands aloft, repeating their prayers in a sing-song chant. Their bare legs and arms might be covered with *namu* (sandflies), but they apparently did not feel their bites. My mother and brother went circling about the *niu* in procession with the rest. As I sat on the *marae* watching the Ngati-Rangiwewehi go round the *niu* I particularly admired one young chief woman named Hikairo. She was dressed only in a beautiful *korowai,* a white cloak of fine dressed flax. It was fastened over her right shoulder, leaving that arm free, and reached to below her knees, and her bare firmly shaped arm was upraised in the gesture of the *Hapa Pai-marire* as she marched with dignified step round the flagpole. She, like the others, was perfectly fascinated by the Hauhau service. When my brother met me on my visits to the village he would greet me in strange words and repeat his Hauhau charms; he explained that he was trying their effect on me and endeavouring to turn me to the new faith. But I told him that I could not place my faith in the Hauhau religion, and he agreed at last that the spells would have no power over one who was so firm an unbeliever."*

A singular night seance in the communal meeting-house at Puhirua was described to the writer by the venerable Heni:—

"One night," she said, "the people tried to put the spirits on me—that is, to influence the Pai-marire gods to gain me as a convert. The spirits, or *nga wini* as they called them [winds, the *hau* of the Maori], were supposed to dwell in the *niu,* but they could be invoked in the *wharepuni* at night. On this occasion a stranger named Nohoroa te Koki was in the village, and as he was not a believer in the Hauhau religion up to that time it was determined to convert him, and at the same time to make a final effort to turn me to Pai-marire. We were told to stand up, and then the people began their prayers and recited *karakia* after *karakia* in chorus to try and draw the *wini* down upon us, to

---

* This *niu* at Puhirua, and one which was erected at Te Kiri-o-Tautini, three miles inland to the north-west, were the only Pai-marire poles of worship set up by the Arawa. The deserted hill *pa* Puhirua is a beautiful spot overlooking the northern and north-west shore of Rotorua Lake, between Awahou and Hamurana (Te Puna-i-Hangarua); the site of the old headquarters of Ngati-Rangiwewehi is now a burial-ground. Te Kiri-o-Tautini was the centre of a collection of small settlements for food cultivation on the southern edge of the great forest which extended northward to the Tauranga district.

lodge upon Nohoroa and myself and charm us into the new religion. But I was a difficult subject; perhaps my English education made me proof against the *tohunga* powers. After a while I began to laugh, and this annoyed the people, who earnestly told me I was very wrong to laugh when they were calling down the spirits. Nohoroa laughed, too, at first; but presently he became still and attentive. Then, as the chants went on, becoming more and more earnest and intense, he began to tremble and shiver, and went into a kind of trance or fit. He opened his mouth and commenced to recite the usual pidgin-English incantations, '*Piki mauteni, rongo mauteni,*' and so on. He was a convert at last. The people were greatly gratified at what they imagined was the miraculous work of the spirits. But they never won me over."

The devotees of Pai-marire professed to regard the Jews as co-religionists; they considered that under Te Ua's dispensation the Maoris were the chosen people of God, just as the Jews were in the Old Testament. This twisting of the Scriptures to suit the exigencies of the day persisted long after Te Ua's time. Te Kooti's favourite theme was the sufferings of the Israelites, to whom he compared his followers; he likened himself to Moses, the deliverer and liberator of the tribes. Te Whiti, the peace-loving prophet of Parihaka, continually preached a similar doctrine. "We are Iharaira" [Israel], he said to me; "we are one with the Chosen People; our ancestors came from the land of Canaan." This fancy was fortunate for more than one colonist of the Jewish race in the war-days; an instance was the immunity from harm of Captain Levy, a coast trader, at Opotiki, when the missionary Volkner was hanged there by Kereopa's band in 1865. The priests of the *niu* sometimes styled themselves "*Tiu,*" or "Jew"; one of these was Tiu Tamehana, mentioned by Heni te Kiri-karamu.

Sometimes renegade white men joined with the Maoris in the ceremonies round the *niu*. One of these runaways from civilization who had "taken to the blanket" was Kimble Bent, a deserter from the 57th Regiment, in Taranaki. He was as thoroughgoing a Hauhau as any of his Ngati-Ruanui companions in 1865–69, and followed all the Pai-marire ritual, marching round and round the *niu* chanting Te Ua's hymns and brandishing a sword—a trophy from the wreck of the steamer "Lord Worsley" on the West Coast.

Heni te Kiri-karamu relates that one day she was astonished to see a white man, a shaggy-haired fellow with tattered clothes, emerge from the bush at Te Kiri-o-Tautini (on the edge of the forest three miles from Puhirua, on Lake Rotorua) and walk up to the *niu* which stood on the *marae*. Walking round it with his right hand raised, he began to chant the Pai-marire service. The people watched the strange *pakeha* in astonishment; then several joined him at the *niu*. It was in self-protection that this man had gone to the *niu* immediately he entered the village; he knew that by doing so he would assure his safety. He was a deserter from the colonial forces at Tauranga, and had already lived a bush life with the Piri-Rakau and Ngati-Raukawa Tribes for some months (1865–66).

One of the first worship-poles set up by Te Ua's followers in Taranaki was the *niu* at Taiporohenui, near Hawera, the principal gathering-place of Ngati-Ruanui in the first Hauhau campaign. In front of the great meeting-house the sacred mast was planted, a *totara* pine flagstaff 50 feet in height, with a yard about 14 feet long; the mast was stayed like a ship's. The war-flags of the Hauhaus were flown from the staff, and the people daily marched around its foot in their Pai-marire procession, intoning the chants their prophets had taught them. It was the old Maori custom, when the centre-pole of a large meeting-house, or the first large palisade post of a fort, was set in position, to place a piece of greenstone, often in the form of an ornament such as an eardrop or a carved *tiki,* at its foot. Similarly, at the foot of the *niu* at Taiporohenui a large piece of unworked greenstone was planted, as the *whatu* or luck-stone of the sacred pole.*

It was an ancient Maori custom to place a human head beneath the central pillar of a scared house. As recently as 1873 there was a recrudescence of the belief in this custom. Mr. James Mackay, Government Native Commissioner in the Waikato, while at Tokangamutu (Te Kuiti) on a political mission to the Kingites after a murder on the frontier, was attacked and nearly murdered in his tent one night by a fanatic Hauhau. This Maori, Ruru, had been incited to the deed by a speech made by a Hauhau priestess, who demanded that the white man should be killed as a sacrifice in connection with the *taingakawa,* or ceremonial opening of a new Hauhau praying-house, at Tokangamutu.

---

* Taiporohenui is a name of great *mana* among the Taranaki tribes. It is a very ancient Hawaikian name. A great Polynesian temple in Tahiti, one of the father-lands of the Maori people, was called Taiporohenui. The original Taranaki meeting-house of the name stood at Manawapou, but in the first Hauhau campaign an even larger house of assembly was built near Hawera; the present native village of Taiporohenui is on its site. Kimble Bent described this *whare* as the largest building of Maori construction he had ever seen. It was constructed of hewn *totara* timber, with *raupo*-reed walls and *nikau*-thatch roof. The house was about 120 feet in length, a size so exceptional that the ridge-pole was supported by four *poutoko-manawa,* or pillars, instead of one or two, as in the ordinary meeting-house. At night five fires burned in the stone fire-places down its long central aisle. The interior of the house was lined with ornamental *tukutuku* work of *kakaho* reeds and thin laths fastened with *kiekie* fibre. At the foot of the first house-pillar was buried a large uncut piece of greenstone, and another block of greenstone was placed at the foot of the *niu.*

THE SURPRISE AT TE AHUAHU, TARANAKI

The entrance of the Pai-marire party into active hostilities in Taranaki dates from the 6th April, 1864. Early on that day No. 1 Company (Grenadiers) of the 57th Regiment, and some newly enlisted Taranaki Military Settlers (No. 9 Company), were despatched from the redoubt at Kaitake—the position captured by Colonel Warre—to the high land above Te Ahuahu, a short distance to the south along the main track from New Plymouth and Oakura southward. The instructions were to destroy all native crops found. Captain Lloyd (57th) who had only recently arrived from England, was in charge of the expedition; the next in command was Captain Page, of the Military Settlers. The force foraged about the deserted settlements and cultivations on the Patua Range, and after destroying a quantity of maize and other crops the main body returned to the foot of the hill at Te Ahuahu and there awaited the return of Lieutenant Mansfield Clarke, who with a detachment of twenty 57th men was cutting down maize on the hill above. Captain Lloyd ordered the men to pile arms while they rested and waited for their comrades. Lloyd was new to Maori warfare, and was quite unsuspicious of danger. The soldiers were sitting round their stacked rifles when a volley was fired from the fern at very close quarters, and next moment a party of Maori warriors leaped from their well-masked trenches and rifle-pits and came charging down with appalling yells, some firing and others wielding long-handled tomahawks. "*Pai-marire—hau, hau, hau!*" they shouted, as they dashed on their panic-stricken foes. To the soldiers, struggling to use their rifles, the "*Hau-hau*" war yells sounded like the barking of dogs. Lloyd ordered the men to take cover and return the fire, but the resistance was short and useless. Those who essayed defence were killed; the rest made for the ocean-beach, two miles away. Seven soldiers were killed, and twelve were wounded. The Maori casualties were slight. Lieutenant Clarke, with the rear-guard on the hill above, escaped northward by a track along the side of the ranges. The firing was observed from the redoubt at Oakura, and a party was despatched to Lloyd's help, but the Maoris had gone, and only the naked and decapitated bodies of Lloyd and his men were found in the fern on the scene of action. The spot is about a mile south of the present village of Oakura, and on the line of the main road. Captain Frank Mace, with some of his Taranaki Mounted Rifles, was the first to make the discovery. When the alarm was given in New Plymouth a column consisting of the 57th Regiment (Major Butler) and the Taranaki Bush Rangers (Major Atkinson) was despatched to Te Ahuahu, and Colonel Warre took an Armstrong gun out to Hauranga, at the mouth of the stream, and thence inland to the foot of the

Patua Range, where some shells were fired into the Maori position.

The soldiers killed, besides Captain Lloyd, were Privates Dooley, Gallagher, and Sadler, of the 57th Regiment, Corporal Banks and Privates Megles (or Neagles) and Bartley, of the Taranaki Military Settlers. (This corps was a battalion raised by the Government at the end of 1863, recruited chiefly in Victoria and Otago, where many of its members had been gold-diggers. The men were enlisted for three years, and on discharge were given grants of land in Taranaki.) Lloyd's headless body was identified by the rather slender hands and wrists.

On examining the ground it was found that a zigzag trench ran down the face of the hill from the abandoned Maori *pa* on the skyline of the range above Te Ahuahu, and that there were other rifle-pits and trenches near the crops and on the face of the ridge near the flat where the troops had halted. These entrenchments were completely masked by the high fern being pressed down over them. It was the practice of such ambush-parties also to tie bunches of fern above their heads to enable them to steal on their enemies unobserved. The affair was an instance of inexcusable laxness and neglect to take ordinary military precautions; and the easy victory of the Maoris over a British force numerically stronger gave an immense impetus to the newly-born Pai-marire religion.

The heads of the slain soldiers, including Captain Lloyd's, were carried by the Pai-marire disciples to their prophets, and several of them were preserved by the ancient smoke-drying process, and were sent from tribe to tribe to enlist Hauhau recruits, as in the Highlands of Scotland the fiery cross was sent from clan to clan. One of the heads was recovered in 1865; it was sent to Taranaki and mistakenly buried as Captain Lloyd's. The Maoris state that Lloyd's head was taken by Kereopa across the Island as far as Opotiki, on the Bay of Plenty; another head, said to have been Gallagher's, was carried by the prophet Patara Raukatauri to the tribes between Turanganui (Gisborne) and the East Cape.

The Pai-marire worship now assumed a more ferocious phase than that which its founder had first given it. Te Ua professed to have received further inspiration from the angel Gabriel, who now commanded him to send the *pakeha* officer's head from tribe to tribe through the Island. When all the tribes had been visited and converted to Pai-marire the Maori people would be endowed with such power and wisdom that they would be able to conquer the white race and restore New Zealand to its original owners. This was to be done with Divine aid, and by implicit faith in the ceremonies and *karakia* of the Pai-marire. In pursuance of this militant programme Te Ua set apart assistants to promulgate the

PATARA RAUKATAURI
Patara, who was one of Te Ua's apostles sent out to spread the Pai-marire faith, was a chief of Oakura and Kaitake, Taranaki.

new doctrine throughout the Island. His principal priests or prophets were Hepanaia Kapewhiti, Matene te Rangi-tauira, Patara Raukatauri, Kereopa te Rau, and Horomona. All of these men but Patara came to violent ends. Hepanaia fell in the mad attempt to assault the Sentry Hill Redoubt in 1864. Matene was killed about a fortnight later in the Battle of Moutoa, on the Wanganui River. Kereopa, "the Eye-eater," as he came to be known, was captured and hanged at Napier for the murder of the Rev. Carl Volkner at Opotiki; Horomona met a similar fate at Auckland. Patara was a man of very different character to Kereopa; his was a milder nature; he was the only one of the band of apostles who lived to see the return of peace to the land. These men in their turn, as they passed from tribe to tribe, delegated their powers to leading converts, who each took up the duties of Pai-marire priest in the tribe. Often an ancient *tohunga* would so far adapt himself to the needs of the hour as to become the priest of the *niu*. The more ferocious spirits among the converts numbered many such men as Te Ao-Katoa ("The Whole World"), the hereditary priest of the Ngati-Raukawa of West Taupo, who had been educated as a *tohunga Maori,* and who in 1865 assumed the position of Pai-marire leader in his tribe.

NOTES

The decapitation of the slain soldiers at Te Ahuahu was the first instance of this mutilation of enemies' bodies in the wars of the "sixties." To decapitation the West Coast Hauhaus added cannibalism in 1868–69. Tamaikowha, of the Ngai-Tama and Urewera, revived the practice of eating the hearts of his enemies (1866–67). The last instance in New Zealand of the beheading of a foe occurred in 1873, after the end of the wars. This was the murder of Timothy Sullivan by Purukutu and his party near Roto-o-Rangi, on the Upper Waikato frontier. The killing was an agrarian and semi-political affair; it was a protest against the occupation by Sullivan's employers of native land for which Purukutu had not received his share of payment. The Hauhaus, after shooting Sullivan, cut off his head, and also cut out his heart as an offering to Tu and Uenuku, the gods of war. The head was taken to Wharepapa, a Ngati-Raukawa village; the heart was carried through the King Country from village to village.

A shrewd excuse for decapitation of foes was made by a Samoan chief after the defeat in 1888 of a German naval column at Vailele, on Upolu Island. The Germans who fell were beheaded. Mr. Carver, a Wesleyan missionary, had occasion to visit Mataafa's camp, and spoke of the practice with abhorrence. "Misikane," said one chief, "we have just been puzzling ourselves as to the origin of the custom. But, Misi, is it not so, that when David killed Goliath he cut off his head and carried it before the King?"

There is a curious parallel to the Pai-marire fanaticism in the history of the North American Indian Messianic rising in 1890. Mr. James McLaughlin, U.S. Indian Inspector, tells the story in his book "My Friend the Indian" (1910). In the autumn of 1890 Kicking Bear, a half-crazed fanatic of the Minniconjou band, left the Cheyenne River reservation and imparted to Sitting Bull, the great medicine chief of the Sioux, the secrets of a new religion which would bring the Indian into the inheritance of the earth. The doctrine took an enormous hold upon many of the Indian people. Sitting Bull had already heard of the new religion, which was said by some to have taken form at the instigation of some south-western Indians who had observed the practices of those descendants of the Aztecs who look to the east every morning in anticipation of the return of Montezuma, who is to redeem them from toil and subjection, and set them to rule over the earth. Sitting Bull, having lost his former influence over the Sioux, now planned to use the new belief to establish himself in the leadership of the people, whom he might then lead in any desperate enterprise. Kicking Bear, describing his journey to the wonderful land of the ghosts, said he and his companions met the Messiah, who showed them the wounds in his hands and feet made by the whites when they crucified Him, and took them to the Great Spirit, saying that He (the Messiah) would come again on earth, and would remain and live with the Indians, who were His chosen people. The Great Spirit said to him, "While my children are dancing and making ready to join the ghosts they shall have no fear of the white man, for I will take from the whites the secret of making gunpowder, and the powder they now have will not burn when it is directed against the red people, my children, who know the songs and the dances of the ghosts; but that powder which my children the red men have will burn and kill when it is directed against the whites and used by those who believe." "We found our horses," continued Kicking Bear, "and rode back to the railroad, the Messiah flying along in the air with us and teaching us the songs for the new dances." The Great Spirit was to make the earth anew, a paradise for the red man.

Sitting Bull kept his people madly engaged in the new dances, and it was evident that he was secretly preparing for some rash movement. That autumn there were strenuous times on the Dakota frontier. The rising, however, was early quelled by the Indian police. The fanatic ghost dancers at Standing Rock, North Dakota, and their chief, Sitting Bull, found that the magic medicine did not save them from the white man's bullets.

Chapter 2

ATTACK ON SENTRY HILL REDOUBT

THE MOST DESPERATE encounter in the first Hauhau campaign in Taranaki was the recklessly daring attempt of a band of two hundred picked warriors to assault a British fort, the redoubt on Sentry Hill, in broad daylight. Only the extraordinary faith which the newly converted disciples of Te Ua reposed in the *mana* and magical incantations of the fighting religion can explain this hopeless charge against a strong earthwork under the fire of scores of rifles at point-blank range. It was the first fight after Te Ahuahu, where the Hauhaus had scored so easy a success that their confidence in the virtue of Te Ua's system of charms and prayers was confirmed, and they advanced upon Sentry Hill fortified by an implicit belief that the *karakia* which they chanted and the cry of "*Hapa, Pai-marire!*" to avert the bullets of their foes, accompanied by a gesture, the right hand uplifted, palm to the front, as if warding off the balls, would secure them immunity from death or wounds.

The redoubt attacked stood on the crown of a round hill called Te Morere by the Maoris and Sentry Hill by the Europeans, near the right bank of the Waiongona River; the site is close to the present railway-station of Sentry Hill, on the Lepperton Junction–Waitara line. The hill Te Morere, one of the numerous rocky mounds of volcanic origin dotted about this part of Taranaki, was a Maori *pa* in ancient times; it derived its name, meaning "The Swing," from a tall swing-tree or "giant's stride" which stood there, with long ropes attached by which the youth of the *pa* were accustomed to go flying out over a swimming-pool in the river—a favourite sport of the olden Maori. In the early days of the war in Taranaki the ruined hill fort was often used as a lookout place by the Manutahi Maoris, and from this circumstance it obtained its English name.

About the end of 1863 Captain W. B. Messenger and 120 men of the Military Settlers built a redoubt on the top of the mound; this earthwork, with a very high scarp of parapet, was presently garrisoned by a detachment of the 57th Regiment under Captain

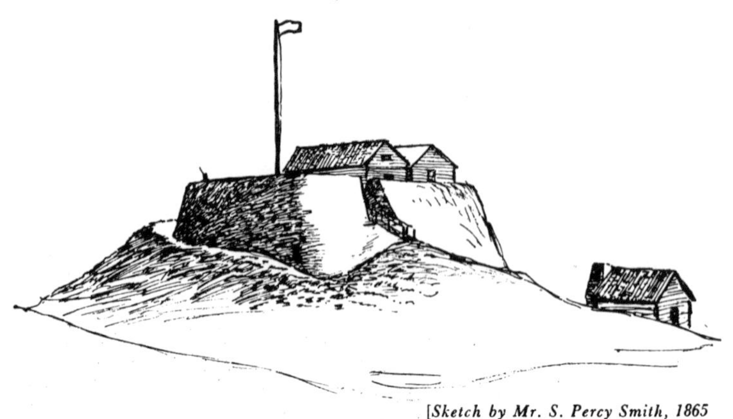

[*Sketch by Mr. S. Percy Smith, 1865*

Sentry Hill Redoubt, Te Morere

Shortt. A wooden barracks with accommodation for over a hundred men was built within the work. Shortt's force was seventy-five strong, with two Coehorn mortars.

The construction of this outpost, so near the Maori position in the bush at Manutahi, was regarded by the Atiawa Tribe as a challenge; it stood on their land. When the Pai-marire religion ran through the land like a fire through felled bush the Atiawa took advantage of this new patriotic impulse to propose the sweeping-away of the obnoxious *Pakeha* garrison on Morere Hill. Their allies eagerly approved this test of battle, and a war-party was formed composed of the best fighting-men on the West Coast from the tribes lately inoculated with the maddening germs of Pai-marire. Two hundred warriors were banded together under the prophet Hepanaia Kapewhiti, one of Te Ua's apostles. They were members of the Taranaki, Atiawa, and Ngati-Ruanui Tribes, with some Nga-Rauru from Waitotara and a number of Wanganui men. Among them were some young lads already used to the scenes of war. The Maori took to the war-path early; a well-grown boy of twelve was considered fit to take his place in a fighting expedition.

From Te Kahu-pukoro,* of Otakeho, probably the last of the Maori warriors who attacked the garrison of Sentry Hill, a dramatic narrative of the battle was obtained (30th August, 1920). This veteran chief was a tall, powerfully formed man, though his frame was bowed with rheumatism. His eyes glittered with some-

* Te Kahu-pukoro died at Otakeho toward the end of 1920. He was the *ariki*, or hereditary high chief, of Ngati-Ruanui, and was closely related to Titokowaru.

thing of the old warrior light as he told the story of his fighting youth. Te Kahu-pukoro was very young—in fact, he was only twelve—when he carried a gun in the ranks of the *ope* which marched against Sentry Hill on the 30th April 1864. Afterwards he was one of the picked fighters of Titokowaru, the "Tekau-ma-rua," in 1868–69, and shared in nearly every engagement of the last campaign in Taranaki. He belonged to the Nga-Ruahine section of Ngati-Ruanui, of which his grandfather Tamati Hone was the leading chief. His father and uncle fell at Sentry Hill, and he himself received two bullet-wounds there.

"Before I was old enough to bear arms," said Te Kahu-pukoro, "I witnessed several of the fights between the Maoris and the British troops; the principal one was the engagement at Kaitake. I also saw the British warships shelling our people at Tukituki-papa on the coast near Katikara. It was at Te Morere (Sentry Hill) that I first carried a gun into battle. I was very young, but a big strong lad, quite able to march and fight. The *ope* which assembled at the Manutahi *pa* [the northern Manutahi, not far from Mataitawa] for the attack on the British redoubt at Te Morere was composed of the best warriors on the West Coast. The Pai-marire religion was then new, and we were all completely under its influence and firmly believed in the teaching of Te Ua and his apostles. Hepanaia Kapewhiti was at the head of the war-party. He was our prophet. He taught us the Pai-marire *karakia,* and told us that if we repeated it as we went into battle the *pakeha* bullets would not strike us. This we all believed.

"Very early in the morning of the day fixed for the attack on Te Morere we all assembled at the flagstaff in the *pa* at Manutahi. Hepanaia led the sacred ceremonies round the *niu.* All the principal chiefs of the Taranaki country were there. Wirimu Kingi te Rangitaake was there; Te Whiti and Tohu Kakahi (afterwards the prophets of Parihaka) were both there. These three chiefs did not use guns; each carried a *tokotoko* (staff), and led his men. Another high chief was Kingi Parenga-renga, of Oakura; he was the leading chief of the Taranaki Tribe Kingi had a big head of reddish hair. He wore it twisted up in a high topknot which was adorned with feathers. He was a tall, splendid-looking man.

"At Hepanaia's call, '*Porini, hoia! Teihana!*' ('Fall in, soldiers! Attention!') we all formed a ring round the *niu,* Hepanaia standing by its foot, and we marched round and round the mast, chanting the incantations which the prophet had taught us, the *Karakia* beginning, '*Piki rewa, rongo rewa, piki hira, ronga hira.*' When the service ended we formed up in order of battle, with our weapons in hand and our cartridge-belts buckled about us, and marched for the British redoubt on Te

Morere Hill, which was not far from our gathering-place at Manutahi. We were armed with guns of various kinds; some had *ngutu-parera,* or flint-lock muskets; some double- and single-barrel shot-guns. The warriors also had tomahawks and stone *patu* in their belts; some who did not carry guns bore *taiaha*, and some *koikoi* (short spears of *manuka*). For myself, I was armed with a percussion-cap gun, and had two *hamanu* (cartridge-belts), one buckled round my middle and one over my left shoulder. I wore a shirt and a *rapaki* (waist-garment).

"Now, had we followed the advice of our prophet Hepanaia we might had succeeded in our assault on the soldiers' fort. Hepanaia proposed that the *ope* should make a sudden attack on the rear of the fort, but Hare te Hokai, a chief of Te Atiawa, insisted that the force should boldly attack the place in front, and this met with the support of most of the other chiefs. Another unfortunate thing was that, as we were marching from Manutahi, one of our men discharged his gun in order to give warning to any Atiawa people who might chance to be in or near the redoubt, for some of that tribe were serving on the *pakeha* side. This gave the soldiers warning of our approach.

"It was perhaps about 8 o'clock in the morning when we attacked the redoubt. Hepanaia led us on. He was a fine man, with a great love for his country and his people. In appearance he was tall and lean; he was stripped except for a short *piupiu* of flax around his waist, and was armed with a gun. We went into battle loudly chanting our Pai-marire service. Fern, about waist-high, and bushes of *tutu* clothed the plain and the lower slopes of Morere Hill, and through this we marched after coming out of the forest. We passed near the spot where the railway-station now stands, and then began the ascent of the gentle slope which led to the mound on which the soldiers' redoubt was built. It was a high, strong earthwork surrounded by a trench; within were the barracks of the soldiers. We did not stoop or crawl as we advanced upon the redoubt; we marched on upright (*haere tu tonu*), and as we neared the fort we chanted steadily our Pai-marire hymn.

"The soldiers who were all hidden behind their high parapet, did not open fire on us until we were within close range. Then the bullets came thickly among us, and close as the fingers on my hand. The soldiers had their rifles pointed through the loopholes in the parapet and between the spaces on top (between bags filled with sand and earth), and thus could deliver a terrible fire upon us with perfect safety to themselves. There were two tiers of rifles blazing at us. We continued our advance, shooting and shouting our war-cries. Now we cried out the '*Hapa*' ('Pass over') incantation which Hepanaia had taught us, to cause the bullets to fly harmlessly over us: '*Hapa, hapa, hapa! Hau, hau, hau!*

Pai-marire, rire, rire—hau !' As we did so we held our right hands uplifted, palms frontward, on a level with our heads—the sign of the *ringa-tu.* This, we believed, would ward off the enemy's bullets; it was the faith with which we all had been inspired by Te Ua and his apostles. I marched along there, calling out in quick, sharp tones, '*Hapa, hapa, hapa!'* with my right hand uplifted—but it did not save me from the *pakeha's* bullets. Our chiefs encouraged us with loud cries of '*Riria, riria!'* ('Fight on, fight on !') '*Kia mau, kia mau, kia mau !'* ('Be firm, be firm, be firm !')

"The bullets came ripping through our ranks. '*Hapa, hapa !'* our men shouted after delivering a shot, but down they fell. '*Hapa !'* a warrior would cry, with his right hand raised to avert the enemy's bullets, and with a gasp—like that—he would fall dead. The *tuakana* [elder brother] in a family would fall with '*Hapa !'* on his lips, then the *teina* [younger brother] would fall; then the old father would fall dead beside them. The bullets actually scorched my face—this cheek, then that cheek, was scorched by the balls, so thick and close did they come. But not until I felt and saw the blood running down my body did I know that I had received my first wound. A bullet struck me in the left shoulder, at a range of about as far as from where we are sitting to that hedge yonder [about 60 yards]. I was just at the foot of the hill on the flat where the road now goes between Sentry Hill and the railway-station. But I was so excited and so possessed by the fury of the battle that I did not feel it at first. I went on, and then I felt my shirt wet with blood streaming down from my shoulder, and in a few minutes another bullet hit me, and passed through my left hip, missing the bone. Then I had to fall back, and I went down to a little stream near-by where I bathed and staunched my wounds, and by this time the attack was repulsed and our people were flying back, and I joined them and managed to get into the safety of the bush.

"Our people fell in heaps. The prophet Hepanaia fell, shot dead, near the redoubt. Another man, Te Wiwini, a very brave young fellow, walked boldly and fearlessly up, firing as he went, until he actually reached the trench below the parapet before he was killed. My father Tiopira was shot dead, and so also was his brother Hapeta. It was for them that my grandfather Tamati Hone composed his great song of lamentation, which you already know. Hare te Kokai was killed; he was the man who had foolishly advocated the frontal attack on the redoubt. Kingi Parengarenga was killed. Mohi Tarakihi, of Kingi's tribe, was killed. He was an old warrior who had been taken captive by the Ngapuhi long ago, and had since then been a Christian *kai-karakia* or teacher.

"About fifty of our *ope* were killed there, besides many wounded. Families fell there. It was a one-sided fight, a miserable fight (*he mate rihariha*), for, in spite of the desperate courage of our warriors, we could not get at the soldiers; they were safe behind their strong walls.

"Titokowaru was one of my relatives wounded in this attack. A glancing blow from a bullet just above one of his eyes destroyed its sight. Tauke, of Hokorima, was wounded in the hand. Te Ua was not present at the fight.

"We survivors all retreated to Manutahi, and there my wounds were bathed with flax-juice, and in about a month I was able to travel again, and I returned to my home at Okaiawa, in the Ngati-Ruanui country. Boiled flax-root water poured on the wounds, and also dock-root (*runa*), well scraped and boiled, were our favourite remedies for gunshot and bayonet wounds."

Such was Te Kahu-pukoro's stirring story of his first battle. The terrible slaughter of Hepanaia's deluded followers temporarily weakened the new confidence in Pai-marire, but Te Ua had a satisfying explanation—namely, that those who fell were to blame because they did not repose absolute faith in the *karakia*. The fanatic religion soon took strong hold upon every West Coast tribe, and was carried by apostles to the east and north, and presently in scores of villages *niu* masts of worship were erected, and daily the wildly excited people marched in procession round and round the pole where the brightly coloured war-flags flew.

The memory of Te Morere is kept ever before the minds of Te Kahu-pukoro's people in a beautiful poem of mourning for the dead, composed by Tamati Hone, of the Nga-Ruahine, for his sons Tiopira (Te Kahu's father) and Hapeta, killed in the charge on the British redoubt. This lament was chanted, too, over Te Kahu himself when the old warrior of the Tekau-ma-rua was laid to rest. I translate from the Maori original, which ends with a comparison of the dead who strewed the glacis of Morere Hill to a wrecked and shattered fleet of war-canoes:—

The lightning's spear flashed redly down
On Turamoe peak,
Omen of warriors' death and women's woe,
Portent that boded forth thy fall,
O Tiopira !
Thou who didst stand in brave array
In the bows of the canoe,
And thou, Hapeta ! cold thou liest ;
Death spread his lure for thee !

Ah me, my sons !
My flock of happy forest-birds
That flew from tree to tree in brighter days—
Now fast in woodsman's snare.

My beautiful, my slender *totara,*
Shattered by wintry gale.
My tall red-painted warrior band,
How grand ye dashed upon the foe,
And I—I saw ye go ,
I, too, rushed naked to the fight,
O sons, at Morere !

O heroes of my house,
How grand that charge,
Beyond Whakaahurangi's woods that day !
Lonely I lie within my home
Beside Kapuni's river-mouth,
And cherish bitter thoughts, and ever weep—
My sons !

Lofty and lone stands Taranaki
In the West ;
So tall and splendid thou, O Kingi—
And now thou'rt gone !
Still o'er the forests, still above the clouds
Towers Taranaki ;
But Kingi's gone. Foremost in council,
Foremost in the fight.
I searched the reddened field; I found him dead
At Morere !

O restless sea,
Beating for ever on the sounding sands
Below the cliffs of Wharau,
Like thee, ever I'll lament.
Oh, sons, arise ! Return ! Return !
Cannot your prophets make you live again—
Restore your breath, and bind your wounds?
Ah me—my hopes !

The billows from the west roll in
And thundering crash on Tataraimaka's shore—
There, too, my children fought,
And red-eyed, furious, leaped in battle-dance.
On lone Morere's hill they fell ;
There shattered lay my tribe, ah me !
O simple ones and brave !
Entrapped in Whiro's snare—
The snare of Fate !

Ye charged along the path of Death !
Ye were deceived—
Beguiled by that false path,
The path of Hau !

How vain your valour, vain your charge
Against Morere's walls !
Lost on that rocky coast of death
Are all my crews—
Tainui, Tokomaru, Kurahaupo, Aotea—
Ah me ! my brave canoes
Lie broken on the shore!

After a sketch by Mr. S. Percy Smith, 1865]

Mataitawa Stockade and Barracks, North Taranaki

MANUTAHI AND TE AREI

Some months after the attack on Sentry Hill the neighbouring Hauhau *pa* Manutahi was captured by the British in this way: On the 8th September, 1864, Colonel Warre, with a force of 500 Regulars and Militia and some friendly Maoris, advanced upon Mataitawa, and found the direct approach blocked by a stockaded fort at Manutahi. The Bush Rangers, under Major Atkinson, skirmished up and were received by a fire from the palisades. Major Ryan, with a company of the 70th, and Captain Martin, R.A., with two guns, came on in support, and on the flank of the position being turned the natives abandoned the stockade. The fortification was of a rather unusual figure. It was nearly 150 yards in length, and the shape was somewhat that of a double concave lens, 20 yards wide in the middle but expanding towards the flanks, which rested on the bush on either side. The place was built across an open fern patch; the track to Mataitawa went through the bush in rear. The *pa* had parapets 8 feet to 10 feet thick in rear of the palisading and casemated covered ways. The troops pushed on without further opposition and secured Mataitawa. The *niu* flagstaff at Manutahi was cut down, and the palisading and *whares* were destroyed. One Maori was killed and one mortally wounded in the encounter.

On the 11th September Colonel Warre, with three companies of the 70th Regiment under Major Rutherford, 150 men under Major Saltmarshe, and an advance-guard of fifty friendly Maoris, marched towards Te Arei *pa,* the fortress which had so long baffled Major-General Pratt in 1860–61. The force got within a few hundred yards of the pa under cover of thick fog. When discovered the troops were fired on by the Maoris on the hill, but the place was soon abandoned. The works were found to be very formidable. There were trenches 15 feet wide, and—a novelty in Maori fortification—a parapet about 16 feet thick, covered by a line of rifle-pits or a covered way, about 40 feet in front of the line of the stockade. Thus, had artillery been used, the Maori defenders, being in front of instead of in rear of the stockade, would have been entirely under cover. The shot and shell thrown into the stockade would have been quite ineffectual, and the garrison would have been able to receive any attacking column after the palisades had apparently been breached. Lieutenant Ferguson, R.E., had the construction of a redoubt on this very beautiful and commanding position overlooking the Waitara.

NOTES

The original of the lament for the dead at Te Morere, as recited to me by Te Kahu-pukoro and Whareaitu, begins:—

E hiko te uira ki tai ra,
Kapo taratahi ana
Te tara ki Turamoe,
He tohu o te mate, na—i.

The poem is chanted to-day on the death of people of the Nga-Ruahine and other clans of Ngati-Ruanui.

Sentry Hill as it is to-day is an example of the unfortunate destruction of a famous national monument. All that remains of the fort-hill is a mere shell, like a hollow tooth. The crest of the mound has disappeared, and Morere has been gutted—cut away by the Railway and local bodies, and spread over the rail-lines as ballast and the roads as metal. When I last visited the place I found only a portion of one of the flanking earthworks as yet undestroyed. If the work of demolition were stayed now it would be possible to save part of the hill as a war memorial, but the celebrated Morere has been disfigured hopelessly.

A famous place in American history which suffered a similar fate to that which had befallen Sentry Hill is Pawnee Rock well described by Colonel Inman in "The Old Santa Fé Trail." This great rock, the scene of many fights between United States troops and frontiersmen and the Indian warriors, has been torn away by the railroad and the settlers, Colonel Inman records, and little now remains of the famous landmark. Recently, however, the Government erected a monument to mark the spot.

Chapter 3

THE BATTLE OF MOUTOA

NEARLY FIFTY MILES up the Wanganui a low shingly island, roughly diamond-shaped and about half a mile in length, lies in the course of the strong river, with rapids above and below and on either side. The upper part of this island—the only one in the Wanganui—is composed of bare shingle and boulders; the lower half is covered with *manuka* and fern, with a few trees. This is Moutoa ("Isle of Heroes"), a famous battle-ground of the river tribes. Many a combat to the death has taken place on the desert island, set in the midst of the rapids, and the most celebrated of all was also the last, the battle of the 14th May, 1864, when the Lower Wanganui tribes routed a picked war-party of the up-river Hauhaus, killed fifty of them, and saved Wanganui Town from invasion. Moutoa lies about half a mile above the large native village of Ranana, and two and a half miles below the settlement Hiruharama (Jerusalem). A short distance above the island, on the right bank, is the pretty little village of Tawhitinui, with its abundant groves of fruit-trees. Here an old native war-track comes in from Weraroa, on the Waitotara River. This village was the rendezvous of the Hauhaus before the battle which decided the political destinies of the Wanganui tribes.

Soon after the surprise and slaughter of the British party under Captain Lloyd at Te Ahuahu, Te Ua and his chief adherents in Taranaki determined to send the heads of the slain soldiers (perfectly preserved from decay by the ancient process of drying with heat and smoke) from tribe to tribe throughout the Island, and the Upper Wanganui people were the first selected for the proselytizing process. Matene Rangi-tauira, who came from the Upper Wanganui, was dispatched with a party to the Waitotara and Pipiriki, carrying Lloyd's head. He found the natives of Pipiriki and neighbouring settlements ready and willing to embrace the Pai-marire faith; they were very bitter over the losses their tribes had sustained at Katikara, Tataraimaka, in the previous year, when the casualties in the storming of the entrenchments by the British force were nearly all

Wanganui men. The kinsmen of the fallen warriors received Matene and his trophy with savage enthusiasm. A *niu* mast was erected under the prophet's directions on the *marae* in the large village of Pipiriki; it stood on the west or proper right bank of the Wanganui, opposite the site of the present hotel and township, which was then a cultivation ground known as Te Kapua, with the flour-mill on the Kaukore Stream. The spot where the pole of worship stood was on a terrace at the landing-place a little below the Rangiahua Hill, the beautiful wooded headland (opposite the steamer-wharf) which is a blaze of *kowhai* flowers in the spring of the year.

Mr. Booth, who was the Resident Magistrate and Government Agent at Pipiriki, and his brother and family were the only Europeans living in the district. They had a very narrow escape from death in the dangerously changed temper of the people, but were at last permitted to leave in a canoe, leaving all their property behind, and reached Wanganui safely. Living under Mr. Booth's guardianship was a little half-caste boy about eight years of age, the son of a British military officer and a chieftainess of the Atiawa Tribe of Taranaki; the mother was dead, and the father had returned to England, entrusting the boy to Mr. Booth for education. Booth endeavoured to take this lad away with him, but the Hauhaus would not permit it, and kept him with them; and he retains to this day a very vivid memory of the thrilling scenes that followed his guardian's departure.*

The white soldier's head (it is known now that it was Captain Lloyd's) was passed round from hand to hand in the Pai-marire ceremonies at the foot of the *niu*. It is described as that of a fair-whiskered man with shaven chin, in the fashion of those days. The head had been thoroughly dried in the *mokomokai* or *paki-paki-upoko* process. Its bearer, the prophet Matene, was a tall

---

* This eye-witness, Mr. H. D. Bates, is a resident of Wanganui. He is the son of Colonel H. Stretton Bates (65th Regiment), who died in England in 1918. Colonel Bates was a subaltern in New Zealand before and during the first Taranaki War, and acquired a good knowledge of the Maori language. He was at one time A.D.C. to Sir George Grey, and in Taranaki and Waikato he was staff interpreter to General Cameron. His wife, a *rangatira* woman of Te Atiawa, closely related to Te Whiti, died when the little son was three years old. She was a granddaughter of the chief Matangi, who was the first to sign the deed of sale of the site of Wellington City to the New Zealand Company in 1839; her father was Manihera Matangi, of Ngauranga, Wellington, a fine-looking well-tattooed chief, who was a great favourite with the pioneer colonists. Colonel Bates was a clever artist in water-colours, and some of his drawings of war-scenes, lent by his son, are reproduced in Volume I of this History.

It was through the help of the Governor, Sir George Grey, that young Bates was recovered from the Hauhaus on the Waitotara and restored to his guardian, Mr. Booth, at Wanganui.

man with long hair and a flowing black beard. He led the people in their newly learned chantings, and round and round the sacred mast the half-crazed devotees marched. In their procession they came closer and closer to the *niu,* until many of them embraced it, one after another, and revolved about it, whirling round and round until they sank at its foot in a fit of giddiness and religious mania. The white man's head was passed from hand to hand among the frenzied worshippers, and there were some extraordinary scenes of fanatic fury. Some of the people, particularly those who had lost relatives in the Taranaki War, gnawed the dried flesh in their demonstrations of hatred and revenge. One, a handsome young woman, who had been brought up in Mr. Booth's family and who had been regarded as a quiet, gentle girl, was so overcome by the new madness that she snatched the *pakeha's* head from her neighbour at the *niu* and bit the flesh of the neck with horrible savagery. The people, indeed, were transformed by Matene's teachings; the appeal to the feelings of revenge swept them along irresistibly, and made them easy instruments in the prophet's unauthorized plan of campaign.

The adherents of Pai-marire, incited by Matene and other leaders, determined upon a bold attack on Wanganui Town, and a flotilla of war-canoes was prepared. Each *waka-taua* was decorated with carved figurehead and streaming plumes after the ancient fashion. A message was sent to the Ngati-Hau Tribe at Hiruharama asking them to join in the attack on the whites. Ngati-Hau were otherwise inclined, and immediately summoned the down-river tribes to their assistance against the Hauhaus.

The people of Hiruharama and other Ngati-Hau villages removed down the river in a body to Ranana, below Moutoa Island. Matene and his Pai-marire host—men, women, and children—embarked in their war-canoes and swept down the Wanganui to Tawhitinui Village, which they occupied and fortified. A message was sent to the chiefs at Ranana, saying that they intended to pass down the river to drive the Europeans into the sea. An uncompromising refusal of the right of way was returned by Haimona Hiroti, Mete Kingi, and the other leaders, not so much out of regard for the *pakeha* of the Town of Wanganui as for the *mana* of their river. Ngati-Hau, Ngati-Pamoana, and the lower-river men were resolved to resist to the utmost the insolent passage of an enemy war-party. " If you attempt to force your way down the river," they replied to Matene, " we shall fight you on Moutoa".

The challenge was accepted, and it was arranged through the messengers between Tawhitinui and Ranana that the issue should be fought out on the following morning, the 14th May.

Both camps were busy all the day before the fight making

cartridges, moulding lead into bullets, and drying gunpowder, spread carefully on cloth, and in the evening there were *hakas* and war dances and fervid *whai-korero* or speech-making. In the Hauhau quarters the Pai-marire ceremonies and chantings were continued nearly all night, and even the children were schooled in their part for the great conflict on the morrow. The women took them in hand, and (as Mr. Booth's protégé of 1864 relates) they were instructed to give a kind of moral support to the warriors by waving their hands, open palms backward toward their shoulders, calling as they did so, *"Hapa! Hapa!"* ("Pass over!"), so that the bullets would fly harmlessly past their champions' heads. The children went into this new war-game with enormous zest, and there was little sleep in Tawhitinui that night.

Very early in the morning the picked warriors of the Hauhau force, numbering about a hundred and twenty, crossed over in state to the island for battle. It was little more than a push-off, but they crossed with all ceremony in their great canoes, carved, painted, and plumed for war. Grounding the canoes on the shingly beach at the upper end of the island, they leaped ashore and lined up for the war-dance, the necessary prelude to battle. The eager spectators, gathered on the green terrace at Tawhitinui, saw their warriors dance their *peruperu,* led off by the big black-bearded prophet, and then watched them move toward the middle of the island and enter the *manuka* thickets.

The loyalist or friendly Maoris had in the meantime posted a selected band of their fighters in the scrub on the island. This party had crossed from the Ranana side of the river at the break of day. It numbered a hundred. Half of the warriors crouched in the thick cover near the middle of the Island; their leader was a chief of great courage and determination, Tamehana te Aewa. The remaining fifty men, under Haimona Hiroti (of Ngati-Pamoana), another good soldier, were posted at the lower end of the island. The main body of the Lower Wanganui men, who had marched over the hill from Ranana, did not cross to the island, but remained as a reserve on the left bank of the river.

The advance-guard of the friendlies allowed the Hauhaus to come some distance in from the beach and then opened fire. The first volley, fired at close range, was too high, and none of the Hauhaus fell. Many of the Kupapas—the Government party—then were seized by sudden fears; they were doubtful whether after all the Pai-marire devotees were not invulnerable to bullets. The Hauhaus came charging on, and the Lower Wanganui men gave way before them, losing several men. Meanwhile the hundreds of spectators on either bank of the river watched with uncontrollable excitement the progress of the battle on the island

Moutoa Island, Wanganui River

below them. The hills echoed with the continuous thundering of the heavily charged double-barrel guns, and the fighting yells of both factions rang across the river, but little could be seen, for the island was soon half-hidden in gunpowder-smoke.

As soon as the first shots were heard all the Hauhau onlookers set to at their magic-working incantations. Seated in rows on the Tawhitinui terrace, they cried their Pai-marire spell prayers. Led by the women, the children waved imaginary bullets back over their shoulders with both hands, exclaiming as they did so, "*Hapa! Hapa! Hapa!*" The old women were crazy with excitement, running back and forward, reciting their high chants, and crying to the young people, "*Kai kaha te hapa! Kia kaha te hapa!*" ("Let your *hapa* be strong!") bidding them redouble their efforts; and into it the children went as hard as they could go, throwing Kupapa bullets over their shoulders—"*Hapa! Hapa! Hapa!*"

Down on the smoke-hazed island the battle was turning against the friendlies. The Hauhaus, encouraged by their first success, were steadily forcing Tamehana te Aewa's party toward the lower end of Moutoa. Some were panic-stricken and were ready to abandon the fight, but the gallant Tamehana, by a desperate effort, rallied his men and stayed the Hauhau advance. After shooting two Hauhaus, one with each barrel of his *tupara,* he killed a third man with a spear, and another with a tomahawk. He continued his fight with another gun, killing a fifth man, when he was put out of action by a bullet which broke his leg, shattering the knee-cap. Haimona Hiroti now dashed into the battle with his supports, and, joined by Tamehana's unwounded men, charged upon the Hauhaus with irresistible force. The combat was hand to hand with tomahawk and gun-butt. The Hauhaus were driven to the beach and into the river; they had no time to think of launching their canoes. More than forty lay dead on the island; some were shot or tomahawked in the water.

The finale to this great tournament was the killing of Matene Rangi-tauira the prophet. He had received a wound, and was swimming across the river to the right bank. Haimona Hiroti, standing on the gravel beach of Moutoa, gave his whalebone club (*patu-paraoa*) to one of his men, Te Moro (afterwards a policeman in Wanganui), and, pointing to the shaggy black head of the struggling prophet, said, "Yonder is your fish." Te Moro dashed into the rapid river and overtook Matene just as the prophet reached the Tawhitinui side of the river and grasped an overhanging shrub in an effort to drag himself out of the water. The Kupapa warrior, seizing him by his long hair, killed him with a smashing blow of his *patu* on the side of the head. Te Moro returned to the island, hauling the dead priest of Pai-marire by his hair, and, dragging the body ashore where Haimona stood watching, said to his chief, "*Ina to ika!*" ("Here is your fish!")

The Hauhaus lost about fifty killed, and had nearly as many of their number wounded. The Kupapa faction lost less heavily; fifteen men were killed and thirty wounded: the dead included the chiefs Kereti, Hemi Nape, and Riwai Tawhito-rangi. The brave Tamehana, who turned the tide of war against the Hauhaus, was taken down to Wanganui with the other wounded, and had one of his legs amputated. The casualties on both sides were extremely heavy in proportion to the numbers engaged. One European lost his life: this was Lay-Brother Euloge, who was a member of the Roman Catholic Mission, under Father Lampila, at Kauaeroa, a mile above Tawhitinui. He was shot while in charge of a small party of the mission Maoris who had been posted on the left bank opposite the upper end of the island.

The battle over, the downcast spectators on the *marae* at Tawhitinui were hurriedly joined by the *morehu,* the survivors of their war-party. In intense sorrow and dejection the defeated braves climbed the bank and stood there before their weeping friends, a long line of weary men. Many had suffered tomahawk-cuts and bullet-wounds, and the blood flowed down their naked chests and limbs. With heads bowed in sorrow and humiliation they stood there by the *niu,* which had lost its magic virtue, for its prophet lay dead on Moutoa. A little old chief, very fierce and wild, ran up and down in front of them gesticulating with his tongue-pointed *taiaha,* shouting himself hoarse, and heaping taunts upon them for their defeat.

The Hauhaus did not remain long in Tawhitinui after their crushing repulse. Had the Kupapas under Hiroti and Mete Kingi followed up the victory on the island and rushed Tawhitinui they could have killed every one, but they rested content with their chivalrous fight on Moutoa. The tribes from up-river, however, feared a renewal of the attack, and so all the women and children were hurried up a wooded valley in rear of the village across country by the war-track to the Waitotara River. They came out at Perekama, a large settlement of Ngarauru on the Waitotara below the Weraroa *pa*. The fighting-men remained awhile at Tawhitinui and followed up as a rearguard. Perekama became the Hauhau headquarters, and the fort on the commanding hill at Weraroa, overlooking the whole of the lower Waitotara country, was enlarged and strongly garrisoned.

Desultory fighting betwen the Upper and Lower Wanganui tribes followed Moutoa, and lasted until early in 1865. Pehi Turoa, Pehi Hitaua, and Topine te Mamaku were among the Hauhau chiefs prominent in the hostilities; on the side of the friendlies the old chief Hori Kingi te Anaua and his kinsmen, Mete Kingi and Hone Wiremu Hipango were the principal leaders. The heaviest fighting was at Ohoutahi, five miles below Pipiriki and near Hiruharama, in February, 1865. Both sides fortified themselves here, and several men were killed. The friendlies lost their leading fighting chief, Hone Wiremu Hipango: his body was brought down to Wanganui and buried with military honours at Putiki-wharanui.

Like the Clan Quhele and the Clan Chattan in the classic combat on the Inch of Perth, the Wanganui men fought for the honour of the tribe. To Mete Kingi, Haimona Hiroti, and their fellow-warriors the chief issue was whether a hostile war-party should be permitted to force a passage down the river. But they fought also to protect Wanganui Town, and their determined stand won the gratitude of the townspeople and the Government. A monument below the old stockade hill of Pukenamu, in Wanganui Town, bears the names of the fifteen Maoris and Lay-Brother Euloge, and the inscription "To the memory of the brave men who fell at Moutoa, 14th May, 1864, in defence of law and order against fanaticism and barbarism."

Chapter 4

THE SIEGE OF PIPIRIKI

SOON AFTER THE Battle of Moutoa Island and the skirmishing at Ohoutahi the military authorities determined to establish a post at Pipiriki, fifty-five miles up the Wanganui, in order to hold the river against the passage of the hostile tribes under Pehi Turoa, Topine te Mamaku, and other powerful chiefs of the Upper Wanganui. Pipiriki was selected because it was a convenient line of demarcation between the Hauhau tribes and those friendly to the Europeans; it was also the point at which overland tracks from the eastern part of the Island reached the great inland waterway. For some years there had been a Church mission school at Pipiriki; there was a flour-mill driven by water-power, and there was a considerable amount of cultivation on both sides of the river. It was a kind of advanced frontier post, beyond which the chiefs of old Maoridom held undisputed rule. The upper waters of the Wanganui were an almost unknown region to the *pakeha;* even in the "sixties" very few except adventurous colonial travellers, missionaries, and occasional military officers had ventured up as far as the Manganui-o-te-Ao or to Taumarunui by canoe. One or two pioneer missionaries, such as the Rev. Richard Taylor, were the only men who were at all intimately acquainted with the geography of the people of this wild part of New Zealand, where the swift river, the narrow gorges, and the roadless ranges were the inhabitants' almost impregnable defences.

The force sent up the Wanganui river to Pipiriki at the end of April, 1865, consisted of Nos. 8 and 9 Companies of the Taranaki Military Settlers, under Captains T. Wilson and Pennefather, and a company of the Patea Rangers, under Lieutenant J. Hirst. Major Willoughby Brassey, N.Z. Militia, a veteran of the Indian and Afghan wars, was in command of the expedition. One of the officers of the Patea Rangers was Captain W. Newland, a young Taranaki-born soldier; he served with great distinction throughout the wars from 1860. Dr. J. B. Suther was the surgeon of the force. The expedition was despatched from New Plymouth to Wanganui, and, after being taken a short distance up the river in the steamer "Gundagai" (Captain Fairchild), marched to Parikino and there embarked in canoes for Pipiriki. The European force, numbering two hundred, was joined by a Native Contingent (Lower Wanganui men), about sixty strong. The canoe flotilla, numbering some scores of long river-craft, laden with men, baggage, and stores, paddled and poled up the swift river, the native crews inspired by the stirring chants of their captains. Major Atkinson, then Defence Minister, accompanied the expedition, and returned to Wanganui after he had seen Major Brassey established at Pipiriki.

The position taken up was on the right (west) bank of the river, close to the Pipiriki native settlement and directly opposite the terrace on which the present township and the Pipiriki Hotel stand. Three earthwork redoubts were built close to each other. The main work, No. 1 Redoubt, was built on the ridge at the bend of the Wanganui near the prominent wooded hill called Rangiahua, overlooking the river; there was a much better site, but it was a Maori *wahi tapu,* or burial-place, and so was not occupied. The second redoubt, Popoia, was built on a spur, a little to the north-west of Rangiahua Hill, nearly opposite the present steamer landing-place; and No. 3 Redoubt was thrown up on the south side, close to an ancient native *pa* called Koanga-o-Rehua, and about 500 yards from No. 1 Redoubt.

The main position was garrisoned by the Taranaki Military Settlers. The Native Contingent, under Kepa te Rangihiwinui (Captain Kemp, afterwards Major), and the Patea Rangers built the other redoubts. After some weeks the Native contingent was ordered down the river again to assist in the operations against the Weraroa *pa,* on the Waitotara.

The arrival of the Government force at Pipiriki and the fortification of the positions commanding the river were accepted by the Hauhaus as a challenge, and before long a formidable body of warriors nearly a thousand strong was assembled in camps on both sides of the Wanganui a short distance above the Pipiriki landing.

The Hauhaus included all the Upper Wanganui *hapus* as high up as Taumarunui, and many men of Ngati-Maniapoto, Ngati-Raukawa, and Ngati-Tuwharetoa. The leading chief was Pehi Turoa, the *rangatira* of highest rank on the Wanganui. The principal position occupied by the natives was Pukehinau *pa,* a commanding fortification on a hill about a quarter of a mile in rear of the terrace on which the present township stands. Another large camp was pitched on a terrace about two miles higher up the river, at a place called Ohinemutu, on the same side as the redoubts. The usual Pai-marire pole of worship was erected on each side of the river. That set up by the Pukehinau force stood near the site of the present Pipiriki Hotel. It was 60 feet or 70 feet in height, with a butt 18 inches in diameter; it was crossed with a yard like a ship's, and was firmly stayed; and from its halliards flew the Hauhau war-flags, in designs of black, red, and white.

No hostilities occurred until well on in July. Meanwhile the Upper Wanganui was lively with warrior crews paddling furiously down to reinforce the Pipiriki camps for a grand assault on the *pakeha* forts. Friendly natives in the village near the redoubts conveyed warnings to Major Brassey, through Lieutenant Newland (who acted as interpreter after Mr. Booth, the Resident Magistrate, had gone to Wanganui). The friendlies predicted an early assault, and the Major took additional precautions. The troops lay down at night fully accoutred, ready to turn out at an instant's call. A picket of six men had been maintained at the store-tent on the river-bank where canoes landed, but on the evening of the 18th July Major Brassey fortunately called in the picket; and this saved it, as was afterwards discovered, from a planned attack which would have annihilated it.

On the morning of the 19th July Lieutenant Chapman, of the Patea Rangers, when walking down towards the picket tent, was attacked from ambush at close quarters, but escaped to his redoubt. This was the beginning of fighting which developed into a regular siege and lasted for twelve days. The Hauhaus seized the *wahi tapu,* or burial-place, and opened a heavy plunging fire on the Taranaki Military Settlers' position (No. 3 Redoubt, called the "Gundagai"). The range was not more than about 30 yards. Other Hauhaus appeared on the ridge in rear of the main redoubt and commenced sniping at the troops. It was necessary to drive the Maoris off Rangiahua at all costs, and this was done by Lieutenant Clery with a party of twenty men, who gallantly stormed the position with the bayonet. Clery was slightly wounded, and two of his men were hit, but none were killed. The Hauhaus lost several shot dead as they fled from the bayonets into the low bush at the foot of the hill. The Maoris had begun to entrench themselves on the hill; these rifle-pits were completed by the captors of the position, and a small field-work was thrown up and defended until the end of the siege.

Meanwhile the position of the Rangers and Military Settlers withstood a general attack by the main body from the broken ground in the rear. The Hauhaus in strong force marched along the right bank of the river from Ohinemutu, and appeared on the side of the range about a third of a mile from Rangiahua. "We had a magnificent view of them as they advanced," narrated Captain Newland. "It was the finest sight I ever saw.

They had fuzzed out their hair in an extraordinary way; none of us had ever seen Maoris do this before. They had wooden trumpets 4 feet or 5 feet long, on which they played some of our bugle-calls."

The greater number of this war-party halted in a gully, and Newland and the Rangers, who had a better view of their enemy than the men in the headquarters redoubt, opened fire at a range of about 200 yards. The fire was effective; the Hauhaus were in close order, and many of them fell. They abandoned their intended assault in force and scattered for cover, dragging their dead and wounded away. Some hastily dug rifle-pits on the hills; others returned the Rangers' fire under cover of the bush and *manuka* and the inequalities of the ground. The earthworks of the corps, however, gave good cover; the parapets were high and well loopholed. The tents were struck when the fighting began, and bundled up on top of the parapet, facing the main body of the Hauhaus, to give additional head-protection.

This frustrated rush in a body gave place to sniping and guerrilla tactics. From the 19th to the 30th July the high wooded hills about Pipiriki swarmed with Hauhau musketeers, abundantly supplied with ammunition, and from entrenched positions on the high ground they maintained a persistently heavy and annoying fire. There was little to fire at in return, except the puffs of smoke from the Hauhau guns, and orders were given to be careful of the ammunition, as the reserve supply was not large. Half a dozen of the best shots of the Rangers were told off to reply to the enemy's fire. Three of the snipers were Sergeant J. R. Rushton (now Captain), Sergeant C. MacDonald, and Private George Foreman. Firing steadily, these sharpshooters kept the Hauhaus well to their cover. Sometimes a reckless fanatic would leap on to a parapet showing on the hillside, and yell Hauhau chants and battle-cries. A prophetess, who apparently believed that her Atua Pai-marire had given her immunity from bullet-wounds, was conspicuous in front of one of the entrenchments on the high ground above the redoubts. She paraded up and down, chanting her songs, and cheering on her warriors with cries of "*Riria, riria!*" ("Fight on, fight on!") Marvellously she escaped death many times. Sergeant Rushton, after an unsuccessful shot, said to his comrade Sergeant McDonald. "I was low; try her at full 400 yards." The marksman fired, and Rushton, watching through his glasses, saw the warrior chieftainess fall. It was learned afterwards that she had been shot through the head.

The Hauhaus frequently changed their positions and dug fresh rifle-pits during the night. On the third morning after the fighting began, Newland was ordered out with twenty of his

Rangers to storm some freshly dug trenches. He advanced the men by rushes, firing, and charged with fixed bayonets, under a heavy fire, from several positions; and the Hauhaus ran. The rifle-pits were filled in, and the party returned to their redoubt without loss.

By day the swarming Hauhaus kept up a continual fire from the whole face of the hills above the redoubts; the nights were unrestful with their Pai-marire chantings and their loud fighting speeches and watch-cries. They sounded bugle calls in imitation of the soldiers; some of them had learned the "Reveille," the "Advance," and other military calls, and played them on their *tetere*—the trumpets made with twisted-up green flax-leaves or hollowed-out *tutu* branches with mouthpieces. Similar bush bugles were used by the garrison of Weraroa *pa,* on the Waitotara. On both sides of the river the Hauhau gunmen were busy, opening their fire at daylight in the mornings. Some of them had good cover in the narrow gorge of the Kaukore, the small stream on which the old flour-mill stands, below the terrace opposite Rangiahua. This flour-mill, driven by the crew, had been built by the Booth brothers for the furtherance of agricultural industry among the natives; it now became the haunt of Pai-marire snipers, who gave the beleaguered force a good deal of trouble. The *niu* which stood on that side of the river at the cultivation ground called Te Kapua, in full view of the redoubts, was the centre of daily gatherings. Hundreds of Hauhaus, in a fury of fanatic exaltation, marched round and round the flagstaff chanting their hymns. The warriors, as they barked out their "*Hau, hau!*" at the end of every Pai-marire verse, brought the butts or the muzzles of their guns and rifles sharply down against the foot of the mast. When the siege was over and the Maoris were dispersed the troops found the *niu*-butt marked with the blows from innumerable guns delivered in this way.*

---

* Captain J. R. Rushton, of Kutarere, Ohiwa, narrates the following incident: "For several days we had been much annoyed by a Hauhau sniper, at about 350 yards from our redoubt, across the river. Just on dusk one evening Corporal David White and myself got across in a canoe unseen, and when under cover we drew him by a shot from our hiding-place. He banged at our smoke, and exposed himself, when we covered him, both firing at the same time. We could not go to look, but he never troubled us again. We made exit quick to our canoe and paddled across the Wanganui."

Captain Rushton adds: "Our enemy Topia Turoa, the chief of the rebels, took the oath of allegiance afterwards and joined Colonel McDonnell's forces in pursuit of Te Kooti in the Bay of Plenty. I was chief scout at Opotiki at the time, and found Topia to be a very good fellow."

The Government positions were completely hemmed in, for the Hauhaus not only held the hills but drew their lines between the redoubts and the river. The Rangers were in bad straits for water. The only way they could obtain it was by crawling down through the bushes at night to a spring on the lower side of the redoubt and bringing up in buckets a scant supply for the next day. Rations ran low—in the end they were reduced to quarter-rations of biscuit and salt meat; but, curiously, there was plenty of grog, and the men got three tots of rum a day. Despite the care exercised in the expenditure of ammunition, the supply was running very short. The position was one of great anxiety for Major Brassey and his small force, outnumbered five or six times by the Hauhau army. It was considered that the natives were sure to make a resolute attempt to storm the redoubts. Probably it was only the fear of the bayonet that prevented such an assault.

Major Brassey now determined to try and communicate with Wanganui. He wrote out a number of messages to headquarters, appealing for relief. Some were written in Latin, some in French, and these were carefully sealed up in bottles and thrown into the river after dark. In each cork a feather was stuck to attract attention. One of these bottle-letters which ran the gauntlet and survived the rapids and the rocks was picked up below Wanganui Town by Mr. G. F. Allen. The message that all were well but ammunition was urgently needed was worded thus: "*Omnes sunt recti. Mitte res belli statim.*" Another Latin message was brought in by a friendly Maori by way of Waitotara; it ran, "*Sumus sine rebus belli satis,*" which was the Major's terse way of informing the authorities that he was running very short of ammunition. These appeals were delivered to the Militia Office in Wanganui.

In order to make sure that the authorities were informed of the garrison's critical position Major Brassey resolved also to communicate with the town by canoe. Volunteers were called for, and two men of the Patea Rangers, Sergeant Constable and Private A. Edgecombe, were chosen for the perilous mission. Taking Major Brassey's despatches, they quietly put off in a small canoe under cover of darkness and made the river passage safely. At Hiruharama they met a relief expedition, under Major Rookes, in a great fleet of war-canoes manned by the Lower Wanganui friendlies.

Meanwhile fighting had temporarily been suspended. The Hauhaus, to the surprise of the troops, hoisted a white flag; they had heard by secret messages from the lower river of the approach of a relief force. A chief came to the Government headquarters with the white flag and declared that Pehi Turoa wished to make peace. After a great deal of talk it was at last decided that Lieutenant Newland, the acting interpreter, should go up to the main camp at Ohinemutu and discuss the terms of peace. Two Maoris poled the plucky Newland up to the Hauhau headquarters. It was so risky an adventure, in view of the unreliable temper of the enemy, that the commanding officer declined to order the expedition: Newland went as a volunteer. A chief who had gone to the troops as messenger was retained as hostage for the safe return of Newland.

The dangerous mission to Ohinemutu was fruitless. Pehi Turoa told Newland that the people had now changed their minds, and did not intend to go down and surrender. The armed natives sitting round, scowling at the white officer, were clearly in a dangerous mood, and as Newland saw nothing could be done he returned to camp in the canoe, after some very anxious moments when it seemed uncertain whether he would be permitted to return or be put to death. On leaving the Popoia Redoubt to go up-river on his perilous mission he had given instructions to his men to shoot the Hauhau hostage if at the expiration of a certain time he (Newland) had not returned. This native was given in charge of a squad with loaded revolvers. "Never was a Maori more relieved," says a veteran of the Rangers, "than this man was when, within two or three minutes of the time stipulated, the small canoe with Newland safe on board shot round the bend of the river just above the Paparoa Rapid."

Lieutenant Newland reported that there were from a thousand to twelve hundred armed men in the great camp at Ohinemutu, besides women and children; there were warriors there from all parts of the Island. They must have been in severe straits for food-supplies towards the last, and many of them had no shelter from the wintry weather but breakwinds of *manuka* and fern and blanket tents. It was evident that the Hauhaus had never intended to surrender, and extra precautions were taken in the redoubts, for it was thought that the warriors might make a final attack that night. But the anxious night passed without the expected Pai-marire charge; and next morning the canoes of the relief expedition were sighted poling up the bend below Pipiriki, and the river-gorge rang with the canoe choruses of the toiling crews.

The force which raised the siege was composed of a company of Forest Rangers under Major F. Nelson George, a company of Wanganui Rangers under Captain Jones, and Kepa's Native Contingent, in all 300 strong, together with several hundreds of the Lower Wanganui friendly tribes. Major Rookes, an ex-Imperial officer with West African service, who was in charge of

From a photo by the Hon. Sir Maui Pomare]

The Last *Niu*

This last remaining relic of the Pai-marire worship was standing at Maraekowhai, on the upper Wanganui River (53 miles above Pipiriki), when Sir Maui Pomare photographed it in 1905. It is the lower mast of a *niu*, or Hauhau sacred pole, with the lower yard.

the forces in the Wanganui district, commanded the expedition, which brought abundant stores of food and ammunition.

After meeting Major Brassey and finding the long-beleaguered posts all well, Major Rookes took a strong force up the river, some in canoes and some marching along the right bank, to attack the Hauhau camp at Ohinemutu. It was found deserted. The other side of the river was also examined, but the Hauhau army had melted away into the up-river fastnesses. Not a Maori was to be found to make a target for the relief force. Ohinemutu was burned, the cultivations destroyed, and the *niu* poles demolished. The main body of Major Rookes's force returned to Wanganui in a few days, leaving George's Rangers to augment

Brassey's garrison. In August all but Captain Wilson's No. 8 Company, Taranaki Military Settlers, were ordered down the river to embark for Opotiki, and soon afterwards Wilson was relieved by Brevet-Major Shortt with two companies of the 57th Regiment: this force held Pipiriki for the rest of the year.

In the whole of the fighting at Pipiriki Major Brassey's force did not lose a man killed, and only three or four were wounded. The troops found and buried six Hauhaus, and it was known definitely that thirteen were killed. The total Maori casualties were probably about twenty killed and more than that number wounded.

Chapter 5

CAMERON'S WEST COAST CAMPAIGN

THE WESTERN SIDE of the Island, from Wanganui to the White Cliffs in North Taranaki, was the spacious scene in 1865 of an indecisive campaign and a number of small expeditionary operations. Immediately after the New Year Lieut.-General Cameron took the field in the Wanganui district, under instructions to take possession of the Waitotara Block, which had been purchased by the Crown but reoccupied by the natives, and to operate against the hostile tribes from the Kai-iwi to Taranaki. The campaign was chiefly remarkable for the slowness and caution of Cameron's advance, and for the acrimonious correspondence betwen the General and Governor Grey on the conduct of operations. The West Coast tribes had concentrated their forces on the south side of the Waitotara River, and built a strong fortification on the summit of Weraroa Hill, a bold flat-topped height overlooking the river and the surrounding country for many miles. The position can be seen from the present bridge at Waitotara Township, looking up the river. Here at the large village of Perekama, on the river-side flat below, several hundreds of Hauhaus from the Wanganui to the Waitara had assembled, inspired by the presence of their prophet Te Ua Haumene; and when it became known that the General was about to open a war for the possession of the coast and for the occupation of the newly confiscated lands in Taranaki a formidable effort was made to bar his progress northward from the Kai-iwi, which was then Wanganui's frontier. The Hauhaus had carried their forays to within a few miles of Wanganui, and had lately murdered Captain James Duff Hewett, a settler who lived near the Kai-iwi, about eight miles from the town. He was the son of Lieut.-Colonel W. Hewett, of the Rifle Brigade, the last English officer who fought at Waterloo. Hewett's body was decapitated, and the head was carried about the Hauhau settlements on a pole. His heart was also cut out and taken away.

Cameron, marching from Wanganui with about two thousand Imperial troops and two field-guns, pitched his first camp (24th

January, 1865) at Nukumaru, in the South Waitotara district, a short distance inland of the coastal sandhills. The position, on a practically open plain, dotted with small lakes, was fifteen miles from Wanganui; to the north-west was Weraroa *pa*. High *toetoe* reeds, with flax and *tutu* bushes, clothed the level land; near at hand on the right flank of the march was the bush. The camp was suddenly attacked, in daylight, by a strong force of Maoris, supported by a large body in cover. The first volley from the *toetoe* and flax laid low about a dozen men, and the warriors charged right into the camp with gun and tomahawk. Lieutenant Johnston, A.A.G., and fifteen men were killed and thirty-two wounded in this sharp encounter. Major Witchell and his mounted men (Military Train) charged with the sword and forced the Maoris back into cover. The native loss was rather more than the British, but the Hauhaus had the satisfaction of surprising a British camp in broad daylight, and, as the sequel proved, of giving General Cameron such a dislike to the neighbourhood of the bush that for the rest of the campaign he kept as close as possible to the sea-coast.

On the following day the West Coast native army made an even more determined attack upon the General's forces, and drove in the pickets, killing several men. There was heavy skirmishing in the open, and the Maoris fought with great determination and considerable tactical skill. Their fighting leader was Patohe, a very intelligent and bold Hauhau soldier.

Among the Hauhaus who fought at Nukumaru was the late Te Kahu-pukoro, the *Ariki* of the Ngati-Ruanui Tribe. Te Kahu-pukoro was then only a lad of about thirteen, but he had already fought and been wounded at Sentry Hill. (See Chapter 2.) Describing the attack on Cameron's camp, the old warrior declared that it was a *pakanga pai* (an excellent fight), in which the opposing armies met in the open and got to close quarters. Armed with a gun, he took part in the charge into the General's camp, and fought again on the following day. It was a more satisfactory battle than the affair at Sentry Hill in the previous year, where all the odds were against the Maori braves who attempted the assault of a walled fort.

Another Maori veteran of Nukumaru, Tu-Patea te Rongo, gave an animated description of the two days' fighting. Tu-Patea, who lives at Taumaha, is the leading chief of the Pakakohi Tribe, of the Patea district; he fought all though the West Coast War, and in 1868–69 was one of Titokowaru's picked fighting band, the *Tekau-ma-rua*. He is a grey-moustached old soldier, of big athletic frame and strong features, a good type of the active fellows who kept the coast in turmoil up to the beginning of the "seventies."

"Nukumaru," said Tu-Patea, "was my first experience of battle. There were perhaps two thousand Maoris assembled on the Waitotara to bar the General's march northward. We all assembled at Weraroa *pa,* a few miles away, and from there marched down towards the sea to attack the troops. Among the warriors were men from the Waikato and Ngati-Maniapoto, besides a great many from Taranaki. Of our tribe, the chiefs were my father Hau-matao, Tu-mahuki Rongonui, Paraone Tutere, and Kahukura-nui. Te Ua-Haumene, the chief prophet of the Pai-marire, was the man at the head of the assemblage at Weraroa, but our fighting general was Patohe. Te Ua was an *atua*—a god. He remained in Weraroa *pa* while the army was out under Patohe engaging the soldiers. I marched with my father—I was only about thirteen years old—to get my first lesson in the art of war. I carried a short-handled tomahawk. My war-path clothing consisted only of a *koka* of flax, a short roughly dressed mat worn as a *rapaki* around the waist.

"The plain at Nukumaru was covered with fern, flax, and *toetoe,* and from the cover of this our men attacked the troops. In the first day's fighting my uncle Tama-kanohi was shot. I watched the fight. One of our warriors, Pita Weka, charged right into an officer's tent in the camp and shot the officer dead. (This was Adjutant-General Johnston.) Pita was killed in the battle at Te Ngaio, near Kakaramea, not long afterwards. He was a big active young man, a renowned *toa taua,* a bold and experienced warrior. Besides his double-barrel gun, he was armed with a whalebone *patu,* worn in his girdle.

"Our warriors rose from their cover and charged on the soldiers at the command '*Kokiritia!*' from the chiefs, and then '*Puhia*' ('fire'), was the word. When the *pakeha* opened fire on us we held our right hands up on a level with the face, palm open, and cried '*Hapa, hapa!*' ('Pass over!'), the charm which Te Ua told us would prevent the bullets from striking us. Those who acted according to Te Ua's instructions in every respect were not hit. He had his two *atua,* the gods Rura and Riki; but he was also, as I have said, an *atua* himself.

"Amongst the Taranaki high chiefs who fought at Nukumaru were Te Wharepouri and Tohu-Kakahi. Te Whiti was also there. Hone Pihama* was not at Nukumaru, and those who have said

---

* Some writers have wrongly credited Hone Pihama, Patohe's younger brother, with the leadership of the Hauhau forces at Nukumaru. Hone was not distinguished as a fighter. The brothers were chiefs of the Ngati-Hine and Tangahoe Tribes. Ngati-Hine, whose lands extended from Wairoa (now Waverley) to the Tangahoe River, were a particularly enterprising warrior tribe. Hone Pihama was conspicuous in the later days of the Taranaki War as a friend of the Europeans.

he was in command there were quite mistaken. Patohe, his elder brother, was the leader there. Hone Pihama was not a war-loving man. Patohe formerly lived at Ngatiki, near Hawera. He had been a captive in Waikato, where he was tattooed.

"The fighting on the first day at Nukumaru lasted well into the night. We had twenty-three men killed. On the second day we attacked again, when the troops were at dinner; we were all determined to prevent Cameron's advance up the coast. There were Maoris there from all along the West Coast from Otaki up to Waikato. One warrior was a near relative of Rewi Maniapoto; he fell at Te Ngaio a few weeks later. There was a British picket near the scrub in a small field-work. The Maoris crept into this with their tomahawks and disposed of the picket."

Lieut.-General Cameron, shifting camp to a more secure position close to the sandhills, remained there until the night of the 2nd February, when he moved northward. His army had now been augmented to 2,300 of all arms. Marching at night with half the force, he crossed the Waitotara near the mouth on a raft of casks, made by the Royal Engineers, early on the morning of the 3rd. The troops camped on level ground on the right bank. A redoubt for 150 men was built on a precipitous cliff on the left bank, and two field-guns were mounted on it.

On the night of the 15th February this force marched to the mouth of the Patea River; the troops were replaced at the Waitotara by the force left at Nukumaru on the 2nd. The General remained for about a week on the left bank of the Patea, where a redoubt for 200 men was constructed. The main body then crossed to the right bank, a short distance seaward of the present Town of Patea, where a good position was selected on the high ground immediately above the river. Here an entrenched line, with a redoubt in the centre, was formed; the entrenchment enclosed a large area of ground, on which buildings were erected some time later for a large depot of provisions as well as huts for 600 men.

Cameron had made no attempt to reduce the Hauhau headquarters, Wereroa *pa,* and his action in moving up the coast and leaving this strong enemy position untouched in the rear excited strong criticism. He informed Sir George Grey that he considered his force insufficient to besiege the *pa* and keep communications open. The Governor was of a different opinion, and the correspondence between Governor and General developed into a bitter exchange of irreconcilable views. Cameron resolutely declined to waste men's lives on the attack of such an apparently strong position, while Grey was equally determined to obtain possession of the *pa,* the key to the occupation of the

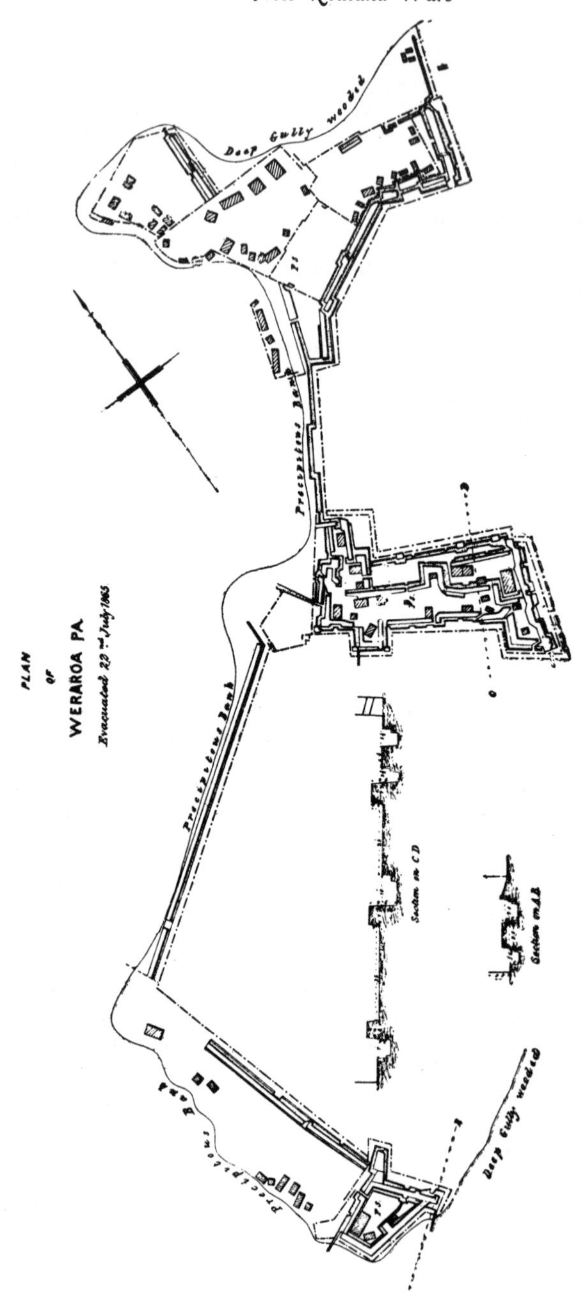

The Weraroa *Pa*, Waitotara.

From a plan, 1865]

West Coast. Cameron's dislike of the operations against the Maoris became very obvious, and many of his officers and men, like himself, had no great desire to be made the instruments of the Colonial Government in what looked to them very like a war of land-plunder.

At the end of January a Government notice was issued proclaiming confiscated native lands in Middle Taranaki as open for settlement under the New Zealand Settlements Act, 1863, and later in the year the confiscated areas of Ngati-Ruanui and other tribal lands were proclaimed. The total area confiscated in the Taranaki–Wanganui district amounted to about 980,000 acres, of which a certain proportion was afterwards returned. The country belonging to Ngati-Ruanui and kindred tribes proclaimed was defined by outer boundaries extending from Mount Egmont to Parikino on the Wanganui River, and thence to the sea, and northward to the Waimate Stream. Including Waikato and other conquered districts, the total area at first proposed to be confiscated was about 8,000,000 acres; but even when this was reduced to 3,000,000 acres there was strong condemnation in some quarters of what was termed the Colonial Government policy of spoliation. The sharp differences of opinion between the Imperial authorities and the Colonial Government on this and other features of the war hastened the day when the people of New Zealand came to rely on their own military resources.

The Wanganui friendly natives requested the Government to permit them to attack the Weraroa *pa,* and, although the Imperial officers discouraged the proposal in every possible way, the Governor presently authorized the expedition and took personal command of the field. The Government also set about enlisting white volunteers for the defence of the frontier and occupation of the confiscated lands, and by the middle of July there were available, besides the Wanganui Native Contingent of about 200 men, two companies of Rangers (with Von Tempsky in command of one) and the Wanganui Yeomanry Cavalry. The Wanganui Maori Contingent was under Captain Thomas McDonnell, with Ensign W. E. Gudgeon as his adjutant—officers who both attained field rank and gave their country distinguished service all through the Hauhau campaigns. The Yeomanry Cavalry was a newly formed corps of frontier horse. The troopers, mostly settlers and their sons, were armed with sword, Terry and Calisher carbine, and revolver; the uniform was Garibaldi jumper, knee-breeches, and long boots. Each man was served out with a waterproof poncho after the Mexican pattern, with an opening in the middle for it to go over his head; it covered not only the rider but his carbine and saddle from the rain. Captain Percy commanded the troop.

The force camped at Maeneene, between Nukumaru and Weraroa, and negotiations, conducted chiefly by Captain McDonnell, were carried on with the Hauhau leaders in Perekama, below the *pa* on the hill-crest. Sir George Grey himself, with the old chief Hori Kingi te Anaua, went up close to the *pa* to summon the garrison to surrender, and was in a position of imminent danger until some of the chiefs persuaded him to retire. The Hauhaus declared they would never surrender. Grey persevered in his preparations, and induced Major-General Waddy to send 400 Imperial troops to Maeneene as a support. On the 20th July a force of about 400 men (Yeomanry Cavalry, dismounted, Forest Rangers, and Maori Contingent), under Major Rookes, executed a skilful turning movement, in very bad weather, by marching under cover of the bush along the Karaka plateau, in rear of the Weraroa, and, in the night, taking up a position commanding the Hauhau villages of Perekama and Arei-ahi. The operation was completely successful. McDonnell and his Maoris surrounded and captured Arei-ahi with all the people, and about sixty fighting-men were taken prisoners, including some twenty warriors of the Ngati-Pukeko Tribe, who had travelled all the way overland from Whakatane, Bay of Plenty, to join in the West Coast fighting, and who were now rounded up just after their arrival. Fifty guns were taken. The prisoners were kept in a stockade hastily run up, and were then, with some others, shipped off to Wellington. There, to the number of eighty, they were placed on board a prison-hulk moored off Kai-wharawhara. Most of them escaped, with their old chief Tataraimaka (who had planned the escape), by swimming ashore one stormy night; many were drowned in the struggle for life. The swimmers devotedly helped their chief ashore; a number of the heroic men perished in the effort.

Weraroa remained to be captured and meanwhile fire was opened on it from the Karaka plateau at a range of 600 yards. A night attack on the *pa* was planned, and a force set out via Perekama* Village, intending to scale the cliff in rear of the fortress. Just before the ascent was begun a Maori brought the news that the *pa* was deserted. In the morning this was found to be the case. The unexpected night march to the rear and

---

* Perekama was the headquarters of the Nga-Rauru and kindred tribes, whose warriors in 1864–65 had a military drill modelled on that of the British soldiers. They had frequent alarms, to accustom them to the emergency of sudden attack, and they had buglers who blew calls on a *tetere,* a long trumpet made of twisted-up green blades of flax. A veteran of the Wanganui Yeomanry Cavalry recalls the fact that on the afternoon and night march via the Karaka plateau the flanking column heard the flax-bugle calls of the Weraroa garrison across the intervening valley sounding very sweet and clear.

the capture of Arei-ahi had convinced the garrison that their stronghold was no longer tenable with safety, and they had slipped out northward and across the Waitotara.

The bloodless capture by means of strategy—otherwise the application of brains to military problems—of a position which General Cameron had declined to attack with two thousand men was a distinct triumph for the Governor, and it tended to widen the breach between him and the Imperial commander. The relief of Pipiriki was the next operation undertaken by the colonial forces.

In the meantime General Cameron had marched in his deliberate way up the coast and had established posts at several places as far as the Wai-ngongoro River. The principal opposition he encountered was at Te Ngaio, in the open country between Patea and Kakaramea. The General, with about a thousand men of all arms, moved out from Patea camp on the 15th March for the Wai-ngongoro. At about two miles from Patea volleys were fired into the column by a body of Maoris posted under cover of a ridge parallel to the line of march, on the right, near the Patea River. The advance-guard was thrown out in skirmishing order, bringing round the left flank to attack the natives. The Hauhaus fell back in good order towards Kakaramea, fighting well in the open, with deliberation and bravery. There were about two hundred natives in action, and for all their inadequate numbers and inferior arms they opposed a manful front to the invading army. Retiring along the swampy ground toward Kakaramea they made the most of their knowledge of the terrain and their native genius in skirmishing, but nearly half of them were shot down. Eighty natives were killed. It was the heaviest blow in point of casualties that the Hauhau tribes suffered in the West Coast War.

Tu-Patea, of Taumaha, describing this engagement of Te Ngaio, which was fought over his own tribal lands, said:—

"I followed my elders into action, armed with my tomahawk. Over two hundred of our people came out to fight in the open. There were five women among them, not armed, but urging the warriors on. One of them, Tutaki's wife, was killed. The principal chiefs were Patohe, my father Hau-Matao, Te Waka-taparuru, Paraone Tutere, and Te Mahuki. Our prophet was the old man Huriwaka, from Otoia, on the Patea. His god was Rura. Huriwaka, before the fight began that morning, prophesied saying, 'To-day's battle will be good; it will be a favourable fight for us.' But we were beaten, and eighty of our people fell on the field of Te Ngaio."

There were many instances of native heroism and daring. An eye-witness, Dr. Grace, surgeon in the force, wrote: "The dignified and martial bearing of the Maori touched the hearts of our soldiers." In the field hospital afterwards General Cameron asked a badly wounded warrior, "Why did you resist our advance? Could you not see we were in overwhelming force?" The Maori replied, "What would you have us do? This is our village; these are our plantations. Men are not fit to live if they are not brave enough to defend their own homes."*

The tribes engaged in the fighting at Te Ngaio were chiefly Ngati-Hine, Pakakohi, and Ngati-Ruanui. It was the final attempt in strength to dispute the right of way with General Cameron. The British casualties were a private of the 57th shot dead and three men wounded.

That afternoon the British force encamped in the captured village of Kakaramea, where a redoubt for 150 men was at once commenced. The position was about six miles from the coast and close to the Patea River; the present Township of Kakaramea is more inland and on higher ground.

On the following day (16 March, 1865) the column moved on and camped at the Maori village Manutahi, three miles from the historic village of Manawapou, on the sea-coast. Detachments were sent to Manawapou, which was on the left bank of the Ingahape River, at the mouth; and, as it seemed practicable to beach boats on the sandy shore on the opposite side of the river, redoubts were constructed on the high ground to cover a depot of stores.

The force, with headquarters, moved from Manutahi on the 29th March, halted for one day a few miles from Manawapou,

---

* "The soldiers," wrote Dr. Grace in his "Sketch of the New Zealand War," "no longer desired to kill the Maori, and disliked more than ever being killed by him." He heard the sympathetic Irish soldiers say, after the exhibition of native bravery at Kakaramea (Te Ngaio): "Begorra, it's a murder to shoot them. Sure they are our own people, with their potatoes and fish, and children. Who knows but they are Irishmen, with faces a little darkened by the sun, who escaped during the persecutions of Cromwell!"

Dr. Grace was in error, however, in a statement that very few of the Maoris were killed in this battle in the flax and *toetoe*. The report of Colonel T. R. Mould, R.E., giving twenty-three as the number killed and mortally wounded, was equally astray. Wells's "History of Taranaki" makes the loss thirty-three killed, left on the field. A list of casualties in Gudgeon's work gives the killed at fifty-six—also under the mark. It was natural that the Maori losses should have been underestimated in the official reports of this and other engagements, as most of the dead were usually carried off the field. It is clear now from the narratives given me by Tu-Patea and other natives that the Hauhaus lost eighty killed at Te Ngaio, besides having many wounded.

A veteran transport bullock-driver who witnessed the encounter at Te Ngaio says: "After the battle I saw the dead body of the biggest Maori I ever set eyes on—he must have been 7 feet high."

and on the 31st March marched through Hawera—then an open plain of flax, fern, and *tutu*—to the Wai-ngongoro River. There was a little skirmishing as the column moved on from Hawera, the Maoris opening fire from the coast ridges, but a few rounds from the guns scattered them, and camp was pitched on the high banks above the Wai-ngongoro without further opposition.* A large camp was formed here, and redoubts were erected on both banks of the river to protect the landing and storing of supplies.

A small steamer managed (8th April) to send a boat on shore at the Wai-ngongoro mouth with some provisions. Surf-boats were provided there and at the Manawapou, but there were numerous capsizes and some fatalities. In a boat capsize in the surf at Manawapou seven men were drowned. These accidents, illustrating the difficulty of working this harbourless coast to land stores for the troops, and the knowledge that the land route towards New Plymouth was difficult as well as hostile, convinced the General that it would be prudent to retrace his steps. Accordingly the force marched down the coast again, leaving 150 men (57th Regiment) in each of the redoubts on the two sides of the river and a force at Manawapou. Cameron left Patea on the 29th April for Auckland to confer with the Governor on future operations. A force of 750 men was left at Patea for the winter.

In April, 1865, the officer commanding in Taranaki (Colonel Warre, 57th) extended his outposts by establishing a strong redoubt at Pukearuhe, near the White Cliffs (the Pari-ninihi, or "Steep Cliffs" of the Maoris), thirty miles along the northern coast from New Plymouth, and one at Warea, twenty-seven miles south, and another at Opunake, fifty miles from New Plymouth. At Pukearuhe Colonel Mulock was in command with 160 of the 70th Regiment and two R.A. gunners. These redoubts brought the length of Taranaki coast-line occupied to eighty-five miles; but the forts commanded practically only the country within rifle-range of their parapets.

* Mr. William B. Adamson, of Hawera, who came up the coast in 1865 as a transport driver in Cameron's army, says: "When we marched through where Hawera Town now stands, on our way to the Wai-ngongoro, we had a skirmish with the Maoris on the sandhills near the mouth of the Waihi Stream, and somewhere near Mr. John Finlay's present farm at Tokaora. We saw fifty or sixty mounted Hauhaus watching us, and as we came up they opened fire, but at long range. Our march that day had been from Kakaramea and Manutahi up through the site of this town—in fact, the troops marched past within 20 yards of where the Hawera Public School now stands. General Cameron advanced his troops in several columns so as to surround the Maoris, but the soldiers did not get up to them. He opened fire on them with his field-guns, and, the shells exploding in their midst, they soon galloped off and crossed to the other side of the Wai-ngongoro."

General Sir H. J. Warre, K.C.B.

General Warre, as Lieut.-Colonel, served with the 57th Regiment (1st Middlesex) in the first and second Taranaki Wars. He left New Zealand in 1866.

In the early part of June a junction was effected between two small British forces in light marching order, one from the Waingongoro and one from Opunake: this was important because it temporarily reopened the coast road from New Plymouth to Wanganui, which had been barred to Europeans since the beginning of the Taranaki War in 1860. This opening of the road, however, was as yet only possible by the use of *force majeure;* not until a considerable time after Titokowaru's campaign, the last war in Taranaki, did the coast road become practicable for anything but an armed force.

Much of the work in Cameron's march up the coast was done by the 57th Regiment, the famous "Die-hards" of Albuera memory, under Colonel Butler. They led the advance on Kakaramea, followed by detachments of the 50th and 68th. They provided the most advanced garrisons, and a strong force of the regiment was encamped at the Manawapou Redoubt for some months. It was from Manawapou that the afterwards notorious Kimble Bent, a private in the regiment, deserted to the Hauhaus, after a military flogging for insubordination. Another private of the regiment, Hennessy, fell into the hands of the Maoris in a different way. He was out foraging for potatoes near the Ingahape, and was captured by a roving party of Hauhaus, who took him to their *pa*. He was kept in captivity, practically a slave like Kimble Bent, for over a year, when he contrived to escape and rejoin his regiment. A court-martial resulted in his acquittal, and he received all his back pay for the period of his involuntary desertion.

There was a good deal of skirmishing in mid-Taranaki in the latter part of 1865. At Whatino, a few miles from Opunake, on the 1st June, several men of the Mounted Corps, part of an escort to Lieut.-Colonel Colvile (43rd Regiment), came into conflict with six natives, who killed Trooper O'Neill and lost three killed themselves. On the 13th June Colonel Warre, with a column working in three divisions, attacked the Taranaki tribes in their villages inland of Warea. The troops engaged were detachments of the 43rd and the 70th Regiments, besides the Taranaki Bush Rangers under Captain Jonas. The villages of Nga-Kumikumi, Okeanui, Nekeua, and Te Puru were destroyed after a little fighting. Nekeua was an old fortified position with a deep trench round it. At Te Puru, where the Hauhaus were engaged in their Pai-marire devotions round the *niu*, there was a slight skirmish. A quantity of plunder from the wrecked steamer "Lord Worsley" was found in the villages burned.

On the 28th July Captain Close (43rd Regiment) and a private were mortally wounded while with a party from the Warea Redoubt gathering firewood in a clearing a short distance inland of Warea. The troops, extending, drove their attackers back. Next day a force of three hundred men left New Plymouth to operate against the Taranaki Tribe in the Warea district, and on the 2nd August a strong body of Imperial troops, with some of the Taranaki Mounted Volunteers under Captain Frank Mace, marched out from Warea to engage the natives in their inland retreats. The force, divided into two columns, totalled about four hundred men, under Lieut.-Colonel Colvile and Major Russell. Marching into the bush and scrub country via Kapoaiaia, the divisions separated, and Captain Cay (70th), with a company of Russell's division, rushed a village and bayoneted eleven Maoris, besides killing and wounding many more by rifle-fire. The 70th had one man shot dead. There was some heavy skirmishing as the force retreated after burning the village. The Hauhaus followed the troops and attacked them in rear and on the flanks until they got out to the open country. Colonel Colvile's wing encountered six natives, and killed five of them. Next day Colvile revisited the scene of the fight and burned some *whares*. The British casualties in this sharp bush skirmishing were a lieutenant of the 70th and four men killed and six wounded.

On the 20th October, 1865, Captain Frank Mace, with a small party of the Taranaki Mounted Corps, rode into an ambush party of about seventy Hauhaus between Warea and the Hangatahua, near the mouth of the river, and had an exceedingly narrow escape. Mace was riding along with three men when a sudden volley was received at close quarters, so close that most of the bullets went over their heads. The Maoris came rushing out of the flax and fern, firing from the hip, as was often their way. One of the troopers, W. Bullot, was lying down over his horse's neck to escape the shots when a bullet partly scalped him, travelling up from the back of his neck and over the skull at the front. The man was dazed by his wound, and went riding round and round in a circle, firing his revolver aimlessly. Captain Mace galloped up and got him away; his horse had been hit and dropped soon afterwards. Mace was wounded in the leg, and several bullets went through his clothes. For this gallant rescue he received the New Zealand Cross. He had been one of the first troopers to join the corps, the Taranaki Mounted Rifles, on its formation in 1860, under Captain Des Voeux.

Lieut.-General Sir Duncan Cameron having resigned the command of the army in New Zealand, Major-General Trevor Chute was appointed to take over the command of operations, and in October of 1865 he arrived in New Plymouth to confer with Colonel Warre on a plan of operations. The self-reliant policy of the Colonial Government having been initiated, the embarkation of the Imperial forces for England commenced. At the end of 1865 the Imperial forces in the colony totalled about ten thousand men, consisting of the 12th, 14th, 18th, 40th, 43rd, 50th, 57th, 65th, and 70th Regiments, two batteries of Field Artillery, and Royal Engineers and Military Train. The first units to sail were the 70th and the 65th. By the end of March, 1866, four out of the ten Imperial regiments had left the colony, and the others, with the Artillery, were gradually concentrated at Auckland for embarkation, leaving three regiments to garrison the Australian Colonies and New Zealand. One complete regiment was, as a temporary arrangement, to remain in New Zealand, but all the outposts were withdrawn, and the towns of Auckland and Wanganui were alone to be garrisoned.

It was Sir Frederick Weld (then Mr. Weld), who had been a settler in New Zealand for twenty years, who originated the new policy in the management of the colony's defences. In

1860 Mr. Weld was elected to the New Zealand Parliament as representative for Wairau; he was then engaged in pioneer work as a sheep-farmer in partnership with the Cliffords. He became Minister for Native Affairs, and in 1861 he went with the Governor to Te Arei *pa,* on the Waitara, to conclude peace with Wi Kingi's Maoris. In October, 1864, Governor Grey sent for him, and asked him to form a Ministry and assist him in saving the country under its overwhelming difficulties. Weld did so on the condition that he should be supported in his "self-reliant" policy. This policy he had lately outlined in these words:—

"I should propose to ask the Home Government to take away all the soldiers, and reduce our forces to about two thousand men, whom I should arm with the best rifles procurable; these I would have trained to bush-work, and employ a part of them on the roads when not required to fight. With regard to the natives, I should not disarm them—it would be equivalent to a war of extermination to insist upon doing so. Their pride would be hurt as well as their fears roused, and we should only succeed with the loyal tribes, who would thus be at the mercy of their enemies. I should pardon all offenders except those convicted of murder, and I should confiscate only enough land to show them that they lost by going to war; and, in order to secure the peace of the country, I should start armed settlements where they were required. But I should leave even the most turbulent tribes more land than they could ever require, which would then be of treble its present value. I should offer every inducement to the defeated tribes to settle down quietly, and enforce their submission by making roads through the most disturbed parts of the country—by force, if necessary. At the same time I should stop the lavish expenditure in presents and bribing the natives to keep quiet. By the policy I have sketched out I believe the expense of the colony might be reduced by one-half."

The Governor having agreed to a new policy based on these lines, Mr. Weld formed a Ministry, in which Mr. J. E. Fitzgerald, who was in perfect accord with the new Premier's views, became Minister for Native Affairs. One of the members of the Ministry was Major Harry Atkinson. Parliament endorsed the new scheme, and gradually the employment of colonial forces succeeded the old method of relying chiefly on the British Regulars. The Imperial Government approved of the colony's intention to dispense with British regiments, and after 1865 the operations against the Hauhau tribes were conducted chiefly by New Zealand troops, white and native. General Chute conducted a vigorous Taranaki campaign in 1866 with mixed forces, Imperial and colonial, but from that year until the close of the wars the Government relied solely on its own officers and men.

NOTES

The Wai-ngongoro Redoubt.

The erosion of the West Coast cliffs between the Wai-ngongoro and the Patea has resulted in the almost total destruction of General Cameron's redoubt at the mouth of the Wai-ngongoro, which was in 1865 the advanced field base of the West Coast Expeditionary Force. The assault of the ocean in strong westerly and south-westerly winds undermines the lofty cliffs on the coast, particularly east of the Wai-ngongoro mouth, and hedges, fences, old historic forts, and grassed land are carried away. All that is now left of the Wai-ngongoro main redoubt (east side of the river) is an indistinct section of earthwork which formed the north-west flanking bastion, with a small portion of the north parapet and ditch. The work is on the verge of the cliff, in the west corner of the Ohawe Domain, above Livingston's Beach. The old military road ran down here—the present road follows approximately this route—and the river ford was a short distance above the mouth. The scenery here is bold: high cliffs towering above the boulder-strewn beach of black ironsand, and the Wai-ngongoro coming down in sweeping curves, with the wooded west and north banks of the river rising into heights crowned by the ruins of Maori *pas* and British redoubts. Above the river-mouth on the east side, and somewhat lower than the redoubt at Ohawe, is the ancient Maori fort Rangatapu, a very large earthwork enclosing a flat hilltop. This was originally the *pa* of the moa-hunters, the ancient race who feasted upon the *moa,* the bones of which were unearthed in great quantities by Sir George Grey and others in 1866 in the hollow below the *pa,* formerly a lagoon enclosed by the sandhills.

On the opposite (west) bank of the river the Maoris, some of whom occupied the bold cliff *pa* Motutapu, standing north-west of the river-mouth, were accustomed to skirmish out and snipe the troops on the flat below. The Wai-ngongoro was then the frontier line.

Chapter 6

CHUTE'S TARANAKI CAMPAIGN

MAJOR-GENERAL TREVOR CHUTE was a vigorous downright soldier who infused new energy into the operations on the West Coast. His tactics were in strong contrast to those of his predecessor. Cameron hated the bush, and consistently kept his troops as near the coast as possible. Chute, on the other hand, boldly entered upon forest operations, and followed the Maoris up into their strongholds, sought them out in their bush retreats and stormed *pa* after *pa,* concluding a successful series of attacks by undertaking a venturesome and difficult march through the roadless forest at the back of Mount Egmont. He proved the ideal commander for a short, sharp bush campaign.

There had been several murders by the Nga-Rauru and Pakakohi Tribes, who, like Ngati-Ruanui, had refused to receive the peace proclamation by the Governor in 1865. On the 1st November Mr. Charles Broughton, interpreter to the forces in the Wanganui district, went to Otoia, on the Patea River, to confer with the Hauhaus on the peace proclamation, and was treacherously shot. Farther north Ngati-Ruanui and their kin gave evidence of their determination to hold their lands against the *pakeha* and to scorn all demands for surrender. On the 4th October a small party of the Military Train was ambuscaded on the track between the Manawapou and the Wai-ngongoro redoubts, by way of Hawera, and one of them, whose horse was shot, was tomahawked.

Chute, having received his directions from the Governor to open a campaign against the West Coast tribes, began operations from the southern side at the end of 1865. He marched out from Wanganui on the 30th December for the Weraroa, the scene of Sir George Grey's triumph of strategy earlier in the year. His force was considerably smaller than that which Cameron had led slowly and cautiously up the coast. Some reinforcements joined him on the Waitotara, and the column he now had at his disposal was a very capable force, consisting of 33 Royal Artillery, with field-guns, under Lieutenant Carre; 280 of the

14th Regiment, under Lieut.-Colonel Trevor; 45 Forest Rangers, under Major Von Tempsky; and the Wanganui Native Contingent and other Maoris, about 300 strong, under Major McDonnell; besides a Transport Corps of 45 men each driving a two-horse dray.

Chute wasted no time at Weraroa. Crossing the Waitotara on the 3rd January, 1866, with three companies of the 14th Regiment and the Maori Contingent, he advanced upon Okotuku, a village on the edge of the high ground about five miles inland from the Wairoa (the present Township of Waverley). On the wooded plain below Okotuku, in the direction of Wairoa, was Moturoa, destined to be the scene of a disastrous fight for the Government forces nearly three years later.

At daylight on the 4th two companies of the 14th and a Maori force under McDonnell advanced upon Okotuku, where the village had been burned the previous day; it was now the intention to destroy the large plantations of potatoes and maize found there. A small advance-guard (Lieutenant W. E. Gudgeon, Ensign W. McDonnell, and Winiata Pakoro, of the Wanganui Contingent) were heavily fired on close up to the *pa,* which was defended by a breastwork of heavy timbers, and took cover in a small hollow until Lieutenant Keogh's company of the 14th, with the Maori Contingent, came charging up to the position. The *pa* was stormed at the point of the bayonet, and three Maoris were killed; three more were killed by the Contingent and the Forest Rangers in the pursuit of the retreating enemy through the bush. The British loss was one killed and six wounded.

The next operation was the attack and capture of a strong Hauhau *pa* at Te Putahi, on high ground above the Whenuakura River. The terrain was thickly wooded, with awkward spurs, where it was easy for a small force to resist an advance. Very early on the morning of the 7th January the British force (detachments of the 14th, 18th, and 50th Regiments, Forest Rangers, and Wanganui Maoris) made a detour under cover of darkness and cautiously ascended through the bush to the top of the plateau on which the *pa* stood. McDonnell and his natives took the place in the rear while the troops advanced to the attack. The Hauhaus were first seen engaged in their morning service round the *niu* pole. Their resistance was determined, but the *pa* was soon taken at the bayonet's point, with a loss of two killed to the Imperial troops. Among the twelve wounded was Major McDonnell, who received a bullet in the foot. The Hauhaus lost fourteen killed in the *pa,* and in the retreat another was shot.

This sharp action drove the Hauhaus inland, and terminated

the fighting south of the Patea. The scene of action now shifted to the Tangahoe territory, in the heart of the rebel country. Here, at the edge of the plateau high above the right bank of the Tangahoe River, the Hauhaus had constructed the strongest fortification built in this campaign.

Otapawa* occupied a very commanding position. The hill on which it stood was the terminal of a long table-land then densely wooded—it is now a beautiful well-grassed farm, with a fringing of bush in the gullies and on the slopes toward the Tangahoe. The river flows in a sweeping curve round the base of the spur, several hundreds of feet below the fortress hill. The *pa* was roughly wedge-shaped, with the apex toward the river. The irregular base of the wedge, on level open ground, was defended

---

* The site of Otapawa is on a farm about five miles from the Town of Hawera, and a mile above the bridge across the Tangahoe on the Hawera-Meremere Road. Much of the beautiful forest still remains on the broken ground in rear of and on the flanks of the old Hauhau fortress. When I explored the place in 1918 with Mr. William Wallace, of Meremere, a veteran of the wars, it was easy to trace the line of the many-angled front parapet and the trenches by the depressions in the ground. The double ditch and triple parapet at the narrow rear were still well preserved. Inside the *pa* there are numerous *ruas,* or food-stores, and the sites of dug-in huts. The place is not fenced or in any way protected from stock, and it is worthy of a little attention as one of Taranaki's most historic spots. A reserve of about an acre would include the whole of the ruined fortifications.

The artillery used in the attack on Otapawa consisted of a 6-pounder Armstrong and two small mortars, under the charge of Lieutenant (afterwards Lieut.-Colonel) G. T. Carré, R.A. This officer, in recounting the incidents of Otapawa, said: "When Major-General Chute ordered the assault, officers who had been used to the cautious tactics of General Cameron ventured to remonstrate. The gallant Chute cried, 'Small force! I tell you, if there was only one man, and that man myself, he should go at it!'" On the General's return past the guns Lieutenant Carré ventured to congratulate him. He shook his head. "Lost too many poor boys! Nearly lost myself," he said, and pointed to his jumper, from the breast of which a bullet had torn the braid. Had he been one step farther it would have gone through his body.

Lieut.-Colonel Jason Hassard, of the 57th Regiment, who died of his wound (a bullet through the lungs) received at Otapawa, was a native of Fermanagh, Ireland. He was the second son of Captain Jason Hassard, 74th Highlanders. He was born in 1826, and in 1844 obtained an ensigncy in the 57th Regiment of Foot. He became a captain in that regiment in 1854. During the Crimean War he was present at most of the battles. He distinguished himself in the storming-columns at the assaults of the Redan and Kinburn. He received in reward the Sardinian, Turkish, and Crimean medals and clasps, the Fifth Class of the Medjidie, and a Major's brevet. He was afterwards at Malta and in India. At the end of 1860 the 57th embarked for New Zealand. In September, 1864, he was gazetted as Brevet Lieut.-Colonel; but he did not live long to enjoy his promotion, for he fell, mortally wounded, while gallantly leading his men to the assault of Otapawa.

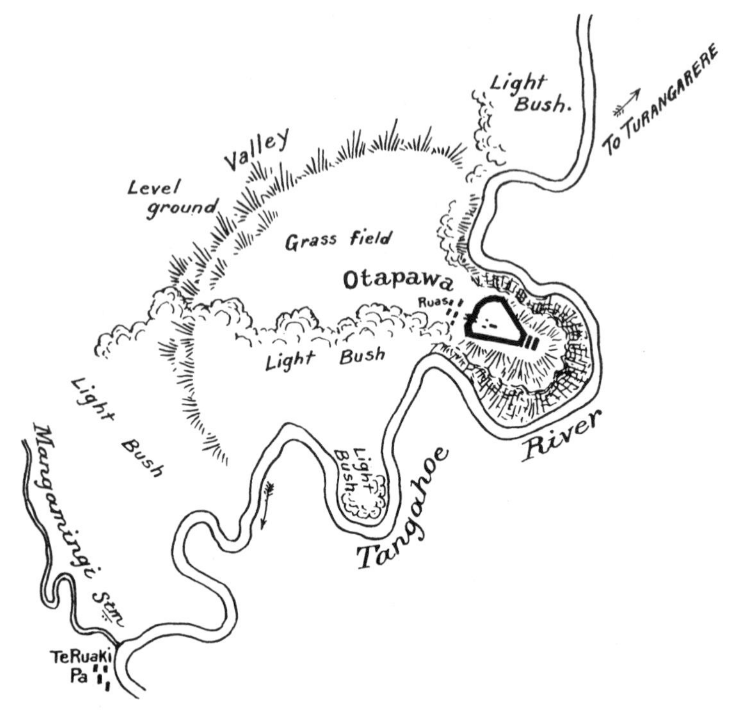

J. C., sketch-plan, 1918]

Otapawa Pa, South Taranaki

by two lines of high palisading and by rifle-pits and well-traversed trenches. On each flank the ground fell precipitously into the forested gorge. From the narrow rear a long forest-covered spur tended steeply to the elbow of the Tangahoe. This end of the fort was defended by two deep ditches and three parapets.

The General selected the Tawhiti, near the present Town of Hawera, as his field base for the advance on Otapawa. The intervening country was fairly level, intersected by small streams with steep banks. At Taiporohenui the large meeting-house of the Hauhau tribes was destroyed. Lieut.-Colonel Butler, with a detachment of the 57th, had now joined the column. On the 12th January Chute moved out across the plain and encamped within easy striking distance of Otapawa, and next day Ensign W. McDonnell and some of the Wanganui Maoris reconnoitred the position. Very early the next morning (14th January, 1866) the General advanced to the attack with a force consisting of 200 men of the 14th Regiment (Lieut-Colonel Trevor), 180 of the 57th (Lieut.-Colonel Butler), 36 of the Forest Rangers (Major Von Tempsky), and 200 of the Native Contingent under Major McDonnell, beside three Armstrong field-guns. The friendly natives were to move to the rear and cut off the retreat, but the General was impatient to attack and did not give them time to get into position in the very broken ground. Fire was opened with one of the Armstrongs from the plateau facing the *pa,* and several shells exploded within the palisades. As no Maori appeared, it was thought by some of the troops that the place was deserted. However, there were over two hundred Hauhaus manning the trenches, waiting until their foes were within close range. The 57th, supported by the 14th, were ordered to advance to the assault. The veteran "Die-hards," led by Lieut.-Colonels Butler and Hassard, steadily breasted the rise leading to the level front of the *pa.* They were within point-blank range when the whole front of the palisades blazed and a heavy volley came ripping through their ranks, followed by another volley as the soldiers rushed upon the stockade with their bayonets at the charge. Slashing at the *aka*-vine fastenings of the palisading with tomahawks and bayonets, the troops were soon in the fort and despatching the Hauhaus who remained to dispute possession. Those who escaped fled down the long steep spur to the Tangahoe, most of them eluding the Native Contingent which followed in chase. On the right flank of the *pa,* where the ground was steep and wooded, Von Tempsky and his Rangers had cleared the bush of some Hauhaus who had opened fire on the Imperial troops as they advanced to the assault.

The Hauhaus lost about thirty killed in this sharp encounter and they had many wounded, who were taken up the Tangahoe to a sheltered spot and there tended. Thence the fugitives, fearing further pursuit, travelled inland several miles, through a wild forest and gorge country, to Rimatoto, on the northern side of the Meremere Hills.

The British loss in the assault was eleven killed and twenty wounded. Lieut.-Colonel Jason Hassard, of the 57th, was mortally wounded. Major-General Chute had a narrow escape; a bullet tore the braid on his coat. The rather heavy casualties, suffered chiefly by the gallant 57th, were due to the impetuosity of Chute's frontal attack. Lieut.-Colonel Butler was indignant at not being allowed to send out flanking parties, but that part of the operation could have been attended to very thoroughly by the Forest Rangers and the Native Contingent had a little more time been allowed.

It was camp gossip after the battle that Kimble Bent, the deserter from the 57th, was one of the defenders of the *pa,* and that it was his bullet that had laid his old officer, Hassard, low. This was incorrect. Bent, however, had assisted, on compulsion, in the building of the fort, and was in the place until two or three days before the assault, when he was sent away with non-combatants to a place of security in the forest higher up the Tangahoe.

The Hauhaus who garrisoned Otapawa were chiefly members of the Tangahoe, Ngati-Ruanui, and Pakakohi Tribes. One of their principal fighting chiefs was the old warrior and priest Tautahi Ariki; another was Tukino. Te Ua, the arch-prophet of Pai-marire, had been in the *pa,* but had ridden away shortly before the day of the engagement.

The principal stronghold of the South Taranaki Hauhaus having been captured, the General continued his advance, concentrating on Ketemarae, a famous gathering-place for the West Coast tribes and the junction of several old war-tracks. The stockaded village of Ketemarae (about a mile from the present Township of Normanby) was attacked by the troops, who occupied it early on the morning of the 15th January. Ten Hauhaus were killed. The Wanganui Native Contingent, in the advance, had some sharp skirmishing when the order was given to clear the various settlements in the neighbourhood of Ketemarae, including Keteonetea and Puketi.

The force moved on past Waihi, taking several settlements, and, crossing the Wai-ngongoro River, captured the large village of Mawhitiwhiti, the principal *kainga* of the Nga-Ruahine Tribe. Here seven of the defenders were killed. The day's work resulted in the destruction of seven villages of Nga-Ruahine and Ngati-Ruanui, including, besides Ketemarae and Mawhitiwhiti, the large *kaingas* Weriweri and Te Whenuku. Most of the fighting fell to the lot of the Native Contingent, and here Kepa (Kemp) te Rangihiwinui (later given a Major's commission) distinguished himself by his activity and dash. The scene of these sharp operations, the first attacks delivered on the Ngati-Ruanui and Nga-Ruahine in their bush homes, is now a beautiful farming district, famous for its fertility, and covered with villages and homesteads. Some of the Maori *hapus* still hold their native soil, and the sons of the old warriors of Nga-Ruahine are even carrying on dairying-work like their *pakeha* neighbours. One of the historic settlements is Weriweri, the home in the war-days of the fighting chief Toi Whakataka, who took a prominent part in the opposition to General Chute and afterwards in Titokowaru's war. His son, Pou-whareumu Toi, is now the leading man of Weriweri.

Dr. Featherston Takiora, the guide Von Tempsky
Major-General Chute
From a drawing by Major Von Tempsky, 1866]

Chute's Column on the March

This sketch represents the start of the expedition from Ketemarae on the march through the forest round the east side of Mount Egmont to New Plymouth.

THE MARCH THROUGH THE FOREST

The vigorous Imperial commander now rounded off his invasion of the Hauhau country by taking a column through to New Plymouth by the most direct route—the difficult, almost unknown, Maori trail through the dense forest on the east side of Mount Egmont. This route was the ancient war-track between Puke-rangiora, on the Waitara, and Ketemarae; to the Maoris it was known as Whakaahurangi, a name which alludes to the gradual ascent to the heights as the eastern ranges of the great mountain are approached. The Whakaahurangi track was the common route in pre-European times between North and South Taranaki, and in the early days of the New Plymouth settlement working-parties sent out by the New Zealand Company's agent in Taranaki had cut a bridle-track along the native trail. In the course of twenty years, however, heavy undergrowth had covered the almost disused track, and Chute's determination to take horses through to New Plymouth made the enterprise one of vast labour for his troops. Chute was determined to vindicate before the eyes of the colonists the capacity of the British soldier to undertake hazardous and difficult bush campaigning, and to demonstrate to the Maoris also the willingness and the ability of troops to follow them up into their most remote fastnesses.

The column set out on the forest march from Ketemarae northward early on the morning of the 17th January, 1866. Chute took three companies of the 14th Regiment, Von Tempsky's Forest Rangers, and a picked body of the Native Contingent, in all 514 of all ranks, including 247 of the 14th Regiment. Each soldier carried a waterproof blanket and greatcoat, and biscuits for two days. The transport service consisted of 67 packhorses, with their drivers, besides 24 saddle-horses. The staff included Colonel Carey, D.A.G., and Lieut.-Colonel Gamble, D.Q.M.G.; and Dr. Featherston, the Superintendent of Wellington Province, accompanied the General. The march through to the open country at Mataitawa occupied eight days; it could have been done in half that time but for the necessity of cutting a track and making bridges for the horses. The first day's march was between nine and ten miles. The only skirmishing was an encounter between the Native Contingent in the advance, a few miles from Ketemarae, and seven Hauhaus on the track; three of these were shot. As the column advanced across the lower spurs of the mountain the country became more and more difficult; the forest undergrowth was dense and matted, and gullies and watercourses continually intersected the line of march. The Forest Rangers in the advance did excellent work as pioneers, cutting the track and bridging creeks and swampy gullies with trunks of fern-trees, which gave good footing for the horses. Half-way through the forest heavy rain set in, and the rest of the march was slow and toilsome in the extreme. The Rangers were now so exhausted by the heavy labour of pioneer duty that working-parties of the 14th, under Colonel Carey, were sent to the front.

On Sunday, the 21st, the force marched only four miles, crossing four rapid streams and fifteen gullies, and went into bivouac early in wet and gloomy weather. That evening it became necessary to kill one of the horses for a meat ration; all the provisions but a little biscuit had been exhausted. On the night of the 20th Mr. Price, of the commissariat, and Captain Leach and Ensign McDonnell, with some Maoris, had set out on a forced march for Mataitawa to get supplies for the troops. The rain fell in torrents, and the struggle through the roadless bush became so exhausting that Mr. Price had to be left under a tree while his companions pushed on to Mataitawa. Reaching the British post at last they obtained provisions, and on the evening of the 2nd Captain Leach returned from Mataitawa with a party of the 43rd and 68th carrying supplies for the half-starved troops. Meanwhile the Native Contingent and some of the Rangers had hurried on in advance to the open country. A second horse was killed on the 22nd before the arrival of the party with food. The weather continued wet, and progress over the gully-dissected forest country was slow and toilsome. At last, on the 25th, after a bush march of sixty miles, the column gladly halted in the Mataitawa Valley, and the sun shone out once more. After drying clothes and blankets the troops marched through to the Wai-wakaiho flat, where they encamped, and next day made a triumphal march into New Plymouth, where the townspeople dined the soldiers, and the General was presented with a congratulatory address, read by the Superintendent of Taranaki Province, Mr. H. S. Richmond. The address described the expedition as the first march on which a large body of regular troops had been led for several days together through the forests of New Zealand, and declared that General Chute's decisive field operations had shown that against British forces, regular and irregular, New Zealand had no impregnable fortresses; that British courage and arms could penetrate wherever man could hide; that there was no security for rebellion, and that the only course open to the hostile natives was frank submission to the terms which the Empire and the colony held out for their acceptance.

Included in General Chute's column on the bush march was a detachment of the Mounted Artillery under Lieutenant G. T. Carré, R.A. (afterwards Lieut.-Colonel Carré). Describing the arduous march, Lieutenant Carré wrote in one of his letters:—

"We started on the morning of the 17th January, 1866, and marched by a well-marked track into the bush with a few native guides and three days' provisions and 300 men. At first the track was all that could be desired, and the first three miles were soon passed over. We laughed at the idea of taking more than three days to do sixty miles, but by degrees the path grew smaller and beautifully less until it disappeared altogether to the sight of any European, though the natives could follow it. After the first four miles we had literally to cut our way with hatchets and billhooks through the most entangled jungle, the undergrowth very thick with plenty of supplejack in it; but what was worse than all this were the innumerable gullies and small rivers. It took us an immense time to get the pack-horses over these obstacles. In most places we had to make steps with fern-trees, both up and down, for them, and we moved at about the rate of a quarter-mile an hour, starting always at 7 a.m. and working till dark. After the third day we were out of provisions, and, to make matters worse, it came down a regular three days' New Zealand rain, drops as large as half-crowns coming off the trees, which were so high and dense that twilight reigned at noon. It began to look certainly very horrible, for no one knew where we were. We had to eat our horses, and the rain prevented our lighting fires to cook that unpalatable fare. But luckily we got succour at last. Captain Leach was sent on with the natives, who would no longer stay with us, taking a dog for food on the way, and in two days got help and returned with some men carrying blankets and food. We were nine days in the bush altogether."

Chute without delay set out on his return march through Taranaki southward by the west coast road, thus encircling Mount Egmont. At the Hangatahua River (usually called "Stony River") Captain Mace's Mounted Corps and seventy men of the 43rd Regiment joined the column; a company of Taranaki Bush Rangers also came up to join in the projected operations against the Hauhaus in the Warea district. Before daylight on the 1st February the General moved out of camp with 450 men of all ranks and followed a track which had been reconnoitred by the Native Contingent scouts the previous day. Advancing through bush and scrub, the force came out on a large clearing five or six miles inland from the Warea–Opunake Road. A *pa,* called Waikoko, was now in sight about 500 yards distant. The troops were extended in skirmishing order, the 14th on the right, the 43rd on the left, and the Rangers in the centre. The order to assault the stockade was given, and under a heavy fire the troops rushed cheering upon the enemy. The Maori resistance was vigorous but short, and the garrison soon took to the bush in rear, leaving four dead men in the *pa*. One man of the 14th was killed, and a sergeant of Corbett's Rangers and two of the Wanganui natives were wounded.

This was the last skirmish on Chute's march. The force went on to Opunake and the Wai-ngongoro, and marched into Patea on the 6th February, 1866. In the five weeks' campaign, beginning at the Waitotara, the force had captured and destroyed seven fortified *pas* and twenty-one open villages, inflicting large casualties.

While the General was on his bush march from Ketemarae northward, Lieut.-Colonel Butler (57th) had some skirmishing with a flying column operating from the camp at the mouth of the Wai-ngongoro. With 200 of the 50th and 57th Regiments and 120 Maoris, and taking two field-guns, he marched inland on the 18th January and went as far as Tirotiro-moana, east of Ketemarae. The *pa* and cultivations there were destroyed. On the 20th he made another expedition, marching northward into Ahipaipa, with 20 of the Military Train as cavalry, 80 men of the 50th and 100 of the 57th, besides the greater part of the Native Contingent under Lieutenant Wirihana. Ahipaipa was found deserted, but as the troops were destroying the *whares* they were fired on. The Native Contingent, pursuing the Hauhaus through the bush, found another large village, a very well built place. A 57th detachment under Sir Robert Douglas came up, and the force attacked and carried the village, after a sharp fight in which five Hauhaus were killed and one Wanganui man was wounded. The village, *niu* flagstaff, and cultivations were destroyed.

The 57th Regiment, after its excellent work in General Chute's campaign of 1866, was sent to Te Awamutu, in the Waikato. There the corps remained for several months and then was ordered to England. Those men who did not take their discharge in New Zealand were despatched to England in the ships "Electra" and "Maori" in April, 1867. Seven officers and sixty-eight non-commissioned officers and men of the regiment lost their lives in the New Zealand campaigns. Many of the 57th veterans joined the colonial forces after their discharge. In the heroic defence of Turuturu-mokai Redoubt in 1868 four of the old "Die-hards" were engaged, and three of them were killed.

Chapter 7

PAI-MARIRE ON THE EAST COAST

IN THE EARLIER campaigns the missionaries had been respected, and often had been free to come and go among the combatants, but the Hauhau no longer regarded them as *tapu*. March, 1865, saw the worst atrocity of the Pai-marire war, the murder of the Rev. Carl Sylvius Volkner, at Opotiki, by Kereopa and his band of fanatics.

Kereopa te Rau (also called Tu-hawhe) and Patara Raukatauri were the two prophets despatched by Te Ua early in 1865 to convert the tribes of the East Coast to the Pai-marire faith. Kereopa was a man of the Ngati-Rangiwewehi clan of the Arawa Tribe, of Awahou and Puhirua, on the north-west shore of Lake Rotorua; he had fought in the latter part of the Waikato War. He was a thoroughgoing old savage, and he quickly plunged into the worst excesses, even cannibalism. He disregarded Te Ua's instructions, which were to conduct a peaceful propaganda through the Island until he reached Hirini te Kani, the highest chief of the East Coast, to whom he was to give Captain Lloyd's head and also Pai-marire flags. Patara Raukatauri, of Oakura, was a man of milder character than the barbarous Kereopa. He was a chief of the Taranaki Tribe, and had been the principal leader in the fighting against the troops at Kaitake, where he had entrenched himself strongly at the end of 1863.

The prophets took with them two deserters from the British forces. One of these renegades was Louis Baker, a French-Canadian-Indian half-breed (the notorious Kimble Bent was also of part Indian blood). At one time in his career Baker had been a stoker in H.M.S. "Rosario." Him they forced to carry Captain Lloyd's head, which was paraded at each place visited as a symbol of the new religion. The prophets pretended that they could make the dead mouth speak.

That the founder of Pai-marire did not authorize murders—or, indeed, hostile acts of any kind—on the proselytizing mission to the East Cape there is documentary proof. The following is a copy of Horopapera Te Ua Haumene's written instructions to Kereopa and Patara before their departure from Taranaki:—

Matakaha, Wahi o Taranaki, Tihema 8th, 1864.

HE whakaaturanga tenei mo te upoko. Ka tukua atu nei kia haere i nga wahi o te motu. Ko te ara, maro atu i konei a Waitotara, ka ahu atu ki uta, te putanga kei Pipiriki, maro atu ki Taupo, maro atu ki te Urewera maro atu ki Ngati-Porou, tae atu kia Hirini te Kani-a-Takirau, te mutunga mai. Kia tika te hari, kaua e whakahengia e te tangata, a penatia me Te Rangi-tauira ritenga whakehe i tera o aku akoranga i te motu. Ko tenei kia pai te kawe i tenei o aku akoranga ki nga wahi o te motu kia tae pai ai kia a Hirini, mana e hoatu pai ki ona whanaunga pakeha i reira.

Ki tenei reta korerotia i nga kaainga katoa, ki te kino i te repo ma koutou e ahua atu ki tetahi pepa hou, kia tae pai atu ai ki etahi kaainga atu, pena tonu a tae noa kia Hirini. Heoi.

NA TE UA HAUMENE.

(Na Te Ua Haumene ki nga kaainga katoa o te motu puta noa i ona rohe katoa.)

[TRANSLATION]

Matakaha, Taranaki, December 8th, 1864.

THESE are directions regarding the head which is being sent forth to the districts of the Island. This is the route to be taken: Go direct from here to Waitotara, then pursue a course inland until Pipiriki is reached; thence go direct to Taupo, and from there to the Urewera, thence on to Ngati-Porou until you reach Hirini te Kani-a-Takirau. There ends the journey. Let your proceedings be correct, not like those of Te Rangi-tauira, whose actions were not in accordance with my teachings in the Island. Let your conduct be good in carrying these my instructions to the various parts of the Island, even until you come to Hirini, who will convey the teachings peacefully to his European relations there.

This letter you must make known to all the villages. Should it become soiled in the swamps, you must copy it on a new paper, so that it may be conveyed properly to the settlements visited, and so until you reach Hirini.

That is all. From TE UA HAUMENE.

(From Te Ua Haumene to all the settlements in the Island, extending to every boundary.)

On his arrival at Whakatane Kereopa demanded that the Ngati-Awa tribes should hand over to him the Roman Catholic priest of their district. Pending their reply he travelled on to Opotiki, accompanied by some of the principal chiefs of Whakatane, including Mokomoko and Te Hura. (Later it was stated that the priest was spared because he was a Frenchman.) The Pai-marire cult was expounded at Opotiki, and nearly the whole of the Whakatohea Tribe became converts. Patara then demanded of the chiefs their missionary, Mr. Volkner, whom he desired to sacrifice to the god of Pai-marire.

This missionary, the Rev. Carl Sylvius Volkner, was one of several German Lutheran clergymen who had come out to work among the natives in New Zealand. He was a member of the Church of England body, and he worked with zeal and devotion to improve the moral condition of the Whakatohea people. He built a fine church in the principal settlement; this church (now known as St. Stephen the Martyr's) is the Anglican place of worship in the town of Opotiki. The Whakatohea had a high regard for their missionary, but Pai-marire everywhere produced a strong revulsion of feeling against Christian ministers. As in other places, even Volkner's church deacons turned against him. (One of these men, Timoti te Kaka, became one of the most desperate warriors under Kereopa, and was afterwards with Te Kooti for two years; he fell to a bullet from Captain Mair's carbine near Rotorua in 1870.)

When Te Ua's apostles reached Opotiki in February, 1865, Mr. Volkner was absent in Auckland. Patara wrote a letter to the missionary ordering him not to return to Opotiki; no missionaries would be allowed to remain among the Maori people. Mr. Volkner's chief offence appears to have been that he had endeavoured to restrain the Whakatohea Tribe from joining in the Kingite War, 1863–64; and he was accused of being a spy for the Government in Auckland.

A *niu* flagstaff of worship was erected in the middle of the principal settlement, Pa-kowhai, facing the entrance to the Opotiki Harbour and the Pai-marire worship was commenced. Kereopa, with Lloyd's head, stood by the foot of the pole, and the trophy of the Te Ahuahu battlefield was flourished before the people as they passed in excited procession around the *niu* and rehearsed the chants of the new religion.

On the 1st March the coasting-schooner "Eclipse," owned and commanded by a Jewish trader, Captain Levy, arrived at the Opotiki landing from Auckland, bringing as passengers Mr. Volkner and a brother missionary, the Rev. Thomas Grace, who had been forced to abandon his station at Pukawa, Lake Taupo. Volkner had been warned in Auckland that it was dangerous for him to return to his charge, in the changed temper of the people; but he could not be dissuaded from what he considered his duty. In his absence his house, some distance from the church, at a spot called Peria (the Scriptural Berea, in Macedonia), had been sacked by the Hauhaus and the contents sold at a kind of auction. The schooner was looted, but Levy and his brother, being Jews, were considered akin to the Hauhaus—whom Kereopa called "Iharaira," or Israel—and were allowed their liberty. The two missionaries were arrested and kept in confinement. Kereopa by this time had thoroughly established his power over the greater part of the tribe, and at a meeting that night it was resolved to hand Mr. Volkner over next day and keep Mr. Grace a prisoner.

On the afternoon of the 2nd March Mr. Volkner was taken out of his prison hut by an armed guard and was marched into

From a drawing, 1865]

The Seizure of the Schooner "Eclipse" at Opotiki by the Hauhaus

his church, which was crowded with the fearfully excited people. Kereopa, standing by the altar, ordered the missionary to be brought before him. He announced that Volkner must die that day, stripped him of his coat and waistcoat, which he (Kereopa) put on, and ordered the minister to be led out for execution by hanging. The armed guard took him to a large willow-tree which stood about a hundred yards away, between the church and the waterside. A line and block had been taken from the "Eclipse"; the block was made fast to a branch of the tree, and the rope was tied round Volkner's neck. He knelt down and prayed, and then shook hands with some of those around him. The executioners hauled on the rope, and the missionary's body hung lifeless from the gallows-tree. It is said, further, that Kereopa shot Volkner after he was run up to the branch. The body was hauled up and down several times, and after hanging for about an hour it was lowered and taken to a spot near the church. Here the head was cut off with an axe by Heremita, and the natives crowded up to catch the blood and drink it. Kereopa had taken from the church vestry the white-metal communion chalice. This he filled with the blood as it spouted forth, and he carried it with the head to the church, followed in procession by all the people.

That scene in "Hiona"—"Zion," as the Opotiki church was called by Volkner's old congregation—was of a character revolting beyond measure. It was as if a devil had entered into the people. Assuredly there was a demon before them there in human form, at once terrifying and fascinating them by his sheer savagery. Kereopa, dressed in his victim's long black coat, stood in Volkner's pulpit, and placed the dripping head on the reading-desk in front of him; by its side he set the communion cup of blood.

"Hear, O Israel!" he cried. "This is the word of the God of Abraham, Isaac, and Jacob! We are the Jews who were lost and have been persecuted. Behold!" Gripping the head, he gouged out both eyes. He held up an eye in each hand between fingers and thumb. "Listen, O tribe!" he said. "This eye is the Parliament of England, and this one is the law of New Zealand!" So saying, he swallowed them one after the other. The second eye stuck in his throat, and he called for a drink of water to help him to swallow it. He picked up the head from the floor where he had dropped it, and set it up in front of him again on the pulpit-desk.

Then the cannibal priest took up the communion chalice and drank of its contents. He passed it to one of his flock, who put it to his lips and took a sip, and then it was passed from hand to hand among the congregation. Some put it to their lips to taste their missionary's blood; others dipped leaves into the cup and sprinkled themselves with its contents. The empty cup was carried back to the desecrated pulpit where the head lay; the stains of the martyred missionary's blood remain in the wood of the reading-desk to this day.

This atrocious deed earned the arch-murderer the epithet "Kai-karu," or "Kai-whatu," the "Eye-eater." Six years afterwards when he was captured in the Urewera Country, he said he knew he would meet with misfortune sooner or later, because one of "Te Wakana's" eyes stuck in his throat; it was an *aitua,* an unlucky happening and a portent of death.

From the church Volkner's head was taken to the house of the Roman Catholic priest, where it was set on the mantelpiece; then it was carried to the murdered man's house, Peria; the object was to *whakanoa,* or "make common" and pollute with blood, all the places sacred to the Christian ministers.

The after-history of Volkner's head is narrated by the natives, up to a certain stage. It was preserved by being smoke-dried over a fire, and when Kereopa continued his travels to Tauaroa, on the Rangitaiki, it was carried with him; the bearer was the renegade Louis Baker, who had carried Captain Lloyd's head from Taranaki. Later it was taken to South Taupo, and it is reported to have been hidden in a cave at Roto-a-Ira or Tongariro.

Not all the Whakatohea participated in or approved of the slaying of Volkner. A member of the tribe who was an unwilling eye-witness of the execution says two sections of the Whakatohea were opposed to putting the missionary to death. Ngati-Ira, of Waioeka, and Ngati-Ngaere both disapproved of it. Ngati-Tama favoured Kereopa's work. This witness, a woman, recalls the abhorrence and fear with which she and some of her companions saw from a short distance Volkner's body hanging to the tree, and then its decapitation. She was taken into the church, " Hiona," with the other people, and saw Kereopa place the minister's head on the *torona* (" throne "—*i.e.*, the pulpit), and she witnessed the swallowing of the eyes. " The prophet," she says, " had to take a drink of water before the second eye went down. Kereopa impressed on the people that by tasting the blood of the missionary when the cup went round the converts would acquire a knowledge of the English tongue, and would be able to work miracles. In the old Maori days the belief was that by the drinking of an enemy's blood his knowledge and *mana* were acquired by his slayers. Mr. Volkner's body was not mutilated except by the cutting-off of his head. Many of our people were astounded by the killing of the missionary who had been with us so long, but although one or two made an attempt to prevent the execution they were powerless before Kereopa and his armed men, and they were also filled with fear of his god and his magic incantations."

The fate of the other missionary, Mr. Grace, hung in the balance for some time. He was publicly accused of having disseminated false doctrines amongst the people. Probably he would have been sacrificed like Volkner but for Patara, who offered to exchange him for Hori Tupaea, the highest chief of Ngai-te-Rangi, who had recently been captured by the Ngati-Pikiao clan of the Arawa at Rotoiti Lake while attempting to join the Hauhaus. Mr. Grace was kept in suspense for a fortnight after the death of his friend, but at last contrived to slip off in the boat of the schooner " Eclipse," which was about to sail for Tauranga and Auckland. The boat, going out, met two armed cutters sent in by H.M.S. " Eclipse " (Captain E. Fremantle, afterwards Admiral), which had just arrived from Auckland to investigate the reports of Volkner's murder. Mr. Grace was then received aboard the warship.

A few weeks after these events at Opotiki the newly recruited Hauhaus at Whakatane cut off a small coasting-vessel and murdered Mr. James Fulloon and two of the crew. Fulloon was a half-caste, a man of great ability, and was in the employ of the Government as interpreter and native agent; he was a surveyor by profession. His mother was an East Coast chieftainess, and he was known among the Whakatane people, to whom he was related, as Te Mautaranui, after a locally famous forefather. When H.M.S. "Eclipse" was sent down the coast to investigate the murder of Volkner Mr. Fulloon accompanied Captain Fremantle. Armed parties landed at Hicks Bay and other places in an attempt to capture Kereopa and Patara. Fulloon then boarded the trading-cutter "Kate," and sailed for Whakatane to inquire into native conditions there. When the cutter anchored off the bar, to await high water, the Taranaki prophet Horomona, one of Te Ua's apostles of Pai-marire, was at Whakatane, and he persuaded his converts to capture the vessel and kill those on board. That night a party of Ngati-Awa, numbering about twenty, led by Mikaere Kirimangu, quietly boarded the cutter in two whaleboats. Entering the cabin, they discovered Fulloon sleeping soundly in his bunk. A young boy crept down and secured a loaded revolver under the sleeping man's pillow. He gave the weapon to Kirimangu, who shot Fulloon dead. Several others each used the revolver in turn and fired shots into their victim. The sailors were simultaneously attacked. The crew consisted of two white men and two half-caste youths. The Europeans were killed; the half-castes were taken ashore and permitted to go free. Mr. Bennett White, who was also an board, escaped the slaughter, as he was married to a Maori woman; one of the half-caste youths was his son.

The cutter was brought into the Whakatane River opposite the settlement and looted, and her mast was chopped through at the deck and taken ashore to Kopeopeo, a short distance outside the main village on the beach. There it was set up as a *niu* under Horomona's directions, and the Patu-tatahi and other *hapus* of Ngati-Awa and the Ngati-Pukeko, newly brought under the maddening influence of Pai-marire, went through their fanatic ceremonies round its foot. The old chief Te Apanui, who was averse to the faith and works of the Hauhaus, was compelled to participate in the worship. He was forced to the foot of the *niu,* and ordered to revolve about it with his raised hands resting on the mast, while his people went round and round in procession, chanting the new service taught them by the white-bearded prophet from Taranaki.

The sequel to these deeds of blood was the despatch, after considerable delay, of Government punitive expeditions, and the ultimate capture of many of those actively concerned in the murders of Volkner and Fulloon. Of these, Horomona, Kirimangu, and three others were tried and hanged in Auckland. The operations of the Government forces are described in the two following chapters.

THE CAPTURE OF HORI TUPAEA

The Ngati-te-Rangi chief Hori Tupaea, to whose capture reference has already been made, was arrested by the Ngati-Pikiao in the bush on the south side of Rotoiti Lake while endeavouring to join Kereopa by a long inland detour. The capture was made in February, 1865, under directions from Colonel Greer, commanding at Tauranga. The following narrative of the capture and of a curious Pai-marire scene in the forest was given by Heni Pore (Te Kiri-karamu), the Arawa woman who behaved so valiantly at the Gate *Pa* in 1864:—*

" In 1865, when the Hauhau religion began to spread to some of our Arawa people (the Ngati-Rangiwewehi), I went to live close to Kahuwera, a strong palisaded *pa* on a high point on the northern shore of Lake Rotoiti, near Otaramarae. I lived there with the family of my uncle Wiremu Matenga te Ruru, of Ngati-Uenukukopako. We camped on the beach below the *pa*. It became known that the Ngai-te-Rangi chief Hori Tupaea—the highest chief on the Bay of Plenty coast—was endeavouring to cross through the Arawa country on his way to join Kereopa or the other Hauhau rebels in the interior, and this move we determined to prevent. Every track was watched, and armed canoe-crews went out daily and nightly to scout the shores of the lake. I carried Matenga's rifle; he was not in good health, and he wished me to accompany him and use his gun whenever necessary, as I was accustomed to war and the use of firearms. We knew that Hori Tupaea intended to join Kereopa and his band, but no one knew exactly where the chief would creep through our district; therefore we kept diligent watch all along the shores of the lake, which lay across Hori's path into the interior.

" Matenga and his wife and several others of us went out daily in a small canoe. One morning as we were closely scanning the coast of the southern side of the lake we saw an empty canoe drifting about near the middle of the lake. The alarm was given, and soon a score of canoes were racing for it. The canoe had evidently been cast loose a very little while before. We concluded correctly that Hori and his party had crossed the lake in the early dawn and were somewhere near the shore in the bush south of us. We paddled ashore to the nearer part of the south coast, and there came on the trail. Matenga's keen eyes noticed a place where the soil had been disturbed a very little while before; it was on the cliff-side between Hauparu and Ruato Bays, and a tuft of grass with earth clinging to the

---

*Statement by Heni Pore to the author, at Rotorua, 1919.

roots had been dislodged from the higher parts of the steep wall.

"We landed and climbed the cliff, and soon we came upon the foot-tracks of a party of people leading into the forest. We followed them up rapidly into the bush south of Ruato, and we soon came upon a number of Maoris with Hori Tupaea among them. An elderly man named Tiu Tamehana ("Jew Thompson") was with them; he was their *kai-karakia* (religious leader) or *poropiti* (prophet). Our chief Matenga called on the party to stop, threatening to fire on them unless they stood fast. Hori and his companions thereupon came to a halt, but made no move to surrender. Instead, they gathered round their prophet and chanted their Pai-marire incantations and called upon their gods to strike us blind. We surrounded them and listened to their *karakia*. Besides Hori and Tiu, there were in the Hauhau party Hori's old wife, Akuhata and his wife and child, a half-caste named Hoani Makaraoti (John McLeod), of Tauranga, Te Hati, Timoti te Amopo, and a number of others, about twenty in all. Timoti was my old friend of the war-path the previous year, the *tohunga* who had saved my life at the Gate *Pa*. He had turned Hauhau, and was guiding the Tauranga people across the country. Having camped for a long time in the bush on the north side of Rotoiti, they had succeeded in crossing the lake unseen, and were making for the Urewera Country when we discovered them. Hori and his people were all unarmed; there was not even a stone *patu* among them. But old Timoti secretly carried a short-handled tomahawk under his shirt; this was discovered afterwards. The party had done their utmost to escape detection, but their tracks were readily found, and their device of dragging brushwood back and forward on the beach at the spot where they landed, to hide their footmarks, only served to put our scouts on their trail.

"The old chief and his prophet, as we approached, cried out to their two *atuas* or gods, Rura and Riki, to blind our eyes and prevent us seeing them. Then the prophet began his Pai-marire chant, as taught by Te Ua in Taranaki:—

Koterani, teihana!
Karaiti titi Kai.
Kopere, teihana!
Rire, rire, hau!

"As they chanted the Hauhaus raised their right hands above their heads, the universal Pai-marire gesture. Then they chanted their fanatic prayers, seeming to believe that their incantations would avert their capture. The prophet began this Maori version of the Benediction, in which all the people joined:—

Kororia me te Pata,
Ranei tu,
Ranei to,
Riiko—e!
Te wai te pikine,
Huoro Pata, hema ta pi,
Wai wi rau te,
Rire rire, hau!

("Glory to the Father and to the Son and to the Holy Ghost, as it was in the beginning and ever shall be, world without end"—and, instead of "Amen," "*Rire, rire, hau!*")

"I well remembered this *karakia* as I heard it then chanted by the Hauhaus with their right hands upraised, but it was not until long afterwards that I discovered what it meant. The Hauhaus believed that when they had learned all these incantations well their gods Rura and Riki would give them power to walk upon the waters and perform other supernatural deeds. Some of us asked, 'Then why did not Hori Tupaea walk across the lake instead of taking a canoe?' 'Oh,' said the Hauhaus, 'he was not well enough versed in the *karakia* then.'

"When we had surrounded the Hauhau party Matenga te Ruru told me to go out to the edge of the bush and fire my gun to let the Arawa know of our discovery. I hurried out to the edge of the bush near the cliff and fired, and then all the canoe-crews who were out scouting came paddling eagerly up to where I stood. The prisoners were brought out to the beach, and we embarked them in a large war-canoe with Matene te Huaki and some of his armed Arawa. We paddled up to Kahuwera, our crew in great excitement, chanting their war-songs in time to the paddle-strokes, and when we reached the beach below the *pa* there was a tremendous commotion. The people dashed out into the water to meet us, brandishing tomahawks over the prisoners and threatening to kill them. Matene te Huaki, who held the steering-paddle, swept the canoe out from the shore and waited until the excitement had subsided before landing the prisoners. Hori Tupaea remained impassive through all this demonstration. He offered to go ashore and brave the anger of the people, and then he betook himself again to his Pai-marire chants, with uplifted right hand, apparently firm in the faith that his Hauhau gods would preserve his life and strike his antagonists helpless. The Arawa loudly taunted him with his condition; he was a prisoner now, and never again could he call himself a *rangatira*.

"The prisoners were brought ashore and were led up to a big tent which was pitched on the point of Kahuwera *pa*. There they were plentifully supplied with food—pork, *kumara*, wild honey, and so forth—but they were very sorrowful and could not eat much. From Kahuwera the people were sent on to

Maketu and Tauranga. Hori Tupaea was kept a prisoner for some time. When my old friend Timoti was searched in Tauranga Gaol his short *patiti* (tomahawk) was found stuck in his flax girdle underneath his shirt. The prophet had ordered that no weapons should be carried on the secret expedition, and when he learned of Timoti's tomahawk he declared that this breach of his instructions was the *aitua* which had brought misfortune on the party."

The arrest of Hori Tupaea led, in a rather curious way, to the prosecution of a man prominent in Maori affairs, Mr. C. O. Davis, of Auckland, on a charge of sedition. Tomika te Mutu and other chiefs of the Ngai-te-Rangi Tribe, of Tauranga, visited Auckland shortly after the capture of Hori Tupaea. Tomika and his friends were indignant at this action, and vented their opinion of the Arawa in a song of derision, which Mr. Davis copied and had printed at his press. The *waiata* was as follows:—

Ko wai te iwi e korerotia kinotia nei?
Ko te Arawa mangai-nui.
He aha tona kino?
He tohe nona ki te whakatutu ki te taha Maori.
He aha te take a kaha ai ki te whakatutu i te taha Maori?
He pati moni, he pati kai.
He aha tona he e kitea nei e nga iwi?
Ko tona pakanga ki te patu i nga iwi i te Awa-a-te-Atua.
Tena tetahi?
Ko te kohurutanga i a Te Aporotanga.
Tena tetahi?
Ko tona whakai ki te hopu huhuakore i te Ariki a Tauranga, i a Hori Tupaea.
Meatia e mutu ai enei he?
Me whakahoki pai-marire a Te Arawa ki tona tupunga mai ki Hawaiki.

[TRANSLATION]

Who are the people that speak words of evil?
The big-mouthed Arawa.
Wherein does their evil lie ?
They urge insistently violence and mischief among the Maori people.
For what reason do they persist in this mischief ?
They are bribed with money; they are bribed with food.
What was their sin in the eyes of the tribes?
They made war upon and slew the people of the Awa-a-te-Atua.
What was another of their evil deeds?
The murder of Te Aporotanga.
And another ?
They surrounded and unjustly seized the high chief of Tauranga, Hori Tupaea.
What can be done to end these evils ?
The Arawa should be returned peacefully to the father-land whence they came, to Hawaiki.

The Government secured the manuscript of the song, and instituted a prosecution on a charge of seditious libel, professing to see in it an invitation to the other tribes to attack the Arawa. The whole thing lay in the interpretation of the Maori words. Archdeacon Maunsell and others gave expert evidence which had the effect of inducing the jury unanimously to acquit Mr. Davis.

Te Aporotanga mentioned in this *waiata* was the Whakatohea chief captured in the Kaokaoroa battle near Matata and shot by Tohi te Ururangi's widow in revenge for the death of her husband.

Chapter 8

THE FIGHTING AT TE TAPIRI

ON THE WESTERN side of the Urewera Ranges, overlooking the Kaingaroa Plain, are the fern-grown ruins of a series of Maori redoubts, the scene of a war drama, hitherto unchronicled, which probably was the most gallant deed of the friendly natives during the wars. These earthwork *pas* of Kupapa and Hauhau are arranged with relation to each other somewhat in the figure of the Southern Cross constellation. They stand on the verge of the high country more than 2,000 feet above sea-level, and 1,000 feet above the plains which stretch away for apparently illimitable distances north and south. The locality is some fifteen miles above Murupara, on the Rangitaiki, and can be reached only by a rough horse-track, fording the swift Rangitaiki near its junction with the Wheao, then following up the latter stream for some distance, and striking into the hills by a narrow and rather difficult trail through the tall *tutu* and fern. As the top of this outermost range of the Urewera *rohepotae* is reached, two small rounded hills are seen on either side of the track, almost within revolver-shot of each other. Each *toropuke* is densely covered with *tutu* bushes, flax, *koromiko*, shrubs, and fern. Only on close exploration is it discovered that these peaceful verdurous mounds are fortified. Breaking through the shrubbery and flax bushes, an oblong fort of trench and parapet is found crowning each of the hills; in some places the parapet is 5 feet or 6 feet in height, preserved from crumbling by its protective garment of vegetation. These redoubts were built and manned in 1865 by the Ngati-Manawa Tribe and the Ngati-Rangitihi section of the Arawa Tribe, who espoused the Government side against the Hauhaus and bravely barred Kereopa's passage from the Urewera Mountains to the Kaingaroa Plain and the Waikato, after his murder of the missionary Volkner and the conversion of the Urewera tribes to the rebel faith. The larger of the two is Te Tapiri; it is the hill on the north side of the track—the left as one approaches from the Rangitaiki Valley. The earthwork here is about 40 yards in length by 18 yards in width, its greater axis lying north and south, the trend of the range. The *pa* on the south side of the trail is Okupu. These were the little forts which blocked the way to the west, and held up Kereopa the Eye-eater and his hundreds of newly made disciples. Looking eastward to the interminable ranges and forests of the Urewera, we observe that we are on the scarp of a tableland, much dissected by gullies and creeks, and that this tableland, now fern-covered, was evidently once populated and cultivated. Clumps of native bush stand here and there, but the edge of the main forest is about three-quarters of a mile distant. Half a mile away, in the direction of the forest, about south-east, is the site of the Hauhau camp Te Huruhuru. Farther in, three-quarters of a mile east from Te Tapiri, is a round hill called Hinamoki, close to the bush. This fortified hill was the headquarters of Kereopa and his gang of fanatics and murderers, with their army of Urewera warriors. Then, turning to the north, where the crest of the range breaks into less gentle outlines, we see the steep mountain-top called Te Tuahu-a-te-Atua ("The Altar of the God"). On this height, distant three-quarters of a mile by air-line from Te Tapiri Hill —the intervening terrain is broken into gully and severely slanting hill-slope—a section of the rebels built a fort which formed the objective of a desperate night raid by the Arawa contingent.

In the late summer of 1865 Kereopa and his apostles, gathering up a large body of Whakatohea people and carrying with them the preserved head of the murdered missionary Volkner, moved inland to the territory of the Urewera. The *niu,* or sacred flag-pole of worship and incantation, rose in the bush villages, and Kereopa and his fellow-prophets of the new and bloody faith exhorted their savage congregations, teaching them the ritual of the *niu* as they revolved about the sacred mast-foot, and assuring them that if they embraced the gospel of Pai-marire, no Government bullet could touch them. Volkner's head was left for the time being at Tauaroa, on the open Kuhawaea Plain, at the foot of Mount Tawhiuau; it was not taken to Te Tapiri, but presently other human heads were set up on the platform at the foot of Kereopa's *niu.* The mountain clans were summoned, and by May Kereopa was preaching his doctrine of blood and superstition to a gathering of practically the whole of the Urewera and Ngati-Whare, assembled near Ahi-Kereru. It was the leader's intention, after spreading the principles of the new religion among the bush tribes, to cross the Kaingaroa to Waikato and convert the Kingites to his creed.

Now it was that Ngati-Manawa determined to make an effort to prevent Kereopa penetrating their territory to reach the Waikato. Te Tapiri and Heruiwi, the routes by which the

Eye-eater would leave the ranges for the Kaingaroa, were Ngati-Manawa lands, and resentment at the threatened passage of the rebel through their country heightened the animosity born of a determination to join forces with other sections of the Arawa against the Hauhaus. A chief of the Ngati-Manawa had fought against the Government and suffered a wound at Orakau the previous year, but that circumstance did not prejudice the clan's adherence to the Queen. The little tribe did not number more than forty fighting-men, but its pluck and determination made it a formidable antagonist to its truculent neighbours of the mountain country. Moreover, the women took a vigorous hand, and some of them exhibited a courage in no degree inferior to that of the heroines of Orakau.

So, in May of 1865, we find the Ngati-Manawa hurriedly raising an expedition to hold the Tapiri track. The business was urgent; there was no time to collect a large war-party. About forty people of the tribe, half of whom were women and girls, gathered at a rendezvous on the Rangitaiki, and, quickly marching up to the ranges, selected a commanding hill as a site for their post. A redoubt was speedily constructed, consisting of ditch and parapet as already described, reinforced with a timber palisade. This *pa* they occupied, and a message was sent to the Ngati-Whare and Tuhoe at Te Whaiti informing them that neither Kereopa nor any of his followers would be permitted to cross Ngati-Manawa land to the Kaingaroa Plain. An appeal for help had already been despatched to Arama Karaka Moko-nui-a-Rangi, the principal chief of the Arawa Tribe at Lake Tarawera, who in his turn sent out to rally the main body of his people; but the only assistance Ngati-Manawa received in time to be of service was a party of about thirty of the Ngati-Rangitihi from Tapahoro, at the eastern end of Tarawera. When these people arrived, the *pa* Te Tapiri proved too small for the united force, and therefore another redoubt was constructed on the adjacent hill Okupu. The forces were then rearranged so that some of each tribe garrisoned each *pa*. Te Tapiri was under the command of Rawiri Tahawai, and Okupu under Peraniko Parakiri Tahawai, both of Ngati-Manawa, and each took in a section of Ngati-Rangitihi.

The larger garrison, that of Te Tapiri, consisted of the following persons, nearly all Ngati-Manawa:—

Men: Rewi Rangiamio, Peraniko Parakiri, Rawiri Parakiri Tahawai, Horomona Rawiri, Waretini te Mutu, Poia te Ririapu, Enoka Unuhia, Te Mau-paraoa, Raharuhi, Kuratau, Heta Tamati Eru te Uru-taia, Ahuriri, Takeke, Ngahere te Wiremu, Ngaharere, Katu Poia, Ngawaka, Nga-Korowai, Rorerika, and Pani Ahuriri (younger brother of Harehare).

Women: Maraea Rawiri, Hinekou, Te Pare Tipua, Te Hau, Ramarihi te Hau, Roka Hika, Erena Horomona, Ruihi Eru, Te Amoroa, Mere Peka, Mere Rangiheuea, Ripeka Harehare, Hana Tia Poia, Raiha Poia (wife of Rewi Rangiamio), Kutia Poia, Waretini Paurini, Mereana Harete Peraniko, Ruihi Tamaku, Mera Peka Tamehana, Te Puaka Huriwaka, Nga-Aikiha Marunui, and Heni (sister of Harehare Ahuriri and the wife of Ngawaka te Toroa).

Among the Ngati-Rangitihi, besides their chief Arama Karaka, were a number of men who had previously distinguished themselves in battle. One of these was a very plucky old man from Tapahoro, named Rorerika. The combined garrisons were armed with single- and double-barrel shot-guns and some ancient Tower flint-lock muskets, called by the natives *ngutu-parera.* Their stock of powder and lead was not large, owing to the haste with which the expedition had been organized, and the chiefs therefore did their utmost to prevent a waste of ammunition. In Te Tapiri *pa* the cartridges were made up by the old men Ahuriri and Rawiri Tahawai.

Among the women of Ngati-Manawa was a highly valuable auxiliary to the fighting force, a celebrated *kuia matakite,* or prophetess and sorceress, by name Hinekou. She was the mother of the two young warriors Te Mau-paraoa and Raharuhi (Lazarus). In her hands rested the direction of what may be called the religious or occult side of the operations. She was of the old cannibal age, and was a sorceress of reputedly terrible powers. She betook herself to her ancient gods, and continually recited *karakia Maori,* incantations of pagan days, read the *tohu* or signs of earth and sky, interpreted dreams, and performed dark ceremonies to confound and defeat the enemy. So wise a woman was a source of enormous strength in stiffening the morale of a Maori war-party.

The hilltop parapets of Ngati-Manawa and their Tarawera friends were still raw from the spade, and the lashing of the palisades had only just been completed, when the first shots were exchanged between the outlying pickets and the scouts of Tuhoe. The Urewera and Ngati-Whare headquarters with Kereopa was barely ten miles distant, and immediately the challenge of the Government party was delivered at Te Whaiti the call to arms was sent from village to village through the gorges and over the ranges to call in the full force of the tribes, and the conch-shell trumpets and war-horns, or *pu-tatara* and *pukaea,* blared their summons from hill to hill. A force of several hundreds of men was quickly on the march to the western frontier to engage and eject the daring Ngati-Manawa. The leading chiefs of the Whakatohea, Tuhoe, Ngati-Whare, and Patu-heuheu, with their people, had been captivated by Kereopa's religion, and the prophet of slaughter found the mountaineers a willing instrument. Added to this newborn fanatic fervour was the desire to pay off old grudges against Ngati-Manawa, and to sweep such a "contemptible little army" from the face of the hills.

Emerging from the forests which blanketed the head-streams of Whirinaki, the Hauhau army fixed its camp at the old clearing of Hinamoki, a stretch of undulating land about three-quarters of a mile east of Te Tapiri, just on the edge of the great *tawa* and *rimu* bush. Here a small round isolated hill which rose about 30 feet above the clearings was seized upon as a suitable site for a fortification; it had the advantage of a convenient water-supply, for a small clear stream flowed in a valley between its slopes and the bush. The hill was trenched, parapeted, and palisaded, and *whares* were constructed within its walls for Kereopa and his disciples and as many of Tuhoe and Ngati-Whare as could find room in the closely packed quarters. The rest built rough shelters on the slopes and levels about the *pa*. Later a smaller camp, not well fortified, was made at Te Huruhuru, about a third of a mile to the south-west of Hinamoki in the direction of the descent to the plains. Above the double palisade of Hinamoki were flown the Hauhau war-flags called "Rura" and "Riki"—the Pai-marire gods of incantation and battle. There was not room on the fortified knoll for the necessary *niu* flagpole, and a spar was planted on the little level space at the foot of the hill, on its northern side. To this day the *turanga o te niu,* the spot where the pole stood, may distinctly be seen. It is a bare circular space of earth from which the surface sods have been removed—in diameter about 6 feet. Here stood the sacred mast of Pai-marire invocation and worship, surrounded by a low fence of stakes. Within this pale none but the priest could stand; and here Kereopa and his fellow-prophet Horomona, a patriarchal white-beard from Taranaki, took up their posts, leading the chants as they stood with their hands on the flag-staff, and slowly revolving about it while their disciples marched around it repeating the rhythmic service in loud chorus. On the stage at the foot of the mast was exhibited the smoke-dried head of a white soldier who had been killed in Taranaki, one of the victims of the surprise attack at Te Ahuahu. This head had been carried from village to village through the heart of the Island; the Pai-marire prophets pretended to consult it as an oracle. Its bearer was the white deserter, Louis Baker. After the murder of Mr. Volkner at Opotiki this white slave was compelled to carry the missionary's head about the country on Kereopa's journeyings, and at each village it was displayed to the people on a kind of tray which was slung in front of him, supported by flax straps about his neck.

Not all the native spectators of those barbarous rites at the *niu* foot were willing witnesses. One at least was a *herehere,* or prisoner, temporarily in the Hauhaus' hands. This was Harehare, a young chief of the Ngati-Manawa, who happened to be at Te Whaiti on a visit to the Ngati-Whare, to whom he was related, when Kereopa and his party began hostilities. Harehare was not permitted to return to his people, but was held captive and taken to the camp at Hinamoki. His life was in danger, if not from Ngati-Whare, at any rate from Kereopa's acolytes among Whakatohea and Tuhoe; but presently he escaped into the night, and after hiding and wandering several days in the bush he rejoined his people on the plains after the last fight.

Kereopa could, of course, have descended to the Kaingaroa, but his Urewera followers determined to eject the daring Queenites.

Several skirmishes occurred between the opposing forces. Ngati-Manawa and their allies for the most part contented themselves with holding their redoubts built across the track and in defying Kereopa. Early in June, 1865, a skirmish was fought in the open ground between the camps. The enemy had cut off Ngati-Manawa from their water-supply, which was a small stream in a gully between the opposing camps. The Queenites made a desperate attempt to recover their source of water and to drive off the enemy who had entrenched themselves above it. Strong Hauhau reinforcements rushed out from the Huruhuru *pa,* and the enemy were led on by Kereopa with the utmost savagery, uttering ferocious cries and reciting Pai-marire charms. The prophet had assured his followers that his incantations and *mana* would render them bullet-proof; nevertheless two of them fell dead, pierced by balls from the Tapiri warriors, and several were wounded. The little band of Queenites fought their way back, losing five killed. These men were Eru te Erutaia, Tamehana te Wiremu Unuhia, Hohepa Matataia, Hemi Tamehana Anaru, and Te Ririapu.

The bodies of the first three named were decapitated by the Hauhau savages; the remaining two had hastily been concealed in the fern by their comrades, and so escaped mutilation with the tomahawk. The hacked-off heads were carried triumphantly to the foot of the *niu* at Hinamoki, and there Kereopa, in front of the people, snatched up each head in turn, scooped the eyes from it and swallowed them. Then, lifting up his voice in fanatic prayer-song, the cannibal priest, his face, hands, and garments smeared with blood, led his people in a burst of Pai-marire chanting round the *niu.* From this deed of ferocity, following upon the crime at Opotiki, the arch-Hauhau came now to be known through the land as "Kereopa Kai-whatu" (or "Kai-karu")—"Kereopa the Eye-eater."

The three heads were set by Kereopa on the stage at the foot of the *niu,* beside the soldier's head, in the ceremonies which followed, and the prophet and his coadjutor old Solomon (Horomona Poropiti) exhorted the maddened tribespeople and prophesied complete victory over all *pakehas* and *pakeha*-favouring Maoris. Overhead flew the war-flags "Rura" and "Riki," hoisted on the sacred mast. Round and round the *niu* again went the host of deluded worshippers, Kereopa the Eye-eater in the inner circle revolving about the pole, and the roar of hundreds of voices in the barking chorus was borne to the ears of the gallant little garrisons of the twin hills on Te Tapiri track.

Next day Kereopa boldly appeared in full view of the redoubts, on a bush-fringed ridge between Te Huruhuru *pa* and the hills of Okupu and Te Tapiri, and considerably more than half-way to the Queenite posts. The prophet was escorted by some of his disciples, who bore the heads of the three slain warriors of Ngati-Manawa. These heads were displayed on short sticks (*turuturu*) stuck in the ground, and over them Kereopa performed his Pai-marire ceremonies, crying his incantations and dancing with many and savage gestures. These insults to their dead infuriated the Ngati-Manawa and Ngati-Rangitihi, who from the parapets of Okupu fired several volleys at the Hauhaus at a range of about 300 yards, wounding a man named Meihana, one of the bearers of the heads. While Kereopa with his Pai-marire spells strove to strike terror into the Queenites, the walls of Okupu were crowded with men and women in an extraordinary state of rage mingled with fear. Their prophetess Hinekou was there, marching up and down the parapet, reciting her spells to *whakaporangitia* (cause madness to afflict) the enemy, and *karakia* to counteract those of Kereopa. While some of the musketeers directed a fire upon the prophet, others hurled curses at him, and some rolled up little balls of dough in their hands and, shouting, "See! I eat Kereopa's eyes!" swallowed them. So the strange scene continued until the volleys drove Kereopa and his head-bearers into cover in the gully beyond.

Ngati-Manawa and Ngati-Rangitihi were now in a desperate situation. Not only was their water-supply cut off, but their food-stores were very small, and their ammunition was almost expended. They were besieged and practically beleaguered, for while the skirmishing was going on on the tableland a party of the enemy had built another *pa,* hemming in the Queenites on the north. This *pa* was constructed on a sharp spur of the Tuahu-a-te-Atua Range, about three-quarters of a mile from Te Tapiri, and separated from it by a deep gully and steep slopes covered with bush and fern. The only way left clear was the western side, the sharp descent to the Rangitaiki Valley and the plains; but the two little garrisons did not intend to retreat until any other course was absolutely hopeless.

The leaders of Te Tapiri and Okupu at a council of war now resolved to launch at least one vigorous blow against their foes before abandoning their positions. Meanwhile Hinekou, the wise woman, waited for a *tohu,* a sign from the gods, and she counselled patience for a little while.

The old seeress watched the heavenly bodies at night and presently announced that the propitious time had arrived. The *tohu* was a small star just above the moon. Hinekou announced dramatically that it represented the small war-party of the Kawanatanga—the Government—while the moon symbolized the large force of the Hauhaus. The sight of the star in the ascendant signified that the Kawanatanga would prevail over the foe. The *kokiri* (the storming-party) had already been selected by the prophetess. One by one she told off the men for the assault. Some volunteers were bidden remain in the *pa,* for Hinekou's gods warned her that they would fall if they ventured forth. Certain eager young men marched out in spite of her admonitions and they were killed, as she had predicted.

The storming-party numbered seventeen men, led by Mauparaoa Puritia, Rewi Rangiamio, and Raharuhi. Armed with double-barrel guns and tomahawks, they left Te Tapiri quietly under cover of the darkness and made a long detour along the fern slopes on the west, facing the Kaingaroa Plain, ascending to the bush just below the *pa* well before the first signs of daybreak. The bush grew close to the south-east side of the *pa,* and the gateway faced the dark growth of timber and fern which sheltered the little forlorn hope. The *kokiri* lay there awaiting the rising of Kopu (Jupiter, or Venus, as morning star), which was to be the signal for the attack. The assault was to synchronize with a series of feint attacks made simultaneously from Te Tapiri and Okupu redoubts against the three positions held by the enemy on the tableland. It was a winter's night, very cold at this altitude (about 2,300 feet), and the scantily clad warriors shivered as they lay in their cover anxiously awaiting the appearance of the morning star.

Suddenly a dark figure emerged from the gateway of the fort and walked down the track towards Rewi Rangiamio, who was crouching in the fern near the front face of the *pa.* The man was the Hauhau sentry. Unconscious of the nearness of his enemies, he moved along the track until he was almost on top of Rewi. That warrior could wait no longer. He fired both barrels of his gun into the sentry, who gave a great bound and fell dead.

Leaping over the body, Rewi charged for the gateway, followed closely by several of his men. The other Queenites, posted at short intervals below the stockade, rushed for the nearest parts of the *pa,* and soon were clambering over the palisade and parapet. The *pa,* though small, was a strong place of defence, and could only have been taken by surprise. It had been constructed by cutting away the top of the sharp peaked hill and enclosing the flattened summit with an earth wall, ditch, and timber stockade. The *whares* of the garrison were built close up against the parapet, with the thatched roofs sloping inwards and the fronts open. Those of the *kokiri* who swarmed over the walls therefore found themselves on top of the huts. They thrust their guns through the flimsy roofs and shot some of the Hauhaus before they had time to rush outside.

There was desperate hand-to-hand work around the *niu* pole which stood in the centre of the *pa.* A man named Mihaere, of the Ngai-Tawhaki *hapu* of the Urewera, was shot at the foot of the *niu.* The surprise was complete; all who remained in the *whares* of the *pa* were shot or tomahawked. Those who escaped engaged the gallant little band as they fought their way back to Te Tapiri in the early foggy morning. Seven Hauhaus had been killed in the *pa,* but the loss inflicted on the enemy outside was much greater. One of the principal men shot was Te Roihi, of the Patu-heuheu; he was the too-wakeful sentry who received the contents of Rewi's *tupara.* Others of his comrades who fell in or around the walls were Karito, Wi Tere (Patu-heuheu), Eria Toko-pounamu, and Ruka te Papaki (Ngai-Tawhaki).

The Queenites' loss was five killed and ten wounded. Rorerika, a fine old man of much courage, was shot through both thighs, and fell in the high fern below the fort. Both thigh-bones were broken, and Rorerika, knowing that his case was hopeless, with his tomahawk and hands scooped out a hole in the earth large enough to conceal his body from the enemy. The dying man then scraped the earth over himself as well as he could, and drew the fern around to hide all traces. So the old hero dug his own grave and saved his body from the mutilating tomahawk. The story of his last moments was plainly to be read by the relief-party of Arawa which arrived some days later, too late to join in the fighting.

Meanwhile the terrain between the Queenite redoubts and Hinamoki and Te Huruhuru was ringing with battle. The Queenites, immediately on hearing the first shots from Te Tuahu-a-te-Atua, delivered swift feint attacks on the Hauhau positions in order to hold the enemy's attention and prevent an effort to cut off Rewi and Raharuhi and their band. The parties told off for these operations took nearly the whole of the man-power of the garrisons; only five men could be spared to defend the forts, besides a number of women. These women, however, were as brave as their husbands and brothers. A courageous chieftainess named Maraea, a tower of strength to the Queenites by reason of her vigour and her prowess with a gun, was detailed to defend the *waharoa,* or gateway, of Te Tapiri *pa.* The attackers, assailed in their turn by hundreds of Hauhaus, were soon compelled to fall back on Te Tapiri, and a fierce fight was waged on the southern and eastern faces of that fort. Kereopa's men were beaten back from the walls after a strenuous attempt to storm. Maraea, the *wahine toa,* distinguished herself by shooting two men who had attempted to rush the gateway.

The members of the *kokiri* who had stormed the *pa* on Te Tuahu-a-te-Atua Ridge had desperate work in fighting their way back to their fort, from which they were cut off by a party of the enemy. They reached their friends at last, after making a long detour through rough and steep fern country. They were encumbered with the bodies of their killed and several men badly wounded—one had received an ounce bullet through his lungs—and finding it impossible to carry the dead off the field they concealed them in the fern, pressing the vegetation down round the bodies in such a manner that the foe never discovered the remains.

When the twelve survivors of the heroic storming-party at last rejoined their friends in Te Tapiri a council was held to consider further operations. Elation at the successful surprise attack upon Tuahu-a-te-Atua was tempered with the thought that if relief did not arrive very soon the position on the range would be quite untenable. Nevertheless, it was determined to hold the fort to the last possible moment.

Several days passed, made painful for the garrison by the want of food and water and the sufferings of the wounded. The one consolation was that they had inflicted so severe a blow upon the Patu-heuheu and kindred *hapus* at Te Tuahu-a-te-Atua that the survivors did not again occupy the hill *pa;* disgusted at their cutting-up, they marched off the field and left the other tribes to continue the siege.

Being now in a desperate strait, with scarcely any ammunition left, and with no prospect of relief, Ngati-Manawa and Ngati-Rangitihi resolved to abandon their posts. So, in the dead of night, having tied up their dogs and left their fires burning, to deceive the enemy, they quietly took the steep trail down through the *tutu* and fern to the Rangitaiki.

Daylight revealed to the Hauhau outposts the fact that the Tapiri redoubts were deserted, and a large force of Hauhaus came in pursuit. The retreating Kawanatanga men and women, however, having a few hours' start, had by that time crossed the

Rangitaiki at a place where a precarious bridge, consisting of a single log, spanned the river, flowing rapidly through a narrow cañon, in places 100 feet deep and only 15 feet to 20 feet wide. This river-gorge, several miles in length, was crossed at three widely separated places by these perilous bridges. The retreating force used the bridge called "Te Arawhata a Noho-moke." Wounded and all safely reached the west bank, and when the last man of the rearguard had crossed, Raharuhi with his tomahawk cut away the earth which supported the end of the *arawhata,* and the log fell into the rushing Rangitaiki. By the destruction of this bridge the pursuers were delayed, and the respite of several hours thus gained enabled the fugitives to continue their march unmolested until they reached the open tableland of the Kaingaroa. The persistent advance-party of the Urewera, however, still followed them, and only drew off when near Pekepeke, two small hills on the eastern side of the plateau, a few miles south of Murupara. Their retirement was prompted by the sight of a body of men crossing the plain to meet the retreating Queenites.

This was the long-expected relief-party, the main body of the Arawa, under Major William G. Mair, who had hurried up from the coast on receiving news of the siege at Te Tapiri, transmitted to Rotorua by the Ngati-Whaoa *hapu* at Paeroa Mountain. Mair took his force up into the range, the enemy retiring before him, and recovered the bodies of the slain friendlies.

So ended the plucky exploit of the friendlies on Te Tapiri Range, an epic of the Maori wars which has not until now found an historian. It was remarkable not only for the gallantry displayed by the small band of men and women who espoused the Government side, but for the observance of the ancient war-customs side by side with all the picturesque ritual of the Pai-marire. The Ngati-Manawa and Arawa expedition, although compelled to retire under pressure of numbers, accomplished its principal object, which was to frustrate Kereopa's plan to cross the plains and raise the Kingites against the Government. It was not long after Te Tapiri that he returned to Opotiki, for we hear of him there in August of 1865 bringing with him several heads of Government natives killed, smoke-cured, and preserved as trophies. These heads, he declared to his followers, would be efficacious as talismans in preventing the Government troops landing at Opotiki. That *pakeha* expedition was at hand. As for the Urewera who had come under the prophet's influence, but whose faith in the infallibility of his *mana* and incantations was somewhat shaken by the fall of so many men to the Kawanatanga bullets, Major Mair, with characteristic fearlessness, presently made a diplomatic visit to their headquarters and persuaded them to refrain from taking further active share in Kereopa's campaign.

NOTES

On the 14th March, 1920, Captain Gilbert Mair, N.Z.C., Harehare and two other men of Ngati-Manawa, and the writer camped in the *tawa* bush close to the Hinamoki *pa,* after exploring the battle-ground, and the old chief related many of the incidents narrated in this chapter. Harehare is now over eighty years of age. He wears the New Zealand War Medal for service on the Government side against the Hauhaus on many expeditions from 1866 to 1871. Other details were gathered at meetings with the Ngati-Manawa in their carved house, "Tangi-haruru," at Murupara. The Urewera versions of the fighting differ from the Kawanatanga natives' narrative on some points.

Hinamoki (or Ohinamoki) was a settlement of Ngati-Whare. The Huruhuru *pa* was built by Tuhoe. It was not strongly fortified like Hinamoki Hill.

Harehare, when pointing out the spot where the Hauhau *niu* stood at Hinamoki, related that as the mountain tribes and Whakatohea were gathered one day on the *marae* surrounding the pole of worship, listening to Kereopa proclaiming the efficacy of his incantations against bullets, the faith of the disciples was rather damped when they suddenly received a volley which killed two of their number. The volley was fired by a Ngati-Manawa party at long range across the Hinamoki Creek. Harehare witnessed this incident.

Captain Mair supplied the following note about the casualties in the Tuahu-a-te-Atua fight:—

"Of the friendlies, Poia Ririapu had his lower jaw smashed; his son Katu was killed. Peraniko Tahawai (Parakiri) was very badly wounded. Ngaharare, Ngawaka's younger brother, was taken prisoner, flung on the ground, and held down while one of the enemy, placing his gun-muzzle (as he thought) on the centre of the neck, fired. The shot only stunned him; he lay still till next night, then recovered his senses and crawled out to rejoin his people. When Te Kooti raided Galatea in 1869 Ngaharare was taken prisoner, and later was shot by one of Te Kooti's men (accidentally, it was said, but really he was jealous of Ngaharare's predilection for his young wife). Of the seventeen men who attacked Te Tuahu-a-te-Atua five were killed and ten wounded. Mau-paraoa killed four or five Hauhaus with his *tupara* as they passed along a high ridge, showing clearly against the sky. He was a greater *toa* than Rewi Rangiamio. Another good fighter was Morihi, of Ngati-Rangitihi. As for the enemy, when I was sitting as Royal Commissioner dealing with Tuhoe lands, a surprising number of Ngati-Whare, Patu-heuheu, and Ngai-Tawhaki men were mentioned in sworn evidence as having been killed in the Tuahu-a-te-Atua fight. The total enemy loss must have been about twenty-five killed and the same number wounded. The loss effectually prevented Tuhoe and associated tribes from going to the Waikato."

Chapter 9

OPERATIONS AT MATATA AND TE TEKO

MANY OF THE men most actively concerned in the murder of Mr. Volkner and Mr. James Fulloon took refuge in the natural fortresses provided by the almost impassable swamps and islanded lagoons of the Rangitaiki, on the east side of the Matata settlement near the mouth of the Awa-a-te-Atua. This Rangitaiki Swamp—now unwanted by the Government drainage-works and in process of profitable settlement—was then accessible only by the tracks along the seaward sandhills, or by canoe along the Tarawera River, the Awaiti-paku, and the Orini River (connecting the Awa-a-te-Atua with Whakatane Harbour) and by the labyrinth of reed-fringed waterways, navigable in small canoes, winding among the islets that rose above the water a few feet and made camping-grounds for eel-fishers and wildfowl hunters. The first fortified positions of the Hauhaus—consisting of Whakatohea, Ngati-Awa, Ngai-te-Rangi-houhiri, and some Urewera—were the palisaded *pas* Parawai and Te Matapihi, on the west side of the Tarawera River, and when driven out of these they took to their island-like forts in the great swamp. The Government despatched Major William G. Mair, R.M., who had served in the Waikato War as ensign in the Colonial Defence Force Cavalry and as staff interpreter, to organize a force of the Arawa Tribe and engage the Hauhaus, and endeavour to capture the principal men concerned in the murders at Opotiki and Whakatane. Major Mair, after initiating a Maketu column and arranging Matata as the rendezvous, assembled his force at Rotorua for the Matata campaign. It consisted of detachments from Tuhourangi, Ngati-Tuwharetoa, Ngati-Whakaue, Ngati-Rangiwewehi, Ngati-Uenukukopako, Ngati-Rangiteaorere, Ngati-Tuara, and the smaller clans of the Arawa. Crossing Tarawera Lake to Tapahore *pa,* a considerable number of Ngati-Rangitihi were enlisted for the expedition, and Mair's force now numbered about four hundred men. He marched down the valley of the Tarawera River, skirmishing on the way, to Matata (Te Awa-a-te-Atua). The position at Parawai was too strong to be taken by assault, so had to be passed by. On reaching Matata the column was augmented by the force from Maketu, made up principally of Ngati-Pikiao and Ngati-Whakaue. The skirmishing which followed on the western side of the river and then among the islands of the great swamps, followed by the siege of Te Teko *pa,* occupied nearly two months. At Tiepa-taua and other places a few miles inland from Matata Mair and his Arawa cut the Hauhaus off from their cultivations on the slopes west of the Awa-a-te-Atua. Te Parawai *pa* was taken. Here, says a native who served in the contingent, Major Mair set a bold example of courage by working right up to the palisades and firing his rifle through the fence. The capture of the strong position at Te Matapihi was the next operation, and the Hauhaus were forced into the swamps. The friendlies settled themselves comfortably in the captured village at Matata Island, where there were many large *whares,* and expeditions went along the beach dunes and maintained a heavy fire on the enemy. Among the Arawa was the warrior woman Heni te Kiri-karamu, who had distinguished herself by her bravery and her humanity to the British wounded at the Gate *Pa* in the previous year, and who was now fighting on the Government side, with her uncle Matenga te Ruru. She was armed with a Minie rifle, and proved herself a good shot. One day, at fairly long range, she killed a Hauhau who was poling a canoe across a lagoon. The fighting grew closer, and for several days there was sharp skirmishing and sniping at a range of about 100 yards until the Hauhaus were driven out. Mair and Heni Pore had the only rifles in the force. The Arawa were armed chiefly with double- and single-barrel shot-guns; some had only old flint-locks and Tower muskets.

The swamp strongholds, Oheu, Otamauru, and Omeheu, inland of the coastal belt were all trenched and palisaded, and in these retreats the Hauhaus, like Hereward the Wake and his Saxons in the fens of Ely, considered themselves safe from conquest by their foes. Mair took them in the rear by quietly and swiftly landing a hundred Ngati-Pikiao on Otamauru, a large strongly trenched and palisaded *pa* about five miles up the Orini Stream in the direction of Whakatane; the stream bounded its east side. The war-party from Matata Island first marched along the sea-beach, under cover of night, taking care to walk just within the edge of the water (it was flood tide) so that their footmarks would not be seen by any Hauhau scouts. The attackers then struck inland, crossed the belt of sandhills, and swam the Orini River, with their guns held high and their ammunition fastened on their heads. They completely surrounded the Otamauru *pa* and took the garrison prisoners. This broke the resistance in the Rangitaiki swamps. Omeheu *pa,* on an island east of the Tarawera River, some four miles inland, was the last place abandoned. The Hauhaus retreated up the Tarawera River in their canoes, and thence paddled along the Motumotu Creek, which then connected the Tarawera with the Rangitaiki River; it ran parallel with the Orini.

The present road between Matata and Whakatane traverses the low-lying country which was the scene of Mair's difficult swamp campaign. Matata Island, once a large and populous place, is passed on the east side of the new mouth of the Tarawera River. Te Matapihi is on the west bank of the Tarawera, about a mile above the present punt-crossing, a short distance from the ocean-beach. The square scarped hillock of Oheu, in the raupo swamp, the smallest *pa* of the series, is seen a little way from the road, on the inland side. In the siege of this stronghold Major Mair shot a Hauhau through the forehead from Te Rangatai, on the opposite bank of the Tarawera River.*

The coastal parts cleared of the Hauhaus, the Arawa went on a foraging expedition to Whakatane by canoe along the Orini River—it was then a deep navigable waterway, but has now been rendered useless by the Rangitaiki drainage-works. Loading their canoes with great quantities of *kumara, taro,* and maize from the deserted cultivations on the lower Whakatane, they paddled back to their base at Matata, and prepared to take the field again.

THE SIEGE OF TE TEKO

Intelligence had now reached Major Mair that the principal body of the Hauhaus had taken up a position at Te Teko, some twenty-five miles inland, where they had entrenched themselves strongly on the Rangitaiki River. The war-canoes were manned and the force was moved up against the strong current, and presently sat down in front of Te Teko and considered the strength of the enemy. The position occupied by the Hauhaus was a large *pa,* with the usual firing-trenches and a stout double line of palisading, abutting on the steep west (left) bank of the Rangitaiki, a mile and a half above the large settlement Koko-

---

* Regarding this man shot by Major Mair, Captain Gilbert Mair said: "The Tarawera bounded the western face of the *pa,* and the body floated down that river into the Rangitaiki and was picked up three days afterwards. The man had been shot fair through the forehead, and on word being sent to the enemy a message came back to say that their man had not been killed but had fallen in and been drowned through a magic spell wrought by an evil *atua* (god). The Major told the messenger that the *atua* had made a curious hole in his head. However, they were ashamed at having told lies, so declined to send for the body.

From a drawing by Major-General Gordon Robley, in "Illustrated London News."]

Matata Pa after its Capture by the Arawa, 1865

In the background is the *niu,* the Hauhau mast of worship, with a carved *rupe,* or dove, on the truck.

hinau. The lines of the fortification can still be traced in a grass paddock about 200 yards in rear of the present hotel and store at the small township of Te Teko, on the main road from Rotorua to Whakatane.

On reconnoitring the Hauhau stronghold Mair saw that it was not practicable to take it by assault, and he therefore decided to approach it by sap. He had closely observed the military engineers' methods in the sap at Orakau in the previous year, and proceeded to apply them to the reduction of Te Teko. His examination of the *pa* showed that the position had been very skilfully fortified. The main palisade, the *kiri-tangata,* stood about 10 feet high, composed of split totara timbers set closely together, and practicably unassailable by a storming-party. The main gateway in the fort faced west. At the rear there was a well-designed covered way to the water, cut obliquely down the bank of the river, here about 20 feet high. It was excavated out of the bank, and it sides were reinforced with strong totara posts; it was roofed over with slabs, which were then covered with earth. There was also a small palisaded dockyard for the canoes at the foot of the river-bank connected with the river gate. The position of the Hauhaus was made doubly strong by the support of a small *pa,* called Pa-harakeke, erected on the opposite bank of the river, within close range of Te Teko. The garrison of Te Teko totalled about one hundred and seventy men and youths; with them were a large number of women and children. Mair's force, drawn from the principal tribes of the Arawa, and including some of the Ngati-Tuwharetoa from Taupo, was between four hundred and five hundred strong.

In approaching the *pa* by sap Major Mair profited by what he had seen at Orakau—and, indeed, improved upon it. He observed that an old river-bed of the Rangitaiki, considerably higher than its present channel, described a great arc westward of the *pa,* curving round from south to north and meeting the river again some hundreds of yards below the enemy's position. This depression he selected as his base of attack. Five lines of sap were opened on the eastern brink of the old river-course (now marked by a grove of tall eucalyptus). Each sap was allotted to a tribe or large *hapu,* and the rivalry thus engendered produced intense competition in the trench-digging. The most southerly line of sap was given to Ngati-Pikiao, the strongest section of the Arawa engaged; and, although it was somewhat longer than the other trenches, it reached the palisades first. It was carried in a zigzag course in a line between Mount Edgecumbe and the south-west bastion of the *pa.* After commencing this sap Mair set his men to work on a trench parallel with the front face of the *pa* and about 100 yards distant from it. This parallel served as a base communication trench, and from it four other saps were opened out at varying distances.

The several lines of approach by sap were allotted to the tribes in this order, beginning with the southernmost trench directed towards the south-west angle: (1) Ngati-Pikiao, Ngati-Uenukukukopako, and Ngati-Tarawhai (of Maketu, Rotoiti, and Rotorua); (2) Ngati-Whakaue, of Ohinemutu, Rotorua; (3) Ngati-Rangiteaorere and some of Ngati-Uenukukukopako (Rotorua); (4) Ngati-Rangiwewehi (of Awahou, Rotorua); (5) Ngati-Tuwharetoa (from Taupo) and Tuhourangi (Te Wairoa, Tarawera). A large number of Ngati-Rangitihi were incorporated with the various trench-parties.

As these saps were advanced towards the stockade, demi-parallels about 10 feet in length were opened out at short distances apart, on either side alternately, and marksmen took post there to cover the work of the trench-diggers. The main communication trench was also filled with musketeers. The head of each sap was just wide enough for one digger; three or four would be behind him deepening it to about 4 feet, while the rest of the people were engaged in keeping down the Hauhaus' fire from the *pa*. Women as well as men toiled and fought. Among the Ngati-Uenukukopako *hapu* who joined with Ngati-Pikiao in driving the southern sap diagonally towards the *pa* was Heni te Kiri-karamu (Heni Pore). When she was not digging she was firing in one of the covering-parties. Another dauntless *wahine* was Ana Pene, from Te Ngae, Rotorua. She was conspicuous for her fearlessness in exposing herself to fire and urging the warriors on. "While the saps were being dug," narrates Heni, "each tribe and *hapu* striving furiously to be the first to reach the foot of the palisade, Ana Pene and several of the other Arawa women climbed on to the roofs of the *whares* built on the level ground outside the trench-lines, and loudly encouraged their men by chanting battle-songs and urging them to be strong and brave. High above all the noises of the battlefield we heard the penetrating voice of Ana Pene. When the firing was hottest she stood on top of a hut, heedless of the Hauhau bullets, shouting '*Riria, e te iwi, riria!*' ('Fight on, O tribe, fight on!') and similar inspiring calls that heartened us all up and gave more vigour to the diggers' arms. Ana's husband and two brothers were among the fighters."

Another exciting scene was a daredevil demonstration made one day by an Arawa named Hakawa. This man, a tall tattooed old fellow from Ohinemutu, came to Mair and asked for some yards of white calico. (This material was used for making bands, which all the Arawa wore about their brows to distinguish them from the Hauhaus when in action.) The commander gave him 4 yards of the stuff. Hakawa stripped naked, painted himself all over with *kokowai* (red ochre mixed with shark-oil), tied the white calico round his head, leaving the great part of it streaming out behind him, and completed his alarming outfit by sticking turkey-feathers in the turban band all round his head. Then, painted like a Red Indian, he rushed out to the open and went dashing at the top of his speed up and down in front of the *pa*, within close range, leaping from side to side, shouting words of insult at the enemy, and uttering short sharp yells or thrusting his tongue out in derision and defiance. Bounding furiously from side to side, he went the length of the *pa*-front several times, his calico head-streamer flying behind him like a pennant. Hundreds of shots were fired at him under the foot of the outer stockade by the astonished Hauhaus in their trench, but he escaped untouched. Major Mair, hearing the cheering and laughing and the great fusilade from the *pa*, went out to discover the cause of the uproar, and with difficulty recalled Hakawa, who was hugely enjoying himself. When Mair demanded the meaning of the remarkable exhibition the old warrior explained, with an amusing naïveté, that his object was to induce the enemy to waste all their ammunition firing at him, so that the Arawa presently would be able to storm the place. He was surprised when Major Mair vetoed his spectacular tactics. Mere crazy bravado as it seemed, however, Mair privately recognized it as a really brave bit of self-sacrifice. Hakawa used to declare afterwards that the rebels wasted three hundred cartridges on him.

It became necessary to silence Pa-harakeke, the small fort on the opposite bank of the Rangitaiki, whose garrison kept up a harassing fire on the sappers approaching the angles of the main stronghold. Major Mair called for volunteers for the task, and a party of about twenty of the best fighters of Ngati-Pikiao crossed the river—several in a small canoe which Mair had captured, and the rest by swimming, using one hand to swim and carrying their loaded rifles, muzzles down, in the other, gripped half-way up the barrel to keep the charges dry. Three of the warriors—Te Pokiha, Mita te Rangi-tuakoha, and another man—on reaching the western bank under the *pa,* went up and demanded the surrender of the place, wishing to obtain peaceable possession of it if possible in order to avoid the necessity of shooting several of their kinsmen who were among the garrison. Maraki, a connection of the Ngati-Pikiao chiefs, was in charge of the *pa.* He and his companions surrendered. Freed from the annoying fire across the river, Mair's sappers pushed on more rapidly. When the fifth sap had passed the north angle of the *pa* (the end nearest the present road) Major Mair worked down the bank and towards the covered way which led to the river and succeeded in cutting off the garrison from their water-supply.

The sappers of Ngati-Pikiao, being the most numerous clan, were the first to carry their trench close up to the stockade. They were within a few feet of the south-west flanking salient, and prepared for the assault. Strong ropes of flax were plaited, and stones of 4 lb. or 5 lb. weight were made fast to them, with the intention of throwing them over the palisades and hauling down sections of the fence by united pulls. In the other saps the men were working away furiously, while the covering-parties continued their heavy fire on the stockade. The defenders of the fort were now running short of ammunition, and they were troubled also by the difficulty of obtaining water.

All was ready for the assault when Te Pokiha (Major Fox, the principal fighting chief of Ngati-Pikiao) called out to the garrison from the head of the sap, " Where are the Tawera ? " He wished to give that *hapu* a last chance to escape the slaughter. " Come out, Te Tawera, that you may be saved ! " The effect exceeded Pokiha's expectations. A white flag was displayed, and the whole garrison surrendered.

Major Mair ordered the Hauhaus to file out and lay down their arms. As they came out of the gateway one by one, headed by their dejected chiefs, their heads bowed in humiliation, the Arawa sprang up from their works, *hapu* by *hapu,* and leaped into the action of a furious war-dance, with choruses of tremendous volume. Ngati-Pikiao and their related *hapus* chanted, as they danced, the ancient battle-song beginning "*Koia ano te peruperu,*" accompanying their tremendous rhythmic shouting with appropriate action, raising their guns, held horizontally in front of them, up above their heads and down again, in time to the words. Then they chanted, in another measure, the famous old war-song "*Kia kutia, au au!*" The Taupo men, with the Tuhourangi, burst into their great battle-song. "*Uhi mai e waero,*" to the action of a leaping performance in which they jumped in perfect time high off the ground, their legs doubled under them like birds on the wing, facing this way and then that, with their guns gripped by the barrel, uplifted at arm's length. Then the tribes united in one grand war-song of triumph, delivered with terrific leap and stamp, in front of their silent captives.

Several of the Hauhau garrison had been killed in the three days' siege, but the Arawa lost no men. Major Mair had a narrow escape. Towards the end of the fighting he was in the head of the Ngati-Pikiao trench, within 5 yards of the outer palisade, when a man fired at him from the trench inside the main stockade. The bullet probably struck a post of the *pekerangi* (the outer stockade) and was thereby given a jagged edge, for in its course it was momentarily entangled in Mair's long beard and tore some of his whiskers out by the roots. The shock and the excruciating pain caused Mair to imagine at first that part of his jaw had been carried away.

The prisoners were escorted down to the Arawa headquarters camp at Matata, where another war-dance of victory celebrated their arrival, and then Major Mair marched about a score of the principal offenders to Opotiki for trial by court-martial. Among the men captured was Horomona (Solomon), one of the Pai-marire prophets from Taranaki, the chief instigator of the murder of Mr. Fulloon. He was a venerable man with long snow-white hair and beard, a mystic and sage of the ancient type. Horomona was born at Moturoa, the present site of New Plymouth. Other Hauhaus captured included the chief Te Hura, and Kiri-mangu and the boy Penetito who had been concerned in the death of Fulloon. Heni Pore described a lively incident which followed the arrival of captors and prisoners at Matata. When the force marched into the headquarters *pa,* Te Hura was attacked by the Arawa chieftainess Puhou, of Maketu, whose nephew Tamarangi had been killed at Mana-Whakatane, opposite Te

Matapihi, in the swamp skirmishing. Puhou, in a furious state of rage and grief, declared that she would have revenge for her young relative's death. Clothed only in a waist mat and armed with a whalebone *patu,* she rushed up to the captured chief Te Hura as he sat on the *marae.* She caught him by the hair, violently rated him, and would have killed him with the sharp-edged club had she not been prevented forcibly. Te Hura said not a word, and made not a move all the time, says an eye-witness; he sat there like a statue.

The Arawa expeditionary force followed up their success by scouring the Hauhau country in the Whakatane Valley and looting horses and other property and foraging for food. They returned along the Orini Stream to Matata with canoe-loads of potatoes, *kumara,* and *taro.* The Ngati-Rangitihi clan and a section of Tuhourangi and Ngati-Tarawhai occupied Matata, which was given them for their military services, and Ngati-Pikiao and the other *hapus* marched home to Maketu and Rotorua.

The trial of the principal captured Hauhaus took place in Auckland, and on the 17th May, 1866, five of the prisoners—Horomona the prophet, Mikaere Kirimangu, Mokomoko, Heremita Kahupaea, and Hakaraia te Ruwhi—were executed in Mount Eden Prison. Young Penetito and Hekara, who had been sentenced to death, were reprieved on account of their youth, and later were pardoned. Penetito in 1922 was living at Te Teko. He served under Captain Preece in the last campaign (1871–72).

Te Uhi, a Whakatane chief with a reputation as a worker of witchcraft, was one of those who surrendered to the European force at Opotiki. For his complicity in the cutting-off of the "Kate" and the killing of Fulloon and the crew he was sentenced to imprisonment. Te Uhi died at Opotiki in 1886; he imagined he was *makutu*'d, or bewitched, by a more powerful *tohunga,* and his fears killed him.

NOTES

The southern trench at Te Teko, which was the longest, is the best marked of all the lines of sap to-day. In spite of repeated ploughings it is easily traceable in a line from the south-west bastion of the *pa* towards the volcanic peak of Mount Edgecumbe, which dominates the landscape. A large blue-gum tree is growing in the olden war-sap, about 60 yards from the *pa.* The south-west flanking bastion towards which this trench was directed is the most distinct section of the *pa*-lines. The line of the main communication trench in the grove of eucalyptus, and two of the other four lines of sap dug towards the stockades, are also still traceable on exploring the ground.

Captain Preece in the early "seventies" occupied Te Teko as a military post with his No. 2 Company of the Arawa Flying Column, and built a redoubt.

Mr. F. Burt, who for many years farmed the Matapihi Block, with the *pa* on it, in the low-lying Matata country, writes as follows on the subject of the fortified places in the great Rangitaiki Swamp: "I have inquired of the natives and they state that Te Matapihi and Oheu are the places to which the Hauhaus went after the Battle of Kaokaoroa. The brother of Wharepapa (of the Tawera Tribe) was killed at Oheu. He was shot by Major Mair as he stood up on the parapet of Oheu *pa*. Major Mair was at a spot called Rangatai. Tamarangi climbed up a peach-tree at Mana-Whakatane, opposite Matapihi (westerly), and was shot from the *pa;* the distance would be half a mile at least. These Maoris must have had some 'go' in them in the old days. From Matapihi to Tiepataua they had a good solid road made. One part ran through the swamp, which was fairly deep, starting from the *pa,* across to Mana-Whakatane. They had a road made across, and a bridge near the end to let the water through; the piles are there now, *totara* and *puriri*. I cut a piece off to see what it was like, and the timber is as good as the day it was put there. Evidently they made the foundation of the road with large pumice blocks and then put earth on top (there is even now a great quantity of pumice boulders round about these parts), but how they carted the earth I do not know. This part of the road is about half a mile long; it is now fairly dry on account of the dredge-cut the Government put up to tap the Awakaponga Stream. I have found the remains of guns and revolvers on Matapihi. The natives tell me when they were spearing eels near the Kohika Lake they came across the remains of an old *pa,* so there was evidently one between Oheu and the Kohika. Omeheu Island is about three or four miles from the Rangatai, and I should say it must have been a great stronghold in the old days, as it is (or was) entirely surrounded by swamp."

Chapter 10

THE EXPEDITION TO OPOTIKI

A PUNITIVE FORCE was despatched from Wanganui and Wellington to Opotiki early in September, 1865, to conduct operations against the murderers of Mr. Volkner. This expedition consisted of two companies of the Taranaki Military Settlers, two companies of Wanganui and Patea Rangers, a troop of the Wanganui Yeomanry Cavalry, and the Wanganui Native Contingent. There was also a company of men from Waikato under Captain George. The strength of the force was about five hundred men, and Major Brassey, the Indian veteran who had distinguished himself at Pipiriki, was in command. The transports which conveyed the expedition up the coast were the steamers "Stormbird," "Ladybird," and "Ahuriri." At Hicks Bay, East Cape, on the 7th September, they were joined by H.M.S. "Brisk," and by the small steamer "Huntress" as a tender for the landing at Opotiki. At 10 o'clock on the morning of the 8th September the fleet arrived off the Opotiki bar, and preparations were made to land the force. The Patea Rangers, about fifty strong, and Nos. 8 and 10 Companies of Military Settlers were transferred to the "Huntress." The little steamer crossed the bar, but grounded on a sandbank, and with the ebbing of the tide she heeled over, with her decks towards the shore. Captain Levy, the coast trader who had been prominent in the episodes at Opotiki earlier in the year, had come up from Wellington with the expedition as pilot and interpreter, and he was at the wheel of the "Huntress" when she took the ground. The Hauhaus on the shore opened fire at long range, but did little damage. An over-confident Pai-marire prophet, strong in his fanatic faith, walked deliberately across the tidal flat to the edge of the channel within close range of the "Huntress," reciting his incantations and making magic passes with his hands. The old priest took his seat on a log regardless of the heavy fire opened on him, which quickly stretched him dead. When the "Huntress's" men at last got ashore they found he had received eighteen bullets.

With some difficulty the small force at last landed on the sandhills opposite the large settlement of Pa-kowhai, the site of the present town of Opotiki. The Maoris, in strong force, opened fire from the left bank. The Patea Rangers (who were accompanied by Captain Von Tempsky as a volunteer) occupied the dunes directly opposite the settlement and resisted strong sorties of the Hauhaus. The north-east wind strengthened to a gale, and the position of the small landing force was extremely uncomfortable. The gale sent the loose sand flying in clouds, and eight men of the Rangers contracted a kind of sandy blight in the eyes as the result. One of the veteran Rangers recalls a curious remedy adopted for this eye trouble: " We had our ears pierced as a cure for it."

From a drawing, 1860]
H.M.S. "Brisk"

The men spent a perishing night crouched on the sandhills, lashed by a cold wind and drenched with torrents of rain. They had no rations, and most of them not only were without their greatcoats, but had not even tunics; the Patea Rangers had gone ashore in the customary fighting-costume of shirt and waist-shawl, and some were barefooted. Shivering, hungry, and sand-grimed, the little party anxiously awaited relief. The gale had compelled H.M.S. "Brisk"* and the three small troop-steamers to put to sea, and they sheltered under

---

* H.M.S. " Brisk " was a steam-corvette, armed with a 68-pounder solid-shot gun on a traversing-carriage mounted in the bow; fourteen 32-pounders of 34 cwt. each, seven on each broadside; a 45 cwt. 32-pounder mounted abaft the mizzenmast (on wooden carriage) to fire on either quarter or right astern. The ship's compliment was 190 officers and men. The " Brisk " was a full-rigged ship with very small coal-capacity, so she nearly always moved about under sail. Her screw propeller, when not in use, was disconnected and hoisted up to the level of the upper deck by stout tackles.

In 1853–54, in the war with Russia, the " Brisk " was sent up to the White Sea with the corvette " Miranda," also afterwards on the New Zealand Station, and the " Eurydice," and she shared in the blockade of Archangel. Admiral Sir Cyprian Bridge was then a midshipman in the corvette.

Volkner's Church, Opotiki

Showing the church entrenched by the colonial troops, 1865

Mou-tohora (Whale Island), off Whakatane. Next day the weather cleared, and when the " Brisk " and her convoy returned the rest of the force landed on the sandhills. As soon as the " Brisk " was near enough she dropped over a keg of biscuits and a small keg of rum to drift ashore to the starving men, and the ship's large pinnace was launched. The boat was swamped in the breakers, but the crew continued pulling, and the Patea Rangers ran into the surf and dragged her bodily up on the sandhills. After a scanty meal the Rangers crossed over to the Opape side of the river-mouth (west), and after a skirmish on the sandhills occupied a low spur of land. The tide was now half-flood, and the Rangers were able to cross a salt-water creek, the Hikutawa-tawa (Mackerel-tail), afterwards called the "Huntress Creek," by a ford on the west side of the present Town of Opotiki, near the house of the martyred missionary. The water was up to their armpits. They sent a message back to their ship for their boots, and when the main body landed they entered the large Whakatohea village. The Native Contingent, immediately on landing in the " Brisk's " boats, engaged the Hauhaus, who were

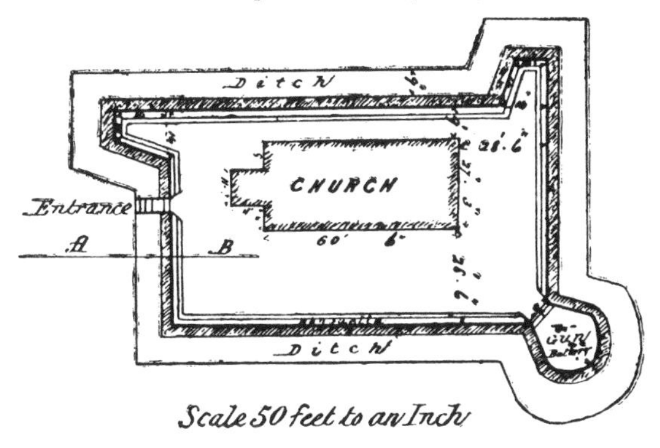

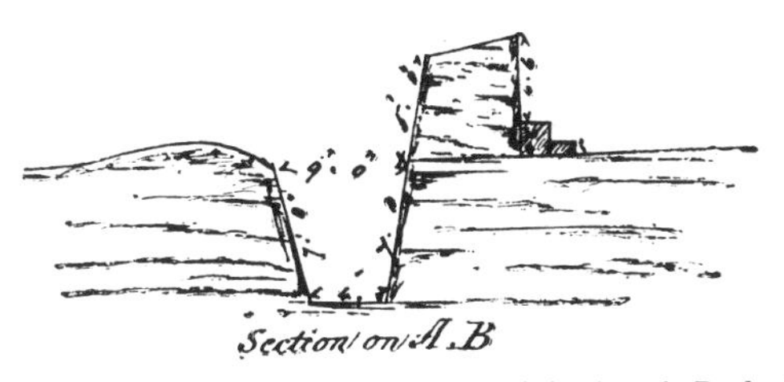

Plan of Entrenchment, Opotiki Church Redoubt.

in strong force on the sandhills, and, headed by Major McDonnell, drove them back several miles, killing six; another Hauhau was shot in the village. A rusty cannon, an old ship's gun, was found emplaced and loaded near the beach, ready to greet the force, but the Hauhaus, for some reason, did not fire it. The projectile consisted of a large stone cut to shape and crammed into the muzzle, out of which the end of it was protruding.

For some weeks thereafter the expedition remained in Opotiki, skirmishing occasionally, and revelling in the abundance of food in the captured settlements. The Whakatohea people were celebrated for their skill in wood-carving, and the alluvial plain of Opotiki was covered with well-built villages containing many beautifully decorated houses. The valley was rich in food crops and in groves of peach-trees. The force was plentifully rationed out of the abundance of meat and poultry, and the *kumara* and potatoes and other vegetables which the fields and gardens of the Whakatane produced. The Wanganui Yeomanry Cavalry were mounted on looted Maori horses, and had the satisfaction presently, of engaging in a cavalry charge on the open plain.

Major Brassey took possession of the murdered missionary's church, which he entrenched and converted into a redoubt. The stores and camp equipment were placed in the church, and the force camped round it. The Patea Rangers, probably the hardiest veterans of the expedition, camped by themselves. They were proficient in the art of food-foraging, and on the march they outdistanced most of the other corps, particularly the less practised men of the 1st Waikato Militia under Major (afterwards Colonel) St. John. The Rangers were always ready on the instant for any emergency. Wherever they camped a rallying-post was appointed, and in the event of an alarm, at the call " Turn out, Rangers ! " they ran to their post, belted and armed. They did not wait to fall in in parade order, but as soon as the officer in charge had a dozen or so about him he dashed off, leaving one man at the rallying-point to give the direction taken. The company of the Wanganui Rangers was another competent workmanlike body, armed like the others with carbine and revolver. Their commander was Captain Ross, who was killed at the Turuturu-mokai Redoubt, Taranaki, in 1868.

The Hauhau *hapus* of the Whakatohea fortified themselves between four and five miles up the valley, on the end of a low spur which abutted on the plain near the eastern side of the entrance to the Waioeka Gorge. The entrenchment consisted of three redoubts close to each other on knolls or terraces, one in rear of the other; two of these works were surrounded by palisading. On the flat below, where the road winds round the foot of the ridge, stood the *niu* flagpole. This fortification was called Te Puia *pa*. A short distance farther up the valley, and closely overlooking Waioeka River from the east, was the hill fort Opekerau. Hira te Popo's village—the present headquarters of Hira's people, the Ngati-Ira Tribe—was at its foot. The Native Contingent and Captain Nelson George's Forest Rangers skirmished close up to the Puia *pa*. In one of the expeditions after cattle Captain John Percy, commanding the cavalry, was severely wounded, near the Puia ridge.

On the 4th October a force under Major McDonnell advanced to the attack of the stockaded *pa* which the Hauhaus had just built at a spot called Te Tarata, on the right (east) bank of the Waioeka River, some four miles from the Opotiki settlement. The terrain here, the Kiorekino plain, is perfectly level; it is now covered with beautiful well-tilled farms. The first report that the natives had built a fort on the Kiorekino levels was brought into headquarters by several mounted men of the Native Contingent; in the meantime McDonnell made a preliminary attack on the *pa* and came under a very hot fire, from which there was little cover. The Patea Rangers dashed off to the scene immediately the news reached the camp. The Wanganui Yeomanry Cavalry troop was soon in the saddle, and passed the Rangers at the gallop. The first of the Rangers to reach the scene of action were Sergeant (now Captain) J. R. Rushton and his inseparable comrade Corporal David White (later Lieutenant), who was killed on the Upper Whakatane in 1869. Taking cover in some flax bushes in front of the *pa,* they were busy sniping at the Hauhaus when the rest of the force came skirmishing up. The troops surrounded the *pa* on three sides—the steep bank of the river, 20 feet high, was on the other flank, the west. A piece of artillery was brought out from Opotiki, a 6-pounder gun from the steamer "Huntress," manned by a crew of bluejackets. It was emplaced commanding the *pa* at close range and loaded with chain-shot and old iron. The fort was a hastily-built double stockade, consisting largely of *whanake* (cabbage-tree) trunks set in closely between posts of heavy timber; inside were the trenches and rifle-pits, connected with each other and well traversed.

The attack on Te Tarata quickly roused the garrison of Te Puia *pa* to action and assistance; the places were in plain view of each other and about three-quarters of a mile apart. Reinforcements from the Otara side, on the eastern flank of the plain, and from the triple entrenchments of Te Puia, after a Pai-marire service round their *niu,* came skirmishing across the plain to make a diversion in favour of their friends. They were met and engaged by the troop of cavalry, who charged through them and killed or wounded about a score.

Describing this engagement, one of the few cavalry charges made in the Maori wars, a veteran of the Wanganui Yeomanry Cavalry, Mr. William Wallace, of Hawera, gave the following narrative:—

"Our small troop engaged in the skirmish on the fern flat at Kiorekino numbered twenty-two, under Lieutenant McPherson (afterwards Captain). Late in the afternoon, just as we were getting ready to skirmish up with the foot troops, it was observed that a party of Hauhaus had left the Puia *pa* and was advancing quickly across the plain towards us. We could see them marching round their *niu* pole on the flat below the *pa,* the preliminary to their dash down to relieve their comrades in Te Tarata. Some of our men had dismounted for the attack on the river-bank stockade. The cavalry method then was to work in formation of threes, not fours as now; it was right, left, and centre, and when working dismounted the centre man had to hold the horses. The order was given to mount and charge the Maori reinforcements. There was a slight dip in the ground between us and the Hauhaus, and they did not see us until we were pretty close on them. With drawn swords we galloped into them and caught them in the short fern, and we killed or severely wounded twenty—nearly a Maori apiece for us. One of our big troopers, Hogan, gave them the point of his sword and ran through three in succession. Others cut at them with the sabre, but the point was the best. I saw one of our troopers, armed with a curved sword or scimitar (most of us had the straight cavalry sword) cutting away at a Maori, but not making much impression, as the sword was so blunt. Another man, Maxwell, whose horse was hit, went flying in one direction and his horse in another, and he was left on the ground. His horse went bolting on ahead, and one Maori escaped by hanging to its bridle as it galloped off. It did not stop until it reached the foot of the spur near the *niu,* and there it dropped dead from two bullet-wounds. A fine big warrior with a great bushy beard who was lying wounded in the fern made an attempt to rise to fire the second barrel of his *tupara* lying near him, but a trooper—Maxwell, I think—reached it first and shot the owner dead with it. We were among those Maoris for a few crowded moments, swords slashing and thrusting, and guns and revolvers popping. The Maoris dodged in all directions. One daring fellow grappled one of our men and nearly pulled him off his horse. The trooper was trying ineffectually to fire his Tranter revolver, but only kept pulling the cocking-trigger, forgetting in his hurry to press the firing-trigger. [The Tranter, unlike the Colt, was cocked by a second trigger, below the chamber and outside the firing-trigger guard.]

"It was wonderful," continued the veteran cavalryman, "to see the way the Maoris parried the sword-cuts. We found one gun afterwards which was hacked across the stock and up the middle of the heel of the butt; the man who used it had parried two sword-cuts in quick succession. Our troops could have done more execution if we had wheeled about at once after the charge and gone through the Maoris again, but we were not quick enough. Just after the fight I saw a Maori lying wounded on the field, and I went to a waterhole and brought him some water in my forage-cap, and I handed him over to the Wanganui Maoris, who took care of him."

After the charge Farrier-Sergeant Duff brought in a lad of the Whakatohea Tribe whose skull had been cleft open with a sword. This youth, Paora Taia, recovered, and was living in 1921.

Taking advantage of the low bushes, the flax clumps, and other vegetation around Te Tarata *pa* on the river-bank, McDonnell's force (Rangers, Military Settlers, and Native Contingent) kept up a heavy and accurate fire until well on in the night. A Maori chief in the *pa* called out, about 8 o'clock in the evening, asking what terms would be given if the garrison surrendered. McDonnell's answer was that the surrender must be unconditional; the men concerned in the murder of Mr. Volkner would be tried; the others would simply be prisoners of war. The Hauhaus requested an hour's truce to consider the question of surrendering. This was granted them, and "Cease fire" was ordered. The defenders, however, did not all employ themselves in accordance with the conditions of the temporary truce. The Rangers and other attackers were by this time lying within 10 yards of the outer palisade. It was a moonlight night, and Sergeant Rushton, intently watching the *pa,* exclaimed to his comrade White, "They're cutting the lashings!" Some of the Hauhaus were chopping away at the *aka* vines used to fasten the horizontal rails to the uprights of the stockade, close to the gateway. Next moment some shots were fired from the *pa,* killing two men. A cloud passed over the moon, and down came a long section of the palisade, thrown outward upon the Rangers by the garrison to confuse the attacking-party and facilitate a retreat. There was an instant heavy rush of desperate Maoris, firing their double-barrel guns right and left as they charged out for liberty. Leaping down over the fallen portion of the war-fence, they met the Rangers hand-to-hand. The Rangers first gave them the contents of their carbines and then used their revolvers. One big Maori pitched right over Private William Kelly's head as he fell in the act of charging out. Carbine and tomahawk clashed. It was hot work for a few moments; when it was over sixteen Maoris lay dead, close to the stockade. Most of the shooting by the Rangers in the mêlée was done with their Dean-Adams revolvers. In the midst of it all the 6-pounder from the "Huntress" was fired, very badly aimed, right over the slight dip in which the Rangers were posted. "The chain and old iron with which it had been loaded," narrates a veteran of the corps, "made a terrific screeching as they flew over our heads; this was just after the escaping Maoris had given us their first volley."

The Maoris dashed for the cover of a small watercourse and across the Waioeka River. Heavy volley firing was directed on the river-crossing, and several Hauhaus were killed as they swam or waded to the west bank. The *pa* so suddenly evacuated was occupied, and next morning the Maori dead were buried in their own trenches. The day's casualties for the Whakatohea, Ngai-Tama, and other Hauhaus engaged were about thirty-five killed and at least an equal number wounded. The Government force lost three killed; one of these, Private Tom Brown, of the Patea Rangers, received a bullet through the forehead as he lay with his carbine at his shoulder about to fire. On the morning after this battle the whole force, under Major Stapp (who had been placed in command soon after the arrival of the troops at Opotiki), advanced to the attack of the threefold redoubt at Te Puia, but the Hauhaus abandoned the place without waiting for the assault. They took to the high broken country in rear, and thence fell back on new strongholds in the Waioeka Gorge.*

Intermittent skirmishing continued in the Opotiki district until November of 1865. The cavalry were useful in reconnoitring and foraging expeditions in the open country, and the Rangers and Native Contingent actively scouted the approaches to the plain and the river-bed avenues to the mountainous forest country in rear. The capture of the *pas* at Te Tarata and Te Puia convinced most of the Whakatohea that it was useless to oppose the occupation of the Opotiki Valley, and in October the Ngati-Rua *hapu* of the tribe, numbering over two hundred, came in and surrendered to Major Stapp. Ngati-Ira, of Waioeka, under Hira Te Popo, remained hostile.

The principal expedition inland undertaken by the troops was a forced march into the Waimana Valley via Ohiwa, in an attempt to capture Kereopa and his band of followers. The force, numbering one hundred and fifty men, was under the command of Major McDonnell. The expedition occupied three days. Early on the morning of the 20th October the force reached the outskirts of a small bush *kainga,* Koingo, on the Waimana River, where Captain W. Newland, of the Military Settlers, was left in ambush with half the force to attack the

---

* One of the Maori survivors of the fighting at Te Puia and Kiorekino is the venerable tattooed warrior Netana Whakaari, now living at Waimana. Netana was one of the Hauhaus in Te Puia, and he was engaged in the skirmishing on the Kiorekino plain when the cavalry charge was made. He narrates that a bullet furrowed the top of his head.

The site of the Tarata *pa,* on the Kiorekino flat, can still be traced. The spot is on a terrace on the east bank of the willow-fringed Waioeka River, four miles from Opotiki Town. A few hundred yards from it, on Mr. W. T. Pile's farm, between the homestead and the main road to Waioeka, is the battle-ground of Kiorekino, where the Wanganui Yeomanry Cavalry charged into the Hauhau reinforcements. On this farm also stood the *niu* flagstaff round which the people of Kiorekino marched in their Pai-marire services.

A mile farther on, near the entrance to the Waioeka Gorge, and close to the east bank of the river, are the grass-grown ruins of the Waioeka Redoubt. This was an outpost of the Opotiki district in 1866–70, when Tamaikowha and his band of Ngai-Tama and Urewera Hauhaus were on the war-path. A hundred yards from the redoubt is the pretty native *kainga* of Opekerau, among its peach-trees on a terrace at the foot of the old hill fort of the same name. The Ngati-Ira *hapu* here are all staunch disciples of the Ringa-tu religion, the offshoot of Pai-marire.

village, while McDonnell with the rest of the men marched cautiously on to some cultivations, where Kereopa, as it developed, was camped with his "twelve apostles."

McDonnell's advanced guard, passing along a narrow bush-track, suddenly encountered Kereopa and his bodyguard. The prophet escaped into the bush, but five of his men were shot. Meanwhile Captain Newland had rushed the village, killing three men and taking several prisoners. The Hauhaus here were the Urewera and Ngai-Tama.

This well-executed attack and other guerrilla activities of the force, chiefly in the Waioeka Gorge, produced the surrender of many of the Hauhaus. Among those who came in was the chief Mokomoko, afterwards hanged in Auckland. Major Mair came in with many prisoners who had been captured at Te Teko, and eighteen Hauhaus were sent to Auckland for trial. In November the Native Contingent returned to the West Coast for the campaign under General Chute; the second battalion of the 1st Waikato Militia, with some Military Settlers, remained in occupation of Opotiki.

One of the expeditions carried out by the Patea and Wanganui Rangers, the Ngati-Hau (Native Contingent), and other corps was a forced march to the Waimana Valley in search of Kereopa, who was known to be in shelter among the Ngati-Tama of that rugged bush district. Captain J. R. Rushton describes this expedition as follows:—

"We marched along the coast to Ohiwa Harbour, and there branched off from the beach and went up through Kutarere. Thence we crossed over the range into the valley of the Waimana and divided our force. The Patea Rangers and Ngati-Hau followed up the branch creek Pae-tawa; the rest, under Captain Ross (Wanganui Rangers), followed up the course of the Waimana River. At 2 o'clock in the morning we Patea Rangers were in a narrow gorge wading up the stream. Major McDonnell, the commanding officer, asked me and Winiata Pakoro, the little Ngati-Hau warrior, to scout on ahead. Towards daylight we came to a place where the stream branched. We took the creek to the left and then ascended a spur on the right. We found a track leading over the range. I said to Winiata, '*Me ata haere taua, ka kino te haere pea*' ('Let us go slowly; the track may be dangerous'). 'No,' replied Winiata, a very impulsive little warrior, 'let us hurry on.' He went up the spur; I followed him, and we looked down through the bush on the top and saw a *niu* flagstaff and the huts of a small village directly below. This, we found afterwards, was a place called Te Kuwini. Winiata did not hesitate, but rushed down ahead of me, and we charged through an opening in the palisade into the *pa,* and across the open space towards the *whares*. The Maoris, thinking a large force was upon them, began to retreat, and my little comrade kept up a hot fire on the running Hauhaus. Not wanting to be caught like a rat in a trap, I slung my revolver by its lanyard to my wrist, and got my back up against a post at the gate of the *pa* with my carbine ready. I kept my eye on a small hut 8 yards or 10 yards to my left. The door opened, and a tall tattooed warrior with a rifle in his right hand came out, rubbing his eyes with his left. I called out, levelling my carbine, 'Drop your gun, and I'll save your life.' The Maori tried to put a cap on his gun. 'You're a dead man now,' I said, and fired, aiming for his breast. Just as I fired, he swerved quick as lightning, but the bullet struck him in the shoulder, and he fell. Just then our force came dashing down the hill to the *pa*. I had to stand over my wounded man to save his life, as the Ngati-Hau wanted to kill him. Winiata wounded Te Whiu, a young Hauhau. (Te Whiu afterwards turned to the Government side and was chiefly instrumental in the capture of Kereopa in 1871.) Te Kuwini was a small place—there were only about twenty Maoris in the *pa*. The spot is about four miles above the present township of Waimana."

Desultory skirmishing continued in the hinterland of Opotiki during 1866 and 1867; several settlers and others were killed, and there were numerous expeditions up the Waioeka and Waimana valleys. The Patea Rangers, who took a particularly active share in the scouting and fighting, were in Opotiki nine months, returning to the West Coast at the end of May, 1866. This very competent little corps was broken up in 1866, through the niggardly treatment of the men by the Government in regard to their grants of land for military services; but many of the good fighters in the corps joined other bodies of volunteers, and their courage and experience in bush fighting made them valuable officers and non-commissioned officers.

Chapter 11

EAST COAST OPERATIONS

HAVING SUCCESSFULLY PROSELYTIZED the tribes of the Bay of Plenty, from the Rangitaiki to Opotiki, Kereopa and Patara in 1865 continued their Pai-marire mission eastward to the tribes of the Tai-Rawhiti (The Coast of the Rising Sun). Kereopa went to Turanganui (now the Gisborne district), where he made hundreds of converts among the Aitanga-a-Mahaki and Rongowhakaata Tribes. The Turanganui Plain around Bishop Williams's mission station at Waerenga-a-Hika was at the time a well-settled, peaceful Maori countryside, covered with cultivations, particularly maize, and rich in fruit-groves. A considerable trade was carried on with Auckland, and numerous schooners and cutters were loaded with produce of the native farms. Into this land of quiet and plenty the cannibal prophet carried his frenzy-exciting religion, and fanaticism, discord, and at last war ruined the long toil of missionaries. The Bishop, in the end, was compelled to abandon the Waerenga establishment to save his life, and the Pai-marire converts reverted to the practices of war and fortified themselves in trenched and palisaded strongholds.

Pata Raukatauri was to some degree a restraining factor; he opposed violence and murder, but he preached Pai-marire throughout the East Cape settlements, and many hundreds of the numerous Ngati-Porou Tribe from Hicks Bay to Waiapu became disciples of the new faith. Hone Pohe was one of the principal advocates of Pai-marire in the Waiapu district, as Pita Tamaturi, of the Aitanga-a-Mahaki, was in Poverty Bay.

One day in the beginning of June, 1865, a large gathering of Ngati-Porou untouched by the Taranaki fanaticism was engaged in the ceremonial opening of a new church at Popoti, near the base of Hikurangi Mountain, when the native minister, Mohi Turei, announced that he had just received a message informing him that a body of Hauhaus had arrived at Pukemaire, in the lower part of the Waiapu Valley. It was at once resolved to make war upon the disturbers of the tribal peace, and an armed party of forty men, chiefly of the Aowera sub-tribe, was selected to march against them. The leaders of the war-party were Makoare Tuatai, Henare Nihoniho, Hika-rukutai, Wiremu Kingi Kuhukuhu, and a very downright and determined man named Ropata Wahawaha, who presently made a great name for himself as a skilful, resolute, and withal ruthless soldier. The small force had only seven muskets and one rifle; for the rest the warriors bore native weapons such as *taiaha* and *patu*.

Setting out next day, the *taua* or war-party reached Mohi Turei's place at Te Hatepe, and in the morning (Sunday, 10th June) continued the march upon the Hauhaus of their tribe. They encountered the fanatics at Mangaone, near Pukemaire, and lost six men killed, including the chief Henare Nihoniho (father of Tuta Nihoniho, who served with distinction on the Queen's side in all the fighting that followed). The Hauhaus' loss was less; nevertheless, although better armed than the Queenite force, they fell back into the cover of the bush. It was in this opening skirmish that Ropata Wahawaha's courage and military genius first attracted the attention and admiration of his tribe.

Several small engagements followed in the Waiapu Valley. The loyal chiefs, headed by Mokena Kohere, Hotene Porourangi, and Henare Potae, appealed to the Government for arms and reinforcements to assist in subduing the Pai-marire revolt, and Mr. McLean (afterwards Sir Donald McLean) quickly sent from Napier a supply of rifles and ammunition, which enabled the Queenite section of Ngati-Porou to take the field satisfactorily equipped for their campaigns. The Government also despatched European forces to the aid of Mokena and his people; these included a company of Military Settlers and some Hawke's Bay volunteers. Brevet-Major James Fraser (late of the 73rd Highlanders) and Lieutenant R. Biggs were in command of the troops, numbering about a hundred men. One of the junior officers was Lieutenant (afterwards Major) Frederick Gascoyne, of the Colonial Defence Force Cavalry, Hawke's Bay squadron. H.M.S. "Eclipse" landed Fraser's force at Te Awanui, near the mouth of the Waiapu River, on the night of the 5th July, 1865, and the men were all in Hatepe *pa*, the stronghold of Mokena Kohere and his friendly natives early next morning. Skirmishing began that day. The "Eclipse" fired a number of shells (some of them 110 lb.) over Te Hatepe into the Hauhau positions.

Some time passed with intermittent skirmishing between the Queenite and Pai-marire factions. Ropata distinguished himself in an affair at Te Horo, where, by making a feigned retreat and laying an ambuscade, he killed several Hauhaus and drove the rest back in disorder. On the 18th July some of Fraser's force had a skirmish in the open, Lieutenant Gascoyne and Ensign Tuke in charge, and inflicted several casualties on the enemy.

On the 2nd August Fraser moved out and made a successful advance on the Hauhau stockade Pa-kairomiromi, several miles up the Waiapu basin. The force was divided into two, taking different routes, and the joint assault on the *pa* was timed for daylight. Ngati-Porou friendlies guided the parties. Fraser and Gascoyne were in charge of the right attacking column (seventy men); Biggs and Tuke took the left (sixty men). At break of day the right wing reached the end of a low ridge in rear of Pa-kairomiromi, which was a large square stockade, with two flanking bastions at diagonally opposite angles. The palisading was about 10 feet high, with loopholes near the ground and a firing-trench inside.

Crossing a small stream unseen by the Hauhaus, the right column fixed bayonets, and Fraser gave the order to charge. Before the flat intervening between the stream and the *pa* had been crossed the force received a heavy volley through the palisading. A number of the enemy had been sleeping in the rifle-trench. Fraser made straight for a gateway with many of his men; Gascoyne and others swarmed over the palisade. There was some sharp fighting at the gateway, where Fraser was using his revolver, and bayonet met long-handled tomahawk. Then Biggs's column dashed up on the right, attacking one of the flanking angles, and the Hauhaus broke and ran. Twenty-five of the enemy were killed in this well-executed affair, besides many wounded, and about thirty prisoners were taken. Eight of the European force were wounded, some dangerously. After pursuing the retreating Hauhaus some distance the force burned the captured stockade and marched back to the Hatepe camp.

In the meantime Henare Potae and his Queenite section of Ngati-Porou, numbering about two hundred men, women, and children, had fortified themselves against the Hauhaus at Tokomaru Bay. Their position was an old *pa* on Te Mawhai, the headland which forms the south head of the bay, above the whaling station known as St. Patrick's Cove. Three old whalers, Waddy, John Henderson, and Cassidy, also took up quarters in the *pa*. The headland was almost an island—it was joined to the mainland by a very narrow neck—and was practically unapproachable except at low water. A short distance inland, facing the centre of the bay, the Hauhaus had strongly entrenched themselves in a *pa* called Pukepapa; they largely outnumbered Potae's loyalists. Another fortified position of the Pai-marire people in the vicinity was Tautini *pa*. During August, Potae and nearly the whole of his fighting-men, who had received arms from the Government, went out along the coast to Anaura and other places to gather in the loyal people, leaving the *pa* temporarily defended by five men and the women; their only arms were muzzle-loading shot-guns.

Discovering the garrison's absence, a large war-party from Pukepapa attacked Te Mawhai at sunrise one morning, when it was low water, clambering up over the precipitous face of the rocks on the seaward side. The few men and women who had guns fought desperately to repel the stormers. Hati te Houkamau, the young chief of Hicks Bay, led the defence, and was most heroically supported by three young women; the three old men in the *pa* kept loading the guns for the brave *wahines*. These young women, Te Rangi-i-paea, Mere Arihi te Puna, and Heni te Pahuahua, shot several of the attackers, whose bodies tumbled to the rocks. The defence was waged with desperate resolution; the gallant handful knew that upon them depended the lives of all the women and children in the *pa*. Some of the older women who had no guns did their part by hurling stones down upon the Hauhaus swarming up the cliff. When the attack was beaten off, thirteen dead Hauhaus lay among the rocks. One of the defenders wounded was Henderson, the old whaler; he was afterwards taken to Auckland, where he died in the hospital.

Henare Potae returned to find all safe. He sent a whaleboat along the coast to Ropata, at Waiapu, requesting assistance. Ropata quickly advanced south with ninety men and joined forces with Potae, and a combined attack was made upon the Hauhau positions, which were garrisoned by four hundred to five hundred men against the loyalists' two hundred. As they advanced upon Tautini the occupants of the *pa* fled to the bush. The hill *pa* Pukepapa was then attacked and captured; most of the garrison evacuated it by night. Ropata dealt out stern punishment by shooting with his revolver several of his tribe, the Aowera, who had joined the Hauhaus and been captured in the skirmishing.

The next encounter (18th August) was near Tahutahu-po, where the Hauhaus had taken up a position, between Tokomaru and Tolago Bay. Henare Potae's force of thirty-six men, on the way back to Te Mawhai from a search for the rebels, met a large body of Hauhaus at Pakura, and fought a sharp action on the edge of a narrow but deep swamp. The two war-parties extended in skirmishing order along two parallel ridges with the swamp between. Potae was outnumbered, and was retreating when Ropata and his ninety Aowera, hearing the firing, dashed up, outflanked the Hauhaus, and decisively defeated them. There were many hand-to-hand encounters, as was the way in those Maori combats. Ropata himself killed two of the twelve rebels who fell. One of these, a wounded man, whom he shot in hiding in the raupo swamp, was the chief Hamiora Rangiuia, of the Hauti Tribe from Tolago Bay.

The defeated Hauhaus abandoned Tahutahu-po and fled southward to the Turanganui country, where they joined the

Aitanga-a-Mahaki and Rongowhakaata Tribes in the Waerenga-a-Hika *pa*. Ropata and his Aowera warriors then returned to the Waiapu Valley to devote their attention to the Hauhaus in Pukemaire *pa*.

Pukemaire was a rather formidable position: a trenched hill with two *pas* connected by a covered way; it stood three miles inland, and was garrisoned by about four hundred Hauhaus. Reinforced by a party of Forest Rangers (about fifty men, under Captain Westrup and Lieutenant Ross), landed from H.M.S. "Brisk" on the 1st October, Major Fraser marched against Pukemaire on the 3rd. It was bitterly cold weather, and the attack was delivered in heavy rain. The forces under Fraser and Ropata numbered 380, which was found sufficient to surround the *pa*. The attackers skirmished up the ridge towards the entrenchments and opened a flying sap. Ropata and twelve of his men got close up under the stockade, and, making fast a rope to a branch cut from a *kauere* tree (*puriri*), one of them threw the bar over the stockade. It caught on the upper cross-rail (*roau*) of the fence, and a quick strong pull by the warriors brought down some yards of the stockade, making a breach. Ropata leaped up into the breach and entered the works. An exceedingly heavy downpour of rain at this moment frustrated the efforts to push the attack home. Ropata himself was half-frozen with cold, but, seeing a dead Hauhau lying inside the parapet, he fastened the rope with which the breach had been made to his feet, and gave the order to haul away, and a great shout arose from his men when they beheld their chief's trophy. The rain continued to fall heavily, and Fraser at last gave the order to withdraw. The European force returned to Te Hapete, bearing the bodies of two dead—one shot, the other the victim of the cruel weather. Nine Hauhaus had been killed. The principal part of the main force went to Wai-o-Matatini settlement for shelter, and awaited favourable weather for a renewal of the attack.

A second attempt was arranged by Major Fraser when the weather cleared. On the night of the 8th October Captain Westrup marched out from Te Hapete to take up a position in rear of Pukemaire, and the rest of the force marched at daylight next morning to attack the front. The place was found deserted. The Hauhaus, well served by their scouts, had escaped just in time. They retreated northward through the rugged bush country, and fortified themselves once more in a hill *pa* called Hungahunga-toroa ("Down of the Albatross"), about twenty miles from Waiapu in the direction of Kawakawa.

This palisaded stronghold, deep in the bush, was surrounded by cliffs very difficult to scale, but Biggs and Ropata, with eight Maoris and a dozen Europeans, occupied a height that commanded the interior of the fort, and, after killing twenty and wounding many others, compelled the Hauhaus to surrender.

During the attack Ropata had captured in the bush a man who was recognized at Pita Tamaturi, one of the chiefs of the Aitanga-a-Mahaki, of Turanganui: he was a leading spirit in the Pai-marire crusade. Lieutenant Biggs, seeing this man in Ropata's grip, asked who he was, and, on being told, shot him dead with his revolver. Mokena Kohere had sent a message to Ropata requesting him to make peace with the Ngati-Porou in Hunga-hunga-toroa; the Hauhaus from outside districts were to be killed. To this Ropata assented, and he called to the *hapus* of Ngati-Porou within the fort to cease fire, and come out and so save their lives. The resistance stopped, and the Ngati-Porou rebels, *hapu* by *hapu,* were called out. But there was no call for the *iwi ke,* the strangers, members of Whakatohea, Ngati-Awa, Whanau-a-Apanui, Te Aitanga-a-Mahaki, and Taranaki, numbering some sixty in all. When the wayward Ngati-Porou had all been summoned out of the *pa,* laying down their arms as they came, the remainder, realizing that they were to be given no mercy, made a rush for the safety of the forest, jumping and sliding down the cliff in the rear of the *pa.* They were out of sight before the Government force discovered their escape.

About five hundred of the rebellious Ngati-Porou were taken here, with three hundred stand of arms. The prisoners were all fighting-men; none of the women or children had been taken to this mountain retreat.

Most of the Ngati-Porou were now in custody, and on being marched out to Waiapu were required to take an oath of allegiance to the Queen and to salute the Union Jack. They were permitted their liberty on parole under the chief Mokena and Captain Deighton, R.M., with a guard of thirty of the Hawke's Bay Military Settlers. The peace thus secured at the East Cape was never again broken, and many of the Ngati-Porou so summarily weaned from the Hauhau craze became in after-years loyal supporters and soldiers of the Government in the campaign against Te Kooti.*

NOTES

[*From MS. letters in Grey Collection, Municipal Library, Auckland.*]

Bishop William Williams, of Waiapu, writing from Turanganui to the Governor, Sir George Grey, regarding the arrival of Pai-marire emissaries on the East Coast in March, 1865, said it had been agreed among the

---

*See Appendices for notes by Captain Preece on the operations on the East Coast.

people that inasmuch as this party was accredited to Hirini te Kani, whom they professed to wish to appoint Maori King, it would be wise to make the most of the influence which was conceded to him. Hirini ordered them away when he came to Taureka. Later he accepted the preserved head of a white man who had been killed, also white prisoners; Hauhau flags and other *tapu* things had been offered him but rejected. However, Te Aitanga-a-Mahaki received and hospitized the Hauhau emissaries.

On the 18th March a second Pai-marire party from Taranaki came to Turanga, accompanied by a number of Kairoa and Ruatahuna natives, who had all joined the Pai-marire. The faith spread quickly among the people. Even the better-disposed natives who had been disgusted at Mr. Volkner's murder seemed "thoroughly spellbound"; "their decision has well-nigh forsaken them," said the Bishop. In the Hauhau party, the Bishop said, there were two principal men. One was Patara, a man who had had much intercourse with the English: he was at Tunapahore at the time of Mr. Volkner's murder, and professed to be much disgusted at Kereopa's deed. "At the same time," the Bishop wrote, "I cannot divest myself of the feeling that he was aware of the intention to commit the murder. The other chief man is Kereopa, a man of the vilest character. At a meeting on the 14th I came in near contact with this Kereopa, who was often endeavouring to excuse himself, saying that it was the Whakatohea who committed the murder. I told him I could not shake hands with a murderer—that I could see the blood still wet upon his hands. Since that time he has made use of threatening language: 'Let the Bishop keep out of my way. He has refused to make peace with me; let him remember that I am a murderer.'

"On the 20th March," the Bishop continued. "on which day the Wairoa party was close at hand, being reported to be four hundred men—though their number turned out to be only half this amount—there seemed to be so many suspicious circumstances about these Pai-marire that I felt it necessary to speak to Mr. Wylie who had the control of the schooner 'Sea Shell,' and suggest that this vessel should lie at anchor in the bay, in case there should be any unforeseen event which might make it desirable to make use of her. I told him that Mr. Leonard Williams and myself would in the meantime go to the Wairoa natives and ascertain the state of feeling. Alarm was taken at remarks made by certain chiefs to a settler's wife, to the effect that they would not be able to protect the settlers, and several families left their houses the same afternoon and made their way to the vessel. It turned out, however, that the second party of Pai-marire who came to Wairoa were of a very different character from those who had been at Opotiki. The principal leader found great fault with Kereopa, and said that they had no instructions from Horopapera [Te Ua] to commit murder.

"There are two prisoners here, one with each party," the Bishop wrote further. "One of these is, I believe, a runaway soldier. He has had the opportunity to escape, but declares he does not wish to leave the natives. The second is a young man, said to be of the 70th Regiment. He is not delivered up to Hirini because those who have charge of him imposed a condition that Hirini should retain him until their return from Taranaki." The Bishop asked for this renegade. The natives, he said, kept a very strict watch over him.

The Hauhau prophet Patara wrote a letter in English to the Patutahi settlers, Poverty Bay, reassuring them. Patara, who signed himself "William Buttler," told the whites to have no fear, that he only wished to make war on the Governor and the soldiers, but added that if the *pakehas* at Makaraka and other places had arms sent to them he would consider them enemies.

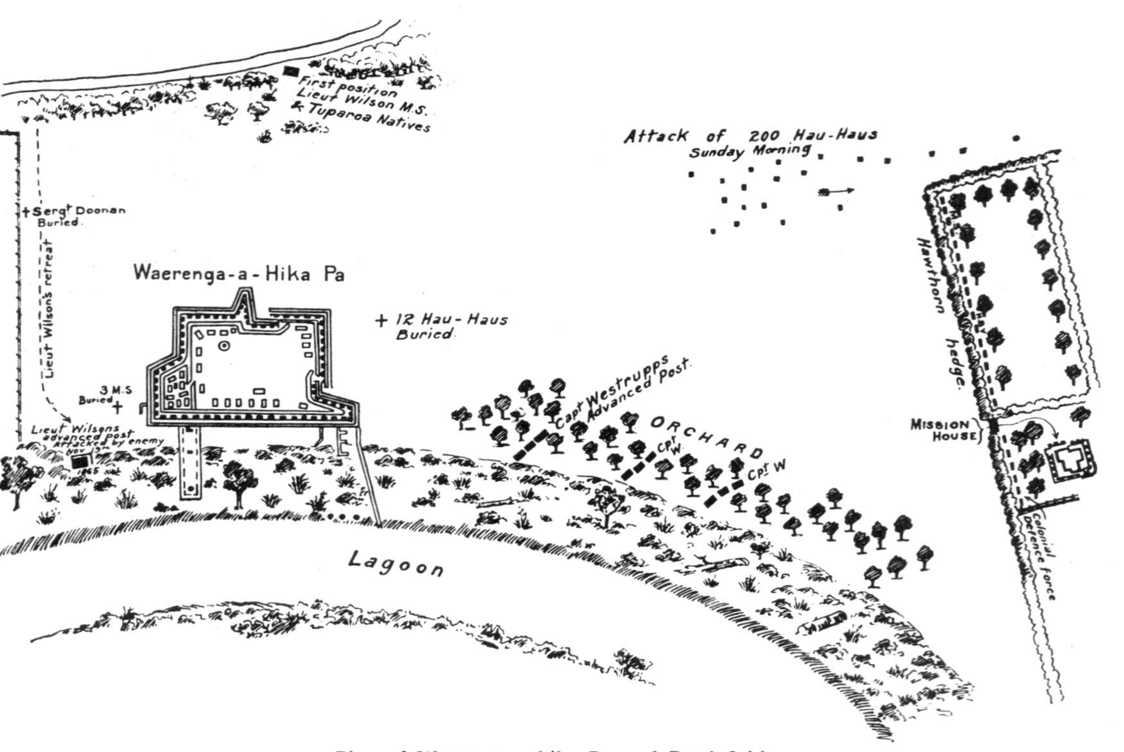

Plan of Waerenga-a-hika Pa and Battlefield

Chapter 12

THE SIEGE OF WAERENGA-A-HIKA

THE NORTHERN PART of the East Coast district pacified, it was now possible to begin operations for the defeat of Hauhauism in the Poverty Bay country. Here the position was serious, for the greater part of the native population had fallen to the fascinations of Pai-marire and accepted the new religion, and several hundreds of men had fortified themselves in a strong *pa* within rifle-shot of the English mission house at Waerenga-a-Hika ("Hika's Clearing"), about seven miles from the present Town of Gisborne. Others occupied two fortified villages further inland, Pukeamionga and Kohanga-Karearea ("The Sparrowhawk's Nest").

At the end of October, 1865, Mr. Donald McLean, Superintendent of the Province of Hawke's Bay, who had urged the Government to take speedy measures against the Hauhaus of Turanganui, visited Tuparoa in order to enlist Ngati-Porou's assistance in the campaign. In the meantime H.M.S. "Brisk" landed at Poverty Bay a force consisting of the Hawke's Bay Cavalry (Colonial Defence Force) under Captain La Serre, and some Military Settlers under Lieutenant Wilson. Major Fraser and Captain Biggs were also despatched to the bay with their East Cape expeditionary force. Mr. McLean met Hotene Porourangi and Ropata Wahawaha and requested their co-operation in the military work at Turanganui, with the result that three hundred Ngati-Porou volunteered and were taken to the bay by steamer. At Turanganui Mr. McLean sent messages by Hauhau chiefs to the rebel sections of Rongowhakaata and Aitanga-a-Mahaki, warning them that unless they came in and made submission to the Government they would be attacked and deprived of their lands and homes. This offer met with no response, and Major Fraser was then directed to begin operations for the reduction of the enemy fortifications.

In the middle of November the Government force, numbering between a hundred and fifty and two hundred Europeans and three hundred Maoris, moved on Waerenga-a-Hika and took up positions on three sides of the *pa*. The fortification was built on level land, with a swampy lagoon in rear; in front was the mission station, 300 yards distant. The Hauhau *pa* consisted of three lines of defence—the outer stockade (*wita*), the main fence (*tuwatawata*), and the earth breastwork (*parepare*). The *wita* was a sloping fence, about 6 feet high, its top nearly touching the *tuwatawata,* its base inclining outward 2 feet or 3 feet. Only the main timbers of the *wita* were in the ground; the rest of the stakes did not touch the earth, but left an opening of about a foot at the bottom as firing-space for the riflemen behind the *tuwatawata,* which was a stout palisade 10 feet high. Inside it was the earth *parepare* about 4 feet 6 inches high. In many forts there was also a *parakiri,* a third stockade, strongly built of stout tree-trunks solidly set in the ground.

Major Fraser occupied the Bishop's house at the mission station as his headquarters, and some of the best shots sniped at the *pa* from the roof. The Colonial Defence Force and Military Settlers entrenched themselves behind a hawthorn hedge which commanded two faces of the *pa,* and the Forest Rangers, under Captain Westrup, took up their position on ground near the lagoon.

The siege of the *pa* occupied seven days. In order to hasten the reduction of the stronghold Lieutenant Wilson and thirty of his Military Settlers were sent to the northern face of the stockade, where a sap was commenced and carried close up to the fort. Here they were attacked by a large body of Hauhau reinforcements from one of the other villages, and came under a very heavy fire from this body as well as from the *pa,* when they charged with fixed bayonets back to the main body. In this dash Wilson's force had six men killed and five wounded.

Next day (Sunday) the Hauhaus, after the devotions round the *niu* pole, moved out from the *pa* in three strong bodies and charged with fanatic determination on the men holding the hawthorn hedge. They came holding up the right hand, palm to the front, in the attitude of warding off or catching the *pakeha's* bullets. Shouting their Pai-marire war-cries, some of them rushed up to the opposite side of the hedge and fired through into the men in the trench. The reply was vigorous, and was supported by the body in camp. The Hauhaus came on almost up to the rifle-muzzles only to be shot down in scores. They were repulsed, leaving about sixty dead on the field. The Government forces lost none.

There were some hand-to-hand encounters during the fighting. On one occasion three Hauhau braves sallied out and challenged their enemies in the open. Young Tuta Nihoniho and two of his Ngati-Porou comrades rushed at them. Tutu was armed with a Minie rifle and fixed bayonet; his opponent had a long *huata* or spear. The Hauhau made a lunge and speared him in the left hand, but Tutu killed his foe with a bayonet-thrust through the body.

After a week's constant fighting Major Fraser decided to try artillery on the *pa*. The only gun he had was a 6-pounder brought ashore from the steamer "Sturt." There was some ineffectual firing in incompetent hands, until Thomas Porter (afterwards Colonel Porter), of the Colonial Defence Force Cavalry, turned his experience as a midshipman in the Royal Navy to account by taking charge of the gun and rigging proper tackle to prevent the recoil capsizing it. There was no shot for it, so salmon-tins were used as cases for shrapnel charges. Two rounds were accurately fired into the *pa*, and this rough-and-ready but efficient bombardment produced the required effect. The garrison hoisted a white flag and surrendered. A number escaped through the swamp in rear of the *pa*, but four hundred laid down their arms and gave themselves up as prisoners.

"They could scarcely be recognized as men as they came out after their long defence," said a member of Ngati-Porou, who had fought at Waerenga-a-Hika; "they were covered with mud, and their hair was long and shaggy."

The Hauhau losses in this siege, which ended on the 22nd November, 1865, were more than a hundred killed, besides several scores wounded. The Government casualties were eleven killed and twenty wounded.

The capture of Waerenga-a-Hika, followed by the destruction of the fortified position, completely settled the Pai-marire revolt in Poverty Bay. The Hauhau fugitives from the district took refuge in the Wairoa district, in the northern part of Hawke's Bay, and it presently became necessary to open a campaign there. Most of the prisoners taken were released, but a number of the most troublesome of the Rongowhakaata and the Aitanga-a-Mahaki were transported to Chatham Island for safe-keeping until the coast was tranquillized.

During the fighting at Waerenga-a-Hika a man of the Rongowhakaata named Te Kooti Rikirangi, serving on the Government side, was made a prisoner by one of the friendly chiefs on suspicion of treachery. It was declared that he had been removing the bullets from his cartridges and firing only blank at the enemy. He was also accused of being in communication with the Hauhaus. Rikirangi, as he was generally known at that time, strenuously denied these charges, and after some time was released. Later, however, he was arrested on other charges, and although not convicted or even brought to trial, was regarded as too turbulent and unreliable a character to be at liberty, and was therefore shipped off to Wharekauri (Chatham Island) with a number of other prisoners of war. This act of punishment, whether justifiable or not, cost the country dear in lives and money, for Te Kooti made his escape two years later and exacted a fearful revenge. The story of his many and often amazing adventures and his campaigns is narrated in this volume, beginning with Chapter 24, in which his escape from exile by seizing the schooner "Rifleman" is described.

NOTE

Captain G. A. Preece, N.Z.C., writes: "Te Kooti was not the only friendly native who was deported to the Chatham Islands on a charge of supplying the rebels with ammunition. In March, 1866, Rewi te Nahu, a sub-chief of the Ngati-Kurupakiaka Tribe, was arrested at Wairoa (H.B.) on a charge of sending ammunition to the Hauhaus. There was a small force of the Native Contingent kept on regular pay at Wairoa and used for despatch-carrying and scouting under Captain Deighton, R.M., and myself. Two companies of the 12th Regiment, under Captains Crawhall and Dawson, were stationed at Wairoa, between the ground where the hospital now is and the Wairoa Hotel; they were only engaged on garrison duty. Rewi te Nahu was arrested and placed in a guard-tent borrowed from the 12th Regiment, and put under a guard of the Native Contingent, pending further action. The Poverty Bay prisoners and the bad characters amongst those who had surrendered to us at the East Cape in October, 1865, were being sent to the Chatham Islands under instructions from Mr. McLean. Rewi te Nahu was sent up to Napier under charge of Privates Kereama and Piha, who formed part of the guard to the Chathams. He remained a prisoner at Wharekauri until Te Kooti escaped. Some time in 1871 he surrendered to the officer commanding at Wairoa, and was always a well-behaved man after that. This has never to my knowledge been published before; it shows that in those days men who were supposed to be friendly and were acting otherwise were dealt with more severely than those who were fighting against us openly."

Chapter 13

THE FIRST WAIROA CAMPAIGN

TOWARDS THE END of 1865 trouble developed among the *hapus* of the Ngati-Kahungunu Tribe occupying the beautiful and fruitful valley of the Wairoa (Hawke's Bay). Pai-marire emissaries in the earlier part of the year spread their doctrine with such success that the ritual of Te Ua became established in many villages, and the arrival of the fugitives from Waerenga-a-Hika brought the temper of the malcontents to fighting-pitch. The chief Te Waru Tamatea, who had fought at Orakau in the previous year, was the principal leader of the Hauhau party. The most vigorous champion of the Government side was Kopu Parapara, of the lower Wairoa, who was supported wholeheartedly by the fine old chief Ihaka Whanga, of Nuhaka and Mahia. The Government, through Mr. Donald McLean, sent arms up from Napier for the loyal faction, and early in December despatched Major Fraser to the Wairoa with a force of volunteers and Hawke's Bay and Taranaki Military Settlers.

The Queenite chiefs of Ngati-Kahungunu also wrote to Ngati-Porou requesting their assistance, and Mr. McLean visited Tuparoa at the beginning of January, 1866, and handed the letter to Ropata and Hotene Porourangi. The writers asked Ngati-Porou to "come and be a backbone for us for a great number of Hauhaus are now assembled here." "Let your coming be speedy," the entreaty concluded; "we are living in fear."

Ngati-Porou's response was prompt. A hundred and fifty men under Ropata and other chiefs embarked in the steamer and reached the Wairoa landing on the 4th. Their pay while on active service was fixed at 3s. per day. Ropata and Hotene were appointed by Mr. McLean to act as assessors of the Magistrate's Court at yearly salaries of £50 each.

In the meantime (25th December, 1865) the European force at the Wairoa, with some of the local Maoris, had fought a sharp action with the Hauhaus at a stockaded settlement called Omaru-hakeke, about twelve miles up the Wairoa River, killing twelve men and losing Captain Hussey (Taranaki Military

From a sketch by an eye-witness, 1865]

The Attack on Omaru-hakeke Pa, Upper Wairoa
(Christmas Day, 1865)

Major Fraser's and Captain Hussey's men are shown in the front. Captain Biggs's detachment was on the higher ground to the left (the Maoris' right flank), and fired on the escaping Hauhaus when Fraser's force assaulted the stockade.

Settlers) and two natives killed. The attacking force consisted of one hundred men of the Hawke's Bay and Taranaki Military Settlers and about an equal number of Maoris under Ihaka Whanga and Kopu-parapara. Dr. M. Scott, who was settled at the Wairoa, accompanied Fraser's force as surgeon. An account of the expedition which he wrote in 1890 is of value for its description of old Wairoa and its lively narrative of a first experience under fire:—

"In these hurry-scurry days, when great Pan has long been dead," wrote Dr. Scott, "few people lived nearer Arcadia than we of Te Wairoa, Hawke's Bay, some twenty-five to thirty years ago. Inhabiting comfortable houses, situated on the bank of a magnificent river which in due season supplied us plentifully with fish, while its lagoons and tributaries contributed wild ducks innumerable, and the forest fringing its banks pigeons and Maori game without end; surrounded by, and not on too intimate terms with our Maori landlords and their *hapus,* who raised wheat and other produce in large quantities, and were then an industrious, happy community, we contentedly ground our flour in our improvised steel windmills, procured our modest supplies of luxuries (otherwise unattainable) twice annually, through my friend Mr. Carroll, from Napier, and, newspaper-, law-, and lawyer-less, lived on happily and took little thought for the morrow. And for many years our intercourse with our native friends was genial and sincere on both sides. They invariably resorted to us in great trouble or calamity which threatened or assailed their quiet, domestic life, consulted us in their little ailments, and gratefully appreciated any kindness rendered them, while I verily believe that all they had, including themselves, was, so to speak, at our behest and service. Indeed, with the exception of a rare squabble among themselves, in which we were never implicated, we lived very peacefully and happily together—Ngati-Kahungunu and ourselves—Maori and *pakeha*. But as the years wore on there gradually fell a shadow between us. Distrust usurped slowly and by degrees the olden confidence; and the Maori King (who has now virtually followed Pan, but unlamented) became an entity in Waikato.

"Events followed quickly. Our quondam landlords and their tribes sold their lands—which was the beginning of evil for our Utopia—and swallowed the proceeds, mostly. Some acres remained, represented by ships which were lost or rotted on the beach, and mills which never saw erection, but were destroyed together with much goodly produce during the ensuing troublous times. From being peaceable, industrious, and at times ridiculously abstinent, the Ngati-Kahungunu at Wairoa became turbulent, drunken, and ripe for mischief, while the Hauhau devilry was brewing in their midst.

"About this time (1865) I was resident at Wairoa with my wife and family, and not a little anxious as to the possible result of affairs, disquieting rumours coming in hourly, the surrounding hills nightly resplendent with signal fires, and our only effective European force consisting of some sixteen men, while the immediately local natives were not only untrustworthy but bounceable to a degree. I was not a little pleased one morning to hear the unwonted sound of a Light Infantry bugle waking the unaccustomed echoes, and was soon shaking hands with the officers of the East Coast Expeditionary Force, who, under their gallant chief, Fraser, had stemmed and swept before them the swelling tide of fanaticism from the East Coast southward to where they stood. From these brave gentlemen and soldiers I soon learned that, *nolens volens,* I was expected now to seek the time-honoured 'bubble' even at the rifle's mouth—to which I was, however, more inclined inasmuch as I had found an old schoolfellow among them, who so infected me with the desire to see a little service in the bush that I gladly acquiesced and joined forthwith. 'Besides, you know,' drawled Norman (Taranaki No. 9 Company Military Settlers: we used to call him 'Cupid'), 'our medico was badly hit at Waerenga-a-Hika, and we must have pills.'

"Behold me, then, a sufficiently unwarlike individual from the banks of the sedgy Cam, with a revolver on hip and haversack full of surgical sundries on back, trudging along, about midway in a line of some 250 fine fellows, rangers, settlers, and Maoris, with an irrespressible and loquacious little Irish orderly trotting alongside, who also bears a satchel with bandages, &c., and all singing 'Old John Brown,' at the top of our manageable voices until we drop into some dense *manuka* scrub, which exercises its influence upon the upper notes; and then ford a creek breast-high, which seems to wash out the vocal ability altogether.

"A bugle sounded ahead, and Lieutenant St. George and I went on at the double to have a look at the Hauhau *niu,* or sacred flagstaff, which, together with its circular site and settlement surrounding it, the Hauhaus had abandoned at our approach, removing, however, only to the opposite bank of the river which flowed beneath the natural mound and plateau upon which it was erected. Thence they shouted, and exhibited defiance after the Maori manner, but hitherto no shot had been fired, though the men, in extended order, were loaded, alert, and ready.

"We utilized the *niu* at once as a means of signalling to the enemy, and Hamlin's white handkerchief having been hoisted as a flag of truce, parleying took place across the river between the native chiefs, friendly and insurgent. But Fraser grew tired of the finessing, and sang out to Hamlin, who was interpreter, 'Tell them to throw down their arms and surrender!' An evasive answer being returned, down came Hamlin's handkerchief, up went the Union Jack (ready bent on), and simultaneously No. 9 gave fire with a tremendous crash, while a mixed force of volunteers, Nos. 3 and 9, and some Maoris, led by Captain Hussey (who was very conspicuous with his 'solar and sword topee'), accompanied by the narrator, forded the river under cover of the fire from the plateau and entered the valley, at the extremity of which the Hauhau stronghold was supposed to be situated. We sang no 'John Brown' now, as we marched somewhat dubiously along a narrow Maori track, bounded on one side by a high fern-clad ridge, and on the other by a deep creek with precipitous banks [the Maru-hakeke]. Crack went a single rifle in front, then another, then three or four, and my attention was claimed by an entirely novel, peculiar, and by no means unmusical singing overhead, while the bugle in advance was rattling away at a great rate.

"'Sure an' it's the assembly, and the double, sirr!' said, or rather shouted, my man; and away we went with the rest, while St. George, Richardson (my old schoolfellow), and Biggs tore past us at the top of their speed, shouting out to the men to come on.

"And we did go on, urged by an undefinable something which seemed to renew our energies as required during that apparently long and most exciting race. Meanwhile the flute-like whistling overhead became less and less melodious at every step, until at last it increased into an intermittent angry hiss. An unconquerable desire to see the worst, for we guessed our people were getting roughly handled, a rush forward between the thick flax and *toetoe* bushes, and the scene is all before me.

"Right in front, and at about 40 yards distant, hangs a dense, opaque mass of fog and smoke obscuring everything, which is momentarily pierced by tongues of vivid flame. Looking down I see miniature furrows suddenly stricken out of the green sward by invisible ploughs, while the tall *toetoe* grass drops its head, and the vibrating flax-leaves shrivel up and bend apparently without cause. Around in every conceivable attitude, and availing themselves of all sorts of cover, our men are loading and firing frantically, for there are but few up as yet, and I find I have unwillingly joined the advance-guard, which Richardson informs me of thusly: 'What the devil are you doing here?'. The opposing fire is very fierce and rapid. But fresh men are arriving every moment, blown, helpless, staggering after their long race; but in a few minutes flat upon the ground or squatting behind a frail screen of *manuka* or *toetoe,* and also contributing to the infernal din around us.

"I had already dropped down behind a log and fired a couple of shots from my revolver—not at anybody in particular, but into the hurly-burly of smoke, flame, and yells before me—when I became conscious of a commotion on the extreme left of the position we occupied, and just then, catching sight of Major Fraser, observed that he was beckoning me. It was a perilous run from cover to cover, for the intervening space was fairly swept by the enemy's fire, but I got across unhurt, and arrived just in time to find poor Hussey dying. A shot had crashed literally through his spine, as, sword in hand, he was urging his men on. A few hardly intelligible words, and a true gentleman and brave soldier ceased to exist.

"Don't let the men know, if you can help it,' Major Fraser said, just as a heavier burst than usual flashed out of the misty thunder-cloud, and Private Hollingsworth toppled over into my arms with a bullet through his shoulder, while the corner-piece of a *whare* close by went scurrying up in the air. 'By Jove, this is getting hot,' Fraser said, as Biggs and Richardson with about thirty men came along at the double, with fixed bayonets, and Bugler Spenser sounding the charge. 'Stop! Down men, all!' shouted Fraser; and as his order was instantly obeyed by nearly all, few casualties resulted from the discharge of the second barrels, which the Maoris had cunningly kept in reserve for the *kokiri,* or rush, which they dreaded. Only Sergeant Hawes (afterwards Captain of the Taranaki Volunteers), being tall and not quite quick enough, got it through the arm, and incontinently tumbled over.

" 'Now,' shouted Captain Biggs (afterwards murdered at the Poverty Bay massacre) in a temporary lull; and with a yell which was not a cheer, though somewhat akin thereto, the men climbed and swarmed over the intervening fence and entered the village [Omaru-hakeke] with a rush. There was wild and terrible work inside for a few minutes, and then pot-shots at the fugitives escaping up the hillside which dominated the settlement. Parthian-like, the Hauhaus fled and fought bravely. In the evening we returned to headquarters, bearing our dead and wounded with us, and we burned ploughs and carts and carved houses, also much maize, and split up canoes and did other mischief."

Among the volunteers from Wairoa in this engagement was Mr. (now Captain) G. A. Preece, who began on the East Coast a career of distinguished soldiering service. In the Christmas Day fight he was with Captain Biggs on the left; his party fired on the enemy as they fled from the frontal attack. Biggs shot one man as he tried to escape up the creek, and one of Biggs's Hawke's Bay volunteers shot another at 300 yards with an old smooth-bore musket. On the Government side the killed, besides Captain Hussey, were a half-caste named Wi Christie and one of Pitiera Kopu's Wairoa men. Next morning (26th December) there was another skirmish at the top of the hill overlooking the Omaru-hakeke Village. In this encounter only the Mohaka Maoris and Pitiera Kopu's Wairoa natives were engaged on the Government side; Preece accompanied Kopu's men. The rebel leader Te Waru was shot in the wrist. Of the loyalists a Mohaka man received a bullet through the lungs. The whole force moved out later, but the Hauhaus had abandoned their position and retired towards Whataroa.

Early in January an expedition moved out from Wairoa against the enemy, who were entrenched at the top of Tikorangi Hill. They abandoned this position in the night. Major Fraser then decided to return and await Ngati-Porou reinforcements.

The Hauhau faction, after this affair, moved up to the southern side of Waikare-moana Lake, where they remained until the stern and vigorous Ropata Wahawaha appeared on the scene. On the 13th January, 1866, a force of friendly natives led by Ropata and other chiefs, and Major Fraser and several of his officers, had a sharp and successful engagement with a large body of the rebels at Te Kopane, a defile between steep hills clothed with high fern and some bush about twenty-five miles from the Clyde Township at Wairoa.

The Ngati-Porou numbered one hundred and fifty men. The Ngati-Kahungunu, totalling two hundred, were led by Kopu Parapara and the gallant Ihaka Whanga, of Nuhaka and Mahia.

The plan of campaign arranged with Major Fraser was to advance upon Onepoto, where the Waikare-taheke torrent issues from Lake Waikare-moana, and deliver an attack on the Hauhaus, who were known to be in the neighbourhood of that place to the number of several hundred, consisting of many Rongowhakaata men from Poverty Bay, some *hapus* of Ngati-Kahungunu, Ngati-Ruapani, and Urewera.

Leaving the Wairoa camp on the 9th January and marching by way of Te Tawa, Manu-tawhiorangi, and Te Koareare, the force early on the 13th approached the entrance to an obviously dangerous place where the track ran along the bottom of a valley between two high ridges, a highly suitable spot for an ambuscade. Ropata had pushed on about two miles ahead of the main body, with an advance-guard intently watching the trail. His leading men discovered a footprint in the dust of the track, no doubt that of a Hauhau scout, and passed the word back to Ropata, who called out to them not to tread upon it until he came up. The advance-guard halted and watched a singular war-path rite. Ropata (according to a Ngati-Porou narrative) knelt down and carefully scooped up with both hands the earth bearing the impression of the scout's bare foot and swallowed the whole of it. (In the Maori narrator's words: "*Aohia ake nga oneone o te tapuae ra, horomia katoatia ki roto o tona puku.*") This done, he said, addressing his unknown enemy, "*Kati noa oti ko to tapuae e pau i au ki roto o taku puku, ko to tinana ano ia ka ngaro atu i au*" ("As your footprint has been consumed by me within my stomach, so will your body be destroyed by me").

This preliminary ceremony satisfactorily performed, the advance-guard was moving forward cautiously, when the first of the foes were descried in the distance on the summit of the height called Raekahu, near the Waikare-taheke River. Ropata ordered a halt until the main body came up, and then allowed Ngati-Kahungunu to take the lead, as it was their district, advising them to fire into places where any enemy was likely to be concealed. This prudent counsel, however, was not followed as the shallow valley at Te Kopane was entered. The Hauhaus were entrenched in rifle-pits and behind earthworks skilfully hidden with fern on the ridges on both flanks of the advance and also directly ahead, where a parapet and firing-trench, not visible at a distance, crossed the flat of the track between the hills. Firing began when this trench was approached, and heavy volleys were poured into the long column of men by Hauhaus in ambush in the fern on either flank. The Ngati-Kahungunu, being crowded closely together, presented a target that could not be missed. Twelve were killed outright by the first volleys, and over a score were wounded. Ngati-Kahungunu were thrown into confusion and replied ineffectively to the enemy's fire. The fearless veteran Ihaka Whanga rushed to the front, calling on his men to charge, but he was not supported. Making his way through the fern, he fired his carbine at the foe, and next moment was shot just behind the hip. He took a rifle from his nearest man and fired again, and then fell with another bullet in the leg. His tribesmen now rushed forward and carried him to the rear.

A retreat was imminent when Ropata, a master of battlefield tactics, came up and ordered the fern on the right-hand side of the gully to be fired. A strong breeze was blowing in the direction of the well-posted Hauhaus. The dry fern was set alight, and the enemy on that flank were compelled to fall back before the onrolling flames and dense smoke. Ropata then led a rush on the hill, shouting "*Kokiri, kokiri! Kua whati, kua whati!*" ("Charge, charge! They fly, they fly!") The rebel Rongowhakaata, hearing that dreaded voice, knew that Ngati-Porou were upon them, and took to flight. Ropata dashed up in pursuit of the retreating Hauhaus and found their camp on the summit of Raekahu Mountain, where some of the people were captured.

The enemy made no further stand, but fled towards Onepoto, near the outlet of Lake Waikare-moana. There most of them manned canoes and took shelter on the north side of the lake, where they were secure from further pursuit. Those less swift of foot were captured in the bush or on the shore of the lake.

Ropata and Hotene proposed to Ngati-Kahungunu that Hauhau members of that tribe captured should be spared, but that any men of the Ngati-Porou, Urewera, or Rongowhakaata taken should be killed in order to prevent rebellious assemblages of tribes from outside districts. The Wairoa chiefs Kopu and Paora te Apatu, however, demanded also the execution of any Wairoa Maoris found in the Hauhau band, and accordingly Ropata shot with his revolver the principal prisoner, Te Tuatini Tamaionarangi, a high chief of the Ngati-Kahungunu. Some sixty Hauhaus were killed in the day's fighting; of the friendly natives fourteen were killed, including Rawiri Hika-rukutai, who was Ropata's uncle, and between twenty and thirty were wounded. The only Europeans engaged at Te Kopane, besides Major Fraser, were Lieutenant St. George (Colonial Defence Force Cavalry), Mr. E. Towgood (who was a volunteer with Ihaka Whanga's natives), Mr. Richard J. Deighton, and Major Fraser's two servants and an orderly.

This decisive battle broke the Pai-marire rebellion in the Wairoa district. Ngati-Porou, to whom the success was wholly due, returned to their homes at Tuparoa and Waiapu, and remained at peace until they were called upon to take the field against Te Kooti in 1868.

Scene of the Engagement at Omarunui, Hawke's Bay

From a drawing, 1866]

Chapter 14

THE FIGHT AT OMARUNUI

THE DISTRICT OF Hawke's Bay south of the Wairoa was not seriously troubled by the Hauhau propaganda until late in 1866. Shortly after the Volkner tragedy at Opotiki in 1865 and the arrival of the Pai-marire prophets in the Poverty Bay and East Cape settlements, Mr. Donald McLean (afterwards Sir Donald) and his colleague Mr. J. D. Ormond took measures to influence the Hawke's Bay native chiefs against the spread of Pai-marire in their territory. McLean, before settling permanently in Hawke's Bay, had acted for many years as native adviser and land-purchase agent under successive Governments, and had won the confidence of the leading men in many tribes. At this time he was Superintendent of the Hawke's Bay Province, and was also the Government Native Agent for the East Coast. Mr. Ormond, afterwards for many years a member of the Legislative Council, had been elected to the House of Representatives in 1861; he was a leading settler in the province and a coadjutor with McLean in his public work. McLean's first step was to call meetings of the Hawke's Bay chiefs and urge them to set their faces against the murderous doctrines of the Pai-marire apostles. The principal *rangatiras* of Ngati-Kahungunu—the old warriors Tareha, Te Moananui, and Renata Kawepo, supported by Karauria, Karaitiana Takamoana, and others—agreed to do their utmost to stay the spread of Hauhau unrest, which they admitted had permeated some sections of their people. The subjugation of the rebellious faction among Ngati-Porou and the defeat of the Poverty Bay Hauhaus at Waerenga-a-Hika produced a good effect among the small doubtful sections of Ngati-Kahungunu, and in fact the only menace to European settlement on the plains of Hawke's Bay did not come from that tribe, but from an outpost of Hauhauism in the interior, on the mountain-track to the Taupo country.

At the beginning of October 1866, the Ngati-Hineuru Tribe, a small but war-loving clan whose principal villages were Te Haroto and Tarawera—on the present Napier-Taupo Main Road—

set out for the East Coast with the intention of delivering an attack on the Town of Napier. This bold scheme was due chiefly to the fiery counsels of the old warrior Te Rangihiroa, the hereditary head of the clan, and the Pai-marire preachings of a prophet named Panapa; and it had obtained the approval of Rewi Maniapoto and other Kingite leaders, to whom emissaries had been sent from Te Haroto. Panapa had sent spies down to the coast to gain what information they could regarding the likelihood of success in a raid on Napier Town. These men went through the town in the guise of peaceful visitors, ascertained where the barracks were, where the arms and ammunition were kept, and returned to Panapa and Te Rangihiroa with the information. A few days later the Ngati-Hineuru war-party, numbering about eighty men, marched over the range at Titiokura and descended to Pohue and the plains. The "Tekau-ma-rua" ("The Twelve"), as the Hauhau war-band was called, irrespective of its numerical strength, included some wild spirits from other tribes, as far away as the King Country. Besides Te Rangihiroa and Panapa, there were four chiefs of Ngati-Hineuru named Kipa and Kingita (who were Rangihiroa's half-brothers), Nikora, and Petera Kahuroa; with them came a powerful and savage fellow from the eastern shore of Lake Taupo, a big black-bearded man named Te Rangitahau, of whom a good deal will be heard hereafter; he was the principal man of Waipahihi and Waitahanui, and was of the Ngati-Tuwharetoa Tribe. From the Ngati-Maniapoto country there was a young warrior named Peita Kotuku, who had fought in Taranaki in 1860 and was one of the gallant three hundred who held Orakau *pa* in 1864.

At Te Pohue the force appears to have been joined by recruits from other parts, including some from the Wairoa district, for before a move was made on Napier the total strength was about one hundred and thirty. The column was divided, Panapa going on to Omarunui, on the Tutaekuri River, six miles from Napier Town, with the greater portion of the force, while Te Rangihiroa remained with about twenty-five mounted men. The plan of attack was that Te Rangihiroa was to make a night attack on the town by way of Petane (Bethany), the settlement near the sea on the north side, while Panapa, Nikora, and Te Rangitahau were to deal simultaneously with the out-settlements of *pakeha* and Maori and then join in the sack of Napier. It was expected that at the same time Wi Hapi and Hauhau sections of Ngati-Kahungunu would march on Porangahau and other settlements in the south of the province. In the event of a successful attack on Napier the Hauhaus in other districts were to rise and descend on the *pakeha* and the friendly Maoris; the Urewera were expected to make forays to the plains, and the Waikato Kingites were to renew the war on their frontier. A disaster at Napier, therefore, would have involved many other parts of the country in razzias and bloodshed.

The arrival at Omarunui of Panapa and a hundred armed men was reported by the friendly natives to Mr. McLean; and Mr. Hamlin, Native Interpreter to the Superintendent, who had been sent out to inquire the intentions of the strangers when they were halted at Petane, was now deputed to warn them to return to their homes, otherwise they would be attacked. For a long time the Hauhaus remained silent. At last Panapa said that peace and war were both good; but nothing more definite could be gathered as to his intentions. The Hauhaus took no notice of the Superintendent's warnings, and it was evident that they meant mischief, although by Panapa's instructions they remained quiet and refrained from any act of violence. The place where they had taken up their quarters, Omarunui, was a fenced village on a flat above the cliffy bank of the Tutaekuri; the chief of the *kainga,* Paora Kaiwhata, with most of his people left and joined Tareha in the strongly stockaded settlement called Pa-whakairo ("The Carved Fort"), about a mile distant.

The people of Napier were now fully alive to the danger of attack, and preparations were made for action against the invaders from the mountains. The armed force available consisted of the Militia, numbering about one hundred and thirty men and youths, and a company of Napier Rifle Volunteers, forty-five rank and file, under Captain Buchanan. A message was sent to Wairoa for Major Fraser and his company of Military Settlers, who had done good service in the East Cape and Poverty Bay campaign. Fraser and his men, numbering forty, and also a party of Wairoa Maoris under Kopu-Parapara and Ihaka Whanga, reached Napier on the 11th October. The Napier forces were under the command of Colonel George Whitmore, who had been military secretary to General Cameron; he had left the Imperial army and was now a settler in Hawke's Bay. He saw that everything was in readiness for action, and detached Fraser and his veterans to guard the approach from the Petane side. Reports had been received that Te Rangihiroa and his party would pass down the valley at Petane on the morning of the 12th, and Fraser was instructed to await them at a point where the track passed through a defile close to the home of Captain Carr (late R.A.), who had a sheep-station at Petane. Simultaneously Whitmore moved on Omarunui to demand the surrender of Panapa's force.

The Napier citizen soldiers, numbering in all about two hundred, including some twenty-five volunteer cavalry, marched out from the town soon after midnight on the 11th October and took up positions on the Tutaekuri in co-operation with the friendly Maoris under Mr. Locke, Native Agent, and the chiefs Tareha, Renata Kawepo, and other tribal leaders. The Omarunui settlement was surrounded by daylight, the Maori contingent taking up a position on the edge of a swamp in the rear. At daybreak the Hauhaus began their fanatic services round the *niu* pole of worship which had been erected in the village, Panapa the prophet standing at the foot of the mast and leading the Pai-marire incantations.

Mr. Hamlin was sent into the village under a flag of truce with a message from Mr. McLean demanding the surrender of the Hauhaus in an hour, otherwise they would be fired upon. Hamlin returned and reported that the natives would not listen to any proposal. After waiting an hour the order was given to attack the village.

The Militia, two companies under Major Lambert, were sent forward to ford the river opposite the settlement and take up a position on the bank. The Hauhaus were still undecided how to act, for they had not intended to take the offensive until the signal was given that Te Rangihiroa was attacking Napier, and there was no word from him. At any rate they permitted the Militia to ford the river, cross the wide shingle bed, and ascend the bank near the village without opening fire, and so lost an opportunity of inflicting heavy loss on their *pakeha* foe. Orders were now given to open fire, and volleys were poured into the village from three sides. The Hauhaus ran for the shelter of their *whares* and the large meeting-house and returned the fire; some skirmished out to the open, but a number fell, and the huts proved precarious cover. Panapa, the war-priest, came out into the open and was shot dead. The firing continued for over an hour, and the Maori casualties grew heavy. At last, seeing it hopeless to hold the village longer, and disheartened by the fall of their prophet, whom they had believed to be invulnerable to bullets, the majority of the survivors decided to surrender. A number of the defenders rushed out in the rear and attempted to escape to the hills across the swamp, but Captain Gordon and his volunteer cavalry galloped round and intercepted the fugitives. All except one or two were killed, wounded, or captured. Those who remained alive in the village hoisted a white flag, and the "Cease fire" was ordered. Nikora was the leader of those who surrendered; he had fought gallantly and received a severe wound. The brothers Kipa and Kingita both were killed. The Hauhaus lost in this short sharp affair twenty-one dead and about thirty wounded, of whom some died in hospital. Fifty-eight unwounded prisoners were taken. Very nearly the whole war-party, therefore, was accounted for by death, wounds, or capture.

Peita Kotuku (Ngati-Maniapoto and Patu-heuheu Tribes), who was one of those captured, described to the present writer (1921) his share in the engagement. " At the beginning of the fight on the river-bank at Omarunui," he said, " I had no gun, but when one of my comrades fell I took his double-barrel gun and his cartridge-belt, nearly full, and fired at the *pakehas* advancing to surround us. I expended all my ammunition here. A bullet struck me in the stomach, but its force, somehow, was deadened by my clothing, and it did not injure me beyond inflicting a heavy blow; it entangled itself in my shirt. Another bullet thudded on my chest just over my heart, but my waistcoat and shirt stopped it from penetrating, or else the angle at which it was fired caused it to glance off. This was at a range of about 100 yards. I saw Nikora shot in the body; two bullets struck him. A number of us retreated across the swamp and took to the hills, but we were surrounded there by cavalry and forced to surrender. All of us who could walk were marched to Napier, and the wounded were taken to hospital there. Then we were shipped off to Wharekauri (Chatham Islands) in a steamer. Kikora and the other wounded men were sent after us when they had recovered in hospital. Only one of my comrades succeeded in returning to Te Haroto: this was a young man named Maniapoto. Three years afterwards he was killed at Te Pononga, near Tokaanu."

Whitmore's casualties were slight. One Militiaman, Private W. Young, and a Ngati-Kahungunu Maori were killed, and Captain Kennedy, eight other Europeans, and five Maoris were wounded.

Meanwhile Fraser's small force despatched to Petane had gained an equally decisive victory. Early on the same morning as the battle of Omarunui (12th October, 1866) the company of Military Settlers, reinforced by Captain Carr and some armed settlers, intercepted Te Rangihiroa's war-party in a narrow pass through which the road ran. The Hauhaus numbered twenty-five, all mounted. Fraser sent some of his men to cut off their retreat, and there was nothing for it but to fight against heavy odds. The encounter was as sharp as that at Omarunui, but much shorter. Old Te Rangihiroa, an inveterate foe of the *pakeha,* was killed, and eleven of his men fell with him; one was wounded, and three were taken prisoners. The only European casualty was Sergeant Fletcher, wounded. Among the Maoris who escaped were two rather noted men, Paora Toki and Anaru Matete. The latter was a most determined fighter. In 1868 he joined Te Kooti, and fought under him in all his raids and skirmishes. Anaru at last surrendered to Captain Ferris at Te Reinga.

Thus the bold enterprise of Ngati-Hineuru and their allies ended in complete disorder, wiping out the fighting strength of a tribe renowned for its war-making proclivities. The total number of the combined Hauhau parties was set down at 128. Of these thirty-three were killed, several died of wounds, and the other wounded and prisoners numbered about eighty. The total disposed of was given as 114, leaving only fourteen at liberty. Most of the prisoners were deported to the Chatham Islands to join those captured at Waerenga-a-Hika.

The explanation of the daring manifested in the attempt of so small a war-party to attack a well-armed European settlement is to be found in its extraordinary confidence in supernatural aid produced by the preachings of the Pai-marire apostles. Panapa's disciples believed that the *Atua* of the Chosen People, who were the Maoris, would endow them with strength to prevail over their enemies; moreover, there was the faith implanted by Te Ua that the *pakeha's* bullets could be averted by the magic incantations and the favour of the gods. The double defeat on the outskirts of Ahuriri convinced the survivors that the Hawke's Bay *pakeha* had not only a more powerful *Atua,* but were endowed with an unexpected capacity for fighting. The lesson was not lost on the tribes when the news of Ngati-Hineuru's ruin spread through the interior, and whatever troubles befell other settlements Napier was never again menaced.

A monument unveiled by the Hon. J. D. Ormond at a jubilee gathering in 1916 now stands on the battlefield of Omarunui, on land presented by Mr. W. Kinross White.

Chapter 15

McDONNELL'S TARANAKI CAMPAIGN (1866)

AT THE CLOSE of Major-General Chute's campaign on the West Coast there was a brief cessation of active military operations, and the settlement of the confiscated lands was begun, but occupation was precarious, for Ngati-Ruanui, Te Pakakohi, and Nga-Rauru were only waiting their time. Areas totalling about 50,000 acres, mostly open land, south of the Wai-ngongoro, were laid out in military settlements; the townships were Kakaramea, Mokoia, and Ohawe. Many of the Military Settlers took up the occupation of the sections to which their period of service entitled them—there were chiefly men who had already had farming experience—but the majority in the end disposed of their grants and left the district.

When the Government in 1866 came to the decision to occupy the confiscated lands between the Wai-ngongoro and the Wai-totara the West Coast portion of the expeditionary Force at Opotiki was recalled, and in June went into camp at Patea. This body consisted of the Patea and Wanganui Rangers, two companies of the Taranaki Military Settlers, and the Wanganui Yeomanry Cavalry. A contingent of the Wanganui friendly Maoris who had been doing garrison duty at Pipiriki now joined the Taranaki column, peace having been established on the Wanganui by a pact with the up-river tribes under Pehi Turoa.

Major Thomas McDonnell was appointed to the command of the force, and shifted camp to Manawapou, a convenient position for operations against the South Taranaki tribes and for covering the survey-parties under Mr. S. Percy Smith and others engaged in the work of laying out township-sites and farm sections in the occupied country. McDonnell opened negotiations for peace with the Ngati-Ruanui and Tangahoe, but their attitude indicated that they intended to resist the confiscation of their lands. This was soon made plain in the usual way by ambuscades and attacks on small parties and on convoys. The newly begun survey work on the plains was carried on under highly adventurous conditions, and on several occasions the Hauhau

Mr. S. Percy Smith, F.R.G.S.

Mr. Smith, who became Surveyor-General of New Zealand, carried out survey work under perilous conditions in Taranaki during the war period. He died at New Plymouth in 1922. His diary narrative of adventures in South Taranaki, 1866–67, is given in the Appendices.

snipers or ambush-parties compelled the working-parties to make for cover.

On the 16th June, 1866, Mr. S. Percy Smith (afterwards Surveyor-General) and several companions had a narrow escape from an ambush-party. "I was riding across the fern plains at Hawera," Mr. Smith narrated, "in company with Mr. Octavius Carrington (then Chief Surveyor of Taranaki), Major McDonnell, and Lieutenant Wirihana, of the Native Contingent, on the way back from the Wai-ngongoro to Kakaramea, when we fell into an ambuscade near where the middle of the Town of Hawera now is. We were cantering along the narrow winding track among the fern and bushes. I had a big horse, a brute to hold in. When we reached a point at the junction of General Cameron's old route with the track that turns off to Ketemarae I heard Wirihana, who was behind me, call out, 'Hauhaus!' I turned my head towards a clump of flax bushes and fern, and there about 40 yards off saw a lot of black heads popping up above the fern. I could not pull my horse up quickly, and while I was doing my best to stop him we got a heavy volley from the Maoris. None of us was hit; it was an amazing escape, for the bullets knocked up the dust in the track about us, and I could hear and see them striking the flax, and saw the tops of the fern snipped off. I got my horse turned round, and we all galloped back the way we had come, with a lot of shots fired after us. Major McDonnell vowed he would get even for these attacks so near his post, and it was a night or two later that he raided the Hauhaus at Pokaikai. There were more than forty Hauhaus firing at us; our escape was miraculous. If it had not been for Wirihana, who saw their heads moving in the flax, we should all have ridden right into the ambush and have perished. We reached the Waingongoro Redoubt safely, and Captain Dawson gave us an escort of ten troopers and fifty of the 18th Regiment part of the way, and from Manawapou we had another escort on to the camp at Kakaramea."

After this ambuscade, which occurred at Te Haumi, between Hawera and the Waihi Stream, McDonnell sent to the Ngati-Tupaea *hapu* at Pokaikai a cartridge, a percussion cap, a bottle of rum, and a white handkerchief bearing the words "*Rongo pai*" ("Good tidings"), asking them which of the emblems they would accept. They retained the handkerchief and returned the other articles, thus signifying their intention to remain peaceful. However, a short time later (1st August) McDonnell suddenly marched on Pokaikai with two hundred men and attacked the village early in the morning, No. 8 Company of Military Settlers charging in with the bayonet. Two men and a woman were killed, and a girl received four bayonet-wounds. There were many women and children in the place. Most of the Hauhaus escaped to the bush down a gully, the majority of them in their alarm leaving their guns in the huts. They received volley after volley as they fled. One of McDonnell's men was killed, a young man named Spain, who had recently left Mr. Smith's survey-party, then camped at Manawapou. According to one report he had gone into a *whare* to bring out a dead Hauhau; another version was to the effect that he was searching for loot. At any rate, he was fired on and mortally wounded. It was reported that he was shot in mistake for the renegade Kimble Bent, who was supposed to be in Pokaikai. Bent at the time was in Taiporohenui Village, Ngati-Ruanui's headquarters, three miles away. Three days previously he had been in Pokaikai, sent there by his chief and owner Tito te Hanataua, but had returned to Taiporohenui at the bidding of Te Ua the prophet, who had had a dream of bad omen, portending some disaster, and had counselled the *pakeha* to leave Pokaikai. The troops captured thirty-five guns of various makes left by the fugitive Hauhaus. The village was burned, and the expedition marched back to Manawapou.

The affair was not very creditable to McDonnell. The natives complained afterwards that they had been lulled into security by the peace messages of the Governor sent through his prophet Te Ua on his return from Wellington (whither he had been taken as a prisoner by General Chute in 1866), and by McDonnell's white-handkerchief message. A Commission of inquiry into the Pokaikai surprise was held, and after taking evidence from both sides the Commissioner (Mr. George Graham) reported that the attack was unnecessary, and that McDonnell's action in lulling the natives into a state of security and then attacking them was "improper and unjust."

This surprise attack was followed by negotiations with the Tangahoe Tribe and a section of the Pakakohi, resulting in many of these Hauhaus surrendering and signing the declaration of allegiance. The greater part of Ngati-Ruanui, however, still held aloof, and in the beginning of September a reconnaissance-party had a slight skirmish near Ketemarae.

In September a redoubt was built at Waihi, and this position became the field headquarters of the South Taranaki force. Captain Newland and a body of Rangers and the Native Contingent who constructed the redoubt had numerous small skirmishes with the Hauhaus, who frequently fired on the working-parties from the edge of the bush half a mile away.

The Ngati-Tupaea and others of Ngati-Ruanui presently exacted *utu* for the attack on Pokaikai. On the 23rd September a cart convoy escorted by three troopers of the Wanganui Yeomanry Cavalry left the post at the Round Bush, near the present Town of Hawera, for the redoubt at Waihi. The cart was loaded with fresh meat and bread, and contained also an invalided Wanganui Ranger, Michael Emerson, formerly of the 65th Regiment. It was driven by Private George Tŭffin (afterwards one of the defenders of Turuturu-mokai Redoubt, where he received five wounds). Two of the troopers, William Wallace and Haggerty, rode ahead, and the third, Michael Noonan (killed near Waikare-moana, 1869), was rearguard. When about half-way between Hawera and Waihi the little convoy was ambushed by a party of twenty Maoris from the cover of high fern and *tutu* bushes. A volley was suddenly delivered at Haggerty, whose horse received six bullets and fell dead. Haggerty was thrown on the track with a wound in the leg, and instantly there was a rush of Hauhaus from the fern and a flash of tomahawks as they despatched him. "They were on him like a pack of wolves," says Wallace, the sole survivor to-day of that escort. Wallace was the target for the second volley, but, as if by a miracle, he escaped. The Maoris then shot the shaft horse in the cart team; a wounded Hauhau rode the leader away. Tuffin, who was unarmed, jumped out of the cart and ran for his life; he reached Waihi Redoubt unhurt. Emerson, who was suffering great pain, got out and appealed to the troopers not to let the Hauhaus get him. "It's all right, Mick," shouted Wallace, "we won't leave you." Emerson was unable to mount a horse, but hobbled along between the two cavalrymen, who kept the Hauhaus off with their carbines and revolvers until a party of Rangers, volunteers, and Wanganui natives came doubling up from Waihi, led by Captain Newland. The Hauhaus secured Haggerty's carbine, revolver, and sword, but had not time to plunder the cart. Captain Smith, commanding at Hawera, was put under arrest for sending so small an escort through perilous country.

Captain J. R. Rushton, of Kutarere, Ohiwa, describes how vengeance was exacted for Haggerty's death. Rushton had been a sergeant in the Patea Rangers, and had resigned, but was now serving as a volunteer without pay. "The Maoris," he says, "now became very enterprising, and often fired from a point of bush about 800 yards away. I think I suggested this trap for them. I took six or seven men out, and when some distance from the bush started a sham survey—that is, I told the men to use their carbines as if cutting lines. I stood at a distance as surveyor, directing them towards the part of bush the firing had come from. A party under Ensign Northcroft had come out of our redoubt unseen by the Maoris, and as we moved forward kept in touch with our flank. Now came what we expected—a heavy volley right at us; but luckily no hits. Our supports now sprang up, charging right into the bush. We thought that our ruse had failed, when our brave little comrade Winiata fired point-blank at a Maori trying to shelter behind a *rimu* tree, and killed him. 'This is *utu* for my friend Haggerty,' cried Winiata, as he ran up to tomahawk the fallen Hauhau. We followed up the rest, who bolted. After this we prepared to attack Pungarehu, as that place and Te Ngutu-o-te-manu were the chief strongholds of the Hauhaus."

The principal engagement of the campaign was fought at Te Pungarehu, a village in the bush on the western side of the Wai-ngongoro and not far from the afterwards celebrated Te Ngutu-o-te-manu. The position of the place was not exactly known for this bush country was unmapped and unexplored by Europeans; but McDonnell's practice was to scout about until a well-marked track was found, and then follow it up. With a force of about a hundred and ten men he crossed the Wai-ngongoro late on the night of the 1st October and marched in past Mawhitiwhiti, following a trail which led to a clearing in the heavy timber. *Whares* were scattered about this clearing, which was found after the fight to be Pungarehu, peopled by many families of the Nga-Ruahine Tribe. Lieutenant C. A. M. Hirtzel (Palmerston North), then in the Wanganui Yeomanry Cavalry, thus describes the attack on the *kainga*:—

"We lay in the bush on the outskirts of the village, after crossing a small creek, until dawn; the cocks were crowing in the settlement as we halted. Just at daylight one of the men's rifles went off accidentally, and so we had to rush the place at once. I jumped up, calling to my corps—the cavalry, dismounted—to follow me, and ran for the village. Our sergeant-major, Duff, dashed past me, and was into the place first, I think. Some men rushed to each *whare,* and McDonnell demanded the surrender of the people. The Maoris opened fire, and we replied, firing into the *whares.* Some of the natives rushed out; others fired at us from the hut doorways. Sergeant-Major Duff was stooping down to look into the doorway of one of the dug-in huts when he was shot and mortally wounded. I saw a woman with a baby in her arms come out of the largest *whare*—the one where Duff was hit—and walk away into the bush on the right flank of the clearing. One of our men was about to shoot her when I stopped him and protected her. She stood looking at me a moment and then disappeared in the bush. I asked Captain Newland to send some men to help me get Duff's body away, and I was just in the act of getting over a fence when I was shot in the back, and after I was carried to the rear I saw no more of the fight. The bullet struck near my spine below the shoulder and went right round the back. Meanwhile there was hot firing, and the village was in a blaze. Ensign Northcroft, as I heard afterwards, ran up and carried Duff off into shelter. The Maoris kept up a heavy fire from the bush at the rear end of the clearing, and more came up from Te Ngutu-o-te-manu to assist them when they heard the firing; they tried to work round on our left flank and surround us, and the withdrawal of our force was risky and difficult, but McDonnell carried it out well."

Five of the *whares* in the village were fortified, according to McDonnell's report. In order to dislodge the occupants, who had fired heavy volleys on being called on to surrender, the troops scraped off the earth which covered the roofs and pulled down the slabs to fire into the defenders. In half an hour the attackers were masters of the position, and firing ceased. Then the force, when engaged in setting fire to the *whares,* was suddenly fired on heavily from the bush, and as this firing increased it was evident that the Hauhaus had been reinforced strongly, and the withdrawal of the troops began. Some casks of gunpowder exploded in the burning houses as the force moved off.

Besides Duff, two men had been mortally wounded, and several others were hit in the heavy skirmishing which followed the first attack, and these were carried off in blankets by the main body when the return march was ordered. Captain Newland, Captain Kepa, Ensign Northcroft, and a few men held the Hauhaus in check while the main body withdrew, and fought a gallant rearguard action with a much larger body of Hauhaus. Those who had escaped from the *whares* in the clearing were reinforced by warriors hurrying down from Te Ngutu-o-te-manu, and they hotly pressed the retiring force through the bush and the gullies. Those who particularly distinguished themselves in this hard-fought affair were Ensign (afterwards Captain) Northcroft, Poma Haunui (of Hiruharama), and volunteers J. R. Rushton and David White. The rescue of the dying sergeant-major from the Hauhau tomahawks was one of a series of brave deeds which earned for Northcroft the decoration of the New Zealand Cross, tardily bestowed on him long afterwards.* Poma Haunui, an athletic deeply tattooed warrior from Hiruharama, on the Wanganui, and several of his comrades had a close-range encounter with double their number of Hauhaus, and killed four of them and secured their arms. Rushton and White, two devoted comrades, had been sergeants in the Patea Rangers. All the men of that corps had resigned owing to the Government's niggardly treatment of them in the allotment of land, but the two sergeants had volunteered for service without pay, seeing McDonnell's great need of experienced men. Rushton had the stock of his carbine smashed at Pungarehu.

The Ngati-Ruanui Tribe, chiefly the Nga-Ruahine section,

---

* Lieut.-Colonel McDonnell wrote as follows to the Under-Secretary of the Defence Office, under date 30th March, 1871: "For the consideration of the Hon. the Defence Minister, I have the honour to state that at the attack on Pungarehu in October, 1866, Ensign Northcroft, of the Patea Rangers, and now a Sub-Inspector in the Armed Constabulary, did, with great bravery, and at the risk of his life, rescue Sergeant-Major Duff, who was mortally wounded and helpless, from the enemy; also at the attack upon Tirotiro-moana, in November of the same year, Mr. Northcroft, being on that occasion in front in the bush with Private Economedes, was met by the enemy, who fired and killed the latter. Mr. Northcroft held his ground until assistance came up, preventing mutilation of the body and the capture of carbine and revolver, besides a considerable sum of money the man had on his person. This officer would have been recommended by me for the above to the Hon. Colonel Haultain as deserving the Victoria Cross could it have been conferred on a colonial soldier." It was not, however, until after the lapse of forty years that Captain Northcroft was awarded the New Zealand Cross for his gallant deeds.

lost about thirty men in Pungarehu and in the bush skirmishing thence to the Wai-ngongoro. Twenty-one dead were counted, and others were buried in the burning ruins when the *whares* were destroyed. One of the fighting chiefs, Toi Whakataka, was wounded in escaping from a large *whare* in the clearing. Young Te Kahu-pukoro, who afterwards became one of Titokowaru's warriors of the "Tekau-ma-rua," succeeded in bursting out of one of the burning huts. Nine of the Nga-Ruahine were taken to Waihi as prisoners, and the victors also captured about thirty stand of arms. Next day the three dead of McDonnell's force were buried with military honours in the little military cemetery at Ohawe, on the south side of the Wai-ngongoro.

After this well-planned and well-executed blow against the bush-dwellers Major McDonnell carried out several surprise raids upon forest settlements, compelling those Hauhaus who did not deem it expedient to make submission to retire farther into the interior. Keteonetea, Te Popoia, Tirotiro-moana, and other settlements (lying to the east of the present railway-line) were the principal objectives of these expeditions. There was a brisk action on the 18th October at Te Popoia. The force advanced to the attack just before dawn, but at a place where the Maoris had felled trees across the narrow bush-track heavy volleys were fired into the advance-party, and, as it was still dark, a retirement was ordered. Captain William McDonnell, who was leading, was severely wounded in the hip.

In another expedition to this place on the 22nd October a detachment of the 18th Regiment from the Wai-ngongoro Redoubt took part; the column was commanded by Major Rocke of that regiment. This was a more successful attack, for it was delivered in daylight. The Maoris made resistance at the barricade of logs, but the troops rushed it, killed two Hauhaus, and destroyed the village. The British had one man killed.

The Hauhaus at this place made use of a curious bush-engine against their enemies. Just alongside the tracks leading to Te Popoia they set some formidable *tawhiti*, or spring traps, formed of growing trees. The *tawhiti* was a sapling of some tough and elastic timber, preferably *matipo*. Such a tree by the trail-side was stripped of its branches and bent down and back without breaking it, until it was lying as nearly horizontal as possible, in such a position as to sweep the road. The end was fastened with a flax-line carried across the track, so laid than any unsuspecting invader coming along the track in the darkness or uncertain light would release the trap and the next instant receive the full force of the rebounding tree. (A very similar device, consisting of a bent sapling, an invisible trap-line, and a spear. has been encountered by explorers and punitive parties in the Solomon Islands and in Papua.) The old Hauhaus of Taranaki claim that some of the Kupapas (Wanganui Native Contingent) were injured by these *tawhiti* in the night advance on Te Popoia; however, any casualties thus caused could not have been serious.*

On the 5th November Major McDonnell took a force much farther inland, intending to surprise the Ngati-Tupaea clan at their village, Tirotiro-moana, by approaching it from the rear. The column had a long bush march, working round over what is now the Eltham district. On crossing the Mangemange Creek, which flows out of the Ngaere Swamp and joins the Tangahoe below Otapawa, the leading files received a volley from a Hauhau party in ambush behind some logs on the high bank. Economedes, a Greek—an excellent soldier—was killed. The force rushed up into Tirotiro-moana Village, which was a short distance above the creek, but found it deserted. Natives were seen in considerable numbers in a clearing, but McDonnell's force was scarcely in condition to follow them up after the long and wearying march, and the order was given to return to Waihi.

Another expedition about this time was of importance because it was the first visit of a Government force to Te Ngutu-o-te-manu, and also because it was the last occasion on which the 18th Royal Irish Regiment took the field against the Maoris. The force included, besides a detachment of the 18th from the Wai-ngongoro Redoubt, the Wanganui Yeomanry Cavalry, a useful little corps which did a great deal of dismounted work in Taranaki. Sir George Grey had come to oversee McDonnell's operations, and he accompanied this expedition. A veteran of the Wanganui Yeomanry Cavalry, Mr. William Wallace (afterwards sergeant in No. 2 Division Armed Constabulary), gives the following account of the discovery of Titokowaru's forest stronghold:—

"In the summer of 1866 we had seen great columns of smoke rising from the heart of the bush, and we knew that in the forest inland of Waihi the Hauhaus were preparing large clearings for growing food; for these we were now searching. After a march through the heavy timber that then covered the plain we came to a wide clearing on both sides of a small watercourse. This we discovered was the stream (the Mangotahi) which formed part of the western and southern boundaries of Te Ngutu-o-te-manu clearing. The place was a little distance to the north of the present Domain paddock. On the northern or inland side

* Kimble Bent, the *pakeha-Maori,* told me that in 1866, when he was living with the Ngati-Tupaea, he saw ten or twelve of these sapling spring traps, or *tawhiti,* set on the tracks just outside Te Popoia.

of the creek many *whares* were scattered about the clearing. The place was quite deserted, but I think the Maoris could not have been very far away. The houses were of a different style of construction to anything I have seen before or have seen since among the natives. They were log cabins much after the pattern of those used in the backwoods of North America. Each hut was built of small unbarked logs laid horizontally on one another, and notched at the ends so as to interlock closely. The sides of the huts were low, not more than 4 feet or 5 feet high; the interior was hollowed out of the earth to a depth of about 2 feet, so that in entering, as in the usual *wharepuni* of those days, one had to step downwards through the low doorway. Loopholes for rifle-fire were cut in the log walls, 2 feet or 3 feet above the ground. The roofs were thatched with *raupo* reeds and *nikau*-palm fronds. There was a large number of these *whares* scattered about on each side of the track ahead. Had they been occupied that day we should have had a very bad time of it indeed, for each hut was a little blockhouse and rifle-pit combined in itself, and each could have been defended independently of the others. Through the gun-apertures in these strongly built huts, impervious to bullets, they could have shot down our men in scores with perfect safety. It was a regular death-trap; and when we discovered the real strength of the apparently unfortified village we were very thankful that the Hauhaus were not at home to receive us that day. We burned the settlement, and returned through the bush without meeting the enemy."*

This log-cabin *kainga* is very close to the place where McDonnell was defeated in the second attack on Te Ngutu-o-te-manu in 1868.

---

* Regarding this unusual type of Maori *whare,* the Rev. R. Haddon (Tahu-Potiki), who is closely related to Titokowaru's family, in a conversation on the subject at Nga-pua-rata, Normanby, said: "I have heard from my old people of this *whare-rakau* or *whare-tuwatawata* settlement. I believe they got the idea in the early days before the war from the Rev. Skevington, the missionary, who lived in a house built in log-cabin fashion down at the Inaha, where the Riverdale Cheese-factory now stands. It was from this *whare* probably that they learned how to notch the ends of the poles and saplings so that they would fit in closely together."

Chapter 16

THE TAURANGA BUSH CAMPAIGN

IN THE EARLY part of 1867 the tribe called Piri-Rakau ("Cling to the Forest"), descended from ancient aboriginal clans, came into conflict with the Government forces in a series of sharp skirmishes along the northern edge of the bush-covered tableland in rear of Tauranga Harbour. These Piri-Rakau, assisted by parties of men from other districts, were all Hauhaus, and the Pai-marire pole of worship was a feature of each village. The edge of the Hautere plateau, much dissected by ravines, at a general altitude of 1,100 feet above the sea, was the scene of engagements in which a few Imperial troops co-operated with the Colonial Militia and a contingent of Arawa Maoris against numerous war-parties of the bush-dwellers. The conditions of campaigning were difficult because of the very broken character of the country, but the Arawa friendlies and a few skilful colonials made conditions so precarious for the Hauhaus by seeking them out in their bush villages and destroying their crops that the little campaign soon convinced the rebels of the futility of active resistance.

Towards the end of 1866 twelve survey-parties began the work of cutting up the confiscated lands for settlement. These lands were on the upper parts of the Wairoa and Waimapu Rivers and in rear of Te Puna. The Piri-Rakau and their kinsmen and allies of the Hauhau faction soon exhibited their hostility by sending warnings to some of the surveyors to remove from the district on pain of death. These threats were followed by armed raids on several camps, and the theodolites of Messrs Graham and Gundry, two of the surveyors, were carried off. About this time a settler named Campbell was murdered on his section near Waimapu.

Besides the resentment of the Hauhaus at the preparations for the settlement of the country taken from them, there was a strong desire to avenge the deaths of the scores of their people who fell in the battle at Te Ranga, 1864. Pene Taka, the Ngai-te-Rangi man who was chiefly accredited with the laying-out of the Gate *Pa* entrenchments, had joined the Piri-Rakau with a number of his people—the majority of Ngai-te-Rangi remained neutral—and he announced that he intended to obtain *utu* for the death of his relative Rawiri Puhirake at Te Ranga. Prominent among the Hauhaus was the old warrior priest, and prophet Hakaraia, from Kenana (Canaan), near Te Puke. A number of Ngati-Porou from the Moehau Peninsula had cast in their fighting fortunes with the Piri-Rakau under the chiefs Te Popata and Te Kewene, and many Ngati-Raukawa and some Waikato also joined them.

The opening action of the campaign occurred on the 18th January, 1867, at the village of Te Irihanga. On the previous day a force of the 1st Waikato Militia was moved out to the Omanawa Redoubt for the purpose of covering the arrest of Pene Taka and others of Ngai-te-Rangi, and Te Kewene and others of Ngati-Porou, on charges of interference with the surveyors by taking their instruments and threatening them with death. On the morning of the 18th the officer in charge of the force at Omanawa crossed over towards Te Irihanga with forty men. This movement, which was premature, quickly brought on a fight. A volley from the Hauhaus, as the small force began its ascent of Te Irihanga Hill, mortally wounded Sergeant-Major Emus of the Militia; he died four days later. On receiving this surprise volley the Militia quickly extended in skirmishing order, and hot firing lasted for about three-quarters of an hour. After an indecisive encounter the Militia force drew off and returned to the Omanawa post.

The next expedition (21st–22nd January) consisted of detachments of the 1st Waikato Regiment of Militia, under Colonel Harrington, and the 12th Regiment, commanded by Colonel Hamilton. The force crossed the Wairoa River at Poteriwhi in canoes and boats (just above the present bridge), and ascended the long fern-clad slopes of Minden Peak, where the 12th Regiment bivouacked for the night. Mr. Gilbert Mair, who was soon afterwards given a commission as ensign and received promotion to lieutenant, was attached to the Imperials as interpreter, but obtained Colonel Hamilton's permission to act in that capacity for Colonel Harrington's force which was in the advance, and which did all the fighting.

Passing through Te Irihanga the Militia skirmished through the belt of bush which separated it from the next settlement, Whakamarama. On entering the large fields of maize and potatoes at Whakamarama the Militia came under a heavy fire from the edge of the forest all round. The tall maize afforded good cover, and no casualties occurred just then. Gilbert Mair was one of the few who were on horseback and led the attack on the village.

Seeing a party of seven Hauhaus making for a slab hut, he galloped up, trying to turn them to the right, where they would have run against Captain A. C. Turner's company of Militia. The enemy reached the shelter first, and fired a volley at short range through the doorway and two open windows. Mair's horse, a heavy one, fell dead, its spine smashed by a bullet, and other shots through its head and heart. In its fall it pinned Mair's left leg and spurred boot so that he could not move. In the meantime the natives rushed out, reloading as they ran toward him, while he kept snapping his revolver, which had been wet through when he swam the Judea estuary at high water that morning. Fortunately one cartridge exploded, wounding the foremost man, which checked the rush, and Captain Turner, hurrying up, extracted Mair from his perilous position. A bullet had cut the peak of his cap, another grazed his sleeve, and another cut the pommel of his saddle. Several 1st Waikato men now ran up, and the party gave chase to the natives. The Hauhaus retired into the bush, and the pursuers got in among some fallen timber. Here Private Henry Jeffs was mortally wounded at close range, and was brought out with great difficulty. While the advance-party was so engaged, the main body of the Militia reached the spot where Mair's dead horse was lying, and Private Burslem, by way of a joke, stood up on the animal and began soliciting bids, when a dozen shots rang out from the edge of the bush and a bullet deprived the self-constituted auctioneer of part of an ear.

At the request of the Government, Major William Mair, R.M. at Maketu, raised a force of two hundred armed Arawa, at a pay of 3s. a day, for the purpose of following up the Hauhaus to their forest villages and dispersing them and destroying their cultivations. Mair was instructed to begin at Te Puke, then the headquarters of Hakaraia's band (Waitaha and Tapuika clans), to destroy food crops there, and then to push on to Oropi. After burning the village and making havoc in the food-gardens the Arawa pushed on along the edge of the bush. The instruments belonging to Mr. Graham, the surveyor, were found at Te Puke. Oropi was found unoccupied and was destroyed. Here a large quantity of loot and some gunpowder was found, and Hakaraia's great flag and other Hauhau banners were discovered in the bush.

On the 4th February a combined attack was made on the Hauhaus assembled at Te Akeake, a short distance inland of the redoubt called Pye's Pa (after Captain Pye, V.C., of the Colonial Defence Force Cavalry) at Otupuraho. The column was made up of the 1st Waikato Militia under Colonel Harrington, Mair's Arawa, and some other Arawa under Captain Walker. The Hauhaus were collected in some strength in a wooded gorge.

After some sharp skirmishing from tree to tree they were driven back into the dense forest. Akeake and Taumata Villages were taken, with five prisoners, from whom it was ascertained that Hakaraia had been there with forty-five men. Gilbert Mair led the attack on the rifle-pits at Taumata, and the Defence Minister, Colonel Haultain, who accompanied the expedition, gave him a commission as ensign of Militia. The work of cutting down and otherwise destroying the food crops in the captured settlements occupied the Militia for three days. From here the Arawa went on inland to Paengaroa, where the Hauhaus retired into the forest after firing a few heavy volleys. The settlement here, too, was burned down.

In the middle of February a strong expedition was organized at Tauranga to attack Te Irihanga and Whakamarama again. On this occasion the force was composed almost entirely of Arawa natives commanded by Major William Mair and his brother Gilbert. Captain H. L. Skeet's company of volunteer engineers, a fine body of young surveyors, all well accustomed to bush-work formed part of the column, and several companies of the 1st Waikato Militia acted as supports. The expedition followed the route taken by the first attacking column, up the right (proper) bank of the Wairoa, fording that river at the lower falls. The first night out was spent in bivouac at Awangarara, near the ford. On reaching the Irihanga village, on the eastern fringe of the forest, on the 15th February, the place was found strongly held by the enemy. The Hauhaus did not fire until the troops got into the open ground near the top of the hill on which the village stood. The summit was about 150 yards from the bush. The fern on each side of the narrow road was 8 feet or 10 feet high. The Hauhaus had cleared a space of about 10 yards wide between the hill and the bush by treading the fern down, and the heads of the fern were pressed over in the direction of the line of march of the troops. This was done in order to enable the defenders of the hill to fire destructive volleys while the attackers were passing over the ground between the summit and the bush—a task of difficulty and slowness on account of the artful manner in which the fern had been pressed over. As the troops approached the hilltop the Hauhaus opened fire. Major Mair's Arawa, who were leading, waited until the enemy had delivered a heavy volley, and then, before the Hauhaus could reload, charged and captured the settlement, and drove the Hauhaus into the bush. The force advanced and penetrated to Whakamarama, the headquarters settlement of the Piri-Rakau and their chief source of food-supplies. (The present sawmill at Whakamarama, fifteen miles inland from Tauranga by the Wairoa route, is close to this spot.) The village and cultivations occupied a beautiful tract of fertile country, with a thin belt of bush on the front and the dense forest and deep gorges of the hinterland in the rear—a perfect retreat and refuge in case of need. The Piri-Rakau had over 100 acres down in food crops, chiefly potatoes and maize; the cultivations occupied a shallow sunny saucer of country slightly inclined to the north-east, divided by a low ridge. In rear there was heavy timber—*rimu, tawa,* and even *puriri,* a tree not often seen on this part of the coast. Comfortable thatched *whares,* with some slab houses, were scattered all over this terrain, among the plots of maize and potatoes; the place had recently been cleared of forest, and burnt logs and stumps were dotted about the fields. A tall *niu,* the pole of worship, stood in the principal part of the settlement; its foot was encircled by a red-painted railing modelled on church altar-rails. There were similar *niu* masts at other villages along the edge of the forest—Irihanga, Oropi, and other *kaingas.* In some cases the mast was painted red as high as the crosstrees.

The retreating enemy were pursued through the belt of forest, about a quarter of a mile in length, separating Irihanga from the eastern end of the Whakamarama village and fields. The strip of heavy timber between the two settlements is still standing; then, as now, it was fairly clear of undergrowth. There was a sledge-track through it connecting the two villages, which were half a mile apart. Mair's Arawa contingent, dashing ahead, fell in with the Hauhaus in the middle of the bush. The enemy made a determined stand behind the cover of some very large trees and logs. Their resistance was broken by Harete te Whanarere, one of a famous fighting family of Ngati-Pikiao, from Rotoiti. On the side of the track, where the huge, densely foliaged trees make a twilight gloom, he pluckily grappled the foremost of the antagonists, a big Hauhau, whom he threw to the ground. The two warriors were engaged in a desperate struggle when another Hauhau dashed out from his cover, and, placing the muzzle of his Tower musket against Harete's body, fired and smashed both the hip-joints. (Though terribly wounded, Harete survived for some years.) Hemana then dashed up and killed the man who had shot Harete. Several of the Piri-Rakau were wounded in the tree-to-tree fighting here. It was typical bush warfare for a few minutes. Only the black heads of the combatants were to be seen now and again, and the muzzle of a gun showing for an instant, followed by a puff of smoke, then an instant dash for another tree. The Hauhaus presently broke and fell back on their main body at the Whakamarama village.

Just after the Piri-Rakau had retreated from the scene of this skirmish midway through the belt of bush Ensign Mair noticed a trail of blood leading down to a deep gorge on the left, or east, in the direction of Poripori. There was a faint track here through the forest to Poripori, which the Piri-Rakau had marked by breaking and doubling over the fronds of the fern called *tu-taumata* (*Lomaria discolor*), which are silvery-white underneath. When doubled over, the white under-surface of the fern showed conspicuously against the dark green of the ferns, moss, and tree-trunks around it. Mair observed that these white fronds were splashed with blood; and, diverging from the route followed by the others, he scouted down to the creek in the gorge. Hot on the trail, he followed the blood-marks to a cave, over the mouth of which a little waterfall came down. A shot rang out from the cave, narrowly missing him. Mair rushed in and encountered a wounded Maori kneeling behind the rocks in the gloom, and shot the man dead just as he was levelling his long single-barrel gun for another shot. Taking the dead warrior's gun and *whakakai* pendant of *tangiwai* greenstone as trophies, Mair hurried back to the scene of the fight. He found by inquiry afterwards that the man he had shot, a big tattooed warrior, was a Piri-Rakau named Rota, one of the leading men of the turbulent tribe.

Ensign Mair soon overtook his brother William, who, with his Arawa, was hotly engaged with the enemy at Whakamarama. The contingent skirmished through the maize-fields, where the corn was higher than a man's head, and forced the Hauhaus back to the western end of the clearing. Here, at their third position, Te Umu-o-Korongaehe, on the edge of the bush, the enemy made a further stand.

One of the Arawa, a man named Kitua, was severely wounded by a curious projectile, a large nail, which lacerated his leg badly; there were several slighter casualties. Gilbert Mair was joined here by several of the volunteer engineers, including Privates Eric Goldsmith, A. Crapp (afterwards Captain Crapp), and Tom Jordan. Lieutenant Horne, of the 1st Waikato Regiment, and others also came up. On ascending a low ridge a number of the Hauhaus were seen behind a large *tawa* tree which was lying across the track. These men fired at about 25 yards, mortally wounding young Tom Jordan in the abdomen. At the same moment Lieutenant Horne, who had taken cover behind a big *rimu* tree, killed the foremost assailant, a stalwart young fellow named Raumati, with a bullet through the eye. His fall so discouraged his companions that the small force were enabled to retire with Jordan's body and rejoin the main division. Raumati was a chief of the Piri-Rakau. He had fought in the Waikato War, receiving a wound at Otau, Wairoa South, in 1863, and he was one of the men who defended the Koheriki trenches, the left wing of the Gate *Pa,* in the battle of 1864.

The work of carrying out the dying volunteer was difficult. He was a big, heavy man, and there were only four to bear him out to the main body, while two others acted as rearguard and kept the Hauhaus off with their carbine-fire. The Piri-Rakau, however, had had enough of it by this time, and their pursuit was not very spirited.

In this skirmishing, in which several hundred Hauhaus were engaged, most of the fighting was done by the Arawa; few of the Europeans got up in time. The crops were ordered to be destroyed, but the area was so large that the troops could only cut down or otherwise destroy a part of the maize and potatoes. The *whares* in the group of villages were destroyed, and the force marched back to Tauranga.

Major William Mair led his Arawa with his customary skill and judgment. A characteristic story is told by an eye-witness as an illustration of his coolness under fire. While he was waiting for his supports to come up under a hot fire at Irihanga some of the advance-party gathered in a grove of peach-trees loaded with fruit. Mair climbed to the top in full view of the Maoris, 40 yards away, to reach the ripest peaches, and the Hauhau bullets brought the fruit tumbling down; but the Major remained there enjoying the peaches and calling down to his brother and other comrades below, " Have you enough, boys ? "

Of this Irihanga-Whakamarama battle (15th February) Mr. H. T. Clarke, Civil Commissioner, wrote in his report to the Native Minister, Mr. J. C. Richmond: " The enemy were not suffered to rest a moment. They were driven from tree to tree through the wood in an incredibly short time. They were then driven through their cultivations at Te Whakamarama to the wood on the other side. The dashing manner in which the Arawa accomplished the work under the direction of Mr. Mair is described by everyone who witnessed it as being very praiseworthy.

On the 19th February the Arawa moved on to Paengaroa and Kaimai; the latter village was found deserted. On the 2nd March Major Mair and his Maoris threw up breastworks at Paengaroa to cover the work of the survey-parties and to watch the Kaimai hostiles. On the 3rd March Gilbert Mair and four men, out foraging, followed up a trail near Te Kaki clearing, in very wild rough country, and suddenly were heavily fired on—" a terrific close fire." A brave young Arawa, Mau-paraoa, fell severely wounded. Mair and the other three men kept up a smart fire until the rest of the small foraging-party came up. He then took the offensive and drove the Hauhaus off, killing two of them. Lieutenant C. Dean Pitt, of the 1st Waikato Militia, who was attached to the Arawa contingent, brought up fifty men in support. The Civil Commissioner in his report on the skirmish praised the activity and courage displayed by Mair and Pitt in this hot bit of work.

Several other hazardous scouting operations into the great forest of the ravine-seamed tableland trending up to the Hautere wilderness were undertaken by the Mairs and their pickel bodies of Arawa. Many Ngati-Raukawa from Patetere and Waotu had joined the Piri-Rakau, but these presently withdrew to share in a strong Kingite attack from the north upon the Rotorua district, left temporarily unprotected by the absence of so many Arawa in the Tauranga operations.

The remnant of the Piri-Rakau still own a large area of the high land on the fringe of the forest and inland to the Hautere plateau. Many of the Maoris employed at the Whakamarama sawmill, close to the principal battle-grounds, are descendants of the Hauhaus who fought the troops here and at Irihanga in 1867.

Chapter 17

HAUHAU INVASION OF ROTORUA DISTRICT

IN MARCH OF 1867 a formidable attempt to invade Rotorua was made by a body of Waikato, Ngati-Raukawa, and Ngati-Haua men, acting at the instigation—or, at any rate, with the approval of King Tawhaio. The object was to exact retribution for the action of the Arawa tribes in barring the way to the East Coast army of reinforcements for Waikato in 1864. The invaders reached the western shore of Rotorua Lake, but did not succeed in their essay to attack Ohinemutu itself.

The first alarm of the Kingite-Hauhau incursion was communicated to the Civil Commissioner at Tauranga by Dr. Nesbitt, the Government agent and medical officer at Rotorua. He reported in March that a force of Waikato Hauhaus, numbering from three hundred to five hundred fighting-men, had appeared on the edge of the Mamaku Forest and had encamped at Puraku, near Tarukenga, sending parties out to Waiteti and to Parawai, near Puhirua, close to the lake. Those at Parawai were said to be under the command of Hakaraia, the Hauhau prophet from Te Puke. It was ascertained later that Kihitu was the principal leader of the Waikato and their allies.

The first to engage these raiders was Ensign Gilbert Mair, with a small body of Arawa, in a skirmish on Sunday, the 17th March, three days before the main body of Militia and Arawa reached Rotorua from Tauranga. Most of the Arawa had been in the Tauranga district fighting the Piri-Rakau and other Hauhau tribes, and there were only a few with Mr. Mair, who had just made a hazardous scouting expedition, alone, into Poripori, discovering there that the Hauhaus were making for Rotorua. As he came along the lake-shore from the Kaituna side he saw in the distance a line of blazing villages on the crest of land south of Rotorua—Paparata, Te Whetengu, and other places along the Tihi-o-Tonga, from the slopes of Ngongotaha Mountain stretching east to the Karaka Hill above the Hemo Gorge. The enemy had come down over the Hautere plateau and were making for Ohinemutu, hoping to capture the chief home of the Arawa during the absence of the fighting-men. Mair hurried on at the double, taking with him the best of his men—and there were very few who were able to keep up with this active and tireless young officer on the war-path. He reached Pukeroa *pa* ahead of all his men, and found only a few able-bodied warriors there; most of the garrison were old men and women and children.

The Maharo Redoubt, on the summit of Pukeroa Hill, had been built under Mair's direction before he left for Tauranga with the main body, and had been placed under the charge of Henare te Pukuatua with twenty-five men. From the western slope of the hill, at Paepae-mohoao, he could now see a long line of men, single file, advancing rapidly over a low ridge which trended across the old battlefield of Mataipuku, of cannibal fame, to the abandoned earthworks of Te Koutu *pa,* the terminal of the ridge, overlooking a small *kainga* of Ngati-Whakaue on the sandy shore of the lake. As was discovered afterwards, this war-party numbered seventy. The invading *taua* was headed by a woman, a circumstance reminiscent of the warlike customs in Samoa, where a high-born *taupo* woman usually led the march into battle. This woman of Waikato was Pare Turanga, a high prophetess and a sorceress or seer of visions (*matakite*).

There was not an instant to lose, for it was clearly necessary to seize and hold the *pa* at Te Koutu before the enemy reached it. Accordingly Mr. Mair, having called on the most active of the men in Pukeroa to join him, rushed off to forestall the invaders. He had now thirty-nine men, a small body to join issue with the strong and evidently well-equipped invading force, who looked a splendid body of warriors as they came marching at a steady walk over the plain, stripped to the waist and armed with guns and tomahawks with numerous cartouche-boxes strapped around them. Mair's men had not a rifle among them. His own weapon was a double-barrel gun; his Arawas were armed with similar pieces and with single-barrel guns and old-fashioned Tower flint-lock muskets.

The little Arawa force forded the Utuhina Stream 200 yards or 300 yards from its point of discharge into the lake. The water came up above the men's waists, and they had their guns and ammunition-boxes over their heads to keep them dry. They could hear the wild music of the Hauhaus' Pai-marire chant, a fanatic chorus, rolling up from the warriors as they marched into battle. Once across the little river the Arawa made direct for Te Koutu through the *manuka* scrub, here pitted with boiling springs and bubbling mud-holes, a nest of perils for an enemy unacquainted with the ground. Racing for the old hill *pa,* they clambered into its ditches on the south and east sides just as the enemy charged and occupied the other two sides. The *pa* was roughly square in shape, about 45 yards in length and the same in width; its outline can plainly be traced to-day, although the olden *parepare* or parapets, trench, and traverses have suffered from the hand of time and the feet of grazing stock. [Later, in the "seventies," Captain Mair, then resident at Te Koutu as Government officer, planted rows of *Pinus insignis* round the ramparts, and the stumps of these trees—which, when 100 feet high and 4 feet through the butt, were felled for timber and rafted round to the Ngongotaha sawmill—remain to-day to mark the limits of the ancient fortification.]

The enemy were led on by Pare Turanga, the chieftainess already mentioned, a handsome young woman, tattooed on chin and lips, attired in beautiful native garments of finely dressed flax—a *huaki* with its double flounce of *taniko* pattern about the shoulders, leaving the right arm bare, and a *korowai* of white flax with dangling black dyed thrums around the waist. Huia-feathers adorned her luxuriant black hair. She wielded a long spear-headed *taiaha,* and this she handled in true warrior fashion as she came running on at the head of her warriors, perfectly indifferent to danger. Yelling their Pai-marire battle-cries, the Waikato Hauhaus made desperate endeavours to wrest the opposite trenches of the *pa* from the Arawa. They attempted to outflank the Lakes men, but this was frustrated by Mair and his comrades, a few of whom dashed up to the south-west corner of the redoubt and enfiladed the enemy holding a portion of the westernmost trench. Meanwhile a number of Arawa, led by Henare Pukuatua and a big black-bearded young warrior chief of the Ngati-Raukawa and Ngati-Whakaue named Arekatera Rongowhitiao, worked round the north-eastern corner and began to outflank the Hauhaus in that direction, the side facing Kawaha. Some of the enemy had crept into the *pa* and occupied some *ruas,* or old food-pits, and other depressions there, and from this cover they kept up a constant and heavy but not very well directed fire upon the Arawa, very few of whom were hit. All that could be seen of most of the enemy were the black shaggy heads popping up here and there across the 20 yards of clear ground in the interior of the *pa,* and a gun hastily raised and discharged.

The sharpest fighting occurred at the south-east angle of the *pa.* Mr. Mair and a man of Ohinemutu named Te Honiana, dashing up the hill, secured cover behind a small but thick patch of *manuka* a few yards from the angle, and from here kept up a steady fire. Some of the enemy had taken cover behind the traverses of the old trench, which were still in usable order Meanwhile a fine young warrior of the Arawa, a man named

Werimana, of the high-born Amohau family, the favourite young chief of the Ngati-Tunohopo clan, boldly stood forth near the parapet, and singling out a foeman across the intervening few yards, shot him. Clubbing his gun he dashed forward "over the top" to despatch his foe, crying as he did so "*Ki au te mata-ika*" ("Mine is the first fish!"—*i.e.*, the first antagonist slain), when he himself was shot through the lungs by Hone, of Ngati-Ahuru, and fell mortally wounded. His fall was quickly avenged by Whiripo, of the Ngati-Tuara *hapu;* he shot and severely wounded Hone, who, after the fight was despatched by a bullet from Rameka's gun as *utu* for Werimana's fatal wound.

Almost simultaneously Mair and Honiana secured a good view of a daring slim lad, conspicuous for his head of yellow-red hair, the ruddy tinge called by the Maoris *urukehu*. Their bullets both struck him, and he fell dead. It is believed he was Netana, of the Ngati-Haua Tribe.

Now the Arawa on the other side of the *pa* succeeded in outflanking the enemy holding the northern face, and these at last broke and fled with the survivors of those who had faced the fire and Mair and his immediate followers. The whole war-party of Waikato turned and made for the cover of the thick *manuka,* fighting as they retired. The last to leave the battle-field—as she had been the first to enter it—was the fearless chieftainess, brandishing her red feather-decked *taiaha,* and rolling her eyes in the warrior grimace of the *pukana* until the shelter of the thickets was reached.

Seven Waikato warriors were killed in and around this *pa* of Te Koutu; their bodies were interred in an ancient *wahi-tapu,* or burying-ground, which is marked to-day by an old willow-tree in the highest part of the redoubt. The Arawa, following up the retreating enemy, killed two more in a clump of *kahikatea* timber called Te Pa-nui-o-marama, on the flat in the direction of Ngongotaha. The pursuit ended at Te Puna-a-Tuhoe (now called the Fairy Spring), close to the base of Ngongotaha Mountain, and here two more were shot, making eleven in all; but the bodies were carried off by the retreating Waikato, who made off round the base of the Kauae spur and fell back on Tarukenga.

The Arawa lost only one man—the brave Werimana, who was carried to Ohinemutu, where he died that night. Five men were wounded. Captain Mair gives the following list of the thirty-nine men who followed him to Te Koutu: Henare te Pukuatua, Te Raika, Manahi Poihipi, Taekata, Te Warihi, Te Werimana (died from wound), Te Tupara Tokoaitua, Whiripo te Puni, Hamuera Pango, Pango Kaingamata te Ore, Ngamahirau, Reupena, Perepe Tapihana, Ieni Tapihana, Arekatera Rongo-whitiao, Poniwahio Pango, Ngakuku, Hona te Ngatete, Matenga

Rangi-whakairi-ao, Paora te Amohau, Te Pimara, Pirika Poihipi, Te Wheuhi Wharekiekie Ngamako, Himaera, Te Rangikaheke (severely wounded), Wehipeihana, Henare Mokoia, Te Hauiti, Te Kowhai, Te Kipihana te Keho, Te Katene Motunau, Whakatau Ngakuku, Whitiana Pako, Te Taotahi, Te Araki te Pohu, Raniera, Hema te Tua, Hori Keretumu, and Manahi te Puango.

Some of these men, such as the Ngati-Tu chief of Te Araki te Pohu—a splendidly tattooed patriarch who died some years ago nearly a hundred years of age—were elderly men, and so could not keep up with the younger warriors in the race to forestall the Hauhaus, but all arrived in time for the fight.

Chapter 18

CAPTURE OF PURAKU PA, TARUKENGA

IMMEDIATELY AFTER THE Arawa repulse of the Waikato Hauhaus at Te Koutu (17th March, 1867) news reached Rotorua that the main war-party under Kihitu had occupied and was fortifying a position at Puraku, a short distance from Tarukenga, on the edge of the wooded ranges west of Rotorua Lake. This place was close to Parahaki, the scene in 1835 of the murder of Hunga by Haerehuka, a tragedy which led to the invasion of the Lakes country by the great warrior Te Waharoa and his Ngati-Haua. Now history was repeating itself in this attack by the Waikato tribes after a lapse of thirty years, but in this later instance the assailants were destined never to set foot on the shores of the famous lake or to reach the palisades or their hereditary foemen's fort. The Kingites established themselves comfortably in their eyrie at Puraku (called also Ahiria, or " Assyria "), whence they could overlook the whole basin of Rotorua, posted as they were on its lofty rim. They hoisted their curiously designed war-flags on a *niu* pole within the walls, and day and night the camp resounded with the solemn music of their Pai-marire chants.

This fortification at Puraku was first built by the local disaffected tribes, the Ngati-Tura and others, and a small section of Ngati-Rangiwewehi. Ensign Gilbert Mair, who was at the time stationed at Rotorua, repeatedly scouted out alone to the lofty north-west spur of Ngongotaha Mountain—the wooded height called Te Tuahu-a-te-Atua ("The Altar of the God"), famous in Arawa fairy folk-lore—and from that post watched the Hauhaus hard at work digging their trenches and erecting their stockade. Then, after the fighting in rear of Tauranga, when the Waikato, Ngati-Raukawa, and other rebel tribes came out of the Piri-Rakau bush country and concentrated for an attack on Rotorua, they took up their quarters with Ngati-Tura and occupied and strengthened the *pa*. Mair's daring scouting exploit, when he went into the forest from Tauranga and found the large rebel force had moved out from Poripori southward, had the result of arousing the authorities to a sense of Rotorua's imminent danger, and a Government column was hurried off to the Lakes via Maketu. On the 20th March Major (afterwards Lieut.-Colonel) T. McDonnell and Major St. John arrived with the 1st Waikato Regiment of Militia. The loyal Arawa co-operated with the troops in the skirmishing which followed.

The principal operation was the attack and capture of Puraku. There was a preliminary reconnaissance in force when the *pa* was temporarily abandoned; it was partly destroyed by the force. Then, at the end of March, the full strength of the European and Maori force marched up the valley of Waiteti Stream, working past the northern spur of Ngongotaha Mountain to the fern-covered terraces and the bush ranges above. Gilbert Mair was detailed to take a hundred men of the Ngati-Pikiao and Ngati-Manawa Tribes and make a long detour to the right in order to work round into the forest in rear of the *pa,* which was a few hundred yards from the bush. The scheme was to surround the *pa* on the forest side, the main body meanwhile keeping the enemy busy on the front facing the lake, then to attack and drive the garrison into the cordon in rear.

Mair, realizing the broken and difficult nature of the country, asked his superior to allow four hours in which to complete the task allotted him. However, he was only given two hours. Mair moved off quickly with his hundred Ngati-Pikiao, accompanied by Ensign Dean Pitt and Sergeant-Major David White (who was killed in 1869 at Te Paripari, on the Whakatane River). As he had anticipated, he had not gone very far before he was confronted by a series of precipitous defiles, the deep gorges Te Uhi and Manurewa, and other rocky gulches. " In the pursuit which followed the fight the Arawa had to go nearly a mile at one of these places," he narrated, " to find a place where they could cross the gorge, so steep were the cliffs."

The force pushed on with the utmost speed, but the two hours allowed were quite insufficient to allow Mair time to cut off the retreat. Meanwhile a heavy fire was opened on the *pa* by five or six hundred rifles and guns, a fire so heavy that the Hauhaus realized their position was hopeless. It was possible now to form an idea of the strength of the Hauhau position, garrisoned by several hundred warriors, whose double-barrel guns and muskets flashed fire from beneath the outer stockade. The *pa* stood on a gentle eminence on the open fern land which sloped down from the forested and gully-bitten plateau (over which the Waikato–Rotorua Railway now runs) to the valley of the Ngongotaha. It was commanded by higher ground on the west, but the interior of the *pa* seemed well protected by a strong palisading; moreover, as was afterwards discovered, every *whare* in the fort was rendered bullet-proof by being built close up against the inner stockade and by the device of heaping up the earth over its dug-in sides and its thatched roofing. The fort was roughly oblong except for a large bastion on its northern side, a salient designed to command the Rotorua–Waikato track which wound up through the valley immediately under this aspect of the defences. A tall *niu* rose above the stockade near from the north-western angle; it had a topmast and yard like a ship's mast, and from the yardarm and masthead halliards flew the Kingite flags. On the north, east, and west sides were *waharoa,* or gateways, closed by solid slabs of timber. Between the two lines of stockade, a few feet apart, was a skilful trench system with traverses and covered ways. On the western and southern sides were fern-covered gullies, hillocks, and ridges, trending to the forest; on the north and east were cultivations and fruit-groves, the food-gardens of the Ngati-Tura *hapu,* most of whom had joined the Hauhaus in the *pa*—the only section of the Arawa nation, besides a portion of Ngati-Rangiwewehi, who showed any sympathy with Hauhauism.

Mr. Mair gradually worked round the right flank towards the rear of the *pa* under great difficulties owing to the broken terrain. He detailed a party of his Maoris under two young chiefs, Hemana (nephew of Major Pokiha Taranui, of Maketu) and Hohapeta te Whanarere, to push on quickly to the eastward and take up a post commanding a deep gorge which the escaping Hauhaus would have to cross. Mair then ran down a fern spur with the rest of his men in order to seize a mound which commanded the *pa* on the west; here was a sentry's rifle-pit. Just as he was in the act of mounting this low hill, his advance was stayed by an incident characteristic of the heroism and devotion which so often marked the Maori warrior.

A tall, tattooed man, in a white shirt and waist-mat, emerged from the west gateway of the *pa* and advanced to meet the white officer. He wore a *hamanu* or cartridge-belt with boxes across his shoulders, and another buckled around his middle, feathers in hair, double-barrel gun in hand. He walked with a deliberate jauntiness across the short fern towards Mair. Halting when within about fifteen paces of his antagonist, he grounded his gun-butt and, placing his hands across the muzzle of the *tupara,* he gazed fixedly with stern defiance straight into Mair's eyes. Ensign Pitt and Sergeant-Major White were just behind Mair. Two of the young Arawa—Whakatau was one—ran up and, dropping to the knee, levelled their guns at the Hauhau.

"*Kauaka !*" said Mair; "*kauaka !*" ("Don't !") gesturing to his men not to fire.

The Maori spoke. "*He aha,*" he asked, "*ta koutou i haere mai ai ki te whakaoho ia matou, i te iwi Kawanatanga?*" ("Why do you come here to alarm us, who are a tribe of the Government?")

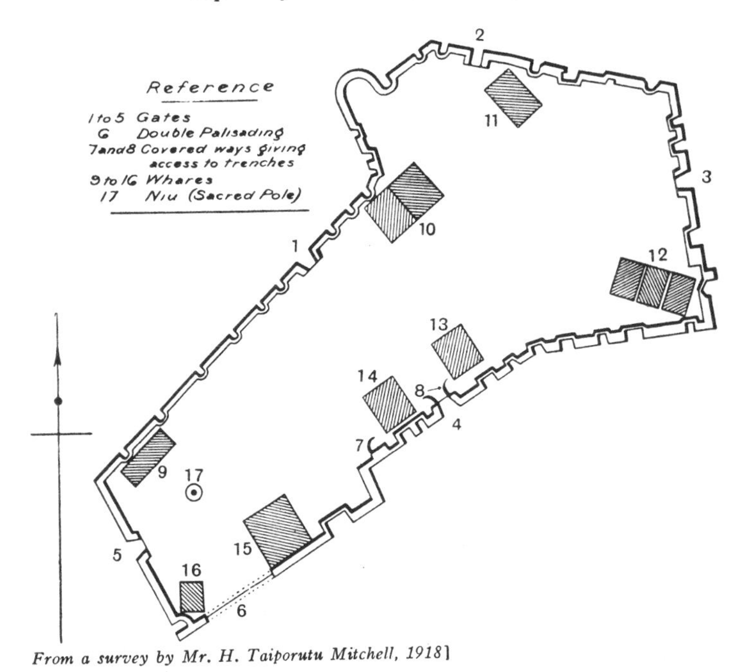

From a survey by Mr. H. Taiporutu Mitchell, 1918]

Plan of Puraku Pa Entrenchment, Tarukenga, Rotorua

"*No Waikato tenei ope*" ("This war-party is from Waikato"), replied Mair.

"*He horihori!*" ("It is false!") declared the Hauhau.

This cool and impudent attitude for the moment puzzled Mair, to whom the thought occurred that possibly the garrison consisted largely of Ngati-Rangiwewehi, an Arawa clan who had been in rebellion but now were known to be anxious to join the side of the Queen and make amends for this disaffection.

There was a further interchange of words, but Mair now perceived that the Hauhau's daring intervention was only a device for gaining a little precious time to enable his people to escape. A few moments more and the Ngati-Pikiao would have gained this mound which commanded the *pa*. The unknown warrior's bold action, however, had given his comrades two or three minutes' grace, and they were quickly racing out of the *pa* for the forest and the gorges under the heavy fire of the Militia force. in which Mair's men now joined. As for the tattooed hero of this episode, he bounded like lightning to the side of the trail, and in an instant he was out of sight in the fern that masked a little trough of a valley just to the south of the *pa* stockade. Miraculously he escaped; a little later he was seen—conspicuous by reason of his white shirt—running over a spur 600 yards to the south. His devotion undoubtedly enabled many scores of his comrades to escape.

Now came the pursuit of the enemy, flying for their lives through the gorges and forests. The Arawa, lightly costumed for the bush, took up the chase of their hereditary enemies, the Waikato and Ngati-Haua, with great zest. Yet here entered in an illustration of that clan-fellowship which so often operated to save a hostile tribe. Puraku was within the territory of Ngati-Tura, a subtribe of the Arawa, and the lake-side people were closely connected by ties of kinship with these dwellers on the ranges. Ngati-Tura had thrown in their fortunes with the Waikato *ope,* and their men, or most of them, were within the *pa* when the attack was delivered. Probably they had no great sympathy with the Hauhaus, but expediency dictated their temporary alliance with the invading *ope*. When the *pa* was evacuated, most of these Ngati-Tura, instead of flying to the forest, concealed themselves in the high fern which densely filled the little valley and covered the ridges immediately to the south of the stockade. In this valley seven or eight of the Hauhaus were shot as they ran, but the canny Ngati-Tura escaped by lying quietly in the fern until the chase had passed on. No doubt they would have been discovered had the Arawa from Rotorua *takahi'd,* or trodden down, the fern, as was the practice in cases of the kind, but the Government's brown allies carefully refrained from doing so, knowing doubtless that some of their unfortunate kinsmen lay trembling there.

As Ensign Mair and Sergeant-Major White stood near the palisade just after the mêlée that followed the capture of the *pa* they saw a tall naked Hauhau, his brown skin shining in the sun, running up the side of a little hill, to the southward of the *pa*. Both threw up their rifles for a shot. "Sight for 600 yards," suggested White. They fired together, and the Maori fell. When the body was examined afterwards it was found that one of the bullets had struck him just behind the base of the neck, killing him on the instant. He was a young man; his name, as was ascertained, was Tu-Wairua.

The main body of the fugitives took flight up a long, narrow gorge, a deep gulch which the present railway-line crosses about two miles on the Waikato side of Tarukenga. Hemana and his party, holding this gorge, killed several men, and one or two more were shot dead or severely wounded at various points on the line of flight. In all, the Hauhaus lost eleven men killed, and had many wounded. Hemana and his men had great difficulty in following up the swiftly-flying foes owing to the rough character of the country; in order to cross the gorge they were compelled to travel along its brink a long distance before they found a practicable place of descent, and then they had to lower themselves down by *aka* vines. The train traveller to-day may gain a fleeting idea of the formidable obstacles presented to troops, even the mobile and lightly-clad Maori, by observing from his carriage-window the numerous sudden gullies on the plateau between Mamaku and Tarukenga. They formed an impediment to the flying enemy, too, but the Hauhaus had the advantage of having been over the ground recently.

Up the straight sides of some of these gulches the Hauhaus clambered by means of the trailing *aka* vines, some as thick as ships' hawsers. Hemana was so hot in chase of one man that the two, fugitive and pursuer, were on the same *aka* together. The Hauhau, struggling desperately upward, was caught by his foeman, who gripped him in his arms, and in the struggle they either lost their hold of the *aka* or the tree-vine gave way under the strain, with the result that the two warriors came down by the run to the bottom of the gully, where Hemana killed his man.

The Hauhau leader, Kihitu, was shot through the hips, and was carried off the battlefield by his men. He lived to reach his home, but died from his wounds about a year later. Many others of the enemy were wounded. Not a man among either the Arawa or the Militia was hit. Had the Hauhaus remained to fight it out, Puraku might have become another Orakau, but they were quick to realize that they were in a trap from which only prompt flight would save them, and so they did not offer the fight that might have been expected from their numbers. Their fire from the *pa* was feeble in comparison with that of the attackers, and only a few returned the shots of their pursuers in the chase.

Rotorua was never again invaded by the Kingites, and enjoyed immunity from raids until Te Kooti attacked it in 1870, when he sustained a decisive defeat at the hands of Mair and his lakesmen. For his services in the Poripori scouting episode and in the actions at Te Koutu and Puraku Mair was promoted to the rank of Lieutenant.

When the Government forces inspected this captured *pa* they found it a marvel of Maori military engineering ingenuity, and even to-day its trenches with traverses and flanking bastions remain almost intact, a monument which should not be obliterated. The double palisading was destroyed by the Arawa, but they fortunately did not take the trouble to fill in the entrenchments. There were two strong palisades, the *pekerangi* on the outside of the trench and the *kiri-tangata* ("the warrior's skin") immediately inside. These stockades had been constructed of totara timber hauled from the near-by forest by the sledge-track which wound up past the *pa.* The trench was about 3 feet wide with a depth of 5 feet. The interior of the work measured 80 paces in length by 45 paces at the widest part, and this space was largely occupied by low huts thatched with *kaponga* fern-tree fronds, the sides and eaves well protected by being earthed up for several feet. The earth floors of these huts were dug in a foot or two below the level of the *marae* outside, a feature which gave their occupants additional safety. The trench, with its numerous traverses and covered ways, was essentially the same as our soldiers' trenches in France and Flanders in the Great War, but in one detail there was a difference. The *pakeha* engineer throws out the earth from the trench in front of his ditch in order to form a low parapet; the Maori cast the earth on the inner side, his rear, lest the bullets of the enemy, striking the loose, soft soil, should throw dirt in his eyes, confuse his aim, and perhaps temporarily blind him. The dug-out soil also formed a *parepare,* or parapet, on the outer side of the main line of palisading, close against the back of which the bullet-proof *whares* were built. On the *marae,* the open space or parade-ground, stood the *niu,* around which the Hauhaus marched chanting their Pai-marire service. There was a low, roughly built railing, a Hauhau altar-rail, around the foot of the mast; within this *tapu* space stood the *tohunga,* the priest of the war-party, who slowly revolved about the pole, leading the chantings.

NOTES

On the 9th December, 1918, the author explored this Hauhau fortification in company with Captain Gilbert Mair, N.Z.C., who pointed out the scenes of the fight in which he led the Ngati-Pikiao contingent. Puraku is easily reached by walking along the railway-track for a mile and a quarter from Tarukenga, crossing the Manurewa Gorge, until a white-painted railway-gate is seen on the left; thence, entering on the fern- and *tutu*-grown slopes on the Ngongotaha or eastern side of the line, a walk of 200 yards down the fern slopes in the direction of some pine-trees that mark a deserted dwelling brings one to the *pa.* There are no bold walls or *maioro* to mark the spot, but the fern-grown mounds which were once the earthed-up sides of *whares* remain in places 3 feet or 4 feet above the general level of the ground. The palisades have vanished, except for one or two burnt butts of *totara* timber. The sites of the three gateways, the principal one on the western side, may still plainly be traced. Except at these gateways and at places where the covered ways ran, the deep narrow ditch of the Hauhau trench is continuous about the roughly rectangular *pa.* Its sides, in places, are as cleanly cut as if they were delved out but yesterday: this is where the scaling of moss which accumulated upon the fern-protected walls has fallen off. The trench is in most places 4 feet deep, somewhat shallower than its original dimensions, but the wonder is that more than fifty years have left the work in so perfect a state of preservation.

The Maori engineer was careful to guard against enfilading-fire, hence the continuous line of the trench is broken by a man-high traverse every few yards. On the northern side, where the ground falls steeply to the old track through the fern—the front attacked by the white section of the force—there is a strong flanking bastion projecting about 25 feet from the main work.

Relics of the Hauhau war-party were still to be found within and about these fern-hidden ditches and mounds when we paced the lines and sketched the entrenchments—a broken gun-barrel of large bore, apparently an old Tower musket; broken iron cooking-pots, and fragments of human bone, *memento mori* of Kihitu's warriors.

Puraku stands on Crown land, a portion of the Okoheriki Block, purchased from the Maoris. The *pa* should be preserved from destruction in the course of settlement, the fate that has overtaken so many fortifications of great historic value. It is the best existing example of Maori skill in entrenchment in the wars of the "sixties."

Captain Mair wrote (11th April, 1919): "The hero in that fine episode when the warrior came out of Puraku *pa* and parleyed with me to gain time was Te Matai Paruhi. He was a member of the Marukukenga *hapu* of Tapuika, who live near Te Puke. He died some years ago."

Chapter 19

SKIRMISHING IN OPOTIKI DISTRICT

THE PERIOD 1866–68 was a time of intermittent skirmishing and bush-marching for the military forces and the settlers in the Opotiki district, which was particularly exposed to forays from the gorges and ranges of the Urewera borders. The principal trouble-makers were the Ngati-Ira *hapu* of the Whakatohea Tribe, under Hira te Popo, and the Ngai-Tama and Urewera, led by the savage warrior Tamaikowha, of Waimana. The Waioeka and Otara gorges were the favourite haunts of the inland Opotiki rebels, and Tamaikowha, when not engaged in raiding the Opotiki frontier, was strongly posted in his ancestral fighting-ground, the narrow valley of the Waimana, the principal tributary of the Whakatane River.

In February and March, 1866, Lieut.-Colonel Lyon, who had been left in charge of Opotiki, led expeditions, chiefly Patea and Wanganui Rangers, up to the Waioeka Gorge in search of the Hauhaus. Several of the enemy were killed in the skirmishes which occurred in very difficult and dangerous country for an invading force. The principal success was at Wairakau, a strong position on a cliff above the rapid river. Captain W. Newland was sent under cover of the bush to scale the cliff while a detachment crossed the river-bed in front. The Hauhaus fired heavily on the latter force, but Newland and his active Rangers rushed the *pa* and cleared the enemy out of it. In the chase which followed four Hauhaus were killed. A large quantity of property looted from the Opotiki settlers was found in the captured *pa*.

Another expedition was one directed against the settlements in the Otara Gorge, where one or two Whakatohea men were shot and others captured and disarmed.

Eru Tamaikowha te Ariari, who now became the chief figure in the principal murderous forays on the settlements, was the most ferocious warrior that the East Coast wars produced, a true type of the olden savage. His forte in military tactics lay in the ambuscade and the lightning raid on unprotected or unsuspecting settlers. His reversion to the methods of ancient Maoridom was

From a photo at Tauranga, about 1895]

Eru Tamaikowha, Chief of Ngai-Tama

complete, for he delighted not only in slaughter and mutilation, but in cannibalism. Tamaikowha was the chief of the Ngai-Tama, an Urewera clan inhabiting the Waimana Valley; he was connected also with the Ngati-Awa, of Whakatane. Before the Pai-marire fanaticism reached the Bay of Plenty he was on the war-path; in 1864, when he was about twenty years old, he fought in the attack of the East Coast tribes on Maketu and in the sea-beach battle of Kaokaoroa, near Matata. Thereafter his fighting-grounds were the Waioeka, Waimana, and Whakatane valleys, and the northern borders of the Urewera Country. To the day of his death a few years ago he was a picturesque old barbarian, clinging to the primitive *rapaki* or waist-shawl long after his people had taken to the garb of the *pakeha*.

After the fight at Kairakau, on the Waioeka, in March, 1866, Tamaikowha took revenge for the death of some of his kinsmen there by laying an ambuscade at the mouth of the Waiotahe River, between Opotiki and Ohiwa, and killing Wi Popata, a Maori of the Arawa Tribe who was carrying mails for the Government between Opotiki and Tauranga. Captain Newland, who was riding along the beach to Ohiwa and Whakatane about the same time, narrowly escaped the war-party. The heart was cut from the Maori mailman's body and was cooked for a cannibal war-rite. Tamaikowha ate a portion of it, after offering part in the sacrifice of the *whangai-hau,* or *whangai-atua,* to his tribal gods Hukita and Te Rehu-o-Tainui; he professed to be the medium and priest of those pagan deities.

At a later date a European was similarly ambuscaded and killed at Waiotahe. This was Mr. Bennett White, who was shot from ambush at a *pohutukawa* grove on the right bank of the river, close to the mouth; the present main road to Opotiki traverses the spot. White was riding from Whakatane to Opotiki when he was waylaid. His head was cut off and stuck on a rock alongside the track, and Tamaikowha had portions of the body cooked for a cannibal meal.

In May, 1867, Tamaikowha and about twenty men crossed the range between Waimana and the upper end of the Opotiki Valley, and carried out a murderous raid on the farthest-out military settlers near the mouth of the Waioeka Gorge. These four men were Messrs. George T. Wilkinson (surveyor by profession, and afterwards Government Native Agent at Otorohanga, in the King Country), Livingstone, Moore, and Begg. They lived in a *whare* alongside the Waioeka Redoubt, which was not then garrisoned. Surrounding the house on a very wet day (21st May), Tamaikowha and his band completely surprised the unfortunate settlers, who had rifles but no ammunition. Dashing out of the *whare,* they ran for the bush, but only two gained it, Wilkinson and Livingstone. The other two men were shot down and tomahawked, and their hearts and livers were cut out by the savages. Wilkinson and Livingstone escaped to Opotiki, after a terrible flight through the bush. The Ngai-Tama burned the house and cooked and ate their trophies of the chase. Tamaikowha offered up a portion of one of the hearts in oblation to the gods of war. The raiders retired across the ranges to Waimana, and heavy floods in the Waioeka and other rivers prevented pursuit by the force sent out from Opotiki.

At this period a number of the military settlers formed a small volunteer corps at Opotiki Henry Mair (brother of William and Gilbert Mair) was captain, David White was lieutenant, and J. R. Rushton ensign. The corps was called the Opotiki Volunteer Rangers, and its members were armed with breech-loading carbines and revolvers. The Rangers were in the advance in an expedition organized by Lieut.-Colonel St. John to follow the Maori raiding-parties into the Urewera Country. The force marched up the Waiotahe Valley and then crossed over into the gorge of the Waimana River. An attack was made on a village about two miles above the present township of Waimana. The Rangers met with a hot reception from Tamaikowha and about a hundred men of the Urewera and Ngai-Tama, but only one of them was wounded; as it happened, he was hit by an old chief of the ancient Kareke Tribe, the father of the young woman Maro Taporangi, who afterwards became Captain Rushton's wife. The attackers encountered a heavy fire from a wooded point at a bend in the river half a mile above the settlement. This was at a place where the river had to be crossed by swimming. Tamaikowha was very strongly posted in the position, and it was decided that further advance would be imprudent. The Urewera were in such a naturally strong position for defence that there would have been heavy loss of life had the attack been carried out.

In this affair at Te Pokopoko seven or eight Maoris were killed. The *kainga* was situated on a flat in the bed of the river-valley. These Ngai-Tama had been concerned in the killing of Moore and Begg at Waioeka. After the skirmish Mair and Rushton attended to an old much-tattooed Urewera man whom Rushton had shot, and gave him a drink of rum; they prevented the Maori contingent from robbing him of his greenstone *tiki*. This warrior was from Maunga-pohatu.

During 1867 there were numerous Hauhau raids on the outskirts of the settled districts and on the friendly natives in the Whakatane and Ohiwa country. On the 12th September an attempt was made to burn the blockhouse at the Waioeka before it could be finished, but the enemy was driven off after a skirmish. Several expeditions into the haunts of the Hauhaus were undertaken by Lieut.-Colonel St. John in retaliation for their forays, but the natural difficulties of campaigning in such a country, where the mobile Maori had all the advantage, prevented any effective operations against Tamaikowha and his marauding bands.

In January, 1868, a large war-party of Urewera raided Ohiwa and Waiotahe, laid ambuscades on the sea-beach track, and terrorized the friendly natives. Lieut.-Colonel St. John early in February followed these men up into the Waimana: he had a force of ninety men (Opotiki Volunteer Rangers and Militia). In a skirmish high up the Waimana (10th February) the Hauhaus lost three killed and five wounded; St. John's force had two wounded. An attack on a village a little later was without success, as large Hauhau reinforcements arrived, and St. John found it advisable to withdraw.

A body of one hundred Arawa was now raised by Major Mair and the Opotiki forces were strengthened by the arrival of a division (company) of Armed Constabulary under Major Fraser. In March Hauhau raiders attacked the friendly natives of Rakuraku's *hapu* (the Upoko-rehe) at Ohiwa and killed an old chief on Hokianga Island, in the harbour. A punitive expedition against the mountain tribes was undertaken; the force consisted of Rangers and Constabulary under St. John and Fraser, and Arawa Maoris (Ngati-Rangitihi) under Major Mair. The column followed the retreating raiders in to Te Ponga, many miles up the Waimana River. The Hauhaus (on the 11th March, 1868) checked the advance at Te Ponga, occupying a steep spur in front, having deserted the Otara *pa* on the flat. Captain Rushton, describing the operations, said: " We rushed the base of the ridge, the top of which the Hauhaus held. The position was such a difficult one that a council of war was held by the officers or the question of whether to advance or retire. Being the youngest subaltern, my decision was asked first. I voted to retire, for I knew that Tamaikowha was strongly entrenched in a very strong position at Tauwharemanuka, a mile and a half or two miles up the gorge. It would have been a death-trap for us. The officers decided not to continue the advance, and this, I believe, saved the force from destruction. We discovered that the Urewera were entrenched on the spurs all round commanding the gorge, and when we had got into the jaws of the narrows, with rifle-pits on both sides, we would have got it hot." The force withdrew to Whakatane and Opotiki. One man, a Tauranga volunteer, was mortally wounded in the skirmishing, and one Hauhau was shot.

A later expedition (May, 1868) followed up Tamaikowha and Heteraka te Wakaunua after a raid into the Lower Whakatane Valley on the Ngati-Pukeko, who were friendly to the Government. St. John and Fraser followed the enemy through Ruatoki and many miles up the Whakatane Valley, but heavy floods in the rivers compelled them to return without discovering the elusive Hauhaus.

Chapter 20

OPENING OF TITOKOWARU'S CAMPAIGN

THE YEAR 1867 was one of comparative quiet in Taranaki, troubled only by Maori interference with the survey of the confiscated lands, and by large gatherings of the Hauhau tribes at Te Ngutu-o-te-manu and other bush villages. It was now that Titokowaru, chief of the Nga-Ruahine Tribe, of the Waimate Plains, became prominent as the priest and prophet of his people, and gradually gathered to himself an enterprising body of warriors, the pick of the fighting-men of Nga-Ruahine, Ngati-Ruanui, Ngati-Tupaea, Pakakohi, and Nga-Rauru. Titokowaru in one of his speeches early in 1867 announced a truce in these figurative words: "*Whakarongo, whakarongo mai e te iwi! Tenei te tau tamahine, tenei te tau o te Rameti*" ("Hearken, hearken, all ye people! This is the year of the daughters, this in the year of the lamb"). But the lamb-like peace was only the prelude to the most ferocious fighting in the Taranaki campaigns. Titokowaru presently employed himself in travelling from *kainga* to *kainga* and explaining the new scheme of campaign, which consisted in making surprise attacks on small isolated military posts, in laying ambuscades, and in enticing the white troops into the depths of the forest, where the Maori warrior would have the advantage. Had such a man as Titokowaru led the Taranaki tribes in the earlier campaigns the task of the British troops would have been infinitely more difficult. He was the most skilful warrior that the West Coast produced in the Hauhau wars; no Maori leader but Te Kooti was his superior in military capacity. He had fought in the first of the Hauhau rising, and had lost an eye through a bullet-wound at Sentry Hill in 1864. A *tohunga* schooled in the lore of ancient Maoridom, he revived the practices of the cannibal era and the half-forgotten rites of paganism, which, conjoined to some of the ceremonies of the Pai-marire, imparted to the campaign under his generalship a new and bitter ferocity. He revived the worship of Uenuku and Tu, the Maori gods of battle—the rite of propitiation of the deities with a human heart torn from the first slain in a battle. Although he himself did not take part in cannibal feasts, for the reason that in his belief the eating of human flesh would impair his personal sanctity, or *mana-tapu,* he encouraged his followers to do so, and on several occasions in the latter part of 1868 and the early weeks of 1869 the bodies of slain soldiers of the colonial forces were cut up, cooked, and eaten in his forest camps. "Even the winds of heaven are Titoko's," said his followers. The *whakarua,* the north-west breeze, was the breath of Uenuku, his war-god and his familiar spirit, and when it prevailed it was a fitting time to despatch a fighting expedition.

In May, 1868, trouble began to develop on the plains. Some of Titokowaru's young men stole several horses belonging to Mr. James Livingston (of Waipapa, near Hawera) and other settlers, and when Mr. Booth, the Magistrate at Patea, went to Te Ngutu-o-te-manu to claim the horses he found the chiefs defiant. (The natives say that the horses taken were really Maori horses looted by the military settlers.) Booth issued a warrant for the arrest of Toi Whakataka and Haowhenua, Titokowaru's two principal fighting chiefs, and requested Colonel McDonnell to execute it. On the evening of the 11th May McDonnell marched in to Te Ngutu-o-te-manu with a hundred men, and, leaving his armed force just outside the village, met the chiefs and discussed the matter of the stolen animals. Peace prevailed for the time, and two of the three horses were brought in to the Waihi camp; but Mr. Booth presently precipitated further trouble by arresting three men on charges of theft. Warnings that war would soon be commenced, in the customary way, by the ambuscading of stragglers or the murder of settlers, reached the authorities, but little notice was taken of them. One officer, however, was on his guard. This was Captain (afterwards Colonel) W. E. Gudgeon, who was stationed with his company at Waihi. "At 3 o'clock one morning in June, in my tent at Waihi," he narrated to the writer, "I was awakened by Katene Tu-whakaruru, the celebrated scout and warrior, who told me he had come to warn me. He said, 'Do not go out to-day or you will be killed.' I had intended to go to a *whare* I had on a section near Waihi. He would tell me no more, but repeated his warning and returned to the Hauhau camp. In the morning I informed Mr. Booth, the Resident Magistrate, and asked him to warn the settlers, as it was evident that Titokowaru's people were about to begin mischief. Booth took no notice of my counsel. That very afternoon Cahill (who had been a sergeant-major under me) and two other sawyers were killed by Titokowaru's men, Katene among them. Katene's warning undoubtedly saved my life, and the others would have been saved had the Magistrate not disregarded my advice."

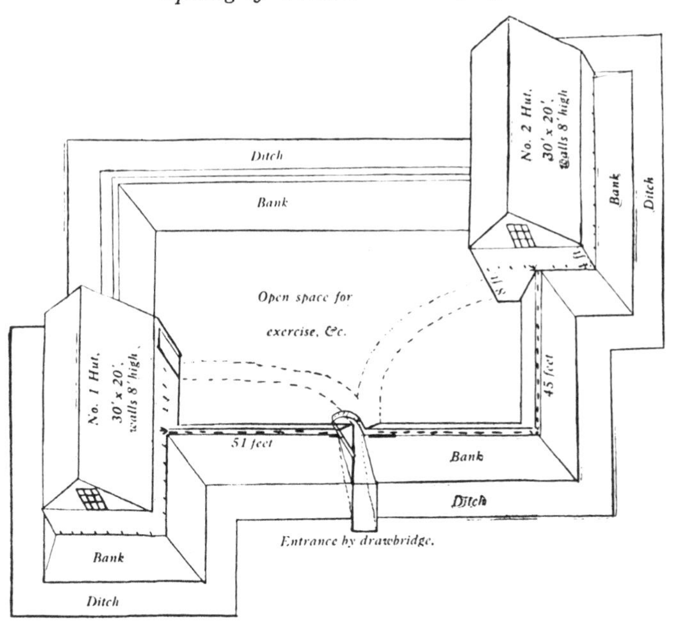

The Manutahi Redoubt, South Taranaki

Several redoubts in Taranaki were built from the design of this one, constructed at Manutahi, between Patea and Manawapou. The redoubt with its two blockhouses was designed by Major M. Noake, and the plan was drawn by Lieutenant R. Blake.

This tragic opening of the new campaign occurred on the 19th June on the block called Te Rauna, a portion of the confiscated lands close to the east side of the Wai-ngongoro River and near the Maori settlement Mawhitiwhiti. The three military settlers, Cahill, Clark, and Squires, were engaged in felling and sawing timber in the bush when they were suddenly attacked by Haowhenua, Katene, and several other men, who fired a volley into them from ambush and then tomahawked them. The Maoris claimed that the timber and the land were theirs, and they were determined to kill intruders. Warnings to quit had been disregarded by the settlers.

When the news of this deed—clearly a prelude to war—reached the Waihi garrison, a despatch was sent off to recall McDonnell, who had gone to Wanganui. The outlying settlers were warned, and preparations were made against an attack. The force in the district at this critical hour was quite inadequate for field operations, and McDonnell, hurrying to Wellington, obtained the consent of the Defence Minister, Colonel Haultain, to enlist immediately four hundred men, including a hundred Wanganui natives, for three months' service. In this way several companies were raised in Wellington and elsewhere and hastily drilled for the imminent campaign.

The slaughter of the three bushmen was quickly followed by the killing and savage mutilation of a man of the mounted corps of the Armed Constabulary within sight of Waihi Redoubt. This man, Trooper Smith, had gone out to the edge of the bush to search for his horse. He was shot down from ambush and tomahawked. A detachment was sent out at the double, but all they found when they reached the spot was half the body of the poor trooper. The legs were lying on the ground, but the upper part of the body had been carried off by the Hauhaus to Te Ngutu-o-te-manu, where it was cooked and eaten. This deed of frightfulness, intended to strike terror into the whites, was the first of the series of man-eating exploits by Titokowaru's warriors, chiefly a few of the older men, who welcomed the revival of the olden practice of *kai-tangata*.

In an intimidating letter intended for the *pakehas,* sent a few days afterwards to a semi-friendly chief at Mawhitiwhiti, Titokowaru boasted of having eaten human flesh, but his use of the first person singular need not be taken literally; he was referring to his cannibal band in general. " Cease travelling on the roads," he wrote; " cease entirely travelling on the roads that lead to Mangamanga (the Waihi camp), lest ye be left upon the roads as food for the birds of the air and for the beasts of the field, or for me. For I have eaten man—I have begun to eat the flesh of the white man; I have eaten him like the flesh of the cow, cooked in the pot; all have eaten him, even the women and the children. My throat is continually open for the eating of human flesh by day and by night."

On the 20th June an ambuscade laid on the track near Waihi for the ration cart convoy resulted in a skirmish in which a sergeant and ten men fought a large party of Hauhaus until reinforcements arrived. Two troopers were wounded, and the Hauhaus had two of their number killed. The garrison of Waihi was now reinforced by the arrival of Rifle Volunteers from Wellington. Many of them were young recruits who had too little time for training before they were called upon for the most trying of all fighting—skirmishing in the bush against practised Maori warriors.

The headquarters settlement of the belligerents of Ngati-Ruanui and Nga-Ruahine from the beginning of 1868 until November of that year was Te Ngutu-o-te-manu (" The Bird's Beak "), a clearing deep in the rata forest, lying about ten miles

From a photo by Mr. R. S. Thompson, 1875]
Waihi Redoubt, Taranaki

from the site of the present Town of Hawera, in the direction of Mount Egmont. The large village was partly palisaded, and some of the hollow *rata* and *pukatea* trees were loopholed and converted into bush redoubts; but the strength of the place lay chiefly in its forest environment, the absence of roads, and the unfamiliarity of the troops with the tracks which wound through the tangled bush. Its front could be approached by a rough cart-track cut through the heavy timber from the neighbourhood of the Wai-ngongoro. The clearings of Te Rua-ruru and Te Ngutu-o-te-manu adjoined each other. The principal building in the latter place was Titokowaru's large prayer-house and assembly-hall, called "Wharekura" ("House of Knowledge"), the term applied to the olden tribal lodges of instruction in religion, history, and genealogies. This sacred house, built of sawn timber, was about 70 feet long. It was a temple not only of the Pai-marire but of the far more ancient rites and ceremonies revived by Titokowaru. Here the war-priest selected, by curious methods of divination with his sacred *taiaha,* the weapon called "Te Porohanga," the warriors of the "Tekau-ma-rua" ("The Twelve"). This term, though generally applied to the whole of the war-party of sixty or seventy, strictly speaking, pertained to the first twelve men chosen, who formed the advance-guard on an expedition and who were strictly *tapu* while out on a foray. The process of selection of the warriors is described in detail in "The Adventures of Kimble Bent," (pages 111–115).* Bent

* "The Adventures of Kimble Bent," by James Cowan. (Whitcombe and Tombs, 1911.)

was living in Te Ngutu-o-te-manu at that time under the protection of Titokowaru, and, although not permitted to fight, made cartridges for the Hauhaus and repaired their guns. He was a runaway soldier of the 57th Regiment, and was practically a slave to the Maoris. His life was frequently in danger at their hands, yet he did not dare to return to the British from whom he had deserted. His story is the most remarkable one amongst those of the many renegade *pakehas* who took up a life with the natives in the war days.

Kimble Bent was an American by birth; his native town was Eastport, State of Maine, U.S.A., and he was the son of a shipbuilder and a young half-breed woman of the Musqua Indian tribe. In his youth he spent three years in a United States training-frigate. In 1859 he enlisted in England in the 57th Regiment, the old "Die-hards"; he was then twenty-two years of age. After the regiment came to New Zealand from India his impatience of strict discipline culminated in insubordination, which brought him to a court-martial in the camp at Manawapou, in South Taranaki, in the early part of 1864. For refusal to obey a corporal's orders he received a flogging of twenty-five lashes at the triangles, followed by a period of imprisonment. This severe punishment sent him to the Maoris as soon as he found an opportunity of deserting. He stole away from the camp in the winter of 1865, and a Maori chief, Tito te Hanatua, who found him, took him to the palisaded *pa* Ohangai, on the Hauhau side of the Tangahoe River. The Ngati-Ruanui Tribe received him with savage ceremonies, and he became Tito's protégé. The prophet Te Ua befriended him, and bade the tribe give hospitality to any soldier who deserted to them from the *pakeha* forces. At Taiporohenui, Keteonetea, Otapawa, and other stockaded villages of the Ngati-Ruanui Bent lived with his *rangatira,* taking his share in all the work of the community; he had imagined for himself a life of leisure among the natives, but he soon found that he was little better than a slave. Among a less intelligent and forceful people than the Maoris perhaps he would have realized his ambition of an easy life and a position of authority; as it was, he found his level, which was that of a servant. He was compelled to labour in the plantations and in the building of fortifications, and all the other heavy labour of the tribal life. His special skill was made use of in repairing the Maoris' guns, and for several years he was Ngati-Ruanui's chief armourer and cartridge-maker. His first Maori name was "Ringiringi," which Titokowaru, his master and protector for many years, afterwards changed to "Tu-nui-a-moa," an ancestral name, by which Bent was known among the natives until his death at Blenheim, in the South Island, in 1917.

NOTES

Waihi and other Redoubts

The field headquarters of the colonial forces in Taranaki at this time was the Waihi Redoubt, an important post of the Armed Constabulary, until the close of the Parihaka trouble in the early "eighties." The site of the redoubt at Waihi, with its loopholed walls, blockhouses, and observation-tower, is now a farm, Section 45, Block V, Hawera Survey District. The first fort was erected in 1866; the second, much larger and more substantial, was completed in the early "seventies." It was a rectangular work of heavy timbers, enclosing a space of 55 yards by 52 yards, and it contained two blockhouses, guard-room, reading-room, orderly-room, magazine (underground), and a well. The two blockhouses were each 50 feet by 52 feet, built of matai slabs, adze-dressed, and about 7 inches thick. They were at diagonally opposite angles, and extended about 8 feet beyond the redoubt walls so as to form flanking bastions. The walls of the stockade were 6 inches thick, and loopholed. The look-out tower, at the northern angle, was 8 feet square and 35 feet high, and was loopholed; the lower rifle apertures were nearly level with the ground.

There were redoubts also at Hawera, Okautiro (Mokoia), Kakaramea, Manutahi, and Manawapou, besides General Cameron's old redoubts at the mouth of the Wai-ngongoro.

From the main road and the railway between Hawera and Patea we see the green hill on which the Okautiro Redoubt was built by the colonial troops in 1867. This ridge, on which the earthworks are still traceable, is about a quarter of a mile south of the Mokoia Railway-station. The redoubt was built by a company of Volunteer Militia taken on for six months in the period between the operations of the Military Settlers corps and the formation of the Armed Constabulary (1868). Captain Page was in charge. One of the members of the Volunteer Militia company was Mr. William Wallace, now of Meremere and Hawera. The corps consisted mostly of old Military Settlers from Pukearuhe, near the White Cliffs. The officers were Lieutenant Gudgeon, Lieutenant Norman (brother of the Lieutenant Norman killed at the Mauku fight in the Waikato War of 1863), and Lieutenant von Rotter, a German baron, who was afterwards Postmaster in New Plymouth. Some time after the redoubt was built Captain Lepper was in charge of the post. There were no troops in it by January, 1868; it was for the use of the settlers in the district in case of trouble. A corrugated-iron blockhouse or hut was built inside the walls. William Wallace was farming at Mokoia, close to the redoubt, in 1868, when war broke out again, and he and five or six other settlers lived in the post for some time until they were compelled to abandon their farms to the Maoris. Thomas Bayley then owned the land on which the redoubt stood.

From a drawing, 1868

Turuturu-mokai Redoubt, Taranaki

On the left are the *whares* occupied by some Military Settlers, and Captain Ross's *whare* (nearest the redoubt). Lennon's canteen *whare* on the extreme right. Mount Egmont in the background, twenty miles distant north-west.

Chapter 21

THE DEFENCE OF TURUTURU-MOKAI

A MILE AND a half north of the town of Hawera, along the Turuturu Road, where the clear trout-stream of the Tawhiti curves round the base of a great parapeted *pa* of ancient Maoridom, is a quiet grassy knoll sacred to the memory of the most desperate combat in the whole of the Taranaki Wars. Within a wire fence on the left that divides the green fields from the main road the traveller may see the slight undulations of the ground that indicate the long-since razed parapets of the Turuturu-mokai Redoubt, the "Rorke's Drift" of Taranaki. No memorial marks the spot where a little band of Armed Constabulary and Military Settlers—nearly all Irishmen—held the fort successfully against Titokowaru's Hauhau warriors though three-fourths of their number were shot down or tomahawked. A monument stands on the battlefield of Te Ngutu-o-te-manu, where Von Tempsky fell; the site of the Turuturu-mokai deserves at least a stone of remembrance. Turuturu-mokai Redoubt was built in 1866 by a company of the 18th Royal Irish Regiment. The Governor, Sir George Grey, on his visit to Taranaki in that year to direct Colonel McDonnell's operations against the Hauhaus, had selected the site for the redoubt. The spot was close to the great ramparts of the ancient walled *pa* Turuturu-mokai, a stronghold with a history dating back more than twelve generations. It was captured about three centuries ago from its builders by the Ngati-Tupaea Tribe, whose descendants now live at various settlements east of Hawera. When the Military Settlers in 1866–67 occupied the country at and around Turuturu-mokai the Ngati-Tupaea went inland a few miles and fixed their headquarters at the terraced *pa* Puke-tarata, now the tribal burying-ground, on a hill above the Mangemange Stream. There are ancient forts on both sides of the Tawhiti Stream; on the south side, close to the road from Hawera, is Te Umu-a-Tongahake, with its ruined parapets and trenches. The British redoubt would have been secure had it been constructed a little farther eastward on the crown of the hill; as will be seen, its interior was open to a raking fire from the slightly higher ground.

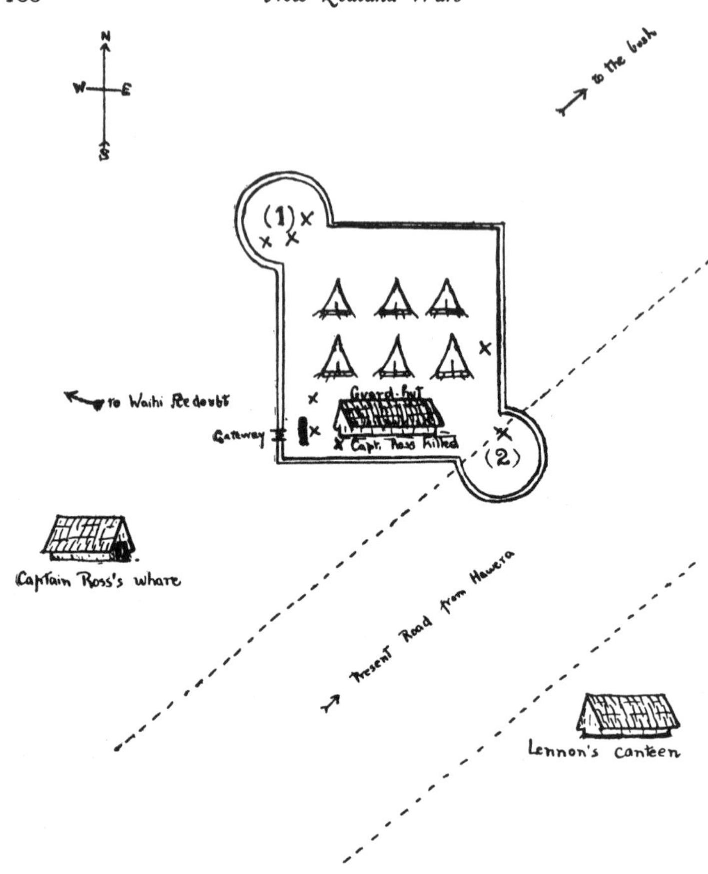

Plan of Turuturu-mokai Redoubt.

(1) N.W. flanking bastion held by John Beamish, Gill, Connors, and others. (2) S.E. bastion defended by Milmoe, Cosslett Johnston, and others. The crosses indicate where various members of the garrison were killed.

By the beginning of 1868 several military settlers had fixed their homes on the fertile plains about Turuturu-mokai, and the redoubt—now without a garrison, for conditions were more peaceful for the time being—was used by one of these pioneer farmers, Mr. Morrison, as a pen for his sheep. Another settler, Cosslett Johnston—a Wexford man, a veteran of the Royal Irish Constabulary and the Taranaki Military Settlers—had taken up his 80 acres grant near Keteonetea, within sight of the deserted redoubt, and had built a *whare*. Up to the edge of the heavy bush on the east and north the gently undulating land was covered with high fern, flax, *tutu,* and *koromiko,* with here and there native cultivations and groves of peach-trees. Maori tracks wound across the plain, through the old cultivation and into the Maori clearings cut from the heavy forest that came close down to Johnston's farm.

After the killing of the three bush sawyers near the Waingongoro, Colonel McDonnell detailed a detachment of twenty-five Armed Constabulary, under Captain George Ross, to garrison Turuturu-mokai and put it in order. The few military settlers in the neighbourhood came in at night, working on their sections during the day. The redoubt was so small that the officer of the detachment had to live in a *whare* outside the work. The parapets were low, and had been broken down in places; they were about 5 feet high, and were surrounded by a trench 6 feet deep. Just inside the gateway, where the ditch was crossed by a plank, there was a small earthwork, a traverse to blind the entrance. The little garrison set to work to repair the redoubt and strengthen the parapets but the work had not been completed when the Hauhau attack was delivered. There were no loopholes, and the parapet was not topped with sandbags, with spaces between for rifle-fire—a most necessary thing in these frontier forts. It was impossible, therefore, for the defenders to enfilade the trench, or, in fact, to fire at all, without exposing themselves over the earthwork. There was a plank walk running along the inner side of the parapet, a fire banquette, but it had not been finished, and it was so wet and slippery on the night before the attack that the men had asked the captain to allow them to do sentry duty outside instead of on the walk.

The redoubt was about 20 yards square, with rounded flanking bastions at diagonally opposite angles, one at the north-west corner, facing the Tawhiti Stream and Waihi, and the other on the south-east, facing the higher ground and the bush. Within the earthwork were several tents, and a thatched house, used as a commissariat store and guard-room, stood in rear of the earthwork curtain near the gateway, in an awkward position, for it masked the fire of the men in the south-east angle, preventing them from properly defending the entrance.

For some time before the attack a kind of truce prevailed, and the Maoris frequently came into camp, selling potatoes and onions to the Constabulary. Daily there were men and women about the place, gossiping and joking with the men, but all the time intently watching the slow work of repairing the redoubt and spying out, as they could with ease from the adjacent ground, the interior arrangements of the post. On Saturday, the 11th July, the day before the attack, some of Ngati-Tupaea visited the camp; a survivor narrated that they were "larking about" and playing games; it was all part of a cunning scheme to put the troops off their guard. At least one of the Constabulary men had some suspicion of the natives. On that Saturday George Tuffin, who was on sentry duty, noticed a Maori walk at a steady pace round the redoubt three times, looking intently at everything. The sentry said to the sergeant of the guard, "That fellow is up to something." "Oh, he's only looking for old clothes," said the sergeant.

In the forest stronghold of Te Ngutu-o-te-manu, seven miles away, the war-chief Titokowaru made his plans for the attack. Turuturu-mokai, as his spies had reported to him, was a poor specimen of a *pa,* and was weakly and carelessly defended; and a picked band of warriors, numbering sixty, the usual strength of the Tekau-ma-rua, was told off for an assault, to be delivered before dawn. In the great meeting-house "Wharekura" ("House of Knowledge") the chief assembled his people and selected the members of the Tekau-ma-rua by means of divination with his sacred weapon, the *taiaha* "Te Porohanga," which was supposed to be influenced by the breath of the war-god Uenuku. Before the chosen sixty set out on the war-path *hakas* were performed by the men and *poi* dances by the girls to "send them away in good heart," as an eye-witness (Kimble Bent) expressed it; and as they marched out of the *pa,* armed with their guns and tomahawks, and with their cartouche-boxes and belts strapped about them, Titokowaru paced up and down with his befeathered *taiaha* in his hand and farewelled his soldiers. "*Patua, kainga!*" he shouted in his great gruff voice. "*Patua, kainga! Kia mau ki tou ringa!*" ("Kill them, eat them! Kill them, eat them! Let them not escape! Hold them fast in your hands!")

The warrior Haowhenua, a chief of Nga-Ruahine and near relative of Titokowaru, led the storming-party. With him was his younger relative Kahu-pukoro and other youthful braves, besides many an old fighter of cannibal days. With the party, too, marched a renegade white man, Charles Kane, a deserter from the 18th (Royal Irish) Regiment. Kane had been punished for insubordination, and had fled to the Hauhaus. He was exceedingly bitter against his late comrades, and Titokowaru permitted him to join the war-party, seeing that the disgraced runaway was anxious to strike a blow against his fellow-whites. Kane was armed with a double-barrel gun, and took part in the attack on the redoubt: he was wounded in the face by a bullet. He was tomahawked some time after by the Maoris on suspicion of treachery. Kimble Bent remained in the *pa* at Te Ngutu-o-te-manu.

It was a bitterly cold, freezing night. Most of the Maoris were very scantily attired, after the fashion of war-parties, and some only wore short flax mats. Passing through the bush and crossing the Tawhiti Creek in the midnight hours, they stole up the gully inland of the redoubt and lay close to each other in the fern, shivering, awaiting the signal for the rush. All this time Titokowaru, sitting on his sacred mat within the praying-house Wharekura in the "Beak of the Bird," was engaged in repeating *karakia* after *karakia*—incantations to the heathen gods, and Hauhau prayers to the Christian Trinity—for the overwhelming of the *pakeha*.

The night dragged on too slowly for the impatient and shivering warriors. Some wished to rush the white man's *pa* at once, but their leaders forbade it till there was a little more light. Several of the younger men began to crawl up through the fern towards the walls of the little fort. The form of a sentry was seen, pacing up and down outside the walls. He could easily have been shot. but the time had not yet come.

In the frontier redoubts it was customary to call the garrison to stand to arms at 3 a.m. and to remain ready till daylight as a precaution against Maori surprise attacks, which, as a rule, were delivered about an hour before daylight. The sergeant or corporal of the guard usually went round and wakened the men quietly by tapping the tents, but on this fatal morning at Turuturu-mokai the corporal omitted the call, and the men off guard slumbered until the first rifle-shots roused them to battle for their lives.

Soon after the attack began, Captain Ross was killed while bravely defending the gateway with revolver and sword. The canteen-keeper, Lennon, also was killed outside the redoubt. Then, in the midst of the fighting, the pagan ceremony of the *whangai-hau,* the offering of a foeman's heart to the gods of battle, was performed by one of the Hauhaus, the young war-priest Tihirua. The heart of the first man slain (Lennon) was cut from the body even before it had ceased to beat. It was the ancient custom to offer the heart of the first victim to Tu and Uenuku, the deities of war. Lighting a match, Tihirua held it under the bleeding heart until the flesh was singed slightly and began to smoke. Then, crying out "*Kei au a Tu!*" (meaning that the supreme war-god Tu was with him or on his side) he threw down the heart, and snatching up his tomahawk, he rushed again into the fight. When Captain Ross was killed, his heart, too, was cut out. A human heart, either that of Lennon or of Captain Ross, was found on the ground outside the fort after the fight. The other probably was carried off to Te Ngutu-o-te-manu as the *mawe* of the battle, a trophy of oblation to the gods. This savage rite, revived by Titokowaru, was carried out on several occasions in the war of 1868–69.

Cosslett Johnston, a veteran of the Military Settlers, gave a vivid account of the attack. "On the morning of the fight, the 12th July," he said in his narrative to the writer, "I and Garrett Lacey (an old 57th soldier, an Irishman) were on sentry duty. My post was at the south end of the redoubt, near the gateway; Lacey did sentry-go on the north side, near the north-west angle. I was armed with a long Enfield rifle and fixed bayonet, and carried eighty rounds of ball cartridge in the big pouch at my hip, besides twenty rounds loose in a pouch in front. The Enfield we used was a good straight shooter—it would kill a man at a mile. The Armed Constabulary were armed with Terry carbines; only the Military Settlers carried the Enfield.

"Suddenly, just before the first faint break of day, I heard Lacey challenge, 'Halt! who goes there?' There was a single shot, and next moment a thundering volley from the enemy in the fern. The Maoris had crept up the gully on the west and north side of the old *pa* Turuturu-mokai, and silently lay in wait not far from the eastern flank, and on the east and south they now concentrated their attack. Lacey was wounded in the shoulder by one of the Maori bullets, and as he thought he was cut off from the redoubt he ran into the fern and escaped to Waihi. At the first shot Captain Ross was up and out of his bed in the *whare,* and in his shirt only, revolver in hand, he ran over the plank and in through the gateway. I took post in the eastern flanking bastion, with Milmoe and others. Milmoe and I were the only two armed with Enfield rifles and bayonets, and I think it must have been the glint of our fixed bayonets as much as anything else that kept the Maoris from rushing us. Our weapons were unhandy—it took a long time to load and cap them—but they shot well. Then at it we went, firing away for our lives wherever we could see anything at which to shoot.

"There was a cry that the natives were coming in at the gateway, and a number of us rushed for the entrance to hold it. I found a dead man, William Gaynor, sitting against the earth-work screen just inside the gateway. He had evidently been in the act of firing over the low parapet when a Maori, who had charged in, killed him with a tomahawk-blow on the temple, as we discovered in the morning. He slid down, turning round as he fell, and remained in a sitting position, his back against the parapet, his rifle resting in the hollow of his arm. Captain Ross was killed near the gateway, and his heart was cut out. Lennon, the canteen-keeper, was killed outside the redoubt. They tomahawked him in two cuts, slanting downwards on his temple.

Then they cut out his heart. They certainly made a clean job of it—trust the old cannibals!

"I was wearing a Glengarry cap—I had no uniform, as I was a volunteer settler. A man fired at me over the parapet at such close range that the explosion blew my cap off and sent me down half-stunned in a sitting position. Now we heard some of the Maoris in the ditch cutting away at the parapet with their long-handled tomahawks in an attempt to undermine it. We shouted out from time to time. 'The troopers are coming,' but the Maoris only laughed fiendishly and continued their chopping and digging. We fought there for two hours, and kept them off till help came from Waihi after dawn—but we had never expected to see daylight again."*

In the other angle, that facing towards Waihi, an equally heroic resistance was made by six men, of whom only one escaped death or wounds. Among these men were two brothers, John G. Beamish and Alexander Beamish, from Skibbereen, County Cork, who had joined the Armed Constabulary in the early part of 1868. The younger brother, Alexander, was mortally wounded in the fight, and the other was severely wounded. "It was quite dark when the Hauhaus attacked us," said John Beamish, standing on the grass-grown scene of his youthful heroism, the north-west angle of the redoubt. "It was between 4 and 5 o'clock in the morning; sunrise was not till about 7 o'clock, for it was midwinter. It had been raining and blowing, and the night was very cold. We were suddenly awakened by a shot; one of the two sentries had seen something move on the slope of the gully just below him, and challenged and fired. Then there was a return volley, and the Maoris jumped up from the fern and charged on the redoubt. They made their first rush on the parapet on the side facing Mount Egmont. When we first heard their yells and shouting as they came up on that flank, and rushed for our carbines and belts, we could scarcely realize that it was an attack. We had been sleeping soundly, and the thing at first seemed like some terrible dream. When we turned out most of us manned the low parapet on the north and east, and fired away there into the darkness, where the yelling and shouting were coming from. After firing a shot we did not wait to see the effect—if we could see—but stooped down under cover of the earthwork and reloaded. Then the Hauhaus worked round to the south-east angle, and presently there was a rush for the gateway. They were quite familiar with the lay of the redoubt, for on the

* Statement to the writer by Cosslett Johnston, of Keteonetea, 17th October, 1918. Mr. Johnston died 23rd June, 1920, aged seventy-nine years.

previous day (Saturday) some of them had been in, having sports close to the redoubt and apparently very friendly. They knew exactly our numbers, and knew all about the weakness of our defences. We had been there a month, so that was ample time to have had the redoubt strengthened. The lowness of the parapet and the want of loopholes were terrible deficiencies that cost us many men. At the first shot Captain Ross ran out from his *whare* dressed only in his shirt, and when the gateway was attacked he headed the defence of it. He fired many shots out of his revolver before he was shot, probably while reloading. After the fight we found his body lying inside the gateway between the earthwork curtain and the guard-hut; his heart had been cut out; we found it lying outside the ditch, not far from his hut. While some of the enemy tried to rush the gateway, others took to the rising ground on the east and south-east, and fired right into the north-west angle in which six of us had taken post; they could rake part of our angle between two of the tents. We, on the other hand, were able to enfilade the ditch on the west flank, and so prevent the gateway being rushed, but to do so we had to expose our heads over the parapet, which was only about 4 feet high above the firing-step. I was firing away there for about an hour, I suppose, before I was hit, and then there was another hour's fighting before relief arrived from Waihi, by that time the sun was up.

"Most of our firing was at very close range; only two or three yards, sometimes less, separated us from our enemies trying to swarm into the place. My brother was shot at close quarters. Both sides were yelling at each other as they fought. I was hoarse with shouting at the Hauhaus to come on, and bluffing them that the troopers were coming. 'Come on, come on!' we yelled, and the Maoris called on us to 'Come out, come out!'

"Some of the Maoris," Mr. Beamish continued, "set fire to the *raupo* huts outside the redoubt. They were armed with muzzle-loading Enfields and shot-guns, and we could now and then see the ramrods going up and down as they sent the charges home. Then sometimes we would see the flash of a tomahawk and catch a glimpse of a black head above the parapets. When they set fire to the huts we were able to take aim at some of them by the light of the blazing *whares*. Then they started to dig and cut away at the parapets with their tomahawks. We could plainly hear them at this work, and I heard one Maori ask another for a match; I suppose he wanted to try and fire our buildings inside the walls.

"One after another our men dropped, shot dead or badly wounded. I had very little hope of ever getting out of the place alive. But we well knew what our fate would be if the Maoris once got over the parapet, so we just put our hearts into it and kept blazing away as fast as we could load.

"My younger brother fell mortally wounded, and before he died he told us he believed it was a white man who shot him. [This would be the deserter, Charles Kane.] I was wounded about the same time. An Enfield bullet struck me in the left shoulder. It took me with a tremendous shock, just as I was stooping down across a dead man to get some dry ammunition. The bullet slanted down past my shoulder-blade and came out at the back. This incapacitated me from firing, or, at any rate, from taking accurate aim, so I had to content myself with passing cartridges to Michael Gill, who kept steadily firing away, and with levelling my unloaded carbine as well as I could with my right hand whenever I saw a head bob up above the parapet. When the fight ended, Gill was the only unwounded man in our angle of the redoubt. Out of the six who manned it when the alarm was given, three were killed and two wounded. One man, Tuffin, was wounded in five places.

"Daylight came, and those of us who could shoulder a carbine were still firing away and wondering whether help would ever reach us. We knew they must have heard the firing and seen the flashes of the guns at Waihi Redoubt, only three miles away. Suddenly the Maoris ceased firing and retired into the bush. Their sentries had given them warning that troops were coming. As they dropped back we rushed out of the redoubt and gave them the last shot, and then Von Tempsky and his Armed Constabulary arrived at the double, and the fight was over. Out of the twenty men who held the place, ten were killed (the captain, sergeant, a corporal, and seven privates) and six wounded; and the only wonder is that any of us ever came out of it alive. My wound kept me in hospital for five months."*

Private (Constable) George Tuffin, Armed Constabulary, who was one of those who made an attempt to hold the gateway at the beginning of the attack, was soon disabled; he received five wounds. He had served in the Wanganui Rangers in numerous engagements. Describing the defence of the little fort, he said:—

"It was a bitter, cold frosty morning. Five minutes after the sentries had been relieved that morning some of our men heard one of the two men (Lacey) who had just gone on duty suddenly challenge and fire. He shouted, 'Stand to your arms, men!' and made for the redoubt, but was cut off from it and had to run for Waihi. He received a bad wound in the shoulder.

---

* This narrative was given to the author by Mr. John G. Beamish, of Patea, on the site of the redoubt, 28th July, 1920. Mr. Beamish, who is the last survivor of the defenders in Taranaki, is now eighty-two years of age.

Our carbines and accoutrements were hung to the tent-pole, and when we leaped up we knew exactly where to lay our hands on them. Besides our carbines we were armed with revolvers. I ran out to the parapet and fired my revolver into the ditch; the other men did the same; a great crowd of Maoris were upon us, close up to the parapet. The dogs around the place had been making a lot of noise that morning, barking furiously, but we thought they were barking at Captain Morrison's sheep, and when the sentry first saw forms dimly moving through the fern he imagined they were sheep. We were all in our shirts, just as we had jumped from our blankets, and it was freezing. The parapets were too low; the earthwork was only up to my waist when I stood up on the firing-step. I had just fired one shot out of my carbine, drew out the flange and put another cartridge in, and was just rising to fire again, when a Maori caught sight of my head and fired at me. The bullet ploughed a deep furrow right across the top of my head, making a bad skull-wound. Captain Ross came up and asked, 'Where are you hit, old man?' I could not speak. Then he asked, 'Where's your rifle?' I pointed to it: he picked it up. 'Come on, lads!' I heard him shout next moment, 'the devils are coming in at the gate!' That was the last I saw of Captain Ross alive. I made my way to the north-west angle. Later on, after the fight, when I was crawling down to warm myself at the blaze of the burning *whares,* I saw a human heart lying on the ground outside the trench; the savages had cut it out of his body. We found afterwards that he must have been killed between the parapet and a *whare* which stood inside the gateway; this was the *raupo*-thatched building used as a guard-room and store-room. Another Ross, a private—no relation to the Captain—jumped the parapet and was killed in the ditch. He was an old 57th Regiment soldier.

"I received four wounds as I lay in the north-west angle. I was shot in the left arm, through the back near the spine, in the right hip, and in the right ankle. When I got to the angle there were five men there. Of these, three were killed outright, including Sergeant McFayden, and one of the Beamish brothers was mortally wounded. My comrades were fighting for quite two hours before we were relieved; I was out of action early in the fight. When relief came I got down to the fires outside: the Hauhaus had set fire to Captain Ross's *whare* and the storehouses and they were still burning. However, I soon came away, because I was so weak from loss of blood that I feared I would fall into the fire if I stayed there longer. As I was going out across the plank bridge when the fight was over—it was full daylight then—I looked down and saw two dead Maoris lying in the trench, one on either side of the plank, feet to feet

Photo by A. E. Watkinson, Wanganui, 1918]

George Tuffin (Armed Constabulary).

Tuffin was one of the defenders of Turuturu-mokai in 1868, and received five wounds.

—their bare feet almost touching each other. Another dead Maori was lying in front of the gateway.

"I have often thought since the fight that we made a mistake in firing off our revolvers at the Maoris in the ditch at the beginning of the attack. We should have reserved them in case of a final rush of the enemy."*

One of the first men killed was Corporal John Blake, who was shot through the head while defending the side nearest the rising ground. Paddy Shields, an old 65th soldier, who was the Captain's orderly, was killed in the angle held by Gill and Beamish. Private George Holden was shot dead between the guard-house and the parapet near the gate.

Michael Gill was one of the veterans who put stiffening into the little band of men; but the youngest recruits, the Beamish brothers, fought as gallantly as any old soldier. Gill was the

* Statement to the writer by George Tuffin, formerly of the Armed Constabulary, at Wanganui, 23rd October, 1918. Tuffin died in 1920, aged eighty-four years.

first to rush to the gateway when Captain Ross shouted for volunteers. "I'll make one, sir," he replied. "All right, Gill," said the Captain. "Any more?" he asked. Henry McLean, Tuffin, Swords, and Gaynor came forward. But all the garrison did not behave with equal bravery. Three men jumped the parapet early in the fight and ran to Waihi. Their names were Wilkie, Burrowes, and Cobb. When they proposed to go, Gill said, "No, there are wounded, and we must protect them." But they thought the place was doomed, and they ran and left their comrades. Gill and Michael O'Connor (or Connors), another fine steady soldier, joined some of the others in the north-west angle and fought there to the end. When John Beamish was hit, Gill said, "You open the ammunition and I'll do the shooting"; and in spite of his bad wound the plucky young Irishman kept handing up cartridges for the Terry carbine. The Terry, the survivors said, was not a good weapon for such an emergency; after a few rounds the breech-block often jammed and was difficult to work.

On the east side and at the north-west angle some of the Hauhaus dug away at the parapet with their tomahawks, endeavouring to cut a hole through or to undermine it. In one place the earthwork was so much weakened that it fell in, but fortunately not before help came.

Five men besides Garret Lacey, the wounded sentry, escaped to Waihi. Two or three of these, who were Military Settlers, were unarmed; they lived in a *whare* outside the redoubt. Another who had tried to escape, a private named Kershaw, was wounded a few yards outside the north-west angle and was found there by the relieving force.

It was 7 a.m. before the relief force of which the garrison had begun to despair arrived from Waihi. For the tardiness of this reinforcement Major Von Tempsky was to blame, but another officer was most unjustly and cruelly made the scapegoat. All the Armed Constabulary at Waihi Redoubt were under arms from 3 o'clock until daylight each morning. The garrison turned out as usual this Sunday morning, and the parade had just been dismissed when firing was heard in the direction of Turuturu-mokai. The men rushed out of their tents, and Major Von Tempsky, the senior officer, called out, "No. 5 this way," and marched his division (company), numbering sixty men, off to the relief. The garrison remaining consisted of sixty of No. 3 Division, half of whom were mounted Constabulary, and about a dozen men of No. 2 Division. The troopers ran to the stables for their horses, which had been saddled at the early morning turn-out, fell in, and numbered off, when Major Hunter came out of his *whare*, which was between the Constabulary redoubt and the work built by the Kupapa, or friendly natives. To the astonishment of the troopers, all anxious to ride off to the rescue, Hunter gave the order, "Dismount and feed the horses." Whether Von Tempsky gave definite orders to Hunter, who was his junior, or whether he hurried off without leaving instructions, is a point on which reports are contradictory. It is clear, however, that Major Hunter was of the opinion that the attack on Turuturu-mokai was in all probability only a feint, in order to draw out the garrison of Waihi and so enable them to capture that post with its valuable stores of ammunition. He concluded that Von Tempsky's sixty men would be adequate for the relief work, and felt that his duty, much as he wished to go to the help of the other garrison, was to guard the Waihi post. But the troopers were indignant at Hunter's order to put their horses away, and some of them expressed their opinion of their Major in such terms that they were put under arrest. When the court-martial sat to inquire into the circumstances Major Hunter was acquitted of blame, for he had obviously acted under a strong sense of duty, being responsible for the safety of the principal redoubt. On the other hand, had Von Tempsky sent off the troopers immediately the firing was heard, Turuturu-mokai could have been relieved an hour earlier than it was, and several lives would have been saved.

The unjust stigma sank deeply into Hunter's soul. He was a high-minded, sensitive man—none braver in the force—and it was undoubtedly in a determination to refute this unwarranted accusation against his soldierly honour that he deliberately threw his life away in the charge against the stockade at Moturoa three months later. His younger brother, Captain Hunter, fell at Te Ngutu-o-te-manu.

As the relief force of Constabulary advanced and, fording the Tawhiti Stream, came doubling up the hill, the Hauhaus retired to the bush on the east, leaving three of their dead on the field. The little redoubt was a frightful scene of slaughter. Ten men —half the defenders—lay dead or dying, two of them mutilated with the tomahawk, and six others were wounded. Only six unwounded men came out to greet their Waihi comrades. The casualties were—

Killed or mortally wounded: Captain Ross, Sergeant McFayden, Corporal John Blake, Privates Ralph Ross, Alexander Beamish, P. Shields, George Holden, Peter Swords, William Gaynor; Lennon (canteen-keeper).

Wounded: Privates J. G. Beamish, Garrett Lacey, Flanagan, Michael O'Connor (or Connors), Kershaw, G. Tuffin.

The unwounded defenders were: Cosslett Johnston, Michael Gill, Milmoe, O'Brien, Stewart, and McLean.

Among the sixty warriors of the Tekau-ma-rua was the young chief Te Kahu-pukoro, who, though only a youth, had already seen four years of war. Describing the attack on Turuturu-mokai he said:—

"Our leader Haowhenua headed the principal assault. Take-take led the attack from the north side, and it was he who shot and wounded the sentry outside, on the flank. Nuku, a brother of Titokowaru, dashed right into the redoubt through the open gateway and killed a *pakeha* there with a short-handled tomahawk. [This was Private Gaynor.] After this first assault we all fired heavily upon the *pakehas* at very close quarters, and some of us cut away a portion of the parapets with our tomahawks, trying to force a way in. Only three of our men were killed, an old man named Papia, Taroai (from Ketemarae), and Uruwhero, a young man whom Titokowaru had warned not to join the expedition. When the *pakeha* reinforcements were sighted coming from Waihi we thought we had killed or wounded all but two of the men in the redoubt. These two men jumped up on the parapet when they saw help coming, and shook their rifles at us and danced a *haka,* and shouted at us in derision, 'Te bloody Maori—*hau, hau!*' As the reinforcements advanced, firing at us, we retired to the bush in the rear, and then worked round home to our *pa* at Te Ngutu-o-te-manu."*

The survivors who particularly distinguished themselves by their gallant bearing and resolute resistance were Cosslett Johnston, Gill, John Beamish, and Connors. Each of these men deserved the highest recognition, and the decoration of the New Zealand Cross, instituted for just such exceptional cases of valour, might well have been bestowed upon them.

This determined attack on a military post quickened the field force into precautions for the safety of the other redoubts. Waihi was strengthened by the withdrawal of Captain Page's company of Armed Constabulary, ninety strong, from the Wai-ngongoro Redoubt: this concentration of troops inland, however, left the middle Taranaki coast from Manawapou northward free to the Hauhaus.

Very shortly after the fight Captain J. M. Roberts took charge of Turuturu-mokai with a detachment consisting of nine non-commissioned officers (including Sergeant MacFarlane, Sergeant Anderson, and Corporal H. Talty) and fifty men of Nos. 2, 3, and 5 Divisions of the Armed Constabulary. Roberts's first care was to repair the redoubt and put it in a proper state of defence. On the eastern side an enemy on the high ground could see right

---

* Narrative given by Te Kahu-pukoro, head chief of Ngati-Ruanui, at Otakeho, Taranaki, 1920.

into the redoubt: this was remedied by increasing the height of the parapet. Bottles were collected and broken, and the trench was strewn with them. A drawbridge replaced the plank bridge across the ditch. Loopholes of timber were made in the parapet; these firing-apertures were masked in the daytime with plugs of fern. (Layers of fern were used by the colonial troops in redoubt-building in order to strengthen and bind the earth parapets. The men were not allowed to cut the fern, but had to pull it, and double it and turn the roots inwards, so as to leave the fern-leaves outside on both faces of the parapet. A parapet when completed had a matting of fern alternating with every foot or so of sods and earth until the top layer was reached.) Captain Roberts told his garrison off in sections, and each section was instructed exactly what portion of the redoubt it was to defend in case of an alarm, without necessity for further orders.

On the night Captain Roberts was given charge of the redoubt Lieut.-Colonel McDonnell who had ridden up from Manawapou and was very excited over the fate of so many of the garrison, asked the young officer to walk outside the redoubt with him. When they had gone a short distance he said, " Sit down." Drawing his sword he extended the blade, gleaming brightly in the winter moonlight, and brought it back up to his lips, kissed it, and said dramatically, " Roberts, I shall have revenge for this." The sequel was the first attack on Te Ngutu-o-te-manu. McDonnell was a man of dashing courage, but he was of excitable temperament, and when skilful leadership was required his impulsive character had its military defects.

NOTES

The site of Turuturu-mokai Redoubt is included in a national reserve vested in the Hawera Borough Council, near the crown of the hill on the east side of the Tawhiti Stream, and about a mile beyond the borough boundary. The road cuts obliquely across the south-east angle of the work, so that the bastion at that corner—the part of the redoubt held by Cosslett Johnston and four others—is just outside the reserve-fence. The complete outline of the entrenchment with the flanking bastions can still be traced plainly by the depression in the ground. The work measures approximately twenty paces square. Small *totara* trees planted as memorials by survivors of the fight grow in the angles. An unsightly wire fence intersects the south-east part of the redoubt inside the road-fence; this should be removed and the place enclosed in alignment with the contour of the work. The scene of this heroic defence should be marked by a fitting memorial, such as that which stands on the battle-ground of Te Ngutu-o-te-manu.

The name Turuturu-mokai (that of the massive old *pa* near the redoubt) embodies a memory of the savage days of Maori warfare. It signifies the short stakes on which the smoke-dried heads of warriors killed in battle were set up in ceremonial display.

Chapter 22

TE NGUTU-O-TE-MANU

THE FIRST ATTACK

LIEUT.-COLONEL MCDONNELL, waiting until he had received a reinforcement of volunteers, consisting chiefly of the newly raised Wellington Rangers and Wellington Rifles, delivered his first blow in avengement of Turuturu-mokai on the 21st August, 1868. Before daybreak that morning, in a thick wet fog, a column numbering about 350 men fell in at Waihi Redoubt, and, crossing the Wai-ngongoro River, struck into the bush to attack Te Ngutu-o-te-manu. McDonnell's force consisted of detachments of Nos. 2, 3, and 5 Divisions of the Armed Constabulary, totalling about 110 officers and men; Wellington Rangers, 66; Wellington Rifles, 83; Taranaki Volunteer Militia, 32; Patea Yeomanry Cavalry, 18; and a number of unenlisted volunteers. The column was divided into two, one under command of Major Von Tempsky and the other under Major Hunter. A French Roman Catholic priest, Father Jean Baptiste Roland, accompanied the force; in the fight in the bush that day his gallant conduct in tending the wounded under fire won him the admiration and affection of all the force.*

McDonnell, in a despatch dated Camp Waihi, 22nd August, 1868, described his operations on the previous day in the first attack on Te Ngutu-o-te-manu. He stated that he paraded the force, totalling 345, at 5.30 a.m., and experienced considerable difficulty in crossing the flooded Wai-ngongoro River. The column entered the bush by the track he had previously used. The rain was coming down in torrents. On arriving at Pungarehu McDonnell left Lieutenant Roddy, with the Taranaki Volunteer Militia, as a connecting-link betwen the main body and the Patea Yeomanry Cavalry outside the bush. He now found that rifle-pits and defensive posts had been made on each side of the

---

* Father Roland was afterwards well known as Dean Roland. He died at Reefton many years ago.

track right up to Te Maru, and they had evidently been used the preceding night, as the embers were still smouldering. On arrival he found that a stockade had been erected since he was last at the place; it commanded the crossing of the creek. This compelled him to alter the original plan; and instead of detaching Major Von Tempsky's division to the left to occupy the bush, and allowing Inspector Hunter to rush his division at the village, he led the advance division right at the new stockade, which did not take five minutes to seize.

McDonnell then directed Von Tempsky to take his men along the track to the left and endeavour to enter the village simultaneously with the men whom McDonnell led round to the large clearing in front. When they reached there they were received by a very heavy fire from the village. As soon as sufficient men were up (they could only come in Indian file), the commander ordered a cheer and a charge. "Never was any order more heartily responded to," wrote McDonnell. "In spite of the destructive fire poured on us from the bush on our right and from the palisading in our front, we went right into the *pa* without a pause." Major Von Tempsky entered about the same time from the left, and the defenders broke and fled in every direction where they could find bush to cover them. As the remainder of the force came up they were extended round the village, at the edge of the bush, while those within the palisading cleared the *whares*. Only one man was found within, and, as he fired and killed one of the men, a hand-grenade was thrown in "to prevent him doing further mischief," as McDonnell put it.

The *whares* were searched for arms. In the large house a considerable quantity of powder was found in flasks, also a good-sized box of Government ammunition of all kinds, and a quantity of breech-loading cartridges, made by the natives themselves. Ammunition was found in almost every one of the small houses. Katene's pouch, quite full, his double-barrel gun, eleven other guns, two swords, two revolvers, tomahawks, and spears were taken, and either brought away or destroyed. The houses were set on fire. The dead and wounded had been brought to the large sawn-timber house Wharekura, and when all had been well cared for by the doctor they were sent on under Major Von Tempsky, with Nos. 3 and 5 Divisions A.C. When they got clear away the large house was fired in several places, and when it was in flames McDonnell, leaving a strong rearguard under Major Hunter, moved out of the stockade.

About this time the natives were reinforced and commenced firing from several parts of the bush, but their fire was promptly returned by the rearguard. McDonnell was anxious to follow them, but could not find any track, and as they seemed to be in forest which he could not penetrate without great labour and loss he thought it better to move out. In several clearings on the track the force was fired on, but the men behaved steadily. Several men were wounded in this retirement, one mortally. On reaching Weriweri a smart fire was opened on the party escorting the wounded, but without effect, and Lieutenant Fookes with a few men rushed up to the *pa* and speedily silenced the enemy. On reaching the Wai-ngongoro River it was found in high flood; and it was a work of danger as well as difficulty to get the force across. The principal anxiety was for the wounded, but volunteers came forward and offered their services, and, after a severe struggle, succeeded in getting them all safely across. The men managed to scramble across, some by the rope and some holding on to the cavalry horses, but a great deal of ammunition was rendered unserviceable. "We reached Waihi about 6 p.m.," McDonnell concluded, "and drenched and tired as the men were they gave three cheers that were refreshing to hear. The losses of the enemy must have been severe. We know of seven bodies."

The European casualties in this engagement were four men killed and eight wounded.

One of the few surviving veterans of the fight, Mr. William Wallace, of Hawera (ex-sergeant, No. 2 Division A.C.), described on the battle-ground some of the details of the action. He said: "It was the second expedition to Te Ngutu-o-te-manu; the first was in 1866, when we burned the village. When we reached the place the log huts we destroyed in 1866 had not been rebuilt, but instead there was a big settlement in a wide clearing just across the head of the creek. It had been raining heavily, and, in fact, it was still drizzling, and the stream was pretty high. Immediately we crossed it, just on the opposite bank before we mounted a slight rise, we came upon a palisading of tall timber constructed in a half-moon shape with the convex side facing us; small manholes were cut in it here and there. It was obviously intended as a kind of outer guard for the village. It was here we got our first salute, wounding two men. The Hauhaus only gave us one volley at this place. I remember crawling in through one of the manholes in the stockade and thinking what an easy target I would be for any Hauhau. Going on, we passed over a large clearing overgrown with weeds. There were many *whares* scattered about the clearing, with here and there some of the *rata* and *mahoe* trees left standing." [In a belt of light bush just north of the Domain paddock in which the military monument stands there are still some of these ancient *mahoe* trees, towering and venerable by contrast with the lighter and younger growth around them.] "We soon came under a heavy fire as we skirmished up across the principal clearing. My brother Richard, a boy of seventeen, who had only lately enlisted in the Wellington Rangers—the corps of which I was then a member—was shot at the southern end of the clearing not far from the belt of *mahoe* trees on the east side of the Mangotahi Stream. Richard was my rear-rank man. We had not been fighting long when word was passed along that one of our fellows was down, and I found it was my brother. I ran back and bent over him, but he was gone in a few moments. He was hit in the jugular vein and bled to death. We had some desperate fighting as we retired, after setting fire to the settlement and the large meeting-house. One of our men, Burrowes (he who had escaped from the Turuturu-mokai affair a few weeks previously), volunteered to throw the hand-grenades we had brought with us, and I saw him lighting the fuses and throwing these bombs into the *whares* through the low doorways."

When the Hauhaus returned to the village they found that some of the huts had not been burned when the troops fired the village, and in the thatch of these *whares* they discovered unexploded grenades. The shells were given to Kimble Bent to handle; the deserter at the time of the engagement was at Turangarere, a settlement near the Tangahoe, whither he had gone to procure gunpowder and paper for the manufacture of cartridges. He drew the fuses, and from each hand-grenade obtained a sufficient quantity of powder to make eighteen gun-cartridges.

Chapter 23

REPULSE AT TE NGUTU-O-TE-MANU

THE SECOND ATTACK by Lieut.-Colonel McDonnell on the Hauhau bush stronghold at Te Ngutu-o-te-manu was delivered on the 7th September, 1868, and resulted in a disastrous defeat for the Government column. The repulse had far-reaching consequences, for it brought large accessions to Titokowaru's band and so weakened the numbers and the morale of McDonnell's force that all the country northward of Patea was soon abandoned to the Hauhaus.

The force, which marched out from Waihi just after midnight in freezing weather, numbered 360, of whom nearly a hundred were friendly natives from Wanganui. Lieut.-Colonel McDonnell's force was in three large detachments. The Armed Constabulary, Wellington Rifles, Wellington Rangers, and some Taranaki Volunteers made up the first and second detachments; the third was composed of the Kupapa, or Maori, force. The detachments were made up as follows: No. 1 Detachment, under Major Von Tempsky—No. 2 Division of the Armed Constabulary, 16 men; Patea Rifle Volunteers, 14 men, under Captain Palmer; No. 5 Division A.C., 59 men, under Captains (Sub-Inspectors) Brown and Roberts; Wellington Rifles, 45 men, under Lieutenants H. Hastings and Hunter; Taranaki Rifle Volunteers, 26 men, under Lieutenant Rowan; Volunteers from Waihi, 2 men: total, 142. No. 2 Detachment, under Major W. Hunter—No. 3 Division A.C., 32 men, Captains Newland and Goring; Wellington Rangers, 65 men, Captain G. Buck, Lieutenant Fookes, and Ensign Hirtzel; Patea Cavalry (dismounted), 11 men, Captain O'Halloran: total, 108. Maori Contingent—110 Wanganui natives (Kupapas) under Captain W. McDonnell and Kepa te Rangihiwinui and other chiefs. Dr. Walker accompanied Von Tempsky's command as surgeon, and Dr. Best was with Major Hunter. The half-caste woman Takiora, a celebrated guide in the war-days, accompanied the column.

Colonel McDonnell's plan was to strike deep into the forest and endeavour to surprise the Hauhaus in their village Te

Rua-ruru, which was believed to be in rear of Te Ngutu-o-te-manu. It was well on in the afternoon, and the column had penetrated the great *rata* forest in the direction of Mount Egmont for seven or eight miles before a sign of the Hauhaus was found. A track was discovered, and this was followed back in a southerly direction. Then one of the Wanganui Maoris climbed a tree and reported smoke about half a mile farther along the track. Maori voices were also heard in the distance. McDonnell advanced, and his leading Maoris surprised a sentry's camp on the track. Here the Kupapas killed a man and two little children. Another child, a small boy, was saved and carried throughout the fight on a Wanganui man's back; he became well known in later years in Taranaki as Pokiha (Fox) Omahura. Up to this time the leaders of the force did not know exactly where they were, but it was presently discovered that they were well in the rear of Te Ngutu-o-te-manu. A break in the interminable forest was seen ahead, and the force moved on cautiously towards the edge of the clearing. Kepa was ordered to take his Wanganui Maoris and work round the *pa* on the left flank, and Von Tempsky's division went ahead towards the *pa,* crossing a small creek (the Mangotahi) which bounded the clearing on the west and north.

As Von Tempsky's men, with part of Major Hunter's division, moved up in skirmishing order through the *rata* and *mahoe* timber to the north end of the clearing a heavy fire was opened on them, at very close range, from Hauhaus well concealed behind the undergrowth and logs and in the branches of several of the *rata* trees. It was now that Captain Kepa came running up and told McDonnell that the place was Te Ngutu-o-te-manu. Casualties became numerous, and McDonnell was undecided whether to advance or retreat. It was a fatal moment of indecision, for he left his subordinates without definite orders, and the units of the force quickly lost touch with each other. Men fell struck down by bullets from unseen marksmen. Lieutenant Rowan was shot in the face, the bullet breaking both jaws. He was carried out of fire by Private J. H. Walker and others, and handed over to the surgeons and Father Roland, the Catholic padre, who had again accompanied the force.

Volleys were fired into the *rata* trees and at the cover on the edge of the clearing, but no advance was made, and men continued to fall fast. It was very clear that defeat was near if the force remained only on the defensive. The seasoned men of the Armed Constabulary were able for the most part to take care of themselves, like the Maoris, but many of the unfortunate recruits of the Wellington Rangers and Rifles, quite unfamiliar with bush-fighting methods and fatally slow in the art of seeking cover, were perfectly useless when pitted against the active foresters of Titokowaru's band. Some of the new levies, chiefly Wellington Rifles, were seized with panic and ran, reaching Waihi camp first and reporting the force as wiped out.

Had the order been given to storm the place the casualties would have been fewer, but McDonnell imagined a far stronger force was opposed to his. Ensign Hirtzel, who was with Captain Buck, of the Wellington Rangers—" Buck's Bruisers " they were called—heard his captain ask McDonnell, " Where are the axes? Why don't we charge the *pa* ? " But no order came, and the force became disorganized under the continuous heavy fire, to which there was no chance of replying effectively except by a charge.

Had McDonnell but correctly gauged the position he scarcely would have hesitated to assault the place. The fact was that there were not more than about sixty men in Te Ngutu-o-te-manu when the engagement began, and that most of these skirmished out into the forest to meet the troops, leaving the *pa* easily assailable by a determined commander. Hunter and Von Tempsky both requested permission to storm the place, but McDonnell still hesitated. At last, seeing how numerous the casualties were and considering it his duty to extricate his force with as little further loss as possible, he ordered a retreat to the Wai-ngongoro. The wounded were sent on under Major Hunter, and McDonnell following with about eighty men. There was no track on the route taken, which was a course through the tangled bush in as direct a line as possible for the open country. Captains Brown, Newland, and Cumming accompanied the larger part of the expeditionary column. A heavy rearguard action was fought. The Hauhaus had now been reinforced by men from some of the neighbouring villages, and pressed the retreating force hotly to the gully at Te Maru. Father Roland took his turn at the toil of carrying the wounded out, and there were bullet-holes through his hat when the day's battle was over. Kepa and some of his best men fought well in keeping the Hauhaus in check. The force took out fourteen wounded, some of them carried on crossed rifles in lieu of stretchers.

In the meantime the senior officer remaining before the palisaded village, Major Von Tempsky, waited vainly for the order to advance against the *pa*. Indignant at not being permitted to charge the place he moved restlessly to and fro, careless about taking cover. He was shot down at last by one of a party of Hauhaus crouching in the undergrowth near the bank of the Mangotahi Stream. Some of the defenders of the *pa* had opened fire from the *rata* and *pukatea* trees—severai of the large hollow trees had been loopholed as redoubts—but soon after the fighting began they rushed out to skirmish in the forest. It is generally agreed by Ngati-Ruanui and Nga-Ruahine that it was an elderly warrior named Te Rangi-hina-kau who shot Von Tempsky. He was one of a party of eight men of the Tekau-ma-rua who sallied out from the stockade and took cover near the creek-side. His comrades were his son Whakawhiria, young Tutange Waionui (of Ngati-Hine and Pakakohi), Wairau, and four others. Taking careful aim at an officer whom he saw armed with a curved sword, he shot him through the head. Other *pakehas* fell, and when the fight was over there were eight or nine men lying near the slain officer, whom the Maoris found out afterwards was the celebrated "Manu-rau," as Von Tempsky was called. After the troops had fallen back before a charge led by Katene Tu-whakaruru—erstwhile on the Government side—one of whose young children had been cruelly killed by a Wanganui Maori, several of the young men dashed forward to tomahawk the fallen whites. Tutange Waionui delivered a tomahawk-blow on "Manu-rau's" temple, and took the dead Major's sword, revolver, cap, and watch. These trophies were afterwards laid before Titokowaru as battle-spoils, and when a division was made Tutange received the revolver as his share and used it in the war. Some survivors of the European force declared that Von Tempsky was shot from a *rata* tree, but this was incorrect. He fell to a bullet fired from ground cover not more than 12 yards away.

All this time within the stockade in the bullet-swept clearing the war-chief Titokowaru remained walking up and down, *taiaha* in hand, reciting prayers to his Maori gods and shouting to his soldiers. "*Patua, kainga!*" he cried; "kill them, eat them!" And again and again he shouted in his far-carrying voice, "*Whakawhiria, whakawhiria!*" bidding the warriors encircle their foes. It was from this battle circumstance that the son of Te Rangi-hina-kau received his name, Whakawhiria. Earlier in the day, as soon as the first shots were heard in the distance, Titokowaru had despatched Kimble Bent out to the forest in rear of the *pa* to join the women and children, and the white deserter had a narrow escape from death as he made his way through the bush, for he was fired on by some of the troops who took him for a Maori, and only evaded them by hurrying down the bed of the Mangotahi Creek.

Soon after the bush battle began, the pagan rite of the *whangai-hau* was performed by two *tohungas,* Wairau and Tihirua, the priest of the burnt sacrifice. The veteran Pou-whareumu Toi, of Weriweri Village (son of Toi Whakataka, Titokowaru's lieutenant), thus described the savage ceremony as he narrated on the spot the episodes of the fight:—

"One of our warriors was the old priest Wairau, whose comrade and coadjutor was young Tihirua, of the Ngati-Maru

Tribe, from Waitara. Both of them shared in the tomahawking of Von Tempsky and other soldiers who fell at the north end of the clearing. Wairau rushed to the body of the first white man killed, cut the chest open with his tomahawk, and tore out the heart, for the ceremony of the *whangai-hau,* or feeding the gods of battle, Tu and Uenuku. Wairau held up the bleeding heart, and Tihirua applied fire to it. The young man carried *pakeha* matches, and, striking these, he held them to the flesh till it began to singe and sizzle and smoke. The smoke (*paoa*) that rose from it was regarded as a *tohu,* or omen. Wairau watched it intently to see the direction of its drift. The smoke rose and drifted out through the trees in the direction of the *pakeha* force. Had it been blown the other way, across or towards the stockade, it would have been a fatal omen for the Maoris, indicating the speedy fall of the place (*ka hinga te pa*). But the breath of the *atua* directed it the other way, and Wairau knew then that the white soldiers would be the vanquished ones that day."

Scarcely any two accounts of European survivors agree as to the events on the battlefield after the withdrawal of McDonnell. The salvation of those who lived to reach the Waihi Redoubt once more, after a terrible night in the trackless bush, was due to the gallant Captain J. M. Roberts (now Colonel Roberts, N.Z.C.), who had been Von Tempsky's subaltern in the Forest Rangers in Waikato. Roberts collected the disorganized remainder of the force, some sixty in number, got them into some kind of order, and with the help of some cool fellows who instilled confidence and hope into the men he made his way out to the open country. His narrative of the engagement and the retreat (a story never before published) is the only connected accurate account of the happenings after the main body moved off with most of the wounded.

"To this day," said Colonel Roberts, "I do not know precisely why Colonel McDonnell decided to retire as he did, leaving the rest of us without definite orders. We could have taken the *pa,* I believe. We were handicapped, however, by the presence of some unfit men, particularly the Wellington Rangers; their officers were very good, but the men should not have been sent into the bush. They couldn't walk in the bush and carry a rifle, far less fight in the bush. The practised bushmen among us, like myself—I had done pioneering bush-work before the Waikato War began—had grown to look on a tree as a friend. The recruits from Wellington knew nothing of the bush, and were easily panic-stricken when required to work in skirmishing order, where a man is necessarily separated from his comrades. They were falling over logs and vines; a man needs to get his bush-legs just as a sea passenger needs to get his sea-legs; he must learn where to place his feet and how to get through the bush with the greatest speed and the least trouble. The new men crowded together, and in consequence made easy targets for the Maoris.

"We had no definite orders after the fight began. The last I saw of Major Von Tempsky was near the creek in rear of the *pa,* some time after the fighting had begun. I remember well that he struck me as being curiously listless. He was cutting away with his sword at a hanging bush vine, not cutting it through, but rather chipping it downwards, cutting shavings off it. He was waiting for orders from McDonnell.* Presently Captain Brown came along and said, 'I've got a job, Roberts, I'm going out with the wounded.' Then, speaking in a low voice as he passed me, he added, 'You get out of this as soon as you can—don't stay here.'

"I had fired a few shots at the palisade," continued Colonel Roberts, "more for the sake of making a noise than anything else, for I could not see a single Maori. Our men were hotly pressed by the Hauhaus' fire from good cover. We were by this time on the east side of the *pa,* firing away, and waiting vainly for orders. I heard Lieutenant Hunter—who had been the life of the camp at Waihi—calling out to his men, 'Give it to them boys, give it to them! I can see the white of his eyes! Give it to him!' and similar cries. I saw him a little time afterwards, poor fellow, lying on the broad of his back, dead, staring at the tree-tops. There were a few men with me; an officer cannot see more than ten or fifteen when he is skirmishing under such conditions. I asked whether any one had seen McDonnell. I then came to the conclusion that he was fighting his way out. In this situation I did a thing which, strictly speaking, really was a great piece of presumption on the part of a junior officer. I ordered the bugler to sound the 'Halt!' and the 'Officers' Call.' I collected all the men I could, and two or three officers appeared. Captain Buck was one of them. I asked them whether they knew where the Major was, and they said they heard he was killed. We had a consultation, and I told them that from the sound of the firing I believed McDonnell was making his way back to Waihi. Then I asked, 'Which of us is the senior?' and on comparing dates of commissions with Buck I found I was the senior officer. When I had collected a few men I formed them into a sort of semicircle with the outer

---

* Lieut.-Colonel McDonnell sent a message to Von Tempsky by his brother, Captain William McDonnell, requesting him to follow No. 2 Division when it retired; but it is doubtful whether, if the Major received the message, he understood it as a definite instruction to withdraw. He certainly remained anxious to attempt the storming of the *pa.*

Lieut.-Colonel Thomas McDonnell, N.Z.C.

Lieut.-Colonel Thomas McDonnell was the son of Lieutenant McDonnell, R.N., who settled at Te Horeke, Hokianga Harbour, in the early part of last century. He served as a young officer in the Colonial Defence Force Cavalry in the Waikato War, and was awarded the New Zealand Cross in 1886 for a daring scouting exploit in 1863, when he and Von Tempsky made a reconnaissance from the Lower Waikato in to the Maori position at Paparata. (See Vol. I, page 271.)

side facing the *pa*. Then I said to Buck, 'You stay here, and I'll go and see what has become of Von Tempsky. If I'm not back in ten minutes or a quarter of an hour you'll know what to do.'

"I worked back through the bush towards the other side of the *pa*, passing some of my men who were still sticking to it. They called to me 'Don't go back, sir! You'll be shot!' They said they believed the Major was shot. I went along the flank two or three chains towards the creek that ran in the rear of the *pa*. I saw nothing of Von Tempsky, but he must have been lying close by. It was all dense bush here, with some very large *mahoe* trees—the biggest I had ever seen—and some *rata*. At last I turned to come back, and just as I did so a bullet buried itself in a sapling behind me. I made my way back towards the place where I had left Captain Buck a quarter of an hour previously, and I found him lying on his back, dead. I got together all the men I could find and disposed them as well as I could to resist the Hauhaus, who were pressing us hard, yelling 'Surround them, surround them!' in Maori. I formed the men into a rough half-moon front, and instructed them to fire volleys—'Blaze away as hard as you can, boys, blaze away!' We fired a number of volleys, and this had a great effect on the Hauhaus, who kept a greater distance after that.

"By this time it was getting quite dusk in the bush, under the close, dense foliage. I came to the conclusion that I had better try to make my way out to camp with the wounded. I had heard firing away on my right and knew it must be McDonnell fighting his way out to Waihi. There were eleven wounded, but most of these could walk. My total strength now was fifty-eight men. Sergeant Russell fell shot through the hip; he was a fine brave fellow. We had to leave him there lying propped up against a tree, with a loaded revolver in his hand. We had some faint hopes of rescuing him later, but the Hauhaus got him, after he had stood them off at first with his revolver. Lieutenant Hirtzel was with us, and another good man was big James Livingston, of Waipapa, Hawera, who had come with the force as a volunteer; he was a splendid fellow, cool and brave, and a first-rate bushman. When we were under a very heavy fire he was picking up the rifles of men who had been killed or wounded and smashing them against the butts of trees, saying that the Hauhaus would never be able to use those guns. He broke Russell's carbine before we left him.

"I kept my men together as well as I could in the bush, and got my wounded along; we went very slowly, occasionally turning to fire. I don't think we were travelling more than half a mile in the hour. All of us were now very exhausted, and I ordered the men to sit down in the bush undergrowth for a rest, waiting till the moon rose, so that I could fix my course. We had two or three friendly Maoris with us, Kupapas from Wanganui. I kept them close by me, for I was depending on them to lead us out of the bush; in fact, I put a sentry over them to make sure they did not give us the slip.

"We were still within cooee of the *pa;* in fact, we could hear the Hauhaus' yells and war-songs all night, we were that close. About 2 o'clock in the morning the moon rose over the tree-tops, and now that I had an idea of the points of the compass I made a start again. I sent the Maoris ahead, telling my man who was keeping an eye on them to make sure that they were not attempting to leave the column. 'If they do,' I said, 'you know what to do.'

"When we started on our retreat we were well in on the

Egmont or inland side of McDonnell's route. By about daylight we got out on to the track leading down to the Wai-ngongoro ford—the track we had come in the morning—and we reached the camp at Waihi about 8 o'clock. Some of them had given us up for lost. My friend Captain Brown (afterwards killed at Ngatapa) was one of those who hurried down to meet us. As he shook hands with me he said, 'Some of them said you were all killed, Roberts, but I knew you'd turn up, because you know the bush.' "*

All the dead and some of the wounded were left on the battle-field. The death-roll numbered twenty-four, of whom five were officers. Twenty-six wounded were brought off the field. One man, Private Dore, of the Wellington Rangers, who was shot through an arm in Robert's retreat, was lost in the bush, and did not reach Waihi until four days afterwards. Of the officers, Major Von Tempsky, Captain Buck, Captain Palmer, Lieutenant Hunter, and Lieutenant Hastings were in the list of dead. Palmer and Hastings were with Roberts's force, and were mortally wounded. Palmer died as he was being carried through the bush, and was left there.

LIEUT.-COLONEL MCDONNELL'S REPORT

Lieut.-Colonel McDonnell, in his despatch to the Minister of Defence (9th September, 1868), said that his intention on setting out from Waihi Camp was to reach Te Rua-ruru through the bush, attack the village, and return by way of Te Ngutu-o-te-manu. On reaching Mawhitiwhiti he struck inland on the main track to Te Ngutu and to seaward of the track that was supposed to exist and was marked on a map as leading to Te Rua-ruru. A very old trail was followed up for some time, then it ceased altogether, and the force headed in the supposed direction of Te Rua-ruru. The country was very rough, intersected with gullies and streams, and the bush was a tangled network of supplejack. About 1 p.m. a bush ridge was ascended, and then on the advice of Hone Papara, the Maori guide, McDonnell struck for the sea to try to hit a track. It was after another hour of this work that the first signs of Maoris were seen and heard, and a little later the track to the rear of Te Ngutu-o-te-manu was entered, and the force came under fire at the creek. The force was soon under fire from the front, right, and rear, but, except within a palisading in the clearing in front, no enemy could be seen. It was now that McDonnell, considering it impossible to

---

* Narrative to the author by Colonel J. M. Roberts, N.Z.C., at Rotorua, 13th February, 1919.

rush the place, or even if successful to hold it—the Hauhaus were not only occupying it, but were on three sides of it—determined to collect the wounded and push out through the forest. After sending the wounded off under Hunter and Newland, with Kepa's men, he returned, wrote to Major Von Tempsky, and desired him to collect the rest of the men to form a rearguard and follow at once. Then he told Captain Cumming to come on with him. During the whole of this time the Maoris were firing on the troops from every quarter. The way had to be cut through supplejack and undergrowth, which, with the eight wounded men on stretchers, was a work of great toil. The creek which runs through Te Maru was reached, but there was still no track.

"Presently," Colonel McDonnell's despatch continued, "news was brought to me that Major Von Tempsky, Captain Buck, Captain McDonnell, and Lieutenant Hunter were shot dead. But just then Captain McDonnell came up and stated that Major Von Tempsky, Captain Buck, and Lieutenant Hunter were killed, and that he had told Lieutenant Hastings that the only chance was to carry out the orders that had been given Major Von Tempsky; at once his reply was that Captain Buck was senior, and he would consult him. Captain McDonnell then went to see Captain Buck, but found that he was killed, and the enemy by this time in possession of the place where the bodies of Buck, Major Von Tempsky, and two men lay. He returned then, and pointed out to Mr. Hastings the necessity of retiring. The fire at this time was very heavy from the front, rear, and right, and from the tops of the *rata* trees. He then followed on my trail with eight natives and ten Europeans, and reported as above. I had now with me about eighty men, including natives—hardly sufficient to carry out the wounded, now increasing in number, and to keep down the fire from our right. Knowing that a large portion of the force was in rear, and several good officers, I moved on, feeling sure they were covering our retreat; but I presently found that the enemy had got between us, and it appears from what Sub-Inspector Roberts tells that soon after Captain McDonnell had left the Hauhaus succeeded in completely surrounding the rearguard, and it was only with the greatest difficulty they cut their way through them. The Hauhaus then left him (as he struck to the left farther into the bush) and came after us, overtaking us before we struck the main track leading into Te Ngutu-o-te-manu. Captain McDonnell meanwhile had taken up a position at Te Maru to keep our front open. Our wounded had by this time increased to twelve, who had to be carried, beside several who had been hit but could walk. The men with our party worked hard, but were so done up as to require every persuasion and advice I and my officers could think of to keep the majority from abandoning the wounded. One man killed I had to leave, and Dr. Best was badly hit in going to ascertain his state. The doctor had to be carried off on rifles, having no more stretchers in my party. The natives now swarmed in our rear, and kept up a heavy fire, which I was obliged to return only occasionally, as my ammunition was very short, Captain Cumming and myself loading and firing now and then. I was afraid the enemy might have got round to the crossing of the Wai-ngongoro River before I could reach it. We attained the opening at Ahi-paipa just at dusk, and here received a parting volley from the enemy. They followed on yelling, and commenced a war-dance in the open ground out of the bush. I caused my men to cheer, and gave them a volley which I should think took effect, as their dance ended rather abruptly, and they did not molest us any more. I may state that for some time I had not heard any distant firing, and therefore concluded the remainder of the force had got in advance of me. I pushed on across the river and found a few friendly natives holding the crossing. We got the men and wounded safely across and reached camp about 10 p.m. A mixed party of natives and Europeans, the latter numbering about eighty, had arrived before me and reported that all the officers were killed or wounded and left behind myself included."

McDonnell emphasized the great need of training and experience in forest fighting. The Wanganui and Ngati-Apa Maoris, who accompanied the force and who, it was known, killed fifteen Hauhaus, themselves suffered no loss; not even a man was wounded. This, he said, was proof that to fight Maoris successfully in a bush where every tree and every track were known to them required men who had been long and carefully trained to such work. Instead of his men dispersing and taking cover, they could not be prevented from huddling together in small lots, making a good target for their enemies. His efforts and those of his officers were in most cases without effect in convincing them of the mistake they were making.

As for the Hauhau losses, McDonnell reported that those known killed by the Europeans numbered thirteen, and by the Kupapas fifteen, making a total of twenty-eight; this was exclusive of losses the enemy must have suffered when the main body was fighting its way out. The Maoris, however, dispute this estimate.

TE NGUTU-O-TE-MANU AFTER THE BATTLE

It is the day after the fight. The square in the centre of the forest stockade is an amazing scene of ferocious excitement. The men with blackened faces, and all but nude, are dancing *hakas* and yelling war songs that can be heard a mile away. The women are screaming to each other, and running about with tomahawks in their hands; dogs are barking; children are screeching. It is a bedlam in the forest. On the ground lie the naked bodies of twenty white men, stripped by the Hauhaus, who had dragged them in from the forest where they had been left when the retreat began. Von Tempsky's body is there. The face had been hacked about with a tomahawk, the work of one of the Maori women —the natives revenge themselves in such fashion upon the head for those of their relatives who fell in the battle—but it is identified by Kimble Bent. The camp is in a fury of exultation over the fall of "Manu-rau" ("Many birds"), the name given to him because of his activity in guerrilla warfare; Von Tempsky was as nimble as the birds of the forest. And there, in front of the heap of slain, stands Titokowaru, the planner of ambuscades and midnight surprises, the victor of Te Ngutu-o-te-manu. Long he stands there, his chin resting upon his two hands, which are crossed on the end of his long tongue-pointed *taiaha,* his halbert-fashioned staff. At last he raises his head, and in a great croaking voice cries to his men that they must *tahutahu* the bodies of the *pakehas*—they must destroy them by fire. And this must not be done within the walls of the *pa.* The slain must be dragged outside the palisades, to the clearing which fronts the fenced village.

When the funeral pyre was prepared by the Hauhaus the body of Von Tempsky was laid upon it in the middle, and the other slain soldiers were piled around and above him, laid cross-ways on each other. As the Maoris cast the Major's body on the pile of firewood Titokowaru stalked forward, his *taiaha* in his hand, and cried his farewell, his *kupu poroporoaki,* to his dead foeman. There were his words (as given by Kimble Bent): *"I nga ra o mua i whawhai koe i tena wahi i tena wahi, i ki hoki koe ka puta koe ki te ao marama. Ka tae mai hoki koe ki au, moe ana o kanohi. Taea hokitia, nau i kimi mate mou naku. Ka moe koe."* ("In the days of the past you fought here and you fought there, and you boasted that you would always emerge safely from your battles to the bright world of life. But when you encountered me your eyes were closed in their last sleep. It could not be helped; you sought your death at my hands. And now you sleep for ever.")

In this not unpoetic fashion did the war-chief of the forest speed his fallen foe to the spirit-land of heroes.

The great pile of firewood—trunks and branches of dry *tawa*— was set alight with a brand from one of the village fires. When the pyre was kindled an old man walked up to it with a long forked pole in his hand. He was Titokowaru's own *tohunga,* or priest,

Te Waka-takere-nui. His wrinkled cheeks were deeply tattooed. The warlock chanted an ancient song, a savage elegy to the dead, as he raked the burning logs together. The black smoke soared straight up from the pyre, and as every now and then the bursting of a body sent up the flames and smoke in thicker volume the bushmen laughed and cried, "*Haere, haere, e koro!*" ("Go, depart, old man!") Like the smoke from a burning Viking dragon-ship, the funeral boat, so rose the corpse-smoke, black, in the midst of the green forest. And so, in that fiery breath, in true heroic fashion, farewelled by the pagan scalds and the tattooed braves, passed the fallen white men of Te Ngutu-o-te-manu.

A CANNIBAL FEAST

One of the soldiers' bodies was cooked and eaten. Pou-whareumu Toi, who witnessed the feast on human flesh, said when he pointed out the place where the cannibals of the bush sat down to their meal: "The body, which was cooked in a large *umu* (earth-oven), was that of a stout man (*he tangata momona*). It was eaten on the *marae* by the people, after it had been carried up in baskets, to the accompaniment of a chant by the bearers. The principal men who ate the human flesh were the old priest Tautahi Ariki (or Tu-Ahi-pa), Kai-taua, and Tohi. Many others shared in the meal. Some abstained, because they were *tapu*."

Kimble Bent, in narrating this episode, said that he saw the *tohunga* Wairau and Katene Tu-whakaruru enjoying the man-meat, which was eaten with potatoes. Katene joined in the meal, partly out of feelings of revenge for the killing of one of his children by a Wanganui Maori. Titokowaru himself abstained from human flesh for the reason that the eating of it would impair his *mana tapu,* his personal sanctity. Describing the process of cooking the body, Bent said:—

"I watched the preparation of the body of the white soldier for the warrior's feast. The head was first cut off with a tomahawk, and then the body was cut open and prepared as a butcher prepares a beast he has killed. The body was laid on the red-hot stones in the bottom of the *haangi* or *umu* (the earth-oven) so that the outer skin could be scraped off easily. This was done by the cannibal cooks with sharp cockle-shells. Water was then poured over the hot stones, to create the steam which was to cook the meal, and green leaves were spread on top of the stones, then the man-meat was placed in the oven. The body was cut up into convenient portions, and arranged so as to cook thoroughly. The oven was 5 feet long and about 3 feet deep, and there were several layers of meat, with green leaves between each. Some of the pieces, such as the rib portions, were set on edge, with hot stones between them. The thickest pieces were the meat cut from the thighs, the *huha*. The hands were laid with the palms uppermost, because when they were cooked they curled up, and the hollow palm was full of *hinu* or gravy, which was a great delicacy to the olden Maori. Mats and other coverings were laid on top again and more water poured over them, and then the earth was laid over all, so that no steam was permitted to escape. The body of the *pakeha* took between two and three hours to cook. Then the oven was uncovered and the contents carried up to the *marae* in small flax baskets with *kumara* and fern-root." "It was usual, too," added the old *pakeha-Maori*, "to cook some *pikopiko*, the young curly fronds of the *mauku*, or ground-fern, with the meat; it added to its flavour."

It was customary also to use *panahe* roots, steamed, as a corrective for the meat. The *panahe* is the wild convolvulus; its roots are long and thin, somewhat like macaroni, and are slightly bitter in taste.

NOTES

The Battlefield To-day

The battlefield of Te Ngutu-o-te-manu, which is reached by the Ahi-paipa or Tempsky Road from the Township of Okaiawa, is a public reserve of 50 acres, partly in grass and partly covered with a tall growth of *mahoe* trees, exotic pines, and oaks. The greater part of the reserve is leased for grazing. Some of the *rata* stumps and logs lie rotting on the ground under the shade of the new growth of *mahoe*, which now covers part of the clearing entered by the colonial troops in 1868. Many of these *mahoe* or whitewood trees (so called because of their gleaming white bark and trunks) are, however, more ancient than the period of the war. The domain, sacred to the memory of a score of colonial soldiers, is entered by a road beneath an overarching thicket of ancient whitewoods, their venerable trunks and twisted limbs glimmering ghostly in the shades. This is part of a belt of *mahoe* which marks the southern end of the Hauhau clearing made in 1866–68. The belt extends eastward into a grassy paddock; there the land is slightly higher than the green expanse of turf where the soldiers' monument stands, bounded on the west and north-west by a strip of timber and a little half-dry stream, the historic Mangotahi. A monument to Von Tempsky and his comrades stands near the northern end of the park, some little distance from the spot where they fell. North of the monument is a plantation bordering the grass field. In this woodland there are some huge *mahoe;* one is just such a tree as that in which Kimble Bent took shelter from the fire of the troops when hurrying from the *pa* on the morning of the attack. It is a twisted, knotty old wizard of a whitewood, its trunk hung with moss and ferns, and in its butt a hollow large enough to conceal one or two men. At the base it was about 8 feet through, a mass of misshapen roots and buttresses. Beyond this pine and *mahoe* wood again is a paddock in which there are many traces of Titokowaru's war-camps.

The old man Pou-whareumu Toi, of Weriweri Village, went with me to Te Ngutu-o-te-manu on the 15th October, 1918, and described many incidents of the fight. He was a child in the *pa* in 1868, and although he did not actually witness the attack on the stockade, as he was sent out with the women and children to a safe place in the forest, he saw all the after-events, including the burning of the fallen soldiers' bodies and the cannibal meal on the day after the battle. Pou described the fortifications, which were not formidable, and could have been taken by a determined assault. "The *pa*," he said, "had a stockade, ditch, and low parapet. The ditch was outside the tall stockade of *totara* timber, and the parapet, just inside the fence, was formed with the earth thrown up by the diggers. The trench surrounded the greater part of the *pa;* it was not dug on the west side, where the Mangotahi Stream, with its abrupt bank, closely approached the stockade. On a low hillock on the west, just above the stream, was Titokowaru's dwelling."

The domain caretaker's bungalow cottage, its veranda festooned with passion-flower and honeysuckle, fronts the site of the olden *marae,* the village square or *campus.* At one side of this *marae,* according to the old chief, stood the large assembly hall Wharekura, Titokowaru's sacred house of incantation and exhortation. It was built of sawn timber, and was adorned with a carved front and lined with ornamental reedwork.

"The place where Von Tempsky was killed," said Pou, "was not at the monument, as some suppose. It was over here," and the old man walked to the north end of the *pa,* past the slight rise in the ground where the rear palisade stood. Passing through a low hedge which crosses the reserve here, Toi looked about him for the stumps of the great *rata* trees of 1868. He pointed out the stump of one, sawn across, just above the bank of the creek near the little footbridge to the park playing-lawns. The other tree for which he was searching formerly stood, he said, in the plantation to the east, near a large cabbage-tree to which he pointed. In those two trees Maoris were posted as sentries—the inner one was the principal lookout place—and as sharpshooters. "But it was not they who shot Manu-rau" (Von Tempsky), said Pou, confirming the narratives of Tutange Waionui and others. "The chief of the soldiers was killed by men who were crouching on the ground outside the *pa,* just under the little fall of ground at the creek-side. It was Te Rangi-hina-kau who shot Von Tempsky; with him were Wairau and others. Kaake, an old tattooed warrior from Araukuku, was shot by the troops at the end of the *pa.*

"Many of the *pakehas* were ignorant of the ways of war," said Pou. "They came marching along upright, staring about them in amazement, very unlike the Maoris, who skirmished crouching, keenly searching the undergrowth, sinking to the ground for cover, and fighting nearly naked.

"There were only thirty or forty men in the *pa* at the beginning of the fight," Pou declared. "The rest had gone out to shoot cattle inland in the direction of Te Rua-ruru, two or three miles away. They heard the firing, and dashed back and caught the troops in a cross-fire, hence the defeat and retreat of the whites."

The place where the bodies of about twenty soldiers were burned in a funeral pyre was pointed out. It was outside the *pa* stockade on a *maara* or cultivation, clear of bush, where the plantation now is, south of the village. The spot is on the right-hand side as the domain is entered from the road. "A great fire was made with *tawa* logs and other timber, and when it blazed up and began to consume the bodies we children were stricken with awe and fear."

I explored the battle-ground on other occasions (1919 and 1920) with Mr. William Wallace, of Hawera (ex-sergeant, No. 2 Division, Armed Constabulary). Mr. Wallace, the son of a soldier of the 65th Regiment, fought in the first engagement at Te Ngutu-o-te-manu as one of the Wellington Rangers. He was of opinion that the great house Wharekura which was burned by the troops that day was in the north end of the large clearing, a considerable distance from the park *marae* where the soldiers' monument stands. The site of an unusually large house was traced in the grass paddock on the north or Egmont side of the plantation, close to an angle formed by two thorn hedges. This ground was a clearing in 1868, with *whares* scattered about it. A short distance northward again, around the head of the Mangotahi watercourse, now almost dry, there were numerous remains of olden dug-in huts and food-stores. This is where the log-hut village previously decribed stood in 1866.

While the veteran recounted those events of half a century ago we explored the clearing and the adjacent bush and fields, and found numerous traces of the olden village. On the north-eastern side of the reserve, in a paddock through which the head of the little stream Mangotahi runs, a farmer's cows were grazing peacefully over the field where Titokowaru's warriors met the whites in battle. Just north of the creek, where the log-hut *kainga* of 1866 stood, there were numerous depressions in the turf indicating the sites of old-time *whares* dug into the earth for greater warmth and snugness, and for defence. There were also hollows indicating the *ruas,* or store-pits, for potatoes. Near the creek were the softly grassed ruins of a parapet and rifle-pit commanding the crossing-place. Numerous rotting stumps of *matai* (black-pine) showed the heavy character of the bush which formerly covered the spot.

On the opposite or southern side of the now dry watercourse—it is near its head—many slight depressions and undulations in the turf marked the site of the old-time refuge-place and gathering-ground of the Hauhaus. In the middle of the track across the paddock the foot struck against smooth stones embedded in the ground, and a little investigation showed that these formed the *taku-ahi,* or hearthstone, which formerly occupied the centre of a *whare.* All had mouldered away, except, close by, two decaying butts of *matai* posts on opposite sides of the site of a dug-in hut. Dairy herds chew placidly in the midst of this conquered sanctuary of the rebel Ngati-Ruanui; and the unheeding foot of the white farmer passes over the long-quenched home fires of the bushmen, whose ashes have been scattered to the winds that have free passage over the plains, for the forest that was their help and refuge has wellnigh all been hewn away.

Von Tempsky's Sword

One day in the early "eighties," long after the war, Kimble Bent visited some of his acquaintances in Parihaka; they lived in a *whare* by the side of the road which led through the village. As he entered the house, stepping over the high *paepae* or threshold, one of them seated within the house said to him, "You have crossed a very rich threshold" ("*He paepae whai-taonga*").

"What do you mean ?" asked Bent.

"Beneath that beam of wood," replied the Maori, "there lies the sword of 'Manu-rau.'"

This was the truth. The owner of the whare had become possessed of Von Tempsky's sword, which was preserved as a sacred relic, a *taumahatanga,* or offering to the gods. It was not displayed in public, but was placed beneath the threshold, to which in Maori eyes a kind of sanctity attached, and beneath which valuable relics were often placed, to assure the security of the house and occupants. The sword was carefully greased and wrapped in flannel before it was laid in its resting-place. Some years later it was buried in the grave in which its Hauhau owner was laid, and there it lies to this day.

Chapter 24

TE KOOTI'S ESCAPE: CHATHAM ISLANDS

Thus saith the Lord: Refrain thy voice from weeping, and thine eyes from tears; for thy work shall be rewarded, saith the Lord; and they shall come again from the land of the enemy.

And there is hope in thine end, said the Lord that thy children shall come again to their own border. (Jeremiah, xxxi, 16 and 17.)

—*Te Kooti's text in exile.*

IT WAS ON the prison-island of Wharekauri, the largest of the Chathams, that Te Kooti Rikirangi, the outstanding figure in the later New Zealand wars, first became prominent as a leader of his people. As has been narrated in a previous chapter, he was arrested on suspicion of treachery during the fighting at Waerenga-a-Hika, and was released, but afterwards re-arrested and shipped off to Chatham Island in the steamer "St. Kilda" early in 1866. Te Kooti's name as a child was Rikirangi; the name Te Kooti, which he assumed in after-years, is simply a transliteration of the English surname Coates. At the time of his transportation to Chatham Island Te Kooti was about thirty-five years of age. He was a man of about 5 feet 9 inches in height, spare of body, but his apparently slight frame disguised a wiry strength which carried him through countless privations and fatiguing marches. When I met him long after the war (1889) he was not an impressive figure: a bowed, rather undersized man, prematurely aged, with a straggly white beard; he was very much reduced in health by his terribly arduous campaigning life and also by his intemperate habits. His features were well cut, his nose aquiline, dominating, his eyes very keen and searching. He was not of high birth, and therefore owed nothing of his extraordinary ascendancy over the people to any *whakapapa rangatira*, or aristocratic pedigree.

Te Kooti was a member of the Ngati-Maru *hapu* of the Rongowhakaata Tribe, of the Poverty Bay district. In his youth he received some education at the Waerenga-a-Hika Mission School. He became a rather notable fellow on the coast for his skill in horsemanship, his ability in handling boats, particularly surf-boats, and also for his rather lawless way with other people's horses and his bold amorous exploits. He saw a good deal of coastwise sailoring life, and was interested in trading enterprises. For some time he was supercargo of a native schooner called the "Henry," running between Turanganui and Auckland, and he occasionally remained over in Auckland between trips of the vessel attending to trade affairs. At another time he was in charge of a small schooner called the "Rua-whetuki," trading along the coast as far as Auckland. Thus Te Kooti by the beginning of the war had acquired a good deal of knowledge of the *pakeha* world in one way and another, and with his natural shrewdness and his well-sharpened wits, added to uncommon force of character, it was easy for him when the opportunity presented itself to take a place of leadership. Superadded, too, was a strain of mysticism, but this does not appear to have manifested itself until the period of exile on Chatham Island.

Te Kooti in a statement made after the war attributed his deportation to Wharekauri chiefly to the influence of Captain Read, then the principal business man at Turanganui, who was jealous of him for taking native trading business away from his (Read's) concerns. There is no doubt that several Gisborne people thought that Te Kooti was a troublesome fellow who would be better out of the way, and the opportunity of sending him off to Wharekauri was too good to be missed. There is evidence that he was in sympathy with the Hauhaus. There is no doubt that he was in arms on the European side against the rebels at Waerenga-a-Hika. According to his own statement, he was beside Captain Ross when that officer was shot through the bridge of the nose, and he declared that he shot two Hauhaus that day. However, he was arrested by the loyal chief Paora Parau, who charged him with breaking the bullets off his cartridges, pocketing them, and firing blank cartridges at the enemy. Apparently this charge, or whatever accusation was made against him, could not be substantiated, as after a short detention he was released. Later —in March of 1866—he was re-arrested on suspicion of treasonable communication with the enemy. Captain G. A. Preece states that a messenger to Anaru Matete, one of the Hauhau leaders—who had formerly been one of Bishop Williams's mission-school teachers—was captured bearing an incriminating letter from Te Kooti, or Rikirangi, as he was then known. This was when a party under Captain Westrup was moving up towards Te Reinga to co-operate with the forces from Wairoa under Major Fraser, against the remnant of the Poverty Bay Hauhaus who were in the back country up the Waipaoa River. Rikirangi's message contained the words "Wednesday is the day, and Te Reinga is the place." The inference was that an ambuscade should be laid by Anaru Matete for Westrup at the time and place indicated. From the messenger also some three hundred and fifty Enfield rifle-cartridges were taken; at this time the friendly natives were only supposed to have seventy cartridges from the Government supplies. Rikirangi accordingly was put in the guard-room once more, and as the prisoners taken at Waerenga-a-Hika and some of those from the East Cape and Wairoa were about to be sent to the Chathams, Major Biggs decided that Rikirangi should go with them. Protesting his innocence he was sent to Napier, where he appealed to Mr. Edward Hamlin, Government Native Interpreter, who was superintending the deportation, to be tried by a Court. Te Kooti in his own statement after the war said he saw Mr. Donald McLean, the then Superintendent of Hawke's Bay, and appealed to him, but "Te Makarini" would not listen to him, and he was sent off with the other prisoners in the steamer "St. Kilda" to Wharekauri. It is clear that whatever charges were made against the man they were not investigated by any tribunal, and he was shipped off to the distant isle of exile untried and unconvicted, nursing a grievance and cherishing a bitterness which grew in process of time to an intense passion for revenge.*

For more than two years the exiled Hauhaus were detained at Waitangi, Chatham Island, where a redoubt had been built and quarters and cultivation-grounds assigned to the prisoners. Captain Thomas, Resident Magistrate, was in general charge of affairs on the island, and Captain Tuke commanded a military guard of twenty-five men. Early in 1868 Captain Tuke was transferred to New Zealand, and the guard was reduced to fifteen men on the instructions of the Hon. W. Rolleston, then Under-Secretary for Native Affairs. The prisoners had been given to understand that if they were of good behaviour they would be returned to their homes at the end of two years; but as there was no sign of this being carried out they began to despair of ever seeing their country and friends again. Several of the principal chiefs were permitted to return to New Zealand; this left the remaining prisoners practically in the hands of Te Kooti, who had by this time assumed a position of importance as a priest and prophet among the people. During 1867 he had announced himself the recipient of a Divine message bidding him establish a new religion for the Maori people and await the time when he should be the instrument to release them from their bondage. He set himself to an earnest study of the

* "I think from what I have heard," Captain G. A. Preece says in a note to the writer, "that there was ample evidence against Te Kooti if he had been tried, but, as is often the case, a little of 'might is right' was carried out in this and also in other cases."

Scriptures, and presently evolved a ritual which replaced the old Pai-marire jargon of his followers and which became known later as the religion of the Wairua-Tapu, or Holy Spirit. This religious cult, founded entirely upon the Bible, exists to-day among the tribes of the Bay of Plenty and the Urewera Country, and numbers many hundreds of adherents; it has obtained official sanction as the Church of the Ringa-tu, the "Uplifted Hand." Te Kooti in framing his services drew upon the Psalms of David, the Books of Job and Jeremiah, and the Proverbs of Solomon. The spirit of the Old Testament appealed strongly to the Maori mind, and the Psalms with their poetry and grandeur of language went to the hearts of the exiles. Most of them had received Scriptural instruction from the missionaries in their home-land, but in their "land of bondage" the mournful beauty of the Psalms thrilled them beyond expression, and the cry for deliverance from enemies was voiced with an earnestness that rose to a frantic fervour. The *karakia*, or form of service, was skilfully chosen from passages specially applicable to the condition of the Wharekauri prisoners, far removed from their friends, and hemmed in by their foes. Te Kooti led the chantings in the services held morning and night in the meeting-house, and there were very few among the people who did not join with intense devotion in the worship. Of the chief sceptic, Te Warihi, more will be heard. The Maoris made lament daily with the Psalmist, "Lord, how are they increased that trouble me! Many are they that rise up against me"; and they chanted the words of the prophet Jeremiah, the consolation and the promise, Te Kooti's favourite text, that head this chapter. The 2nd Psalm, in after-years used as a service before going into battle, was another portion of the meeting-chants. Pai-marire as a form of worship was superseded by the new faith, but one ceremonial in Te Ua's religion was retained, the upraising of the right hand to a level with the face at the invocation of the *Atua*.

Te Kooti gradually obtained overmastering control of the people by his fervent exhortations and his peculiarly attractive and appropriate ritual of worship, and by the beginning of 1868 they were in a state of mind that lent itself perfectly to the scheme of escape he was formulating. The gaunt black-bearded prophet did not rest content with the Bible service for properly impressing the prayer-gatherings. He must needs introduce stage effects the more to enthral and mystify the devotees. One of his methods, highly successful in the dimly lighted church or the meeting-house, was to smear his fingers with phosphorus and then at the right moment to display his outspread hand above the pulpit or in some other position, a hand of pale flame, gleaming there in the sacred gloom. It was the hand of the

Holy Spirit, a sign of a token from the unseen. Again, he would draw up slowly, by a thread above the pulpit, a small cross made of thin laths of wood, plastered with a mixture of flax gum and the phosphorus of match-heads. By such devices, in the half-light or sometimes the complete darkness of the church, he obtained a reputation for working miracles. A latter-day *tohunga,* he borrowed ideas from many sources to excite the imagination of his followers and enhance his priestly *mana.* It was the beginning of a strange career in which his sway over the Maori mind of a certain bent, though often beaten to the ground by defeat, ever rose resilient, and, in spite of his defects of character, remained strong to the end. On his death a quarter of a century after the escape from Wharekauri—the flight of the Israelites from the land of bondage, as he described it—he was venerated as a god by the faithful, and that tradition persists to this day among his old flock.

Dissatisfaction among the prisoners was so strong towards the end of 1867 that reports of their condition reached the New Zealand Government, and Mr. Rolleston was sent down to investigate the position. He reported very unfavourably regarding their treatment in some respects, particularly in the matter of the medical examination; this had been carried out in such a manner as to arouse the just resentment of the women among the exiles. The discipline of the military guard was very bad, and drunkenness was common. A sergeant (Elliott) admitted having kicked some prisoners who refused to turn out when ordered; and the conduct of some of the other men towards the people was calculated to provoke a revolt. Te Kooti however, always declared that Captain Thomas, most of the troops, and all the civilian inhabitants of Wharekauri were very kind to the exiles.

When the guard was reduced to fifteen men and a non-commissioned officer under Captain Thomas, as the result of Rolleston's recommendations, Te Kooti saw his way clear to a successful rising; the only thing wanting was a vessel in which to escape to New Zealand. He prophesied that an "ark of salvation" would presently arrive—knowing that a vessel with stores was nearly due. There was a doubter in the camp, Te Kooti's uncle, the old man Te Warihi Potini, of Turanganui. He had scoffed at his nephew's tricks with the phosphorized cross and the ghostly hand in the dim religious gloom of the prayer-house, and had told some of the Europeans about the new *karakia* and Te Kooti's prophesyings. Warnings, however, were lost upon Captain Thomas and his fellow-whites, who could not believe that so patient and well-behaved a community of prisoners would attempt anything so violent as a rebellion.

On the afternoon of Tuesday, the 30th June, 1868, the

From a sketch by Mr. S. Percy Smith, 1868]

Waitangi Bay and Settlement, Chatham Island

The redoubt seized by Te Kooti in 1868 is shown on the edge of the cliff above the beach.

ketch "Florence" arrived in Waitangi roadstead from Wellington, and on the Friday following the three-masted schooner "Rifleman" arrived from the same port under charter to Captain Hood, of Chatham Island. She brought stores and was to load a return cargo of wool. The arrival of these two craft had been prophesied by Te Kooti in an oracular utterance in which—according to the Maoris—he announced that a large vessel and a small one would reach Wharekauri; the large vessel was the one in which, with the aid of the *Atua,* they would return to their native land.

The prophet's words thus confirmed, the intensely excited people awaited with perfect obedience Te Kooti's scheme of escape. He carried out his dramatic coup on Saturday, the 4th July. He and some of his men had been engaged, as was customary, as boats' crews in unloading the vessels; Te Kooti himself was at the steer-oar of one of the surf-boats. Two parties of picked men were quietly told off, one to surprise the guard and capture the redoubt, the other to seize the Government boat engaged in working the "Rifleman." Te Kooti gave explicit instructions that there must be no bloodshed.

From a drawing by Mr. A. H. Messenger]

The Schooner "Rifleman"

This picture of the vessel in which Te Kooti and his fellow-exiles escaped from Chatham Island to the east coast of New Zealand is drawn from a description and sketch by the late Captain M. T. Clayton, who was Lloyd's surveyor at the Port of Auckland for many years.

The plan was executed with complete success on the Saturday forenoon. The sentry at the redoubt was seized and disarmed, and the whole of the guard were rushed and tied up in a few moments. Captain Thomas was thrown down like the others, and bound hand and foot; afterwards, at his appeal that the bonds were hurting him, he was untied and handcuffed, and locked up in a cell. Only one man was killed—and this was in disregard of Te Kooti's order. Tamihana Teketeke tomahawked a private of the guard named Michael Hartnett, who was on duty at the magazine. Tamihana appears to have had a private grievance against Hartnett, and in the heat of the struggle he could not resist squaring accounts with his *patiti*. The redoubt armoury and magazine were ransacked, and on Te Kooti's order Captain Thomas surrendered the key of the safe in which the money was kept. The sum of £397 8s. 2d., Government money, was taken from the safe, and some private moneys were seized; in all Te Kooti secured £522 in notes and coin. The arms and ammunition captured in the redoubt and in private houses were 32 rifles, 29 bayonets, 1 carbine, 8 guns, 7 revolvers, 1 pistol, 3 swords, 4,584 rounds of rifle-ammunition, 200 revolver-cartridges, and 6,670 percussion caps. A bugle was also taken; it was appropriated by Peka te Makarini, who had previously induced the bugler to teach him the various military calls. This knowledge he turned to account in the war up to the time of his death at Captain Mair's hands in 1870.

Meanwhile the "Rifleman" had been boarded and seized. Captain Christian, the master of the vessel, was ashore with Captain Thomas at the time. He was captured by the Maoris, but was not tied up; his captors allowed him his freedom on his promising not to interfere with the seizure of the schooner. The ketch "Florence" was also seized; the master (Captain Priest) and crew were sent ashore. The vessel was looted, and the cable cut. The vessel drifted ashore and became a wreck; this prevented any news of the rising being sent to New Zealand.

The settlers' houses having been ransacked for arms, money, clothing, and other things likely to be useful to the Maoris, Te Kooti prepared for the voyage to New Zealand. Mr. Payne, the mate of the "Rifleman", and the crew were informed that their lives would be spared if they worked the vessel to New Zealand, and that she would be given up to them after the fugitives had been landed. On this understanding Mr. Payne agreed to navigate the schooner to the East Coast, and the crew carried on at their usual duties, assisted by some of the Maoris who had a knowledge of the sea. Boat after boat came off crowded with Maoris—men, women, and children—until the decks of the schooner were packed with excited and exultant escapees, prisoners no longer. It was found that there was a large quantity of flour, sugar, and other stores on board, and more food and water were brought off from the shore.

On the evening of the 4th July the anchor was weighed and the "Rifleman" beat out of Waitangi roadstead. Mr. Payne was ordered by Te Kooti to navigate the schooner to Turanganui, Poverty Bay. There were in all 298 Maoris on board—163 men, 64 women, and 71 children. Armed guards were told off to keep watch on deck, and men assisted the cook in his galley in the heavy task of preparing food for the people. Head winds compelled the vessel to return to the anchorage; and when a start was made again next day little progress was made. "We were three days in sight of the land after we first weighed anchor," said Te Kooti* in a statement after the war. "I was in great fear lest a Government steamer should come from Wellington and capture us." Strong westerly winds prevailed, and for three days the schooner was tacking continually. Most of the people suffered from sea-sickness. So the voyage went

---

* Te Kooti in a statement made in 1873 to Mr. James Mackay at Tokangamutu (Te Kuiti) said: "The sailors in the schooner were treacherous, and I found out that they were steering for Wellington instead of for Poverty Bay. I know how to steer, and understood the compass from my experience in coasting-vessels. I told them to go the right course or they would be thrown overboard."

J. C., photo at Taringamutu, King Country, 1921]

Peita Kotuku

Peita fought against the British troops at Puke-takauere, Taranaki, in 1860, and was one of the defenders of Orakau *pa* in 1864. He was captured at the engagement at Omarunui, near Napier, in 1866, and was transported to Chatham Island with the other Hauhau prisoners. He escaped with Te Kooti in the "Rifleman" in 1868, and fought against the colonial forces until 1870. He was one of Te Kooti's best warriors and scouts.

on until the afternoon of the 9th of July, when the vessel was about a hundred miles east of Hawke's Bay.

Now befell the first episode which exhibits Te Kooti in a grim revengeful character. He declared to the people that there must be a Jonah (*Hona,* in the Maori) in the "Rifleman"; it was a saying he had heard sailors use; this was the cause of the long spell of head winds. He professed to consult the *Atua* as to the identity of this Jonah; then it was revealed unto him that it was his old uncle Te Warihi Potini. The sequel to this professed supernatural discovery was narrated to the writer in the dramatic manner of the Maori by one of the "Rifleman" escapees, Peita Kotuku, who had been captured at the Omarunui engagement in 1866. Describing the voyage to New Zealand and the manner in which Te Kooti wreaked his will on Te Warihi, this old scout and warrior said:—

"When the schooner came into the bay at Wharekauri from New Zealand I was away working on a sheep-station inland, and so I did not witness the actual seizure. As soon as the vessel had been captured Te Kooti immediately sent messengers out to bring in all the exiles who were working in various outside places. Then, until the vessel was ready to sail, I and a number of others did duty as guards to prevent the Europeans in the principal settlement communicating with those living in other parts of the island, who did not as yet know of the successful rising of the prisoners. When Te Kooti was ready we went on board, and we took a supply of water in casks from the shore. The 'Rifleman' had plenty of stores in the hold, which had been intended for the use of the station; there were about 20 tons of flour, biscuit, sugar, and other provisions. Our ship of deliverance was a three-masted schooner, painted black; she had square topsails on her foremast, besides carrying a large lower squaresail for running, and she also had a square topsail on the main; for the rest she was fore-and-aft rigged.*

"Our voyage to New Zealand, after putting back once owing to head winds, occupied four days. As the captain had been seized and left on shore, the mate of the schooner was the navigator. I and several other Maoris were sailormen during the passage, and helped the white crew in setting and trimming sail. There were more than two hundred of us on board—men, women, and children.

"I witnessed the throwing-overboard of one of our people, an elderly man named Te Warihi. He was an elder relation of Te Kooti. The principal reason for the execution was that Te Warihi had given information to some of the European people about the *karakia,* or religious worship, practised by Te Kooti and his exhortations to the prisoners. The vessel was hindered by head winds on the voyage, and on the third day she was not making any progress. We were tacking frequently. Te Kooti had resolved that Te Warihi must suffer death, and he told the people that he was desirous of taking him to New Zealand and executing him there, but his (Te Kooti's) *Atua,* his god, was not willing that the offender should be taken to the mainland. The schooner, the *Atua* told him, would not reach the shore so long as Te Warihi was kept on board. Therefore he must be cast into the sea (*whiua ki te moana*).

"At this time it was late in the afternoon, and the sun was setting over the windy ocean. I was on deck helping the sailors with the ropes. We saw a great wave, a billow like a mountain, rolling towards us. It would surely overwhelm us when it reached us. It was about as far from the spot where we are sitting to those *kahikatea* trees on the bank of the Taringamutu" [about

---

* This was illustrated in a rough sketch. The part square rig on the mainmast as well as the foremast was frequently adopted in old-time three-masted schooners, though never seen nowadays in those vessels. Technically the "Rifleman" was a three-masted two-topsail schooner.

Te Rangi-tahau

This East Taupo chief was captured at the Omarunui engagement, near Napier, in 1866. He escaped from Chatham Island in the schooner "Rifleman," and was with Te Kooti in all the fighting until the early part of 1870. He was a most savage and ruthless warrior. (See note to Chapter 31.)

300 yards away] "when the condemned man was brought up on deck from the hold, where he was sitting with his old wife. He was marched aft by Timoti te Kaka. The wave towered up like a mountain-range; it looked on the sea-line like Hikurangi Mountain yonder" [the crest of a range on the north of Taringamutu]. "Te Kaka, pushing Te Warihi to the rail, attempted to lift him over, but he was not strong enough. Then a powerful Maori standing by, a man from the Wairarapa, seized the old man, lifted him over the rail, and dropped him into the sea. Te Warihi did not make any outcry, nor did he struggle. He fell into the water and went down like a stone." ["*Whenei me te kohatu*" were Peita's words.] "He did not swim after the ship. And we, who were in fear that the great wave sweeping along towards us would break on the ship and sink us, saw in that moment that we were saved. The billow did not break, and the schooner rode safely on the sea. The sun shone out from the clouds for a few moments before it set. Te Kooti told us we would sight land next morning.

"It was early in the morning that we caught sight of the east coast of New Zealand. There were nine of us on deck at the time—six sailors and three of us Maoris (Rawiri, Tuari, and myself) who were helping the crew. The wind had come fair after Te Warihi went overboard; it was blowing strongly, and the schooner was going along well with all sail set. Many of the Maoris had been making bets in *pakeha* fashion as to when land would be sighted; some would stake £5, some £6, some £10." [A large sum of money had been secured on the Chathams at the time of the rising.] "The mountains of the North Island were seen just after the sun rose, and there was loud rejoicing among the people."

The land sighted that morning (10th July) was the snow-covered high country inland of Poverty Bay. Te Kooti ordered a course to be steered for the coast a few miles south of the Bay, and at dusk the "Rifleman" sailed into the small sheltered bay Whareongaonga, seven or eight miles south of Young Nick's Head. Te Kooti led chants of thanksgiving for the safe return to the home-land, and the complete success of the bold enterprise confirmed the popular belief in his superhuman powers. Joyfully the escapees pulled ashore and pitched camp close to the beach, and next day all the stores required were landed. The mate, Mr. Payne, and his crew were given their liberty, and the schooner put to sea. Instead, however, of putting in at Turanganui and warning the people there of Te Kooti's landing, Payne steered for Wellington, and as the vessel was delayed by head winds he did not reach there till the 23rd July. The place where the ex-prisoners landed was on the run of Mr. Woodbine Johnson, a pioneer settler, and there were not many natives resident in the vicinity of Whareongaonga. The nearest Maori village of importance was Maraetaha, near Young Nick's Head, and Te Kooti's first step was to send an armed party there and requisition arms and ammunition. So opened his new and marvellous career as a military leader in a land where for fifteen years he was to be a refugee, a reiver, and an outlaw.

NOTES

Captain Gilbert Mair, N.Z.C., writing to me from Tauranga, October, 1921, reagarding Te Kooti's career, said:—

"So far as Te Kooti's guilt was concerned, I am perfectly certain that no charge could have been substained against him in any Court of competent jurisdiction prior to his deportation, untried, to the Chathams. In January, 1868, it was proposed to install me as Commandant at the Chathams, and I accompanied the late Hon. William Rolleston, then Under-Secretary for Native Affairs, to Wharekauri. Captain Thomas, then in charge, had urgently applied to be relieved of his command. The steamer 'St. Kilda' made a special trip for us. We found matters in a most scandalous state. Captain Thomas appeared to exercise no control whatever. The 200-odd native detainees were out of hand and in an excited state. Of the twenty-five men comprising the guard, we found more than half under arrest for drunkenness, disobedience, and bad conduct towards the interned Maoris. We had several interesting meetings with the internees, and I heard more than enough to convince me that the position was scandalous, and decided me against my previous strong desire to take charge. Most circumstantial details were given in every case, mainly by Te Kooti, seconded by the big half-caste Peka te Makarini, whom I heard playing the bugle everlastingly, and who desired to be second only to Te Kooti in powerful influence over the people. Peka went to great trouble to hire me a horse, and secured me a magnificent upstanding chestnut with a big star, which he bounced the Moriori owner into hiring at 2s. 6d. per week. He also cadged most unblushingly for carvings and curios, of which the prisoners gave me a sackful, all of which were subsequently confiscated by Mr. Rolleston, who seemed put out at me—a subordinate—being so favoured while nothing was presented to him. It may have been that the prisoners had heard I was to be the new Commandant, but mainly, I think, because I showed them sympathy and tried to soften Mr. Rolleston's rather harsh declarations. We had our meetings in the nice little dimly lighted church. Te Kooti made a most eloquent speech at every meeting regarding his wrongs, the jealousy of Captain Read, at Gisborne, and several chiefs; how he had proved his loyalty by serving under Major Fraser, and how he had unavailingly demanded to be given a trial on every possible occasion. He also spoke scathingly of the insults to the men and women by the colonial soldiers, also about the sergeant's behaviour. One of his complaints was that every difficulty was placed against them using the church. I was told years afterwards that second to Read's objections to Te Kooti was the fact that Te Kooti was the Poverty Bay Don Juan, and had numerous love affairs with the wives of prominent chiefs, who joined Read in prejudicing Sir Donald McLean against him.

"Looking back on my Chatham Islands trip," concluded Captain Mair, "there is a remarkable coincidence in my association with Peka te Makarini and Patara te Whata. The latter Maori Rolleston and I found confined in gaol—I am not sure that he wasn't handcuffed or ironed—being charged with committing an assault on Dr. Watson, the surgeon. It is curious that I should have put a bullet through each of these men in after-years."

[Captain Mair shot Peka te Makarini at the foot of Tumunui Mountain, in the Rotorua district, in 1870, and Patara te Whata at a camp on the Waipaoa River, east of Waikare-moana, in 1871.]

Te Kooti's *tapu* manuscript ritual book, containing the heads of Old Testament passages forming the Ringa-tu or Wairua-Tapu services, was shown to Colonel Porter and the author some years ago by Eria Raukura, who was for some years Te Kooti's chief priest, and is now the leading minister of the Wairua-Tapu religion. The book, which is in Te Kooti's handwriting, contains twelve services, chosen chiefly from the Books of Job, Jeremiah, Zephaniah, Proverbs, and the Psalms.

When prisoners were being led out for execution by Te Kooti's "butchers," in 1868–70, the verse Proverbs ii, 22, was recited over them: "But the wicked shall be cut off from the earth, and the transgressors shall be rooted out of it."

Chapter 25

FIRST ENGAGEMENTS WITH TE KOOTI

THE EUROPEAN INHABITANTS of Poverty Bay did not learn of Te Kooti's landing until two days later. Captain R. Biggs, Resident Magistrate at Matawhero, on the Turanganui Flat, immediately called out the only available force, the Mounted Rifles, under Captain Westrup, formerly of the Forest Rangers, and sent a chief of the Rongowhakaata Tribe, Paora Kati, to Whareongaonga to demand that the escapees from Wharekauri should give up their arms and remain peaceably at Whareongaonga until the Government sent instructions regarding them. Te Kooti made reply refusing to surrender his arms. He declared that he only desired an open road to the interior of the Island; he intended to go to Waikato and set up a new king of the Maoris. Biggs's messenger returned and reported the failure of his mission. On the morning of the 15th July Te Kooti and his people began their march inland through the bush. They had been joined by a number of armed Maoris from the adjacent settlements. The Captain, with a force of about eighty whites and Maoris, arrived at the landing-place too late to intercept them. He then decided to hurry inland across the more open country and cut them off at Paparatu, commanding the spot where the Hauhaus must emerge from the bush and cross the Arai Stream on their way into the shelter of the Urewera Mountains. Messages had been sent to Wairoa and Napier for assistance, and Biggs marched for Paparatu with about forty of his European volunteers and thirty friendly Maoris under Henare Kakapango. Lieutenant (afterwards Major) F. J. W. Gascoyne, lately of the Colonial Defence Force Cavalry and the Military Settlers, had offered his services to Biggs, and he very gallantly took a despatch to Wairoa, delivering it after a perilous ride and walk of forty hours through hostile country. Soon after he rode off he heard firing at Paparatu. This was on the morning of the 20th July, 1868.

Captain Biggs meanwhile had started back to Gisborne to hurry up supplies, as his force had been five days out and were now without rations. As for ammunition, they had only thirty rounds per rifle. Colonel Whitmore had just arrived at Turanganui with a few volunteers. Te Kooti delivered his attack while Biggs was absent, and with his strong body of men, well supplied with ammunition, he surrounded a hill which Westrup was holding. This was a height at the head of the long spur along which Te Kooti advanced his force. The European force lost two killed and several wounded in the hot fighting, and was cut off from the baggage and equipment, which had been left in the camp in the valley below, together with reserve ammunition and rations which had just arrived. Most of the friendly Maoris had quickly retreated when Te Kooti made his vigorous attack, and it was left for Westrup and Wilson with about forty men, carrying seven wounded, to make their retreat by night across the hills and ravines to the open country. It was fortunate for them that Te Kooti did not pursue them, but remained contented with the capture of the valuable camp supplies, besides the horses of the expedition. This easy victory, in which the Hauhaus suffered no casualties, was the first of a long series of military successes which Te Kooti attributed to Divine assistance. Coming so quickly after the seizure of the "Rifleman," it confirmed the prophet's followers in their belief in his supernatural powers. Whitmore, writing of the Paparatu engagement, said: "Undoubtedly the extraordinary prestige this remarkable man afterwards acquired sprang from this brilliant, and to the Maori mind inexplicable success."

On the day following the fight Te Kooti moved on towards Whakapunake Mountain. Whitmore marched from Turanganui the same day to reinforce Westrup, but only to meet the defeated and dispirited force returning along the Arai Valley. Whitmore urged the Poverty Bay men to return with him and attack Te Kooti, but most of them had had enough of it, and were exhausted by the rough marching and the want of food. He therefore halted to await reinforcements, consisting chiefly of No. 1 Division Armed Constabulary, under Major Fraser, and a new body of volunteers to be organized by Biggs and Westrup.

The operations of a hastily organized body of volunteers, *pakeha* and Maori, from Wairoa will now be described. Soon after Te Kooti's landing, Captain Deighton, R.M., was holding a Court at Wairoa, accompanied by Mr. (now Captain) G. A. Preece, his interpreter, who had seen service as a volunteer in the East Cape and Upper Wairoa fighting in 1865. The first news of the Chatham Island rising was brought by a messenger, who came in with a brief note to Mr. Deighton from Captain Briggs, stating that he was at Whareongaonga and asking for assistance. The old chief Ihaka Whanga had arrived in Wairoa, and he offered to gather his men from various settlements and wait at Te Mahanga until ammunition could be brought from Wairoa. Some months previously Major Fraser with No. 1 Division Armed Constabulary had been sent from Wairoa to Opotiki to assist Major St. John in that district against Eru Tamaikowha and the Ngai-Tama and Urewera, and Wairoa was left defenceless; only one man had been left in charge of stores and arms and ammunition.

Captain Deighton and Mr. Preece at once went to get ammunition, sending the Maori messenger back to Captain Biggs to inform him of what they were doing and of Ihaka Whanga's plans. Mr. Preece was sent with a small party taking packhorses laden with ammunition for the friendly Maoris. Travelling all night, they reached Te Mahanga early next morning. The party was just about to start when a messenger arrived with a letter from Captain Biggs to Captain Deighton, reporting that the enemy had escaped through his lines during the night and were moving across country towards the head of Te Arai Valley, and asking the Magistrate to get a force together at Wairoa to intercept the Maoris at Te Reinga or Waihau lakes. After consulting with Ihaka Whanga, Mr. Preece decided to return to Wairoa at once to assist Captain Deighton in organizing a party. At Wairoa the chiefs were called together, and it was arranged that Paora Apatu with a hundred men should start next day. Meanwhile some twenty old Military Settlers from Lieut.-Colonel Fraser's disbanded force were got together under Mr. Clement Saunders, a former member of the Colonial Defence Force Cavalry, who had just joined a Volunteer corps as lieutenant, and twenty picked Maoris under Mr. Preece. The little force set out late that afternoon and reached Opoiti the same night, then pushing on to Whenuakura, where Ngati-Kowhatu (former rebels), under their chief Te Rakiroa, had been allowed to settle. When these people were informed of the escape of the Chatham Island prisoners they pretended that they had heard nothing of it; afterwards it was concluded that Te Kooti had communicated with them.

It was decided to scout towards Hangaroa next day and await the arrival of the Wairoa natives. That night Lieutenant F. J. Gascoyne arrived with despatches for Captain Deighton, and getting a fresh horse rode on to Wairoa. He said he had heard firing in the direction of Paparatu. Captain Richardson soon arrived with Paora Apatu and the promised hundred Maoris and four European volunteers. Lieutenant Gascoyne returned and went on to Poverty Bay.

The advance-party under Richardson and Preece moved on, in wild wintry weather, and at the second crossing of the Hangaroa met Lieutenant Wilson, of Poverty Bay, and a Maori named Netana. Wilson had been out scouting the tracks, and he brought instructions to Richardson from Biggs to return to Whenuakura.

Accordingly the force marched on the back trail. Towards evening of this day (24th July) Te Kooti's force, many of the men mounted, was observed advancing along the Ahimanu Range, above Waihau lakes. Richardson's small force—he had only thirty or forty men with him at this time—was soon hotly engaged in the position on Te Koneke ridge. Among those in the advance-party were Mr. Saunders, Mr. John Carroll (elder brother of Sir James Carroll), Dr. M. Scott (of Wairoa), and Tom Marsh. The few Maoris present—good picked men—were commanded by Karaitiana Roto-a-Tara and Ahitana. (Both these fine young chiefs of Ngati-Kahungunu were afterwards treacherously murdered at Whataroa.)

The main body of the friendly natives from Wairoa had not appeared, and an expected force of Mahia Maoris, under the staunch old Ihaka Whanga, did not arrive in time for the fight. Richardson and Preece and their gallant few engaged their foe spiritedly, but it was soon realized that the position was hopeless. The range, however, was held until nearly dark. The Hauhaus now worked up along the gullies on either side, and as there were not sufficient men to oppose this flanking movement a retreat was ordered. Ammunition was failing, and the small force was without rations. A rearguard action was fought, and Richardson skilfully extricated his force by sending the less active and experienced men on first to cross the gully in rear while the commander and Preece, Carroll, Karaitiana, and a few other good shots kept up an accurate fire on the Hauhaus. The first party, on reaching the next hill, now halted and opened fire, enabling the brave little rearguard to cross the valley under cover of their rifles. In this way an orderly retreat was carried out, with the loss of only one man, one of Karaitiana's Maoris, who fell early in the fight with a broken thigh and had to be left on the field; another native had his hand blown off by the accidental explosion of his rifle. The force reached Mangapoike that night and camped there, and next day marched back to Wairoa. It was afterwards ascertained that the Hauhaus had suffered eight casualties. One of their mounted scouts was captured at the beginning of the action. It was only the good work of the few sharpshooters and the approach of darkness that saved the little band from destruction. The locality of this engagement, Te Kooti's second success, was on the proper left (east) side of the Wairoa River, a short distance eastward of the Reinga Falls, at the junction of the Ruakituri and Hangaroa Rivers. The present Township of Tiniroto is about two miles to the north.

At this time Lieutenant Gascoyne, accompanied by Dr. Scott, made another gallant ride with despatches, taking a message from Mr. Deighton, the Magistrate at Wairoa, to Colonel Whitmore at Te Arai, and also a report as to Captain Richardson's whereabouts. On the track Gascoyne and Scott met Paku Brown, a half-caste, carrying a despatch from Whitmore to Richardson. Half an hour after they met him Brown was intercepted by Te Kooti's men, and was shot and tomahawked; his little dog was also shot. The despatch-carrier's remains were found near the track at Pukewhenua a few days later by Colonel Whitmore's force on the march to Ruakituri.

The next engagement with Te Kooti, one still more unfortunate for the Government forces, was fought on the 8th August on the Ruakituri River, a short distance above the present crossing on the mountain-road from Waikare-moana to Poverty Bay. The two preliminary successes had brought the rebel leader many recruits, among them Te Rakiroa, the chief of the Ngati-Kowhatu, at Whenuakura, who had recently been armed by the Government, with some of his people. He deserted to the rebels during the fight on Te Koneke ridge, saying he was going for a drink of water. Te Kooti's line of march was across the high forested range between the Hangaroa and Ruakituri branches of the Wairoa River, and thence up the Ruakituri Valley in the direction of Te Papuni. There was an ancient hill fort called Puketapu ("Holy Hill") overlooking the dry shingle bed of the olden Lake Papuni, and there the leader designed to establish himself. His march was slow, with several halts at small settlements, and Whitmore therefore was able to overtake him while he was making his way up the rocky Ruakituri. Whitmore's force consisted of about two hundred men, of whom half were the Napier Division of Armed Constabulary, and some volunteers and Maoris; the other half were Poverty Bay volunteers and Maoris. The weather was bitterly cold, with rain and snow, and the rivers were flooded, and the march to the Hangaroa was toilsome in the extreme. At the Hangaroa the European volunteers from Poverty Bay declined to go farther, informing the Colonel that they had reached the boundary of the district in which they were liable for military service. Whitmore therefore left these men to take charge of the horses and camp gear near the Waihau lakes, while he pushed on in pursuit of Te Kooti. On the morning of the 6th August he crossed the force over the Hangaroa in canoes, and followed hard on the Hauhaus' trail through the fern. The force now totalled 118, of whom 76 were Europeans, most of them Hawke's Bay men.

On the 8th the force was well up the gorge-like valley of the Ruakituri, and the advance-guard led by Mr. Davis Canning, a gallant settler from Hawke's Bay, was hot on the trail of the Hauhaus, who were heard shooting pigeons in the distance. Early in the afternoon Captain Carr (Hawke's Bay), who had been an officer in the Royal Artillery, reconnoitred through the bush along the river-bank, and reported that the Hauhaus were halted a short distance up the river. The swift and ice-cold river was forded several times and the European and Maori force advanced to the attack. Captain (afterwards Colonel) Herrick with part of the force moved on to take the Hauhaus in flank and reverse, and when his men were in position Whitmore directed the advance-guard to push forward. It was soon driven back, leaving both Canning and Carr dead on the field. The former was shot dead while gallantly leading the men. Whitmore moved quickly forward and recovered the ground; but the Hauhaus were now retiring through the thick forest, and night was coming on. There were several wounded, and it took sixteen men, eight on each side, to steady each bearer of a wounded man in crossing the rapid river. Whitmore lamented the approach of night, which prevented further pursuit; but the hardships of the winter marching had told severely on the men, and they were not in fit condition for the bush chase; moreover, they were quite without food. The return march to the camp occupied all night. Lieutenant Gascoyne came to the rescue near the Hangaroa with four packhorses loaded with provisions from Turanganui, and the force encamped at Whenuakura. Major Fraser, who had been on the Hangaroa with his No. 1 Division Armed Constabulary, was sent to Wairoa with the Wairoa men, and the Gisborne volunteers marched home. The wounded, including Captain A. Tuke, who was shot through the shoulder, were sent to the Wairoa. Whitmore himself, after soundly scolding the Poverty Bay men, rode in to Turanganui, and left for Wellington in the steamer "Sturt"; he was presently engaged in reorganizing the defences on the West Coast.

In the meantime Captain Richardson and Mr. Preece, with a party of picked Europeans and natives, and a few Mohaka volunteers under Ensign Lavin (afterwards killed in the Mohaka massacre, 1869), marched to Opoiti and scouted thence to Te Reinga and Whenuakura. The latter place was found deserted. It was afterwards discovered that Te Kooti's party and Rakiroa's men were then at Pukewhenua, some four miles away. The weather being terribly bad and all the river flooded, and no news having been received from Poverty Bay, Captain Richardson decided to fall back on Wairoa. On the night of the 5th or 6th August a mounted man named Munu arrived with a despatch from Colonel Whitmore, at Pukewhenua, to Captain Richardson, stating that he was pushing on in Te Kooti's trail, and instructing Richardson to move up to Whenuakura with as many men as he could get, bringing packhorses with provisions and ammunition, and to follow his (Whitmore's) route. Lieutenant Preece, who knew the country well, advised Captain Richardson not to go via Whenuakura, but to move up the Mangaaruhe Valley by way of Te Tuhi, striking the Ruakituri higher up, and thus cutting off an angle and saving more than a day's march. Richardson, however, said he must carry out the orders as given. Accordingly a picked force of whites and Maoris, about seventy men, moved up on the 7th August to Opoiti, reaching Whenuakura next day. Constable Solomon Black (who afterwards won the New Zealand Cross at Ngatapa) had been sent on, following up Whitmore's track, with a depatch for the Colonel informing him that the reinforcements with provisions and ammunition were moving up.

On the morning of the 9th a very early start was made from Whenuakura, and at about 3 p.m., as the force was descending towards the Ruakituri, it was met by about thirty of the Ngati-Porou, under the chief Hotene Porourangi, who reported the engagement at Ruakituri, and stated that Lieut.-Colonel Fraser with the Armed Constabulary Force, and the Hawke's Bay natives under Mr. F. E. Hamlin and Urupene, were moving back on Wairoa via Te Tuhi with the wounded men, and that Colonel Whitmore would return to Poverty Bay via Whenuakura next day. Captain Richardson then fell back on Whenuakura, having rationed Hotene's men and left further provisions for Colonel Whitmore. Had the advice of Mr. Preece and the natives been acted on by Captain Richardson, and had the force marched via Te Tuhi, so saving a day, Colonel Whitmore would have had a reinforcement of seventy men before engaging with Te Kooti, and would have had a fresh supply of provisions and ammunition. Richardson's force could have caught up to him at Erepeti, where he camped on the night on the 7th August.

The European losses at the Ruakituri were six killed and five wounded. Among the Hauhau casualties were Te Kooti himself; he was wounded in the foot. He made good his retreat to Puketapu, where he rested and recruited his strength in a fortified camp, and gathered in many warriors from the surrounding tribes, including the brothers Te Waru from the Upper Wairoa, some of the Rongo-whakaata people, and many Urewera from the mountain villages of the interior. Now well supplied with food, arms, and ammunition, and with between three and four hundred fighting-men at his command, he laid his plans for a surprise descent upon the plains and a raid of vengeance on his foes in the Poverty Bay settlements.

Early in October Karaitiana Roto-a-Tara, the young chief already mentioned as having distinguished himself in the fight at Te Koneke, was sent up the Wairoa with his comrade Ahitana and two other men to visit Whataroa (or Erepeti), Te Waru's village, and gather what news they could about Te Kooti's movements. The older Te Waru was absent, with his son Tipene (the one who had lost an arm at Orakau)—they had joined Te Kooti—but Reihana te Waru entertained the four scouts, and gave them food and a sleeping-hut. In the middle of the night Reihana, his sister, and others stole into the *whare* and killed the sleeping men with tomahawks. Karaitiana's heart was cut out and was taken by Reihana to Waikare-moana, where it was offered to the war-god Tu with the ancient Maori ceremonials, and was deposited at the *tuahu* or sacred altar of Whakaari *pa,* on the northern shore of the lake. When Te Kooti visited the *pa* some time later he ordered the heart and *tuahu* on which it was placed to be destroyed.* Te Waru and Reihana afterwards (1870) surrendered to Captain Preece at Horomanga, on the Rangitaiki side of the Urewera Country, and were exiled to Waiotahe. Neither of them dared return to Whataroa, where they would have been attacked by Karaitiana's people in revenge for the murder.

Mr. Donald McLean, Government Agent at Napier, had arranged for two hundred Ngati-Porou, under Ropata and Hotene Porourangi, to come down from Waiapu to Wairoa, and for a large contingent of Hawke's Bay Maoris, under Tareha, Henare Tomoana, and other chiefs, to move on from Wairoa to Te Kooti's stronghold at Puketapu. The combined force was under Captain Tuke, who was accompanied by Captain Bower (in charge of stores and ammunition) and Lieutenants Ferguson and Preece, with about forty Armed Constabulary. The column left Wairoa on the 27th October via the Waiau River instead of the usual track by way of Mangaaruhe, the idea being to attack the rebels in flank if the settlement was fortified. The force was well up the Waiau Valley towards Whataroa when, to the surprise of all, Colonel Lambert (who had been sent to Wairoa to take charge of the district) overtook them and assumed command. Marching all night, the force reached Whataroa next morning and captured one old man and a woman. They stated that Te Waru and all his people had joined Te Kooti, that Puketapu had been abandoned, and that Te Kooti was moving on Poverty Bay. The bodies of the murdered scouts were exhumed. It was seen that all had been tomahawked, and that Karaitiana's heart had been cut out. A scouting-party went to Orewha, overlooking Erepeti and the nearest point towards Puketapu, but could see no fires in that direction.

Ropata and Hotene strongly urged Colonel Lambert to move on, but he said the country they had to go through gave the

---

* A grandson of this brave chief Karaitiana Roto-a-Tara was a sergeant in the Great War, and was awarded the Military Medal for services in France.

enemy every advantage for laying ambuscades, and that severe loss might result. Ropata's retort was: "We do not expect to return with the same number of men with which we started." Lambert then held a consultation with the European officers, who all favoured the advance. The Colonel, however, ordered otherwise; and, after remaining a day, the column returned to the Wairoa via Orewha and Mangaaruhe, reaching Wairoa about the 3rd November. A despatch was sent by the mailman on the coast road to Major Biggs at Poverty Bay. Had the force gone on from Whataroa to Puketapu it would have found Te Kooti's *pa* abandoned, and could have followed his well-defined cut trail towards Poverty Bay. Thus he would have been attacked unexpectedly from his rear, and the terrible massacre at Matawhero would have been averted.

Chapter 26

WHITMORE'S DEFEAT AT MOTUROA

THE REPULSE AT Te Ngutu-o-te-manu, the loss of valuable officers, and the disgust in the ranks at the mismanagement of the expedition had reduced McDonnell's field force to a state of disorganization and semi-mutiny. Many good men left the force in disgust; the Wanganui Kupapas returned to their homes strongly impressed by Titokowaru's *mana,* and the troops remaining in Taranaki were so weakened that it became imperative to shorten the front, and in the end to withdraw from the occupied country north of Patea. McDonnell's reverse, with its train of misfortunes for the Government cause on the West Coast, seriously embarrassed the Ministry in power (Mr. Stafford's Cabinet), which was hard put to it not only for funds, but for men to serve in the field. McDonnell resigned, after withdrawing the whole of the force to Patea, but fortunately a good soldier was found to take his place, a man of energy and initiative, with a professional training which McDonnell lacked. This was Colonel George Whitmore, who had arrived from the scene of the first operations against Te Kooti on the East Coast. There was some slight skirmishing before McDonnell gave up the command, and the Hauhaus spread over the country, menacing the communications and cutting off stragglers. Waihi and Manawapou camps were abandoned in September, and the redoubt at Kakaramea was also evacuated.

An incident of the withdrawal to Patea from the plains was a skirmish at Turangarere, near Manutahi, complicated by two Government detachments firing on each other. A force of sixty men, under Captain Smith, was on the way from Patea to Manawapou to shift the camp stores, while a down convoy of about fifty was advancing from the opposite direction. The detachment from Patea sighted a body of armed Maoris on Turangarere Hill; the Hauhaus were coming down to burn the bridge over one of the streams. The Maoris fell back firing, and just then the convoy from Manawapou arrived, and, mistaking the Patea detachment for Maoris, shot and killed one of them. Describing the affair William Wallace (ex-sergeant No. 2

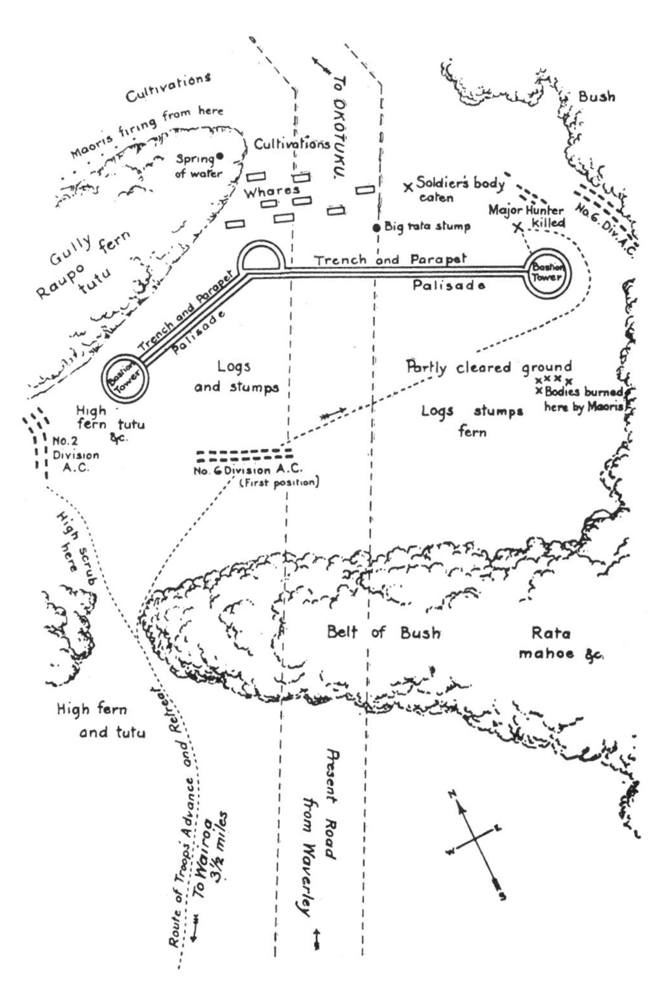

J. Cowan, sketch-plan, 1921]

The Battlefield of Moturoa

This plan of the scene of the Moturoa or Papa-tihakehake engagement (1868) shows the site of the Maori stockade, as described on the ground by Tu-Patea te Rongo, who fought there on the Hauhau side. Other map details were furnished by Colonel Roberts, N.Z.C., and Mr. William Wallace.

Division A.C.) said: "I was in Captain Smith's company from Patea. The Maoris fell back from the crest of Turangarere as we advanced, and while they did so and while we were ascending the gentle southern slope of the hill the Manawapou convoy was approaching from the opposite side. Our advance-parties suddenly sighted each other and opened fire, and we were also under the Maori fire. Our leading man was Smith, one of Von Tempsky's veterans, and as soon as he reached the brow of the hill he was shot in mistake. Each force of troops thought the other was a Maori war-party. As for the Hauhaus themselves, they were on our right front; we gradually drove them back, and went through to Manawapou. That day the Hauhaus burned down the *whare* of Mr. Maxwell, a settler in the district."

At Kakaramea the Hauhaus came down and attacked the redoubt built there after the attack on Turuturu-mokai. They fired heavily into the place at night. The flashes of the guns were seen at Patea camp, and rockets were sent up, a prearranged signal system, asking whether the Kakaramea garrison was in need of help. The reply, with rockets, was that no assistance was required. When the post was abandoned the Kakaramea Hotel was burned.

It became necessary for the outlying military settlers to come into Patea, and the abandoned huts of the pioneers, like some of the redoubts, were speedily burned by the Hauhaus. One man was cut off. This was Alexander McCulloch, who was mate with another military settler, R. B. Hamilton, of Manawapou. When William Wallace, Hamilton, and other soldier settlers abandoned their farms in October, 1868, and the troops left the district, McCulloch did not come in. Long afterwards the story of his death was gathered from the Maoris. He was chased, and hid in the *raupo* swamp below Turangarere Hill.* The Hauhaus

---

* Turangarere Hill, the scene of the convoy affair, is on the Patea-Hawera Road, about two miles from Manutahi. Below it on the north is Flaxbridge Creek, so called because in the pioneer days bundles of flax were thrown into the small creek as fascines for a crossing. It was at this swampy creek, a little way seaward of the road, that the Maoris poured a volley into the *raupo* and killed the settler "Sandy" McCulloch, who was hiding there.

The old-fashioned wayside hotel at Kakaramea close to the stock saleyards—a great gathering-place for farmers on cattle-sale days—stands on the site of the first hotel, which was burned down by the Hauhaus in 1868, when the troops evacuated the coast. On the crest of the hill about 250 yards in rear of the hotel are the grassed-over traces of the Constabulary redoubt. A boxthorn hedge now runs across part of the redoubt-works on the crown of the hill. The place from which the Hauhaus came and fired into the camp at night is the hill north-east of the redoubt, and 500 or 600 yards distant, near the present road leading inland from Kakaramea. They threw up a breastwork on the hill.

searched, but could not find him. They discovered his two dogs and shot them. McCulloch when he heard the shots could not resist crying out in his place of concealment among the reeds, and a volley was fired into the *raupo*. He was crouching with only his nose and mouth above the surface of the water. The volley killed him, but the Maoris could not find his body, and it was long afterwards that his bones were discovered in the swamp.

Colonel Whitmore, on assuming command at Patea, set vigorously to work to reorganize the small force at his disposal. The levies from Wellington and Nelson took their discharge and went home; Von Tempsky's division (No. 5) had been disbanded, and all that was left as a nucleus of a new field force were No. 1 Division A.C. from Napier, fifty strong, and the remnants of Nos. 2 and 3 Divisions. Titokowaru had abandoned Te Ngutu-o-te-manu and marched south, gathering the Pakakohi and Ngati-Hine Tribes as he advanced, and after a stay at Otoia *pa* crossed the Patea River and established himself in a new camp which presently became the objective of Whitmore's attack. There was a preliminary demonstration at Otoia on the 21st October; a newly raised contingent of Wanganui Maoris marched out, and some Armstrong shells were thrown at the Hauhaus on their hill post at a range of 1,200 yards.

Whitmore got rid of all the irregular troops, resolving to work only in future with enlisted men, and he urged the Government that in future all recruits should be enrolled in the Armed Constabulary and not as temporary volunteers.

At the beginning of November it was discovered that Titokowaru with his conquering Tekau-ma-rua had reached the Waitotara River, gathering in the Hauhaus of the Nga-Rauru Tribe as his followers, and that the settlers on the lower part of the river had narrowly escaped slaughter. Whitmore thereupon transferred his heaquarters to Wairoa (now the Town of Waverley) with all the available Armed Constabulary (only seventy at that date) and some Patea Volunteers, besides some Kupapas. His object was to prevent Titokowaru making raids into the settled districts south of the Waitotara. At Wairoa the settlers had enrolled in a corps of militia and built a good redoubt. The Wairoa company numbered about sixty, under Captain Hawes. This officer, who became of great service to Whitmore because of his knowledge of the country, reported that Titokowaru had now fixed his camp at Moturoa ("Long Bush"), between three and four miles inland of Wairoa, on the level land below Okotuku Hill, the scene of an engagement in 1866 in General Chute's campaign. The Colonel determined to attack at once before the Hauhaus had time to erect a strong fortification.

Recruits for the Armed Constabulary were now coming in, and a newly raised company, No. 6 Division, 100 men, arrived at Wairoa on the 6th November, coming up late in the afternoon when Whitmore had decided upon an attack before daybreak next morning. The Colonel was greatly pleased with the appearance and eager spirit of the new division, and with the captain in command, J. M. Roberts, who had distinguished himself on the retreat from Te Ngutu-o-te-manu three months previously. Roberts's division were mostly young fellows from Auckland and the Thames goldfields, with a number of men who had already seen service. "The Young Brigade," as it came to be called, was ready for action in spite of the sea voyage and the long hot march, but Whitmore told Roberts that as his men were tired from their march he would want them only as a "moral support" on the expedition against Moturoa. As it happened, No. 6 was called upon to take a leading part in the operations.

At midnight, in misty, showery weather, the attacking column marched from Wairoa inland in the direction of Moturoa and Okotuku. Whitmore's force consisted of detachments of Nos. 1, 2, 3, and 6 Divisions of Armed Constabulary, some Patea Rifles, Patea Cavalry (dismounted), Wairoa Militia, and a contingent of Wanganui Maoris under Captain Kepa te Rangihiwinui. The European portion of the force numbered about two hundred and fifty; there were some three hundred Wanganui Maoris, but only seventy of these, under Kepa, entered the fight. Shortly before daylight (7th November) the Colonel halted about three miles from the camp, on rising ground outside the bush called Moturoa, and directed Captain Hawes to use his Militia in throwing up a small earthwork as a protection if the force was compelled to retire and to form a reserve to guard the ammunition. The force left blankets and haversacks at this point, and then moved on cautiously towards the bush. No. 6 Division, carrying ammunition, was to have remained there, but was now required in the bush operations.

The road entered the bush and high *tutu* scrub by a cleared bullock-track 12 feet wide. This tract of timber was a narrow belt of tall bush, largely *rata,* extending like a long tongue from the forest on the east—the right flank of the advance—towards the Kohi Valley on the west, and masking the partly cleared ground on which the Maori camp was built. The terrain was the watershed between the Kohi Stream (which flows into the Whenuakura) and the Mou-mahaki (a tributary of the Waitotara). A very short distance separates the valleys of the two rivers at this place. On the left flank as the troops marched out to Moturoa the wooded valley of the Kohi was skirted, and as the Hauhau position was approached the deep precipitous gorge of the Ngutu-wera opened up on the left front. A small wooded gully, where a little watercourse has its source, was in the right rear of the Maori camp, and a level expanse of forest land spread out on the right. In rear again, about a mile away, was the high wooded tableland of Okotuku.

The Maori fortifications were in an incomplete state when the attack was delivered, and had the place been reconnoitred properly beforehand the issue might have been very different. One of Titokowaru's warriors, Tu-Patea te Rongo, describing on the spot the details of the battle, said:—

"I helped to build this *pa,* which after the battle became known as Papa-tihakehake, because of the events on the battle-ground, when the place was strewn with the dead Europeans. Before it was constructed we had a temporary settlement here with some potato cultivations. Our war-leader, Titokowaru, came down from Te Putahi and inspected the village, which stood yonder, just on the edge of the gully. He had a foreboding that we would be attacked here by the soldiers, and he ordered us to fortify the place and protect our large cultivations, because he said he was sure the *pakeha* scouts would find us sooner or later. So we set to work—felled and split timber and dug trenches, and made earthworks. We had been at work four days when we were attacked, and did not have time to finish the fortifications. We had only one side done, besides three *taumaihi* (towers or redoubts), one in the elbow of the work and one at each corner. The palisade on the south side was the only line finished; the second stockade of timbers on this line had not been completed when the troops found our retreat. The *pa* was not closed in; the stockade erected commenced above the gully on the west, running east to this roadway, and then turning slightly and continuing towards the edge of the standing bush. The length was about 5 chains."

The front of the *pa* presented a concave face to the approaching attackers; some of those who reached the place described it as roughly half-moon in shape. The western wing of the stockade was about 2 chains in length, and the main line 3 chains, extending towards the thick belt of forest on the east. (The line of this main defence is now intersected at right angles by the road which runs north-north-east towards Okotuku.) In rear of the defences were the *nikau* and fern-tree huts of the Hauhaus, with their cultivations on either side of the head of the gully. The stockade for the greater part was a single fence, built of heavy split timbers and whole tree-trunks, set 3 or 4 feet in the ground and standing 12 feet high. Within this palisade was a trench 6 feet wide and 6 feet deep, with traverses and fire-step and a parapet. At each end of the stockading and in the angle

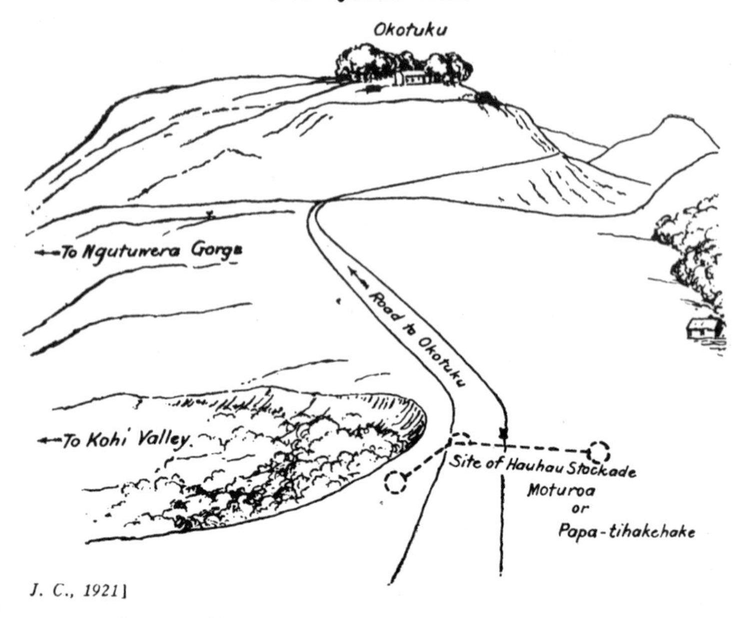

Sketch of the Moturoa Battlefield

Okotuku, on the high ground looking north from Moturoa, was the scene of fighting in 1866, when Major-General Chute's force captured a Maori position. (See page 62.)

where the two wings joined, a strong *taumaihi* or redoubt-like tower had been erected, an item of defence partly borrowed from the design of *pakeha* redoubts; this kind of bastion was afterwards used in the building of Tauranga-ika *pa*. Each *taumaihi* was a small fort in itself. Tu-Patea described it as roughly circular in figure, built of earth and layers of fern in the usual manner of field-works; it was about 15 feet in diameter and 20 feet in height. Timber ladder-ways gave access to the top, and the sides were palisaded and loopholed. Each of these small redoubts would hold about twenty men, and could be used both as watch-tower and as citadel. It was reached by a covered way from the main trench. The *taumaihi* at the eastern end was held by the Ngati-Hine Tribe; their principal warrior was Paraone Tutere, an experienced old fighter and a good shot. The middle tower was garrisoned by the Tangahoe men, and the south-west one, just above the edge of the gully, by Ngati-Ruanui. The *whares* and food-stores of the garrison were grouped on the bank of the gully near this spot.

We return now to Whitmore's attacking column, which advanced at grey dawn along the avenue through the bush and took cover behind logs and stumps and in the edge of the bush, waiting for the order to charge. Whitmore detached No. 1 Division and the contingent of Wanganui Kupapas under Kepa to move round to the right of the *pa,* directing them to get close up to the palisade and attack it on that flank while the main body assaulted in front. No. 6 followed the other divisions after a short halt outside. Roberts was at the edge of the bush with his "Young Brigade" when Major Hunter passed him with his division detailed for the storming of the *pa.* As Hunter passed he said to Roberts, "Follow me up like the devil!". No. 6 was at first extended on the left, but quickly was in the thick of the assault. A signal had been arranged when Kepa and No. 1 Divisions were in position on the right.

Meanwhile the defenders of Moturoa were on the alert. Their sentries were in the *taumaihi* before dawn, and that hero of many fights Katene Tu-whakaruru, was the first to catch sight of Whitmore's advance-guard as it emerged from the bush. It was a damp, misty morning, and the figures were indistinctly seen moving from tree to tree and sinking down into cover. Katene quietly warned his comrades, and in a very few moments the trench and *taumaihi* were crowded with warriors, waiting with death-like silence for the soldiers' charge.

Whitmore, crouching behind a stump at the edge of the ragged clearing, noticed that no dogs barked, and that there was no sign of the women moving to collect firewood as was customary in a Maori *kainga* in the early morning; and other officers shrewdly surmised that the Hauhaus had been forewarned. Kepa and his men (fifty Wanganui natives, besides twenty-five of No. 1 A.C.) were on the edge of the clearing on the extreme right of the *pa,* where the long palisade could be seen extending westward to the broken ground. In front of the *pa* and on the right the ground was covered with low fern and with stumps and burnt logs; on the left there was a tangled tract of low bush on the edge of the gully.

At last the signal for the assault was given, and Major Hunter rushed for the palisades with his storming-party of fifty Armed Constabulary (No. 3) and some of the Patea men. Hunter, who was determined to refute the unjust aspersions cast on his soldierly honour after Turuturu-mokai, had requested the duty of leading this forlorn hope. The Maoris waited until the first of the stormers were within 10 or 12 yards of the stockade, and then opened fire in a thunderous volley. The whole front of the *pa* blazed. "I never saw the like of that sheet of fire," said a survivor of the party. "Men went down all round me." Whitmore

Major Kepa (Kemp) te Rangihiwinui, N.Z.C.

Kepa, who was Captain of the Wanganui native contingent in the Battle of Moturoa, was awarded the New Zealand Cross for his gallantry. He was the best of the Wanganui Maori soldiers who fought on the Government side, 1865–70, and was regarded by his *pakeha* fellow-officers as an able and skilful leader. He was one of several native officers who received swords of honour from Queen Victoria.

was with the stormers. Hunter, seeking a likely spot to enter the work, ran on past the front of the palisade and had just passed the eastern angle when he was shot down by Paraone Tutere from the *taumaihi* which formed the bastion at that end of the unfinished fortification. Others fell before the fire of the well-hidden Hauhaus, and soon there were a dozen men lying dead or wounded on the bullet-swept open ground. Kepa did not get far towards the rear, and returned to Hunter's help; several of his men were hit in the close-quarters firing at this point.

Roberts with his No. 6 Division now came up in support. When he was waiting for the word to charge in, the young commander formed up his men and said to them, "Now, when you see me do that," and he held up his carbine, "you all follow me, and every man for himself till you get across to the other side—don't look behind you!" The word was given, and No. 6 ran the gauntlet of the Hauhau fire across the open ground and reached the eastern end of the stockade. The men dropped to cover behind logs and stumps and were at once hotly engaged, holding the position after the stormers had been repulsed.

The fighting on the right flank was now fierce and deadly. Hunter had been shot in a vital place, the femoral artery, and it was impossible to stanch the wound. He was only 8 or 10 feet from the stockade corner when he fell, just in the act of turning to the nearest men to bid them take cover. He died very soon after being carried off and laid under a *mahoe* tree. The rescue of his body from the Maori tomahawks was a gallant deed. Several men were wounded in the attempt, but Captain Gudgeon, Privates Kelly and Foote, and one or two others succeeded in getting him clear of the palisades.

Whitmore soon came to the conclusion—a quite erroneous one—that the *pa* was too strong to be taken, and he ordered a retirement. This was carried out with judgment and gallantry, and more than one New Zealand Cross was earned that day.

When the bugle sounded the "Retire" the Maoris left the shelter of their stockade and fire-trenches and charged out to skirmish with their foes in the open. One Hauhau was shot down—the natives declare that he was the only man of the defenders who was killed that day—after a desperate rush on the troops with his tomahawk. This was an old tattooed savage, Te Waka-taparuru; he leaped right over the palisade from the inner parapet and dashed on his foes in a fit of *whakamomori* (recklessness). Here, as at Te Ngutu-o-te-manu, the battle-rite of the *whangai-hau* was observed. The body of the second Constabulary man killed—shot by Pikirapu, of Ngati-Hine—was lying close to the stockade at the eastern bastion. The young warrior Tihirua (otherwise Te Rangi-puaweawe) rushed out with his tomahawk, and making three great cuts in the dead man's breast thrust in his hand and tore out the heart. This was the *mawe* of the battlefield. At his waist, buckled to the flax girdle, was a leather pouch, such as was generally used for carrying percussion caps; in this he had some matches. Tu-Patea te Rongo described the ceremony which followed:—

"I saw Tihirua light a match and hold it underneath the

slain soldier's heart, which he held up in his left hand. As the flame of the match singed the heart the *paoa* (smoke) rose into the air. The old man Tu-mahuki, who had rushed out with Tihirua, watched this intently, for it was a divinement to determine the issue of the battle. The smoke rose and drifted out from the *pa* in the direction of the soldiers. Then Tu-mahuki cried 'Kokiri!' ('Charge!') and we all rushed out and engaged the *pakehas* in the open. Had the smoke of the burnt sacrifice been blown towards the stockade it would have been an evil omen for us; the fort would have fallen to the enemy. There was very little wind, but what there was sent the *paoa* towards the soldiers, and by that token we knew that we should be the victors. Tihirua, his divination ended, cast the human heart away to one side as a *taumahatanga,* a sacred offering to the gods. After Tihirua's ceremony we charged determinedly upon the enemy. We skirmished with them in the bush, and I shot five men there that day."

After holding the position on the east flank of the *pa* until the wounded had been carried off through the bush, Nos. 1 and 6 Divisions retired in excellent order, fighting a hard rearguard action. No. 1, as Whitmore reported, retired through the bush with great regularity and order, and then No. 6 covered the retreat. Each division halted in turn and kept the Maoris in check while the others withdrew through it. Colonel Roberts, describing this operation, said: "I came across Goring there; he fought well that day. I said to him, 'You try this billet for a change.' 'All right, mate,' replied Goring, in his drawling way, and he coolly and competently commanded his division in turn in holding the rear." Colonel Whitmore in his account praised Roberts and his young soldiers for their share of the operation: "No. 6, retiring skirmishing, was now attacked by the enemy almost all along the line, and nearly hand-to-hand. Through the jungle the voice of the gallant commander rang out continually, 'Be steady, my men, stick together,' and each time a cheery reply, 'We will, sir,' might have been heard in answer from the 'Young Division.'"

Meanwhile on the west flank a small detachment of No. 2 Division, all of them veterans of either colonial or Imperial service, were engaged in sharp fighting with a considerable body of Hauhaus outside the *pa.* This part of the day's work was described on the battlefield (1921) by one of the survivors, Mr.
Meanwhile on the west flank a small detachment of No. 2
Division. He said:—

"When we marched out from Wairoa a detachment of us, numbering twenty-two, under Captain George McDonnell and Sergeant Bassett, was sent off to the left flank to engage the

Mr. William Wallace, a Veteran of Moturoa

William Wallace (who was the son of an Imperial soldier) served from 1865 to 1869 in the colonial forces, and fought in some of the heaviest actions of the Hauhau wars. He was a sergeant in No. 2 Division, Armed Constabulary, at the close of the campaign. His narrative of the Moturoa engagement is given in this chapter.

Maoris on that side (near the west end of the *pa,* above the gully). The object was to keep the Hauhaus from working round through the gully on that side and outflanking us. We had some hot fighting there. We fired across the fern and *tutu* that filled the valley. Whenever we saw a puff of smoke we fired at the spot, and the Hauhaus kept up a fire as sharp as ours. I never saw the *pa* at all that day; we were quite close to it, but some bush and scrub intervened: our special job kept us quite busy enough. Our officer and the sergeant left us early in the action and joined the rest of the force, and we were left there long after the retreat of the main body began. We were quite without orders, so had to carry on the fight to the best of our own judgment. Corporal Talty took charge of us —he was the senior non-com. left—and he deserved the New Zealand Cross for his gallant and skilful work that day. Talty was a veteran Irish soldier, late of the 57th Regiment, with

Crimean and Indian Mutiny service. He had fought in the bush battle at Te Ngutu-o-te-manu after joining the colonial force. Our small detachment of No. 2 Division was a picked body of men; all of us had seen a good deal of service, and several were old Imperial soldiers. The lance-corporals beside myself were R. B. Hamilton (now of Manawapou) and George Cooper (who died recently in Auckland); the constables (privates) included Anderson and Savage (missing), M. Gill and H. McLean (both survivors of the Turuturu-mokai defence), Stewart, John Dunn (an old Forest Ranger), Charles Timms, and Dennis Coffey (ex-57th Regiment). Captain Scannell was in command of No. 2 Division, but he was not at Moturoa. After holding the edge of the gully for a considerable time we fought our way out, and we held the edge of the bush after the rearguard had gone on; in fact, we were really the rearguard—the others did not know we were there. Corporal Talty handled us as coolly as if he were on parade. We retired by sections, each one in turn keeping the enemy engaged while the other reloaded and retired a certain distance. Of our twenty-two, about twelve, including those I have named, fought out with us at the end; most of the others had retired early. We lost Anderson and Savage on the retreat. No one knew exactly what became of them; no one saw them fall. They probably were shot, and were lost in the thick fern and scrub. If we had remained a little while longer in the bush our small detachment would have been done for, as the Maoris were nearly all round us. It was Hamilton who went out first and came back and told us the retreat had begun. As we fought our way out of the scrub and fern we were so far behind the rest that the friendly Maoris on the parapet hill (just west of the present road about three-quarters of a mile from the *pa*) made sure we were the Hauhaus and opened fire on us. The Hauhaus were now in possession of the belt of bush on our left, and they kept a close and hot fire on us, so we were under the bullets of foe and friend alike. The Hauhaus followed us towards Wairoa, and some of them burned down the settler Ritchie's *whare,* near the Mangatangi Creek (where the dam now is for the Waverley electric-light supply, three-quarters of a mile from the township). The force brought out an Armstrong field-gun from the redoubt and fired a few shells at them, and they retreated.

"I had only two rounds of ammunition left when I got out to the open, besides the one in my Terry carbine. I remember that I tried to put one of these in, thinking I'd be able to sit up and have a final smack at the Hauhaus if I was wounded, when I found my carbine already loaded. I fired close on sixty rounds in that day's fight.

"The first man shot at Moturoa was Sergeant Kirwin (No. 6 Division A.C.), who was accidentally wounded on the morning march into the bush; a comrade's Enfield rifle, carried at full cock, went off and struck him in the back of the neck. He was put on a stretcher to be carried out, but he was left in the retreat, and the Maoris got him and killed him."

No. 2 Division brought out two badly wounded men who had been left on the bush track. One of these was very gallantly recovered by Lance-Corporals Hamilton and Cooper and Private Monrod, who went back for him on hearing from a man, who ran on, that there was a wounded man down the track.

The retreat of the force emboldened the Hauhaus to follow them almost to Wairoa. When the various detachments had reached the entrenchment on the hill held by Captain Hawes, Whitmore re-formed the divisions, and ordered the commanders to retire slowly by fours along the Wairoa Road. Alternately each division from the front extended, knelt down, and prepared to relieve the rearguard as it retired skirmishing, and as each rearguard passed its relief it formed fours again and rejoined the column. Carts had been sent for to Wairoa to take away the numerous wounded. The last man wounded was one of the Wanganui Maoris who was sitting down at the parapet on the hill; the bullet (which penetrated his lungs) had been fired at Lance-Corporal Wallace, of No. 2. Captain Roberts had a narrow escape after reaching the entrenchment. An ounce bullet from one of the pursuing Maoris struck the side of the plate on the butt of his carbine, which he was carrying at the trail. The force of the blow was such that it sent him down on his knees. The Armstrong guns were brought out from the Wairoa Redoubt about three-quarters of a mile and opened fire, and most of the Hauhaus then drew off, but several daring spirits followed the troops out so far that some of their bullets fell in the redoubt.

The return of the victorious Hauhaus to their palisaded camp was a scene of terrible savage exultation. They came in dancing, yelling, shouting war-songs, and brandishing the arms and equipment of the slain soldiers. The dead Constabulary men were collected and dragged to the camp, stripped of their uniforms, and then burned in a great funeral pyre—all but one body, which was eaten. Tu-Patea te Rongo, who was in the forefront of the day's hot work, thus described that cannibal meal:—

"I saw the body of one of the soldiers cut up, cooked, and eaten. The body was hauled in behind the fence and cooked in a big *hangi*, as a sheep would be cooked. Some of our old warriors cut off the legs and part of the breast for their meal, and hung up other parts of the man-meat in a tree for future use. We young men were filled with wonder and fear when we saw the elders seated there feasting on the human flesh. There were five of them at least whom I knew—men who had previously eaten human flesh in the old Maori wars. Titokowaru did not share in this man-eating; nor would he allow those who participated in it to come near him at meal-times, for this would infringe his *tapu*. *Timoti,* of Nga-Rauru, was one of them; Tama-kanohi was another. The old tattooed *tohunga* Tautahi Ariki also ate a portion of the soldier's body. The reason why we young men did not share in this *kaitangata* meal was that we were afraid of the *wairua* (the spirits) of the dead soldiers."

It appears probable, from accounts gathered, that the body cooked and eaten was that of a young man named Kenealy, of No. 3 Division A.C.; he had been a private in Captain Palmer's Patea Rifle Volunteers, and had fought at Te Ngutu-o-te-manu. William Kelly, a veteran of No. 3, stated that he saw Kenealy fall close to the palisades in the first assualt, and the Maoris dragged him off; he was a fine young fellow of about twenty-one.

So ended the Battle of Moturoa, the worst reverse the troops had suffered in the West Coast war. It certainly was Whitmore's one great blunder. The hard-fighting little Colonel made few mistakes in the after-campaigns; Moturoa was a ghastly and effective lesson. An officer who distinguished himself in the rearguard action says: "I could never understand why we left the Maori position at Moturoa so soon. We had the day before us. We should have surrounded it and stayed there. Losing a few men was no reason for retreating; we should have stuck to it. It was bad management—you couldn't blame the men; they all behaved well. I don't know to this day why we retreated. We would not have had a better fighting-ground. We were only three miles and a half from our base; we had a good force and plenty of ammunition. It was easy country, mostly open and level, and only a little bush. Te Ngutu-o-te-manu was different; there we were far from our base in dense bush. Guns could easily have been taken in along the bullock-track through the belt of bush right up to the Moturoa clearing."

Another veteran of the engagement says: "Undoubtedly Colonel Whitmore made a great mistake in retiring from Moturoa so soon in the day. If we had to retreat we should have waited till dark. We should have stayed there. We always put the set on the Hauhaus when we stayed with them in the bush and fought it out."

Whitmore in his despatch greatly underestimated his losses. According to his account the returns showed: Killed, 5; wounded, 20; missing, 11, of whom 3 were killed. As a matter of fact, all the missing were killed. A veteran says: "My estimate of our casualties at Moturoa is thirty-three killed, wounded, and missing; the Maoris got at least a dozen of these."

Another veteran (No. 3 Division) said: "We left twenty-six men on the field at Moturoa."

Colonel W. E. Gudgeon, asked for his estimate of the casualties, said: "For the numbers engaged Moturoa was the most desperate engagement fought in the Maori War. My line of charge was on Hunter's right flank, and we had good cover, but I had two killed and five wounded out of say, forty Maoris. Whitmore's return did not give nearly our casualties. I made it at the time fifty-two out of fewer than two hundred actually engaged."

Still another estimate gives the numbers as—Killed and missing, 19; wounded, 20, including 5 Wanganui natives.

Colonel Whitmore now decided to fall back behind the Waitotara River in order to place his force between Titokowaru and the Wanganui out-settlements. Leaving No. 1 Division and some other men to defend Patea, he crossed the Waitotara and took post at Nukumaru, where he formed an entrenched camp. The Wairoa Redoubt was occupied by the local settler-volunteers, and was victualled for a month. The Weraroa Redoubt, overlooking the Waitotara, was garrisoned by fifty Militia from Wanganui.

Whitmore wrote to the Defence Minister offering to resign, but the Government decided to support him in his command. The position at this juncture was exceedingly critical. Titokowaru continued his victorious march, and commenced an elaborate fortification on the edge of the bush at Tauranga-ika, on Whitmore's front, commanding an outlook over the coast lands for many miles. Whitmore had at Nukumaru only about one hundred and sixty men, including No. 6 Division. However, recruits soon began to come in, and the Defence Minister arrived at Whitmore's headquarters, followed by a new division of Armed Constabulary, No. 7, under Sub-Inspector (Captain) Brown. The Weraroa garrison was heavily fired into at night, and the Wanganui lads under Captain Powell replied, keeping up a fire all night, and behaving with admirable coolness and confidence considering that it was their first fight. Whitmore, however, considered the redoubt not worth retaining, owing to the difficulty of keeping up communications across Titokowaru's front, and the Defence Minister (Colonel Haultain) accordingly ordered it to be evacuated. All stores that would otherwise fall into the hands of the Hauhaus were ordered to be destroyed. Fortunately for Whitmore's small force, with its untrained recruits, and for the Wanganui settlements, Titokowaru remained inactive, contenting himself for the present with making his army comfortable at Tauranga-ika.

Whitmore had increased his force at Nukumaru camp to 350, and was busy drilling the recruits, when he suddenly received (in the middle of November) imperative orders from the Defence Minister to fall back with all his troops to the south side of the Kai-iwi River, and so dispose them as to hold that line of defence. The reason for this unexpected and, in fact, astonishing order was not made known to the Colonel at the time, but he carried out the Government's instructions, and then was informed that Te Kooti and his Chatham Island escapees had raided Poverty Bay and massacred many of the inhabitants. It was necessary to take the field at once against these men, and the defence of the West Coast against Titokowaru was left to the local forces, with some Armed Constabulary and the two companies of the 18th Royal Irish Regiment in garrison at Wanganui. After assisting the settlers on the Waitotara and at Nukumaru to remove their stock and other property, Whitmore hastily arranged the defences along the Kai-iwi, ordered out all the available cavalry to communicate with Wairoa Redoubt, which was found satisfactorily garrisoned and supplied, and then prepared for the East Coast campaign. The only posts remaining under the British flag from the Wai-ngongoro to the Kai-iwi, a distance of fifty miles, were Patea and Wairoa, which commanded only the ground within range of their rifles; all the countryside, with the homes of scores of settlers, was given up to the Hauhaus.

For the patrolling of the Wanganui frontier line Whitmore placed his chief reliance on the two local Cavalry Volunteer corps, one troop under Captain Finnimore and the other (the Kai-iwi Cavalry) under Lieutenant (afterwards Captain) John Bryce. These mounted corps, largely composed of farmers and their sons, proved highly competent. Of Bryce's troop Colonel Whitmore wrote that it was "for all the duties of frontier mounted infantry absolutely perfect." John Bryce was destined to occupy a distinguished place in New Zealand politics; and in Finnimore's troop rode John Ballance, afterwards Premier of the colony. These yeomanry cavalry bodies actively scouted the border, occasionally skirmishing with Titokowaru's raiders and preventing many homesteads from being looted and burned. One of the small encounters in front of Tauranga-ika was close to Mr. John Handley's wool-shed on the flat at Nukumaru. Here some youths from the *pa,* out foraging, were engaged in killing geese when a party of the Kai-iwi Cavalry, headed by Sergeant-Major Maxwell, came down on them and sabred or shot six. A few weeks later Maxwell himself was mortally wounded under the palisades of Tauranga-ika.

On the 2nd December, 1868, Colonel Whitmore left Wanganui by steamer for Poverty Bay with 212 Armed Constabulary.

During his absence large reinforcements arrived at Wanganui, and the Armed Constabulary camp at Westmere was a scene of daily drilling in preparation for the renewal of the campaign against Titokowaru. Meanwhile an expedition northward was made by Colonel William Lyon and Lieut.-Colonel McDonnell. Lyon fired some Armstrong shells into the Tauranga-ika stockade, and then marched on to Wairoa and Patea, inspecting the garrisons and finding all well. From Patea he went up as far as Ketemarae, burning the large village at Taiporohenui on his way, and returned to the Westmere camp. McDonnell, with a force of mounted Maoris from Wanganui, visited the abandoned redoubt at Waihi and the deserted bush village at Te Ngutu-o-te-manu. It was evident now that Titokowaru's strength was concentrated at Tauranga-ika.

NOTES

The site of the Moturoa ("Long Bush") engagement, known among the Taranaki Maoris as Papa-tihakehake, is about three miles and a half inland from the Town of Waverley (formerly Wairoa) by the road to Okotuku. The exact spot is not marked on any existing survey map or plan, but the study of the ground and an examination of a county map enable the place to be fixed with accuracy. The south-west end and *taumaihi* of the *pa,* on the edge of a gully, were on the ground now known as Section 282, and the other (east) end of the *pa* was on Section 74, Okotuku Parish, Wairoa Survey District. The engagement was fought over this ground and also on what is now Section 73. The main road intersects the *pa*-site. The line of the front entrenchment may still be traced by a slight depression in the ground on the main road running at right angles to the roadway, but this faint undulation would be unnoticed by the ordinary passer-by. In the adjoining paddock no trace of the olden defence exists, but a remnant of the bush (*rata, tawa, karaka,* and *mahoe*) which covered the plain on the eastern flank remains near a homestead which stands about 300 yards from the *pa* ground. A relic of the site of the fortification is an ancient *rata* stump, about 8 feet high and 5 feet in diameter, on the east side of the road, alongside the fence, a few yards in rear (north) of the stockade-line. This *rata* butt will be found a useful guiding-mark by any one wishing to locate the exact scene of the battle.

My last exploration of the scene of the engagement (4th March, 1921) was in company with two veterans of the battle—Mr. William Wallace, of Hawera (No. 2 Division, Armed Constabulary), and Tu-Patea te Rongo, the principal chief of the Pakakohi *hapu.* These old warriors fought on opposite sides at Moturoa. Tu-Patea pointed out the line of the incomplete fortification, the spot where Major Hunter was shot by Paraone Tutere, the place where the body of the A.C. man was eaten, and the spot where the other bodies were placed in a heap and burned in a funeral pyre. The locality of the last-mentioned incident is on the east side of the present road, in the paddock on the right hand, going from Wairoa to Okotuku; it was in the clearing a short distance south of the easternmost angle of the stockade.

The old Hauhau bush fighter dramatically showed the action of the *whangai-hau* ceremony which he witnessed. Tihirua, the young priest of the battlefield sacrifice to the god of war, was the son of Tu-mounga, the last tattooed man in Taranaki, who died at Ratapihipihi recently. The tribe is Ngati-Maru. Tihirua died at Ohangai, near Hawera, in 1907, at the age of about sixty-five years.

"I was not in the engagements at Te Ngutu-o-te-manu," said Tu-Patea. "I joined Titokowaru at Manutahi after the last fight at Te Ngutu. The principal fighting-men of Pakakohi who joined the war-chief with my father, Hau-matao, and me were Pita Tara-tu-te-Rangi, Tutange Waionui, Te Moanaroa, Tamawhero, and Parata Opu. On the night before we were attacked by the troops our chief Titokowaru went round the camp and warned us, '*He po kino tenei po*' ('This is an evil night,' meaning a night of danger). 'Be vigilant,' he ordered, 'and keep a keen lookout for the enemy.' So we were ready for the soldiers when they attacked us at daylight in the morning. In the fight here I used a *hakimana* (a single-barrel percussion-cap gun). Afterwards, however, I was armed with a *purukumu* (breech-loading carbine). I took it from a soldier killed in the battle. The *pakeha* Ringiringi (Kimble Bent) was with us there. He was very clever at making cartridges for our breech-loaders. For want of the *pakeha* covering (goldbeater's skin) for the carbine-cartridges, he used the *tonga-mimi* (bladder) of various animals—cattle, sheep, and pigs—and also used the floats and bladder of eels for the same purpose."

Major William Hunter, killed at Moturoa, and his brother Lieutenant Henry Hunter, who was killed at Te Ngutu-o-te-manu less than three months before, were natives of Antrim, Ireland. William Hunter, who had been trained in the Militia in Ireland and at Hythe, became Captain and Adjutant in the 1st Waikato Regiment of Militia in 1863. He was for some time assistant clerk in the Auckland Provincial Council. Henry Hunter served in the 1st Waikato with his brother before going to the West Coast. Both brothers were excellent soldiers, and one of Major Hunter's fellow-officers in the A.C. describes him as the bravest man in the force.

Colonel Roberts, in discussing the engagement, said: "Most of our fellows were first-rate men and fought well. There were very few exceptions—and, in fact, I only remember one. There was a slightly wounded man who was being carried out on a stretcher. When he heard that the Maoris were close up he jumped out of the stretcher and ran for his life out to the Wairoa Redoubt. The stretcher-bearers were too slow for him. He afterwards exchanged into a mounted force, and when he asked for leave to enlist in that corps I told him I thought it would suit him very well because he would be able to get away faster on horseback than on foot."

Alongside the post-office in the main street of the Township of Waverley stands the green wall of the Wairoa Redoubt, from which Colonel Whitmore's force marched out to Moturoa. After the withdrawal of the forces from the coast at the end of 1868, when the whole coast was temporarily abandoned to the Hauhaus, Wairoa was the only post which held out between Kai-iwi and Patea. The redoubt is overgrown with trees and shrubs; the centre is a roughly kept grassy lawn. The vegetation has helped to preserve the work. The parapets are in places 9 or 10 feet high, and one of the small flanking bastions still stands. The land is a Post and Telegraph section. The redoubt is the only one on the West Coast still in existence in the heart of the town of which it was the nucleus, and it should be preserved as a place of great historical value.

Chapter 27

THE POVERTY BAY MASSACRE

TURANGANUI, AS THE present Town of Gisborne was known in its early years, was a small township in 1868; it consisted of a few stores, an hotel, courthouse, post-office, and several other buildings, on the Waimata River, close to its mouth. Captain Reid's store was the principal place of business. On the opposite (east) side of the river were two military redoubts. Five miles inland was Matawhero, the principal farming district, with numerous homesteads scattered over a wide fertile plain extending to the Waipaoa River. The European population of Turanganui and Matawhero at this time was about one hundred and fifty; the Maoris in the district numbered some five hundred. Most of the prominent settlers, including the military officers, lived at or near Matawhero; among these were several men against whom Te Kooti nursed an undying grudge for his deportation to Wharekauri.

Te Kooti occupied the month of October, 1868, in gathering in his forces and perfecting his arrangements for a terrible blow at the Poverty Bay settlements. In his fortress on Puketapu he preached his gospel of fire and blood, supporting his warrior creed with Scriptural quotations, such as the promise from the Book of Joshua: " . . . And the Lord your God He shall expel them from before you and drive them from out of your sight; and ye shall possess their land, as the Lord your God hath promised unto you." In such wise were the *pakeha* population and the Kawanatanga Maoris of Turanganui to be served.

Many messages of warning—some definite, some vague—had reached the people of Poverty Bay. Unfortunately the most serious warning of all was disregarded. The military authorities kept nine men on duty as scouts to watch for the approach of Hauhaus from the interior. Lieutenant Gascoyne was placed in charge of these scouts, and with the approval of his commanding officer, Major R. Biggs, he fixed his main camp about twenty miles from Gisborne, where the main track to Wairoa approached the Hangaroa River. In the daytime he kept a lookout from a commanding hill and patrolled for many miles above his post.

One day he was informed by an old Maori that Te Kooti would most probably use an ancient track a considerable distance to the right of the scouts' camp for his march on the bay, in preference to that via the Hangaroa Valley and Waerenga-a-Kuri. The track Gascoyne's informant thought would be used, though much overgrown, was by way of the Wharekopae and Patutahi Valleys; although a long and difficult detour, it would enable the attackers to approach their objective unseen, by an unexpected route. Gascoyne scouted in the direction indicated and found a deeply worn track grown over with high *manuka* in a valley some eight or ten miles to the right of his camp, and leading to a ridge overlooking the Manga-karetu Stream. From the hilltop he sighted smoke rising out of the timber some miles inland; his Maori companion thought it was probably the fire of a party of native pig-hunters, as there were no villages in that part of the country. Gascoyne rode in to the settlement of Makaraka and reported to Major Biggs what he had learned and seen. He requested leave to keep three of his men watching the old overgrown track, but Biggs did not approve of this proposal; he said he knew that Te Kooti was restless, and that his scouts kept him informed of the rebel leader's movements. He felt sure that Te Kooti would use the more familiar track by the Hangaroa, and directed Gascoyne to return to his post and not to leave it himself until further orders. "Keep a sharp watch and scout toward Wairoa daily," concluded Biggs. "If you see armed men or are fired at, all of you are to gallop in at once and give the alarm by scattering your scouts; but come yourself to me as quickly as possible." Such were Major Biggs's final instructions. Less than forty-eight hours later he and his family and neighbours were slaughtered by Te Kooti, who came by the old track scouted by Gascoyne, and crossed the Patutahi ford of the Waipaoa River. Some settlers watched this ford for several nights, but Biggs vetoed this, too, as unnecessary.

On the 8th November Te Kooti and his fighting column from Puketapu, moving by the difficult inland track, reached Pukepuke, near the Patutahi ford. The Patutahi Maoris, who were friendly with the Government, were taken prisoner, and three of the chiefs were ordered for execution by Te Kooti, and were led away and shot.

Then, having obtained from one of his spies exact information as to the position of the various settlers' homes, he divided his force—numbering a hundred men—into *kokiri,* or striking-parties, of varying strength to attack the several houses, His principal lieutenants were Nikora, Te Rangi-tahau, Nama, Maaka, and Te Waru Tamatea. The largest *kokiri*, which Te Kooti himself accompanied, was detailed to attack Major Biggs's house.

Wherever possible only the tomahawk or other hand-weapons or the bayonet were to be used; as will be seen, however, there was considerable firing at two or three of the homesteads.

Shortly before midnight on the night of Monday, the 9th November, 1868, the Hauhau force, all mounted, forded the Waipaoa River at Patutahi and rode into Matawhero. One of the farthest-out settlers was Mr. Wyllie, against whom Te Kooti nourished hatred; Wyllie had been instrumental in some degree as Government interpreter in his deportation in 1866. The Hauhaus saw Wyllie writing at his table as they silently passed his lighted room; he was writing letters for the English mail, which was to leave on the following morning. Te Kooti ordered that he should be left for the present and despatched on the return from the home of "Te Piki" (Major Biggs); thus Wyllie escaped the fate of his friends, for he and his immediate neighbours were aroused before the Hauhaus rode back toward the Waipaoa.

Peita Kotuku (of the Ngati-Maniapoto and Patu-heuheu Tribes), who shared in this raid, stated that the *kokiri* in which he marched was led by Petera Kahuroa, of the Ngati-Hineuru Tribe. Peita was armed with a rifle and bayonet. The first people captured were killed by a man of Ngati-Kahungunu, who stabbed them to death with his fixed bayonet. The leaders in the attack on Major Biggs's place were Nikora and Te Rangi-tahau. Peita witnessed the slaughter of the Major and his family. Volleys were fired into the house after the door was broken open, and Biggs and his wife and child and several occupants of the place were killed with rifle-shot and bayonet. Next the home of "Wirihana" (Captain Wilson), a mile or more away, was surrounded and fired into, and after the place was set on fire the Wilsons were killed in the same way as the Biggs family. "The principal man appointed to kill the Wilsons," said Peita, "was Rawiri, of the Rongowhakaata Tribe, and it was not, as some have said, the half-caste Eru Peka or Wi Heretaunga, although both shared in the attack. Other men appointed to kill prisoners in the raid were Te Rangi-tahau, of Taupo (usually called Tahau)—who had been captured with me at Omarunui (1866) and sent to Wharekauri—and Timoti te Kaka, of Opotiki. Tahau's weapon in these executions was a *patu* (the sharp-edged stone club). Te Kaka used a *patu-paraoa* (whalebone club). In our expeditions such men were told off specially to slay those taken prisoner. Some used the tomahawk. As for myself, I never liked killing men with the tomahawk. I disliked such work —I preferred the gun."*

---

*Statement to the writer by Peita Kotuku, at Taringamutu, King Country, 23rd February, 1921.

The attack on Major Biggs and his family was delivered about 2 o'clock on the morning of the 10th November. Biggs was still up writing. (Major Gascoyne states that he was writing out orders for all the settlers to assemble at Gisborne Township on the following day as a precaution against a sudden attack.) Te Kooti surrounded the house with his men, and knocked at the front door. Biggs, after calling out "Who is there?" got his revolver, and when the Maoris burst in the door, he fired at them. He was shot down and bayoneted. Mrs. Biggs and her baby were killed, and also two servants, a married couple. A half-caste girl was killed outside the house. A boy named James escaped by the back door, and succeeded in warning many of the neighbours, including the Bloomfield family, and thus enabling them to evade the Hauhaus. This boy's mother, Mrs. James, who was living near Mr. Goldsmith's house, was roused by the shooting at Wilson's and escaped with her eight children.*

After setting fire to the Biggs's home the Hauhaus mounted and galloped on to Captain Wilson's house, which a party under Nama had already surrounded and set on fire. Nama and his men on reaching the house had called out to Wilson, who had been sitting up late writing letters. On discovering they were Hauhaus he opened fire with his revolver; by this time he probably had heard the firing at Biggs's. His servant Moran came to his assistance. The attackers battered the door down and fired into the house. After some shooting, the raiders set fire to the house at both ends, and Wilson and his family were forced to leave it after he and Moran had held it as long as possible. Some of the natives wished to spare the Wilsons, and it seems from what can be gathered that when the family came out from the burning house the captain was under the belief that he and his wife and children were being taken into safety. However, after they had been led about 200 yards in the direction of Mr. Goldsmith's place, their captors suddenly fell on them with the bayonet. Captain Wilson, who was carrying one of the children, was bayoneted in the back, and fell dead with the little boy in his arms. Mrs. Wilson was then savagely bayoneted, and was left for dead, stabbed in several places. Three of the children and the servant Moran were killed; the little boy, James

---

* Major Gascoyne in his reminiscences ("Soldiering in New Zealand") wrote thus in vindication of Major Biggs, whose courage, prudence, and energy he praises: "He was mistaken in supposing that Te Kooti would advance by the Reinga road, but the information at his command made him feel certain that he would do so. Blame for the surprise must lie on the niggard policy which only gave him, in spite of his strong representation of the danger, one small party of men to watch an extent of country that required six such parties to watch it efficiently."

Major R. Biggs

(Killed in the Poverty Bay massacre.)

Wilson, whom the father was carrying when he fell, was the only one who escaped unhurt. He hid in the scrub, and after wandering about for two days he returned and discovered his mother still alive; she had crawled into a shed. The poor lady contrived to write a note and despatched her son with it to Turanganui, but the little fellow lost his way and was found at last near Makaraka. After lying in the shed for several days Mrs. Wilson was rescued by the search-parties and taken to hospital at Napier, but died from her terrible wounds.

After the slaughter of the Wilsons the scattered homesteads on the Matawhero were quickly attacked by the mounted raiders, and one family after another was slaughtered. The friendly natives were simultaneously pounced upon, and many were despatched with rifle, bayonet, tomahawk, or *patu*. House after house was looted and burned after its occupants had either been killed or had almost miraculously eluded the murderous *kokiri* bands.

Those who were killed on that fatal night and morning of fire and blood included Messrs. Dodd and Peppard (two sheep-farmers who had a station some miles distant from Matawhero), Lieutenant Walsh and his wife and child, Mr. Cadel (storekeeper at Matawhero), Mr. and Mrs. McCulloch and child, Mr. and Mrs. Newnham, Mr. J. Mann and his wife and child, and many others. In all, thirty-three Europeans and thirty-seven friendly Maoris were slaughtered.

Those who escaped in the grey dawn, warned by the firing at their neighbours' houses or by some gallant men who rode from one house to another warning the inmates, ran across the fields or along the beach towards Turanganui. The plain was ablaze with burning homes, and the blood-maddened Hauhaus were galloping over the country, shooting indiscriminately, looting, and destroying.

Lieutenant Gascoyne, out in the scouts' camp on the Hangaroa track, received the news of the raid from one of his native scouts who galloped in from the bay. Gascoyne and his few men immediately raced in to headquarters, but were cut off from Turanganui by Te Kooti's force and had to abandon their horses at the beach, jump into a boat, and pull across the bay to Turanganui. There Gascoyne, now the only officer in the bay, found a scene of terror and confusion. " Men and women," he wrote, " were eagerly inquiring of every newcomer for information of their missing friends; mothers were weeping alone for their children, wives for their husbands, and husbands for their wives." All the people had crossed to the east side of the Waimata River to seek safety in the redoubt. The Hauhaus were in full possession of the country on the other side of the river, and could be seen burning the remaining houses. A number of settlers near the Waipaoa, including Messrs. Wyllie, Hawthorne, Firmin, Stevenson, and Benson, with their families, found themselves cut off from Turanganui, and were forced to retreat in the other direction, and finally were picked up by the ketch " Eagle " near Mahia, whence they were shipped to Napier. The schooners " Tawera " and " Success," which had just left the bay for Auckland, were communicated with by a lucky chance, as the wind was very light, and they returned and took all the women and children away from Turanganui to Napier. In Hawke's Bay the " Tawera " transhipped a number to the s.s. " Lord Ashley " for Auckland.

Captain Westrup and Captain Tuke soon arrived from Napier with some European volunteers and a large force of friendly natives. Te Kooti leisurely retired, taking with him a large number of native recruits and captives from the Turanganui *kaingas,* and a great quantity of plunder of all kinds, including many good horses, besides about a hundred rifles and guns, some revolvers and swords, also a good deal of ammunition. The various raiding-parties united at Patutahi, after sweeping out all life from Matawhero, Makaraka, Repongaere, Makauri, and other settlements. From the Patutahi village Te Kooti marched on inland, taking several hundreds of new allies and prisoners. At Pukepuke he ordered out three of the captive chiefs for execution.

Westrup and Gascoyne and an armed force searched the devastated settlements and buried the dead. Gascoyne was then despatched inland on Te Kooti's track, with the Ngati-Kahungunu friendlies under Renata Kawepo, Karauria, and other chiefs. The force numbered about four hundred and fifty, but its fighting-value was not great. On the first day's march beyond Patutahi (20th November) a party of Hauhaus was surprised and two men were shot. The line of retreat was then followed north-east over the ranges in the direction of the Wharekopae and Ngatapa. Two more days' marching enabled Gascoyne to engage Te Kooti's pickets on a fern ridge above the Wharekopae River at Makaretu. In a hot skirmish—literally so, for the Hauhaus set fire to the high dry fern on the ridge in the face of Gascoyne's advance—the friendlies drove the enemy's pickets back and by digging a wide shallow shelter-trench on the burned ground kept up a heavy fire on the supports from the main body until dark. The Hauhaus then drew off to their entrenched position on the river-bank below. The Ngati-Kahungunu in this action lost four or five killed and had about a dozen wounded, who were attended to by Dr. Murray Gibbs. The Hauhaus lost several men killed. During the night, after sending back for ammunition, Gascoyne entrenched about 300 yards of the ridge, presenting the convex side of a half-circle to the Hauhau front. Te Kooti rifle-pitted two hills that flanked Gascoyne's ridge about 800 yards away. For three or four days indecisive skirmishing was carried on between the opposing forces while Gascoyne awaited necessary reinforcements and supplies.

In the principal encounter the old Hawke's Bay chief Renata Kawepo made a plucky charge on a party of the Hauhaus who had advanced up the gully on Gascoyne's right. The heavy fire forced his men back, and the old warrior was left alone, but Gascoyne and Karauria rushed forward and drove the enemy off. Karauria, one of the very few good fighting-men from Hawke's Bay, was mortally wounded. So the skirmishing went on until Ngati-Porou and other reinforcements arrived. A clever *coup* was carried out about this time by Te Kooti, who sent a force round to Gascoyne's rear to capture the stores and ammunition depot at Patutahi, ten miles away. The convoy from Gisborne was forced to gallop off, and the depot was captured. In this daring raid the Hauhaus secured twelve thousand rounds of ammunition—of this amount, however, eight thousand rounds were afterwards recaptured—and all the provisions for which Gascoyne's half-starved force was anxiously waiting.

Chapter 28

THE SIEGE OF NGATAPA

IMMEDIATELY ON HEARING of the Poverty Bay massacre and the retreat of some of the settlers towards the Mahia Peninsula, Colonel Lambert, commanding at Wairoa, sent Lieutenant Preece up to Whangawehi, on the north side of Mahia, with instructions to give what assistance he could and to report himself to Captain Westrup. Preece found two steamers at Whangawehi, one going to Napier and one to Poverty Bay. Captain Westrup instructed him to go to Turanganui with Ihaka Whanga's men, numbering about sixty. On arrival at the bay Preece found that Lieutenant Gascoyne had escaped the massacre, having been out scouting at the time, and had taken command. The whole country was smoking with the fires of burning homesteads. Captain Westrup returned next day with Captain Tuke and some Armed Constabulary men and Captain Tanner and a number of his Hawke's Bay Cavalry Volunteers. Lieutenant Preece remained at Turanganui a day and returned to Whangawehi by steamer, thence overland to Wairoa, where he reported to Colonel Lambert. Captain Westrup said he would await the arrival of a large force of Hawke's Bay Maoris, which he expected in a day or two, before taking the offensive. At Wairoa measures were taken to get a force ready to start from that point, and provisions and ammunition were collected. About the 25th November 200 Ngati-Porou men under Ropata Wahawaha and Hotene Porourangi, and 170 Wairoa natives under Lieutenant Preece, started in pursuit of Te Kooti via Te Reinga. The force had to move slowly as it was taking a good supply of ammunition and provisions. Information had reached Lieutenant Preece that the Hawke's Bay natives under their own chiefs and Lieutenant Gascoyne had engaged the enemy at Makaretu and held them there. On the third day of the march the Wairoa force reached the last crossing of the Hangaroa River. Here a consultation was held on the question of moving direct for Makaretu across country or taking the track to Patutahi, which was the base of operations for the troops. The latter course was decided on. From Patutahi a forced march was made, the column reaching the Wharekopae Stream, four miles from Makaretu, the same night. Next morning Ropata and Preece communicated with Gascoyne and planned the attack. The Wairoa natives were to move to the right, and at a given time attack the enemy on its flank. On the 3rd December the Hauhau position was assaulted in a most determined manner. Preece and his Wairoa men charged up one of the rifle-pitted hills on Te Kooti's flank and carried it, driving the Hauhaus out and killing three of them. Then Ngati-Porou and Preece's men, with Gascoyne and a few European volunteers and Ngati-Kahungunu, made a combined attack on the *pa*. "It was a beautiful sight," wrote Gascoyne, "a line of fire and smoke half a mile long, with both flanks thrown forward, rapidly descending the hill." The men closed on the centre as they approached the Hauhau entrenchments, and a deadly fire was concentrated on the camp. The Hauhaus fought well until the final rush, when they dashed out of their entrenchments and across the river into the forest, leaving about two score dead and dying in the captured position. A number were shot in the river immediately in rear. Among those who fell was the notorious Nama, who had been concerned in the murder of Karaitiana and his three comrades at Whataroa; he was mortally wounded by Henare Kakapango, one of Gascoyne's scouts.

Among the Hauhaus who fought at Makaretu was Peita Kotuku, some of whose war experiences have been related in the preceding pages. Describing his escape from Ngati-Porou, he said:—

"When the final assault on our *pa* was delivered I hastily filled all my pockets with cartridges, in a tent, and ran out with a rifle slung over my shoulder and another in my hands. I ran to the edge of the cliff above the river. The bank was perpendicular and about 50 feet high. It was no use staying to fight then; the enemy were in our lines. I jumped from the brink of the cliff into a deep pool of the river. As I dashed for the cliff I was fired at. Nama, who was near me, was shot. I got across the river and escaped into the bush, but many of my comrades were shot in the water or on the banks. There was high *manuka* growing on the other side of the river (the Wharekopae), and I crept into this. There I was seen by Huhana (Susan), one of Te Kooti's wives, who had escaped with him. She called to me from the bush, and I joined her and Te Kooti. Our leader was suffering from a wounded foot, which had been injured in the rocky bed of the river, and Huhana and I took turns in carrying him off on our backs in the direction of Ngatapa, where we made our next stand against the Government."

In the fighting at Makaretu the total Hauhau loss was about

From a drawing by the Hon. J. C. Richmond, 1869]

Ngatapa Fortress from the East

Te Kooti's strongly fortified *pa* is shown on the summit of the mountain. (See plan.)

sixty killed. On the Government side two Europeans were wounded and one Ngati-Porou was killed in the final engagement.

During the operations at Makaretu Te Kooti was prudently preparing another and stronger position six miles in his rear, the mountain fortress Ngatapa. While he held up the Ngati-Kahungunu on his front, working-parties were busy renovating the defences of this stronghold, an ancient trenched *pa* long deserted, on the crest of a narrow and precipitous range more than 2,000 feet above sea-level. The scarped fort towered high above all the surrounding country, the most picturesque and most formidable position occupied by the Hauhaus in the war. On being driven from Makaretu Te Kooti and his fugitives, numbering about three hundred fighting-men, besides many women and some children, took up their quarters in Ngatapa and hastily strengthened the lines of entrenchment.

The weak feature of this *pa,* as in most Maori forts, was the lack of a water-supply within the lines. The front of the position, the face of the ridge, was defended by three parapets and trenches; the ditches were connected with each other by covered ways. The lowest and outermost line was about 250 yards long, with very high scarped walls terminating on the cliff at either flank of the fort. The second line of parapets was about 10 feet in height, and the third, protecting the huts built on the summit, was 16 feet high, surmounted with flax baskets filled with earth, a substitute for the European plan of sand-bags. The place was very difficult of approach; it was compassed about with gorges and dense forest, and the rear of the position was a sharp ridge like a knife-back, falling away precipitously for several hundreds of feet on each side.

The first attack on Ngatapa was delivered on the 5th December by Ngati-Porou and the Wairoa natives, two companies of about one hundred and fifty men each. The right column was commanded by Ropata and Preece, the left by Hotene and others. Ropata and Preece, with a few men, leaving their main body in the valley, clambered up the steep face of the cliff and gained the end of the trench on the left front of the *pa* immediately in rear of the front wall. There was no flanking bastion here, and Ropata was able to enfilade the trench for some distance, firing along it as fast as he could discharge the loaded rifles which Preece passed on to him. There the gallant Maori officer and his white comrade remained for some time in a most precarious position, keeping up a hot fire, supported by their best men. In the afternoon a portion of the outer works was captured, with a loss to the Hauhaus of three killed, but ammunition now ran short, and it was impossible to do anything more in the absence of support from the main body of Ngati-Porou. Those who stuck to Ropata

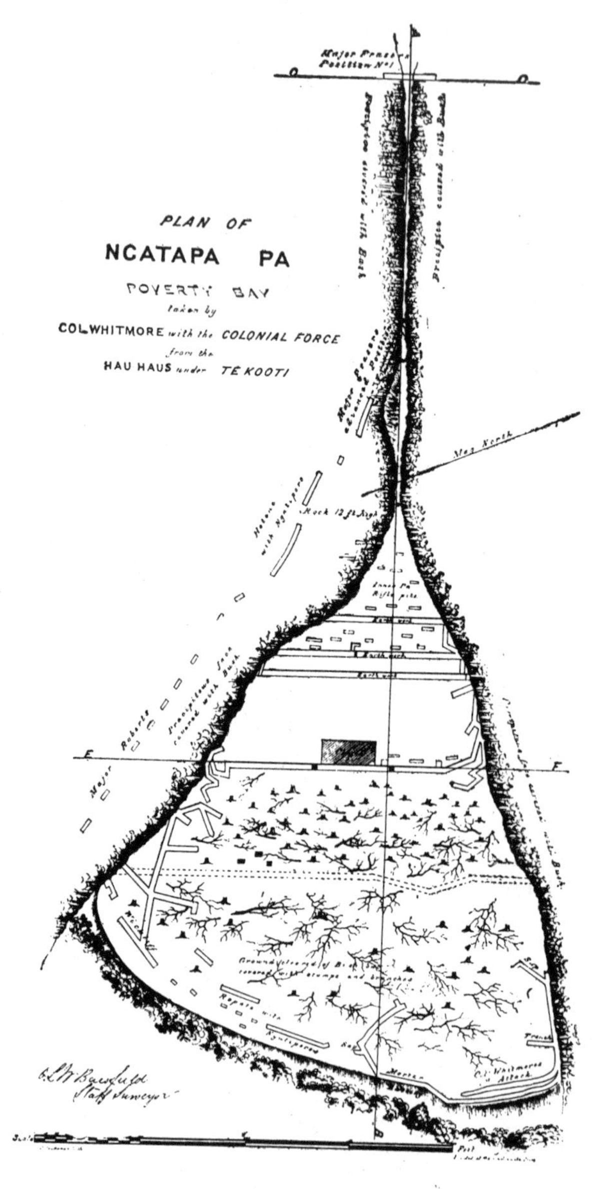

Plan of Ngatapa Hill Fortress (Captured 1869)

were chiefly his near kinsmen of the Aowera clan; conspicuous among them was Ruka Aratapu, a fearless fellow who kept up an accurate fire on the Hauhaus from the branches of a tree which he had climbed. Preece went down several times and endeavoured to get Ngati-Porou to come to his assistance, but without much success. The small party under Ropata accordingly was compelled to withdraw for want of support, after holding the perilous position all night; and next day the force retired on Turanganui, meeting Colonel Whitmore and three hundred Armed Constabulary at Patutahi.

On the recommendation of Colonel Whitmore both Ropata and Preece were awarded the decoration of the New Zealand Cross for their exceptionally brave attack at Ngatapa.

Ropata was disgusted at the defection of the main body of Ngati-Porou; and he wished to recruit fresh men. Whitmore was anxious to attack Ngatapa at once, but on the advice of Ropata and Gascoyne further operations were deferred until an adequate force was gathered to deal with Te Kooti. The European forces therefore remained in camp at Makaraka for nearly a month, while Ropata returned to Waiapu and strengthened his contingent for the new operations.

NOTES

Further details of the operations in the first attack on Ngatapa show that on the 4th December, the day following the final fight at Makaretu, the combined Ngati-Kahungunu and Poverty Bay force, Ngati-Porou under Ropata and Hotene, and the Wairoa men, moved out by the ridge overlooking the Wharekopae Stream. The enemy's position on the crest of Ngatapa was seen in the distance, and, having located it, it was decided that the force should return to camp and march against Te Kooti next day. That night, therefore, was spent in the Makaretu camp, and next morning the leaders moved out with Ngati-Porou (200 men who had come from Wairoa), also the Wairoa natives and some of the Mahia men. It is said there had been a quarrel between Ropata and the Hawke's Bay Maoris under Tareha over a prisoner, and the latter party refused to march. Lieutenant Preece was with the advance-guard. There was a long narrow ridge to climb from a conical hill about two-thirds of the way up to Ngatapa fortress, and the men in the advance had to expose themselves to the enemy's fire. This hill was afterwards called the "Crow's Nest"; it was some 700 to 1,000 yards from the *pa*. Just below there was a stream. There was a lot of felled *manuka* in front of the *pa,* and when the force reached the edge of this Mr. Preece halted and sent some men round the edge of the clearing with instructions to observe the position from that point, but not to show themselves, and on no account to fire on the enemy if they saw them, unless they were fired on. These men disobeyed the instructions. One of them fired when he saw some of Te Kooti's men, and this brought a murderous fire from the enemy. The men sent to the right came rushing down the hill, and numbers of Preece's men followed their example. Just then Ropata came up, and he and Preece stood across the track and threatened to shoot the next man who ran. This stopped the panic. Then the two leaders moved up to the left with only a few men, and held the advanced position at the end of the trench on the left immediately in rear of the front wall of the *pa*. Mr. Preece went down several times to try and bring up men who had been crouching round a fire during the day about 500 yards below his position. He and Ropata and a few others had taken the enemy's outer works, and were firing from there into the inner part of the *pa*. The only men who were killed in this attack were four of their party. One man was wounded, and, with assistance, Preece took him down to where the men were at the fire. He left him there with instructions that he was to be carried to camp. [It was ascertained afterwards that this order was disobeyed, and that the man was abandoned by his people, and was killed by the enemy after the withdrawal.] No attack was made on the right side of the *pa* that day. In Ropata and Preece's bold attack the killed men's guns were loaded as well as their own, and were used to keep up a constant fire. Very late in the afternoon Ropata said to Preece: "We can take the *pa* if we are supported. Go down to the main body and ask Gascoyne to get assistance." The young officer went down with two men. When they got to the foot of the hill it was dark. They decided to follow the Wharekopae, and reached Lieutenant Gascoyne's camp at Makaretu at 8.30 or 9 o'clock that night after a very rough march down the stream, a slippery *papa*-rock river with gravel in places. Preece reported to Gascoyne that Ropata wanted immediate assistance. Gascoyne could not induce the natives to move that night; they said they would start at daylight in the morning. Tareha and his men had moved off on their return march. At daylight Gascoyne's Maoris were just ready to start when Ropata, who had held his position all night, came in, and he was so disgusted at not getting the much-needed help that he decided to return to Waiapu and recruit a new force. Lieutenant Gascoyne had done his utmost before Ngatapa to induce the retreating natives to return to the attack, but without avail.

Captain Preece narrates this incident to show how Maoris are affected by superstition: "Hemi Tapeka was a man whom I had seen distinguish himself at the attack on Pukemaire (Waiapu) in September, 1865; there he went right up to the flanking angle, killed one of the enemy, and held his position until others got up to him. He had been a good fighter, too, in the Upper Wairoa in 1866. When I went to get men to go up to the attack at Ngatapa I found him crouching by the fire (500 yards below the *pa*). I said: 'Well, why are you here? You are not a coward.' He replied: 'No; but if I go up to-day I shall be killed. I had a dream last night. My thigh twitched; that is a *tohu aitua'* [evil omen]."

THE SECOND ATTACK ON NGATAPA

It was late in December before Colonel Whitmore had perfected his arrangements for the reduction of Ngatapa. In the meantime the Hauhaus had been active, making several raids towards Poverty Bay. A party from Ngatapa came down one night and killed several people at Pipiwhakao, five miles from the Constabulary camp at Makaraka. The advance on Te Kooti's position was begun on the 24th December. Whitmore had four divisions of Armed Constabulary, totalling about four hundred men, and Ropata followed him up with three hundred and fifty Ngati-Porou who had been brought down from Waiapu by steamer. By the

31st December the force had reached a hill on the same long ridge as the *pa,* but separated from Ngatapa summit by a deep gully; the distance between this post—which the Constabulary entrenched—and the *pa* was nearly half a mile. From this hill —which was a base of operations, named the "Crow's Nest"— as detachments were sent out to encircle the *pa,* shell-fire was opened on the Hauhau position with a Coehorn mortar, which had been brought up from Turanganui with great difficulty. It was seen that Ngatapa had been greatly strengthened since the first attack. A considerable area of ground in front had been cleared by felling and burning the bush so as to afford less cover to the attackers. A high wall, loopholed, had been built across the front, and another timber palisade had been built on the inner side. The flanks also had been stockaded. The *pa* was roughly in the form of a wedge, with the apex to the rear on the highest part of the mountain; the incline at which the ground lay enabled the gunners to shell the interior of the fort with accuracy. The first or outer line of entrenchment on the front covered the spring from which the garrison drew the water-supply. It was not possible to scale the steep flanks with a sufficient force to rush the place; in fact, the sides were scarcely scalable at all, although the bush and shrubs gave hand-hold for part of the way; and the attackers' attention was directed chiefly at the entrenched and stockaded front, with bodies of Constabulary and Maoris posted at various positions along the flanks and in rear. The first attempt to capture the Hauhau entrenchments was carried out by Captain W. Gundry and Captain T. W. Porter, the former leading a recently enlisted division of Arawa Maoris (Ngati-Whakaue, Ngati-Pikiao, and Tuhourangi), and the latter leading a picked party of Ngati-Porou. The force was detailed to surprise the Hauhaus' outer wall, and this was done with complete success, cutting the garrison off from the water-spring. The defenders withdrew to their inner lines, and the Constabulary and Ngati-Porou took possession of the outer line from cliff to cliff and commenced regular siege operations by opening flying saps directed towards the new wall. Shells were thrown into the fort by the Coehorn mortar, and many casualties, as was discovered afterwards, were inflicted by the bursting projectiles. On the Hauhaus' right flank the investing line consisted of No. 6 Division Armed Constabulary under Major J. M. Roberts, nearest the front; then a line of Ngati-Porou under Hotene; and in the rear Major Fraser and his No. 1 Division. On the Hauhaus' left front and part of the flank were some friendly Maoris under Mr. Edward Hamlin.

The siege continued for three days and nights. The very narrow ridge in rear, falling steeply from the *pa,* with several

Major Ropata Wahawaha, N.Z.C.

Ropata, leading the Ngati-Porou native contingent, and his comrade Lieutenant G. A. Preece were both awarded the New Zealand Cross for their distinguished bravery in the first attack on Ngatapa. Ropata was the most vigorous and successful of all the Maori officers who served the Government. He fought the Hauhaus on the East Coast and in the Urewera Country from 1865 until the end of 1871.

scarps scarcely climbable, was pluckily held in the face of a very heavy fire by a few Constabulary men, including Benjamin Biddle and Solomon Black, who performed such gallant and determined work in holding their position that they were both awarded the New Zealand Cross. Casualties became numerous among the Government detachments. Captain Brown of No. 7 Division was killed, and Captain Capel of the same Division was shot through the shoulder. The weather became very wet soon after the siege began. Sapping was discontinued, and a heavy fire of shells and rifle-bullets was poured into the Hauhau citadel. Late on the last day of the siege Captain Gascoyne led a forlorn hope of thirty men of No. 7 Division against the *pa,* and in the teeth of a gale with rain and under a heavy fire he secured a position close under one of the outer parapets and remained there all night waiting for dawn to continue his assault with shovel, axe, and rifle. On the same afternoon (4th

January, 1869) Colonel Whitmore, after consultation with Major Ropata, detailed a storming-party of fifty Ngati-Porou to surprise and seize the second line of defence by assault on the Hauhaus' left front at an angle above the cliff. Captain Porter and a chief of Te Aowera *hapu* were given command of this party. Descending into the ravine under cover of the thick bush, the stormers advanced unseen until immediately under the high cliff, which they scaled with great gallantry, securing climbing-hold with one hand, rifle in the other. The precipice was composed largely of loose rock and gravel, and a secure grip was difficult. When near the top of the ascent they came under the Hauhaus' rifles, but the accurate fire from the covering-party below enabled them to scramble up into the allotted position with some loss. One of the Ngati-Porou who was shot, a man named Rewai Tauranga, fell on Captain Porter, and both rolled to the foot of the cliff. Porter quickly rejoined his men. An enfilading fire was opened along the second trench, and the face of the parapet was quickly manned, causing the defenders to retreat within the innermost line. This position captured, the whole force moved forward, and arrangements were made for blowing up the inner parapet with gunpowder and storming the citadel of the *pa* next morning.

The night was wet and windy. Te Kooti, realizing that the position was hopeless, had given orders that the fort should be evacuated under cover of the darkness, and late that stormy night and very early in the morning hours the garrison escaped down the precipitous mountain-side on the right flank of the *pa*. A section of this side, between Hamlin's Maoris on the right of the attack and the lines of Fraser's No. 1 Division in the rear, had been left unguarded; the cliff here was perpendicular for some distance and then slanted very steeply down into the dense bush. Peita Kotuku, narrating his escape with the other Hauhaus, said:—

"The fall of Ngatapa was due chiefly to the fact that the Ngati-Porou cut us off from the spring which was our water-supply. The fort was taken because we were without food or water. (*I mate ai tera pa na te kore-kai, na te kore-wai.*) When our position became desperate and it was decided to retreat to the forest under cover of night, we let ourselves down the cliff on the flank of the *pa* by means of *aka* (bush vines, lianes) cut from the trees just outside the fort. The part of the cliff where I went down on an *aka* rope was about 60 feet high. I escaped into the deep forest, but many of our people were captured and shot."

Shortly before dawn (5th January, 1869) it was discovered that the Hauhaus had abandoned their mountain-hold. The voice

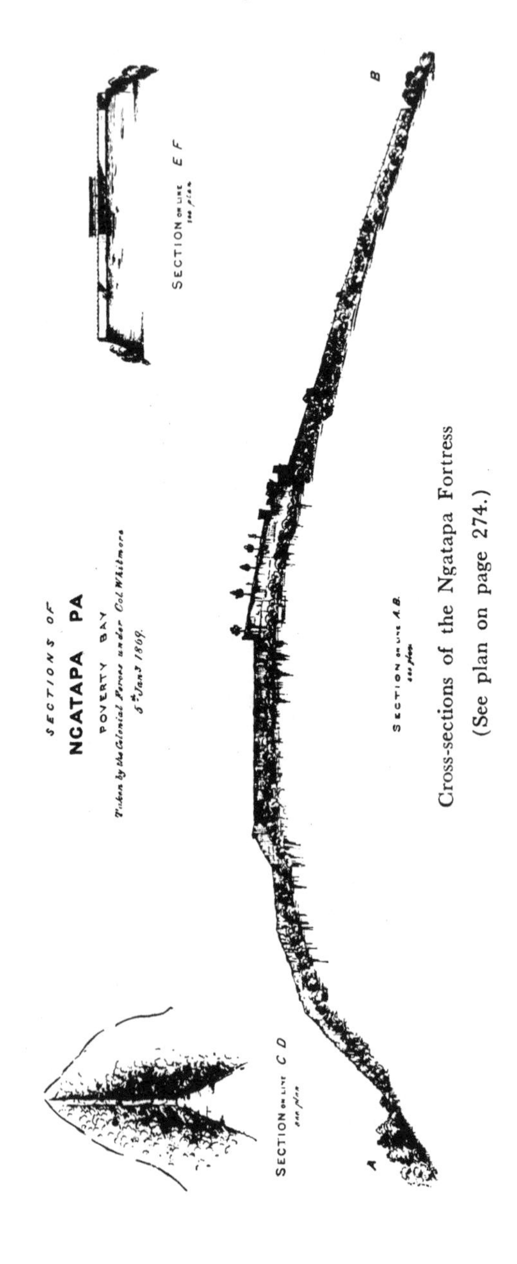

Cross-sections of the Ngatapa Fortress

(See plan on page 274.)

of a woman was heard through the howling of the gale calling out that Te Kooti had escaped down the cliff. Mr. Hamlin, on the right of the attack, who was the first to discover the fact, went in just at daylight and found that all the able-bodied people had disappeared into the bush, leaving only women and some helplessly wounded men in the *pa*.

Immediately the abandoned fort was occupied by the Government force a pursuit was ordered, and Ngati-Porou and the Arawa Division went in chase of the fugitives. The Hauhaus had scattered into small parties, taking different trails in the effort to throw their foes off their track. Ropata adopted similar tactics, and ordered his men to break into small detachments each following up a trail.

Te Kooti and his immediate followers escaped, but a great many of the people, weakened by want of food, were captured before they had gone very far. Every male prisoner taken was shot—some on the spot, some near Ngatapa, where they were taken for execution. An Armed Constabulary scout who shared in the bush chase said: "All the men taken were despatched. We just stood them on the edge of a cliff and gave them a volley."

Ropata's methods in ordering the summary execution of all the Hauhaus captured by Ngati-Porou may have been ruthless, but the memory of the massacre at Poverty Bay was still raw in every mind. The principal chief overtaken and killed was Nikora te Whakaunua, the head *rangatira* of the Ngati-Hineuru Tribe, of Te Haroto, on the Napier–Taupo track. He was one of the prisoners taken at Omarunui in 1866. In the siege of Ngatapa he had been severely wounded.

Te Kooti lost quite half his fighting force at Ngatapa and in the relentless forest chase. The estimates of the Hauhau casualties vary somewhat, but the most reliable reports give the total killed as 136, of whom 120 were summarily executed after capture, either singly or in batches. The wounded (excluding those killed in the captured *pa* by Ngati-Porou and the other Government Maoris) and the prisoners saved totalled about 150; most of the prisoners were women and children, many of whom had been carried off by Te Kooti from the coast. Adding to the Ngatapa losses those sustained at Makaretu, about sixty, the Hauhau leader's force was weakened by approximately two hundred men. Many of those who fell were recent recruits from the Poverty Bay district—some of them compulsorily converted to Te Kooti's tenets—and from the Urewera Country. Those who escaped from Ngatapa and found secure refuge in the forest of the interior could not have exceeded two hundred, including a number of women who survived the terrors and hardships of the bush fight.

The casualties of the Government force at Ngatapa in the second attack beginning on the 31st December and ending on the 5th January numbered eleven killed and the same number wounded. Of the killed, five were members of the Armed Constabulary force and the rest Ngati-Porou and other Maoris.

Te Kooti's power having been shattered for the time being, Colonel Whitmore transferred the Armed Constabulary, including the new division of Arawa, to the West Coast in order to carry out the long-pending operations against Titokowaru.

Te Kooti's refuge-place for nearly two months was a well-concealed camp in the great Te Wera forest, on the headwaters of the Waioeka River, in the exceedingly broken and mountainous country to the westward of the present road via Motu from Gisborne to Opotiki. The camp when discovered two years later by the Ngati-Porou under Captain Porter contained thirty thatched houses roofed with totara-bark. It was naturally defended on three sides by cliffs, forest, and water. Here the fugitives were gradually reinforced by recruits from the Urewera, Whakatohea, and other tribes, and supplies of ammunition were brought in chiefly from the Opotiki district and Ruatahuna. By the beginning of March Te Kooti was in a position to renew the campaign of foray, plunder, and revenge which he had begun in the previous November. His *mana* as a priest and prophet, the founder of the new religion, grew apace; his magnetic personality and his skilful use of Scriptural passages applicable to the condition of the Maoris drew to him men from many a tribe who saw in his leadership, favoured by the gods, hope of successful war against the *pakeha*. He never really recovered from the blows inflicted upon his force at Makaretu and Ngatapa, yet so shrewd a soldier and a strategist was he, with a perfect genius for delivering lightning assaults in unexpected places, that he was able again and again to take the field and to maintain his resistance to the Government for more than three years.

NOTES

Captain J. R. Rushton, of Kutarere, Ohiwa, supplies the following note:—

"That good soldier Major Mair was in command at Opotiki at the date of the capture of Ngatapa. In addition to the Waioeka redoubt, a blockhouse had just been built to protect the Opotiki settlement, near the entrance to the Otara Gorge. I was ensign in charge of this Otara blockhouse with twenty-five men—about half Maoris—and have good reason to remember the fall of Ngatapa. About 10 o'clock on the morning of the 7th January, 1869 (two days after its capture), I was reading in my room when a Maori with a double-barrel gun walked in. I sprang upon him, grasping hold of his gun, and pressing him down upon the floor. I threw him a loaf of bread, and with carbine at full cock and my Tranter revolver slung on my wrist I ran out calling for the sergeant of the guard. He came running up from just below the blockhouse. I said, 'Where the hell are your men, and where is our sentry?' I then called out for all to stand to arms, and 'be damn quick about it.' The sergeant, when shown the Maori in my room, turned as white as a sheet. We found the European sentry at the end of the blockhouse standing like a log, with his carbine between his legs, but a kick with my boot upon his posterior brought him to his senses. I sent out two of my best Maoris to watch the narrows of the gorge until nightfall. As I thought, the Maori was an escapee from Ngatapa, having deserted Te Kooti when they retired from the *pa,* and being related to Wi Kingi's tribe, the Ngaitai, made his way out by the Otara Gorge. I took him in to my commanding officer, Major Mair, and he told me that the Maori's arrival was of great importance because of the information he gave. This incident put an end to the growling I had from two or three grumbling Europeans of the garrison regarding my care in not allowing the door to be opened in the morning without all standing to arms; they called it funk. The occurrence showed how easily a post might be taken through carelessness of the sentry and guard."

Colonel T. W. Porter, when Captain in the Ngati-Porou contingent, obtained from a prisoner the following account of Te Kooti's camp discipline and habits in his Urewera and Tahora forest retreats:—

"It is Te Kooti's custom, when arising from sleep in camp, to call his followers to *karakia* (prayers), when the 32nd and 34th Psalms are sung, altered by Te Kooti to suit himself. After prayers, parties are ordered out to hunt food, &c. When pigs are to be found, the men are instructed to cut off the ears of the first pig caught and to offer up thanks to the *Atua* (God). In all cases where food is obtained thanks is given, and men going out are particularly instructed not to eat, drink, or smoke until they return to camp, lest the *Atua* should be offended. Should a party return unsuccessful, blame is attributed to one of them having disobeyed the orders given; for this sin the *Atua* has kept the food from them. The offender, if pointed out by his companions, is punished by Te Kooti, who in strong terms will sentence him to be deprived of the opportunity of hunting food by confining him to camp. *Karakia* (service) is held four times a day; the last is the prayer for sleep when retiring to rest, after which no one is allowed to move about, and silence is kept by all. No one dare approach Te Kooti's *whare* after that time. Te Kooti will often start out alone in the early morning bird-hunting with a decoy *kaka* parrot on his shoulder, or with a tomahawk to get honey from hollow trees. It is a practice of his to go out and reconnoitre the surrounding country, climbing to the tops of the highest ranges, not returning to the camp till evening. He professes that all his expeditions to murder or plunder are by the inspiration of his *Atua,* as when he was inspired at the Chathams to deliver his people from bondage. When so inspired he will often arise from his sleep and call his followers together to prayers, after which he informs them that the *Atua* has given something to him during his sleep, but whether food, man, or woman he cannot tell. A party is then despatched in a direction indicated by him. If a man or food is found, well and good; if a woman, she is to be brought to him. Should the party return unsuccessful the man to whom charge of the mission was given is tied up and confined in a *whare* for days without food or fire. Should a messenger or a man having been absent from camp some time return, no one dare hold conversation with him until he sees Te Kooti. He is led up to the chief's *whare,* and remains outside waiting the word to enter. It is a strict rule; no one approaches his house without permission.

"It is Te Kooti's practice to have intercourse with his followers' wives, by telling the men to send them to him—that his *Atua* has said they should become enceinte. Whatever men may think of this, they seldom dare refuse, or Te Kooti will at some future time profess that his *Atua* has revealed to him a traitor, and will request that man's death. He is never at a loss for a pretext to dispose of any one obnoxious to him.

"When thunder is heard, his men will inquire the words of the *Atua;* he will then reply to the effect that the *Atua* tells him that there are men among them desirous of escaping to the Government, and that they will be killed. A rainbow is another favourite sign of the *Atua* to him, denoting many things, as it suits him. He threatens future punishment for all men escaping to the Government; however long they may live in imagined security, judgment will come for deserting the *Atua.* He asserts that all the Government people will be delivered into his hands, and great power given him, when all seceders will be put to the sword. When a man is put to death, a Psalm is chanted over him, and then he is led to execution. When on the march or the war-path no one is allowed to smoke or eat till the word is given by Te Kooti. All fresh converts to his *Atua* are rechristened by him with Scriptural names."

Chapter 29

FINAL CAMPAIGN AGAINST TITOKOWARU

THE REDUCTION of the Ngatapa mountain fortress accomplished, Colonel Whitmore withdrew most of the Armed Constabulary from the East to the West Coast, where it was necessary to dislodge Titokowaru and his large force of Hauhaus from the stronghold at Tauranga-ika.* This *pa*, the best-designed fortification yet built by the hostile tribes in the country between Wanganui and Taranaki, occupied a commanding position at the edge of the bush on the road leading from the Kai-iwi to the Waitotara. In front the garrison overlooked the open country sloping gently to the Nukumaru lakes and the sandhills of the coast ; in rear was the roadless and almost trackless forest. Tauranga-ika was of large size, defended with trenches and rifle-pits, parapet, and a double line of stockade. Its design was skilful, as will be seen from the plan, and it was so built as to give the defenders an enfilading fire along each flank. It measured about 450 feet each way. The large posts of the palisade were from 6 to 12 inches in thickness and stood 10 to 15 feet above the ground, and the spaces between them were filled in with saplings set upright close together and fastened to cross-rails with supplejack and *aka*-vine ties. As was usual in Maori stockades, the saplings of the outer fence did not quite reach the ground ; only the posts of this line were sunk in the earth, and the defenders in the trench were enabled to fire under the foot of the fence. In rear of the inner or main stockade there was a parapet 6 feet high and 4 feet in thickness formed by the earth thrown out of the trench. The interior of the

---

* The site of Tauranga-ika stronghold is now occupied exactly by a native village (Nga-Rauru Tribe). On the *marae* and the adjoining ground within the high hedge of the village the outlines of the *pa* can be traced in the uneven turf. The Maoris point out the spot where the tall watch-tower stood near one of the *koki*, or flanking bastions, on the north-west side of the *marae*. Tauranga-ika is eighteen miles from Wanganui, alongside the main road to Taranaki; the *pa* is on the north or inland side of the road.

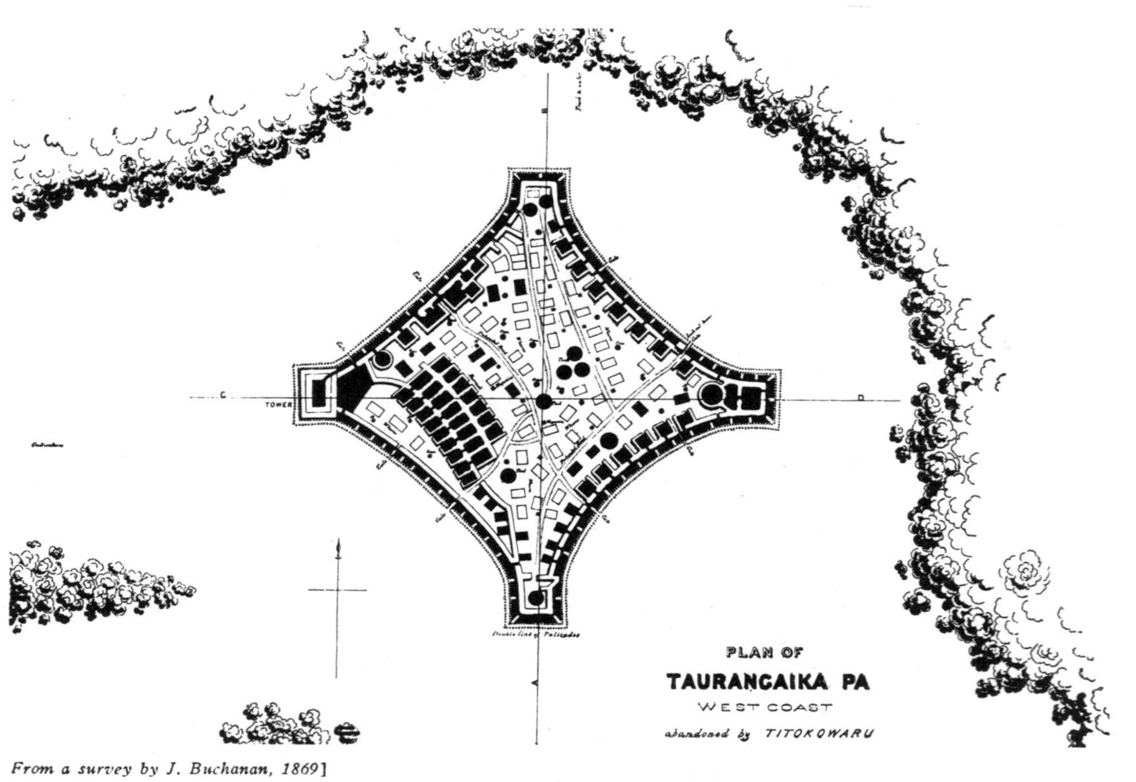

From a survey by J. Buchanan, 1869]

Plan of Tauranga-ika Pa, West Coast

work was pitted with trenches and covered ways and shell-proof underground shelters roofed with strong timbers and *toetoe* and *raupo* covered with earth ; even galvanised iron taken from the plundered settlers' buildings was used as roofing. At one of the flanking angles was a conspicuous watch-tower (*taumaihi*) over 30 feet high, constructed of stout timbers. In front, outside the palisading, stood a flagstaff on which the Hauhau war-flags were hoisted. Two gateways in the rear stockade gave access to the bush and the water-spring. Titokowaru occupied a tent near the rear of the *pa*.

While Whitmore was absent on his East Coast campaign recruits for the Armed Constabulary came pouring in from the South Island and Australia, and all December of 1868 the officers and non-commissioned officers at Westmere Camp and at Woodall's Redoubt on the Kai-iwi were busy drilling the new men. Titokowaru meanwhile was also strengthening his force and his defences, and he sent two men into Woodall's under a flag of truce bearing a letter in which he declared his intention of driving all the *pakehas* into the sea. The Maoris were detained and sent into Wanganui.

Colonel Whitmore arrived at Wanganui on the 18th January, 1869 and at once prepared for the advance on Tauranga-ika. His force consisted of about eight hundred Armed Constabulary and the Wanganui and Kai-iwi Mounted Corps, besides some two hundred Wanganuui Maoris under Kepa. Lieut.-Colonel William Lyon was second in command under Whitmore. The Kai-iwi River was bridged by an advanced column, and on the 25th January the whole force was moved across it to the right bank. There already was a road for the greater part of the way to the Waitotara. About the end of 1864 a large number of unsuccessful gold-diggers at the Whakamarino (Whanga-marino), in Marlborough, were brought across from Picton by the Government and given contract work on the formation of this West Coast military road, which was completed from Goat Valley, near Wanganui, to the Waitotara, passing Tauranga-ika. General Cameron did not take this road, but kept close to the sandhills on the coast. The inland route was too near the bush for his liking ; in fact, it passed through the bush at the Okehu Gorge and other places, highly likely spots for ambuscades. Whit-more's road parties put the road in repair for the passage of his large transport body and built bridges where required.

Whitmore now formed a small body of picked scouts, officially styled the Corps of Guides, for special work in advance of the column. This corps numbered at first seven, and seldom reached a dozen in number. It was at first commanded by William Lingard, a young trooper of Bryce's Kai-iwi Cavalry,

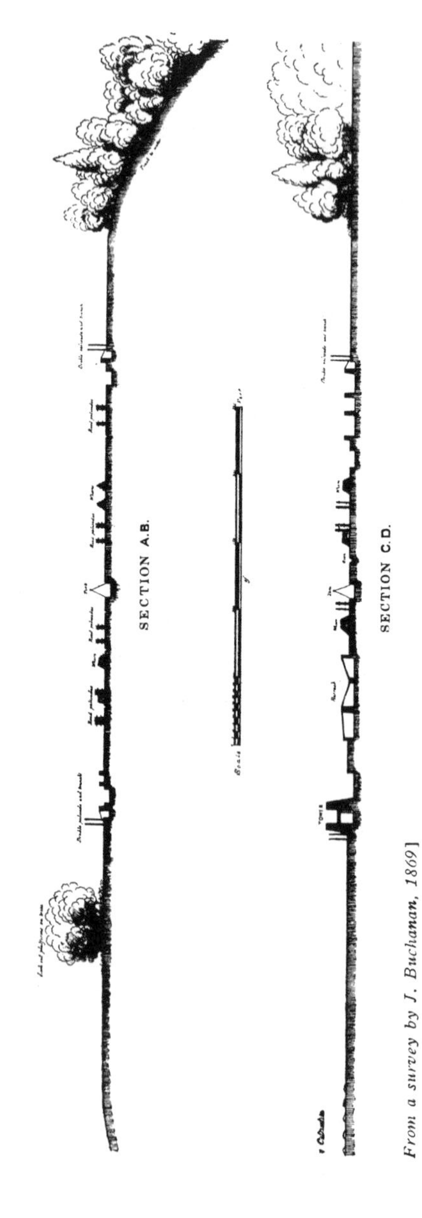

Cross-sections of Tauranga-ika Pa

From a survey by J. Buchanan, 1869]

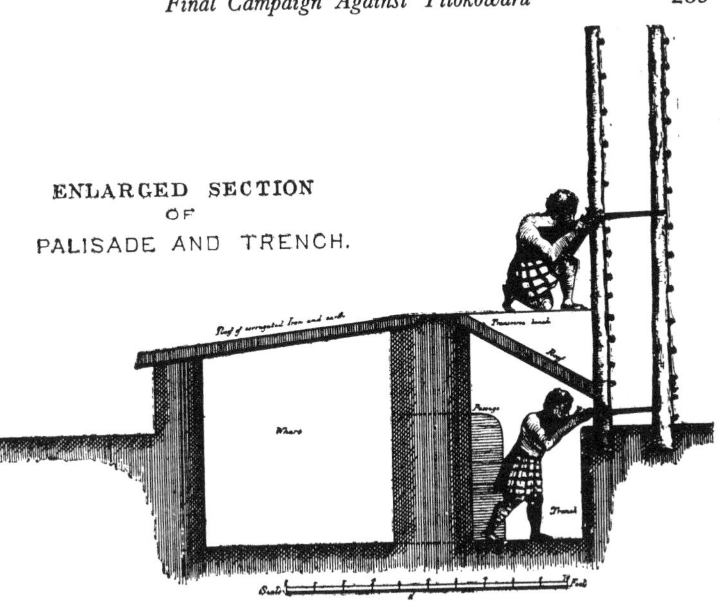

Section of Entrenchments, Tauranga-ika Pa

who had lately won the New Zealand Cross by a gallant deed at Tauranga-ika, when he rescued from the Hauhau tomahawks a comrade whose horse had been shot, falling on him in front of the palisades. Lingard's fellow-scouts were Christopher Maling (afterwards Captain), Williams, Powell, Mackenzie, and two Frenchmen named Herri and Pierre de Fougeraud. Lingard was disabled by illness at Patea after serving a few weeks, and Maling was then placed in charge as sergeant, and commanded the useful little body of scouts until June, 1870, when the European forces were withdrawn from the pursuit of Te Kooti.

Immediately after crossing the Kai-iwi on the 25th Whitmore ordered out the Guides to scout the wooded gorge-like valley of the Okehu, as he intended to take his force through it next morning. When night fell Lingard, Maling, and their five comrades left the camp for their risky night's work. They were shod in moccasins like Indians for noiseless marching; this was the idea of Mackenzie, a dark-skinned old soldier, a veteran of the Indian Mutiny, who had come out to Canterbury from India with Sir Henry Cracroft Wilson. The moccasins were made from the skin of a horse which Mackenzie had shot that afternoon ; the skin while warm was fitted to the men's feet with the hair inside, and was firmly laced with horse-skin thongs. As events proved they made excellent footgear for scouting-work. This Mackenzie was dexterous in the use of his favourite weapon, a double-edged Afghan knife-dagger.

It was a very calm night and bright moonlight. Mackenzie, whose senses were uncommonly keen, declared to Lingard, some time after they took post in the thick fern at the edge of the ravine, that he could smell the Maoris in the bush below. The scouts were posted at intervals above the gorge. About daylight two of them, working cautiously down, discovered a large body of Hauhaus, who were attempting to burn the bridge over the Okehu. The men were fired on, and, turning, made for the open country and the camp at top speed. Maling and Lingard, finding that they were almost surrounded by the Maoris, concealed themselves in the high fern alongside the track, with their Terry carbines ready ; they bit their cartridges for reloading, as was necessary in those days, and put their percussion caps in their mouths for instant use. Just before they did so they shook hands and promised to stick by each other to the end. A moment later a body of armed Hauhaus raced past their place of hiding, and presently they heard heavy firing from the direction of the camp. The troops had turned out and were covering the retreat of the scouts. The two comrades in hiding now found that they were under the fire of their own men, for the bullets were cutting through the tall fern above their heads. They decided to run for it and chance the Maoris, who were firing away on their left.

As they ran they came upon Mackenzie's dead body lying on the track. His head had been smashed in, and his carbine and ammunition and Afghan sheath-knife were gone. Taking a short-cut across the fern, Lingard and Maling safely reached the camp. The one life lost was that of the brave Mackenzie ; the previous day he had a presentiment of his end, and told his comrades that he would never see another sunrise. The surgeon was of opinion that he had fallen dead from heart-seizure before the Hauhaus overtook him.

The unmasking of the Hauhau ambuscade in the gorge was a good night's work. The Hauhaus fell back, and the Colonel marched his men through the dangerous defile unmolested.

By the 1st February Whitmore was at Nukumaru, and next day pushed on the cavalry and brought the infantry up towards the left flank of Tauranga-ika under cover of the bush. Camp was pitched 800 yards from the *pa,* and a body of Constabulary advanced and dug themselves in in a half-moon formation within 100 yards of the stockade ; some of the divisions had the shelter of a ditch and bank on the south flank of the *pa*. Whitmore scarcely displayed his accustomed skill and energy in the operations against the stronghold. If he really intended to capture Titokowaru and his Hauhaus by siege he could readily have surrounded the *pa* with the large force at his command. As it was, the attack is well described by a veteran, who says that the command "tackled Tauranga-ika in a half-hearted sort of way." The Volunteer Cavalry had scouted all the open or lightly timbered country around the place, and Whitmore came to the conclusion, apparently, that there was no urgent need to envelop the position as the enemy would remain within the stockade for the present. The two Armstrong guns were brought up towards the evening and placed on an eminence on the left front of the *pa* 500 yards away, and without orders from Colonel Whitmore the officer in charge began to shell the position. The commander had not intended this; he wished to reserve all his means of attack till next morning. The bombardment did small damage to the fort and very little harm to the garrison, who were all in secure quarters in the trenches and shell-proof *ruas*. The advanced divisions of the Armed Constabulary opened fire on the stockade in reply to the Maori volleys, and some of the force crept up within about 50 yards and entrenched themselves.

The Constabulary in their trenches enlivened the early hours of the night with bivouac songs, and the woods rang with the rousing choruses of "Marching through Georgia" and "Oh, Susannah." The Hauhau musketeers enjoyed the soldiers' music. "Go on, *pakeha,* go on," some of them shouted; "give us some more." But when it grew late the *pa* became remarkably silent; and when at break of day the Colonel began to move his men round the rear of the right flank of the position it was too late to envelop the enemy. The Coehorn mortars opened fire to get the range; the divisions told off to complete the surrounding movement moved on, and the Armstrongs threw some shells into the stockade. Some of the Armed Constabulary pushing on in advance, however, reconnoitred the *pa* and found it empty. It had been deserted during the night. The Hauhaus—men, women, and children—with their *pakeha-Maori,* Kimble Bent, had quietly slipped out into the wooded gully in rear and were already some miles away in full retreat for the Waitotara.

The explanation of this sudden decision to abandon the fort was given by Kimble Bent long after the war. His chief, Titokowaru, he said, had entered into a *liaison* with the wife of another *rangatira* of the *pa,* and this intrigue, soon detected, was considered fatal to his prestige, spiritual and temporal. He had trampled on his *mana tapu,* as the Maoris phrase it; he was no longer the invincible war-priest and war-captain of his people.

At a council of the chiefs it was resolved that the garrison should abandon the *pa;* it would be courting disaster to remain. No doubt the spectacle of Whitmore's army entrenched in front and the arrival of the first of his Armstrong shells clinched the popular decision. The people in silence struck into the bush. Titokowaru with forty men covered the retreat.

Whitmore ordered an immediate pursuit. He pushed the Volunteer Cavalry on to Weraroa by the track across the open country, and sent his best bush corps (No. 8 Division Armed Constabulary) and Kepa's Wanganui men to follow the retreating enemy's trail. Whitmore, in writing of this episode, endeavoured to mask his disappointment at his failure to hold Titokowaru. "I was not sorry," he said, "that Tauranga-ika had thus fallen without resistance. My object was to regain possession of the district, and if I could do this without loss and without putting too heavy a strain on my raw troops they would be encouraged, while an equal advantage would accrue to the country." Certainly Titokowaru's escape saved some lives, probably many lives, but it prolonged the campaign.

The Hauhau rear-guard was overtaken on the Karaka table-land immediately above the left bank of the Waitotara River by Kepa and his advance-guard of Wanganui men. The retreating force turned to fight and planted an ambush, resulting in several casualties among Kepa's men, including a sub-chief named Hori Raukawa, who was killed. Kepa with his few men broke through the Hauhaus and fell back on Captain Porter and his No. 8 Division, Arawa and Ngapuhi Maoris, with a few good European bushmen. Porter quickly extended the supports across the flat, mostly fern country, with some bush, and he and Kepa engaged the Hauhaus till dark, when they drew out to Weraroa. In this skirmish the Hauhaus had three killed. They took *utu* for their losses by decapitating Kepa's comrade, whose body was left on the field, and cutting out the heart and liver, which made a cannibal meal for some of the savages that night.

Next day (4th February) the enemy could not be found, and the most mobile corps in the command were despatched on re-connoitring expeditions. The Waitotara was crossed and an expedition went as far as Moturoa, the scene of Whitmore's defeat in November of the previous year. The headquarters remained at Nukumaru, and Nos. 1, 2, and 8 Divisions Armed Constabulary, under Lieut.-Colonel T. McDonnell, encamped at the Karaka plateau on the left bank of the Waitotara overlooking the bend of the river at Papatupu. Strong reconnaissance-parties under McDonnell, Porter, and Kepa were out daily seeking for traces of the Hauhaus, who were believed to be near the Moumahaki Stream, which flows into the Waitotara near Papatupu.

Nothing definite was known of Titokowaru and his band until the 18th February, when a party of nine men of No. 2 Division Armed Constabulary, under Sergeant Menzies, was cut off by Big Kereopa (a herculean savage of the Nga-Rauru Tribe) and an ambush-party at a peach-grove on the opposite side of the Waitotara to the Karaka camp. The sergeant and his nine men had obtained permission to cross the river in a canoe in order to gather peaches in a large grove on the north side about 300 yards from the river. The foragers had scarcely reached the peach-grove when they were fired on by a large force of Maoris; the shrewd Hauhaus knew that the fruit was a tempting bait, and had laid an ambuscade in the edge of the bush above the grove and about 60 yards from it in the expectation of a visit. The Constabulary men raced for their canoe, but most of those who escaped the first volley were overtaken and tomahawked. No. 1 Division, hearing the firing, hurried to the assistance of their comrades, but it was too late to do anything but exchange a few volleys with the enemy. They had killed Sergeant Menzies and six of his men; three only escaped. Tutange Waionui, a young warrior of the Pakakohi Tribe, felled the sergeant just as he had jumped into the canoe to escape. Tutange struck him on the temple with a *manuka* paddle which he snatched up from the canoe, and when the sergeant dropped back into the canoe stunned or dead a Maori named Toa-wairere slashed off his left leg with a tomahawk and carried off the leg into the bush, where it was cooked and eaten by Kereopa and some of his comrades.*

On the following day No. 8 Division Armed Constabulary (native) under Captain Porter, and the Wanganui men under Kepa, were sent across the Waitotara at Papatupu to hunt up the Hauhaus. They scoured the bush, and following up the enemy's trail, found the fire in which the sergeant's leg had been cooked and the calcined bones. Some skirmishing followed, but the

---

* These details were related to the author in 1908 by Tutange Waionui, then living at Pariroa, on the Patea.

A curious story also is narrated regarding the killing of Sergeant Menzies and the mutilation of his body. A Hauhau named Paramena was severely wounded in the Ngaio engagement near Kakaramea (1865). He was shot in an arm and in a leg—which was shattered—and he was also cut about the head as he lay wounded by the drummer-boys of the Imperial regiments when they were passing him. His smashed leg was amputated. Sir George Grey saw him afterwards and jokingly told him that he ought to get a pension. Paramena took the Governor's persiflage seriously, and actually applied for a pension—for having fought against the Government. His one-legged condition did not prevent him from joining Titokowaru in 1868 and fighting till the end of the war. He wanted a boot for his one foot, and when the sergeant's leg was carried into the bush Paramena appropriated the boot and wore it.

Hauhaus, well acquainted with all that roadless forest, were able to evade their pursuers, who returned to camp.

After a considerable amount of bush reconnaissance work carried out by No. 8 Division and Kepa's Maoris it was discovered that Titokowaru had moved on to the Patea River. By this time, as was learned afterwards, the Hauhaus were in want of both food and ammunition, and fearing discovery by the native contingents —they were in wholesome dread of Kepa's fierce soldiers—they scattered in parties and sought safe camping-places in the deepest parts of the great forest. Kimble Brent related that he and his native comrades were reduced to existing upon the pith of the *mamaku* fern tree, the *wharawhara* and other edible mosses, the mushroom-like *harore* that grew on the trunks of the *tawa* trees, *hakeke* or wood-fungus, and the *huhu,* the large white wood-grub. They did not dare to light a fire in the daytime for fear of betrayal by the smoke rising above the forest-trees. Powder and lead were in short supply, and percussion caps were very scarce and precious.

THE FIGHT AT OTAUTU

Early in March of 1869 Titokowaru had established himself in a bush camp at Otautu, on the left (east) bank of the Patea, about ten miles by the river route from the heads.

Here he gathered most of his people together, but did not fortify the village, which stood on a small area of level ground close to a steep declivity some 200 feet above the river. A party sallying out from here lay in wait on the sandhills at the mouth of the Whenuakura River and attacked (10th March) a dray convoy under Lieutenant and Quartermaster Hunter on the way to Patea. The attack was repulsed without loss to the small Government party. On the following day Colonel Whitmore established himself at Patea, and thus once more occupied the positions abandoned after the disaster at Moturoa in November, 1868.

On the night of the 12th March he marched to attack Titokowaru, whose camp at Otautu the scouts had at last located. Two columns of European and native troops were employed on this expedition. The right wing, four hundred strong, which Whitmore commanded, took the trail up the left bank of the Patea, while Lieut.-Colonel St. John took the other, numbering two hundred, along the right or west side of the river by a rough track. It was a very dark night, and as early morning approached a dense fog enveloped the forest and the river, shrouding from sight every sign of the sleeping camp. No. 8 Division was leading, with No. 1 in support; the advance necessarily was in single file. Suddenly a Hauhau sentry was surprised half asleep under a flax-bush. Ben Biddle, one of the best of the Armed Constabulary scouts, was the first to see the scout, and was about to tomahawk him without noise when an officer stopped him, saying it was an Arawa. The movements of the force alarmed the Hauhau, who was fired on but escaped, and in a moment the slumbering camp was in commotion. The village could not be seen, but as Whitmore rushed up his men through the fog he found his force under fire from invisible musketeers. The camp was not palisaded or otherwise protected, but the Hauhaus found perfect cover at the edge of the small plateau, where the ground dipped suddenly in a ravine to the Patea flowing far below. Sheltered by the dip of the ground they swept the clearing; some of them, too, fired from the lowermost branches of the *rata* trees. Most of them fired from a lower level than the attackers, and the majority of the Government men shot were hit in the head.

This singular battle in the fog developed rather seriously for Whitmore's force, for man after man fell dead or wounded, while the enemy was invisible. Meanwhile the women and children and the non-combatants of Titokowaru's band were escaping down the wooded ravine to the bank of the Patea, and to give them time to retreat to a place of safety the warriors fought a determined action, with all the odds in their favour, until the fog began to lift. Captain Gascoyne, with No. 1 Division, observed that the pall of vapour was becoming less dense, and suggested to Colonel Whitmore that No. 6 should be advanced on to the somewhat lower ground on the right, which would flank the enemy. This was done, and after a quarter of an hour's further skirmishing and an advance at the double the Hauhau rear-guard withdrew rapidly down through the bush to cover the retreat of their people. St. John's column on the other side of the Patea was not of any use in intercepting the flight of the enemy, who, hearing some volleys fired by the left wing near Otoia, struck off inland, and, as customary, scattered into parties. The Government force lost six men in the engagement, besides twelve wounded. Among the mortally wounded was a young half-caste lad, Arthur Gundry, brother of Captain Gundry of No. 8 Division. The Maori loss was slight. Tu-Patea te Rongo, who fought in the engagement, states that only one Hauhau was shot at Otautu, a man named Muhumuhu, from the Waikato. Kepa, however, overtook and killed two or three of the less swift-footed on the retreat. The fighting-men crossed the river and joined the non-combatants, and, travelling deep into the forest, moved on in the direction of Whakamara, a large settlement of former days some ten miles to the north-west.

The Hauhaus had made a plucky resistance at Otautu, favoured by the fog, to save their women and children. They only relinquished the fight when their ammunition was exhausted.

As for the Armed Constabulary, a veteran non-commissioned officer of No. 2 Division says: "It was splendid to see the way the boys in blue went at it that day. Our recruits by this time were getting well up in their work and were beginning to understand the tactics of bush skirmishing."

At Whakamara Village, on an open clearing within the bush, near a fortified position, Titokowaru's half-starved followers found many pigs and other food supplies, but were not long left in peace. Whitmore sent out his native contingents scouting, and Kepa on the 16th reported that he had discovered the Hauhaus at Whakamara. Lieut.-Colonel Lyon at once marched direct for the place with about three hundred Constabulary and Maoris, travelling by night across a rough country with numerous deep gorges. Whitmore meanwhile moved round with some mounted men by way of Mokoia, whence a horse-track led to Whakamara. A mounted Hauhau scout, Tutange Waionui, who was riding back along the track for a swag of blankets he had left, discovered the approach of the advance-party through the high fern and galloped off firing his revolver to give the alarm. Titokowaru and his whole force immediately abandoned their camp without attempting a defence. Kimble Bent and some of his companions, "racing like wild pigs before the hunters," as he described it, made no halt in their flight till they found themselves in an old refuge-place, Rimatoto, near the left bank of the Tangahoe, which here runs in a deep gorge. The main body also presently reached Rimatoto after a severe forced march, with Kepa's force relentlessly on their heels.

The Whakamara *pa* was built on a narrow neck of high land with a flat in front and in rear and deep gullies on either flank. The Hauhaus were camped on the rear flat near some peach-groves when the attack was delivered. It was to Whakamara that many of the natives retired after their defeat at Te Ngaio (Kakaramea) in 1865, and it was a gathering-place of the Hauhaus in the period 1866–68. Here the expedition under Whitmore found a tall Pai-marire flagstaff, probably the largest pole of worship ever erected by the natives. Tu-Patea te Rongo, of Taumaha, Patea, says:—

"Our *niu* at Whakamara was a lofty *rimu* mast, 4 or 5 feet through at the butt. We had felled the tree in the bush a mile away, and, after squaring it, hauled it to the camp. It was set up on the open *marae* in the front of our camp. The strong *pa* of Whakamara was in the rear; the troops did not attack it when they came, but pushed on in pursuit of us. The flag-mast was set up like a ship's mast, with topmast and crosstrees and four yards. The lower yard was crossed about half-way up the lower mast. At the crosstrees on the lower-mast head two yards were crossed at right angles to one another, and then a little way below the topmast-head there was another yard, a small one. The topmast-head was over 80 feet above the ground. At every yard-arm there was a block with rove halyards which led to the ground, and on all these halyards except the lowest, Maori war-flags were flown. A dozen flags, or more, were displayed. Some were British flags, Union Jacks, given to the Maoris before the war; some were flags bearing the words 'Tiriti o Waitangi' and 'Kingi Tawhiao'; some bore stars and other devices. Several of the flags dated back to the time of the Treaty of Waitangi; others had been

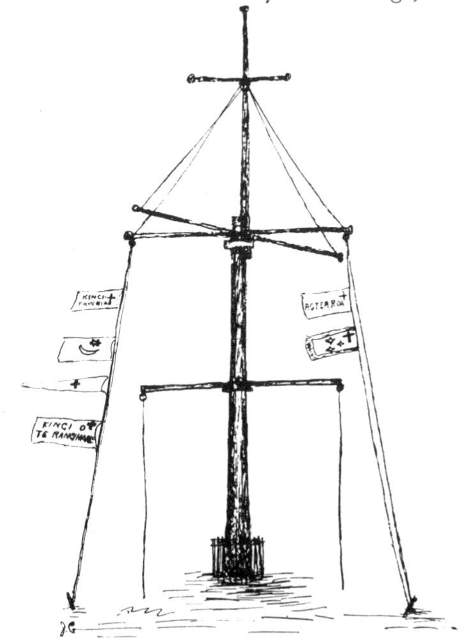

The *Niu* Mast at Whakamara

(Drawn by the author from descriptions given by Maoris.)

given to Taranaki by Waikato and King Tawhiao. The priest of this pole of worship was Te Whare-Matangi."

Mr. William Wallace, ex-sergeant No. 2 Division Armed Constabulary, says:—

"We cut this *niu* down when we captured Whakamara in 1869. We had seen the flags flying on it from a great distance off long before the fight. It was the tallest *niu* mast I have ever seen. It was a great pity, I think, that it was destroyed."

A GREAT BUSH CHASE

The forest chase from Whakamara terminating near Tai-porohenui was the most arduous duty of the whole campaign. The pursuing column was commanded by Major Kepa; it was the first time in the history of the wars that European officers and men volunteered to serve under a Maori officer. Kepa's reputation for skill, energy, and bravery was so high that the *pakeha* troops willingly offered for the service when volunteers were required for the flying column. Kepa's force was about two hundred and fifty strong, consisting of his Wanganui Contingent, the Arawa-Ngapuhi Corps (No. 8 Division Armed Constabulary), under Captain Porter, and sixty white Armed Constabulary of various divisions under Captains H. W. Northcroft and Watt. Sergeant Maling and eight scouts of the Corps of Guides accompanied the column. The advance-guard numbered twenty-five Maoris, some of whom were Wanganui and some Arawa, with Porter and native officers. The noted bushman and scout Tom Adamson marched with the advance.

On the afternoon of the first day's chase (18th March) the Hauhau rear-guard laid an ambush for the pursuers in a deep, densely wooded gorge. The concealed enemy let the advance-guard pass through and opened fire from both sides on the main body of the Armed Constabulary and the Wanganui Contingent. Kepa and his men, however, attacked swiftly and determinedly, and the advance-guard turning about, the Hauhaus were taken in flank and dispersed. They retreated so quickly after delivering their fire that only one was killed. This was the last attempt at resistance made by Titokowaru's followers.

The country traversed, trackless and densely wooded, was dissected with many gullies and gorges, one of which was many hundreds of feet in depth. This great ravine was encountered when the foremost pursuers, including Captain Northcroft and the most active of his bushmen-soldiers, were close upon their foes. It was so narrow that the rifles were sighted for only 200 yards when the Constabulary were firing at the Maori rear-guard laboriously climbing up the opposite side. The force had to descend to the bottom of this defile, through which a small stream ran, and the traverse was so difficult that it took the men from noon—the hour when they were engaging the enemy across the gulch—until 8 o'clock at night to reach the top of the cliff on the other side. The two forces camped that night only about three-quarters of a mile from each other.

Next day at the Kaka-pirau Creek the first stragglers were caught and killed. The chase went on through the dim and pathless forest under an endless canopy of green. Every male

Captain H. W. Northcroft, N.Z.C.

Captain Northcroft began his military career at the age of sixteen years as a guide to the Imperial troops in Taranaki in 1860. He gained a commission in 1864, and served throughout the Maori campaigns with great distinction. He was awarded the New Zealand Cross in recognition of repeated acts of bravery, particularly his devotion to mortally wounded comrades at Pungarehu and Tirotiro-moana, Taranaki, in 1866. (See page 149 and Appendices.) For many years after the wars he was a Stipendiary Magistrate, and after his retirement from the Bench he was for some time New Zealand Government Resident at Rarotonga, Cook Islands.

prisoner was killed and decapitated. This barbarous reversion to old Maori methods of warfare was ordered by Major Kepa, through a misunderstanding of Colonel Whitmore's offer of a reward for Hauhaus killed or captured. After the skirmish on the Karaka plateau, at the Waitotara River, the Colonel had agreed to a request made by Kepa, who was greatly angered by the mutilation of his kinsman Hori Raukawa by the enemy, that rewards should be paid for loss inflicted on the Hauhaus, and had offered £10 a head for chiefs and £5 for ordinary men. The

Wanganui therefore entered into the bush chase with great zest, and spared no man captured. Three Hauhaus were shot and decapitated on the first day, and eight others at various stages of the pursuit. The principal man killed was a young chief named Matangi-o-Rupe, of Titokowaru's own clan, Ngati-Manu-hiakai. Captain Porter, who witnessed the deeds of the Wanganui, was powerless to prevent the head-taking except so far as his own men, the Arawa, were concerned. He asked the Wanganui men to bury the heads, and suggested that they should take only the ears if they wished to claim the Colonel's reward. But they answered, "No; Witimoa said 'heads,' and if he doesn't get the heads he may not pay us!"

A veteran of the Arawa section of the advance-guard, Pirika Hohepa, of Rotorua, thus described some of the incidents in the bush pursuit:—

"The force to which I belonged, the Arawa and Ngapuhi Division of the Armed Constabulary, was always called upon to lead the column in any dangerous work in the bush, and it became a saying among us that although we were Number Eight Division on parade we were always Number One when we were moving into action against the enemy. Before we started out on the forest chase there was a meeting of the Arawa committee in a *wharepuni* at Whakamara, and at this council it was stated that Colonel Whitmore had given direction to decapitate all prisoners taken and bring in the heads. [This, of course, was a misconstruction of Whitmore's statement.] We followed the fugitives through the forest. On the top of a hill we came suddenly upon a man and two women and some children resting. When the man saw us he ran and crouched down between the two root-buttresses of a *pukatea* tree. One of our Maoris shot him and he fell. A European [Tom Adamson, Major Kemp's *pakeha-Maori*] rushed forward, and, lifting up the fallen man's head, he stretched the neck across one of the root-flanges of the tree, and snatching out a short-handled tomahawk from his belt just behind his right hip he chopped the Hauhau's head off. This was not fair to the man who shot the Maori; the European bushman, however, kept the head, and actually obtained a reward for it from the Colonel. The Maori thus killed and beheaded was Matangi-o-Rupe, a chief of the Ngati-Ruanui. Further along the forest-track one of our Government Maoris shot and decapitated Pinoka, another Taranaki warrior. Those were the only rebel heads I actually saw taken on that expedition, but other Maoris, I know, were killed and beheaded.

"The heads of the slain Hauhaus were dried and preserved in the olden Maori fashion, and I shall describe to you what I saw. It was the Ngati-Hau, the Wanganui tribe, who carried out this process; we Arawa did not take part, but we crowded round to watch the *tohunga,* or expert, at his work. The *tohunga* who carried out the process of *pakipaki-upoko* was an old man named Teoti, from the high country near Tongariro. He had dug a hole in the ground and in it made an oven (*hangi*) with stones on which he placed wood. When the wood was mostly consumed he raked the burning sticks away and left the red-hot stones. Above this glowing oven the head was placed on the end of a stick, and flax mats and other garments were heaped closely over all to retain the heat. From time to time the old man removed the coverings to smooth the skin down and wipe off the moisture. The intense heat made the skin very white (*kiritea*), like the complexion of a European, and this showed up the tattoo-lines prominently. The process was repeated with the other heads, and old Teoti really made a very good job of it!"

The column divided when Titokowaru's followers were found to have scattered into small parties and the pursuers' food-supplies were exhausted, and the Constabulary and Kepa's division marched independently for the open country, finally emerging near Taiporohenui. Colonel Whitmore had encamped at that place, and the officers reported their operations in the forest and the final dispersal of the Hauhaus. The Wanganui warriors and two of the white bushmen, Tom Adamson and Donald Sutherland, brought in their flax kits of heads. Eleven Hauhaus had been decapitated, and the Maoris came up in a body to Whitmore's tent and poured in head after head on the floor, to the amazement of the Colonel, who had forgotten all about his promise of a reward, and who, in any case, had not intended his words to be interpreted so literally. "*Na, Witimoa, to upoko!*" ("There, Whitmore, are your heads!") exclaimed the hunters of men as they turned out their ghastly trophies of the chase. The Europeans did not deliver their heads in such unceremonious fashion; nevertheless, a tally was kept and all were paid for, mostly in orders for clothes and other necessaries. Whitmore at once issued orders that no more heads must be taken. However, the Wanganui men did not get another chance.

In a note on these incidents of the chase Captain Christopher Maling, who in 1869 was sergeant in charge of the Corps of Guides, wrote: "The whole matter of the head-hunting was due to a misunderstanding on Major Kepa's part. I was present when the heads were brought in to Colonel Whitmore. We had just arrived, having come by a different track to that taken by Kepa, and I was telling the Colonel about the barbarity of the thing. He told me that he had never authorized anything of the sort. He said he had told Kepa that the Governor had authorized a reward of £1000 for the capture of Titokowaru, and that he would recommend a reward of a small sum for prisoners captured. This was for the purpose of getting information, as the Hauhaus were breaking away in *hapus* and it was desirable to find out their various destinations. He was perfectly amazed when he saw those heads brought in."

THE RETREAT TO TE NGAERE AND THE WAITARA

Titokowaru's power was finally broken. He never fought again; and no doubt the ruthless methods of Kepa's men struck terror into the hearts of his people. He was without food and ammunition, and some women who were taken prisoner on the bush chase described the sore straits to which the fugitives had been reduced. One woman had died from exhaustion on the flight from Whakamara, and her body was concealed in a hollow *rata* tree. [The skeleton was found there long after the war.] The women prisoners gave the information that Titokowaru was retreating on the Ngaere, the great swamp in the heart of the forest country eastward of the Whakaahurangi track leading from Ketemarae to North Taranaki. Whitmore consulted Kepa regarding the line of pursuit, and on his advice moved the force on across the open country to Keteonetea and entered the bush at that point, crossing the Mangemange Stream and marching on the Ngaere by way of Tirotiro-moana.

It was seen, on reaching the edge of the far-stretching morass, that Titokowaru's reported refuge was secure from any sudden attack and was very difficult to reach. The Maori camp, a sanctuary of old for the Ngati-Tupaea and other tribes in time of war was on a long peninsula, practically an island, extending into the middle of the deepest part of the *raupo* and flax fenland. Whitmore's advanced force, cautiously reconnoitring the swamp under cover of the bush along its edge, found that at the narrowest part a quarter of a mile or more of quaking and treacherous bog, threaded by a deep sluggish stream—the source of the Mangemange River, which flows into the Tangahoe near Otapawa —separated the mainland from the islanded village in the centre of the swamp.

Whitmore keeping his men carefully concealed from the view of the enemy, set the force to work making fascine hurdles, formed of long saplings and cross-pieces interlaced with supplejack and *aka* vines, for the purpose of crossing the swamp near a point where there was a large eel-weir. The troops were enjoined to keep as silent as possible; no fires were permitted to be lighted by day and only very small ones at night under cover of the forest. The Maoris could be heard speaking and shouting in the *kainga,* unsuspicious of their enemy's presence.

By the night of the 24th March all was ready for the crossing. Fifty light-going Wanganui and Arawa Maoris were sent across first, and the force then quietly laid the fascines in a line over the swamp, and all crossed the quivering bog in safety and silence before daylight in the morning. Leaving Lieut.-Colonel Lyon with some of the Constabulary to hold the bridge-head and cover the retreat in case of need, Colonel Whitmore pushed on through the belt of bush between the swamp and the Maori *kainga.* The surprise would have been complete and Titokowaru and seventy of his men who were in the camp would have been compelled to fight or to surrender, but at the moment when an attack was about to be made the advance was observed by some of the natives, and several called a welcome to the troops, while to Whitmore's annoyance and embarrassment, two Wanganui friendly chiefs and Mr. Booth, R.M., were discovered among the people of the village. Mr. Booth had called on the people to surrender, and his unnecessary intervention and the duplicity of some of the Wanganui men saved Titokowaru. While Whitmore was vainly endeavouring to discover the truth from the natives, who declared that the Hauhau leader had left the *kainga* three days previously, scores of men, women, and children were seen escaping into the bush and the swamp on the other side of the settlement clearing. As it was thought these were neutrals, no order to fire was given. Too late it was discovered that Titokowaru and most of his warriors had once more eluded the Government force.

A pursuit was ordered, but the Hauhaus had a long start, and it was impossible to overtake them. They retreated northward at their utmost speed, and, abandoning their own district altogether, travelled through the almost trackless forests and over the ranges to the Upper Waitara. There Titokowaru found secure sanctuary at last in the territory of the Ngati-Maru tribe. He established himself at the Kawau *pa,* on a long tongue of level land with steep banks in a sweeping bend of the Waitara. At the Kawau and other *kaingas* in its neighbourhood he remained until the year 1875, when part of the Ngati-Maru country was purchased by the Government. Kimble Bent and about forty other fugitives had broken off from the main body after the operations at Whakamara and had found shelter in the depths of the forest at Ruku-moana, on the Upper Patea. There they remained until they heard that the dreaded Kepa and his Wanganui head-hunters were still scouring the forests, and with the utmost caution they set out for the Ngati-Maru territory. The journey occupied two days; the country traversed was the wildest and most broken part of Taranaki. They did not dare to light a fire on the march, and wherever possible they walked in running water in order to conceal their trail.

Colonel Whitmore, after the fiasco at Te Ngaere, considered it unnecessary to trouble much further about Titokowaru, whose power for rebellion was definitely broken. A company of Ngati-Porou natives had arrived from the East Coast, and these he left at Waihi Redoubt to patrol the country and intercept any parties attempting to return.

Lieut.-Colonel Lyon was given command of the South Taranaki district, with headquarters at Patea. Taking most of the Constabulary, Whitmore then transferred his activities to the Bay of Plenty. One column under Lieut.-Colonel St. John marched to New Plymouth by way of the Whakaahurangi track, on the east side of Mount Egmont, the route traversed by General Chute in 1866. The left wing marched to Opunake and embarked in the Government steamer "Sturt" for Onehunga via Waitara, the s.s. "St. Kilda" taking the other part of the force.

THE MASSACRE AT PUKEARUHE REDOUBT

Colonel Whitmore, before going on to Auckland an_ the East Coast, gave consideration to the question of military operations against the people of the Ngati-Maniapoto at Mokau Heads in avengement of a shocking massacre by a raiding-party of that tribe. On the 13th February a small war-party from Mokau, led by the chiefs Wetere te Rerenga and Te Oro, suddenly appeared at Pukearuhe Redoubt, the northernmost Taranaki outpost, established in 1865 on the site of an ancient Maori stronghold, the key of North Taranaki. The raiders slaughtered the white inhabitants and also a venerated missionary, the Rev. John Whiteley, of the Wesleyan Church. The military outpost at Pukearuhe (Fern-root Hill) had been established in 1865 in order to command the only practicable route along the West Coast between Mokau Heads and Taranaki, and its existence there, blocking the passage of recruits from Ngati-Maniapoto and Waikato to the camps of the Taranaki Hauhaus, was a continual source of annoyance to the Maoris at Mokau, for it was regarded by them as a direct challenge. In 1869 it was temporarily defenceless; the military settlers in the district were working their bush farms, and the vulnerable condition of Pukearuhe was a temptation which Wetere and his section of Ngati-Maniapoto at Mokau Heads could not resist. Lieutenant Gascoigne and his family and two men were the only people at the post, and, although armed natives were sometimes seen passing along the coast, they considered themselves secure.

Among the pioneer soldier settlers in the district was Captain William B. Messenger, who, in 1869, was working his farm near the mouth of the Mimi River, about six miles south of Pukearuhe

Drawing by Mr. A. H. Messenger]

Pukearuhe Redoubt, from the North

This drawing shows the horse-track up the cliff from the beach. The Armed Constabulary post at Pukearuhe was the key of North Taranaki. All Maoris travelling along the coast had to use this route, because of the precipitous cliffs, and the redoubt completely commanded the track.

and nine to ten miles from the Pari-Ninihi (" Steep Cliffs "), the huge precipitous wall, rising in places 800 feet sheer above the sea, usually called the White Cliffs. On the afternoon of the 12th February two armed Maoris suddenly appeared at Captain Messenger's house, and his wife, who met them at the door, at the first glance felt distrustful of them. They demanded to know where " Wiremu " was, and Mrs. Messenger called her eldest son, a little boy, and told him to call his father from his work.

Meanwhile the Maoris stood regarding her intently, and there was something in their savage appearance that convinced her danger was impending. When Captain Messenger arrived he questioned the two men closely. They told him they were on their way north to the Mokau, and wanted him to put them across the Mimi in his canoe. This he did, and after they crossed the river he watched them disappear along the track to Pukearuhe.

Mrs. Messenger's fears were justified on the following day when a friendly Maori came galloping down to the Mimi ford with the news that the little garrison at Pukearuhe had been wiped out. " Will you come back with me and see what has

The Original Redoubt at Pukearuhe

This picture of Pukearuhe Redoubt was drawn by Mr. A. H. Messenger from a sketch by his father, the late Colonel W. B. Messenger, who with his Taranaki Military Settlers garrisoned it in the early “ sixties ”. A blockhouse was afterwards built in the redoubt, and the work was enlarged. Pukearuhe was occupied as a frontier Armed Constabulary post until the year 1885.

happened?" asked Captain Messenger; but the Maori refused, saying that they would be killed. He promised, however, to see that Mrs. Messenger and the children were taken through to New Plymouth, and they immediately set out on horseback, the Maori walking ahead and leading his horse. Captain Messenger started at once for Pukearuhe, and, riding hard, soon came in sight of the cliff-top post, where columns of smoke rising from burning houses showed him that the Maori's report was true.

Realizing that nothing more could be gained by a close inspection, and that the Hauhaus were probably waiting in ambush for him, he turned and galloped off towards the Waitara, with the feeling haunting him that this was only the beginning of a great organized raid on the North Taranaki settlements. On the track to Urenui and the Waitara Mrs. Messenger was being urged to haste by the Maori escort. "Hurry, missus," he kept saying; "Hurry—they'll catch us if we don't hurry!" Continually he looked back apprehensively, expecting every moment to see some of the war-party in pursuit. However, his fears were needless, and he took his charges safely into town. The strange Maoris seen, it was afterwards discovered, met the Ngati-Maniapoto party from Mokau.

On news of the attack reaching New Plymouth an expedition was organized and went up to the White Cliffs by sea. The bodies of Lieutenant Gascoigne, his wife, and their four children were found, lightly covered over with sand. All had been tomahawked. The body of the Rev. John Whiteley was found at the foot of the hill on the inland side of the redoubt; he had been shot at close range, and there were seven bullet-wounds in his body. The bodies of two military settlers, Milne and Richards, who lived at the redoubt, were also found. The blockhouse and other buildings in the redoubt had been set on fire before the raiders returned to the Mokau, twenty-five miles away. The bodies were taken to New Plymouth by steamer and buried in the cemetery at Te Henui.

It was some time before the story of the massacre was obtained from the Maoris by Captain Messenger. The Ngati-Maniapoto war-party appeared on the beach below the redoubt on Saturday morning, the 13th February; the advance detachment only was seen from the post, the main body had halted out of sight. The leading natives went up to the redoubt, and finding two men there (Milne and Richards) induced them to go down to the beach by saying that they had a drove of pigs for sale. They descended the steep path separately and were killed one after the other. The whole of the war-party then ascended to the redoubt and found that Lieutenant Gascoigne and his family were out in their field of potatoes and maize.

The Gascoignes' Home, Pukearuhe

This photograph, taken shortly before the massacre at Pukearuhe Redoubt, White Cliffs, in 1869, shows Lieutenant Gascoigne standing in front of the house, and Mrs. Gascoigne in the doorway carrying one of the children.

On seeing the Maoris at the blockhouse he went to meet them, carrying his youngest child, and Mrs. Gascoigne following him with the other three children. They received him with apparent friendship and repeated the story about pigs for sale. Suddenly he was struck down, and his wife and all the little ones were tomahawked. Towards evening the missionary, Mr. Whiteley, was seen approaching on horseback along the track from the Waitara. He had ridden from the Wesleyan mission station at New Plymouth on one of his customary visits to the outposts of settlement. He had been engaged in work among the Maoris at Kawhia and in Taranaki for more than thirty years, and no clergyman was regarded with more respect and affection than "Te Waitere." But the Mokau men were on the war-path, and were intensely excited by the murderous deeds at the blockhouse and on the beach; moreover, they were Hauhaus and fanatics. They intercepted Whiteley in the dusk of the evening and ordered him to turn back. Perceiving that some disaster had occurred at the redoubt he insisted on going on. His horse was shot down, and, freeing himself, he knelt down to pray, and while doing so was shot by several of the Maoris and fell dead. The murder of the good old missionary horrified even Ngati-Maniapoto when the *taua* returned to Mokau Heads. Although the leaders of the King party at Tokangamutu tacitly approved of the proposed

The Pukearuhe Blockhouse Destroyed by Wetere's War-party, 1869

(Drawn by Mr. A. H. Messenger from a sketch by his father.)

raid on Pukearuhe, they had no intention of encouraging the slaughter of women and children, much less of a missionary whose work and character were familiar to and respected by all.*

Soon after the discovery of the bodies a party of men under Captain Messenger scoured the ranges in rear of Pukearuhe and in the direction of the Mokau, and on one occasion nearly caught Wetere and several of his war-party, who were in the act of preparing their evening meal when their pursuers came on them at twilight in the bush. The surprise would have been complete but for the uncertain light. There was a rush of Maoris into the gloom of the forest, followed by a few hasty shots, and that was all. Wetere was an outlaw with a price on his head until 1883, when he was included in the Government's amnesty to those concerned in the war. He always denied having killed the Gascoignes or Mr. Whiteley. After the massacre Pukearuhe was garrisoned by Armed Constabulary under Captain Messenger, and remained an important military post until the demobilization of the field force in 1885.

In April, 1869, Colonel Whitmore made a reconnaissance of Mokau Heads preparatory to suggested reprisals for the raid on Pukearuhe. The troop-steamers "Sturt" and "St. Kilda," employed in conveying the Constabulary to Onehunga, went in close to the mouth of the river, and the "Sturt," commanded by Captain Fairchild, landed three boatloads of men

---

* For the Maori narrative of the massacre, see Henare Piripi's confession in Appendices.

The Later Blockhouse at Pukearuhe Redoubt

This sketch shows a blockhouse, still in existence, erected at one of the angles of the Pukearuhe Redoubt, after the destruction of the original building by Wetere te Rerenga's raiding-party. The inset shows detail of the rifle loopholes. The drawing was made by Mr. Messenger in 1916.

near the present site of the signal-station inside the heads. Some volleys were fired at the Maori *kainga*, Te Kauri, on the opposite side of the river, which was hidden by the cliffs from observation at sea, but only a few people were seen in the distance; most of Wetere's people had taken canoe up the river. Several shells were fired from the "Sturt's" brass gun in the direction of the native *kainga;* these were the last artillery shots fired in the Maori wars. It was decided that operations at Mokau were unnecessary, and Whitmore, therefore, assured that the nine years' war on the West Coast had ended at last, gave his attention to the campaign against Te Kooti on the other side of the Island.

CAPTURE OF THE PAKAKOHI TRIBE, PATEA

Although actual fighting had ceased, several important expeditions were carried out by the colonial forces in the South Taranaki and Waitotara districts during April, May, June, and July, 1869. The Pakakohi and Nga-Rauru Tribes, who had not remained with Titokowaru after the final defeat at Whakamara, had taken shelter up the Patea, Whenuakura, and Waitotara Rivers, where they considered themselves safe from further molestation. In April a force of sixty men, under Major Noake, Captain Kells, and Captain John Bryce, ascended the Waitotara by canoe for many miles in pursuit of Nga-Rauru, but found only deserted settlements. Captain Hawes, of the Wairoa, with ninety men, chiefly Ngati-Porou, scouted the banks of the Whenuakura, and Colonel Lyon examined the Patea country. The Ngati-Porou company, searching the bush along the Patea, shot four Hauhaus. Colonel Lyon was highly pleased with Ngati-Porou; he wrote of them "as the best body of natives it had ever been my fortune to command." In June Major Noake made a canoe expedition up the Patea, taking two hundred and seventy men in his flotilla, and captured the old chief Nga-waka-taurua and many of his Pakakohi Tribe. The warriors surrendered their arms, and were taken out to Patea. Gradually other sections of the tribe were rounded up on the Patea and the Whenuakura, until practically the whole of the fighting-men of the Pakakohi were captured, to the number of over a hundred, besides most of the women and children. The men, to their great disgust, were transported to Otago, and were not released until peace was thoroughly established on the West Coast. Had the Pakakohi anticipated this imprisonment it is extremely unlikely that they would have surrendered as they did.

Narratives by two veterans of the West Coast forces describe the principal canoe expeditions in search of the Pakakohi Tribe. Mr. R. B. Hamilton, of Manawapou, Manutahi, who served in the Colonial Defence Force Cavalry in the Waikato War and afterwards in the Wanganui Yeomanry Cavalry and the Patea Rifles, stated that in June, 1869, a force of about one hundred and thirty men set out up the Patea River in canoes in order to attempt the capture of the Hauhaus. "Major Noake," he said, "sent me on ahead in a small canoe with two other men to scout the river and report to him if I saw any Maoris or indications of their whereabouts. We were a day and a half working up the river with paddle and pole, a long way up past Otautu. We in our small light canoe got on well ahead, but we encountered trouble at the first big rapid. I was in the bow with my carbine pointing out over the gunwale ahead, as I worked along, now paddling, now poling. When we reached this rapid I advised my companions to keep to the still water under the bank, but the steersman sent the canoe right into the middle of the rapid, and before I knew where we were we had capsized and I was over my head in the swift water. I had a narrow escape from drowning, for I had two hundred rounds of ammunition at my belt in the heavy old-fashioned pouches, my

Major M. Noake

carbine, and an army revolver. After a lot of scrambling we got out and righted our canoe. Fortunately I had a bottle of whisky, and a good tot of this helped to put warmth into us after our ducking in the icy-cold water. When we had put things to rights and partly dried ourselves we went on up and round the bends of the winding river, under high banks covered with heavy forest. At last we saw blue smoke rising from the green bush far ahead, and we went on cautiously, always expecting attack. We landed below the place where the smoke was seen, tied up our canoe, and scouted cautiously up the bank and into a good-sized village. It was quite deserted. Evidently the people had only just left, and it was an eerie feeling that came over me, knowing that armed men must be lurking in the trees about us. Suddenly a Maori, unseen by us but quite near, called out, and Tom Adamson, who was with me, found that the Maoris wanted a *korero* with the white authorities and were willing to make peace with us. We returned to our canoe and paddled down the river as fast as we could go, and when I met the flotilla I reported to Major Noake. The end of it was that 128 of the Pakakohi Tribe surrendered and came down with us to Patea. The men were shipped off to Otago, to tame them.

Old Nga-waka-taurua was the chief of this tribe. He was a fine aristocratic type of Maori, of patriarchal appearance. Of course, had the Maoris wished they could have ambuscaded us at any one of a hundred places on the river and cut up our expedition very badly."

William Kelly, of Stratford, Taranaki, who had been an American man-of-war sailor before he enlisted in the New Zealand forces, gave the following account of the last expedition after the remnant of the Pakakohi, who were sheltering on the upper part of the Whenuakura River:—

"In July, 1869, a detachment of twenty of us (Patea Rangers and Armed Constabulary), under Captain Kells, went up the Whenuakura River in canoes in order to try and capture the chief Te Onekura, who was concerned in the murder of Mr. Broughton, the previous Government interpreter, on the Patea in 1865. Te Onekura was supposed to have taken the Government money—a large sum—with which Broughton had intended to pay for a block of land. All the members of our expedition were experienced canoe-men. I had learned to paddle and pole when we were at Pipiriki, on the Wanganui. We reached a good-sized settlement some miles up the river, and took the Maoris there by surprise, but there was no firing except by way of 'bluff.' We found an old Maori there, one of the Hauhaus, who, we thought, would be able to tell us something. Captain Kells, Tom Adamson, and I took him out into the bush a little distance from the settlement, within gun-shot sound. We stood him out there and told him that we'd shoot him unless he told us where Te Onekura had hidden the stolen money. The old man could not or would not tell. He maintained a stubborn silence. We told him he was about to be killed for his failure to answer us, and I slowly levelled my carbine and fired just past his ear. The plucky old man never moved. The shot was heard in the village as we intended; the idea was to compel the Hauhaus to divulge the secret of the money and to impress them with the belief that we had shot the old fellow for his obstinate silence. We kept the first Maori back in the bush a while, and dealt with another Hauhau in the same way, but with no success. Returning to the settlement, we got a boy to show us the track down through the bush to another place on the river-bank. There we took the people by surprise; they were all gathered in a large *wharepuni*, which was partly dug out of the ground, with the sides earthed up, so that the floor was a foot or two below the level of the ground outside. We interrogated these people also, but to no effect; the Government never recovered the looted money. We took a number of prisoners here and brought them down to Patea."

Chapter 30

TE KOOTI'S RAID ON WHAKATANE

IN THE CAMP of refuge in the deep forest of Tahora one of Te Kooti's daily petitions appropriate to his condition was the 64th Psalm. "Hear my voice, O God, in my prayer," he recited; "preserve my life from fear of the enemy. Hide me from the secret counsel of the wicked; from the insurrection of the workers of iniquity: Who whet their tongue like a sword, and bend their bows to shoot their arrows, even bitter words. . . . But God shall shoot at them with an arrow; suddenly shall they be wounded." The fugitive chief was preparing one of those arrows; presently he launched it, a *kokiri* against the *pakeha* and the friendly Maoris on the Bay of Plenty plains.

With recruits from the Urewera and Whakatohea Tribes, Te Kooti gradually restored his shattered forces, and in March, 1869, he made his first attack on the Bay of Plenty settlements. Marching down the headwaters of the Waioeka, he crossed over to the Waimana, and emerging on the alluvial plain of the Whakatane at Ruatoki he set about his work of bloodshed and plunder in the territory of Ngati-Pukeko. This tribe, whose lands bounded those of Tuhoe at Taneatua, on the Waimana, was comparatively rich in horses and cattle, and cultivated wheat and maize largely, and its villages and the seaport settlement of Whakatane, where a section of the Ngati-Awa Tribe lived, were tempting objectives for plunder.

The Hauhaus first visited Ohiwa Harbour, where a party raided the friendly natives, and a surveyor, Mr. Pitcairn, was killed on Uretara Island, where he was camped shooting *kuaka* (godwit). Wi Piro and Rangi-tahau were in this band.

At the Ruatoki settlements Te Kooti was hospitably received by the Urewera, and many men joined him there for his attack on Ngati-Pukeko and the port township at Whakatane. Among those who had lately reinforced his fighting band was the chief Wirihana Koikoi, of Taupo. The Hauhaus then advanced on Rauporoa pa, Te Kooti detaching a party to take the flour-mill and small redoubt at Te Poronu. These operations will be described in detail.

THE DEFENCE OF TE PORONU

About three miles and a half south of Whakatane Town, close to the main road leading to Taneatua and Waimana, can be seen the grassy mounds which indicate the site of an old Maori flour-mill, driven by water, and a small redoubt which stood alongside it. This spot, Te Poronu, was the scene in 1869 of an heroic fight against overwhelming odds, one of the most valiant defences in the Maori wars. The site of the historic mill is on " Mill Farm, " a beautiful area of level land between the steep hills on the east and the Whakatane River. Crops of maize and potatoes grow luxuriantly in the surrounding paddocks, and the olden mill mound and the adjacent earthworks of the little square redoubt are covered knee-deep in grass and clover. A small clear stream, the Poronu, crosses the main road a hundred yards away and flows down on the east side of the mill-site; a venerable willow-tree on the opposite bank will help the traveller to fix the spot. This stream was dammed by the building of a bank across the shallow valley, and a large pond was formed above the mill, extending up towards the present road-line. This dam supplied the water which turned the mill-wheel, and there was a spillway between the mill and the redoubt; this was crossed by a plank serving as a bridge. Another flood spillway was cut on the other side of the redoubt.

The mill was built about 1867 to grind into flour the wheat largely grown by the industrious Ngati-Pukeko. The machinery was a gift from the Governor, Sir George Grey; a considerable sum of money was expended under his régime in supplying the native tribes with flour-mills and other appliances of civilization. To supervise the construction of the mill and to work it when complete the tribe employed a Frenchman named Jean Guerren. Captain Gilbert Mair, N.Z.C., who knew Guerren well, describes him as a man of about forty-five years of age at this time, short and stout; he was very neat and methodical in his habits. He was an excellent mechanic; his mill and his little house which stood alongside it on the mound were models of efficiency and neatness. There was a garden of old-fashioned flowers, and there was also a little vineyard, from the produce of which Jean made wine for his household and his *pakeha* guests. His Maori wife, a young woman named Erihapeti (Elizabeth)—called " Peti, " for short—was the daughter of Manuera Kuku, a chief of the Warahoe Tribe, of the Upper Rangitaiki. With them was Peti's sister Monika, whose name was usually abbreviated to " Nika "; she was a pretty girl of sixteen or seventeen. Jean had lately been living at Otipa, on the Rangitaiki River, near the foot of Mount Edgecumbe, where he had been trading, and had built a similar mill for the Warahoe. The Maoris called him Hoani te Wiwi ("John the Frenchman").

About the end of 1868 the military authorities sent a detachment of Armed Constabulary out to Poronu and built a small redoubt as a means of defence for the mill; the Ngati-Pukeko had appealed for protection in consequence of threats to burn the place having been made by the Hauhaus of Ruatoki and other Urewera settlements. This was the result of Heketoro's fight and escape, an affair which occurred at Puketi, an ancient hill fort which stands a short distance south of the present Township of Taneatua. Heketoro and a companion had escaped after a remarkable adventure, in which a leading chief of the Urewera was killed. The Armed Constabulary garrison was soon removed, and when Te Kooti swooped down from the mountains the place was in a defenceless condition.

A pitiful incident marked the march of the Hauhau war-party on Rauporoa and the mill. At Te Puapua, the advance-guard, headed by Te Makarini te Waru, a stout reddish-haired almost Eskimo-featured Tuhoe warrior, suddenly came upon a woman in their path. She was a handsome young chieftainess named Ripeka Kaaho, the niece of a friendly chief named Tahawera. She had a number of pet pigs, and these she was feeding with boiled potatoes, some distance from her village. It was considered ill-luck for a war-party to spare any person whom they met on their path when engaged in an expedition of this kind, even through the stray person encountered was one of their own tribe. In this case the girl belonged to the Ruatoki people—in fact, her own brother Te Tupara ("The Double-barrel Gun") Kaaho, of the Tuhoe Tribe—he is still living at Ruatoki—was, one of the foremost young warriors in the *ope*. Te Makarini, the leader, was the girl's brother-in-law; his wife was her sister Rora.

The war-party, after seizing the girl, took her back to Te Hurepo, near Te Pa-a-te-Kapu, and sent back word to Te Kooti that a prisoner had been taken. "We have caught Tahawera's daughter: what shall we do with her?" The savage chief's epigrammatic reply was delivered by his chief lieutenant, the half-caste Peka Makarini (Baker McLean): "*He maroro kokoti ihu waka-taua*" ("A flying-fish crossing the bows of the war-canoe"). This figurative expression, anciently brought by the Maori ancestors from the tropic South Seas, likens to the luckless flying-fish striking the bow of a canoe the incautious wight who is found in the direct advance of a war-party. It meant that the girl must die. Thereupon she was killed with stone *patu* and tomahawk by two of her close relatives. This terrible deed did not content some of the savages of the *ope;* they must needs chop the poor girl's body into pieces, which they threw to her own pigs.*

Continuing their march the Hauhaus laid siege to Rauporoa pa, after being balked in their first attempt to capture it by treachery. Meanwhile a special war-party (*kokiri*) of a hundred men, under Wirihana Koikoi, a big tattooed fellow, was despatched to attack the mill. It happened that at this juncture there were only seven or eight people in the redoubt and mill, including, besides Jean and his wife and sister-in-law, a young man named Tautari and a dumb man of weak intellect named Te Mauriki—both of the Ngati-Pukeko Tribe. There were also two women, one named Maria te Ha (wife of Kaperiera) and the other Pera. Most of these people were in the redoubt, but Jean, on seeing the approach of the armed Hauhaus, remained in his mill, which he determined to defend to the utmost, while the others shut the gate of the redoubt and prepared for the hopeless task of holding it against the *kokiri*.

Jean possessed a good double-barrel gun and plenty of ammunition, and when firing began he gave the enemy a taste of his marksmanship. The attack was opened from the edge of a terrace on the hillside about 300 yards north of the mill. Here the Hauhaus dug a row of shallow rifle-pits; these can still be seen, though partly filled and grass-grown, on the roadside, on the right hand (west) going out from Whakatane by the main road to Taneatua. Jean was a dead shot, and he made the position there too warm for his enemy. After each shot the Hauhau snipers kept their heads up above the trench to observe the effect, and that was the Frenchman's opportunity. Firing through his loopholes he shot several Maoris, most of them, it is said, through the head. The Hauhaus then drew off into the bush and fired volleys into the mill from a higher level on the hillside. Jean was supported by Tautari and the

---

* The place where this tragedy occurred, Te Hurepo, is a curious little artificial island *pa* in the swamp, just below the ancient hill fort called Te Pa-a-te-Kapu, seven miles from Whakatane, on the right hand (east) side of the road to Taneatua. It was built, say the Maoris, ten generations ago (250 years) as a place of refuge and security by the Ngati-te-Kapu, a *hapu* of Tuhoe, whose principal fort was on the trenched hill opposite. The land on the flat, now drained, was then a deep swamp, and this islet of refuge was formed by carrying earth in baskets from the east side of Te Pa-a-te-Kapu Hill, about a hundred yards away. The excavation in the side of the hill is still to be seen; the present road passes close under the hill-cutting, and the island, a low oval mound in the reclaimed swamp, is seen a little over a chain from the opposite side of the road. The artificial islet was surrounded by a line of fern-tree trunks and was then stockaded. In later times it was used as a cultivation plot. To this mound in the morass Ripeka was taken for execution after her capture at Te Puapua.

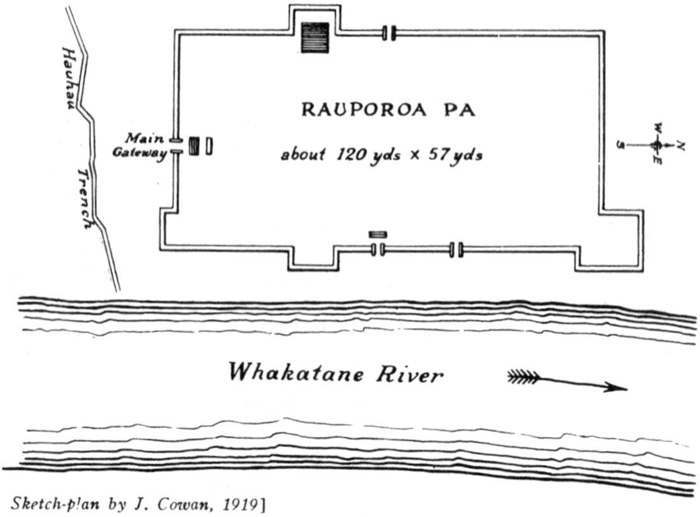

Sketch-plan by J. Cowan, 1919]

Rauporoa *Pa,* Attacked by Te Kooti, 1869

others in the redoubt, who had five guns. The sisters Peti and Nika handed out cartridges and helped to load.

For two days the little garrison in the mill and the redoubt kept the Hauhaus off. The defence was so active and well sustained that the raiders imagined at first that there was a considerable number of men in the place. At last, however, when the Hauhaus ascended the near hills of the range on the eastern side of the valley, a few hundred yards from the mill, and were able to see down into the redoubt they discovered the weakness of the garrison. The attack was then pressed home. The Hauhaus skirmished up close to the walls. While some tried to set fire to a large *raupo* hut which occupied the middle of the redoubt, others endeavoured to scale the parapets. Jean was forced to abandon the mill, and rushed into the redoubt to join his people. For a time he defended the gateway, a narrow opening on the east side of the work; then he was shot and fell dead across the entrance which he had held with such valour. Before he fell he killed Wirihana Koikoi and another chief, Paora Taituha. Now the Hauhaus swarmed over the earth walls in through the gateway to tomahawk the hapless defenders. Two of the garrison, of whom Te Mauriki the *heahea* (half-witted person) was one, jumped the rear parapet and ran towards the Whakatane River and Raupora. Mauriki escaped; the other was overtaken and tomahawked. A few moments after Jean was killed, his wife Peti and Nika were surrounded by the murderous gang of savages. Peti flung herself down and clasped the knees of the man who had seized her, Te Rangihiroa, from Tarawera (on the Taupo-Napier track), begging him to save her and her sister. Rangihiroa protected her and the sister for the time; the others were killed.

After the sacking and burning of the mill, Rangihiroa took his captives across the Whakatane to the leader's camp before Rauporoa pa. When it was reported to Te Kooti that he had saved two women, the ruthless leader sent for him and ordered him to take Peti as his wife and to kill her sister. The young girl had refused to tell where the Frenchman had hidden his gunpowder [Jean had buried it under a *whare*]. So little Nika was tomahawked by Te Rangihiroa, who took Peti to Tarawera after the Whakatane raid. She lived there with him until her death a few years ago.*

The *kokiri* lost about seven killed. A few days after the fight, Captain Mair found the bodies of Wirihana Koikoi and Paora Taituha in the mill-dam.

No stone, no memorial of any kind, marks the spot defended by "John the Frenchman" with such heroic valour. In a few years, but for this record, the memory of Jean Guerren's gallant stand would have perished. New Zealand should mark as one of its national monuments the ground made sacred by the story of a brave son of France, who defended his post to the death.

THE ATTACK ON RAUPOROA PA

The well-preserved remains of the Rauporoa *pa*, the Ngati-Pukeko redoubt besieged by Te Kooti's force in March, 1869, stand three miles south of Whakatane Town, on an alluvial plain thickly dotted with *ti* trees of great size. The place is surrounded by Maori and *pakeha* cultivations; the native villages Poroporo and Te Rewatu are near by, and the Whakatane flows past the rear of the work beneath masses of weeping-willows. Within rifle-shot on the opposite (eastern) side of the

---

* Captain Mair wrote from Tauranga (14th February, 1923): "There was a most pathetic and pitiful scene when Te Rangihiroa approached to carry out Te Kooti's cruel sentence. Twisting the thong of his hatchet round his wrist, he called out, '*Tu mai, e Monika!*' ('Stand up, Monika!') The poor girl flung her arms about her weeping sister, asking, '*E Peti, tena e roa te whakamamaetanga?*' ('O Betty, will the suffering be long?') '*Kaore,*' answered Peti, '*he poto noa iho*' ('No, it will be quite brief'). Then the girl said, '*Mau e pupuri i oku ringaringa kia manawanui ai ahau*' ('Hold you my hands that I may have courage'). Peti did so, averting her face while the terrible blow fell."

river are the grass-grown ruins of the Poronu Redoubt and the earthworks of the water-mill made memorable by Jean Guerren's defence. The Rauporoa *pa* is a rectangular field-work consisting of an earth parapet and a surrounding trench; the height of the scarp above the bottom of the ditch is still 7 to 8 feet, and inside the work is 4 or 5 feet high; the ditch is 4 feet wide and about the same depth. Its dimensions are about 120 yards in length (parallel with the course of the Whakatane River, immediately under its rear wall) and 55 yards in width. There are two large salients, which form flanking bastions against enfilading fire, one on the western flank, to the south of a gateway; the other is an angle near the river. Another flanking work, a bastion 8 yards on its longest alignment, projects from the opposite (south) end of the eastern face, and there is a small salient near one of the gateways facing the river. The *pekerangi* and *kiri-tangata*, the outer and inner palisades, consisting of *totara* posts, *manuka* stakes, and *ti* or *whanake* (cabbage-tree) trunks, have long since disappeared. The parapets, however, remain in an almost perfect condition. In the opening which was once the gateway facing west an enormous and many-branched *whanake* is growing—a cabbage-tree of great girth. This tree says Te More Takuira, the head man of Rauporoa, was originally one of the stakes of the fence—a young tree cut down, sharpened at the butt, and driven into the ground; it took root and grew. Another gateway, that facing the south, is blinded inside the entrance by a short parapet with a rifle-pit in the rear. It was this entrance that Te Kooti's force attempted to rush in their first attack. The ground on the west face of the work is thickly covered with the depressions indicating *kumara* or potato pits, the food stores of the garrison. On the south side, about 30 yards from the gateway, there is a shallow uneven trench running across the face of the *pa* and nearing it as it approaches the river. This was where the Hauhaus dug themselves in after the failure of their first effort against the fort. In the rear wall there are two openings, gateways, which gave access to the river. As a memorial of the Maori wars Rauporoa ("The High Reeds") is of exceptional interest because of its excellent condition at a day when most of the forts of the 1860-71 period have been demolished.

Against this tribal stronghold of the loyal Ngati-Pukeko Te Kooti launched about four hundred warriors, East Coast men of various tribes—many of them escapees from Chatham Islands—reinforced by Urewera and Taupo Hauhaus. They came forward in a solid column, treading the ground with a heavy resounding tramp, their rifles, carbines, and guns held at the " ready." Their threatening march gave the obvious lie to the white flag borne by one of their front-rank men. The flag of truce was Te Kooti's favourite stratagem for lulling the suspicions of Government Maoris. Some of the people in the *pa*, however, were so credulous, or so anxious to avoid fighting, that they were ready to open the gates and admit the enemy. One of these who reposed faith in Te Kooti's flag was an old church lay-reader, Ihaia te Ahu. He cried out, " It is peace, peace; there is the white flag." Another Ngati-Pukeko deceived by the long streamer of white was Hori Tunui, one of the chiefs of the *pa*. He was in the act of pushing open the heavy sliding-door, fastened by wooden pegs, which formed the gate of the south side, and the advance files of the enemy were almost within the defences, when another chief, Tamihana Tahawera, who was not deceived by the flag of peace, ran to close the door. He was struggling with the foolish old man when a young Urewera warrior named Mehaka Toko-pounamu fired at him at a range of a few paces. The bullet missed Tahawera and struck the unfortunate pacifist Hori, who fell dead just inside the gateway. The door was made fast, and the baffled Hauhaus retired under fire to dig themselves in. Mehaka's shot was returned by Hirini Manuao in the *pa* trench; his bullet broke the staff from which the white flag was floating.

Now the Hauhaus found themselves under a heavy fire from the whole south face of the *pa* and the flanking bastion on the west side. The terrain was level and devoid of cover; the plain was covered to the river-bank with the Ngati-Pukeko cultivations of corn, potatoes, *kumara,* and *taro.* The only likely shelter that presented itself was a large *raupo*-thatch house twenty paces in front of the *pa.* Behind it the attackers took cover, but it was soon riddled with bullets. The rebels scooped out rifle-pits behind this *whare*, and secured a little head-cover. They then extended the trench eastward towards the river-bank, beginning at a point 30 yards from the palisades, and working nearer the *pa* as they drove it toward the Whakatane.

The attack now steadied down into a regular siege, but the Hauhaus, curiously, did not push their attack on any but the south face of the pa. Sheltered in their trench and shallow rifle-pits, they maintained a heavy fire on the Ngati-Pukeko defenders. There were a number of women in the *pa*, but it was not strongly garrisoned, since most of the men had gone to the coast with Hori Kawakura, a capable leader, to attend the burial of an old warrior, Te Pierieri, when the attack was delivered. On the alarm being raised in Whakatane by refugees from Rauporoa, Hori hurried up to the besieged *pa,* and entered it under the enemy's fire with his party of about twenty men. As ammunition was running short, he came out again at great risk, with a few men, and took back a supply of powder and bullets. This fine deed was performed under heavy fire.

Te Kooti's force possessed superiority not only in numbers but in arms. The Hauhaus had many good rifles and carbines besides their shot-guns. The defenders of the *pa* had nothing but muzzle-loading single- and double-barrel guns, some of them old-fashioned flint-locks. They endeavoured to burn out the attackers who were posted behind the large *whare* on the south by tying burning rags to stones and throwing them on to the thatched roof, but the Hauhaus extinguished the fire. Several dead bodies of Hauhaus lay between the stockade and this house. The second Ngati Pukeko man killed was Heremaia Tautari. He was shot while standing on the parapet of the south-east angle, calling out across the river to his children, who were at that moment defending the redoubt at the Poronu flour-mill against the final rush of the Hauhaus, bidding them retreat to the *pa*.

Hori Kawakura's little band of fighting men, Ngati-Maumoana, formed the backbone of the defence; but, stoutly as they and their fellow tribesmen fought, their plight was hopeless, for their ammunition was failing. For two days and two nights the garrison had resisted the well-armed rebels. It was now the early morning of the third day (11th March), and although urgent messages had been sent for help there was no appearance of reinforcements.

Major Mair, R.M., at Opotiki, immediately on hearing of the invasion, despatched Captain Henry Mair with the Opotiki Rangers and Captain Travers with some Armed Constabulary—in all about eighty men. At the same time Lieutenant Gilbert Mair was hurrying to the rescue with a column of Ngati-Rangatihi from Matata. Fears that the *pa* had been stormed and Ngati-Pukeko left to the savagery of Te Kooti and his Chatham Islands band spurred him to the utmost exertions. He had spent a day of annoyance and suspense at Tauranga. A native messenger, Sergeant Mikaere te Kati, had arrived with news of the raid on the Whakatane Valley, and all day (the second of the siege of Rauporoa) Mair was anxiously awaiting permission from the Acting Civil Commissioner in charge of the district to leave for the relief of the friendlies. The civil officer was in a state of indecision, but at last he yielded to Mair's urgent persuasion and authorized him to raise a force of natives at Matata. Mair was ferried across the Tauranga Harbour to Matapihi, where he hired a Maori horse for his night ride along the beach. An accident delayed him for some hours. Near Wairake he was caught in

Captain H. A. Mair

(Opotiki Volunteer Rangers)

Captain Henry Abbott Mair was the third son of Mr. Gilbert Mair, who settled at the Bay of Islands a century ago, and brother of Major W. G. Mair and Captain Gilbert Mair, N.Z.C. In 1868 he raised the Opotiki Volunteer Forest Rangers, and served in a number of skirmishes in the Opotiki, Waimana, and Whakatane districts. He afterwards went to the South Sea Islands trading, and with Mr. Handley Bathurst Sterndale established a pearling-station on Suwarrow Island. Later he was engaged in labour-recruiting in the Western Pacific for the Fiji Government. He was treacherously killed, with several of his boat's crew from the recruiting schooner, by the natives of one of the islands of the New Hebrides on the 12th November, 1881.

a quicksand, and in scrambling out his horse threw him, and the stock of his carbine struck him on the head, stunning him. When he came to his senses the tide was lapping the sand near his feet. Feeling very sick, he tramped along the beach in search of his horse, which he at last caught in a swamp among the sandhills. Mounted again, he rode at a gallop along the beach in the night, fording or swimming the rivers, until just after daylight he reached Matata. He rode through the large village two or three times shouting to the natives, "*E ara, e ara! Maranga, maranga! Tatua, tatua!*" ("Rise, rise! Up, up with you! Gird yourselves!") In a few minutes a force of

Ngati-Rangitihi natives—a " scratch lot " as Mair described them, however, for most of the best fighters were inland—assembled in the *marae*, and in an hour 130 men had crossed the Awa-a-te-Atua. At the Orini Stream, without waiting to strip, they plunged in and swam across, holding their belts and rifles above their heads with one hand. They used drift-wood from the beach to make rafts for some of their heavier equipment.

Moving rapidly across the flax swamps and the *manuka* flat, and pushing over the marshy plain of Otahua, near the Whakatane River, Mair now met the first of the fugitives from Rauporoa. The *pa* had fallen, but whether there had been a terrible massacre or not was as yet uncertain. The first Ngati-Pukeko refugee met was an old fellow named Te Noho-waka; he was running hard, in great distress. He cried out to Mair, *" Kua tahuri te motu nei, kua tahuri te motu nei ! "* (" The island has been overturned ! ") Mair's men opened their ranks to let the fugitives through. Near a *raupo* swamp south of Te Poroporo settlement the first of Te Kooti's men came in sight. The pursuing force consisted of about seventy men, all mounted, many of them armed with breech-loading carbines.

Mair extended his men, tired after their heavy forced march, and kept Te Kooti's horsemen in check, while the Ngati-Pukeko non-combatants retreated; the Rauporoa fighters turned and assisted the relief force. There was good cover along the edge of the flax and *raupo* swamp and among the *manuka*. Mair advanced skirmishing up the valley until Rauporoa *pa* was reached. There it was discovered that there had been no heavy losses except on the part of the Hauhaus. The *pa* had been captured, but not until nearly all the defenders had made their escape on the north side. Only four friendlies had been killed in the attack; two of these were an old man and an old woman outside the *pa*.

Te Kooti's main body crossed the Whakatane River and advanced rapidly on the Ngati-Awa and European settlement at the mouth of the river, under the cliffs. Mair, having a rather weak and exhausted body of men, returned to the sand-hills at the coast to await reinforcements and to protect the fugitives. Meanwhile a Hauhau party, chiefly Urewera, raided Whakatane* and looted the *pa*, and many of the warriors got

* When the Urewera attacked and looted Simpkins's store at Whakatane, amongst the spoil obtained were a number of red Garibaldi jumpers. These blouse-like garments were eagerly seized on by the Hauhaus, who uniformed themselves in them, and when on horseback resembled a body of red-coated cavalry. From the hills above Whakatane Major Mair's men were astonished to see these red-tunick'd horsemen galloping about the plain, some of them armed with swords, the bright scabbards flashing in the sun.

drunk on the grog they discovered in Mr. George Simpkins's store. The raiders burned the store and most of the other places in Whakatane.

Next day a Colonial Government steamer came into Whakatane and landed some European reinforcements, and Major William Mair with the forces from Opotiki attacked Te Kooti's men on the plain. There was some skirmishing also on the hills immediately in rear of the Whakatane settlement, and the raiders were forced to draw off.

Crossing over into the valley of the Rangitaiki, Te Kooti now occupied Tauaroa, on the Kuhawaea Plain close under the towering peak of Tawhiuau, on the western wall of the Urewera Mountains, and near the entrance to the Horomanga Gorge. The spot is conspicuously marked to-day by a line of tall pines growing along the olden earthworks and trenches. Tauaroa was a strongly palisaded *pa* with three lines of timber stockading. The bush on the right—looking from the Rangitaiki—grew to within about 60 yards of the fort. When Te Kooti retreated from Whakatane and took post in Tauaroa Major Mair and his brothers Henry and Gilbert Mair, with a force of Maoris and one hundred and fifty of the 1st Waikato Militia and other corps, followed him up and attempted to surround him. Some of the force worked round between the *pa* and the bush, but Te Kooti had placed about half his men (who numbered four hundred to five hundred in all) in the bush, and so the Government men were between two fires. They had not sufficient to surround the place completely, and no entrenching-tools with which to dig in. Te Kooti spent one night in the *pa*, and then made his escape into the mountains to Ahikereru. In one of the angles of the *pa* the Hauhaus killed a fine young Arawa scout, Te Tohea, whom they had captured. Gilbert Mair had crept up close to the palisade and heard Te Tohea's cries as his face was being battered with a shingling-hammer by one of the enemy, but was unable to help him. The Ngati-Manawa Tribe, of Tauaroa, on Te Kooti's approach, had fled to Motumako, on the Kaingaroa side of the Rangitaiki River, and would have been followed and attacked but for the Government force's arrival, which compelled the Hauhaus to retreat into the Urewera mountains.

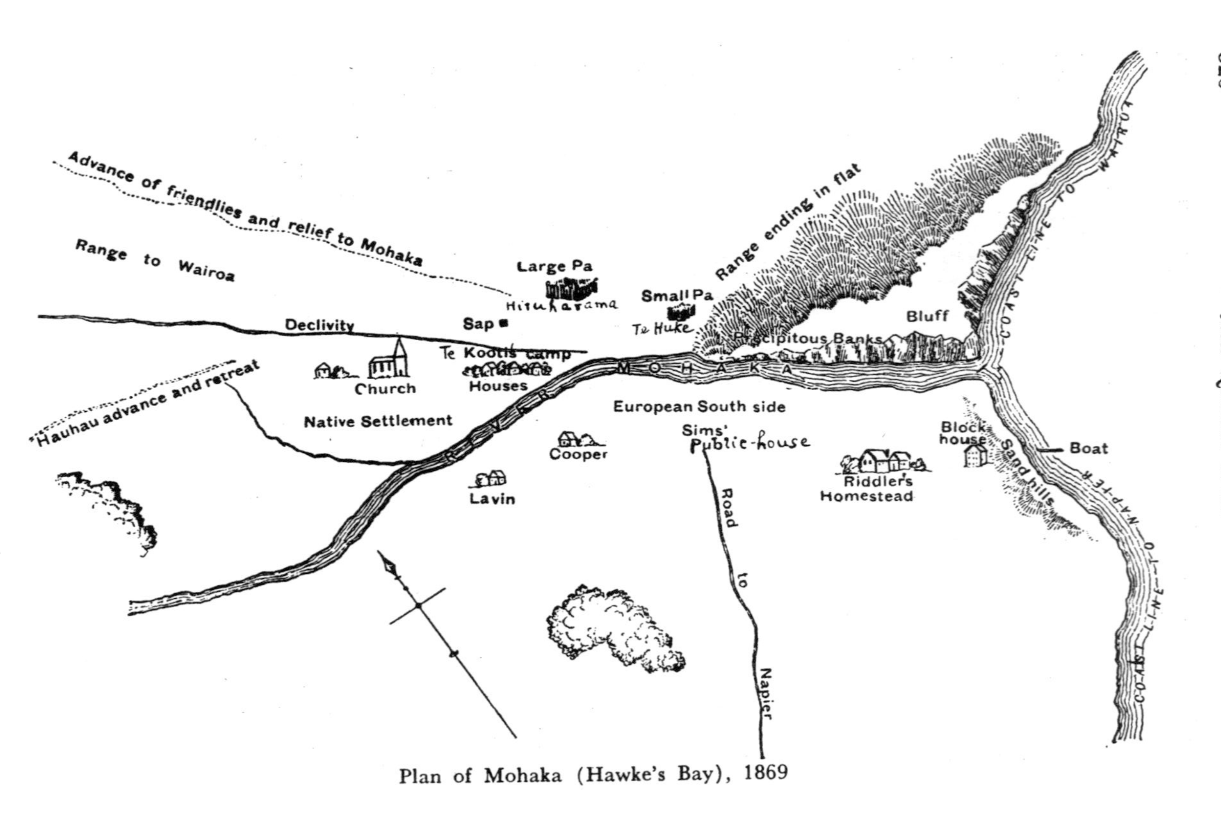

Plan of Mohaka (Hawke's Bay), 1869

Chapter 31

TE KOOTI'S ATTACK ON MOHAKA

AFTER EVADING THE combined European and Arawa force at Tauaroa, on the western border of the mountains that present a sierra-like wall above the plain of Kuhawaea and the Rangitaiki, Te Kooti led his warriors by a forced march through the Urewera forests and gorges to Lake Waikare-moana. It was a march toilsome in the extreme even for the hard-trained Urewera in the war-party, over lofty ranges by the ancient fighting-trails, through gloomy ravines, and across swift streams innumerable. Little rest was given until the shore of the lake was reached at a settlement on the long peninsula on the northern side which makes of the Wairau-moana arm almost a separate lake. Here Te Kooti announced that Mohaka and the Wairoa were the objectives of his expedition. "Te Kooti's intention," says Peita Kotuku, who was a member of the war-party, "was to avenge himself upon the Ngati-Pahauwera Tribe, of Mohaka, and the Wairoa people because they had opposed our march inland after our landing from the schooner in which we had escaped from Chatham Island." Moreover, the ammunition known to be stored at Mohaka, and the prospects of other plunder, were strong attractions.

The force crossed the lake in canoes to the southern shore. One party of men, forty in number, set out in a large canoe, the "Tarake," before the leader had given his orders for the crossing of Waikare-moana. The canoe, too deeply laden, was caught in a sudden southerly squall outside Tikitiki headland and capsized in deep water. The men reached the shore by swimming, but lost all their guns and had their ammunition spoiled. Te Kooti, angrily reprimanding the culprits, made the accident his text for a sermon on the necessity for implicit obedience to his commands. The capsize of the canoe and the loss of the firearms were the Atua's punishment for disregarding the commands of their leader.

On the southern shore Te Kooti divided his force, sending one under Te Waru and Nepia to raid the valley of the Wairoa River, while the other, the main body, he led due south to Mohaka, Hawke's Bay, by the Putere track. The expedition against

Wairoa, which was the first to leave the camp on the lake, met with no success, as it encountered a force of Ngati-Pahauwera which had been despatched against Te Waru's settlement on the Upper Wairoa, and was driven back with the loss of several killed. Te Kooti began his vengeance on the Mohaka people by attacking the Maoris at Ara-kanihi and the neighbourhood and massacring all who were captured. Most of the murderous work was done with tomahawk and bayonet. Early on the morning of the 10th April, 1869, the war-party was divided into two companies, and while one surprised the European settlers and Maoris at the crossing of the river opposite the homesteads of two sheep-farmers, Lavin and Cooper, the other division, under Te Kooti, went along the east side of the Mohaka and advanced against the two stockaded villages close to the mouth of the river. On the west or Napier side seven Europeans were slaughtered by the first division. The whites killed were Mr. and Mrs. Lavin and their children, a man named Cooper, and an old man named Wilkinson. Another settler named Sim (who had a public-house and store besides his run) had gone out early to work on his land, and so escaped; and his wife and several young children took to the bush in time to elude the raiders, having been warned in time by a friendly Maori woman who was afterwards killed. Another settler, Mr. Hudson, escaped to Napier. Dr. M. Scott, formerly of the Wairoa, was now settled at Mohaka, but happened to be away at Napier at the time of the raid. His half-caste wife and family took refuge with many others, chiefly women and children, in Hiruharama (Jerusalem), the larger of the two *pas*. Others ran to Te Huke, the smaller fort. Those in the small out-settlements who were surprised by the advancing force were mercilessly killed. Many were shut up in a wool-shed, and as they were brought out one by one they were tomahawked or bayoneted. Peita Kotuku says: "It was the Tuhoe (Urewera) men chiefly who killed these people, because they and Ngati-Pahauwera were ancient enemies." Timoti te Kaka—Volkner's ex-deacon—Te Rangi-tahau, of Taupo, and the ruffianly half-caste Eru Peka Makarini (Edward Baker McLean) were also among the executioners.

Te Kooti laid regular siege to the two stockades in which the Ngati-Pahauwera had taken refuge. As most of the fighting-men of the tribe, numbering eighty to a hundred, under Hoani te Wainoho, Paora Rerepu, and Iehu te Kupa, were absent at Te Kiwi, near Waikare-moana, the defence devolved upon a very few able-bodied men, assisted by some old men and boys and the women. Each *pa* consisted of strong palisades with trenches inside; from earth banquettes the garrison in the trench could fire through the interstices of the stockade on the ground-level. The houses within the forts were in a measure safe from enemy fire, as their floors were dug out to a depth of about 2 feet below the level of the surrounding ground. The smaller or more compact *pa,* Te Huke, was well situated on the precipitous left bank of the Mohaka River, and about 300 yards seaward of its sister fort, Hiruharama. It was unassailable except immediately in front and on a small part of the right and left flanks, and there the palisade was very solid and strong, backed by a parapet. Te Huke was an ancient fort which had successfully withstood all attacks. Hiruharama had the disadvantage of being rather straggling of figure and requiring a large garrison to man its trenches.

When the alarm was given that the Hauhaus had come down on Mohaka, about a dozen able-bodied men took post in Hiruharama to protect the large number of women and children who flocked to the *pa,* besides some men past the active fighting age. Te Huke was occupied by a stronger garrison, though small in numbers; it consisted of the remainder of the Mohaka warriors who had not marched in the Wairoa expedition. In this *pa* was the Government store of ammunition, buried under the house of the native sergeant of police. From the stockades the Ngati-Pahauwera beheld the burning of the European settlers' houses on the opposite side of the river, and heard firing in the out-settlements where stragglers were being sought out and slaughtered. Te Kooti, mounted on a white horse—recently looted—now appeared with a large body of his armed followers, while about one hundred and fifty skirmishers advancing along the Wairoa road took up positions under cover and opened fire on the two forts. The main body camped near the bank of the river and set about enjoying the loot from its plundered settlement. "When the public-house on the south side of the river was looted," says Peita Kotuku, "some of our men got very drunk on the rum they found, and when they joined in the attack on the stockades they behaved so recklessly, heedless of cover, that several of them were shot dead. Te Kooti was very angry at his men getting drunk while they were fighting. They should have waited until we were on our return journey; then we halted at Ara-kanihi, a short distance inland, and remained there several days to enjoy the liquor we had carried away."

Heavy fighting continued for some hours between the small garrisons and the Hauhaus on the front and flanks of the strongholds. Te Kooti's men dug numerous rifle-pits and also started a trench just under the fall of the ground near the Mohaka so as to command the river face of Hiruharama. The occupants of this *pa* fought particularly well. Boys, women, and old men kept up a steady fire and effectually swept the glacis with their rifles and double-barrel guns. A storming-party rushed at Te Huke, and, getting right up to the palisades, threw a chain over some of the stakes and tried to drag them down and make a breach. After a desperate fight they were beaten off.

Discovering that the place was too strong to be carried by assault, Te Kooti adopted different methods. He sent some of his men forward with a white flag, and, calling for Ropihana, the son of the chief Paora Rerepu—who was absent with the Wairoa expedition—proposed terms of peace. Ropihana warned the people that it was a *rongo patipati,* a deceitful peace; but Rutene Kiri-huruhuru, the native policeman, it is said, was persuaded to make a truce, and he and some others went out at the invitation of the Hauhaus and joined them at grog on the flat below the *pa.* Rutene had been at the mission college at Waerenga-a-Hika, Poverty Bay, and knew Te Kooti well. After grog, the Hauhaus entered Te Huke, in spite of the opposition of some of the people. The invaders professed peaceful intentions, but Ropihana, or one of his comrades, more alert than the others, detected a sign to commence the slaughter of the *pa* garrison, and fired at one of the Hauhaus. The enemy then threw off all pretence of friendship, and the massacre began. The foolish Rutene was killed, and nearly the whole of the occupants of the *pa*—men, women, and children—were shot down or tomahawked. Ropihana escaped by jumping over the bank on the flank facing the river, receiving a severe wound in the shoulder as he fled, and reached Hiruharama *pa.*

After slaying all the people they could find, the Hauhaus set fire to the place. They secured a number of guns and some ammunition, but the Government store of gunpowder was not discovered; it exploded when the house under which it was buried was burned.

Te Kooti now concentrated his attack on Hiruharama *pa,* which was stoutly defended by the garrison firing from their rifle-pits through the narrow openings in the palisades. So the fighting went on for some hours. Te Kooti, anticipating the arrival of natives from Wairoa, had posted a portion of his force on each side of the track from Wairoa, in a wooded ravine some distance north of Mohaka. A force of over one hundred Wairoa friendlies, under Major Withers, was engaged here; their principal chief was the brave old Ihaka Whanga, from Mahia. The majority did not behave well, and fell back, deserting Ihaka Whanga when he was pluckily leading them on; these were some of Ngati-Kurupakiaka. But a small party of natives skirmished most determinedly through the bush and along the track over the hills, and then charged down past the Hauhau rifle-pits. They gained Hiruharama without losing a man killed; few

George Hill, N.Z.C.

In recommending George Hill for the New Zealand Cross, Colonel Whitmore wrote: "Constable (now Sergeant) George Hill, No. 1 Division A.C., accompanied the Wairoa natives who under Ihaka Whanga proceeded to relieve Mohaka, then being attacked by Te Kooti. A party volunteered to run the gauntlet of the enemy's fire and to dash into the Jerusalem *pa*, then sorely pressed. This was a dangerous service, and it was in a great measure due to the example set by Constable Hill, who led that party, that it was successfully carried out . . . Hill animated the defenders by his exertions, and contributed greatly to the repulse of Te Kooti; and his conduct is spoken of in admiration by the natives themselves."

(See notes at end of this chapter.)

suffered wounds. With them came a plucky *pakeha* soldier, Trooper George Hill, of the Armed Constabulary, a veteran of many campaigns. Hill had been sent out on horseback from Wairoa to reconnoitre Mohaka and ascertain if it were true that Te Kooti was in the neighbourhood, and had sent the news back to Wairoa and then joined the returned expedition. He charged down into the *pa* with the Maoris, shooting a Hauhau on the way.

These reinforcements saved Hiruharama. The defence was carried on with redoubled energy, and a sortie was made by some of the garrison. Sallying out from the *pa,* they charged the Hauhaus and drove them from their advanced rifle-pits, but the fire from the main body was so fierce that the Mohaka fighters were compelled to fall back with several wounded. George Hill was now the life of the defence. He had the palisade strengthened with some bullock-chains, so that they could not be pulled down readily with rope and cross-bar, and he kept up an accurate fire from one of the angles. The Hauhaus had begun to sap towards the stockade from the west side, but their progress was slow. By this time several of Te Kooti's men had been killed, including an Urewera chief named Kereopa (not the prophet of this name, the murderer of Mr. Volkner). The small garrison—there were only about forty able-bodied men in the *pa*—were continually on the alert to beat back an attack. Well the defenders knew that if the enemy once screwed up their courage to the assaulting-point they could soon have beaten down all resistance and tomahawked every soul. "I could have done for at least three with my rifle and a double-barrel gun the Maoris had brought me, if it came to a final scrimmage," said Hill, narrating the incidents of the siege, "but there would not have been time to reload." But the dreaded charge never came, and this mercy was undoubtedly due to the spirit infused into the defence by the fearless ex-man-of-war's-man.

Such was the position when early on Tuesday, the 12th April, the first relief expedition appeared off the mouth of the Mohaka. This was a party of fourteen armed men in the Napier lifeboat. The news of the attack had been taken to Napier by a wounded and exhausted Maori. Captain Cellem, the Harbourmaster at Napier, was in command of the lifeboat, which was manned by twelve volunteers, including some masters of vessels; with them was Dr. M. Scott, armed like the others with rifle and sixty rounds of ammunition. On arriving off the mouth of the river the crew watched the attack on Hiruharama, and saw the explosion of the gunpowder in Te Huke *pa*, which was on fire. Captain Cellem called for volunteers to land, in order to rescue any fugitives, when it was discovered that the blockhouse, although apparently deserted, was occupied by Hauhaus who were preparing to fire on the landing-party. Captain Cellem pulled out, and was about to sail northwards along the coast to investigate the position when the hidden Hauhaus opened a heavy fire on the boat from the blockhouse loopholes. The crew at the same time found themselves under fire from the cliff above the beach. Cellem and Scott returned the fire over the stern of the boat while the crew pulled out of range. It was now dark, and the party decided to return to Napier.

Some of the Hauhaus rode along the beach for several miles following the lifeboat and firing on it as it ran south under sail close inshore. When Napier was reached it was found that all the available local mounted men, numbering about eighty, under Captain Towgood and Captain Tanner, had been despatched to Mohaka. Dr. Scott returned to Mohaka at once in the cutter "Grayling," which was conveying military stores, and on reaching the devastated settlement discovered his wife and children safe in Hiruharama *pa*. The palisades of the fort were seen to be thick with bullets which had failed to penetrate the timber. The fighting was over. Te Kooti had retreated on discovering the approach of assistance. His men, all mounted on horses looted from the Maoris and the European settlers, carried off all the plunder they could take, including the liquor from Sims's hotel. The Hauhau war-party halted and camped at Te Arakanihi, and there set to at the grog. Had they been followed up promptly and attacked, a deadly revenge for Mohaka could have been exacted.

The officer in charge of the relief expedition, Colonel Lambert, was extraordinarily lacking in military enterprise. He had a force of Constabulary and Mounted Rifles numbering over a hundred, besides the Mohaka and Wairoa natives. The Mohaka men, burning to take *utu* for the slaughter of their relatives, were ready to follow up the enemy, and the white troops were eager for action, but nothing would induce the cautious Lambert to move inland.

The Constabulary recovered and buried the bodies of the Lavin family and others who perished in the raid. Mrs. Lavin was lying on the ground, shot dead. Her husband lay by her side with his left arm under her as if he had been protecting her when he was killed; his revolver was in his outstretched right hand. The Lavin children, according to the veteran Armed Constabulary scout Ben Biddle, who was one of the first to find the bodies, had been killed by being thrown up in the air and caught on the points of the Hauhaus' bayonets, just as the Sepoys cruelly impaled white children in the Indian Mutiny. "The little ones' bodies were all over bayonet-wounds," said Biddle.

The Hauhau camp at Ara-kanihi, six miles inland, was reconnoitred by Ben Biddle alone. On his return he reported to Colonel Lambert that the Hauhaus were in a drunken condition from their looted grog, and could be cut up with ease if a vigorous attack were made. The scout urged the Colonel to attack at once. Lambert's reply was that he would consider it. Major Richardson would have attacked without hesitation, but Lambert was in command, and the opportunity for ending Te Kooti's career passed, much to the disgust of the force. The plucky Biddle (who had won the New Zealand Cross at Ngatapa) followed up the Hauhaus by himself, and near Te Putere scouted up to an enclosure where the looted horses, numbering about one hundred and fifty, were kept. At night he broke down part of the fence to let the horses out, and nearly all of them returned to Mohaka. The Hauhaus only succeeded in taking ten away to Waikare-moana.

After enjoying themselves at horse-races on the beach at Waikare-moana, close to the Strait of Manaia, which connects the main body of the lake with the very beautiful western arm, Wairau-moana, the Hauhaus crossed in canoes to the north side, swimming the horses across the half-mile channel. At the fortified settlements Tikitiki and Whakaari, on headlands dominating the approach to the Urewera track, Te Kooti and his men remained for some time resting. While here, news came of Colonel Whitmore's march into the Urewera Mountains from the north, and of his capture of Ruatahuna. Te Kooti hurried a portion of his force on to attack Whitmore, who was expected to march to Waikare-moana. Peka Makarini, the ferocious half-caste, led this advance force. Te Kooti followed and prepared an ambush for the troops in a deep gorge through which they would have to pass on their way to the lake. The story of Whitmore's well-executed expedition into the heart of the Urewera Country is told in the next chapter.

NOTES

Constable George Hill (No. 1 Division A.C.), popularly known in the New Zealand forces as Rowley Hill, received the rare decoration of the New Zealand Cross for his share in the defence of Hiruharama *pa* at Mohaka. His fighting career was one of extraordinary variety and adventure. A native of the famous little Devonshire town of Dawlish, he joined the Royal Navy in 1851 and saw over ten years' service as a blue-jacket. He was in H.M.S. "Leopard" at the bombardment of Sebastopol, and on returning to England from the Black Sea in 1856 he joined H.M.S. "Shannon" and went out in her to the China Station. When the Indian Mutiny broke out in 1857 the "Shannon" was ordered to Calcutta, and Hill was in Captain Peel's famous Naval Brigade which took a battery of 32-pounders into the heart of India. He fought at the taking of Lucknow, where he was slightly wounded, and at Delhi, and in the desperate battles at Cawnpore, under Sir Colin Campbell. In 1860 he was in the Mediterranean in H.M.S. "Hannibal," and with three shipmates took French leave at Palermo and enlisted, like many other British bluejackets, in Garibaldi's Army of Liberation. After a brief campaign in Italy, where he was wounded, he rejoined his ship—the desertion was overlooked, for English sympathy with Garibaldi ran high—and afterwards served in H.M.S. "Euryalus." On coming to New Zealand in 1863 he joined Von Tempsky's No. 2 Company of the Forest Rangers and fought in many actions in Taranaki and in the Hauhau campaign on the East Coast. Later he was in Major Fraser's No. 1 Company of Military Settlers in Hawke's Bay, and then for several years in the Armed Constabulary: last of all in the submarine mining section of the New Zealand Permanent Force at Auckland. He was living at Devonport, Auckland, at the date of writing.

It was at Mohaka in 1869 that Hill met the native girl who became his wife, Harata Hinerata, who, with her three sisters—Lucy, Lizzie, and Amelia—half-castes of the Ngati-Pahauwera, took a gallant part in the defence of Te Huke *pa*. When Te Kooti first attacked the place these girls used their double-barrelled guns, and it was Lucy who shot the slayer of her grandfather, a venerable chief who was killed in the act of trying to sever with a sword a chain with a cross-bar attached which had been thrown over the palisades by the Hauhaus in an attempt to pull down a portion of the fence. In the final slaughter, when the enemy gained entrance to the fort by falsely promising to spare the defenders, the sisters escaped by climbing over the palisade at the rear and sliding down the cliff and then swimming across the Mohaka River. Two of them carried children tied in a shawl on their backs. The plucky Harata in making her escape received a heavy blow on the back from the butt of a Hauhau's rifle. When Te Kooti retreated from Mohaka, Hill set off to take the news to Napier, and after swimming the river near the mouth travelled along the beach until he met the advance-guard of the cavalry from Napier. It was on Colonel Whitmore's recommendation that he was awarded the New Zealand Cross.

The Government blockhouse at Mohaka, from which the Hauhaus fired on the Napier lifeboat crew in April, 1869, was of rather unusual construction, being octagonal in form. It was of two storeys, with a double wall, filled in with gravel and sand, and both storeys were loopholed. A stockade, with a ditch on the inner side, surrounded the blockhouse.

Te Tupara Kaaho, of Ruatoki, states that he was one of the Tuhoe (Urewera) men who joined Te Kooti at that settlement early in 1869 and accompanied him to Mohaka. The Tuhoe lost two of their chiefs, Ihaia and Kereopa, in the fighting at Mohaka. Tupara looted a horse in the raid, and it was one of the ten which were swum across Waikare-moana at the Strait of Manaia. Some of the horses were taken right through to Ruatahuna over the Huiarau, but several were killed in the rough traverse of the unroaded ranges.

Te Rangi-tahau, of Waipahihi, Lake Taupo, was one of the leaders in the butchery of the Ngati-Pahauwera, captured at Mohaka. He had been shipped to the Chatham Islands as a prisoner after his capture at Omarunui in 1866, and fought as one of Te Kooti's lieutenants from 1868 until the beginning of 1870. Many stories are told by the Maoris regarding his energy and fearlessness in battle and his callousness in the execution of prisoners. His favourite weapon for such tasks was a *patu-okewa* (or *patu-kara*), a sharp-edged hand-club of hard black stone. It was his practice on occasion to slay prisoners by throwing the *patu*. Singling out a man, perhaps sitting in a row of people in a house or on the village square, he would hurl the weapon at him with unerring aim and kill him with a blow on the temple.

I met Tahau, as he was usually called, at Whakarewarewa, Rotorua, in 1900, when he told me something of his history. He was by repute a powerful *tohunga,* and had been brought up from Taupo to conduct the ancient ceremony of *whai-kawa,* or removing the baneful spell of *tapu* from a carved house, a rite which a number of us witnessed. He died suddenly a few days afterwards; in popular belief he was a victim to the spells of witchcraft (*makutu*) directed against him by a rival *tohunga* who also took part in the ceremonies at Whakarewarewa, the venerable Tumutara Pio, of the Ngati-Awa Tribe. But old Pio himself did not long survive his antagonist. Tahau was a very powerful athletic fellow, with a head that may accurately be described as shaped like one of the old-fashioned round bullets; his grim features were partly tattooed. At the time of his death he was about seventy years of age.

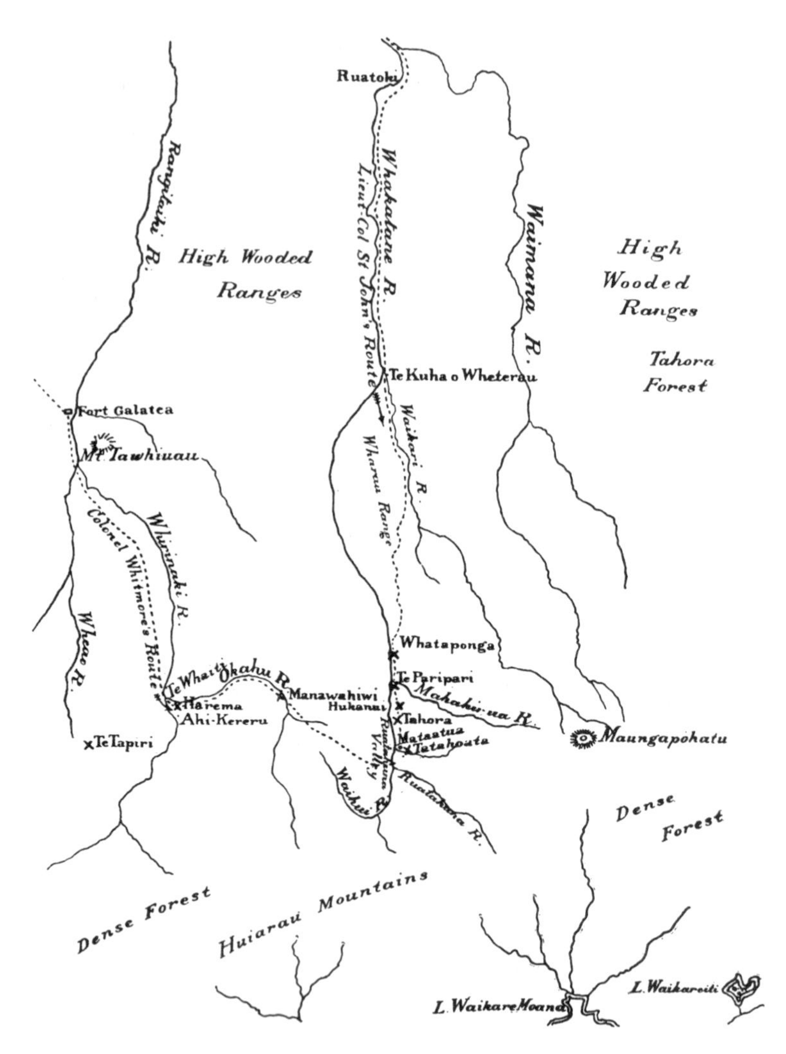

Sketch-map of the Urewera Country, showing routes of march of Colonel Whitmore and Lieut-Colonel St. John, and scenes of engagements, 1869

Chapter 32

INVASION OF UREWERA COUNTRY

COLONEL GEORGE WHITMORE, having transferred his Armed Constabulary field force from Taranaki to the Bay of Plenty, in April of 1869, organized a threefold expedition against the Urewera Tribe and their kin who had supplied Te Kooti with many recruits and sheltered and abetted him after Ngatapa. The war-loving clans of the wild tract of forest highlands between Lake Waikare-moana and the Bay of Plenty plains were intractably hostile, and their villages in the heart of the mountains were ideal refuge-places for the Hauhau raiders. From Ruatahuna and Maunga-pohatu districts, then all but unknown to Europeans, Te Kooti could descend at will upon the Bay of Plenty settlements by way of the Whakatane, Waimana, and Waioeka Rivers, and upon the East Coast via Waikare-moana or the rugged trails across the ranges and down the Ruakituri or the Hangaroa. Whitmore, after discussion with Mr. J. C. Richmond, who had come to the Bay of Plenty to acquaint him with the wishes of the Government, formed the conclusion that the only sound military policy lay in boldly entering the mountains and destroying the food-supplies and the Native strongholds, and forcing Te Kooti to come out to the open country.

The difficulties, however, were considerable: the Urewera region was practically a blank on the map; the only roads were difficult foot-trails, the ancient Maori war-tracks; all supplies would have to be carried on the men's backs; and the winter was approaching with its floods and snowstorms. A rough map of the territory was made by Mr. Richmond and the Colonel from the accounts available, particularly information and a sketch-map supplied by the Rev. Mr. Preece (father of Lieutenant G. A. Preece, who was on Whitmore's staff as interpreter), and from the notes of a journey made through the Urewera Mountains some years previously by Mr. Hunter Brown.

It was decided that three separate columns should be used, entering the ranges at different points and meeting, if possible, at Ruatahuna simultaneously. The Bay of Plenty force, which had marched from Tauranga to Matata, was divided into two columns, one of which was to penetrate the enemy country from the Rangitaiki Valley, while the other was to advance up the Whakatane Valley and gorges the whole way. The third column, which Mr. Richmond undertook to send forward from Wairoa, was to cross Waikare-moana by boat and canoe and march across the Huiarau Mountains by the Native trail to Ruatahuna. This third force (Colonel Herrick's), as it happened, proved useless, not being able to cross the lake in time.

The right wing of the Matata force, under Major Roberts, marched up the valley of the Rangitaiki and encamped at Karamuramu, on the left (west) bank of the river, where a large redoubt was built; this was named Fort Galatea, after the British warship in which H.R.H. the Duke of Edinburgh was then visiting the colony. Here there was a convenient ford of the Rangitaiki. On the opposite side loomed the forbidding blue sierras of the outer Urewera Ranges. The right wing was composed of a hundred Armed Constabulary, with a small but very useful Corps of Guides, and about two hundred Maoris of the Arawa Tribe, under Gilbert Mair, Te Pokiha Taranui (Major Fox), Matene te Huaki, and the Pukuatua brothers. The force marched from Fort Galatea on the 4th May, 1869. The men carried six days' provisions, besides spare ammunition, and the Arawa bearers were each loaded with 40 lb. of bacon or 400 rounds of ammunition. The route taken from the Kuhawaea Plain, on the east side of the Rangitaiki, was into the ranges by way of Ahi-kereru, the Rev. Preece's mission station (then abandoned) in the valley of Whirinaki, thence up the Okahu Stream in the direction of Ruatahuna. The first objective was a fortified position known as Harema (Salem), a short distance from Ahi-kereru. Colonel Whitmore accompanied this column.

The left wing, moving in from Whakatane, was commanded by Lieut.-Colonel St. John, and consisted of about 250 Armed Constabulary—Nos. 1, 2 (part), 4, and 8 Divisions—and a Native Contingent numbering 180, from the Ngati-Pukeko and Ngaitai Tribes, under Major W. G. Mair. The Government steamers "St. Kilda" and "Sturt," which had brought a portion of the force to Whakatane, landed stores and ammunition, and the column encamped at Opouriao, on the Whakatane Plain, in readiness for the entrance into the mountains. On the 4th May St. John began his difficult and perilous march into unknown country, guided by natives of the Ngati-Awa Tribe. The place of rendezvous arranged with Colonel Whitmore, the Ruatahuna clearing, containing the principal settlements of the Urewera *hapus,* was about fifty miles inland by way of the Whakatane River, which had

Major-General Sir G. S. Whitmore

Before coming to New Zealand Major-General Sir George Stoddart Whitmore had seen considerable service in South Africa as a young officer in the Cape Mounted Rifles. He served in the Kaffir wars, 1847 and 1851–53, and in the fighting with the Boers, 1848. On his return to England he passed through the Staff College with the highest credit. In 1861 he arrived in New Zealand as military secretary to General Cameron, and, after the Waikato War, retired from the Army and settled in Hawke's Bay as a sheep-farmer. He was requested to take command of the colony's military forces in the field in 1868. After the successful expedition to the Urewera Country in 1869 he retired from active service through ill health. He afterwards was engaged in sheep-farming on the East Coast, and was for many years a member of the New Zealand Legislative Council.

to be forded innumerable times. The route to-day, after the lapse of more than half a century, is as rough and primitive as it was in the days of the first British military expedition up the gorges of the Urewera.

The work of the right wing will first be described. Whitmore and Roberts had a comparatively easy march for the first twelve miles, taking a trail used by Mr. Preece in former years. The route was over the hills on the proper left bank of the Whirinaki River, after crossing the Rangitaiki River at Fort Galatea. Gilbert Mair and ten of his Arawa Maoris pushed on rapidly ahead of the main body with the object of seizing

Te Pato, on the range called Te Tairi, over which the native track passed to Te Harema and Ahi-kereru. It was feared that the Hauhaus of the Ngati-Whare Tribe would have posted men to watch for the approach of the Government force and to sound an alarm on a tree *pahu,* or drum, at Te Pato. This *pahu* could be heard for a distance of several miles. Mair reached the place without opposition, and found signs that a picket had been posted in the bush on the slope below the summit on which the *pahu* stood, and also that a sentry had been sleeping behind a large tree; these outposts had been withdrawn shortly before the Arawa scouts' arrival. The drum or gong was a hollow totara tree, one side of which, about 60 feet in height, and reaching to within 3 feet of the ground, had been cut into the form of a long narrow tongue. The end of this tongue, when beaten with a stick or a club, gave forth a penetrating resonant cadence which filled the air with its throbbing and reverberations, carrying far over the valleys and ranges. Mair waited on the forested range at Te Pato until the main body came up. He was then given a force of Ngati-Pikiao sufficient for operations, and was sent on to take Harema *pa* in the rear.*

Mair and his Arawa men forded the Whirinaki River about half a mile below where the Okahu River joins it at the base of the massively scarped old hill fort Umurakau, and marched up the rocky bed of the Okahu, passing under the bluffs of Umurakau, for about half a mile. Then they climbed up a steep bank and entered an old *pa* at Te Puhi-a-Kapu, in rear of Te Harema. An old man, a *tohunga* named Matiu Whatanui, was sitting in front of his hut on the brow of the hill. He fired a shot at Mair, but missed, and the officer took him prisoner, intending to save him; but Hemana Moko-nui-a-Rangi, of Maketu, fired and shot him, greatly to Mair's anger. Matiu fell, and next moment he was tomahawked by the Arawa. His wife and family were made prisoners. Curiously enough, these shots were not heard at Te Harema *pa,* which was not far away; a thick belt of bush (part of which is still standing) intervened between Matiu's home and the fort. The Arawa ran through this bush, Mair thinking that he had given the main body sufficient time to reach the front of it by the native track. The force was not there, and the Arawa therefore had the honour of storming the *pa.* Mair

---

* Harema *pa,* a stockaded position occupied chiefly by the Ngati-Whare Tribe, was situated on a hill about a mile beyond the present settlement at Wai-kotikoti, Te Whaiti. The site of the *pa,* now densely overgrown with *manuka,* is seen on the left of the present road to Ruatahuna shortly after crossing the Whirinaki River and before the Okahu Gorge is entered.

and Te Pokiha dashed up the hill with their eager Ngati-Pikiao soldiers, and the contingent in a few moments swarmed over the palisades and the place was in their hands. Four Hauhaus were killed, and forty-five people were made prisoners; the rest escaped into the bush and the ranges. The occupants of the *pa* were commanded by old Hamiora Potakurua, and numbered about eighty, half of whom were women.

The Armed Constabulary main body was in time to pursue some of the escaping Ngati-Whare, but although there was a great deal of firing not much damage was done. Hundreds of shots were fired at long range at a daring fellow named Paraone te Tuhi as he ran up a steep bare spur of Titokorangi Mountain in rear of the mission station at Ahi-kereru. Paraone turned deliberately now and again to make gestures of defiance at his foes, and made his escape untouched into the forest on the summit of the range. The Constabulary had carried in from Galatea a Coehorn mortar and some shells, but artillery was not required. The mortar was left at Ahi-kereru until the expedition returned.

After the capture of Te Harema (6th May), Colonel Whitmore and his officers made the old mission station at Ahi-kereru their headquarters. The large house, built of heart of *totara* in 1849 for Mr. Preece, the missionary of the district, was found in perfect order. Mr. Preece had left the place in 1853, removing to Whakatane, but visiting the place at intervals up to 1856, when he left for another district. The house and contents had been given into the charge of the native teacher Hamiora Potakurua. The missionary's son observed that the old home was undamaged, with some furniture and crockery, just as it had been left thirteen years previously. It was afterwards ascertained that when Te Kooti reached Ahi-kereru after his attack on Whakatane in March, 1869, he threatened to burn down the mission house, but old Hamiora stoutly opposed him, saying, "That place was given into my charge by my father" (meaning Mr. Preece); "if you burn it down you burn it over my head." The result was that Te Kooti abandoned his intention.

After the capture of Te Harema, a woman named Ripeka (Rebecca), whose husband was killed in the *pa,* and who herself had been nursemaid in Mr. Preece's home, hearing that a son of his, who had been her *potiki* (child), was in the force, rushed up to Lieutenant Preece and threw herself at his feet, embracing his legs and crying in a most pathetic manner.

The column spent one night in camp at Ahi-kereru, and on the following morning (7th May) resumed the march to Ruatahuna, and up the gorge of the Okahu Stream. The Corps of Guides led the way, followed by Mair and his Arawa and

"Big Jim," the Scout

(Hemi te Waka, mortally wounded in the ambuscade at Manawa-hiwi, Urewera Country, 7th May, 1869)

Roberts with the Constabulary. The Guides (or scouts, as they were usually styled) were commanded by Captain Swindley, with Sergeant Christopher Maling (afterwards Captain Maling, N.Z.C.) as next in charge. They numbered thirteen. Among them were the stalwart Tom Adamson and his brother Steve, both experienced and hardy bushmen, as active as any Maori in the forest. Steve had lost his right arm in an accident; nevertheless he was very smart with either carbine or revolver. The brothers had lately served in the bush chase of Titokowaru, after the capture of Whakamara in Taranaki. They marched barefoot. Steve's bush uniform consisted of a blue jumper and a pair of trousers cut short at the knees. Another scout was a Taranaki Maori named Hemi te Waka, usually called "Taranaki Jim" or "Big Jim"; he was a tall athletic fellow, wearing the forage cap of an Imperial regiment (the 43rd) perched on his curly hair. He had been a Kingite in Taranaki in 1860, but had turned to the

British side and assisted the troops as guide in the Waitara district. He fought well in many engagements with the Hauhaus, and proudly carried a presentation revolver, given him by the officers of the 57th Regiment for his services after the ambush at Te Ahuahu in 1864.

Describing the march on the 7th May, the principal incident of which was an ambuscade at Manawa-hiwi, near Ngaputahi, Steve Adamson, the veteran scout, said:—

" When we moved off from Ahi-kereru we of the Guides were warned to look out for escapers from Te Harema. These were two or three fugitives who had made off for Ruatahuna to give warning of our approach, and some of the Maori women who had been captured at Te Harema told us to beware as we marched through the gorges. A Maori who was with us was very cautious, often taking cover behind a tree as we advanced up the Okahu ravine, and when we chaffed him about it he said meaningly, '*Taihoa, taihoa!*' ('Wait and see!') We had marched very cautiously into the ranges from Galatea on our way to Ahi-kereru, and we were not allowed to fire at anything, although native birds, especially pigeons, swarmed in the bush, feeding on the *miro* berries. However, 'Big Jim' quickly made a spear and got three or four pigeons on the low branches, and we were not long in cooking and eating them. We came to a very narrow part (Manawa-hiwi) where a big landslip had come down and dammed up a part of the creek, and on the soft mud there 'Big Jim' observed the prints of naked feet. He was stooping to examine the marks closely, and was pointing them out with the butt of his gun to Captain Swindley, when all at once a shot came from the bush half a dozen yards away. Two or three shots followed in quick succession from our hidden foes, and 'Big Jim' received two bullets through the chest and lungs. Captain Swindley yelled to us to take cover, when a great volley came into us, crashing like thunder through the gorge, and Bill Ryan, a big man like the Maori, fell shot through one of his knees. He lay with his legs in the water of the creek. My brother Tom was shot through the right wrist, and another bullet struck one of the two Dean and Adams revolvers he wore slung on lanyards from the neck, crossing each other in front—we each carried two revolvers—and flattened out on the chamber, putting the revolver out of action; the blow cut his chest, although that bullet did not actually hit him. From whatever cover we could find we gave the Maoris a volley from our carbines. A dozen or so of the Hauhaus appeared and made a rush out upon us, but we took to our revolvers. They thought to dash in upon us while we were reloading our carbines. With our brace of revolvers each we fired heavily on them at close quarters and drove them back.

Bill Ryan was lying partly in the water, and I saw a Maori with a tomahawk crawling through the bushes and round a log to despatch him. I quickly shoved a cartridge into my carbine, capped and fired, and nipped him in the bud. I put the bullet through his chest. He was carried off the field wounded or dead. After the skirmish I found the flax mat he had been wearing, and there was a bullet-hole through the back of it. We drove the Hauhaus off. Their retreat was hastened by the terrific yells of the Arawa, under Lieutenant Gilbert Mair, who came rushing up as soon as they heard the firing. The main body of Constabulary was half a mile or a mile behind us, but they soon hurried up and joined us.

"As it was now late in the afternoon we did not follow up the chase, but halted for the night on the scene of the fight. 'Big Jim' died in two or three hours. We sewed him up in his blanket and buried him there. The men who had ambushed us, we learned later, were reinforcements coming down to Te Harema from Ruatahuna. Pickets of Arawa Maoris were sent out for the night, twenty or twenty-five on each side of the gorge in which we were camped. They climbed the precipitous walls through the bush, cutting steps in some places with their tomahawks, and held the heights above us to protect us from a night attack. Some of the Arawa were very nervous in the bush, and every now and then during the night a shot would be fired at some shadow, followed by a whole thundering succession of shots. We would douse our fires with water from the creek at each alarm of this kind; we extinguished the fires two or three times during the night."*

In this ambuscade Sergeant Maling had a very narrow escape from death. The range at which the Hauhaus fired was so close that his face was burned by the gunpowder, and he had several bullets through his clothes. The dead scout Hemi was buried where the road now goes, and the Arawa Maoris made a fire on his grave, as if a meal had been cooked there, a native war-device for preventing the enemy discovering the body and digging it up.

The morning following the ambuscade at Manawa-hiwi Whitmore's force continued the march to Ruatahuna. The trail was extremely difficult and rough. On the 7th the Okahu Stream, running in its tree-shadowed deep ravine of cañon-like narrowness, had been crossed over fifty times. On the 8th the route, leaving the ravine, turned to the left, and led over a succession of steep ridges, densely forest-clad. By 2 o'clock in the afternoon the Guides and the Arawa at the head of the

---

* Statement by Steve Adamson, at Hawera, 1920.

column had reached the summit of the lofty level-topped Tahuaroa Range, forming part of the watershed between the head streams of the Whakatane and the tributaries of the Rangitaiki. The Upper Whakatane, locally called the Waihui, flowed through the forest a thousand feet below. The long narrow valley of Ruatahuna, with its clearings and villages, was spread out before the eyes of the first white armed invaders to break into the mysterious heart of the Urewera. Far in the distance, at the foot of a range on the eastern side of the valley, a fortification could be seen with a large number of men moving about it. This was the Orangikawa *pa* at Tatahoata, and the men were Lieut.-Colonel St. John's Constabulary, who had just captured it after a sharp fight with the main body of the Urewera. Some of Whitmore's people, doubting whether St. John was in possession, imagined the men in the *pa* were the Hauhaus; but the commander and his staff rightly concluded that St. John had driven out the enemy. But for the delay caused by the skirmish at Manawa-hiwi the two forces would most probably have effected a junction that day (8th May), as arranged, in time to fight a combined action.

The descent of the precipitous Tahuaroa Range occupied four hours, and it was dusk when the force reached the old Oputao settlement at the foot of the mountain. Whitmore was anxious to meet St. John that night, and, leaving the column under command of Major Roberts in bivouac, he pushed on for Orangikawa. He took with him only a small party consisting of about twenty officers and men. These were Captain F. Swindley, Lieutenant Preece, and the Corps of Guides, besides a native guide, an Urewera man named Matiu. This man got nervous at one point on the bush tramp in the dark, and declared that his knowledge of the country ended there. However, "a little moral persuasion"—as Captain Preece puts it—restored his recollection of the trail. When Whitmore reached the ford of the Whakatane opposite Ruatahuna he ordered his bugler to sound the "Officers' call." In a few moments an answering call was heard, blown by St. John's bugler, and the loud cheering by the men of that officer's column announced their pleasure and relief at the welcome sound of Whitmore's signal. The distance traversed in the dark by the small party from the right wing was about four miles, through bush in which the Hauhaus lurked. A party of Urewera actually let Whitmore and his companions pass, within a few feet, without firing; this was near the ford of the Whakatane. When the startling sound of the bugle was heard the Hauhaus in ambush imagined the whole force was close up. Whitmore reached the captured *pa* at Orangikawa about 10 o'clock at night. "A great cheer went

J. C., photo, 1921]

The Lower Gorge of the Whakatane

This view, on the Whakatane River, in the gorge above Ruatoki, shows the wooded mountain-cliff of Karioi, near Tunanui. The route of Lieut.-Colonel St. John's troops here was up the river-bed, crossing and recrossing the Whakatane frequently.

up to the heavens from our whole force when he came in," says a veteran of No. 2 Division in St. John's column. "We were beginning to know the little Colonel by this time."

At daylight next morning (9th May) Preece, Maling, and ten of the Corps of Guides were sent off to Oputao, with instructions from Colonel Whitmore to Major Roberts to come on and join the other body; and the battle-ground at Tatahoata was the field headquarters for about a week while the surrounding settlements and cultivations were scoured by foraging-parties. Whitmore's main object was the destruction of the food-supply in the mountains, and this was carried out in all the potato-grounds that could be discovered.

WORK OF THE WHAKATANE COLUMN

The left column under St. John had had much heavier fighting than Whitmore's force on the march into the interior. St. John's principal officers were Lieut.-Colonel James Fraser and Major William Mair, R.M.; the latter commanded the Native Contingent. The force, 425 strong (including 180 Maoris), was very heavily loaded with ammunition, biscuits, and bacon. A Constabulary veteran recalls the fact that when the march began his swag weighed 70 lb. There was no road into the interior but the river-gorge, and St. John's men, laden like packhorses, found that the easiest travelling often was in the water. The first day's march up the Whakatane, crossing the river many times, brought the column to Tunanui, about twenty miles from Opouriao. There was no sign of the enemy as yet. On the 5th the force reached Waikari-whenua, five miles up the gorge of the Waikari, a large tributary of the Whakatane, flowing in from the ranges of Maunga-pohatu. On the 6th the exceedingly difficult traverse by the Wharau Range was accomplished. This ascent, the most arduous day's work in the hard march inland, involved a climb of more than a thousand feet up a densely forested mountain-side; the ascent was necessary in order to avoid an unfordable part of the Whakatane where the river ran between high cliffs a short distance above the junction with the Waikari at Te Kuha-o-Wheterau. Descending again to the Whakatane Valley, the advance-guard of the column came suddenly down into the small village Whata-ponga, on the proper right bank of the river. Here the first shots were fired. Lieutenant David White, leading the Guides, and Captain Gundry, with some Ngapuhi and other Maoris of No. 8 Division, rushed into the *kainga* and surprised the few natives who inhabited it. Gundry went in pursuit of a Maori, an old man, who was running away with a little boy on his back in a shawl or blanket. He shot the boy and brought the man down wounded, and ran up and tomahawked him. Sergeant William Wallace (No. 2 Division A.C.) witnessed this barbarous deed and remonstrated with Gundry, saying that it was not right to slaughter in this fashion. "I was taking *utu* for my brother," said Gundry. His young brother Fred, a lad of about fifteen, had been killed in the fight at Otautu, Taranaki, on the 13th March. Gundry was a half-caste Maori, a surveyor by profession. Another member of the column exacted *utu* for a slain relative, regardless of the fact that

J. C., photo, 1921]

Te Paripari on the Upper Whakatane, Urewera Country

Lieutenant David White was shot from the opposite bank of the Whakatane River (the bush-covered terrace shown) when in the act of stepping into the water in the foreground to ford the river, leading his party of scouts, 7th May, 1869.

the victim was innocent of offence. This man was Tahawera, a chief of the Lower Whakatane. He killed a woman with his whalebone *patu,* in revenge for his niece Ripeka executed by Te Kooti's orders in the recent raid on Whakatane. The death-roll at Whata-ponga was three men, two women, and the little boy. Lieutenant White was slightly wounded.

The force camped for the night in the captured village, and next morning (7th May) continued the advance southward up the narrow valley of the Whakatane, pent in by lofty forest-blanketed ranges. About a mile above the scene of the skirmish the force passed through the Ngati-Rongokarae village Ohaua-te-rangi, the principal settlement between Waikari-whenua and Ruatahuna. It was not occupied; the firing on the previous day had given the alarm, and it was realized that the Urewera were lying in wait at some of the narrows farther on. The force moved up the river, crossing from side to side of its gravelly bed. At Te Paripari ("The Cliffs"), about a mile above Ohaua-te-rangi, the expected volley from ambush was received. Here a small stream, the Mahaki-rua, flows in from the direction of Maunga-pohatu, joining the Whakatane at a ford facing a wooded terrace. St. John's advance-guard had descended to the eastern (right) bank of the river, and Lieutenant David White had just stepped into the water when a volley was fired by a large party of Maoris in ambush on the wooded bank on the opposite side, Te Pari-pari. The lieutenant fell in the water mortally wounded, and was picked up and was carried to the gravel-spit on the east side just above the junction of the two rivers. Heavy skirmishing now began, and lasted for several hours. White's body was buried on the *manuka*-covered flat in the river-bed, and Major Mair read the burial service, under a continual fire from the Hauhaus, who were in good cover, chiefly in the bush on the eastern side of the river.

Te Tupara, of Ruatoki, says that it was a man named Waikite who singled out and shot Lieutenant White, who was leading the scouts.

The Constabulary divisions chiefly engaged in the heavy skirmishing here were Nos. 1 and 2, under Captains Withers, Scannell, and Northcroft, and part of No. 4, under Captain Travers. The force advanced up the east side of the Whakatane and encountered sharp resistance on the march up over the Hukanui Hill, a steep bush ridge abutting precipitously on the right bank of the river. Low bush, scrub, and fern covered the lower part of the hill, and the defenders were strongly posted in the forest above. A party of Constabulary was detached to outflank the enemy's left, and this operation was carried out successfully. The ascent of the range was so steep that steps had to be cut with tomahawks in places. The Urewera abandoned their position on Hukanui, and fell back in the direction of Ruatahuna. Crossing a deep wooded gully, where a small stream joined the Whakatane on the east side, they took post in Te Whenuanui's *pa,* a strong earthwork redoubt called Tahora, about a mile beyond the top of Hukanui. The *pa* occupied a commanding position on a fern ridge trending at right angles to the valley of the Whakatane.

St. John halted his men for a meal on gaining the crest of Hukanui, and then moved forward to attack the Tahora work.

J. C., photo, 1921]

Junction of the Whakatane River and the Mahaki-rua at Te Paripari

This view shows the Mahaki-rua Stream coming in on the left, joining the Whakatane River opposite Te Paripari, which is on the proper left bank of the Whakatane. Lieutenant White was buried, under the Urewera's fire, on the manuka-clothed shingle-bank in the middle distance.

He sent Fraser with No. 1 Division and some of the Maoris to outflank the place on the left, and Nos. 2 and 8, under Scannell, were ordered to work round on the right. The centre was commanded by St. John himself. The Constabulary and natives descended into the intervening gully, across which there had been a good deal of firing at long range, and worked into the position allotted, but not in time to engage the Urewera closely. The defenders hurriedly evacuated the *pa* and took shelter in the bush. It was now getting late in the day, and the force encamped on the Tahora spur for the night. Not far from the captured *pa* was a small stockaded earthwork, a miniature *pa,* a few yards square; it crowned a narrow part of the Tahora ridge, alongside the track. This was a highly *tapu* spot, for it was the grave of Mura-Kareke, the most revered ancestor of the Urewera people. The Ngaitai Maoris who formed a portion of Major Mair's contingent desecrated the grave by making an *umu* or earth-oven there and cooking some pork for their evening meal. This was by way of revenge for the death of one of their comrades, a young man named Maehe, who had received a mortal wound in the Paripari-Hukanui fighting. The Urewera in their turn seized an opportunity of retaliation in kind for this act of sacrilege a few days later, when, at Te Kooti's order, they disinterred the bodies of Captain Travers and others killed in the Orangikawa engagement: "Let them be food for the beasts of the field and the birds of the air," said Te Kooti.

CAPTURE OF ORANGIKAWA PA

The column had now entered the lower part of the partly cleared valley known generally as Ruatahuna, a saucer of undulating and gully-seamed country rimmed by high wooded ranges of steep and broken contour. The advance was resumed on the morning of the 8th May, and by mid-day, after an easy march, St. John found himself close to the village Tatahoata, with its stockaded and entrenched *pa* Orangikawa. Mataatua Village, the present mountain headquarters of the Urewera, was passed on the right of the advance, with the Upper Whakatane a short distance away on the same flank.

The Orangikawa *pa,* an oblong work with trench, parapet, and stockade, stood on the lower part of a long slope below the high wooded range Arai-whenua and close to Tatahoata village and cultivations; its lower end was near the steep right bank of the Manga-o-rongo Stream. It was by no means a suitable site for a *pa;* the only feature to recommend it as a place of defence was the close proximity of the bush. When St. John's force was reported by the scouts a portion of the garrison took up a position in the bush on the north-east of the *pa,* where a small watercourse came down the valley. Captain Travers, with No. 4 Division of the Armed Constabulary, was sent in that direction to work round the higher side of the *pa,* while Major Mair, with some of his Maoris, was sent down to the south-west end to take up a position between the Hauhau fort and the Manga-o-rongo, and intercept the natives if they attempted to escape from the rear of the place. Mair got up within

10 feet of the palisades near the river, and could have shot many of the people in the *pa,* who were packing up in readiness for the retreat, but he waited in vain for Travers to complete the investment of the *pa.* Maori outposts on the opposite side of the river saw Mair's force so disposed, and sounded a loud alarm on a *pahu,* or tree-drum, and on the conch-shell trumpets called *pu-tatara.* By these signals they conveyed a warning to their friends in the bush above and in the fort that a body of the Government men was lying in wait in rear of the *pa.* Captain Travers was killed while engaging the Hauhaus at the edge of the bush on his flanking advance. He fell under a volley fired at very close range, about 30 yards from the thick undergrowth. He was busy making his men take cover, but mistakenly declined to take similar care of himself, saying in answer to remonstrances, "A British officer never takes cover." One of the principal Hauhau fighters at this point was Paraone, a Ngati-Awa and Ngaitai man. He was shot dead, some veterans say, by Captain Travers's batman.* Paraone had been a sailor. When his body was carried down for burial it was observed to be covered with beautiful tattooing in the designs of the Eastern Pacific. Curiously, it was a brother of this man (Mair's scout Maehe) who was mortally wounded in the fight on the river the previous day; the brothers were serving on different sides. St. John got within 10 yards of the *pa,* on the Mataatua side, with No. 8 Division and a subdivision of No. 2, and intended to start a sap, but before the tools could be brought up the Maoris evacuated the place. In the skirmishing the Government force lost five killed and six wounded. The Maori casualties were about the same number. The garrison of the *pa,* covered by the fire of their people outside in the bush, escaped along the small watercourse with wooded banks on the east side of the *pa,* and in the dense bush which extended down the hillslopes to within a few yards of the northern and eastern flanks. They retreated through the forest to the range of Arai-whenua above, and remained there shouting defiance to the troops and sounding their doleful war-trumpets.

Captain Travers and his fallen comrades were buried on the 9th May just outside the front gateway of the *pa,* on the east-north-east side, facing the hills.

After the force left the district the Urewera disinterred the

---

* Captain G. A. Preece writes: "A few days after this engagement I heard from W. A. Thom, who was one of Lieutenant White's scouts and afterwards one of Maling's, that Captain Travers and Paraone fired at each other at the same moment, Paraone being killed by Travers's bullet and Travers being mortally wounded by Paraone's shot."

After Fifty Years

This photograph, taken by the author at Orangikawa *pa,* Tatahoata, Urewera Country, in 1921, shows Captain Gilbert Mair at the grave of his old comrade Captain Travers and the men of the colonial forces killed in the attack on the *pa* fifty-two years previously. When Captains Mair and Preece marched into the Ruatahuna Valley in 1871 in search of Te Kooti and Kereopa they had the remains (which had been exhumed and scattered by Te Kooti's orders) reinterred with military honours near the gateway of the *pa,* and the poplar tree shown in the photo is one of two which were afterwards planted to mark the spot.

bodies, and, after their savage custom, decapitated them and decorated their palisade posts with the heads. When Captain Gilbert Mair and Captain Preece entered Ruatahuna with their Arawa column in 1871 they found some of the skulls stuck on the posts. That of Captain Travers, his old comrade Mair recognized by the gold-filled teeth. The remains were collected and buried in a grave 10 feet deep, Mair reading the burial service and the Maoris firing three volleys over the grave. The spot is marked to-day by a tall poplar-tree which Captain Mair planted there in 1872. The stump of another poplar stands beside it.

(Near this *pa* and close to the Manga-o-rongo Stream, on the lower or Mataatua side, are the ruined earthworks of another fort: this is the Kohimarama *pa,* a redoubt built by Major Ropata and his Ngati-Porou in 1871.)

The united force remained at Ruatahuna until the 14th May, 1869. Several skirmishes were fought during this time. Whitmore was anxiously awaiting the arrival of Colonel Herrick's column from Waikare-moana. The Native Minister, Mr. J. C. Richmond, had relieved him of the organization of this force, and had gone to Wairoa (H.B.) to push it forward. Whitmore knew that Te Kooti was somewhere about Waikare-moana, and as the days went on he began to fear that Herrick had met with a reverse. On the 11th May he ordered a reconnaissance in force up the narrow valley on the south leading towards the Huiarau Mountains and Waikare-moana. The column despatched on this service consisted of one hundred Armed Constabulary, under Major Roberts, and one hundred of the Ngati-Pikiao and other clans of the Arawa, under Gilbert Mair and Pokiha Taranui (Major Fox, of Maketu).

Pokiha, in the lead, encountered Te Kooti's advance-guard at Orona, a fern hill in the bush, about two miles from Tatahoata. This force had been hurried up by Te Kooti from Matuahu, on Waikare-moana, on hearing of Whitmore's invasion of the Urewera Country; it was commanded by the ruffianly half-caste Eru Peka te Makarini (Baker McLean), the bugler of Chatham Island fame. Gilbert Mair and Pokiha, leading the Arawa, charged and drove back the Hauhaus. The Native Contingent occupied Orona Hill, but withdrew, and Peka and his men took possession of it. On the following day a strong force of Constabulary marched out to assault the position, but the hill was found deserted. Peka drew off his men southward, leaving a rearguard in ambush. The sharp actions which followed along the Waikare-moana track and at Te Wai-iti are thus graphically described by Captain Mair:—

"Before commencing the ascent of Orona Hill, which is an open fern ridge, the track is intersected by a narrow gulch perhaps 40 feet deep. This gully we had to cross by a large fallen tree in the bush; it lay across the gully, which was over 30 feet wide. I was leading, and when half-way across the log I saw a Hauhau rise up behind the big stump of the tree on the other side and take a deliberate aim at me. I could not cut for it, so I made a pretence of aiming, which evidently disconcerted him, for his bullet sang past me quite wide of the mark. We got on top of the hill without further opposition, and there was a general halt while further movements were discussed. Sub-Inspector George McDonnell with fifty or sixty of his company of Armed Constabulary went forward as directed, taking up positions on the ridge. Colonel Whitmore directed me to go forward and feel for the enemy. I called on Matene te Huaki with his *hapu* of the Ngati-Pikiao Tribe (Ngati-te-Rangiunuora) to follow me, and advanced with some thirty of them. Passing McDonnell and his men, all lying down and taking it easy, I said, 'Back me up, Mac., if you hear any firing.' I took the lead, with Matene close behind me. A large body of Hauhaus was in concealment behind a thick bank of the drooping *kiokio* ferns (*Lomaria procera*) which fairly overhung the track. This was at a point about 80 yards from McDonnell's men. The trail ran along a deep rut on the side of the hill, which sloped steeply to the left. There must have been eighty or more of them, as I judged afterwards from the beaten-down growth extending to where the trail branched. Directly we got a few yards past a tree on the left we received a volley from thirty or forty guns. A bullet cut one of Matene's ears clean off, and we were half-blinded by flame and smoke, so close was the volley. Some of the Hauhaus poked the muzzles of their breech-loaders through the *kiokio* ferns, firing at a few paces. My Maoris were so staggered that they bolted to a man. At this moment a large piece of oily rag (the wrapping of a bullet) fell on my neck, setting fire to my shirt and making a most painful burn on my neck half as big as my hand. Then I saw the Hauhaus jumping down out of the dense mass of *kiokio* into the track (the trail to Waikare-moana), I suppose, 30 to 35 paces off. I jumped behind the tree I have mentioned, shouting to McDonnell to come up. To my horror my carbine jammed, and I could only whip out my revolver and empty it at the dozen or so of Hauhaus in the track. Most of them were reloading; several potted at me. Suddenly they disappeared like magic along the track. Not being supported, I immediately ran back, and McDonnell looked as if it was my ghost. My remarks were brief and appropriate.

"As for Ngati-Pikiao, seeing the stream of blood from their pet chief Matene, they set up a ghastly howl.

"Suddenly, from an eminence not more than a hundred yards way, we heard the notes of a bugle. It was Peka te Makarini, who was commanding Te Kooti's advance-guard; he used the bugle he had taken when he escaped from Chatham Island. Then he called out in a loud clear voice, '*Kua mate rawa i a te pakeha pahau-roa!*' ('The white man with the long beard has been killed!')—meaning me. In the ambuscade I had no doubt dropped flat, my usual trick when the flash of a gun came at close range. Then Peka shouted, '*Kua tahia e au a Turanganui, marakerake ana; kua purumutia e au a Mohaka. Apopo ka mitikia ake ohe!*' 'I have swept Turanganui [Poverty Bay] bare; I have swept out Mohaka. To-morrow you will be licked up!')

"I was in a furious rage, probably I could hardly speak, so angry was I at McDonnell's failure to come to my assistance. I managed to gasp out that the Hauhaus were just along the track.

"Then a few gallant fellows got round me—Henare Pukuatua, Arekatera Rongowhitiao, Pore Motunau, Rangiriri Ngahere, Te Honiana, and other *toas,* about twenty in all, including two or three of Te Pokiha's young relatives—and away we went at our utmost speed to engage the Hauhaus. When we reached the place where the trail branched [see × × on the sketch-map at the end of this volume] I urged them to go down there and make a detour to the left; we might thus round up the ambuscading-party and also those who had taunted us about the 'long-bearded man' and the massacres at Turanganui and Mohaka. My Maoris nearly all got ahead of me, and we had not gone far when they signalled back and left the track, turning slightly to the left. I could then see, down a clear little glade in the forest, seventy or eighty Hauhaus kneeling on the ground, while an elderly man, dressed in a full suit of navy blue, was addressing them in warlike terms—'*te korero o te toa.*' When we got abreast of them Henare, Arekatera, and the leaders made a sharp turn to the right up the little hill, fell on their faces, and let fly a volley—all too soon. I do not think I got a chance to fire, but dashed forward over several bodies and soon found myself in a small deep *kahikatea*-pine swamp, with a heavy fire coming from the enemy.

"Then came a bugle-call, and my comrades ran in highly excited. They had picked up quite a lot of delicious cooked pork, dropped by Te Kooti's advance-guard in their flight, and we all made a hasty meal there in the swamp. Henare's men with their tomahawks decapitated several of the Hauhaus, and we marched back, feeling very elated, the Maoris brandishing the bleeding heads about, swinging them by their long hair. On the way up they left two of the heads on stones in the creek-bed, not knowing how the Colonel would take this bit of barbarity. But they made a great display of those they carried into Orona, posturing before Whitmore and their chief Te Pokiha." *

One of Mair's soldiers conspicuous in this savage parade of enemy's heads was a youth whom the troops called "Red-head," because of his *urukehu* or ruddy-tinged head of hair. He came dancing in with the head of a man he had shot at Wai-iti. This young warrior, Captain Mair relates, was Ngahere te Wiremu, of Ngati-Manawa (Rangitaiki district). In 1867, during the bush campaign inland of Tauranga against the Piri-Rakau Hauhaus, he greatly distinguished himself by his dash and fearlessness, though only fourteen years old at the time. The 12th Regiment, at Tauranga, wanted to adopt him; the soldiers called him "Ginger." In February, 1870, when Gilbert Mair encountered Peka Makarini's ambush-party at the foot of Tumunui Mountain,

---

* Letter from Captain Mair, 4th June, 1923.

after Te Kooti's attempted raid on Rotorua, this *urukehu* fighter, Rewi, and Te Warihi were the only men of the Arawa who were with Mair at the moment.

The scene of the skirmish in which the Hauhau heads were taken was Te Wai-iti, a valley, with a small native *kainga,* through which the present track passes from Ruatahuna to the north shore of Waikare-moana. On the same day as Gilbert Mair's sharp action his elder brother, Major William Mair, led the Ngati-Pukeko, Ngati-Awa, and other Maoris of the Bay of Plenty contingent in an attack on the lofty hill above Mataatua Village, the locally celebrated Manawaru. The official accounts confused the two brothers, and referred to Gilbert's work at Orona and Wai-iti as the Major's action. The gallant Major himself, however, never got sufficient credit for his own good work in the campaigns. It happened that he was nearly always his own commanding officer, and so many of his fine deeds necessarily passed unrecorded by a superior.

Whitmore was desirous of pushing on to Waikare-moana, a mountain and gorge march of about twenty miles, and tried to persuade the Arawa to undertake the expedition. The Maoris were by no means eager for this perilous march through a country quite unknown to them and bristling with dangers. Peka Makarini and his experienced bushmen were certain to lay ambuscades in a region so suitable for defence against invasion, where the only road was a narrow trail through ravines and up steep mountain-sides, everywhere smothered in forest, or crossing and recrossing the rapid mountain-streams. Pokiha and sixty of his men volunteered to accompany the Constabulary, but on further consideration withdrew their offer. Whitmore had divided his force into two columns, one to march across the ranges to join up with Herrick at Waikare-moana, and the other to return to Fort Galatea with the wounded. He could not, however, move without the co-operation of the friendly Maoris, who urged the lateness of the season and the shortness of food and ammunition as reasons for immediate return to the open country. Henare te Pukuatua spoke of the difficulties of a march through the snow on the Huiarau Range. "Tell him," said Whitmore to his staff interpreter (Lieutenant Preece), with a dramatic wave of his hand—"tell him that my men come from a land of snow." But the Arawa were not impressed. They were determined to march home. The Armed Constabulary were quite ready to go on, in spite of the hardships of the expedition. It was ascertained afterwards that Te Kooti had prepared a trap for the expedition, an ambuscade in a gorge where scores of the Government men could have been shot down by the Hauhaus posted in perfect cover. It happened also that there could have been no support from Colonel Herrick, who was preparing to build boats at Onepoto instead of attempting the march round the eastern end of the lake to the Huiarau trail. Whitmore's force had exhausted the provisions carried, and was practically out of ammunition. Potatoes formed the chief article of food, and many of the men were offering the Maoris 5s. apiece for small cakes made from *kaanga-wai* (steeped maize) and grated potatoes.

Whitmore's final decision to abandon the proposed march to Waikare-moana and to return to Fort Galatea by the way he had come was a relief to the whole force, and particularly to the experienced officers, who realized that a disaster in the mountains would have brought hundreds of recruits to Te Kooti and altered the aspect of the war. On the 14th May the return march was begun. After leaving Ruatahuna the column was divided, Whitmore with the main body going as he came via Ahi-kereru, while Major Mair was sent out with the wounded by way of the Horomanga Gorge, emerging on the Kuhawaea Plain close to Tauaroa. Mair was given a detachment of Armed Constabulary besides the greater number of the native auxiliaries —Arawa, Ngati-Awa, and Ngaitai. Colonel Whitmore was taken seriously ill and had to be carried out in a litter by native bearers. At Ahi-kereru the force was joined by Major Cumming, who had been left there with some Armed Constabulary, and arrived at Fort Galatea on the 16th May. Major Mair had an anxious and perilous march with his wounded. The Urewera and other Hauhaus followed up his column and fired upon it at long range. The two nights in the mountains were a trying time, for the friendlies were eager to get out of the hostile country. The safe arrival of this column at Galatea was an intense relief to Whitmore and his officers, who feared for the safety of the sick and wounded.

This expedition, the first European force that had ever penetrated the Urewera Country, did a great deal to dispel the mystery which had enveloped that savage region, and to demolish its reported impregnable character. For the first time its physiography became accurately known, and, despite the formidable natural obstacles, it was proved that the country was not inaccessible to white troops. The tactics of ambush in which its tribes excelled did not deter the Government forces from traversing the most forbidding country, where the gloomy gorges and the all-enveloping forest gave a thousand opportunities for murderous ambuscades. The plains Maoris, naturally nervous of the bush on their first expedition, saw that under skilful leadership, and given sufficient supplies, they could fight their way anywhere through the ranges. As for the Armed Constabulary, in the words written of them by Colonel Whitmore, " Six months' continuous marching and fighting in the bush had destroyed its terrors, and they were now able to do anything except to run as fast as their naked native opponents, and as regards their pluck, constancy, discipline, and use of their arms they were better beyond comparison."

Colonel Whitmore, leaving the district in charge of Lieut.-Colonel St. John, went on to Matata and thence to Wellington via Wairoa, where he consulted Colonel Herrick with regard to further operations. Whitmore was crippled with rheumatism and unfit for further active service in the field. He left orders to advance the main camp to Opepe or Taupo, concluding rightly that Te Kooti must soon leave the shelter of the Urewera Mountains and emerge on the Kaingaroa Plain on his way to Taupo and the King Country.

THE FIRST WAIKARE-MOANA EXPEDITION

Lieut.-Colonel J. L. Herrick's column operating at Waikare-moana, shortly after Te Kooti's raid on Mohaka, numbered about five hundred, half of whom were Maoris (chiefly Ngati-Kahungunu). No. 2 Division Armed Constabulary joined it after the Ruatahuna expedition. Herrick's officers included Major Scannell and Captains Gudgeon, Newland, Northcroft, Richardson, Handly, Stopford, and Spiller. Dr. Gibbs was surgeon of the force. Herrick had previously acted well in a subordinate capacity, but was lacking in energy and initiative as a commander. The object was to cross Waikare-moana and penetrate the Urewera Country to Ruatahuna as soon as possible, in order to effect a junction with Whitmore's two columns from the Bay of Plenty side. Herrick's expedition was late in starting, partly owing to the difficulties that Captain Bower, Commissariat Officer, encountered in getting supplies over the Wairoa bar. After much delay Waikare-moana was reached without opposition from the Hauhaus, and the force settled down to build boats and pontoons at Onepoto in which to cross the lake, instead of going on round the eastern and northern shores. Many weeks were thus wasted.

A change of Ministry took place, and Colonel Herrick being unable to say when he would reach his objective, the expedition was recalled. Two large boats were sunk in the lake, and one whaleboat was buried on the shore, where it was discovered by the Hauhaus soon after the force returned to Wairoa. This expedition is considered to have been the most useless ever sent against the Maoris; at the same time it was one of the most expensive. The only shots were fired by the Hauhaus (10th June), when they ambushed and killed Trooper Michael Noonan, who was carrying despatches between the lake and Wairoa.

The Armed Constabulary were transferred to Napier, whence they marched to Taupo, leaving detachments on the way to build fortified posts at Te Haroto, Runanga, and Tarawera, guarding the line of communication between the Taupo country and Napier.

NOTES

On the march of Colonel Herrick's column from Wairoa to Lake Waikare-moana some good scouting-work was carried out by Mr. J. T. Large, who had joined the force as a volunteer. He was a settler in the Wairoa district, and was an excellent bushman; he had already performed some valuable scouting service, and served on several expeditions after Te Kooti's landing in 1868. A few days after the force reached Te Ariki, where the Waiau and Waikare-taheke Rivers join and where a redoubt was built, Colonel Herrick led a strong reconnaissance to feel for the enemy between there and the lake, as signs of their recent presence had been observed. After crossing the Waiau the track wound over the Tukurangi Hill, beyond which was a belt of forest. Shortly before the bush was reached the column was halted, Captain Spiller, who was with the advance, reporting numerous fresh Maori tracks, with indications of an ambuscade prepared in the bush ahead. Mr. Large, who was riding behind Colonel Herrick, jumped off his horse and, running to the front, ascertained that the enemy had moved off. He then led the column through the bush. The force returned to camp for the night, and later on reached Waikare-moana unmolested. At the lake Colonel Herrick set his men to work building boats and pontoons, though Mr. Large, who scouted the district thoroughly, reported to the commanding officer that there was a fair native track right round to the eastern end of the lake, Whanganui-a-Parua. Herrick had an excellent force of Armed Constabulary, besides native auxiliaries, and he could have cut a horse-trail round the lake to the landing where the mountain trail to Ruatahuna began, and could thence have gone right through to the heart of the Urewera Country as originally planned by Colonel Whitmore. But the force effected nothing, to the great disgust of Herrick's officers and men. Two large boats built at great expense were sunk in the lake when the expedition was abandoned—so deeply that it was found impossible to raise them afterwards—and two others were buried; one of these, a whaleboat, was found later on by the Hauhaus, and was captured from them in the following year. Herrick's expedition came to an inglorious end, redeemed only by the willing work and zeal of his Armed Constabulary subordinates, particularly such good men as Northcroft and Scannell. Mr. Large distinguished himself by his daring scouting enterprise. When Onepoto was abandoned in the spring he spent three days alone scouting in the bush in the enemy's country, and had been given up for lost when he came in and reported his work.

After the return of Colonel Whitmore's expedition from the Urewera Country, Whitmore and his staff left Matata for Auckland in the steamer "Sturt," as the commander wished to consult the Defence Minister, Colonel Haultain, regarding further operations. He remained in Auckland three days, then returned to Matata, and shipped No. 2 Division Armed Constabulary (under Scannell and Northcroft) round to the Wairoa district to reinforce Colonel Herrick's force at Waikare-moana. The small corps of Guides, under Sergeant Maling, was also sent. The troops were landed at Whangawehi, and marched from there to Wairoa, thence to Onepoto.

Captain Swindley, of Whitmore's staff, was sent to consult with Colonel Herrick, for Colonel Whitmore was too ill to travel and there was no possibility of his seeing Herrick personally, as the bar at Wairoa was too unsafe for the " Sturt " to attempt to enter. Colonel Whitmore then went on to Wellington, accompanied by Lieutenant Preece. Captain Swindley was sent in from Napier to establish the first post towards Taupo, at Te Haroto.

Drawing by Mr. A. H. Messenger]

The Steamer " Stormbird," Troop Transport

The " Stormbird," which was engaged in the trade between Wellington and Wanganui for about half a century, frequently carried colonial troops around the coast during the Hauhau wars. She was one of the small transports used in the Opotiki expedition in 1865. (See page 105.)

Chapter 33

THE SURPRISE AT OPEPE

COLONEL WHITMORE, BEFORE leaving the Bay of Plenty for Wellington, had instructed Lieut.-Colonel St. John to move the headquarters camp forward from Fort Galatea to a position between the Urewera Ranges and Taupo, and indicated Opepe as a suitable point. There the Napier–Taupo track intersected the main trail from the Rangitaiki and the Urewera Country, and the strategic value of the spot was enhanced by the abundance of grass and wood. Whitmore's proposal was to make Opepe the principal inland depot for stores, which could be brought up from Napier on packhorses. But St. John delayed his preliminary expedition until it was too late, for Te Kooti was just about to move across the Kaingaroa on his mission to the King Country to enlist the sympathies of Ngati-Maniapoto and Waikato. When at last a move was made on Taupo a tragic prelude to the campaign was the surprise and slaughter of a small Volunteer Cavalry detachment encamped at Opepe. This party, consisting of fourteen of the Bay of Plenty Cavalry troop, was unexpectedly attacked by the advance-guard of Te Kooti's column on the way from the Urewera Ranges to Taupo, and nine were killed.

This detachment of cavalrymen, under Captain Moorsom and Cornet Angus Smith, left Fort Galatea, on the Rangitaiki, on the 4th June, 1869, for Tapuae-haruru, as escort to Colonel St. John, who was on his way to select positions for military posts. Most of the troopers were young settlers at Tauranga and Opotiki; the sergeant-major, Slattery, was an old Imperial soldier. The march occupied two days. St. John and his escort on the first day's ride passed Ngahuinga, at the junction of the Wheao River with the Rangitaiki, and encamped a short distance above two of the primitive native bridges which spanned the Rangitaiki. The first of these bridges (*arawhata*) was Te Arawhata-a-Nohomoke, about four miles above Ngahuinga; there the river is very narrow. The next footbridge, formed of three or four long *manuka* poles with a handrail, was thrown across

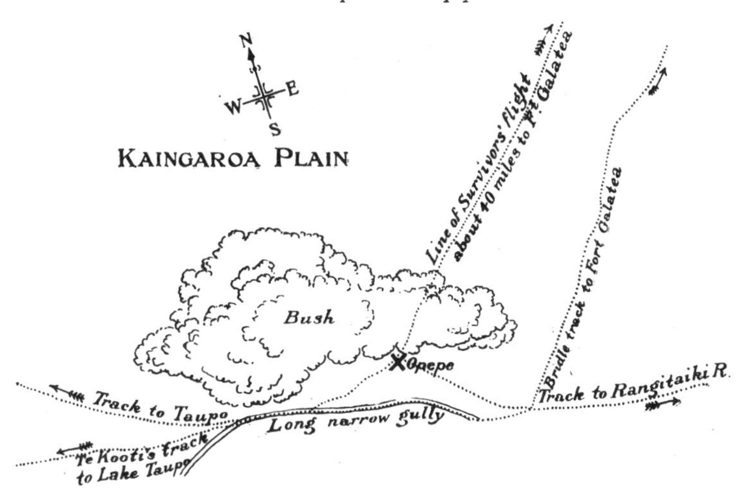

From a sketch-map by Mr. Thomas Hallet]

Opepe, the Scene of the Surprise Attack

(7th June, 1869.)

the river some miles farther south, where the strong stream is still more restricted. Above this again was the spot where St. John forded the river and encamped on the eastern side, close under the Heruiwi hills, on the western border of the Urewera Country, where Te Kooti was lurking.

The force was guided by a Maori, who in the light of after-events is believed to have been in secret sympathy with the Hauhaus. One of the only two survivors of the detachment, George Crosswell, of Opotiki, says: "After dark, at our first camping-place, the guide lit several large fires, and I remember well that I had some suspicion of him all the time. I remarked to my comrade George Stephenson that it was strange the Maori should have been allowed to light the fires, which were not needed; they were quite apart from our cooking-fire. I have no doubt that the fires were intended as signals to Te Kooti's scouts on the ranges above, on the left flank of our march, and that our Maori was in collusion with the Hauhaus. Colonel St. John seemed quite unsuspicious."

On the following day (Saturday, 5th June) the cavalrymen continued their march up the eastern side (right bank) of the Rangitaiki, and when well up the river towards Runanga they forded it again, and rode across the Kaingaroa Plain westward for Taupo. That night they reached the Opepe bush, a belt of timber about a mile in length, one of the sparse remnants of the ancient forests which covered the great plain. In the lee of this bush, on a small pumice plateau, a few hundred yards off the main trail, there was a deserted Maori settlement, consisting of four or five huts built of saplings and fern-tree trunks, and roofed with fern-frond thatching or long strips of *totara* bark. The spot was about a quarter of a mile west of the junction of the tracks from Fort Galatea and Runanga to Tapuae-haruru, and was reached by a turn-off track to the right up a gully. On two sides of the village plateau there was a pumice valley, and the belt of bush was immediately in the rear. Here in the old Maori settlement Colonel St. John left his escort, instructing them to camp there, while he, Major Cumming, Captain Moorsom, and one or two others rode on to Tapuae-haruru. As for the Maori guide, he rode off in the direction of Runanga after he had watched the detachment go into camp at Opepe, and that was the last seen of him by the troopers.

Ex-Trooper George Crosswell, who had a marvellous escape from death in the events which followed, gives a very clear and connected account of the occurrences at Opepe after the troopers off-saddled there on the evening of the 5th June. He first joined the colonial forces at Tauranga in 1865 as a bugler in the 1st Waikato Regiment of Militia. Later, at Opotiki, he carried a rifle and obtained a grant of land, and was settled on his section when he joined the Bay of Plenty Cavalry.

" I believe," narrates Crosswell, " that Colonel St. John before leaving us was asked if the camp was a safe place, and he replied that we were as safe there as we would be in London. This assurance put to rest any anxiety about the Hauhaus, and we set to work to make ourselves comfortable in the *whares* at Opepe, after turning out our horses in a broken-down paddock at the edge of the bush. On Sunday some of us rambling about got three sheep, probably strays from one of the out-stations on the ranges to the east, and we killed them and hung them up in the camp. However, we never had the pleasure of eating them —the Maoris got them. On the following morning (Monday, 7 June) I went in search of my horse, which had strayed in the direction of Galatea, and after an unsuccessful search I returned to camp. It was raining, and I was wet through by the time I got back to the *whares,* so I took all my clothes off and put them to dry at a big fire which we lit in one of the smaller huts, built of ponga fern-tree trunks. In the largest *whare,* the door of which faced north, towards the bush, there were seven men; in another were three half-caste troopers from Tauranga, and I and the others were in the small hut.

" I had returned to the hut about an hour, and it was now

about 4 o'clock in the afternoon. I was lying on my blankets reading a paper, when I heard voices outside, and, looking out, saw a Maori, a stranger, who had come up from one of the gullies on our flanks. Some of our men called to him, and the troopers came out of the large *whare* to talk to him; they took him for a friendly native. I heard more voices, and, getting up, was confronted at the door by two Maoris in fighting trim, with Enfield rifles capped and cocked.

"The Maoris shook hands with me, and allowed me to pass outside. I had just got up from my blanket, and had not a stitch of clothing on, as my uniform was not yet dry. I had a suspicion now that something was wrong. I did not attempt to take my arms. Passing the natives, I walked towards my comrades, most of whom were now outside the huts. Then all with one accord, realizing that the Maoris were enemies, made a rush for the shelter of the bush, which was perhaps a chain away. Not a single one of us had any arms; our carbines, revolvers, and swords were all in the huts.

"When we made the dash for the bush the Maoris did not fire immediately, as they were on both sides of us, and they could not fire without endangering their own party. The instant, however, that the troopers ran the gauntlet a heavy volley was fired after us. The shooting continued as long as any of us were in sight; there were a great many shots fired. I had only time for a hasty glance about me when I realized that we were trapped, but long enough to see that the place was full of Maoris. Immediately the first volley was fired into us I took a different direction from that of the others, and dashed by myself for the bush, making to my left; they ran to the right. Bullets were poured after us; I saw them knocking up the earth all about me as I ran. As I was racing over the short distance between my hut and the belt of bush I received a skin wound; a bullet grazed my left arm, but I scarcely felt it. I plunged into the bush and made my way through it as fast as I could travel, and when I had gone four or five chains I met Trooper George Stephenson, of Opotiki. We kept together, and just at dusk—it would then be about 5 o'clock—we got out of the bush, which was a belt of trees and undergrowth about a mile in length and half a mile in width. Stephenson was fully dressed, but had no arms, not even a revolver; and I don't think any of the others had had an opportunity to get their weapons—our one impulse was to get to the cover of the bush.

"After coming out of the bush to the tussock country we lay down and rested for about ten minutes. We could hear nothing either of the Hauhaus or of our comrades. We rose and continued our flight, making for Fort Galatea, forty miles

George Crosswell, of Opotiki

(Ex-trooper, Bay of Plenty Cavalry, and survivor of the attack at Opepe.)

away to the north. We travelled on all night, and after a time found a beaten horse-track underfoot, leading in the direction of Galatea. We hurried on all the next day, and kept on along the left bank of the Rangitaiki, avoiding the open track in the daytime wherever we could.

"It was very cold, raw weather—the middle of winter—but the excitement and the speed at which we were travelling kept me from feeling it as much as I would otherwise have done in my naked condition. My feet suffered most—they were terribly cut about by the fern and the pumice track. We reached Fort Galatea at last that evening and gave the news of the attack on the camp. My feet were quite poisoned by the rough journey, and it was a long time before they were right again.

"Three more survivors straggled in long after us. Sergeant Dette and Trooper Lockwood reached Fort Galatea after spending three nights and two days on the Kaingaroa Plain. Neither of them saw the other all this time. Cornet Angus Smith, our officer, did not come in till ten days after his escape from the camp; he was in a very bad way when he was found wandering outside the redoubt by a search-party.

"When we made that dash for the bush I believe the three half-caste troopers from Tauranga were lying down in their *whare,* and they may have been killed there. I heard long afterwards, from a Maori in Opotiki who had been one of Te Kooti's men at Opepe, that our big sergeant-major, Slattery, was the only one who made much of a fight. He picked up a stick or stone from the ground, and was only killed after a struggle. Most of the rest killed were probably shot as they ran, and were not killed with the tomahawk. So far as I can remember they were all fully clothed—I was the only one whose uniform was drying; but when they came out to speak to the first Maori who appeared they left their weapons in the hut, and other Maoris quickly came up on both sides between them and the huts, so that they were quite defenceless.

"It was, of course, a most foolish and imprudent piece of work altogether. Our subaltern officer, Cornet Smith, had no sentries out and took no precautions whatever, but I believe the chief blame must rest on Colonel St. John, for Smith understood from him that the place was perfectly safe. I believe the Hauhaus must have seen me out by myself when I first let my horse go and when I was searching for him, but they did not ambuscade me because they did not wish to alarm the camp until they had us all trapped. When they attacked us they came up from where our horses were grazing on the grass near the bush."*

The first discovery of the tragedy at Opepe was made by Mr. Thomas Hallet, of Napier. He was with his brother and Mr. Henry Mitchell, who had just finished the survey of a block of land near Taupo and were on their way back to Napier via Runanga. They were riding past from Taupo on the morning of the 8th June—the day after the attack—when they decided to turn off the main track to visit the Opepe camp, of which they had heard in Taupo. Mr. Hallet was riding ahead, and on ascending from the gully to the flat on which the camp stood he saw the smouldering ruins of the *whares* which had been fired by the Hauhaus. Then he discovered the naked bodies of two of the troopers lying between the *whares* and the bush. Two more bodies were found just within the edge of the bush. The surveyors turned and rode into Tapuae-haruru to inform Colonel St. John of the fate of his men. A body of Taupo Maoris from Poihipi's *pa* at Tapuae-haruru came out with St. John and buried the bodies of the nine men in two graves.

The cavalrymen killed were—Sergeant-Major Slattery, Troopers Ross, Lawson, McKillop (trumpeter), Cooke, H. Gill, Johnson, Bidois, and C. Poictier (Potie).

---

* Statement to the writer by George Crosswell, of Opotiki, at Rotorua, 2nd February, 1921.

Those who escaped were—Cornet Angus Smith, Sergeant Dette, Troopers George Crosswell, George Stephenson, and Lockwood.

Trooper Harry Gill was a Tauranga lad, the son of Judge Gill, of the Native Land Court. Johnson, Bidois, and Poictier were half-castes from Tauranga. The rest of the detachment were from Opotiki.

The Hauhaus stripped the dead of their uniforms, and secured the whole of the arms and equipment of the detachment—fourteen Calisher and Terry breech-loading carbines, and the same number of revolvers and swords, besides the horses and saddles. The ammunition captured was about twenty rounds per carbine. With these weapons Te Kooti was able to complete the equipment of his mounted men, and, as he had already at various times captured troopers' carbines and swords, he had by 1870 a small body of cavalry dressed and armed like our own men.

Cornet Angus Smith received the New Zealand Cross as the result of the Opepe affair. This was regarded as a gross misuse of the decoration, for Smith was guilty of an inexcusable neglect of ordinary military precautions in omitting to post sentries and guard against surprise. The chief blame, however, rested with Colonel St. John whose conduct in establishing camp in such a dangerous position alongside the bush, and in leaving the detachment with the assurance that the place was safe, was careless and unsoldierlike in the extreme.

The most remarkable feature of the episode, probably, was the extraordinary physical endurance of Trooper Crosswell, who travelled across the desolate wind-swept Kaingaroa Plain from Opepe to Galatea, a journey of almost forty miles, in the depth of winter, in an entirely naked condition. Mr. Crosswell, who is a good example of the wiry, hardy pioneer, is still (1923) living at Opotiki.

Very shortly before the Opepe surprise two orderlies riding with despatches from Galatea to Taupo to overtake Lieut.-Colonel St. John were ambuscaded by the Hauhaus on the trail, and one of them was killed. These troopers, Donald MacDonald and Alexander Black, were hurried from Galatea soon after St. John's party had gone, with information brought in by Captain Mair's scouts that Te Kooti was at Heruiwi waiting to descend on the plain. Trooper MacDonald was the bearer of the despatches, written by Mair and others. While the cavalrymen were on their way up the Rangitaiki Valley on the eastern side, close under the ranges, they were observed by three Hauhau scouts, Peita Kotuku, Te Makarini, and Porekapa. The scouts, who were mounted, intercepted the troopers near Te Tieke, an isolated clump of bush at the foot of the hills. Peito was fired at by one of the troopers, and the bullet struck him on the breast but was deflected by some of his equipment. Peita, describing the encounter, said:—

"The troopers got off their horses and, to our surprise, retreated. Had they been Maoris or experienced soldiers they would, of course, have taken cover and skirmished up to us, for there were only three of us. I was armed with a carbine and revolver. I fired at the man who had fired at me [this was MacDonald], and my carbine-bullet struck him in the right thigh and smashed the bone. He fell, and as he lay there disabled Te Makarini shot him dead. This Makarini (McLean) was a Tuhoe man, an elder brother of Te Whakaunua, who was killed in the flight from Ngatapa. The other trooper escaped, after abandoning his horse and carbine. We took the arms and equipment and reported to Te Kooti, and immediately afterwards we all set out from Heruiwi on the march for Taupo and surprised the camp at Opepe."*

Alexander Black, who left his horse and carbine and rushed down the track towards the Wheao River, succeeded in escaping to Fort Galatea.

Peita Kotuku stated that the advance-guard of Te Kooti's force on the march across the Kaingaroa Plain to Opepe and Taupo was led by the chief Te Rangi-tahau, who, like Peita, was an escapee from the Chatham Islands in the "Rifleman." Tahau was familiar with all the tracks, as this was his territory. Peita was with the main body, which was under the command of Eru Peka, the half-caste. It was the advance-guard, he states, that surprised the troopers at Opepe†. Peita confirms Crosswell's belief that the soldiers' guide gave information to the Hauhaus. The

---

* Statement to the author by Peita Kotuku, at Taringamutu, King Country, 23rd Ferbruary, 1921.

† Captain Preece, writing from Palmerston North, December, 1921, said:

"We afterwards heard from the natives who were with Te Kooti that they had no idea that our forces were moving towards Taupo. When they came on the tracks and saw there was only a small party they decided to cut it off. They worked their way round to the Opepe camp through the edge of the bush, sending by the track a friendly native who had been taken prisoner by Te Kooti at Tauaroa, when he retired from Whakatane, to get into conversation with our people and put them off their guard. The plan acted well. Trooper Gill, knowing the man as a friendly native, but unaware that he had been taken prisoner by Te Kooti, got into conversation with him, and was told that he was with some other friendly natives who had come to scout. A few more came up and engaged our men in talk, thus giving the main body time to surround and attack them. After-events proved that Colonel Whitmore's policy which planned the occupation of Taupo was the right one, but it was unwise to send forward a small body of men a distance of over forty miles from their base. The withdrawal of the troops from Fort Galatea to Tauranga was another insane act."

man, who belonged to the Ngati-Tuara sub-tribe, of Pakaraka, near Rotorua, met some of the Urewera followers of Te Kooti as he was riding back along the Rangitikai, and informed them that the cavalrymen had encamped at Opepe.

After the slaughter of the troopers Te Kooti led his force to Waitahanui, on the eastern side of Lake Taupo, and went on to the southern end of the lake and gained the friendship of Te Heuheu Horonuku and other principal chiefs of Ngati-Tuwharetoa. From the Taupo district he travelled on to the King Country and met the Waikato and Ngati-Maniapoto at Tokangamutu, now Te Kuiti.

Lieut.-Colonel St. John immediately returned to the coast. Colonel Whitmore, in discussing these events in his book on the Maori wars, blamed St. John severely for his tardiness, for his assurance given to the escort that they had nothing to fear at Opepe and that a sentry was unnecessary, and for his conduct in withdrawing after an incident which in itself was not of great military importance, and by failure to advance at once, permitting Te Kooti to obtain great influence over the doubtful tribes. In Whitmore's opinion St. John should have collected every available man for a Taupo expedition, and his failure to do so resulted in an enormous increase of Te Kooti's *mana*.

Chapter 34

THE TAUPO CAMPAIGN (1869)

FOR A FEW weeks in the winter and early spring of 1869 active hostilities were suspended, and Te Kooti made the most of the peaceful interlude by recruiting among the Ngati-Tuwharetoa Tribe and visiting the Waikato and Ngati-Maniapoto at Tokangamutu (Te Kuiti). He secured the adherence—not altogether willing—of Te Heuheu Horonuku, the hereditary head chief of Ngati Tuwharetoa, and most of the members of his tribe at Tokaanu and Waihi, on the southern shore of Lake Taupo. At the northern end of the lake the majority of the people under Poihipi Tukairangi, of Tapuae-haruru, and Hohepa Tamamutu, of Oruanui, were friendly to the Government. Te Kooti made Tokaanu his headquarters, and his followers revelled in the soft waters of the hot springs there, and the abundance of food after their short commons in the Urewera Ranges. At the northern end of the lake Captain St. George commanded the friendly natives, whose post was the palisaded *pa* Tapuae-haruru, on the western bank of the Waikato River at its point of exit from the lake. A little later a redoubt (which is still well preserved) was built by the Armed Constabulary on the opposite side of the Waikato; it was the nucleus of the present township of Taupo.

After Colonel Whitmore's departure for Wellington, in ill health, Colonel Harrington, with headquarters at Tauranga, was given command of the Bay of Plenty district. Harrington's first act was a grave blunder. He ordered the Armed Constabulary to abandon the redoubts at Matata, Fort Clarke, and Fort Galatea, and instructed the whole force to fall back on Tauranga, where he intended to put them through a course of drill for a few months. Lieutenant Preece had been sent to Patea with a new contingent of Ngati-Porou who had been enrolled for service in the Armed Constabulary on the West Coast. After handing the men over to Major Noake at Patea he returned to Wellington and there received instructions to go to the Bay of Plenty with Colonel Harrington.

Te Kooti, having more or less compulsorily recruited Te Heuheu and his people, went on to Tokangamutu, in the King

Country. A Turanganui chief named Wiremu Kingi, of Te Aowera *hapu* of Ngati-Porou, who was compelled by Te Kooti to accompany him throughout the war and who was captured at Maraetahi (on the Waioeka) in 1870, gave Lieut-Colonel St. John and Captain Porter an account of the meeting at Tokangamutu with Waikato and Ngati-Maniapoto. Wiremu said:—

"We had about two hundred people in our party which visited the Maori King's country. At the meeting the chief Manga (Rewi Maniapoto) welcomed us, and chanted a song which appealed to the people to hold the land and keep up the fighting. Concluding, he handed Te Kooti a sword, with which he was to sever Manga-tawhiri and Hangatiki (*i.e.*, to beat the Europeans out of the Waikato). Te Kooti answered: 'Here is the sword; take it back. It will remain in front of the King. If he gives the sword I shall take it; if not, let him keep the sword and I will go elsewhere. The King is in the centre with his sword and I am on the outside.' Te Kooti's reason for going to the Upper Waikato was that he wished to gather all the tribes—the people of Waikato, of the Wairarapa, of Wanganui, of Taranaki, of Tauranga, of Hauraki, and of Ngapuhi; then to consider and determine upon the matter of attacking the white man until he should be quite destroyed.

"By the mouth of Tamati Ngapora (King Tawhiao's cousin) came the answer to the words spoken by Te Kooti to Manga and others of the King's representatives. The answer was a refusal. The words were that the people did not consent to Te Kooti's proposals; that his purpose in coming amongst them was to lower their chieftainship, and to destroy their *Atua,* their god, and that they would not bow down to his *Atua.* But when Tawaio heard of the reply he was wroth. He asked, 'Why did you not agree with Te Kooti? What are his crimes? You have robbed me of my dignity as King. My duty is to rise in hostility against the white man.'"

Then, according to Wiremu Kingi (not to be confused with the celebrated Taranaki chief of that name), there was mention of white men who were in active sympathy with the Hauhaus.

"Te Kooti asked if there was not a European in correspondence with the King. The custom of this *pakeha* was to be in opposition to the Queen. His name was 'Hakara Mihara,' and he was chief of the Irish, of the French, and of the Germans! The Mataura Ngati-Porou, living on the Coromandel Peninsula, where the European mentioned had leased some native land, were the bearers of his messages. These are enemies of the Queen, and said they would join Te Kooti. The white man was with Te Hira, whom he asked to concede the land at Ohinemuri to dig for gold, which would make the Government jealous, and afford a pretext for his people to rise up against the whites."

"Later," Wiremu continued, "Te Kooti had correspondence with the *pakeha* mentioned. After we left Tokangamutu some few men of Ngati-Porou arrived from Mataura bringing gunpowder and percussion caps, with a message from the *pakeha*. Te Kooti wrote to him, and the letter was sent to the *kainga* of Hera te Kaki. It was in consequence of the letter that the men brought the powder and caps. They were sent back again. The King and Te Hira acknowledged Te Kooti, and consented to worship his god, and Te Kooti wrote and sent presents of clothing. The King wrote to Te Kooti, 'Go and do your work. You are a man of labour. There are two men in the Island: one is a man of labour, the other is a man of idleness.'"

By the "man of labour" Tawhiao meant Te Kooti; the other was himself. In this fashion the Maori King encouraged Te Kooti to continue the fighting. As for Rewi Maniapoto, or Manga, as he was more generally known then among the Maoris, he accompanied Te Kooti back to Taupo, intending—if conditions were propitious—to join him in the campaign in the district south of the lake. Few of Rewi's people, however, supported him in his warlike plans.

It was early in September, 1969, before active measures were taken to deal with Te Kooti, who had returned from the King Country to Tokaanu. Lieutenant Preece had been sent up from Tauranga to Tapuae-haruru to join Captain St. George in command of the friendly natives, and soon after his arrival there it became known that a large war-party of the Ngati-Kahungunu Tribe, under Renata Kawepo and Henare Tomoana, was advancing from Napier, and also the Armed Constabulary field force under Colonel Herrick, withdrawn from Wairoa. Colonel Thomas McDonnell had now been appointed to the command of operations in the Taupo country, and there was general satisfaction among the Europeans and Maoris at the prospect of fighting under so energetic an officer.

In September Captain St. George and Lieutenant Preece were ordered to cross Lake Taupo by canoe and co-operate with Colonel Herrick's Constabulary and the Ngati-Kahungunu at the south end. Henare Tomoana, however, pushed on with his men—about one hundred and twenty, all mounted—and marching from Runanga reached the old *pa* at Tauranga-Taupo on the east shore of the lake on the 9th September, and were attacked by Te Kooti and his Hauhaus before the Tapuae-haruru contingent arrived. The canoe flotilla under St. George and Preece and the chiefs had been delayed by adverse winds. Te Kooti's men assailed the Ngati-Kahungunu entrenched position on three sides, but after several hours' firing withdrew with the loss of three killed. The fighting was renewed next day, but was inconclusive, and Te Kooti

From a photo, about 1883]

Te Heuheu Horonuku

(Died 1888.)

To Heuheu, the paramount chief of the Ngati-Tuwharetoa Tribe, of Taupo, joined Te Kooti in 1869, but made submission to the Government shortly after the fight at Te Porere. In 1887 he presented to the Crown the summits of the volcanic mountains Tongariro, Ngauruhoe, and Ruapehu, his famous tribal peaks, forming the nucleus of the Tongariro National Park.

then returned to Tokaanu, taking with him all the horses of the Hawke's Bay contingent. St. George joined up with Tomoana soon after this skirmishing. By the middle of the month McDonnell and Herrick, with all the Constabulary and the Maori contingents, were in camp at Tokaanu. Te Kooti had retired southward over the Pononga saddle to the west end of the lake Roto-a-Ira. McDonnell moved round the east end of the Pihanga Range and fixed his field headquarters at Poutu, on the east end of Roto-a-Ira, where he built a defensive work. With McDonnell were the old chief Renata Kawepo and a party of Hawke's Bay natives who had come up via Moawhango.

Te Kooti's force took up a position on the crest of the Pononga ridge, the steep saddle of land, mostly covered with forest, which connects the Kakaramea Range with the extinct volcanic mountain Pihanga, forming the divide between the south end of Lake Taupo and Roto-a-Ira. On the morning of the 25th September the scouts discovered the presence of the Hauhaus there, and were fired on from a spur closely commanding the track from Tokaanu across the flat. Lieutenant Preece, hearing the firing, immediately moved out with the Arawa and Taupo contingents. Captain St. George had ridden out to Poutu to meet Colonel McDonnell. Preece did not think at first that the Hauhaus were in force, but on crossing a swamp and ascending the north face of the Pononga Hill, which was covered with high fern, he found that the enemy were numerous and were entrenched in rifle-pits at the edge of the bush. A sharp engagement followed. Henare Tomoana came up with his men, and, advancing in skirmishing order, the Hauhaus were driven back from point to point. Captain St. George now came hurrying up with reinforcements and gave the order to charge. The skirmishing Hauhaus were driven back on their line of rifle-pits, where Te Kooti made a stand, but Lieutenant Preece with his Taupo and Arawa Maoris charged them in dashing fashion and cleared the entrenchments. Several lay dead in the rifle-pits, and others about the ridge. Among the Hauhaus killed was Wi Piro, Te Kooti's near relative. [The spot where he was shot is pointed out by the Taupo natives, close to the left-hand side of the horse-track as one rides over the crest of the Pononga saddle from Tokaanu to Roto-a-Ira, just before the bush is entered.] Wi Piro had escaped from Chatham Island in the "Rifleman"; he had been conspicuous in every raid and engagement since the landing at Whare-ongaonga, and was one of those who took a savage delight in slaughtering prisoners. The Government force had two killed and four wounded. One of the fatal casualties was Maniapoto, a young chief of Ngati-Hineuru; he had been a Hauhau and fought at Omarunui, near Napier, in 1866, when he was one of the very few who escaped from the field.

This fight at Te Pononga, in which only Maori troops were engaged, carried important consequences, for it stripped Te Kooti of much of the military *mana* which he had acquired in the Taupo country, and it convinced Rewi and some of his Ngati-Maniapoto, who were awaiting the result of the battle, that the Government forces were likely to come out victors in the inland campaign. Rewi went home to Tokangamutu, and renounced all intention of assisting Te Kooti.

Colonel McDonnell came up in time to see the end of the fighting on the Pononga Range and to congratulate St. George and Preece on their success. On the return to camp at Tokaanu it was found that No. 2 Division Armed Constabulary, under Captains Scannell and Northcroft, had arrived from Napier.

Shortly before this encounter Te Kooti had ordered the execution of four scouts sent out by the friendly chief Hare Tauteka, who were captured in a *whare* near Roto-a-Ira. They were killed, mutilated with tomahawks, and thrown into a swamp, where the remains were found.

THE FIGHT AT TE PORERE

A few days were spent in scouting the enemy's position by Captain Northcroft, Lieutenant Preece with some natives, and Sergeant C. Maling with the Corps of Guides. It was ascertained that the Hauhaus occupied the settlement Papakai, under the western slopes of Tongariro. Seventy Wanganui natives arrived under Major Kepa and Captain William McDonnell, and the whole force moved up to Roto-a-Ira. On the 3rd October McDonnell advanced with combined columns, only to find that the enemy had retired from Papakai and was holding two hills and a strong earthwork redoubt at Te Porere, on the tableland at the edge of the bush north-west of Tongariro. It was arranged that Major Kepa was to move to the left under cover of a low ridge, and that after he had had two hours' start he, with the Constabulary in the centre and Ngati-Kahungunu on the right flank, was to make a swift attack on the three positions. The two advanced positions were soon taken; one of these, Roipara, was on the right bank of the Wanganui River, here a small stream issuing from the west side of the Tongariro volcanic range. Just as the force was fording the river Captain St. George ordered Lieutenant Preece to take the Arawa to the right flank. This was done, and the Hauhau redoubt was determinedly assailed on three sides. The forest extended to within a short distance of the *pa* on the west and north-west sides, and McDonnell was not able to extend his force completely round the position in time, otherwise Te Kooti would have been cut off from the refuge of the forest, and his career would have ended on the battlefield of Te Porere.

A party of the Hauhaus took post in the edge of the bush and opened fire on the left flank of No. 2 Division as they were advancing to the assault. McDonnell detached a party to deal with them and launched the rest against the *pa*. Captain St. George and a force of Constabulary and friendly Maoris came at the double up the easily sloping hill on the east and rushed at the front of the work. St. George was leading on his men gallantly, charging through the short fern, when a bullet fired by Peita Kotuku, pierced his brain and he fell dead. But a very few moments later the walls were stormed and the Armed Constabulary and Kupapas, with bullet and bayonet, took abundant revenge for their slain. Just before the final assault the chief and most of his men escaped to the bush in the rear; Te Kooti himself was wounded, for a bullet had cut off one of his fingers and passed through his side.

Peita Kotuku, describing the defence of the *pa,* said:—

"Our redoubt was a massive earthwork—it is standing there to-day—but it had one defect, which resulted in our defeat. In making the loopholes (*huarahi-pu*) in the sod and pumice walls, interlaid with fern, we made them straight (horizontal), and could not depress the muzzles of our guns to fire into the ditch. The Government troops, *pakeha* and Maori, got up under the parapets, and many of them snatched up lumps of pumice (*pungapunga*) and stuffed up the firing-apertures with them. We therefore could not see our nearest attackers unless we exposed ourselves over the top of the parapet.

"It was I," continued Peita, "who shot a *pakeha* officer as he was leading his men in a charge up to the front of the *pa*." [This was Captain St. George.] "I was just behind the short parapet (*parepare*) covering the gateway immediately inside the entrance. My weapon was a breech-loading carbine. When the officer, rushing ahead of his men, was about twenty paces from the entrance I fired and shot him dead. It was not Te Kooti who shot him, as some have said. At that stage of the fighting Te Kooti was in a rifle-pit in an angle on the left flank of the *pa,* some little distance from the *kuwaha* (gateway). He was sitting there surrounded by a bodyguard of women."*

Sergeant W. Wallace, No. 2 Division, narrating the incidents of the attack, said:—

"The first shots fired in the Porere fight were from the top of a hill just to the Roto-a-Ira side of the Wanganui. I saw the flash of a gun-barrel there, and called out, 'We'll get a volley directly,' and so we did, but none of us was hit. We crossed the river and skirmished up to the *pa.* The redoubt held by the Maoris was built of pumice, earth, and ferns, and their bullets sent the pumice from the ground around flying into our eyes. I had some good shooting there as they were retreating, running out of their gateway, into the trench, and then making for the bush. Pompey, of Wanganui, was with us; he ran around the east angle of the *pa* to get a better shot, and was killed between that point and the gateway. I was trying to get one fellow who wore a smoking-cap. Lying flat on the ground I got a splendid shot, and he disappeared. I don't know whether it was I or some

* Statement to the writer by Peita Kotuku, at Taringamutu, 1921.

one else who got him, but I don't think I missed; our Terry carbines were very good up to 400 yards. This man at whom I was shooting was armed with a spear consisting of a bayonet fastened on a long pole."

All the Hauhaus found in the *pa* when the attackers at last succeeded in rushing it were shot or bayoneted. Thirty-seven Hauhaus were buried within the walls after the fight. The Government loss was four killed and four wounded. One of the killed was Komene, an Arawa sub-chief. The two Wanganui natives who fell, Winiata Pakoro and Pape (Pompey), belonged to the Ngati-Hau Tribe, and were fighters of exceptional activity and bravery. Winiata was shot dead while firing down into the Hauhaus from the top of their own parapet. Colonel McDonnell had ordered him to come down, but Winiata, who had been firing shot after shot into the crowded *pa,* said, "Only one more shot," and fired; the next moment he fell from the earthwork, shot through the heart. His brother, Tonihi, had him buried in a running stream; the watercourse was diverted, a grave was dug in the gravel, and the stream was then allowed to return to its channel. This was done lest the Taupo Hauhaus should disturb the remains of Ngati-Hau's hero. Renata Kawepo, the old warrior chief from Hawke's Bay, was severely handled by a young Taupo woman, the wife of Paurini, a chief who had been shot in the attack. In the tussle she gouged out one of his eyes. This occurred in the edge of the bush where Renata was pursuing some of the Hauhaus who had left the *pa.*

The death of Captain St. George, killed while charging up to the *pa* front, was a source of deep sorrow to all his friends. Major Gascoyne wrote of him, "He was brave to rashness, and the finest horseman I ever knew." St. George and Gascoyne had both joined the Hawke's Bay squadron of the Colonial Defence Force in 1863. The gallant soldier was laid to rest on the shore of Roto-a-Ira; two years afterwards Gascoyne brought his remains out to Napier, to be interred there with military honours.

Te Heuheu Horonuku, who had been compelled by Te Kooti to join him in Porere *pa* and who had escaped to the bush, came in a few days later and surrendered to Colonel McDonnell. The Colonel had sent him a message by one of the women prisoners warning him to leave Te Kooti and come in with his people. With him was his little son Tureiti te Heuheu, then a boy of between four and five, who became the head chief of Ngati-Tuwharetoa on Horonuku's death in 1888. Tureiti was well known in late years as Te Heuheu Tukino; he was a man of great personal charm, very proud of his ancestral traditions, and deeply schooled in the ancient lore and poetry of his race. He was a member of the Legislative Council of New Zealand when he

Captain J. St. George
(Killed at Te Porere, 1869.)

In Mr. Alfred Domett's epic poem "Ranolf and Amohia" (1872) there are some lines on Captain St. George, who was the statesman-poet's stepson. "For kinship's sake" Domett wrote in memory of the young soldier:—

"... Who sleeps the sleep no more to wake
On earth, 'mid loveliest scenes afar,
Where Tongariro's snows disgorge
Their flames by blue Te Aira's lake—
Young, kindly, chivalrous St. George!
Whose honour-fired aspiring brain,
Before that instant-blighting ball,
Flashed into darkness without pain.

* * * *

So swiftly his bold course was run,
That ardent spirit's duties done."

died in 1921. Although so young at the date of the battle, Tureiti had a vivid recollection of the attack on the *pa* and of his escape, carried off to the bush by his elders.

The *pa* at Te Porere, the last redoubt constructed by Te Kooti, is in a very fair state of preservation to-day. Diverging from the Waimarino–Tokaanu Road near the foot of Tongariro volcano we follow a horse-trail parallel with the Wanganui—here a little brawling brook—in the direction of the great forests which stretch far away to the west. A short distance from the road we come to the scene of the conflict on the edge of the tableland, close to a thick belt of bush. This *pa* is locally known as Mahaukura; Te Porere is the general name of the district. Its earth walls and rectangular flanking-works at the angles are in nearly as good order, except that their straight lines have been softened by bushes of flax and thick growth of fern, as when the rebel leader and his musketeers built the *pa* in 1869. The redoubt measures about 25 yards in length by 20 in width. The flanking bastions, devised to enfilade the outer side of the high parapet, would each have held about twenty men. The walls were built of sods and pumice, interlaid with fern, and square loopholes for rifle-fire were made in the parapets and kept open with pieces of timber. These loopholes, however, had been constructed without allowing for depression, so that when the Government men lined the outer ditch the Maoris within could not hit them without exposing themselves over the top of the parapet. The parapets are 8 to 10 feet high and 5 to 6 feet thick. The gateway on the eastern side of the redoubt is cleverly covered by earth parapets or traverses just within. In the interior of the work a long grassy mound marks the grave of nearly forty of Te Kooti's warriors.

SCOUTING EPISODES

During the next few weeks the force made numerous expeditions through the surrounding forest country toward Tuhua, West Taupo, and had some small engagements up to the middle of January 1870. Colonel Herrick had left, and Colonel McDonnell remained in command. Kepa returned to Wanganui to get more men.

Two very brave actions performed at this time by members of the native contingent are worthy of record. It was necessary to send a despatch to the Premier, Mr. (afterwards Sir William) Fox, who was at Hiruharama, on the Wanganui River. Lieutenant Preece, in charge of the Arawa and Taupo contingents after the death of Captain St. George, was instructed by Colonel McDonnell to send a native orderly with a despatch to Hiruharama, a distance of more than ninety miles, of which thirty were open to the enemy. None of the Taupo natives knew the road (or they pretended they did not), so Preece said to Te Puia (who was partly an Arawa and partly a Wanganui native), "The Colonel wants a despatch carried to Hiruharama; do you know the country?" He replied, "Yes; give me a trooper's horse, and let me take any horse I see on the way." He faithfully carried out his instructions, and on his return got through in one day and part of one night; he had used five horses on his way there and back, picking up his troop-horse to get to camp at Tokaanu. Lieutenant Preece often quoted this man's action as an example to other natives, but they only replied, "That is not bravery; he is a fool; he did not know he was in danger."

The other incident occurred when the officers were anxious to secure accurate information as to Te Kooti's movements. He was known to be in the neighbourhood of Taumarunui, and two men of the Ngati-Tuara Tribe (Rotorua), Te Honiana and Wiremu, volunteered to go through on a scouting expedition. Armed with carbines and revolvers, they travelled the open part of the track by night, and the bush by day, a distance of forty miles, mostly forest. They reached the ridge just above the settlement of Taumarunui, where, lying hidden part of a day, they heard all the speeches of the enemy and ascertained their movements. At the end of five days they returned to report that the rebels were about to move along the west side of Lake Taupo, making for Tapapa, inland of Tauranga. Colonel McDonnell was so pleased with the information the scouts had gained at a very considerable risk that he presented them with the carbines they took with them on the expedition. These brave services and those of Te Puia certainly should have been recognized, but in the strenuous service in which the troops were engaged they were overlooked.

Te Kooti now marched through the Tuhua country, West Taupo, passing near Titiraupenga Mountain, and via Mokai to the Waikato River. Crossing to the east side of the river he joined his Ngati-Raukawa allies in the Patetere country.

TE KOOTI AT MATAMATA

In January Te Kooti with his armed band ventured out from the bush and visited Matamata, on the Upper Waihou River, where Mr. J. C. Firth was then engaged in working his large estate. Mr. Firth received a message from Te Kooti saying that he desired to meet him (Firth). The latter replied by messenger, "I will meet you unarmed, at Wi Tamehana's monument." Mr. Firth, describing the interview, at which he endeavoured to persuade Te Kooti to make peace with the Government, put on record a pen-picture of the rebel leader as he then appeared.

"As I approached the monument [at Turanga-moana]," he wrote, "a Maori advanced to meet me, raising his hat and saluting me as he approached. I dismounted on learning that Te Kooti stood before me. He was attended by two half-caste youths, fully armed, Te Kooti himself being unarmed. His height is about 5 feet 9 inches; he is about thirty-five years of age, stoutly built, broad-shouldered, and strong-limbed. His features are not repulsive; a rather large development of jaw and chin conveys the idea of a man of strong and resolute will. He has no tattoo; hair, black and glossy; wears a black moustache and short black beard. His dress consisted of woollen cords, top-boots, and a grey shirt; over the latter he wore a loose vest, with gold chain and greenstone ornaments. I noticed that he had lost the middle finger of the left hand." [This was his wound received at Te Porere.]

Mr. Firth urged Te Kooti to surrender to the Government, but the war-chief refused, saying, "If they let me alone I will live quietly; if not I will fight."

"During the conversation," said Mr. Firth, "his followers had formed in a half-circle at his back. They were all well armed, some with short Enfields, some with breech-loaders, and one or two double-barrel fowling-pieces, all apparently in excellent order. A well-dressed woman about twenty-five years old, of a handsome but melancholy cast of countenance, sat at Te Kooti's feet during the interview. I learnt afterwards that this woman was his wife."

THE FIGHTING AT TAPAPA

News reached Colonel McDonnell at Tokaanu that Major Kepa (Kemp) te Rangihiwinui and the Upper Wanganui chief Topia Turoa (who had recently left the Hauhaus to join the Government side) were on their way via Pipiriki to reinforce the Constabulary with two hundred men, consisting of Wanganui, Ngati-Hau, and Nga-Rauru (Waitotara). McDonnell moved off in advance in pursuit of Te Kooti, marching along the eastern shore of the lake and crossing the Waikato River at Taupo, and recrossing it at Whakamaru on the track to the Tokoroa and Patetere plains. At Whakamaru he halted and awaited the arrival of Kepa and Topia.

Lieutenant Preece was sent on through the bush with an advance party to locate the enemy, and managed to surprise and capture a party of Ngati-Raukawa—local Hauhaus. They said that Te Kooti was at Tapapa in great force, but that they did not want to join him, although some of the tribe had done so. They themselves only wished to be left alone. Lieutenant Preece sent back to inform the Colonel that he thought it advisable to stay where he was and keep the natives under control. He camped there and kept a good guard. Late in the night the sentries heard a call some way off their front. They challenged, and after a little while heard an English voice, to which they replied. The stranger in the night was Sergeant Maling, who, with a native orderly named Raimona, had been sent from Tauranga by Colonel Fraser with despatches to Colonel McDonnell. The pair had crossed Te Kooti's trail on the Tokoroa plains and got between

From a photo, 1901

Topia Turoa

This Upper Wanganui chief fought against the troops at Pipiriki in the first Hauhau War, and for several years opposed the Government, but at the end of 1869 he turned to the *pakeha* side, and in 1870 led a contingent of his tribesmen in the operations against Te Kooti. Topia was one of the high chiefs present at the great Maori gathering of welcome and homage to the present (1923) King and Queen at Rotorua in 1901.

McDonnell and the Hauhaus. This was only one of Sergeant Maling's many plucky acts. He was afterwards awarded the New Zealand Cross.

Two days later (24th January, 1870), lying low by day and marching by night, the force attacked and took Tapapa *pa*, a village of Ngati-Raukawa, on the bush track from Rotorua and Tauranga to the Waihou and Matamata. [The place is passed on the present vehicle-road through the forest of the Mamaku-Hautere Plateau, between Rotorua and Okoroire, and north-east of Putaruru.] One man belonging to a Hauhau picket was killed. On the following day Te Kooti reversed the order and attacked McDonnell just as he was about to move out against the enemy. It was fortunate for the force that he attacked when he did, for if McDonnell and Kepa had moved off he would only have found a small body in camp. He attacked from the bush under cover of a fog. One of the Wanganui contingent was, with others, gathering potatoes when he was killed by a blow with a *mere pounamu* (greenstone club) by a man who approached from the forest. [It was ascertained afterwards from Hapurona Kohu, a chief of the Urewera, that it was he who killed the forager.] The alarm was given by the man's companions, and the fighting became general. Te Kooti's people were flying the Union Jack and were at first mistaken for the Wanganui natives, and some of them got between the Wanganui contingent and a point of the bush where McDonnell's men were engaged with the enemy. Lieutenant Preece was instructed to clear this place, when a Maori passed just in front of him at the edge of the bush. Thinking he was a Wanganui native, Preece asked which way the rebels had retired. The Maori pointed in front of him, jumped behind a tree and fired, missing Lieutenant Preece but mortally wounding Private Etherington, of the Corps of Guides, who was a few paces behind him. The Government force drove the enemy off, killing six Hauhaus and wounding several. McDonnell's casualties were one European and three Maoris killed, and four wounded. Kepa and his men captured all Te Kooti's horses, about a hundred in number.

Te Waru, a sub-chief of the Arawa (Ngati-Whaoa *hapu*, of Paeroa, near Waiotapu), was Te Kooti's principal lieutenant in this bush skirmishing. He was well acquainted with the forest tracks, and led the early morning attack on the camp at Tapapa.

Lieut.-Colonel McDonnell, in his narrative of the Taupo–Tapapa campaign, gave the following account of this bush engagement:—

"On the evening of the 24th January I told off those who were to remain in camp, amongst whom were the Nga-Rauru. [This tribe, from Waitotara, had recently been under Titokowaru.] Early next morning, while I was seated on a log eating some breakfast—the men preparing to fall in—the camp being wrapped in a thick fog, three of the Nga-Rauru were sent by their chief to the bush, some 200 yards off, to get some firewood. Hiroki, and the two with him, as they approached the bush, stumbled upon Te Kooti's war-party, who were on the point of charging up to our camp. They shot one of the three; but Hiroki—who some eight years afterwards shot a man named McLean in a survey-party on some confiscated land at Waitotara, and who was executed for what was called the murder—protected his other companion, and shot two of the enemy, and brought into camp one of their guns, a Terry breech-loader, that was recognized as having belonged to one of the unfortunate troopers who had been slaughtered by Te Kooti at Opepe. This action had checked the advance of the enemy, but their first volley came whistling into camp about our ears. I ordered our fellows to take cover, and let the Nga-Rauru protect their own side of the camp. I feared to let No. 2 Division rush at the enemy, lest they mistook the Nga-Rauru for them, or intentionally mistook them. Our men who had been ambushed at Waitotara ten months before had belonged to this division, and one of the men had come to me during our march up and told me that the chief had the rifles which had belonged to Sergeant Menzies and Corporal Horsepool, two of the men who had been tomahawked on that occasion, and I knew that nothing would have pleased them better than to have a slap at them. Privately, I had no objection, but it would not have suited just then, and I had to be careful. The temptation, however, was great.

"The Nga-Rauru fought well, but were thrown into disorder and retreated on our Europeans, to whom I now gave the word to 'Make ready.' The wife of Pehimana, a Nga-Rauru chief, mounted a high *whata* (food platform) and, regardless of the bullets that flew round her, waved her shawl, crying out at the top of her voice, '*Tahuri, tahuri, E Rauru e! Riria e te iwi, riria! Ngakia to mate! Ngakia! Riria e Rauru e, riria!*' ('Turn, turn, O Rauru! Fight on, O tribe! Fight on! Absolve yourselves from sin! Clear yourselves, fight on, fight on!')

"The exhortation to absolve themselves was referring to their having fought against the Queen, and now they were to do their best to prove their sincere sorrow for the past. The attitude of the excited woman was a perfect picture. Not one rap did she care for the bullets. Then the Nga-Rauru rallied, and with one wild yell charged at the enemy.

"Meantime I slipped round with some of the Arawa to our left and came upon the flank of the reserve of the enemy, who were kneeling at the rear of our camp, one man of them holding a staff with Te Kooti's flag on it. We opened fire on them, and after one volley, which knocked over three, they gave us one in return, and then broke and fled to the bush. One of the Arawa I had with me was mortally wounded. We joined the Nga-Rauru, who had beaten back their foes and chased the enemy to the bush, but the fog now rolled up more dense than ever, so that it was useless to follow them up farther."

After Te Kooti's retreat from Tapapa McDonnell's force had a number of small skirmishes in the forest of the Hautere country, a plateau very much dissected with ravines, extending from the Patetere plains to the highlands inland of Tauranga. Expeditions by detachments under Captain Morrison, Lieutenant Preece, Kepa, Topia Turoa, and other leaders were made in various directions through the bush, and there were skirmishes with parties of Hauhaus, several of whom were killed without loss to the Government forces. Owing to the dense and jungly character of the forest and to the numerous gullies and ravines this work of scouting and pursuit was one of great difficulty, and Te Kooti once more succeeded in eluding his hunters. His trail was picked up by Kepa, leading in the direction of Whakamarama-Oropi country above Tauranga. Meanwhile Colonel James Fraser, with a mixed force of Armed Constabulary and Maoris, had advanced into the bush from the Tauranga side. At Paengaroa his advance-guard, under Sergeant Ben Biddle, was ambuscaded by a strong body of Te Kooti's men led by Peka Makarini, the half-caste. Four men of the advance-guard, one a European, were shot down in this affair, and Biddle had a personal encounter with Peka, receiving a bullet through his swag of pork rations. Fraser failed to support his greatly outnumbered advance-guard, and the Hauhaus escaped without loss. Te Kooti then, having evaded both McDonnell and Fraser, turned about and made for Rotorua, intending to attack the Arawa headquarters at Ohinemutu in the absence of most of the fighting-men, and then to return to the shelter of the Urewera Mountains.

Chapter 35

DEFEAT OF TE KOOTI

THE HARASSING AND indecisive character of the campaign against Te Kooti in the early part of 1870 was relieved by a truly brilliant action on the part of that most gallant young officer Lieutenant Gilbert Mair, a deed rewarded by a captaincy and the decoration of the New Zealand Cross. Mair's running engagement with the Hauhaus, fought in the neighbourhood of Rotorua on the 7th February, not only saved the Arawa people at Ohinemutu from massacre in the absence of most of their fighting-men, but deprived Te Kooti of some of his best warriors, and inflicted so severe a blow that he never again risked a battle in the open.

Te Kooti had formally *kanga'd,* or pronounced a curse upon, the Arawa for their unswerving adherence to the Government and their persistent pursuit of himself and his band. He had also announced that his *atua* would deliver them into his hand, and that he would "hew them in pieces." It is true that his strong supporters, the Urewera, including the chiefs Te Pukenui, Te Whenuanui, Paerau, Te Ahikaiata, and others of Tuhoe, who accompanied him on this campaign, were related to the Rotorua tribes, but it is not to be supposed that any intercession on their part would have saved the Arawa from his wrath. Moreover, only a few months previously their own country had been invaded by an Arawa contingent with Colonel Whitmore's force, and their villages and cultivations had been devastated by men led by the very chiefs most nearly related to Tuhoe. Not a *whare* had been left standing or a potato-store unspoiled in the mountain settlements.

The rebel chieftain's movements after his attack on McDonnell's camp at Tapapa were intended to throw his pursuers off his trail and disguise his matured intention to attack Rotorua. His scheme was cleverly laid. He sent one of his chiefs with a small force off northward, and he himself made in that direction, inducing the belief, as he intended, and indeed announced, that he was making for the Ohinemuri district. After a skirmish in the forest behind Okauia he made a sudden deflection to his right, and caused it to be known that his objective was Tauranga. This threat induced Colonel James Fraser to leave Rotorua unguarded and make his ill-managed expedition in to Paengaroa. Fraser ordered Lieutenant Mair to go to McDonnell's assistance at Tapapa, neglecting Rotorua, which was Te Kooti's real objective. Mair, much against his own judgment, had to report to McDonnell at Tapapa, all the time knowing that the Arawa settlements were in grave danger, most of the fighting-men being away in one or other of the forces. Mair had two hundred and fifty men with him. He strongly urged the necessity for returning to Rotorua at once, and on the morning of the 6th McDonnell and Commissioner Brannigan consented to his departure; and he slipped away at once with a smaller number of men than he had taken there. The forest track between Tapapa and the lakes had not been trodden for many years, having been *tauarai'd,* or closed to war-parties, and the trail consequently was so overgrown and jungly that rapid marching was impossible. It was night before the Arawa column reached Te Ara-piripiri, near the edge of the great forest of the Mamaku plateau above the Rotorua lake-basin, and camped at the source of the Waiteti River. No fires were lit, lest the Hauhaus should discover them. The men's supper was a pannikin of water each, with a little sugar in it, and some biscuit.

At daylight next morning (7th February) the march was resumed, and Te Kooti's trail was picked up at the edge of the bush. It was only by accident that it was observed, for the cautious rebels had jumped across the track, one after the other, so as to leave no trace of their passage. Then it became clear that Te Kooti's movements in the forest country of the Hautere highland had all been designed with the object of drawing off the military forces from the Rotorua district, and Mair's men were frantically anxious to reach their homes and families in time to avert the impending ruthless blow. Just before the enemy's trail was discovered Mair had detailed his Arawa for duty in the following order: Fifty men of Ngati-Pikiao, under Ieni Tapihana (Hans Tapsell, son of the old Danish trader of that name at Maketu), to guard the Kaharoa and Taheke tracks; fifty men to guard the country north of Rotorua Lake from Puhirua to Waerenga and the Ohau channel; a small party to patrol the Roria Road through to Hamaria; and Ngati-Rangitihi and Tuhourangi Tribes to take post at Pari-karangi and patrol as far as the face of Horohoro Mountain. It was now a rush to get to Rotorua and forestall the desperate foe. Mair had just reached the level near the lake when a messenger came with news of the capture by the Arawa of the deserter Louis Baker (a French Canadian, lately a stoker in H.M.S. "Rosario"), who had been with Kereopa in 1865 and who afterwards joined

Te Kooti. The rebel leader was on the range at Paparata above Rotorua and delayed descending to Ohinemutu until he had received a reply to a letter he sent to the Arawa chiefs by Baker (who had signed the Tuhoe chiefs' names) promising peace. Mair immediately made his dispositions to attack. He ordered the men up to Ohinemutu from Puhirua, and sent the Tuhourangi and Ngati-Rangitihi off at their utmost speed to Pari-karangi, to guard the track which came out there from the wooded ranges of Te Raho-o-te-Rangipiere and Paparata, in order to block Te Kooti's attempt to reach the Kaingaroa by that route.* Mair himself with all available men dashed off for Ohinemutu: he and his force were on the run the whole way.

Te Kooti meanwhile had emerged from the bush with his whole force, about two hundred armed men besides some women, and surprised a party of Ngati-Whakaue women and girls who were out gathering potatoes in a cultivation on the edge of the bush on the Tihi-o-Tonga slopes, south-west of Rotorua. Kiri-Matao (afterwards locally celebrated as "The Duchess") and some other women were captured, but most of them made their escape, although fired upon.

The enemy now lit large fires all along the edge of the forest between the upper Utuhina Stream and the settlements on the Tihi-o-Tonga, destroying the Arawa houses and crops. Mair, rushing on with the most active of his men, got up to the Utuhina soon after midday, and, running on in advance toward Pukeroa Hill, where the Maharo Redoubt stood, met the chiefs Petera te Pukuatua, Te Amohau, and others going out in a procession to meet Te Kooti, carrying a white flag. Te Kooti's advance man was also bearing a white flag. The Urewera, at Te Kooti's order, had offered terms of peace to the Arawa, to whom many of them were related. Te Mumuhu and Kepa te Ahuru.

---

* Captain Mair writes as follows (22nd February, 1923) in reference to the share of the Tuhourangi Tribe in the day's work:—

"The Tuhourangi made straight for Pari-karangi to protect their women and children there, and had they tried to cut off Te Kooti the moment they heard our firing at the Hemo Gorge he would have been badly mauled; but their principal man, Te Konui, persuaded them against getting athwart Te Kooti's track, lest he take the short, straight route through Te Wairoa and between Tarawera Lake and Rotomahana, and destroy the Wairoa Village *en route*. Had Te Kooti been so deflected, the Tuhourangi villages at Epeha, Te Wairoa, Moura, and Te Ariki could all have been destroyed, and he would have marched over Puke-kaikahu and Te Kai-whatiwhati, two famous battle-grounds where Tuhourangi and Ngati-Rangitihi were destroyed a hundred years ago. Maoris will never fight over a ground where they have once been defeated. I remember how hard it was to get some of them to come up to the scratch at the little Koutu fight (1867), on account of their sanguinary defeat by Te Waharoa on the 7th August, 1836. Neither of these defeats had ever been avenged."

Photo about 1880]

Captain Gilbert Mair, N.Z.C.

The *New Zealand Gazette* (1st April, 1886) announcing the award of the New Zealand Cross to Captain Mair for his distinguished bravery in the fight of the 7th February, 1870, stated: ". . . During this engagement, which lasted many hours, Captain Mair, by personal example and devoted gallantry, inspired his men to come to hand-to-hand conflict with Te Kooti's rearguard, himself killing the notorious Peka McLean, and driving the rest before him in disorder."

In decorating Captain Mair with the Cross at a Volunteer parade in Wellington (1887) Major-General Whitmore said: ". . . New Zealand has the proud distinction, not enjoyed by any other of Her Majesty's colonies, of having this honourable order of valour to bestow on her citizens for brave deeds such as were performed by yourself. By Royal Warrant Her Majesty was graciously pleased to direct that this decoration should rank equal to her own Victoria Cross, and next in precedence. The particular action for which the New Zealand Cross has been awarded to you was the turning-point in the war, and but for your gallant conduct on that occasion Te Kooti and the rebels under his command would have long continued their career of bloodshed."

of the Arawa, had been up to see Te Kooti, and they had returned with a Rotorua lad named Te Korowhiti, who had been taken prisoner by Te Kooti at Tauaroa in 1869. Petera and the other chiefs, completely deceived by Te Kooti's specious proposals for peace, were about to invite him to Ohinemutu, where undoubtedly the tragedy of the Mohaka massacre would have been repeated on a more terrible scale, had it not been for Mair's timely arrival and resolute intervention. Running up, Mair remonstrated with Petera for his foolishness in trusting to such a treacherous fellow as Te Kooti. He tore the white flag out of Petera's hands, and, throwing it on the ground, jumped on it. Then he called on his young men to follow him and attack Te Kooti, whose advance-guard was then about 300 yards away. The Arawa chiefs endeavoured to prevent their men from obeying Mair, crying out that Te Kooti's followers were the Tuhoe Tribe and relatives of the Arawa. Tohe te Matehaere (now living at Weriweri, Waiteti) was the first to break past the elders, who barred the way with their *taiahas;* and he joined Mair, who fired the first shot near the spot where the Rotorua Presbyterian Church now stands. Then the leader dashed at the Hauhaus, who had turned to retreat. Tohe outstripped his officer in his eagerness to engage the enemy, and Mair had to call him back.

The enemy column now hastily retreated southward over the hill on the west side of the Hemo Gorge, passing through a bush called Te Karaka, on the summit of the ridge which trends along to the Tihi-o-Tonga. They then crossed the Puarenga Stream and followed up the valley parallel with the Wai-korowhiti. From here they struck in to the south side of the Waitaruna Stream and traversed a long level *wiwi*-covered valley called Te Wai-a-Urewera, which leads down into the Tahuna-a-Tara River. Thence they retreated across the Kapenga Plain and over some rough ground to the base of Tumunui Mountain. All this way they were hotly pursued by the gallant little band of Arawa led by Mair, who sometimes found himself so far in advance that only two or three of his men could come to his support. The black-bearded chieftain galloped about the plain in advance, shouting to his followers and waving his revolver. He wore a grey shirt, riding trousers, and high boots, and a bandit-like hat. In high contrast were his soldiery—a half-naked body of savages, whose brown skins glistened in the warm sunshine as if they had been oiled. They had that day killed a number of pigs, and many of them had greased their bodies well with pork-fat in anticipation of a running fight through the clinging fern and *manuka.* The clothing worn was in most cases a shawl or piece of blanket or a flax mat round the waist. Each man wore cartridge-belts—some had three or four—buckled round him; some were armed with revolvers as well as breech-loading rifles, carbines, or single- and double-barrel shot-guns. The first Hauhaus killed in the pursuit were shot east of the Puarenga, just after passing the Hemo Gorge; some distance farther on one or two more were killed, and near Ngapuketurua (opposite

Owhinau Hill) several were shot. At every knoll or ridge Peka Makarini and a detachment of the rearguard turned and made a stand, or laid an ambuscade, and once or twice they charged determinedly with clubbed rifles. It was only Mair's personal coolness and accurate shooting that saved his Arawa party, who were greatly outnumbered by the Hauhaus. At Ngapuketurua, six miles from Rotorua, the principal encounter took place. The spot on which this fight occurred is a long steep ridge or tableland rising directly above the Wai-taruna Stream; the present main road to Waiotapu and Taupo runs on the opposite (north) side of the small river. There is an old crossing, called Te Kauaka, over the Wai-taruna at this point. Mair was considerably in advance of his men here, and as he ran he was heavily fired on, under cover of the scrub and the uneven ground. He knelt down and fired ahead and right and left, and presently a few of his men came up and joined in the combat. It was here that Mair shattered Timoti te Kaka's jaw with an expanding bullet from his Westley-Richards carbine. Seven Hauhaus were shot dead. Some of those killed were tumbled down by their comrades into the crater-like depression in the north side of the ridge at Kauaka, a short distance from the stream; these saucer-shaped hollows are formed by springs, and the green growth masks a morass. In one swampy depression Lieutenant Mair, running on in chase of the Hauhau rearguard, suddenly noticed the corner of an embroidered Maori mat showing above the muddy ooze. He stopped and hauled on it, and in doing so dragged up a big Hauhau, still gasping for breath. He had fallen mortally wounded in the rushes a few moments previously, and his comrades, thinking him dead, had hastily trodden him down underneath the surface of the swamp, in order to conceal his body from the Arawa.

The scene of the Ngapuketurua or Te Kauaka encounter, where a track from the ridge to the creek descends a steep bare ridge between two of the hollows mentioned, can be seen from the main road, less than 200 yards away. A short distance eastward the ridge rises to a height of about 300 feet, crowned by an ancient trenched and walled *pa*: this is called Kuharua. Just below it on the north two small spurs slope down and converge, and enclose a kind of saucer with steep sides. Below, again, there is a narrow gorge called Whaowhaotaha, its sides covered thickly with *tutu* and fern; through this gorge runs a small tributary of the Wai-taruna. Near a waterfall here Mair and his men two days afterwards found Te Kaka nursing his shattered jaw. Above this spot the main road runs along the winding valley known to the old Maoris as Te Mania-ia-tote. On the left are the slopes of Owhinau plantation, golden with young larches. The upper part of the Wai-taruna Stream is here known as the Hine-uia. Round its head (at about eight miles from Rotorua) goes an overgrown old track striking southward; this was Mair's packhorse track in the early "seventies" to the redoubt at Te Niho-o-te-Kiore, on the Waikato River near Atiamuri.

After the repulse on the ridge above Te Kauaka—in this sharp affair Mair fired eleven shots—the Hauhaus turned to the right and made direct for the shelter of Tumunui Mountain, across the plain and valleys of Te Kapenga, passing about three miles on the south side of the Pakaraka native settlement. The pursuit continued relentlessly, Mair running ahead of his men and firing whenever a good chance offered. He had twenty-five or thirty men here, as opposed to at least double that number in Te Kooti's rearguard. The Tuhourangi and Ngati-Rangitihi men came up near Pakaraka, but instead of taking the enemy in front or flank they joined Mair's party in the rear. The Hauhaus travelled so fast that only the athletic Mair and a few of his strong runners could keep up with them, and by making a short stand at every suitable spot they were enabled to keep their women in the advance and lead off the wounded.

The final scene in the day's battle was near the great masses of grey volcanic rock fallen among the fern and *manuka* on the precipitous western side of Tumunui, the volcanic square-cut pile, with its cliffs and forests, which can be seen well from the main road to Waiotapu after passing the old *kainga* and remnant of bush on the tableland at Pakaraka. Under the cover of rock and scrub Peka Makarini and the thirty men who now comprised his rearguard lay in wait for Mair and gave him a volley. Mair's nearest man was on a rise of ground some 50 yards behind him. Peka leaped up from his cover, fired a shot, and, clubbing his rifle, rushed at Mair, followed by some of his men; he was a herculean savage, 6 feet 3 inches in height, and exceedingly powerful. The issue of the day's combat depended on Mair's coolness and straight shooting. When Peka came charging at him after firing, Mair, kneeling in the short *wiwi* grass, let him come to within fifteen paces and fired. The bullet struck the half-caste in the right hip and passed out at the left, smashing the bones. He lay there after being deprived of his revolver, with which he attempted to shoot Mair, and a little later Te Warihi finished him by putting a bullet through his head. When Peka fell, his men ran for cover in the thick *manuka* on their left (south). Mair advanced with a few men, and presently found himself under a heavy fire from Te Kooti's main body, posted behind the rocks at the base of the mountain. This stand was only brief, but it gave time for the women and the wounded to escape into the bush-filled gorge on the mountain-side. The pursuit now ceased

Photo by Mr. Mundy, 1870]

Captain Mair and some of His Arawa Soldiers

This photograph was taken at Kaiteriria camp, Roto-kakahi, shortly after Gilbert Mair's defeat of Te Kooti in the Rotorua-Tumunui action.

as it was nearly dark, and Mair, with his handful of exhausted men, returned to Kaiteriria camp at Rotokakahi.

The Hauhaus, after travelling hastily up the forested gully on the north of Tumunui, retreated direct for the Kaingaroa and the Urewera Country. Crossing the Waikorua Valley (Earthquake Flat) and passing the Pareheru bush, they took a trail on the north side of Maunga-kakaramea (the sharp-topped height called Rainbow Mountain), and camped for the night on the northern side of Lake Okaro. Mair, after a visit to his camp for food and ammunition, followed the Hauhaus up in the night, and at 2 o'clock in the morning he found their camp. He had only nine men with him. Creeping up as near as he could to the camp, he gave them a volley. The Hauhaus fled in confusion, leaving behind them some guns and many swags of clothing and food.

Mair had sixty rounds of ammunition in his pouches when the day's action began. When it ended he had only two cartridges left. His war-path uniform consisted of woollen shirt, blue tunic, knickerbockers, long stockings, and a short waist-shawl, Maori fashion. He had marvellous escapes from death in the close-range fighting, but his only wounds were lacerated legs from the hard run through the fern and *manuka*. For this day's good work he received his captaincy and (in 1886) the decoration of the New Zealand Cross for personal valour in the field.

J. C., photo at Weriweri, Rotorua, 1921

Tohe te Matehaere.*

About twenty Hauhaus were shot in the running fight. On the Arawa side Te Waaka was mortally wounded, and Tame Karanama, a young man of Tuhourangi, had his knee shattered by a ball. Three others were wounded.

The big half-caste Peka Makarini, who fell to Mair's carbine, was a man with an atrocious record. It was estimated that he had been guilty of over thirty murders. He carried a bugle, and was accustomed to sound field-calls for his force. He had

* Tohe was one of Captain Mair's most active young soldiers in the running fight described in this chapter. He served for several years in the Arawa contingents operating against the Hauhaus in the Bay of Plenty, Taupo, and the Urewera Country.

learned the military calls from the guard when in exile on Chatham Island; and, in fact, the bugle he used [now in the Auckland Museum] had been taken by him when the redoubt on the island was captured and the white force overpowered. A curious trait in his otherwise savage character was revealed when he lay dying in the fern at Tumunui. At the Mohaka massacre he had taken possession of a little dog, a terrier, which had belonged to one of the settlers killed there. This dog he carried with him on all his marches in a kind of wickerwork tray or basket made of *manuka* twigs, which he fastened on top of his swag. It was probably the only living thing he loved. When Mair ran up to take his revolver from him, the dog ran at him and bit him in defence of his master.

The Arawa displayed great satisfaction at the death of Te Kooti's most notorious lieutenant. Two or three days after the fight they dragged Peka's body down at a horse's tail from Tumunui to the Kapenga and tied it upright to a tall cabbage-tree. There it remained all that summer, desiccated to a mummy by the dry, hot weather of the plains.

Two days after the fight Mair and his men discovered the wounded Hauhau chief Timoti te Kaka in the Whaowhao-taha gully, near the little waterfall on the stream which flows into the Waitaruna. Te Kaka was suffering agony from his shattered jaw; he had contrived to pound up some flax-root and make a dressing of it, which he had tied under his terrible wound. Mair gave the man in charge of one of his Arawa soldiers, and ordered him to take him to the camp at Kaiteriria; he then continued his search for dead and wounded. When the man returned to the camp he had no prisoner. He said that after going a little distance Te Kaka refused to walk any further and wanted his captor to carry him on his back. The dispute was ended by the Arawa shooting his prisoner dead. In punishment, Mair fined the man several months' pay and dismissed him from the force. This Timoti te Kaka was one of the most ruthless and thoroughly barbarous of Te Kooti's desperadoes. His was a remarkable reversion to primal savagery under the influence of a fanatic impulse. He had been one of Mr. Volkner's deacons or Church teachers at Opotiki, and for some time strenuously opposed the onsweep of Pai-marire. But at last he became a convert to the gospel of fire and sword, and after sharing in the murder of his old pastor he plunged into the rebellion. He was one of Te Kooti's "butchers" told off to slaughter prisoners and mutilate them with swords and tomahawks.

Among the Hauhaus wounded at the Kauaka, opposite Owhinau, was Kewene, an old soldier-of-fortune of the Ngati-Porou Tribe, from Mataura, on the Coromandel Peninsula. He had been on the war-path ever since 1863, when he fought in the Waikato War; he was reputed to have led the attack on the Trust family at Mangemangeroa, near Howick, in that year. He also served in the defence of the Gate *Pa*. Mair shot out one of his eyes.

Following up the enemy's trail on the 10th February Mair took a small party of men across country to the Okaro and Rerewhakaitu Lakes, and finding that the tracks of Te Kooti's force led in the direction of the Kaingaroa Plain and Motumako, near the Rangitaiki Valley, he returned to Kaiteriria. Te Kooti had gone through to Ahi-kereru and thence to Ruatahuna.

This decisive defeat of Te Kooti was most creditable to Mair (or "Tawa," as he was universally known among the natives) and to the handful of men of the Arawa who supported him in the arduous and exhausting chase. The Arawa soldiers whom Mair reported as having behaved particularly well were: Kiharoa, Tohe te Matehaere, Te Raika Metai, Hie, Hori, Te Waka, Marino, Tari, Taekata, Te Waiehi, Hakana, and Tupara Toko-aitua. "I hope," he wrote, "the Government will feel satisfied with the effort these men have made; and had they only been supported by the others, the enemy would have suffered more severely. With the small force under my command it was impossible to guard every point. The enemy mustered at least two hundred fighting-men, well trained and accustomed to fighting, while I was never able to get up to him with more than forty."

An incident of the rebels' retreat to the Rangitaiki was a highly plucky exploit on the part of a man of the Ngati-Manawa Tribe named Tiwha te Rangi-kaheke, who with his wife, Hera Peka, was living at Motumako. When Te Kooti continued his retreat along the old war-trail past Lake Rerewhakaitu leading to the Rangitaiki River near what is now known as Galatea, he detailed a large party of his mounted men to visit Motumako—which is a settlement on the edge of the Kaingaroa Plain near a small bush three miles south-west of Galatea—in order to obtain pigs and potatoes, as the force was in great need of food. Tiwha was the only man in Motumako capable of bearing arms; there were a number of old women and young children in the village. Tiwha and his brave wife sallied out with their guns to meet the enemy, and by rapid firing and the use of shouted derisive epithets they gave the Hauhaus the desired impression that there was a strong force under cover on the low hills. These energetic and skilful tactics were successful. Te Kooti's men drew off, and the column moved down to the Rangitaiki and crossed the river at Te Taupaki ford. The column was heading for the Horomanga Gorge when the dauntless Tiwha boldly showed himself on the opposite (west) bank. Te Kooti ordered some of his men to recross the Rangitaiki and kill the Ngati-Manawa warrior, but

Tiwha made such accurate shooting with his old "Brown Bess" that the Hauhaus would not face the crossing. Te Kooti ordered the retreat to be resumed, and marched off for the Urewera Mountains looming a few miles away, while Tiwha triumphantly made demonstration of his contempt for the enemy that could be routed so easily, and danced his war-dance on the bank before returning to the little settlement he had saved from destruction. This gallant Maori had been badly wounded in 1867 in the engagement at Te Koutu, Rotorua, between Gilbert Mair's Arawa and the war-party of Hauhaus from the Waikato.

The month of March, 1870, saw a new policy initiated in the field operations against Te Kooti and Kereopa and their followers in rebellion. The Taupo-Patetere campaign was the last in which the Armed Constabulary were engaged in the expeditions in chase of the Hauhaus. The Government decided that future work in the bush could best be carried on by bodies of Maori troops under a few European officers and their own chiefs, such as Ropata Wahawaha and Kepa te Rangihiwinui, and the duties of the Constabulary were confined to the garrisoning of the various redoubts in the disturbed territory and the guarding and maintenance of lines of communication.

After Te Kooti had been driven out of the Hautere forests and the Rotorua country the Government forces were moved to Matata with the intention of working against Te Kooti simultaneously with the advance of the Ngati-Porou, under Major Ropata and Captain Porter, from the Poverty Bay side. Operations from the Bay of Plenty side were to be conducted by way of Waimana or Ahi-kereru and Ruatahuna. The Wanganui natives, under Major Kepa, had moved to Ohiwa, and Colonel McDonnell went from there to Opotiki to interview the Defence Minister, Mr. (afterwards Sir Donald) McLean. Captain Preece was instructed to go to Tarawera and then on to Fort Galatea with a body of Arawa, and, as soon as a column arrived, to make a movement on the Urewera through Ahi-kereru. Soon Preece was ordered back to Tarawera, and then to Te Teko. It had then been decided by Mr. McLean to relieve Colonel McDonnell of his command. The field force of Armed Constabulary was sent to occupy a line of posts at Taupo and several points on the Bay of Plenty.

NOTES

The country between Rotorua and Tumunui Mountain over which Captain Gilbert Mair fought his gallant running battle with Te Kooti's force in February, 1870, was traversed by Mair and myself on horseback on the 7th and 13th December, 1918. Much of it was very difficult to travel, for the reason that the plains and hills, clothed chiefly in short *wiwi* grass fifty years ago, were now densely overgrown with *manuka* and high fern, and the old tracks were in places impenetrable. The route of Mair's chase of the Hauhaus is parallel with the present main road from Rotorua Town to Waiotapu, and at one point, opposite Owhinau Hill, in the State forest reserve, it closely impinges on the road, from which it is separated only by the Wai-taruna Stream. As we rode along, picking our way through the scrub and crossing swampy gullies, Captain Mair pointed out the spots where he and his men from time to time dropped some of the Hauhau rearguard, where ambuscades were laid, where desperate rushes were made by Peka Makarini and his fellow-rebels, to give time for the main body to retreat, and where Timoti te Kaka and other desperadoes were shot. The final scene was near the foot of the Tumunui cliffs.

The Kapenga tableland over which we travelled along the old fighting-trail, a gully-seamed broken plateau, is covered with a thick growth of *manuka* and *monoao* shrubs, *tutu,* and fern, with many *ti* or cabbage trees and tall flax in the gullies and swamps. Another shrub growing in abundance is the handsome flowering-plant called by the Maoris *hukihuki-raho,* because of the obstruction it offers to travellers on foot. In olden days the Kapenga Plain was celebrated for its special quality of *harakeke* (flax), much used in making strong, tough *ihupuni,* or war-mats, which were worn as a kind of armour in hand-to-hand battles. At the time of the fight in 1870 its clothing of vegetation on the open parts was chiefly *wiwi* grass and fern.

(See sketch-map and Captain Mair's narrative in Appendices.)

Lake Waikare-moana

This view of Waikare-moana is a drawing by W. H. Burgoyne, in 1869, during the first military expedition to the lake. Lieut.-Colonel Herrick's camp at Onepoto is shown in the foreground. On the opposite side of the lake, at the entrance to the northern arm, are the Hauhau strongholds and villages Matuahu, Whakaari, and Tikitiki.

(See map at end of book.)

Chapter 36

OPERATIONS AT WAIKARE-MOANA

THE SECOND MILITARY expedition to Lake Waikare-moana (May and June 1870) was a purely native one, a contingent of about three hundred strong with a few white officers. Major J. T. Large, then a young volunteer, was one of the most energetic spirits in the contingent. Another member of the native force was young James Carroll (now Sir James Carroll); he was a boy of only thirteen, but he carried a Terry carbine and played a manful part in the campaign. The expedition consisted of the Ngaietu, Ngati-Hikairo, Ngati-Rakaipaka, Ngati-Kurupakiaka, Ngati-Matewai, Ngati-Mihi, Ngati-Pahauwera, and other *hapus* of the Ngati-Kahungunu Tribe inhabiting the Wairoa district from Te Mahia to Mohaka. They were under the command of Mr. Edward Hamlin, Government interpreter, of Napier (afterwards Resident Magistrate at Maketu, Bay of Plenty), and Lieutenant J. W. Witty, formerly of the Hawke's Bay Military Settlers, second in command, while each *hapu* had its own chief, subordinate to the European leaders. Dr. M. Scott, of the Wairoa, accompanied the force as medical officer. Mr. Large joined it as a volunteer with the Ngaietu *hapu,* which took a leading part in the operations. The force was encamped on the border of a small lake named Kiri-o-Pukai, separated from Waikare-moana by a narrow ridge. The Maoris had already raised a small boat buried by Colonel Herrick at Onepoto, which had escaped the search of the Hauhaus, but the other one—a whaleboat sunk near Onepoto—the Hauhaus had found, and daily paraded before their foes on the lake. In order to provide additional means of transport Hamlin's force made two canoes out of large white-pine trees, and these were hauled over the ridge and launched on Waikare-moana, with the object of crossing the north-east arm, Whanganui-a-Parua. The chiefs Paora Apatu, Hamana Tiakiwai, and Toha were opposed to any forward movement of that kind, and urged the natives to go back to Wairoa, and not court disaster by attempting to cross the lake in winter. Mr. Hamlin, who was a forcible Maori speaker, always silenced these croakers. Neverthe-

Major J. T. Large

Major Large began his military career as a volunteer and scout in the early operations against Te Kooti, and served with distinction in the arduous bush expeditions until the close of the fighting in the Urewera Country. Later he was for some years New Zealand Government Agent and Resident Magistrate on the Island of Mangaia, Cook Group.

less, in the face of their opposition, no openly organized advance was practicable. The heavy westerly winter gales blowing right across the Waikare-moana made weird sounds amongst the trees and rocks, which the superstitious natives declared were the wailings of Haumapuhia, the deity of the lake, warning them to return.

One day the Hauhaus in their flotilla of canoes and the whale-boat sallied out from the beach below Matuahu *pa* and made for the middle of the lake. Mr. J. T. Large and a party of the best men in the Native force manned the two Government canoes and the dinghy and went out to meet the Hauhaus. As soon as the two miniature war-fleets came within range of each other sharp firing commenced. The accurate fire of Large's canoe-men and dinghy crew proved too much for the enemy, who were forced to return to their stronghold on the north side of the lake. The Government force suffered no casualties.

On the 21st May an armed party of Ngaietu volunteers, under the command of Mr. Large and accompanied by the chief Peneamine, went out scouting in a canoe around the shore of the Whanganui-a-Parua arm of the lake. They were all picked men of their tribe, practised hands with the paddle, adepts in canoe-work, and mostly good shots. Dr. Scott thus described the encounter which followed:—

"Cautiously coasting along the inequalities of the shore, with their rifles loaded and ready to hand, the canoe-men achieve the distance to the end of the bight without incident, when suddenly, near a small cultivation and a *whare* or two, they sight two Urewera men scouting, like themselves, in a canoe. Chase is given, but the Hauhaus paddle frantically for the shore, and the chance of drawing the first blood will be lost if they once gain the bush-clad strand. Peneamine resolves upon a long shot, and with a word, steadying the canoe, adjusts his rifle-sight and fires. One Maori drops listlessly over the side of the canoe and remains there; the other jumps overboard, reaches the shore, and seeks safety in the bush, whither it would not be prudent to follow him. A cry of triumph rises from the perpetrators of the apparently cowardly but absolutely necessary deed. As the first blood had been shed on the right side, the omens are propitious, and they exultingly shout '*Mate rawa!*' ('Quite dead!') as they cautiously land and inspect the corpse and canoe, and proceed to visit the *whares,* carefully, however, leaving a sufficient guard on the canoes, and advancing with rifles cocked, bated breath, and that stealthy yet quick pace which was particularly noticeable in the after-skirmishing of this sub-tribe. They do not find much loot, however—some £2, with a beautifully bound English prayer-book, a gun or two, and other miscellaneous articles; only one gun, a dead man, and two paddles remain in the canoe. Rather disappointed as to the spoils, but jubilant in the first success, they return to camp, and that evening the war-dance echoes and re-echoes over the lake-waters, responded to by the firing of musketry, braying of horns, and derisive yells from the Hauhau villages."

The next day (22nd May) two Hauhaus came off from Matuahu in a canoe under a flag of truce, and, lying off the camp at Onepoto, opened negotiations with the Government side. In response to a demand for surrender they replied that they would hold a consultation at their *pa* and report the result next day. All this, however, was only a ruse to gain time or to reconnoitre Hamlin's position, for shortly afterwards the outlying scouts reported the passage of eight canoes, four of them very large ones, and the whaleboat, all fully manned, from Tikitiki to Matuahu, and thence to Ohiringi, on the south side of the lake, thus menacing the rear of the Government position and the communications with Wairoa. Lieutenant Witty counted twenty-five men in one canoe, and the whole detachment was probably about one hundred and fifty. However, the Hauhaus made no attack, and quietly returned to hold their main positions at Matuahu and Tikitiki.

The principal men of the native force were very much averse to crossing the lake and attacking the Hauhau positions. However, the officers contrived by stratagem to get the better of the chiefs. "Our leaders," writes Major Large, "gave out that on the morrow we were going foraging for food amongst the plantations on the Wairoa side of the lake; but we took care that none but the best men were of the party, which was under the command of Lieutenant Witty. Having launched our two canoes and the dinghy, we started round the east side of the lake in the direction of Whanganui-a-Parua, the north-east end. On reaching the prominent headland Matakitaki we made a dash for the opposite shore. It was a race and I and three Ngaietu men—Pine Pape, Teira Morutu, and Hirini Kereru—in the dinghy were the first to land in the enemy territory, closely followed by the others in the canoes. By great good fortune the Hauhaus did not anticipate that we would cross at that place, and were not there to oppose our landing, otherwise they might have inflicted heavy loss on us before we got to the shore. On landing we advanced in skirmishing order through the bush with which that side of the lake was covered, going in the direction of Matuahu, a well-fortified *pa,* on a headland. We met with no opposition till we got to an old clearing named Taumataua, when we received a rattling volley from the top of a cliff commanding it. However, it did little damage, as we had cover. Lieutenant Witty soon had the Hauhaus outflanked, and we drove them back. Here we camped, and sent the canoes and boat across to Onepoto for reinforcements and supplies, and our surgeon, Dr. Scott, arrived. The following day the Hauhaus attacked us again, but we repulsed them. Amongst their casualties was the chief Enoka, who was killed. The day following we advanced in force on Matuahu, the great stronghold of the enemy, which we found evacuated."

The contingent spent over a month at Matuahu, where the whole force concentrated. A small party of the Waikare-moana Hauhaus, under Hona te Makarini and Hori Wharerangi, came in under a flag of truce and surrendered. They reported that some of their people had perished in the snows of Huiarau, the mountain-range between Waikare-moana and Ruatahuna, in retiring from the Government force.

The following song was composed and sung by the Ngati-Kahungunu friendly Maoris as an accompaniment to a *haka taparahi* danced at Tikitiki *pa,* on the northern shore of Lake Waikare-moana, after the capture of the Hauhau strongholds when

Hona te Makarini and Hori Wharerangi came in and made submission:—

Taku whakatakariri
Ki nga upoko-kohua
O Ngati-Matewai
I huri atu ra
Ki te Hauhau—e!
Pehi ra waiho te Kawana
Tu ana tono atu
Kia kite ia i nga wai-kopikopiko
O Waikare ra!
Toia tu ana taku haere
Ki te whakawhitianga ki Whakaari,
Te mauri aroha tiaki
Na taku pa i Tikitiki.
Ko wai ra kai roto?
Ko koe na, Hori.
E tapu ra koe.
Ka whana atu au
Ka haere ki te rapa
I taku hara ia Te Kooti,
Na te oma Te Waru,
I rere ai,
I ora ai,
Rere hiwi
Rere pari
Rere manga tamoe
Hukarere—i—i!

[TRANSLATION]

Great is my anger at those cursed ones of Ngati-Matewai who have turned them to the Hauhaus. Leave them to the Governor standing there, waiting to see the many-armed waters of the sea of Waikare. Pull away! Here we go crossing the lake to Whakaari *pa.* Jealously, lovingly, this our *pa* is guarded at Tikitiki. Who is within? 'Tis Hori! Thou'rt sacred now, safe from our guns. I go in chase of him who led the tribes to war, Te Kooti, with whom Te Waru fled. They're flying now, flying for life, by mountain-peak and cliff, by deep-hidden waters, and through the snowy wilderness.

"Now we were in the enemy's country," narrated Major Large, "our forward movements in force were retarded by the want of proper means of transport, as we had still only our two canoes and the dinghy; this small boat had been damaged. So a number of our young bloods, weary of our somewhat long period of inactivity, conceived the idea of making a dash to the head of the western inlet at Mahungarerewai and capturing the big canoes and whaleboat from the Hauhaus encamped there. So choosing a dark night, they filled the two dugouts with as many men as they would carry, and, without consulting the leaders, quietly started up the inlet. I was the only white man they took with them. We surprised the Hauhaus, who offered no resistance, and we came back in the morning in triumph to Matuahu with four or five large canoes and the whaleboat.

The Hon. Sir James Carroll

Sir James Carroll whose native place was the Wairoa (H.B.), served as a boy of thirteen in the Waikare-moana expedition of 1870. He received the New Zealand War Medal and a special Government bonus of £50 for his services.

Hamlin was angry with us for undertaking this enterprise without orders, which several of us supposed he had given. Of course, we should not have moved without orders. The leaders contemplated going into Ruatahuna, and they said that our action prejudiced their project. But they could not have moved the force without adequate means of transport, and our capture of the enemy's canoes and boat supplied the one thing most needed for the purpose, and gave them the command of the lake. As to going into the heart of the Urewera Country in winter with our small force, we could not muster more than two hundred good reliable men for the purpose, while the enemy were numerous, and in strong positions. We would simply have been cut to pieces, and there would have been no *morehu* (remnants of a slaughtered tribe) left to tell the tale. This I found out afterwards when I was at Ruatahuna with Ngati-Porou."

The force now had abundant means of transport, and made raids to the Wairau and Marau branches of Waikare-moana. Parties visited all the settlements round the borders of the lake, destroying *whares,* canoes, and other property of the Hauhaus, and bringing away the food, in retaliation for the forays on the coast settlements.

After this short and successful campaign, conducted under winter conditions, the native contingent returned to the Wairoa and dispersed to their homes. Later an Armed Constabulary station was garrisoned at Onepoto and remained an outpost of importance until the final flight of Te Kooti from the Urewera Mountains in 1872.

NOTES

The Occupation of Matuahu

The captured Hauhau position at Matuahu was described as follows in an account written by Dr. Scott shortly after the war:—

"Matuahu, Te Kooti's so-called impregnable fortress, did not by any means sustain its formidable reputation. The bold promontory, jutting out precipitously into the lake, surmounted landward by a lofty bush-clad hill, constituted a natural defensive position of great strength, which, with a few artificial adjuncts, might have been rendered really impregnable to ordinary means of assault from the lake, while a few rifle-pits, barricades, or stockades of fallen trees on the steep of the wooded hill would have effectually protected the rear. The Hauhaus had commenced the formation of an earthwork on the crest of the hill and on each flank of the ascent, but, cowed and apparently demoralized by the certainly remarkable failure of their ambuscades and volleys at short range, together with the loss of one of their most determined leaders (Enoka), they evacuated them on our advance, without a show of resistance, as also the adjacent *pa,* and retreated in boats and canoes to the opposite headland and settlement, Tikitiki.

"The Matuahu Village, including Te Kooti's *runanga* house, a large and spacious building elaborately carved and embellished, consisted of from fifteen to twenty houses of various kinds, mostly of the *wharepuni* type, but in many instances of a kind peculiar to the lake denizens and the inhabitants of the cold mountainous Urewera Country. These subterranean abodes were usually built under a projective bank in the side of a declivity, or were otherwise heavily earthed over, and possessed no means of ventilation other than that afforded by a sliding door of small dimensions, impossible to enter except in a stooping position. No windows, of course, enlightened these troglodytic dwellings, to which the Urewera resort during the stormy winter months. The much-vaunted fortifications—so formidable in aspect from the other side of the lake—simply did not exist in their apparently efficient defensive completeness, resolving themselves mostly into the natural sharply defined contour of the edge of the rocky cape, or, at most, hollow-ways, banks, and rudimentary earthworks evidently thrown up by the wily Urewera more with a view to affect the vision of spectators from the other side than for actual military use.

"Snugly ensconced in one of these recesses hollowed out in the bank, and affording from the parapet formed by the excavations a wide view of the opposing *pa* of Tikitiki and of the neighbouring arms and inlets, I found the officers of the expedition and the Armed Constabulary orderlies. They had rigged a tent, consisting of the united oil-sheets of the party (seven in number), fastened securely to the parapet and stretching to a sapling of corresponding length secured to two stout uprights in front, thus forming a tolerably comfortable domicile and defensive earthwork combined. In front blazed a large fire of logs, while scattered over the peninsula burned numerous other fires indicating the bivouacs of the many sections of tribes and *hapus* of which the field force was composed. The glare of so many large fires within so circumscribed an area shone refulgently in the dark starless night clouds, and Tikitiki, Matakitaki, and Onepoto, where the enemy, our rearguard, and Sergeant Monahan's party lay respectively, all contributed their lesser blazes to the stupendous veil of billowy, vaporous crimson which floated heavily over the lake.

"Morning dawned, and with it broke upon us one of those violent winter storms for which Waikare-moana is notorious, the sleet and rain-laden gusts of wind rushing down the ravines of the mountain-ranges with tremendous force and literally tearing up the surging lake-waters, hurling them against the cliffs and high into the air, while the whole surface of the *moana* was whitened with foam. Under such circumstances marine communication with Onepoto and Sergeant Monahan (in charge of supplies) was quite impossible, and as overland communication was equally out of the question, I speedily obtained some enlightenment as to the ways and means of our officers' mess. The fare was ample, though without much variety, and the cuisine an unvarying success, inasmuch as it was impossible for it to be otherwise. The rations consisted of potatoes (*ex preterea nihil*), or, as Mr. James Carroll, sen., the facetious one of the party, observed: 'Potatoes for breakfast, spuds for dinner, and Paddy's apples for tea.' And when it was considered that among the two or three hundred men encamped within the narrow confines of the peninsula not a grain of salt was to be had, and that they had all subsisted on the like fare since the occupation of the lake, some idea may be formed of this not very agreeable phase of our expeditionary experiences.

"But fortunately the storms of mountainous regions, though extremely violent, are usually of short duration. We were not long in relieving Sergeant Monahan and Messrs. Davis and Banks of their charge—three hundred sheep and other provisions for the force. The Maoris, after refreshing the inner man after their manner for a day or two, began to think (stimulated as usual by their European leaders) of further aggressive movements. An assault by lake and land on Tikitiki was being organized, when the display of a flag of truce on that promontory signified a desire on the part of the Urewera to treat for peace. Consequently, on the 16th June, 1870, while two heavily armed canoes were kept under the shadow of our headland, fully on the alert and prepared to dart out and across the lake if any treachery was manifested, Mr. Hamlin crossed over to Tikitiki, meeting there the three Urewera chiefs Te Makarini, Moko-nui-a Rangi, and Hori Wharerangi. After an amicable conference the chiefs departed for Ruatahuna bearing the Government ultimatum of unconditional surrender to Paerau, Te Whenuanui, and the Urewera there assembled."

While the negotiations were going on, the Government force explored all the arms and inlets of the lake by boat and canoe, and the various overland tracks were noted for future use if necessary. Immense quantities of potatoes—one estimate was a sufficient amount to sustain a thousand men for fifteen months or more—were destroyed by the native parties. More than a hundred cultivations were destroyed by process of breaking down the fences and turning up the potatoes to the frost. The whares in all the villages were looted and burned; indeed, the whole lake-shore was devastated.

It was towards the end of June that Mr. Large's secret expedition to Mahungarerewai and Hereheretaua, at the head of the northern outlet of the lake, revealed the fact that the enemy had all gone inland to Ruatahuna, leaving their large canoes and whaleboat at the landing-place at Hereheretaua.

Colonel Herrick's futile expedition to Waikare-moana is 1869 cost £42,000. Hamlin and Witty's native force, which subjugated the Hauhaus of the lake district, incurred an expense of only £3,000.

Chapter 37

EXPEDITIONS TO UREWERA COUNTRY

THE FOREST WHICH clothes with its dark-green blanket the steep slopes of Maunga-pohatu, the "Rocky Mountain" in the heart of the Urewera Country, is a mysterious, gloomy place. Day is semi-darkness in the tree-shadowed depths of the ravines which scar the mountain-sides, so thick is the screen of leaves and so closely do the boughs of the native pines and beeches interlace themselves overhead. Streamers of grey and white moss in many places drape the ancient trees; these pendulous mosses, hanging there in the silences, look like rows of Druid beards, and the half-light heightens the fancy. Underneath the foot there are dense beds of ferns, and, except where the narrow horse-tracks or foot-trails wind up the valleys and over the ridges, the jungly undergrowth needs work with tomahawk or slasher. The castellated limestone ridges of Maunga-pohatu are seldom free from mists or rain-clouds; the old Maoris say it is the *tapu* which has clung to the Rocky Mountain for centuries, enveloping the sacred burial-mountain of the Urewera from the profaning gaze and tread of the invader, and particularly the white invader. Even to-day in the summer it is a rough place and hard to travel; in winter it is often snow-bound. Yet the Colonial Government forces campaigned over this inhospitable country in winter as well as in summer in the war-days of 1870-71. They were Maori forces, with but three or four white officers, and they spent months in penetrating these almost trackless wilds, always in danger of sudden ambuscade by the Urewera hillmen, whose gorges and forests were their chief defences. Colonel Whitmore's campaign of 1869 did not touch the Rocky Mountain; it was left for a purely native expedition, with one European officer, to break for the first time the *tapu* of Maunga-pohatu.

A Ngati-Porou contingent, about three hundred and seventy strong, marching from Poverty Bay in February, 1870, via the Ngatapa Valley and the Ruakituri, was well in the heart of the Urewera forests by the second week in March, tramping its way slowly up the wooded slopes that led to Maunga-pohatu. Major

Photo by Mr. A. N. Breckon]

Maunga-pohatu Range, Urewera Country, from the North

Ropata Wahawaha led the force, with Captain T. W. Porter second in command. The Maoris were a savage-looking band, for all their Government backing and Government equipment; they were shawl-kilted; they wore tomahawks stuck in their waistbelts. They carried rifles, and each man had a hundred rounds of ammunition. Their heavy *pikau,* or swags, held supplies of biscuit, bacon, sugar, and tea.

Porter was shawl-kilted, like his Maoris; he carried a swag on his shoulders, and was armed with a Terry carbine with gun-stock; round his neck, by a lanyard, sailor-fashion, he wore a Colt's six-chamber revolver. With him he had a guide, spy, and bodyguard, a Maori named Hori Niania, a Hauhau whom he had captured at Te Reinga some time previously, and who now proved a reliable and useful guide. It was this man who described to Porter the situation and defences of the strongholds on the sides of the Rocky Mountain. On the 12th March the Government war-party, weary with the long march, had camped in the forest close to a Hauhau *pa,* which, however, they could not yet see. They did not dare light a camp-fire, for fear of their advance being detected by Te Kooti's scouts. They ate a ration of biscuits and the bacon which they cooked at their last camp. Ropata and Porter questioned their Hauhau guide, and ascertained from him that the *pa* stood on a tongue of land at the junction of the two steep-banked mountain-streams. It was a stockaded village, and its front and sides were so well palisaded that it would not be an easy place to storm. At the rear of the *pa* the mountain rose steeply, and the forest grew close up to it; it was named Horoeka, which is the native name of the lance-wood, because of the abundance of that small tree in the vicinity. Higher up the range, and more to the west, were the Urewera villages Te Kakari and Toreatai. In the "Lancewood" *pa* dwelt the principal families of the Ngati-Kowhatu (the "Tribe of the Rocks"). Toreatai was the capital and citadel of the savage Ngati-Huri, whose chief was Hetaraka. Ngati-Huri belonged to Maunga-pohatu, but Ngati-Kowhatu was an Upper Wairoa tribe; the principal chief was Te Rakiroa, an old-time rebel. Both tribes were strong supporters of Te Kooti.

"You attack Horoeka," said Ropata to Captain Porter; "I shall push on to Toreatai. I leave you Henare Potae and a hundred of the Whanau-a-Rua and a hundred of Te Aowera. That will make two hundred; they should be enough for Horoeka. I shall go on with the rest, and you must join me when you have taken the *pa*."

When the old Maori soldier had moved off with his column Porter made his disposition of the division under his command. He determined, after again questioning Hori Niania, to attack the stockade from the rear. It was a rough and difficult march in the darkness through the dense bush and across the water-courses. Porter guided the force by compass. At last the column came out near the place where the two streams, as described by Hori Niania, made junction. Dimly looming there, Porter saw the sharp-topped palisade of timber that surrounded the village. The glimmer of a fire could be seen, and voices were heard.

As Porter had previously arranged, he took the rear of the *pa* himself, with a hundred Aowera men, intending to make the assault as soon as daylight came. The other hundred, under Henare Potae, he sent to form the cutting-off parties, on either angle of the tongue on which the village stood.

"Go down the creek-bed," he instructed Henare; "have your men ready when you hear us charge in, but don't fire a shot or make the slightest noise until then, or you'll spoil it all."

With the utmost caution, the force surrounded the Hauhau position. Just before daylight the cordon was complete, and Porter and his immediate followers crouched behind some logs close to the rear gateway of the stockade.

As the dawn began to creep over the sleeping forest Porter suddenly saw a figure before him. It was an old Maori woman

Colonel T. W. Porter, C.B.

Colonel Porter, who gave his country distinguished service in the Maori wars and in South Africa, was the son of Lieut-Colonel Porter (7th Bengal Native Infantry), who died in India during the Mutiny, and nephew of Sir Hugh Rose, afterwards Lord Strathnairn, who at one time was Commander-in-Chief of the British Forces in India. On his mother's side he was of ancient Scottish Highland stock, the Roses of Kilravock Castle, Geddes, Nairnshire. He entered the Royal Navy in 1857 at the age of thirteen, and served as a midshipman in H.M.S. "Hercules" in operations against pirates on the coast of China. In New Zealand in 1863 he joined the Colonial Defence Force Cavalry as a trooper, and won commissioned rank in the East Coast Hauhau campaigns. He was continuously on active service from 1868 to the end of 1871 in operations against Titokowaru and Te Kooti. In the South African War, 1900–2, Colonel Porter commanded the Seventh New Zealand Contingent of Mounted Rifles in the Transvaal, Orange Free State, and Zululand, and later the Ninth Contingent. For his services in veldt warfare he received the high commendation of Lord Kitchener and was created a Commander of the Bath. He was afterwards for some time Acting Under-Secretary for Defence in New Zealand. Colonel Porter died in Wellington in 1920 at the age of seventy-six years.

with a bundle of firewood on her back; she had been collecting wood at the forest-edge for the early morning cooking-fires.

The woman, scenting danger, stopped and looked intently into the dim forest, and cast a suspicious gaze all around. She turned to go again, and then, looking quickly back over her shoulder, she saw Porter in the act of rising from the ground.

The old woman gave a startled cry, but next moment, at Porter's shout, "*Me kokiri!*" ("Charge!") the Government men were up. The Aowera, running over the *wahine* in their rush, dashed in through the open gateway. Porter called, "*Hangaia te ngutu o te pu ki nga whare!*" ("Thrust the muzzles of your guns into the houses!") The woman's cry had apparently not alarmed the camp, for the people were talking in a large meeting-house which stood on one side of the *marae,* or village square, and there was not a soul out-of-doors but the one old woman. On the opposite side of the square to the large *whare* were a number of small huts, half-buried in the earth and roofed with *totara* bark.

Porter rushed to the meeting-house, and his men thrust their rifle-muzzles into the door and window. All the houses were similarly covered. It was a complete surprise for Ngati-Kowhatu.

"Come out!" Porter shouted. "Come out, all of you, or I'll fire into you! Pass your guns out first and come out!"

There was a vociferous babble of voices within. Ngati-Kowhatu were boiling with anger and chagrin. They had all been listening to an oration by a notorious Hauhau from the Bay of Plenty, one Iharaira ("Israel"), who had arrived in the *pa* the previous day; he was one of the murderers of Bennett White at Waiotahe in 1867. "Israel" had been narrating his deeds and glorifying Te Kooti and his exploits. Porter had caught him very neatly, without firing a shot.

The people sullenly filed out from the *wharepuni,* passing out their guns, butt first, as they came. All the force was now in the *pa,* and as the captured villagers fell in on the *marae* they were surrounded by armed guards. Porter himself took charge of Iharaira, who surrendered a fine greenstone *mere* which he had been carrying under his flax mat. [This trophy Porter returned to its owner a few days later, in token of trust, when that rebel was sent on a diplomatic mission to the headquarters of the Urewera. Iharaira vanished, *mere* and all, and that was the last that was heard of him.] Rakiroa, it was found, was away with Te Kooti.

The Tribe of the Rocks would have fired upon Porter and his followers had they had but a few moments' warning. But too well they knew what would be their fate if they attempted resistance now. There were ninety-three prisoners, about half of whom were women and children. Few of them had any European clothing; most of them wore rough Maori mats: a shaggy-headed, rude clan of the mountains.

Just as Porter had assembled and disarmed the bushmen of Horoeka heavy volley-firing was heard. It came from far up the foggy ranges, in the direction of Ngati-Huri's villages. Ropata was engaged in a severe fight. The volleys rolled thunderously through the mountain-gorges. Then the firing suddenly ceased.

Ngati-Porou looked at each other and wondered what the result was. Porter himself was anxious about it, but he did not think that Ropata could have been "wiped out" or even beaten, because had he been unsuccessful in his attack the firing would not have ceased so suddenly.

Captain Porter decided to march his prisoners through the bush and join Ropata at Toreatai. It was an undertaking attended with considerable risk, but he guarded against that as far as was possible. "You must walk in front of me," he said to Iharaira, "and be very careful or you'll have a bullet through your head." Each of the other prisoners he placed in front of a Ngati-Porou man so that in the event of any trouble the rebels could quickly be shot.

"Now," he said to his prisoners when the column stood ready to march, "listen to me. We are not going to kill you if you behave yourselves and march quietly. But if any of you gives trouble or attempts to escape, that one will be shot."

Horoeka was left deserted. One of the prisoners guided the column. All the mountain villages had been alarmed by this time, and the Urewera had taken to the bush. From ridge to ridge their sulky war-horns (conch-shells) and *pu-tatara,* or wooden trumpets, echoed. But they did not attack his column; and so that afternoon the two divisions met. Ropata had had a sharp fight and lost one of his men killed (Pene Kerekere) before driving the enemy out of their position at Te Kakari, which he was now engaged in strengthening with parapets in anticipation of an attack by the bushmen.

Ropata went on next day to Tauaki *pa,* where a prisoner was taken, and sent out sortie-parties, who ascended Maunga-pohatu and scouted the rugged country in pursuit of Ngati-Huri. It was then decided to march out down the Waimana and meet Kepa and his Wanganui Contingent, who were supposed to be in that direction. Ropata also intended to attack Tamaikowha on the Lower Waimana.

Ngati-Porou had a harassing march out toward the Waimana, for they were attacked flank and rear by the Urewera. Porter commanded the advance-guard, while Ropata took charge of the rear-guard, which had most of the fighting. Several men were hit, but none seriously. The Urewera ceased to worry their foes when Ngati-Porou had crossed a ridge at Tawhana which divided them from the Waimana headwaters.

Some stragglers of Ngai-Tama were met on the Upper Waimana, and they reported that Kepa had visited Tauwhare-manuka and made peace with Tamaikowha. This by no means pleased Ropata, who would have dealt with the savage chief of Ngai-Tama in a very different fashion.

Solomon Black, N.Z.C.

Constable Black (No. 1 Division Armed Constabulary) was awarded the New Zealand Cross for his determined gallantry in holding, with a few comrades, the precipitous ridge in rear of Ngatapa hill fort, 1869. Benjamin Biddle, of Whakatane, also received the Cross for that service.

(See page 278.)

The leaders met Tamaikowha at his *kainga* and learned from him that Te Kooti with a strong force was in occupation of Maraetahi *pa* high up in the gorge of the Waioeka River. Ngati-Porou marched out to Ohiwa, where Kepa was found encamped with some of his Ngati-Hau; the rest were at Opotiki. The Nga-Rauru, from Waitotara, who had fought so well at Tapapa were included in Kepa's force.

Ropata went on to Opotiki, while Kepa and Topia Turoa with four hundred men made a detour inland to take Maraetahi in the rear. The Wanganui Contingent reached the wooded heights above Maraetahi on the 23rd March. Three small settlements were captured with all their inhabitants during the night, and very early in the morning Kepa, with three hundred men, surrounded and charged into the Waipuna *pa,* where most of the Hauhaus were. The murderer, Kereopa, was there, but escaped in the confusion. The action was short and sharp. Nineteen men of the rebel band were killed, including a number of prisoners summarily executed on the river-bank. One of those killed was old Hakaraia, a notorious Hauhau leader belonging to the Ngai-te-Rangi, Piri-Rakau, and Ngati-Raukawa

Thomas Adamson, N.Z.C.

Adamson was one of three stalwart brothers who joined the colonial forces at Wanganui. He was celebrated for his skill and hardihood in bush scouting and warfare after the Maori manner, and was awarded the New Zealand Cross in recognition of several daring expeditions in Hauhau country. He served with Kepa's Wanganui Maori Contingent and in Whitmore's Corps of Guides, 1869–70, and was wounded at Manawa-hiwi, Urewera Country, 7th May, 1869.

Tribes. Tom Adamson, the big scout with the Wanganui men, took a ruthless hand in the execution of the principal prisoners. Most of the Whakatohea people lately captured at Omarumutu and Opape by Te Kooti were recaptured in this *pa,* and over a hundred Hauhaus were made prisoners. Ropata and Porter and their Ngati-Porou now arrived from Opotiki, having marched for many miles up the bed of the Waioeka River, camping one night in the gorge. A short distance below the Maraetahi settlements they drove back a picket guarding a narrow part of the gorge. Maraetahi *pa* was then assaulted and taken. Te Kooti was there, but with his usual luck escaped to the bush. The Hauhaus took to flight just before the final rush and scattered in the forest, losing only one man killed.

The Government parties lost no men in these operations. The combined force, numbering now six hundred and seventy men, marched back to Opotiki, whence the Wanganui Contingent

Photo at Opotiki, 1871]

Captain Porter and a Party of Ngaitai Maori Auxiliaries

was shipped home by steamer. The operations against Te Kooti and Kereopa and their Hauhau bands now devolved chiefly upon Ngati-Porou—who went home to prepare for another expedition—and upon the Arawa, with the help of some of the friendly Bay of Plenty tribes.

Te Kooti took refuge in the exceedingly rugged bush wilderness of Te Wera, at the source of the Waioeka River, north-east of Maunga-pohatu. From his hiding-place here he suddenly made one of his lightning raids down to the coast. His objective this time was Tolago Bay (Uawa), about fifty miles due east of his camp in the mountains of Te Wera. Some of the people of this place, the Aitanga-a-Hauiti, who had joined Te Kooti, induced him to descend on the district and obtain further recruits for his band. He captured a few people in the inland villages and shot one man, whereupon the Hauiti Tribe at Uawa turned out to resist him, and sent a message to Turanganui appealing for help.

Major Pitt and Captain Richardson, of the A.C. force, and Captain Porter, hurried up to Tolago Bay with a small party of volunteers, and were joined by the Hauiti. This composite body marched at once on Te Kooti's return trail. For three days the pursuit continued in very wet, wintry weather. Te Kooti at last was found in bivouac at Te Hapua, on the bank of a stream in the forest. The officer in command made his dispositions to surround the Hauhaus, and Te Kooti would in all probability have been killed or captured but for a premature shot fired by a Hauiti man, most probably as a warning to the enemy. Next moment the whole force was blazing away into the camp, but once more the rebel leader escaped without loss and vanished in the trackless forest. Captain Porter captured one of his wives, a woman named Huhana (Susan), who had accompanied him on many raids; at Makaretu, in 1869, she had helped to carry him off to Ngatapa when he was disabled.

The search for Te Kooti was continued by Ngati-Porou during May. Ropata and Porter scoured the country between Te Reinga and the Urewera Mountains and captured several families of the Ngati-Kowhatu and other rebel tribes and removed them to the coast. The few members of Ngati-Kowhatu remaining in the field under Rakiroa—who had joined Te Kooti in 1868—soon afterwards came in and surrendered themselves and their arms. Towards the end of 1870 Ropata was requested to make another expedition into the heart of the Urewera Country in order to secure control of the various *hapus* and prevent them joining Te Kooti on any further raids or affording him shelter in their mountain villages. He enlisted two hundred of the Aowera and other *hapus* for this purpose, and arranged to set out on the march early in the new year. Meanwhile, on the western side of the ranges the newly enrolled Arawa Contingent, under Captains Mair and Preece, was scouting the borders of the Urewera in search of Te Kooti, who was now expected to make an endeavour to cross the Kaingaroa Plains and gain sanctuary in the territory of Ngati-Raukawa and Ngati-Maniapoto.

The operations of the Arawa Constabulary will be described in the next chapter.

Chapter 38

EXPEDITIONS OF ARAWA CONTINGENT

TOWARDS THE END of March, 1870, Captain Gilbert Mair and Captain G. A. Preece received instructions to disband the Arawa and Taupo native contingents, and to enrol a special corps consisting of two companies, each of not more than one hundred picked Maoris, who should be drilled in the same way as the European force. Captain Preece was to be stationed at Te Teko and work from there as a base; Captain Mair would be stationed at Kaiteriria. Both officers were under the officer commanding the Tauranga district. They were ordered to act together and meet at Fort Galatea, patrolling the country, and at the same time to keep in touch with Major Roberts, commanding the Taupo district; but a good deal of discretion was allowed them. Captain Preece picked his recruits from all tribes and avoided choosing any chiefs, in order to have the men under his own control; in his own words he had had "a sickening" of native chiefs. He met with considerable opposition from the chiefs, but selected good men in spite of them, and was fortunate in getting some excellent European and Maori non-commissioned officers, and never regretted the composition of the force. The men worked well together; the Europeans were experienced Armed Constabulary men, and one of the Maori sergeants had been many years in the Auckland police and was well drilled. The corps was styled the Arawa Flying Column; Mair commanded No. 1 Company, and Preece No. 2. For two years, working usually in combination, both companies carried out a great deal of difficult work under trying conditions, particularly in the Urewera Country, and it was an Arawa party under Preece that finally engaged Te Kooti in February, 1872.

From the 6th April, 1870, onward Captains Mair and Preece led their Arawa companies in a number of expeditions on the borders of the Urewera Country, and had a few unimportant skirmishes with the enemy in different places. On the 17th April a Ngati-Whare man named Paraone te Tuhi, and four others who had been in one of the skirmishes, came in under a flag of truce and surrendered. Paraone said, "I am the rope; pull me and the horse will follow"—meaning that he was the first to give himself up, and that if he were sent back to his tribe they also would surrender. Shortly after this the whole of the Ngati-Whare Tribe from Ahi-kereru, under their chiefs Hapurona Kohi and Hamiora Potakurua, came in and laid down their arms at Fort Galatea. Under instructions from the Government they were conveyed to the coast at Putere, near Matata, and located there. Later, natives of the Warahoe Tribe surrendered under their chiefs Wi Patene and Manuera, and were settled near the redoubt at Te Teko, the Government providing them with food until they could gather their crops from the seed supplied to them. In all cases they gave up their arms.

When Major Kepa and his Wanganui Contingent advanced from Ohiwa up the Waimana River, Tamaikowha, the Urewera chief of Waimana, who had been the leading spirit in the rebellion in the Opotiki country in 1867 and 1868, met Kepa and made peace. He declared that he had never joined Te Kooti, and promised that the Government troops could go through his country in pursuit of the rebel chief without being molested by his men. After the junction of Kepa's party with Ropata's and their successful fight at Maraetahi, and after they had left the neighbourhood, Colonel St. John, who then commanded the district, heard that rebels were afoot, and made a raid on Ohiwa, where Tamaikowha's father unfortunately was killed. This naturally caused trouble, because Tamaikowha said that the Government had made a treacherous peace and then attacked him. Colonel St. John was removed from the district, and Major Mair was sent to try and patch matters up. His efforts were successful, and Tamaikowha was ever afterwards a firm friend of the Government officers. Captain J. R. Rushton, now of Kutarere, Ohiwa, who was a member of this expedition, gives the following account:—

"Lieut.-Colonel St. John was induced by the chief Tamehana Tahawera, of Ngati-Pukeko, and Wi Maihi Te Rangikaheke, of the Arawa, to organize an expedition against Whakarae, the *pa* of the Urewera chief Rakuraku, on Ohiwa Harbour. Both the chiefs mentioned had had relatives killed by Te Kooti and his people, and their object was to obtain revenge by capturing the Hauhau leader Tamaikowha, who was with Rakuraku. We reconnoitred up to Whakarae and arrived there about two hours before daylight with the intention of surrounding the *pa*. I was ahead on the track leading up to the village with two Whakatohea scouts. Suddenly an old man appeared and came right up to us; he had a calabash in his hand, and was going down to a spring for water. He passed on, and Tamehana Tahawera led him down the track, and before we could prevent the deed he had killed the old man with a whalebone *patu.* It was a deliberate murder; it was Tahawera's way of obtaining revenge for the murder of his niece Ripeka on the Whakatane in 1869. Tamaikowha and his party, hearing the noise made by our people, retreated from the *pa* down a cliff into the Nukuhou River, seaward of the present road. The old man killed was Tepene, father of Tamaikowha; and, as Tamaikowha had already made peace with the Government, the expedition was a mistake. It was simply a scheme by the two friendly chiefs to make use of the Government forces and secure revenge for their family losses. St. John shortly afterwards was removed from the command of the Opotiki district."

In July, 1870, Captain Rushton, who was acting intelligence officer and scout at Opotiki, hearing that some of the Whakatohea Tribe were in communication with Te Kooti, rode to Ohiwa, and explained the position to Colonel McDonnell. At his request Rushton went to Omarumutu, on the coast near the mouth of the Wai-aua River, and found all the Whakatohea mustered in the large sheds which held their whaleboats. He secured the Maoris' guns at Omarumutu, and Sir Donald McLean gave him his captaincy for the work. This was just before Te Kooti came down and captured the large Omarumutu *pa,* which surrendered at once, and led the people off as prisoners. After taking the tribe inland Te Kooti sent back a party of fifty or sixty men, who killed two Arawa scouts, Te Awaawa and Heteraka te Rangikaheke; the latter, a son of the Rotorua chief Te Rangikaheke, was shot by the half-caste Peka Makarini. This brought Ngati-Hau and Ngati-Porou on Te Kooti's trail, and the engagement at Maraetahi followed. All those taken away from Omarumutu were recaptured; they numbered two hundred and seventy men, women, and children.

This ended the war against the Urewera, although a small section of them from Maunga-pohatu under Te Whiu were still out with Te Kooti at Te Wera or Te Houpapa. Among them was Kepa te Ahuru, N.Z.C., a trooper of No. 1 Division A.C., who had been made a prisoner by Te Kooti at Rotorua just before Mair's engagement in February, 1870. This man afterwards escaped and made his way through the country to Maunga-pohatu, and surrendered to Captain Preece at Horomanga, near the Rangitaiki. He was sent to Tauranga to report himself to Colonel Moule, who, having satisfied himself that he was forcibly detained and had taken the first opportunity of escaping, sent him back to duty and gave him his back pay. Kepa was then attached to Captain Preece's force. He served in it for several years, and was in all the expeditions of 1871–72 through the Urewera Country.

Te Waru Tamatea and his tribe of Wairoa (H.B.) natives, who dared not show themselves in the Wairoa district on account of the treacherous murder of Karaitiana Roto-a-Tara and his three fellow-scouts at Whataroa in October, 1868, just before the Poverty Bay massacre, surrendered unconditionally to Captain Preece at Horomanga and laid down their arms. They were informed that any murderers would be tried for their offences according to law. They were being sent to Tauranga under strong escort when Mr. Clarke, the Civil Commissioner, intervened, and the Government decided to place them on the coast at Maketu under charge of the loyal Maoris. They were afterwards settled at Waiotahe, near Opotiki, on land allotted to them by the Government, but were never allowed to return to the Wairoa district.

The Urewera mountain tribes were now growing weary of allowing themselves to be used by the rebel leader. Early in May 1870 Captain Preece heard that the Urewera chiefs Paerau te Rangi-kaitipuake and Te Whenuanui, of Ruatahuna, were inclined to break away from Te Kooti, who, after his defeat at Maraetahi, had taken up a position with the remnant of his followers at Te Houpapa, in the bush at the headwaters of the Waioeka and Hangaroa Rivers, about midway between Opotiki and Wairoa on the Hawke's Bay side. Preece accordingly sent letters by a surrendered Ngati-Whare chief, telling them that if they would come in and give up their arms the Government forces would merely go through their country in pursuit of Te Kooti and would not harm them. They replied that the peace made with Tamaikowha had resulted in blood being spilt, and that they would not surrender. However, shortly after this Te Whenuanui met Major Mair at Ruatoki, and peace was made with his party. A little later Paerau te Rangi-kaitipuake met Captain Preece at Ahi-kereru, and his people made peace and opened their country to the Government. After these important surrenders the only chief of the Urewera on the Ruatahuna side of the country who supported Te Kooti was Kereru te Pukenui, who occupied the lower end of the Ruatahuna clearings and Maunga-pohatu. A chief of Maunga-pohatu named Tutakangahau had previously surrendered with Ngati-Whare.

On one of the many expeditions made by Captains Mair and Preece during the latter part of 1870, scouring the western borderland of the Urewera, they intercepted a party of Te Kooti's men trying to get through to Waikato, and drove them back into the bush between Heruiwi and Te Tapiri. One of these men, Paora Wakahoehoe, was afterwards killed at Waipaoa (August, 1871). Another, named Maaka, was captured by Captain Ferris in the early part of 1872; he was one of Te Kooti's "butchers" who committed the atrocities in Poverty Bay in November, 1868. Maaka was tried in Napier and condemned to death; the sentence, however, was commuted to

Captain Preece, N.Z.C.

Captain G. A. Preece is a New Zealand-born officer who won the highest distinction in the Maori wars. His father was a pioneer missionary who laboured among the natives in the very early days, and was the first to establish a station in the Urewera Country. Captain Preece began his military career in 1865 in the operations against the rebel faction of Ngati-Porou on the East Coast. At the first attack on Ngatapa (1868) he and Major Ropata rendered exceptionally gallant services for which each was awarded the New Zealand Cross. (See Chapter 28, p. 275.) In 1869 he served as staff officer and interpreter to Colonel Whitmore in the Urewera expedition and in the operations on the West Coast. He commanded No. 2 Company of the Arawa Flying Column (Constabulary) in the arduous pursuit of Te Kooti through the Urewera Mountains. When settled conditions came, Captain Preece was appointed Resident Magistrate at Opotiki, and for many years served the country as R.M. in the North Island.

penal servitude for life, and after serving ten years he was released.

From April, 1870, to April 1871, Mair and Preece with their respective contingents patrolled the country from Te Teko as far as Heruiwi, and through the bush from Waiohau to Horomanga and Ahi-kereru, keeping in constant touch with the Armed

Constabulary under Major Roberts at Taupo and Major Mair at Opotiki. Then orders came that they were to hold themselves in readiness to take the field against Te Kooti, as it was reported that he was making for Waikare-moana to avoid Major Ropata and Captain Porter, who were moving up towards Te Houpapa from Poverty Bay.

On the 27th May, 1871, Captains Mair and Preece started from Fort Galatea on their first expedition after Te Kooti through the Urewera territory. They had about fifty men of each Arawa Contingent (Nos. 1 and 2 Companies), and had brought up three weeks' rations from Te Teko. They arrived at Ahi-kereru the following day, and then got deep into the Urewera Mountains, where the knowledge of the country that they had gained on Colonel Whitmore's Ruatahuna expedition in 1869 was of great service to them. On arrival at Ruatahuna they were welcomed by the natives under Te Whenuanui and Paerau te Rangi-kaitipuake; this was the first visit of troops to the mountain clans' country since peace had been made with them in 1870. The force camped at Ruatahuna for a night and day, and buried the remains of Captain Travers, A.C., and five men whose bodies had been exhumed by Te Kooti's orders in May, 1869. With the expedition was old Hapurona Kohi, who had fought at Orakau and had killed one of Nga-Rauru with a *mere pounamu* at Tapapa in January, 1870. He was the chief of the first Urewera who surrendered in April, 1870. Hapurona was a man of great influence with the Urewera, and could be trusted to give reliable information. The passage through the country was not without risk of opposition from the more irreconcilable members of this wild hill tribe. Indeed, before Mair and Preece left Ruatahuna they received a defiant message from Kereru te Pukenui, a chief who occupied the Whakatane Valley below Ruatahuna, warning them not to return or they might get into trouble; this man's influence extended as far as Maunga-pohatu.

After leaving Ruatahuna the first march was over the Huiarau Range, and thence through rugged country and down the river-bed to Hereheretaua, on the northern shore of Waikare-moana. The officers had previously sent an Urewera native with a message to Hona te Makarini, the chief who had surrendered to Mr. Hamlin in the latter part of the previous year, bidding him have canoes to take the Arawa over to his settlement and to be ready to meet them. The canoes were provided, and Preece, having crossed to Waitohi, sent them back for Captain Mair and his men. On the following day the two commanders took the men over to Tikitiki, Te Makarini's settlement. Captain Mair remained there, while Captain Preece, Sergeant Bluett, and twelve men, with a prisoner named Hone Pareha—one of Te Kooti's men who had recently turned up at Tikitiki—went out to Wairoa to get further provisions and boots for the men. Though they had exceptionally bad weather they got back ten days later with a good supply.

Now Mair and Preece, taking with them Hapurona Kohi, who proved very useful as a guide, crossed the lake to the Whanganui-a-Parua arm and marched for Maunga-pohatu. After a very laborious journey they surrounded the settlement Te Kakari. This was the place where Ropata had had an engagement in 1870, losing one man killed. It was a strong position, about two miles west of Maunga-pohatu peak, which was separated from it by a deep ravine in which a tributary of the Waimana flowed. The forest grew close up to the *pa* on the south-east side. The force crept up to the palisade surrounding Te Kakari Village one afternoon in dull overcast weather, and Mair entered the place unobserved and called on the people to lay down their arms and have no fear. Hapurona told the natives that the Government had no quarrel with any but Te Kooti's and Kereopa's people. There were about seventy men, women, and children in the *pa;* most of the young fighting-men were away in the direction of Opotiki. The inhabitants of Te Kakari made an attempt to retreat, but found each gateway blocked by the Arawa. The surprise was complete; submission was the only course, and the Arawa made them their unwilling hosts. It was discovered too late that Kereopa had been in the *pa,* but escaped from an unguarded side when the place was entered. The force remained at Te Kakari next day (19th June), and on the following morning marched on to Tauaki, a *pa* several miles below Te Kakari. There they met the notable warrior Tamaikowha, with some seventy of his tribe. Tamaikowha received the force in a very friendly manner; Major Mair's diplomatic visit to him the previous year had had the effect of allaying his anger over the slaying of his father, Tepene. Peace was cemented with the assembled people; in the symbolic phrase of the Urewera, the *tatau pounamu,* the greenstone door, was erected—an expression for a lasting peace.

The two commanders had intended pushing on from Maunga-pohatu to the forests of Te Wera, at the head of the Waioeka and Hangaroa Rivers, where Te Kooti was believed to be in hiding. But bad weather set in, and when the force moved on to Tauaki, Tamaikowha advised that the expedition to Te Wera should be abandoned for the present as supplies were running low, and that the Arawa should go down the Waimana through the Ngati-Tama settlement and make for Opotiki. It was now well on in June, and as the conditions were so wintry,

Mair and Preece followed their new-made friend's advice. They went on to Opokere *pa,* on the high range, and from there to Te Whakaumu, where the track to Te Wera branches off, thence to Tawhana, at the junction of the Tauranga and Tawhana Streams, which form the Waimana Valley. The next point reached was Tauwhare-manuka, in the gorge of the Waimana, where Tamaikowha had built a large meeting-house. It had been named " Runanga " to commemorate the making of peace, but he, with grim humour, renamed it "Tepene," after his father, who had been killed at Whakarae. A long march down the river, which was crossed forty-two times, took the force into the Lower Waimana. On the 26th June the Arawa arrived at Opotiki, and after another march in bad weather reached their headquarters at Te Teko on the 2nd July.

The force had been over a month going through the most rugged terrain in the North Island of New Zealand, and although Mair and Preece had not achieved much in the way of fighting, they had shown the Urewera that they could get through their country in the depth of winter. After-events proved that it was fortunate they did not go to Te Wera, for Te Kooti was close to Waikare-moana at the time the force was there, and, in fact, had a distant view of Captain Preece's small party as it returned from Wairoa.

Chapter 39

NGATI-POROU'S SEARCH FOR TE KOOTI

THE THIRD EXPEDITION of Ngati-Porou to the Urewera Country, under Major Ropata Wahawaha and Captain Porter, started from Turanganui on the 14th January, 1871. The route taken was in the direction of Te Wera, the immensely broken country in which the Waioeka, the Hangaroa, and many other mountain-rivers have their sources. Te Rakiroa, the ex-Hauhau chief of Ngati-Kohatu, guided the column, which numbered about three hundred men. Several deserted camping-places were found in the great forest of Te Wera, but no definite trail was picked up. The force, after about three weeks' marching and searching, moved down into the upper valley of the Waioeka, and Captain Porter with eighty men went out to Opotiki for food-supplies. Ropata marched across the ranges to the Upper Waimana to meet Tamaikowha. After a *korero* with the savage chieftain of Ngai-Tama, who, as usual, made truculent speeches but ended the meeting with expressions of friendship, the united force marched into the ranges again, and at Tawhana and Te Kakari met the principal chiefs of the Urewera, who had declared that they would not allow booted feet to pass the boundaries of Maunga-pohatu. Ropata discovered that Te Kooti had been at the Tauaki settlement, a few miles from Te Kakari, some weeks previously; he was believed to be in a well-concealed refuge-place in the neighbourhood of Te Houpapa, at the head of the Hangaroa River. A track was picked up and followed, but the men were suffering from the lack of food, and Porter took a party out to Wairoa to procure biscuit for the main body. Supplies having been brought in, the search for Te Kooti was continued.

At Wairoa Lieutenant (afterwards Major) J. T. Large, who had seen some rough service in previous campaigns, and who was an excellent bushman and scout and a good Maori linguist, joined Porter's company as a volunteer, and served thenceforward in the expeditions to the Urewera Country. Describing the further operations of this expedition and the exceedingly rough conditions of bush campaigning, he wrote:—

"The Ngati-Porou were accustomed to take two or three week's rations with them when they went into the back country, and it was a sight to see their immense swags of food, clothes, and ammunition. I had to do likewise and carry a heavy *pikau* on my back. We had literally to be beasts of burden, for no horses, or even mules, could go through the country we were to traverse—high forest-clad ranges, with precipitous gorges and creeks, containing deep pools alternating with rapids and falls. Beyond the strip of occupied country next to the coast there were no tracks, and we had to force our way through high fern, scrub, or bush as best we could.

"We first went up the Wairoa River to Mangaaruhe, thence across the Orewha Ranges, descending to the Ruakituri River—a branch of the Wairoa—at Erepeti, where our advanced guard captured one of Te Kooti's followers named Tautata, who had been left behind. As far as he knew his leader was at Te Houpapa, high up at the head of the Hangaroa. We accordingly made our way across the Waimaha country in that direction, much delayed by wet weather and floods, which made the fords of the creeks and rivers difficult and dangerous, so that we had to camp a good deal. By the time we got to Te Houpapa—one of Te Kooti's far-inland bush settlements—which we found deserted, our European rations (hard biscuit, bacon, sugar, cocoa, and tea) were done, though for some time past we had eked them out with bush food. The principal native edibles we had to depend on were *aruhe* (fern-root), which when roasted and beaten is not unpalatable to a hungry man; *tawa* berries, with a turpentine flavour, not nice; and *whinau* berries. The *whinau* (or *hinau*) pulp is of a floury nature when separated from the kernels by pounding; it was made into a sort of bread (called by the Urewera *te whatu-nui-a-Rua*), and when eaten with fat pork it was fairly nutritious, though coarse. Then there was the *mamaku* fern-tree, the pith of which when cooked in a native oven and flavoured with wild honey is not bad, though it has no strength in it. A rather good bush vegetable is the *pikopiko,* the curled shoots of the *mauku* fern. The natives have long given up the use of these bush foods; but we had on several expeditions to eat them or starve, and when we were on short commons we always had a raging appetite; in fact, we even enjoyed being roused up at night to munch a piece of boar's hide an inch thick when it had been boiled long enough for us to get our teeth through it. Our hunters who operated in the rear of the column caught many pigs, principally in the fern country.

"As we were disappointed at not finding Te Kooti at Te Houpapa, our leaders decided that the force should go out to Poverty Bay to recuperate after our hardships, and escape part of the winter. We accordingly marched out by way of Ngatapa. When skirting a high mountain named Moko-nui-o-rangi our vanguard captured a small party of the Poverty Bay Hauhaus in hiding, and their chief Tamati te Rangi-tuawaru. Their refuge-place was betrayed by the chattering of one of their pet *kaka* parrots. In one of the songs composed by the Ngati-Porou descriptive of our wanderings in the primeval forest this incident is alluded to as follows: *He mokai kaka ka rangona te ngete-ngetetanga* (The chattering of a pet *kaka* parrot was heard). We crossed the Makaretu, then went down the Whare-kopae, and out by the Waipaoa to Turanganui (Gisborne), where we rested and enjoyed good living after our hardships."

The white officers in these expeditions observed many primitive customs among the Urewera people. Particularly interesting were the various devices by which the mountain tribes captured the birds of their forest-covered country. Major Large, describing these bird-taking methods, said: "The *waka-kereru* was perhaps the most common. This was simply a wooden trough filled with water, round the sides of which snares were fixed. These were tied up in the trees frequented by the native pigeon, and caught many when they came to drink. Then, there was the *tutu-kaka*. A handy tree was chosen, the small upper branches of which were cut short. On these were fixed perches, called *mutu-kaka*—carved, as a rule—on which rested loops of string arranged in such a way that when pulled taut by a man hidden in a leafy screen underneath they caught by the leg any unwary *kaka* that happened to light on the perch. A decoy bird served to entice his fellows. Smaller birds were killed with a long stick switched along a pole stuck in the ground at an angle of 45 degrees. A decoy bird was fastened to the upper end of this pole to attract the birds by its calls."

In the chase after Te Kooti and his band in 1871 it was no easy matter keeping on the trail of these outlaws, who were thorough masters of bush craft. "They adopted all sorts of dodges to conceal their trail," narrated Major Large. "One trick was to keep on wading in the bed of a creek, then step from the water on to a fallen tree, thus leaving no mark. But we had a splendid tracker named Kuare, who had been one of themselves, and he knew all their tricks, and when we lost the trail soon picked it up again. The slightest impression or discolouring on stone or wood, a broken leaf or twig, a bit of moss rubbed off, were sufficient for his practised eye. The Hauhaus also scattered in various directions, in order to mislead pursuit, coming together again at an appointed place.

"Wading in the water so much, crossing and recrossing creeks and rivers, we found the *rapaki,* or waist-shawl, infinitely superior

Photo by Mr. A. N. Breckon]

The Urewera Mountains

• This view, in the central part of the Urewera Country, illustrates the extremely rugged character of the highland region through which the Government expeditions searched for Kereopa and Te Kooti, 1870–72.

to trousers. Our boots had eyelet-holes to let the water out, as it was impossible to keep the feet dry. And after wading all day perhaps in that high country, and having made our camp in the evening on the banks of a creek in the bush, we had to wait, often shivering, till after dark before we could light fires, and also had to put all fires out before daybreak to prevent our smoke betraying us to the watchful eyes of the enemy. And how we did enjoy the fires in our low-lying camps when wet and cold! The Maoris obtain kindling-wood in the most unpromising places. One capital fire, which did not take up much room, was the *ahi poporo,* being slips of rimu-bark bound in a bundle, like shingles, and lit on top. It burnt steadily downwards till there was nothing left, diffusing a generous warmth all round."

The fourth expedition of Ngati-Porou, starting from Poverty Bay in June, 1871, was divided into four companies of fifty men, each of which could work independently if necessary. The leaders were Ropata, Porter, Henare Potae, and Ruka Aratapu. After scouring the bush country about Whakapunake Mountain, the detachments marched in the direction of Te Wera, scouting a wide area of country and finding nothing of the Hauhaus but their abandoned camping-grounds. The food carried was soon exhausted, and the men were reduced to living on *hinau* berries, pounded up—a food hard to digest. The weather was wet and wintry—it was now the middle of June—and three men were lost in the bush and died from cold and exhaustion. The inhospitable recesses of Te Wera were again searched, but Te Kooti had deserted this part of the country. News came at last that he was near Waikare-moana, and the united column marched for Wairoa.

After resting there and obtaining supplies the force once more entered upon the toilsome chase. A hundred men under Ropata marched for the southern and western sides of Waikare-moana, while Captain Porter and Lieutenant Large with 150 men marched in the other direction, going up the Ruakituri and then striking towards Maunga-pohatu. Porter and Large were engaged on that march during August, when they were overtaken by Captain Preece, who gave the news of an engagement with Te Kooti a few days previously, and set them on the outlaw's trail once more. This engagement (Waipaoa) is described in the next chapter.

Chapter 40

TE KOOTI DEFEATED AT WAIPAOA

ON THE 17th July, 1871, a telegram was received by Captain Preece at Te Teko stating that Te Kooti was at Waikare-moana, and that Major Ropata and Captain Porter were seeking for him in that direction; Major Cumming and fifty men were also going to Waikare-moana. Captains Mair and Preece were instructed to keep a sharp lookout on their side of the Urewera Ranges. On the 19th instructions came that they were to go in to Ruatahuna. Preece's force started the same day for Fort Galatea, where Captain Mair joined with his No. 1 Company of the Arawa from Kaiteriria. Very bad weather was encountered. Flooded rivers forced the joint contingent to make a detour of over twenty miles before they could cross the Rangitaiki River by the natural bridge at Te Arawhata, just above the junction with the Wheao River, and then they were compelled to fell trees to make a crossing over the Wheao. They had to send to Major Roberts at the Opepe post for a further supply of rations.

In spite of the weather, which continued very bad, the Arawa were kept constantly busy. Captain Mair started with twelve men to scout the ranges southward towards Runanga stockade, where Captain W. E. Gudgeon was stationed, and Captain Preece sent a sergeant and party to scout towards Ahi-kereru. Mr J. D. Ormond telegraphed that Te Kooti was supposed to be at Ruatahuna. Captain Scannell now arrived with a body of Armed Constabulary to take up a position at Okoromatakiwi, between the Arawa and Captain Gudgeon, to prevent Te Kooti breaking through to the plains. On the 29th the rations arrived by pack-horses from Opepe. In the meantime, in reply to a message which Captain Preece had sent to the Urewera to inquire if Te Kooti had been heard of near Ruatahuna, word came that he had not been in that locality, but that it was reported that he had disappeared from Waikare-moana. On the 31st Captain Mair returned from Runanga; he had found no traces of the rebels in that direction. On the same day a telegram arrived instructing the force to march into the Urewera Country for

Waikare-moana with the least possible delay by whatever route was thought advisable.

Mair and Preece started at once, making for Pareranui through the bush. They had about eighty men. Besides the officers there were only three Europeans in the contingent—Sergeant H. P. Bluett and two buglers, Crimmins and Kelly. The Whirinaki River (a tributary of the Rangitaiki) was flooded, and they had great difficulty in crossing, but in the open country of the Whirinaki they found good marching for about five miles. They then took to the bush again, up the Okahu Gorge, and camped at Manawahiwi. The next day they marched over the ranges to Oputao, in the Ruatahuna Valley, and thence to Whatakoko, where they camped. A message was sent to Paerau te Rangi-kaitipuake telling him to keep his people together for fear Te Kooti should get hold of them. Starting at daylight next morning the force marched through the bush, crossed the Huiarau Range, and came out at Hereheretaunga, on Lake Waikare-moana.

There were no canoes there, although a telegram had been sent to Wairoa before they started that canoes were to await the arrival of the force. Consequently the Arawa had to cut their way through the bush skirting the lake, over very rough country, to Mahungarerewai, where they fired guns to attract the attention of Te Makarini's people at Tikitiki. No other course was open to them. It was impossible to get farther round the lake owing to the nature of the country; they had, therefore, to take the risk that Te Kooti might hear the guns and make off. Two men came across in canoes. They reported that Major Cumming was at Onepoto camp, on the other side of the lake, and though his men had followed Te Kooti's trail on the Whanganui-a-Parua arm of the lake they could see no fires. All that night and all the next day it snowed heavily, and there was a heavy sea on the lake. Fortunately the Arawa camp was on a point which had been an old potato cultivation, and the men were able to get a few potatoes by digging through the snow.

On the 4th August two men arrived at the camp in a small boat with a letter from Captain G. McDonnell. Captain Mair remained in camp, and Captain Preece went in the boat to arrange with Major Cumming for rations. He was unable to get to Onepoto owing to the heavy sea on the lake, and remained at Te Makarini's *pa* at Tikitiki for the night. Early next morning he crossed to Major Cumming at Onepoto, secured three days' rations, and arrived at Captain Mair's camp to find his people nearly starving. Next day the force moved across in canoes to the Whanganui-a-Parua, where ten men were left to guard the canoes, and the contingent started through the bush to the range from

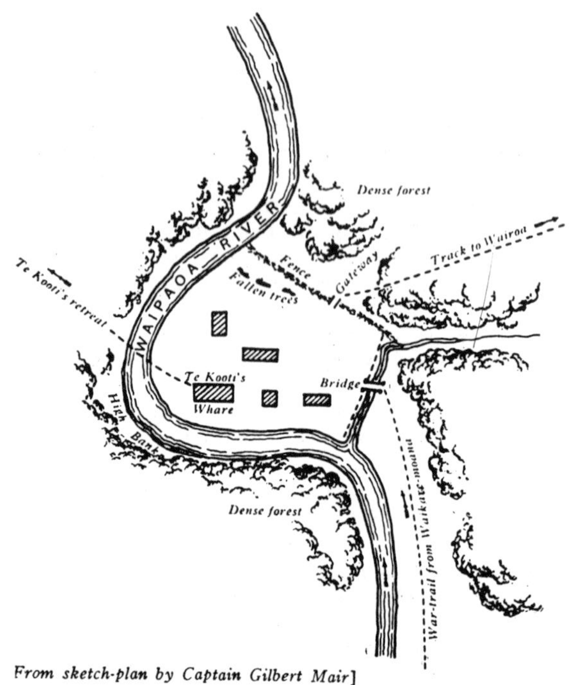

From sketch-plan by Captain Gilbert Mair]

Te Kooti's Camp on the Waipaoa River

(Scene of the engagement on 15th August, 1871)

(Note.—The small creek in front of the camp was usually crossed by a plank or log at the place marked "Bridge," but this had been drawn in by Te Kooti's men before the attack was made.)

where Waikare-iti could be descried. Sergeant Bluett was the first white man who ever set eyes on that lonely and beautiful little lake with its seven wooded islets. He climbed a tree eastward of the lake and called down to the officers that he could see it.

Thinking it likely that Te Kooti might be making toward Waikare-moana, Captain Mair returned with ten men to search the edges of the lake towards Te Onepoto, while Captain Preece went over the range and followed the trail of one man until it joined the others and at last brought him to a camp which appeared to have been deserted about four days. From there he sent word back that he was on the trail. That night the Arawa caught a dog, and then knew that they were not far from the enemy. Early next morning they started to follow the trail, and had not gone far when a volley was fired at them as they were going up a ridge. There were no casualties, as the Hauhaus fired too high. Preece's men returned the fire, but the enemy got away into the bush. The force followed for some distance, but found they had scattered, and as there was only food for one day it was deemed advisable to let the foe know that the Arawa had retired. It was evident that the rebels were making along the Matakuhia Range. Knowing the country well from former experience in fighting in the district, Captain Preece thought that if he and Mair returned to Onepoto and got fresh supplies they could make in the same direction as the enemy by keeping on the Waikare-iti side of the range, while the force would avoid ambuscades if they did not follow directly in their enemy's track. At Onepoto, to his surprise, he found Captain Mair with Sergeant Bluett and the whole of his force, and it was decided to go back over the ground with all the men. After a forced march the column came upon a camp of Te Kooti's at the base of Matakuhia Range, and there found a letter from him, which ran as follows:—

Ki nga Kawanatanga katoa.

E HOA ma, he kupu tenei naku kia koutou, me mutu te whawhai i au, notemea kei toku nohoanga ano au e noho ana, kei te puihi, engari ka puta au ki te moana, whaia. Ko tenei mahi kohuru a koutou me te kiore te kete ana ki te hamuti, me whakarere he whai na koutou i au. Tonoa mai he tangata kia haere atu au ki waho na tatou riri ai; ka pai.

He kapu ke tenei, ko taku mahara ko te maunga-rongo te oranga ko te mahi kai hoki. Kati, kei te whakarite ahau i enei mahara kia oti. E hoa ma, ko tena mahara a tatou ko te riri kaore ano i tae mai ki au, engari ka tata ahau te whakarite ia koutou mahara, engari kia tupato kei ki koutou kaore. Heoi ano.

E hoa ma, i tonoa atu e au aku tamariki ki te kawe i taku pukapuka whakahoki mo koutou, tahuri ana koutou te whawhai. Kati, kauaka hei haku ki to koutou matenga. Ko aua tamariki hoki ko Hata Tipoki ko Epiha Puairangi, ko Patoromu, ko Ruru, he tamariki ena i tohia ki te tohi o Tu, i whangaia ki te whatu-nui-a-Rua. He tamariki hoki e whakaaro nui ana ki te whenua. Heoi ano. Ki te kino koutou ki ena korero, me aha ? Mo koutou mo koutou ano ia.

Na to koutou hoa riri,

NA TE TURUKI.

[TRANSLATION]

To all Government men.

SIRS,—This is a word of mine to you. You must give up chasing me about, because I am dwelling in my own abiding-place, the bush. But if I come out to the coast, then pursue me. This murderous purpose of yours in pursuing me is like a rat roasting in dung; you must give it up. Send a man to tell me to come out to you in the open where we can fight. That would be fair.

This is another word: My thought is that in the maintenance of peace and in the cultivation of food is safety. I am trying to carry out these thoughts and to accomplish them. Sirs, that idea of yours that we should fight has not come to me yet; but I am about to adopt your idea, so beware. Do not say it will not be. That is all.

Sirs, I sent to you some of my young men to carry my letter warning you, and you attacked them. Cease then, to complain about your own killed. These young men, Hata Tipoki, Epiha Puairangi, Patoromu, and Ruru, were young men consecrated by the rites of Tu [the God of War] and fed with the bread of Rua [made of *hinau* berries]. They were young men who loved their country. That is all. If you dislike these words, what does it matter ? All the worse for you.

From your enemy,

TE TURUKI.

The force camped for the night, but, not wishing to attract the attention of the enemy, did not light fires until 9 o'clock, and then only with dry supplejack to boil tea. On the following morning Mair and Preece went forward with forty men without swags and came to an old village a few miles from Erepeti, on the Ruakituri River. They struck back into the bush where they heard a dog bark, but, not finding it, kept along the bush parallel with the track. Traces of people who had been pig-hunting were found. Te Kooti's party appeared to have broken up in small parties in their usual way, and the pursuers were at a great disadvantage in not being able to get supplies without going back for them.

On the following day Captain Preece went out with Sergeant Bluett and thirty men. They climbed the Matakuhia Range, and, after crossing several gullies, at length struck the enemy's trail, which they followed until they found his camp. It seemed to have been abandoned three days earlier. The trail appeared to go down towards Papuni, but scattered again. On a very high point on the Matakuhia Range they came to an ancient Maori *pa*, with massive earthworks and large carved posts; large beech trees were growing in and around the fortress. The men returned to camp, and the following day Captains Mair and Preece decided to go back to Onepoto for a fresh supply of rations, and to follow the course that they first thought of as the only means of overtaking the enemy—namely, to start from Whanganui-a-Parua and work across country in rear of the Matakuhia Range towards the Waipaoa River. On the 13th August they drew ten days' rations from Major Cumming at Onepoto, intending to get across the lake next day; but the sea was too high, and they were obliged to make their way round the lake through wildly broken country. They then struck through the trackless bush, guided by compass and cutting their way, till they reached a high table-land where there was no undergrowth, and travelling was easier. Heavy snow fell, and it was necessary to camp early and prepare wood for fires at night, as it was unsafe to light them in daytime. It was very difficult to get a fire in that mountain-beech country. On the following day they marched through an enormously rugged region of mountain, gorge, and forest. The men complained of cold, but were still cheerful, believing that they were making for Maunga-pohatu.

Next morning it was still snowing heavily when the force, travelling along the high ridge in a north-westerly direction, reached its highest point, and obtained a comprehensive view of the valley of the Waipaoa (a tributary of the Ruakituri). Two of the keenest men, Huta and Rokoroko, called out from a tree-top, to the great delight of the force, that they saw smoke some miles down the valley. Mair and Preece joined their scouts in the tree, and, sure enough, the faintest spiral of bluish smoke could be seen rising amidst a hundred almost similar mists. Taking careful compass bearings, they made as straight for the smoke as the very rough country would permit. The men had to cut across sharp spurs, and in two places to lower themselves down with vines.

About four hours' travelling brought the force to the proper right bank of the Waipaoa, a noisy, rocky torrent which increased in size as they followed down its course; it was, moreover, in heavy flood through the recent heavy fall of snow and rain. At last Te Kooti's well-beaten trail was struck; it led to a camp the fires of which were still alight.

Coming to a small rivulet entering from the right-hand side, Mair noticed the water was quite muddy, and asked the natives the meaning. "Wild pigs," said they, "rooting." "Pigs would never root or enter water with snow lying deep," Mair answered.

The pursuing force halted, and Captain Mair, taking Kepa te Ahuru, one of Captain Preece's best men, scouted cautiously up the little stream a short distance, guided by the murmur of a small waterfall. At a circular pool at the foot Mair caught sight of a closely-cut head of black hair bobbing up and down. The Maori (sex for the moment unknown) was kneading a kit of *pikopiko,* the young curling fronds of the fern *asplenium* (or *Aspidium Richardi*), to get rid of the hairy scales. [The *pikopiko* when prepared is a vegetable much like asparagus.]

Mair and his man, carbines in hand, got up to within a few yards unobserved, the noise of the falling water drowning any sound of their footsteps. They found it was a woman, clothed in only short shaggy flax waist and shoulder mats. Mair told her to keep quiet and not to fear. He recognized her as Mere Maihi, the wife of an officer stationed at Opotiki; she had been carried off with the Whakatohea Tribe when Te Kooti had made his raid on Opape settlement. She had afterwards been forced to take a Hauhau husband, one of Te Kooti's best fighting-men, Patara te Whata. The poor woman was overjoyed at being among friends, and answered all questions readily and intelligently. She gave Mair a clear idea of the enemy's position and strength. Te Kooti's camp, she said, was in a bend of the Waipaoa River partly fenced with palisading; this was the place from which the smoke had been seen. Te Kooti was in fear of an attack that very day and had tried to persuade his followers to move on, and upon their pleading fatigue and unwillingness to shift he warned them that the Almighty would punish them for their disobedience. She said, moreover, that a number of men were out pig-hunting and might discover the trail at any moment, in which case they could signal to Te Kooti by firing their arms, when he would break camp immediately, and, by spreading out like a fan, leave hardly a trace whereby to follow. His force numbered about forty men.

As the evening was closing in, Mair and Preece decided to surround the camp at once, if possible; so, detailing thirty men to guard the baggage, and leaving behind everything that would make a noise, such as pannikins, the attackers moved on quickly, guided by the woman. It was found impossible to cross the river, as it was in high flood, so the only course was a frontal attack. The enemy's position was almost surrounded by water and a high bank, and a strong fence made of *kaponga* (fern-tree trunks). Within were some large *whares* of *kaponga* stems. The place evidently had been used formerly as a place of refuge. A small waterfall came over a bluff at the right, forming a deep ditch or moat, about 8 feet wide. The noise of falling water enabled the attackers to approach close up to the gateway.

Captain Mair, closely followed by his faithful Arawa soldier Te Korowhiti, took a running leap and jumped the broad ditch. Immediately he landed he shot a man who was on sentry duty just inside the gateway. This Hauhau (Patara te Whata, as was afterwards discovered) turned and was in the act of putting a percussion cap, which he had taken from his vest pocket, on his Calisher and Terry carbine when Mair killed him at a few paces distance. Into the *pa* came the Arawa, with Preece at their head; a few had leaped the ditch, but most of them, finding the jump too great, had to scramble up the slippery bank. Mair rushed straight on, reloading as he ran; Preece turned to the left and saw two Maoris coming out of one of the large *whares*. One of them was Te Kooti. He was armed with a Spencer carbine, an eight-shot repeater (American make), as was afterwards learned. This he carried in his right hand; in the other he clutched his waistcoat and a cartridge-belt. He wore a shirt and blue-serge trousers. Running to the bank, he dashed into the river; he left behind his waist-coat, shawl, gold watch, and ammunition-belt. The latter, an officer's silver-mounted belt, had a pouch which contained about twenty copper cartridges.* [As it proved afterwards, the rebel leader's repeater was useless to him after this fight, since he could not procure any more cartridges for it.]

Most of the Hauhaus in the camp had bolted for the river at the first shot. Mair saw a very tall man near him running for the butt of a large fallen *rimu* tree. In another instant the Maori would have reached cover and have had his white foe in the open at fifteen paces distance. Mair took a running shot at him, aiming low. The Maori jumping over a log at the moment, the bullet hit him in the left leg and smashed the knee-cap. Mair gave him into the charge of Sergeant Huta, who took him to the large *whare,* where the few prisoners taken were placed under a guard. Meanwhile Te Kooti and his companion had jumped down the bank at a place where a mass of drift-wood made a kind of bridge across the deep and rather sluggish river. The two fugitives scrambled across on this timber and swiftly climbed the opposite bank, Te Kooti ahead and his companion pushing him up the steep declivity. Nikora te Tuhi (Captain Preece's servant) dashing to the cliff edge of the *pa,* aimed for the middle of Te Kooti's back. His bullet missed Te Kooti, but blew off the top of the head of the second man, who fell into the stream. Te Kooti gained the top of the bank, turned, and from behind a tree fired a shot, the only one in his gun, and then vanished into the forest.

The sharp encounter lasted only a few moments. Three Hauhaus were killed and several wounded. The pursuers found considerable difficulty in crossing the river, but contrived to reach the other side on a fallen tree. They could not go very far, as night was falling, and the buglers were ordered to sound the recall. Te Kooti's escape was an exceedingly narrow one. Had the attackers not been delayed a little scrambling up the bank of the small creek in the first rush they must have got him either in the river or before he reached the top of the cliff. One of the three killed was a Ngapuhi named Mehaka (or Mita) Hare, who was shot by Te Korowhiti. This rebel was a son of James Tautari, a Ngapuhi sailor and trader who owned two schooners sailing between the Bay of Islands and Auckland in the early " fifties " and " sixties," and who also cruised to Rarotonga in the " Sea Breeze." Tautari understood navigation, and was thoroughly trusted by all settlers and traders. The son had married an Opotiki woman, and it was in that way he came into contact with the Hauhaus.

Had not most of Te Kooti's men been away foraging at the

---

* Te Kooti's shoulder-belt, which probably was that formerly belonging to Captain James Wilson, who was killed in the Poverty Bay massacre, is now to be seen, with the cartridges therein, in the Museum at Palmerston North, where it was deposited by Captain Preece some years ago.

time, the attackers' success would have been greater. Four women and two children were taken prisoners. The arms captured were nine Enfield rifles, two breech-loading carbines, four revolvers, and four fowling-pieces.

The women and the wounded prisoner, who was found to be a notorious deperado named Wi Heretaunga, were lodged in one of the *whares*; a side of this house was pulled down and a large fire lighted to keep them in full view. Another fire was made by the deep pool, and after many trials the body of the third man killed was brought up out of the river. It was that of a big, highly tattooed man whom Preece at once recognized as a chief of Waikari (near Mohaka) named Paora te Wakahoehoe. He had been mailman between Wairoa and Napier, and joined the Hauhaus at Omarunui the day before the fight there in 1866. This was the man sent by Te Waru to Te Kooti in 1868 bearing a famous greenstone *mere* called "Tawatahi," and accompanied by Te Waru's daughter Te Mauniko; the understanding was that the acceptance of Te Kooti of the young woman as his wife and taking the greenstone heirloom would imply an obligation on his part to attack the Gisborne settlements and so avenge the death of the son of an important chief, Raharuhi Rukupo, who had been killed in the assault on Pa-kairomiromi, Waiapu, by Major Fraser's force in 1865. How well Te Kooti carried out his part of the compact the massacre at Matawhero shortly afterwards testified. The greenstone weapon mentioned was found in Te Kooti's hut in the *pa*.

It was a wild camp scene when darkness fell. The fires illumined the snow-covered battle-ground in the forest and the figures of the shawl-kilted Arawa moving about the thatched huts in the captured *pa*. The victors found, on searching the *whares* and examining the prisoners, that they had captured Te Kooti's headquarters camp.

After the evening meal Captain Mair was told that Wi Heretaunga was suffering greatly from his smashed knee-cap, so he got his small satchel, containing laudanum, chloral, surgical needles, and bandages, and went to the guard hut, where the prisoner sat. Wi was a fierce truculent fellow of powerful frame, over 6 feet in height, with a great bushy head of hair and a black beard. He was identified as the most ruffianly savage in Te Kooti's band; his only peer in ferocity had been the half-caste Peka Makarini, who fell to Mair's carbine the previous year in the Tumunui fight near Rotorua.

Kneeling down by Wi Heretaunga's left side, Mair opened his medicine-case, and was preparing a dose to alleviate the pain, before dressing the wound, when Sergeant Hohepa Rokoroko, who was standing by with grounded carbine, suddenly cried out,

"*Kapene, ka mate koe!*" ("Captain, you'll be killed!") and threw himself upon the Hauhau. That ungrateful miscreant, thrusting his right arm under Mair's, was in the act of drawing a long knife which he wore in a sheath under his left arm. He jerked viciously at the knife in an effort to stab Mair, but the cross-bar of the haft was caught in the sheath, made of closely woven *whitau* flax-fibre. The sergeant of the guard placed the muzzle of his carbine against Wi's head, while Mair threw himself backward out of reach. The knife was taken from Wi Heretaunga.

The Arawa soldiers were furious at this treacherous attempt and begged that Heretaunga be shot immediately. In the meantime the women prisoners had informed Captain Preece of the dangerous character of the prisoner. The two women, Mere Maihi and Maora Irirangi, described Wi Heretaunga's atrocities in the killing of the Wilsons at the Poverty Bay massacre, his deeds in the Mohaka massacre, and his recent cruel murder of his wife at Tauaki in the Urewera country. It was decided, therefore, that the prisoner should be shot, and this summary execution was carried out.

It was ascertained from the prisoners that Te Kooti had had some premonition that the Government forces were close on his trail, for he had early that morning given his followers orders to prepare to march on to the mountains. The order was not popular; the weary, war-worn people, like the Israelites, were beginning to murmur against the interminable moving-on from hiding-place to hiding-place, but they had a Moses whom to disobey was death. That morning, at Te Kooti's orders, some of the men had scattered out to *patu-kai* or "kill food"—hunting the wild pig and spearing and snaring *kaka* parrot and pigeon. They had dogs which they had cleverly trained to hunt silently and catch wild pigs without uttering a bark.

The force camped in the captured village the next day and night, as it was snowing and raining, and after two days' hard marching got out of the bush into the fern country. Their camp was made in an old potato cultivation; this helped the rations out, as the men were again getting short of food. The officers had made arrangements with Major Cumming at Waikare-moana to send a party with packhorses and supplies along the open country towards Whataroa, as they knew they should have to make for that district, and, seeing fires in that direction, a corporal and nine men were sent to meet the party and advise them of the main body's whereabouts. In the meantime, as the men had had a very hard time, Mair and Preece determined to communicate if possible with Major Ropata and Captain Porter, who were believed to be in the vicinity of Te Papuni with the Ngati-Porou contingent, and set them on Te Kooti's trail.

It was decided that Captain Preece with forty men should make a forced march up the Ruakituri River and endeavour to overtake them. He knew the country well, having been through it during the fighting in 1865 and 1868. Heavy rain prevented him getting away before the 22nd, and he was again delayed on the 24th at Erepeti by flood. The party crossed the Ruakituri by felling a tree and bridging the river at a narrow place, and had a hard march over the hills by Colonel Whitmore's track of 1868. Then, cutting a track to avoid the flooded river, they met seven sick men of Ngati-Porou, who reported that Major Ropata and Captain Porter were ahead. On the morning of the 25th August Preece reached Papuni. Leaving Sergeant Bluett in charge of half the men there, Captain Preece with twenty men pushed on and caught up to Ngati-Porou on top of a range nine miles from Papuni. Ngati-Porou had just found the trail of one man; it led into a larger track, which they were following up slowly. After reporting the Waipaoa engagement to Captain Porter, and telling him that he thought Te Kooti was making for Maunga-pohatu, Preece returned to Papuni that night, covering six Ngati-Porou camps in one day. The information he gave Porter enabled that officer, with Lieutenant Large, to follow up Te Kooti and defeat him at Te Hapua soon afterwards.

On the 27th August Captains Mair and Preece marched for the Wairoa, taking the arms they had captured from the enemy, also the native women and children, and by evening reached Omaruhakeke (the place where Captain Hussey was killed on Christmas Day, 1865). On the 28th they marched into Wairoa, after having been constantly on the move from the 17th July, carrying their supplies on their backs. The force remained at Wairoa waiting for a steamer, the weather being very bad, until the 2nd September, when instructions were received to march for Whangawehi, at the Mahia, and ship in the Government steamer "Luna" for Whakatane. Captains Mair and Preece reached their respective camps at Te Teko and Kaiteriria on the 8th and 9th September. They had travelled some of the wildest country in the Island, amid snow and flooded rivers, and often suffering severely from want of food. But their exertions had a most beneficial and far-reaching effect, for they showed the disaffected natives that their rugged and almost inaccessible country would no longer, even in winter, prove a safe refuge. The Government force's greatest difficulty was the obsolete weapon with which they were armed, a heavy muzzle-loading rifle, whereas the enemy had many breech-loaders—carbines captured at the Chatham Islands or in the field.

When the contingent was at the Wairoa the local natives, hearing that the captured greenstone *mere* "Tawatahi" was in their possession, offered Mair and Preece £100 for it; but the officers decided to present it to Mr. J. D. Ormond, then administering the Government in Hawke's Bay, as an acknowledgment of his solicitude on their behalf while in the field. Indeed, but for Mr. Ormond's good offices the expedition would have fared badly more than once for want of supplies.

ANOTHER ARAWA EXPEDITION

On the 22nd September, 1871, Captains Mair and Preece started from Fort Galatea on another Urewera expedition, taking the trail up the Horomanga Gorge. Their way lay over rough country to Omaruteangi, on the Whakatane River, one of Kereru te Pukenui's settlements. There they were met by Paerau te Rangi-kaitipuake, Te Whenuanui, and other Urewera chiefs, but not by Kereru, who continued hostile. On the 26th they received a letter from Te Purewa, the old chief at Maungapohatu, saying that he had found Te Kooti's trail and was following it. They reached their former camping-ground at Te Kakari next day, and were well received by the Urewera Maoris, who reported that some of Te Kooti's men who had left him had procured guns and rejoined him. The contingent then started for Neketuri to hunt up Kereopa, who was reported to be there, and to endeavour to pick up Te Kooti's trail. Sergeant Huta and ten men went in another direction; but Te Kooti had had four weeks' start, and the heavy rain had obliterated his tracks. For several days the men were divided into small parties under Captain Mair, Captain Preece, Sergeant Bluett, and Sergeant Huta, each going in a different direction through the bush from the *pa* at Te Kakari. On the 30th September Mair sent word that he had found a trail leading towards Ruatahuna or Waikare-moana, and Sergeant Bluett came in with his party and reported that Hemi Kakitu and twenty men of Tamaikowha's tribe had joined in the pursuit of their own accord. The commanders now spread their men out in three parties to follow up the trail, Captain Mair moving by Tatahoata with the main body. One day two camps were passed. Te Kooti had about twenty followers, and was avoiding the settlements of the Urewera, keeping well away from the tracks.

When Preece's force reached Tatahoata it was learned that a trail had been found at Paterangi, inland of Ahi-kereru, and that Captain Mair had started by the ordinary track with thirty men and intended to sleep at Tarapounamu. Within an hour Preece's party was off once more, and reached the Tahuaroa Range that night. On the following morning Preece made an excellent march over the ranges to the foot of Pukiore, where he found that, though Mair had not passed, Paerau te Rangi-kaitipuake with ten men had gone by. The river being low, it was decided to go along the bed of the Okahu Stream. Captain Mair caught his comrade up about a mile and a half from Ahi-kereru, and the the force arrived there at 11 a.m. Paerau and his Maoris there reported that the enemy's trail had been seen on the 30th on the Okahu Stream beyond Paterangi, evidently several days old. Sending the sick to Fort Galatea under Sergeant Matutaera, the column at once marched for Whataroa. It was apparent that Te Kooti was making for the Kaingaroa and Waikato.

Heavy rain set in, and the force had trouble in crossing the Whirinaki River. Captain Mair went with his company by way of Te Tapiri, and Captain Preece struck through the bush by an old track. At Ohihape he found a trail, but it was old. After following it for some time one of his men caught sight of a Maori, but his tracks were lost, though a place was found where Te Kooti had camped about six days before. The man seen was evidently in search of Te Kooti and had camped there the previous night. Captain Mair now joined Preece. He went off again with thirty-five men, and Sergeant Bluett with ten; Captain Preece started with the column for Te Arawhata to communicate with Captain Morrison at Opepe and get fresh supplies of food, and went on to Ngahuinga. Next day Captain Mair had a brush with Te Kooti in the bush. There were no casualties on either side, but the pursuers now knew at least that the foe had not escaped to Waikato.

The weather continued very bad for several days, and the men had so little food that they could not move from the Rangitaiki. Starting again for the bush on the 10th October in very cold weather with snow and hail, they soon found a trail of Te Kooti's people in small parties of twos and threes. It was followed until the Arawa lost it in the open ground. Tamaikowha with twenty Urewera now joined the force. His men reported that they had seen signs of the enemy in a creek in the bush and had followed them until night. Rakuraku, another of the Urewera chiefs, went to Ruatahuna to cut in ahead of Te Kooti in case he should double back that way. Next day the column followed the trail through the dense bush along the ranges beyond Ahi-kereru. In the afternoon they came to Te Kooti's abandoned camp, where they slept. It was believed that he would be at Weraiti by that time. As food ran short Captains Mair and Preece decided to return, leaving Tamaikowha to follow up the trail, and took their men out into the open country to wait supplies from Opepe.

On the 17th October news was received that Hemi Kakitu (an ex-Hauhau) had attacked Te Kooti on the upper part of

Drawing by the author, at Waimana, 1921]

Netana Whakaari

This veteran warrior of the Urewera and Ngai-Tama Tribes (over eighty years of age when this sketch was made) is one of the very few tattooed men of the Maori race now living, and is a good type of the old Hauhau scouts and bush fighters. Netana is the younger brother of the late chief Rakuraku, of Waimana and Ohiwa. He was often on the war-path during the Bay of Plenty and Urewera campaigns from 1864 to 1871. In 1864 he fought against the Arawa natives at Maketu and Kaokaoroa, and in 1865 he took part in the fighting against the Government forces at Opotiki, where he was slightly wounded. He shared in numerous forays in the Opotiki, Waimana and Whakatane districts with his relative Tamaikowha and the Ngai-Tama. In 1870 he turned to the Government side when peace was arranged with Tamaikowha by Major Kepa (Taitoko) at Tauwhare-Manuka, and in 1871 he assisted in bringing in the Urewera people for the final peace-making.

the Okahu Stream, in rear of Ahi-kereru, wounding one man and capturing one rifle, besides taking a woman prisoner. The spot was a short distance from the track to Ruatahuna, and not far above the junction of the Manawahiwi Stream with the Okahu. Captain Preece went to Ahi-kereru with forty-three men and interviewed the captive woman Huhana (Susan). She said that Te Kooti was trying to get to Waikato, but that some of his men were not willing to venture the journey.

Scouting-parties were sent out right and left. Sergeant Huta, finding traces of three men, for several days scoured the bush at the back of Ahi-kereru and towards the head of the Okahu Stream, but came on no more signs of the rebels. On the 24th October some of the scouts returned and reported a trail up the Okahu Valley leading towards Te Weraiti. It was followed for three days beyond Weraiti, in rear of Ruatahuna. The force met the Ngai-Tama warrior Netana Whakaari, Rakuraku's brother, who said that his party had surprised three men; they had, however, escaped down the creek, leaving cooked food behind them. At Ruatahuna one of Te Kooti's men had surrendered to the chiefs. He was a young Urewera chief from Maunga-pohatu, named Te Whiu Maraki. The Urewera were not inclined to hand him over, and as they had given help in the chase and promised to be answerable for his future behaviour Captain Preece allowed him to remain with them. It was this Te Whiu who shortly afterwards was chiefly instrumental in the capture of Kereopa.

Heavy rain set in and lasted several days, and the column was obliged to make for Ahi-kereru once more. Mair returned to his camp at Kaiteriria with his men. Preece, starting again from the head of the Whirinaki Valley, crossed the ranges at the head of the Ngamate and Okahu Streams, and the dividing range above the source of the Waiau River. The heavy rains, the flooded streams, and the shortness of food made it risky for the men to remain in the bush, so Preece marched back to Ahi-kereru, and on the 4th November went out to the plains and returned to Te Teko, leaving some men at Fort Galatea. On the 22nd November news reached him that Major Ropata and Captain Porter had been to Ruatahuna and had captured Kereopa, who was being sent out to Wairoa, Hawke's Bay.

Chapter 41

PORTER DEFEATS TE KOOTI

A YOUNG MAORI in shirt and waist-shawl, with a tomahawk stuck in his flax girdle, was perched like a monkey in the branches of a *tawai* tree, 50 feet above the ground, far up the slopes of the lofty wooded mountain-range called Tikitiki-o-Rotari, in the heart of the Urewera Country. He made an eye-survey of the wild country around, then quickly parted the branches immediately above him and shouted,—

"Smoke—I can see smoke over there, lying on the tree-tops."

" Where is it ? " came a voice, in Maori, from the shadowy ground below.

" There, over to the west—not far—perhaps three miles, perhaps four."

" Come down quickly and point me out the direction of the smoke."

The Maori scout descended, dropping from bough to bough with the agility of a wild cat. Reaching the mossy ground he picked up his carbine, and stood before his captain, surrounded by an eager company of Maoris, armed like himself with carbine and tomahawk, and bearing heavy *pikau,* or swags. The tall, bearded leader, Captain Porter, and his companion, Lieutenant J. T. Large, were the only two Europeans in the band. Both, like the Maoris, wore coloured shawls strapped round their waists; their blue uniform jackets were torn and frayed by weeks of bush exploring; there was little to distinguish them from their comrades but their silver-braided forage-caps and the revolvers which they carried besides their short carbines.

The tree-climber pointed to the west, indicating the spot where he had seen the smoke, and Captain Porter took a bearing by prismatic compass. The place was on a spur of the Maunga-pohatu Ranges. The order to march was given, and in a few moments the column of a hundred Ngati-Porou friendlies was moving smartly along the wooded mountain-side, animated by the prospect of a speedy fight.

It was nearly three weeks since Porter's column had marched

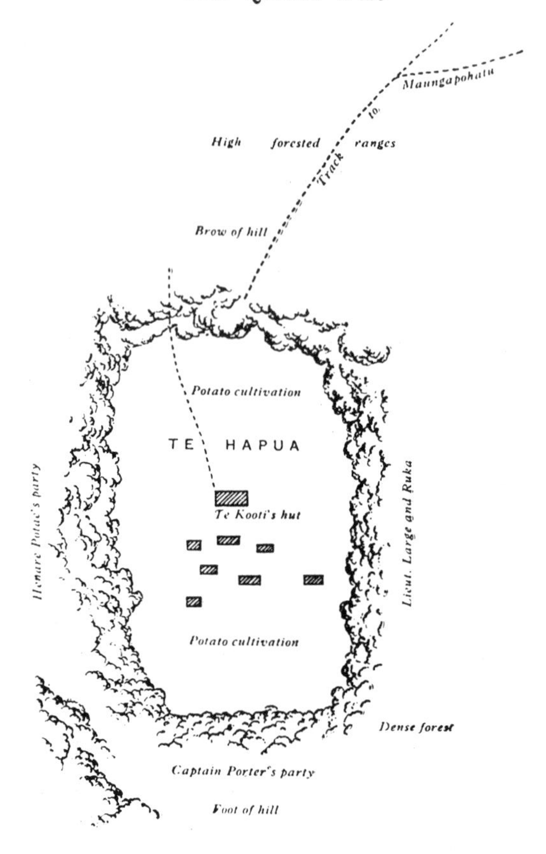

Scene of the Defeat of Te Kooti at Te Hapua, Urewera Country
(1st September, 1871.)

(See Major Large's explanatory notes in this chapter.)

from the Wairoa, Hawke's Bay, in renewed search of Te Kooti, who with the remnant of his band was supposed to be somewhere in the neighbourhood of Maunga-pohatu, the "Rocky Mountain," the natural citadel of the Urewera Country, the refuge-place of Hauhau war parties after every raid and every fight. The pursuers—the fourth expedition of Ngati-Porou—worked up into the higher ranges, crossing and recrossing cold, swift torrents innumerable times, and scaling with infinite labour, swag-laden as they were, the steep ridges and rocky cliffs that continually confronted them. The best trackers were with Porter in the advance-guard, following up a trail after Captain Preece had overtaken their force in the mountains and reported the Waipaoa engagement and the flight of Te Kooti.

Now there was no doubt that the smoke reported by the scout was from Te Kooti's camp. It was wintry weather—the last day of August, 1871—and the fugitive Hauhaus must have suffered, like their pursuers, from the cold and the wet in those stormy ranges, and would be reluctant to leave a comfortable camp.

Travelling quickly through the bush until he considered he must be close up to the smoke-betrayed camp, Porter ordered a halt, and sent two men forward to scout and discover what they could of the position of the Hauhaus and their probable strength. In a very short time the young warriors returned and reported that it was indeed Te Kooti; he was encamped in a small clearing in the bush on the face of the range. There was a large hut of *totara* bark in the middle of the clearing—an old Urewera potato plantation—and this they believed, from what they could see, was occupied by Te Kooti. There were a number of smaller temporary *wharau,* or lean-to's of saplings and bark, scattered about the clearing; on the edges of the cleared ground were masses of fallen timber.

Porter determined to surround the camp and attack at daylight next morning. It was now dusk, and it would be useless assaulting the place in the night-time.

It was a long, cold night, and the half-stripped Ngati-Porou, crouching in the bush, shivered and crept close to each other for warmth, and thought regretfully of the warm clothing they had left in their camp half a mile in the rear. At last the foggy day began to break. With the first faint glimmer of light Porter sent his men out, extending either wing so as to surround the camp. Henare Potae and his tribe were on the left, while Ruka Aratapu—a noted *toa* of Ngati-Porou—and Lieutenant Large were to surround the other side and upper end of the cultivations so as to prevent Te Kooti from escaping. It was difficult work, for the ground was rough and the fallen trunks and branches formed an almost impassable *chevaux-de-frise.* The greatest caution was observed, for the crackling of a branch would be enough to arouse the light-sleeping Hauhaus. Dim figures crept through the bush, and the white commander and his own men lay, tensely waiting, behind some logs at the lower end of the clearing, commanding the bark hut in which Te Kooti was believed to be, with his bodyguard of Maori wives.

Suddenly the bark of a dog was heard, and Porter feared that he was discovered. A voice—it was Te Kooti's—was heard from the central *whare.* "What's that dog barking at?" he asked.

"*Aua!*" ("I don't know") replied a woman, who emerged from the *whare* to gather firewood. "There is no one about."

"Light the fires," called Te Kooti; "we must move on quickly."

At this order the women in the camp began to get the fires ready for the morning meal. Although Porter did not know it at the moment, the party in ambush had already been discovered by one of Te Kooti's Hauhaus. This man had gone out from the camp at the first streak of dawn to examine the *tawhiti-kiore,* or rat-traps made of supplejack, set along a run for the now-extinct native rat—an article of Maori diet—which led up towards the hills. This alert fellow detected figures moving in the bush, and realized instantly that a Government force was stealthily surrounding the place. To have uttered a sound then would have been fatal; so he turned and made his way silently towards the camp to give the alarm to his chief, when the silence of the bush was suddenly shattered by a gunshot. One of the force had fired without orders; the culprit's identity was never definitely established, but it was strongly suspected that a man who was related to Te Kooti was guilty of thus treacherously warning the camp. The cordon of Porter's men was not quite complete, and that premature shot saved Te Kooti's life.

Then what a hubbub there was of yelling Hauhaus and screaming women and cracking carbines! Shaggy-haired fellows, some stark naked, some with scarcely any clothing but rough flax shoulder-mats, raced for the bush; others returned the fire of Porter and his men as they came charging into the camp. Ngati-Porou charged from the front and the two flanks, firing as they ran, and, indeed, their firing was so indiscriminate that there was a danger of their own party suffering by the cross-fire. Ruka and Large rushed on and outran all the rest of their party in the pursuit, but in vain, for Te Kooti escaped.

That wily warrior had snatched up his carbine at the first shot. Divining on the instant that the front of his hut would be covered by his enemy, he broke out through the bark covering at the back near the edge of a steep bank. Leaping behind a tree, he shouted to his followers that it was Ngati-Porou who were up on them. "Save yourselves!" he cried. The next moment, with bullets whistling about him, he jumped down the bank and disappeared in the forest like a flash, with several of his bodyguard following him. Meanwhile the Hauhaus went down before carbine and tomahawk in the smoky clearing. Ten were killed and a number were taken prisoners; amongst the captives was one of Te Kooti's wives. This woman was Oriwia (Olivia); she had shared many of Te Kooti's bush adventures. Before the fight began Porter had observed her, wearing only a waist-shawl, come out of the large *whare;* his guide, Hori Niania, a recently captured Hauhau, told him it was Oriwia.

There were hand-to-hand combats with gun-butt and tomahawk, and Ngati-Porou came out victors in each. Among the men captured in the chase was a ruffian whose face was as savage and ugly as his character—one Wi Wehi-kore, of which the English is "Fearless William." He had amongst other deeds murdered his own wife and children, because, as he explained, they were an encumbrance to him in the bush. "Shoot him!" was the order, and a Ngati-Porou bullet gave him the despatch he deserved.

The scene of Porter's engagement was Te Hapua, also called Ruahapu; the date was the 1st September 1871. Porter and his hundred of Ngati-Porou, burying the dead, and gathering their prisoners together, resumed their march, and that night camped in the deserted clearing, Opokere, on the wooded range above, only half satisfied with their morning's work, good as it had been. It was very bleak weather and heavy snow began to fall. Next morning it was impossible to move on, and the force was snowed in at the Opokere camp for some days. Porter told Large and Ruka that he would mention them in despatches for the active part they had taken in the attack and pursuit of the fugitives.

Among the Urewera Hauhaus in this fight was Eria Raukura, of Ngatapa, now the chief priest of the Ringa-tu or Wairua-Tapu Church, founded upon the ritual originally laid down by Te Kooti. Eria, describing the skirmish, says that he carried a rifle, but the attack was so sudden that the Maoris had little opportunity of making resistance. He escaped into the forest, where the fugitives were broken up into small parties. Te Kooti, with only his wife Heni and five men, fled through the bush towards Ruatahuna, and later reached Ahi-kereru; thence he made for the refuge of the unpeopled bush on the Waiau, west of Waikare-moana. When at last, in 1872, he escaped to the King Country, Eria joined him at Tokangamutu, close to the present town of Te Kuiti; there in the waters of the Manga-okewa Stream Te Kooti in 1881 ordained him after his own fashion, with baptismal ceremony, as high priest of the Ringa-tu religion.

NOTES

Major J. T. Large supplied the following notes explanatory of the sketch-map of the fight at Te Hapua camp (1st September, 1871):—

"Te Hapua was a bush clearing, containing *whares* and potato plantations, on the side of a forest-clad range; higher up was Opokere, on a branch range of Maunga-pohatu. The trees around the edge of the clearing had been felled with their heads outwards, forming a kind of *cheval-de-frise* very difficult to penetrate.

"Foot of plan: Captain Porter and his men were on this side, at the bottom of the clearing, where a track led to the camp. It was said that it was one of the ex-Hauhaus who accompanied the party that fired the treacherous shot which alarmed the camp and gave Te Kooti the opportunity of escaping; at any rate the shot came from the lower end shown on plan.

"The right side was the position assigned by Captain Porter to Ruka Aratapu and myself, and the figure marks the point which we had reached when the treacherous shot was fired that alarmed the camp. Ruka and I, with some of our party, raced up the hill through the tangled and matted vegetation as fast as we could to intercept Te Kooti, all the time exposed to the shots of Henare Potae's men and the left of Porter's party, but though the two of us outran our men we never caught sight of the outlaw, who slipped over the brow of the hill and escaped, his followers—or those of them who were not knocked over—scattering in all directions. Several Hauhaus dashed through on the right. One fired at me at a very short distance, but missed; he was out of sight in a flash before I could reload and fire.

"The left flank was the position assigned to Henare Potae and his party. Captain Porter did not have much faith in these men. They reported soon after they started to take up their position that a cliff obstructed them from advancing farther in that direction.

"From the upper end of the clearing a track led to Opokere, a branch range of Maunga-pohatu.

"It had been arranged that when Ruka and I got to the top of the clearing Ruka was to call out to the Hauhaus to surrender, as they were surrounded. But the premature shot spoiled all our plans, and our arduous pursuit and hardships and the careful scheme to surround the position were all in vain. It was a bitter disappointment."

MAJOR ROPATA'S OPERATIONS

Major Ropata in the meantime had travelled west and north from the Wairoa, working up into the almost unknown Waiau country, an unpeopled region of ranges, gorges, and forests to the west of Waikare-moana. Reaching the lake he visited some settlements, captured a few Hauhaus, and crossed by canoe to Onepoto, where the Armed Constabulary redoubt stood. Marching from there to Orewha and Pounui he was compelled to halt through sickness, and remained ill in his camp in the forest during September. His men became anxious to return to Gisborne, and made an *amo* (litter) for the purpose of carrying their sick chief out. He refused to be moved or to abandon his mission, and sent a hundred men out for supplies of food. By the time they returned Ropata was better, and at the end of the first week in October he was able to resume his march. He decided to go to Maunga-pohatu and join Captain Porter, who he knew would be anxiously waiting him in that district. Following Porter's route he reached the Tauaki *pa*, where he inquired of the Urewera the whereabouts of the other contingent. He was informed that Porter had been out to Opotiki (for supplies) since the fight at Te Hapua, and was now at Maunga-pohatu.

Ropata then marched off on Porter's trail, and, finding he had just left for Ruatahuna, fired volleys. These were heard and replied to by Porter's contingent, who turned about and met Ropata. The two commanders narrated the incidents of their respective marches, and completed arrangements for ensuring the good behaviour of the Urewera, who were now wearying of the association with Te Kooti and Kereopa, and expressing their willingness to capture the outlaws. At Maunga-pohatu Ropata drew out the lines of a *pa,* and earthwork redoubt with strong stockade, which the combined columns speedily built. The purpose of this *pa* was to guard the district and enable a watchful eye to be kept on the actions of any Hauhaus in the neighbourhood. It was garrisoned by a strong detachment of Porter's Ngati-Porou. The fort was named Kohi-tau ("Gather the years"), an allusion to the length of time the contingents had been in search of Kereopa and Te Kooti. The main body then marched to Ruatahuna, where Ropata met Tamaikowha. Most of the Urewera in that district had taken alarm at his approach and scattered into the forest, fearing an attack. Ropata sent out reassuring messages. To Tamaikowha, who inquired his intentions regarding the Urewera, he explained that he only wished to find the two chief rebels and murderers, and he requested the fugitive tribespeople to return to their villages. In family groups and *hapus* they gradually came in until about four hundred were assembled at the principal Ruatahuna settlement. After war-dances (*peruperu*) and ceremonial speeches on each side, Ngati-Porou and the Urewera established friendly relations, which were never broken. All the chiefs of the Urewera or Tuhoe were now at Ruatahuna; the principal men were Paerau, Te Whenuanui, Te Haunui, Tutakangahau, Te Purewa, Hataraka, and Te Puehu. The last-named man, hitherto a bitter foe to the *pakeha*, announced that

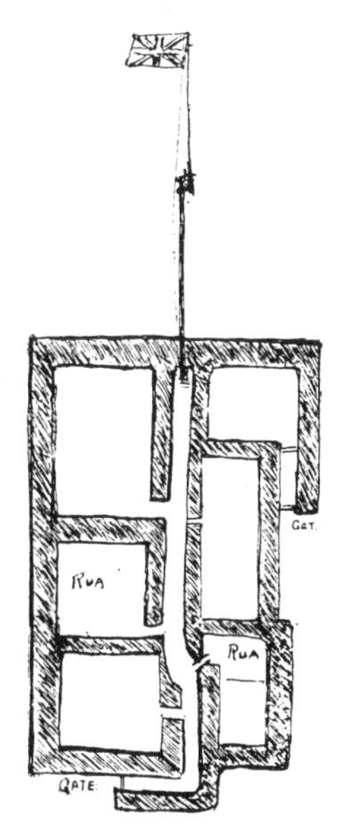

Kohitau Redoubt,
Maunga-pohatu*

* This sketch-plan of the *pa* built by Major Ropata at Maunga-pohatu, Urewera Country, in 1871, is from a pencil drawing made at the time by a Maori of the Ngati-Porou contingent.

he would have nothing more to do with Te Kooti or Kereopa or other evil men. Ropata constructed a redoubt here similar to that at Maunga-pohatu; the site was on the right bank of the Manga-o-rongo Stream, a little below the Orangikawa *pa* at Tatahoata (captured in 1869). The *pa* was given the name Kohi-marama (" Gather the months "), carrying a reference similar to that bestowed upon the fortification at Maunga-pohatu.

THE CAPTURE OF KEREOPA

The Urewera, seeing that Ngati-Porou were determined to remain in the mountains until their mission was accomplished, now made efforts to catch the two outlaws. A small party under Hemi Kakitu went out in search of Te Kooti, and Ropata was informed that Kereopa was at or near Tuapuku, on the Upper Whakatane. Ropata sent out requesting the Government's instructions in case he encountered Te Kooti or Kereopa the Eye-eater in hiding. The reply received, after a long wait was " Capture them."

Ropata now set himself the task of catching Kereopa, keeping his arrangements secret from the Urewera lest some warning should reach the wanted man. Three detachments were quietly despatched down the valley under cover of night in the direction of Ohaua-te-rangi, a large settlement of the Ngati-Rongokarae clan, on the Whakatane, about seven miles below Mataatua *kainga.* Te Whiu Maraki, the young chief of the Ngai-Tama and Urewera who had lately surrendered and espoused the Government cause, offered to guide Ngati-Porou to Kereopa's haunts. The outlaw was believed to be at Te Roau, a small bush village in the vicinity of Ohaua-te-rangi. Te Whiu, who had been the most active of Urewera *toas* against the Europeans and was anxious to atone for his recent rebellion (" *kia murua te hara,*" as Ropata phrased it), accompanied one of the detachments, or *kokiri.* One of these *kokiri,* consisting of thirty men led by Matiu Kahawai, followed the bed of the Whakatane River. The second *kokiri,* twenty men, went down the track on the east or right bank of the river; and the third, twenty men commanded by Erueti Rena, marched down the west bank, a difficult traverse because of the steep and broken character of the country immediately above the Whakatane on that side. Ropata, who remained with the main body at the camp close to Tatahoata, gave instructions that if either of the *kokiri* succeeded in capturing Kereopa two volleys should be fired as a signal to the others. Te Whiu, marching with the centre detachment down the river-bed, led the *kokiri* to one of the small *kaingas,* called Te Roau. The village was

J. C., photo at Ruatoki, January, 1921]

Te Whiu Maraki

Te Whiu Maraki, a very active Urewera scout and warrior of Te Kooti's days, fought against the Government, 1866–70. In 1871 he surrendered to the expeditionary forces in the Urewera Country, and guided the Ngati-Porou party which captured Kereopa at Te Roau, on the Upper Whakatane, near Ruatahuna. He pursued and caught Kereopa when the old rebel attempted to escape. Te Whiu died in 1922.

quietly surrounded in the early morning, and Te Whiu was sent up to the *whares*. As he reached the village he announced loudly the arrival of the Ngati-Porou. Kereopa was in one of the huts, and hearing Te Whiu's shout he rushed to the front of the *whare*.

He ran out in an attempt to escape, but the war-party had encircled the huts, and Te Whiu, who was reputedly the fastest runner in his tribe, seized him and brought him down before he could use his weapons. Kereopa was armed with a loaded gun and a *kope* or horse-pistol.

When Kereopa was secured two thundering volleys went up from the guns of the *kokiri* in announcement of the capture of the desperado who for six years had evaded all the efforts of the Government to bring him to justice. The united force of seventy returned in triumph to Tatahoata, where the rejoicing Ngati-Porou fell in for a great war-dance in celebration of their success. The tattooed, grey-bearded ruffian crouched dejectedly on the ground under guard, while the warriors threw themselves into the frantic action of the *peruperu*.

Kereopa was guarded closely in the Kohi-marama Redoubt while arrangements were made to take him out to the coast. Meanwhile the chief Kereru came in with sixty of his tribe and had a friendly meeting with Ngati-Porou. Captain Porter and seventy men set out for Waikare-moana across the ranges, taking the prisoner for surrender to the civil power. Kereopa informed his captors that he knew when he stood in the pulpit in Mr Volkner's church and swallowed the missionary's eyes that he would meet with misfortune, because one of them stuck in his throat; it was a *tohu aitua,* an evil omen. Major Large, who was with the escort, said: "Every time we rested on the way to Wairoa Kereopa would exclaim, '*Kaore oku hara, kore rawa, kore rawa*' (Emphatically, 'I have not sinned'), meaning that what he had done was in accordance with the Maori custom in war-time." Arriving at Mahunga-rerewai, on the northern shore of Waikare-moana, Porter and his party took canoe across the lake to Onepoto, whence they marched to Wairoa. From there twenty men escorted the prisoner by steamer to Napier, where Porter had the relief and satisfaction of handing him over to the police. The reward of £1,000 offered by the Government for Kereopa's arrest was paid over to Porter, who returned to the Urewera Country, and the money was distributed among Ngati-Porou at Kohimarama Redoubt. The officer's share was £25 each, and the rest of the force concerned in the capture received £10 per man. As for Kereopa the Eye-eater, he was tried for his crimes—after an unsuccessful attempt at suicide with a razor—and was convicted and hanged.

Kereopa te Rau
(Called Kai-whatu, or "Eye-eater.")

Ropata now had all the Urewera assembled at Ruatahuna, and addressed them in a final speech of advice and warning. "Farewell, the Urewera," he said. "The Government has made peace with you, and has required you to withdraw your thoughts and sympathies from the deeds of the Hauhaus; that work must cease entirely. You must refrain from strife and cease to follow the makers of trouble. You must dwell quietly in your country and follow only the paths of peace."

At the close of the speech the British flag hoisted at the redoubt was given over to Kereru te Pukenui in token of the establishment of peace and loyalty among the Urewera. The garrison at the Maunga-pohatu fort having been withdrawn, Ropata and Captain Porter and all their Ngati-Porou marched out to the coast by way of the Whakatane Valley, and were returned to the East Coast by steamer in December of 1871.

Chapter 42

THE LAST UREWERA EXPEDITIONS

AS THE SUMMER drew on the conditions of bush travel improved, and in December, 1871, the search for Te Kooti was renewed from the western side of the Urewera Mountains. On the 7th of that month Captain Preece sent Sergeant Raimona out with a small party from the Rangitaiki to scout the last track followed, with instructions to go farther on towards the head of the Okahu, in the ranges, and then turn down-stream. Instead of adhering to these instructions the scouts crossed the range into the Waiau Valley, where they lost themselves. Then, going down the Waiau for four days, they came out at the western end of Lake Waikare-moana, and managed to communicate with Captain G. McDonnell at Onepoto. There they were supplied with rations, and got back to camp on the 15th, just as Captain Preece was starting with a party to search for them. They had followed the tracks of two men and a woman in the Waiau, and this gave a clue to the whereabouts of Te Kooti.

A month passed quietly by, and on the 18th January, 1872, Captains Mair and Preece made an expedition up the Horomanga Gorge, following a rumour that Te Kooti was in the vicinity of Tutaepukepuke. They captured two men, who denied that he had been in the locality. However, they detained them and surrounded the settlement at daylight next morning. The people were very indignant at being made prisoners, and stoutly denied all knowledge of Te Kooti; and after they had prepared plenty of food for the force, and invited Mair and Preece to remain a month and search the country, they convinced the officers of their good faith. The column scoured the whole country for days without result. On returning to the plains news arrived that Te Kooti had burnt Mr. Dolbel's wool-shed at Maunga-haruru, inland of Mohaka.

On the 31st January, 1872, Captain Preece with Sergeant Bluett and forty men left Ahi-kereru, travelling by the trail used in the previous October, then through rough rocky country, cautiously following the bed of the Upper Waiau River. On

Photo in 1874]

The Armed Constabulary Redoubt at Onepoto, Waikare-moana

the following day, going down the rapid river, they discovered a hot spring just above the junction of a creek with the main stream, and then several other boiling springs, a hot creek, and one place where hot water burst up in the middle of the river. The Waiau proper comes in on the left, rising near the headwaters of the Whakatane behind Ruatahuna. Old Hapurona Kohi, who accompanied the force on this expedition, informed Captain Preece that the boiling springs were well known to the old natives, and also that the range between the two branches of the Waiau had in old times been a well-known hunting-ground for the *kakapo* (night-parrot or ground-parrot) and the *kiore maori* (the indigenous rat), considered by the natives a great delicacy.

After visiting the deserted camp which Sergeant Raimona had found, the searchers on the following day found the tracks of a man and a dog, and then came on a plantation of potatoes. For two days the tracks were followed, and a new camp only two days old was discovered, but the clues then were lost. Striking Sergeant Raimona's trail, Preece and his men now

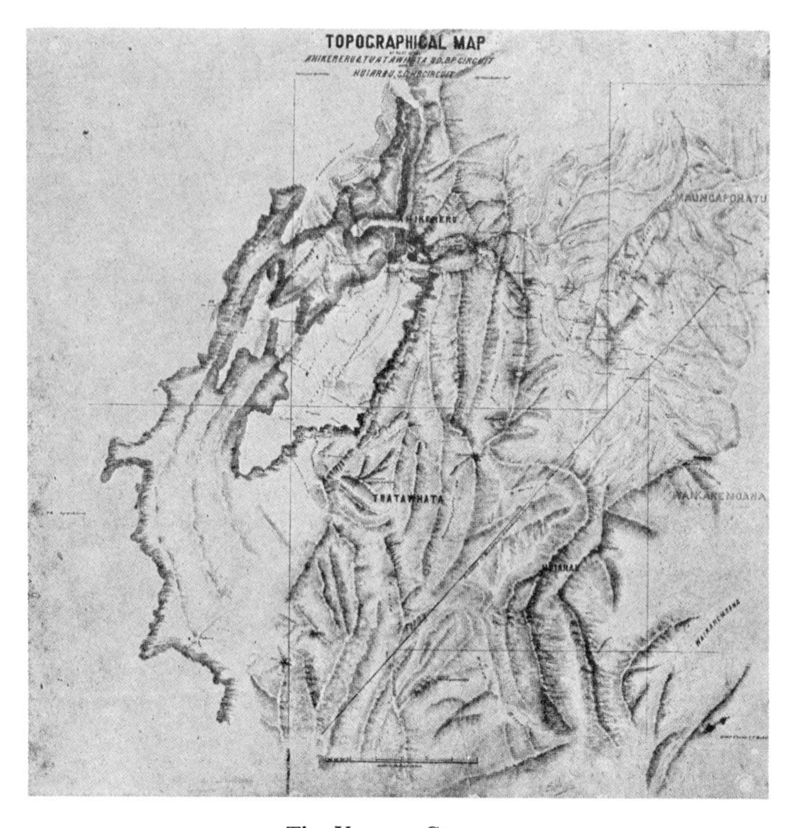

The Urewera Country

This topographical map of the central, southern, and western parts of the Urewera Country, reduced from a large-scale map, is given to show the extremely broken contour of the region which the Government native columns scoured during 1870–72. The map was the first one made of the Urewera district by the New Zealand Survey Department; it was drawn by Mr. M. Crompton Smith (now Chief Draughtsman, Survey Department), who was cadet and topographer with Mr. J. Baber in 1883. The party carried out the pioneer survey of the Urewera in that year in the face of considerable opposition by the Maoris.

made for the Marau Inlet, at the end of Wairau-moana, the western arm of Lake Waikare-moana, and found traces of natives there. On arrival at the Marau shore they lighted a fire, the first they had had in daylight for six days, and followed the Maori tracks to a canoe. Taniora, an Urewera, and his wife, seeing the smoke of the fire, came across the bay and told Preece that the last tracks found had been made by their people; those seen in the Waiau were not theirs. On learning this Preece sent a message by canoe to Captain Ferris, at Onepoto, and arranged with him to take his men along the other side of the lake and work in concert with the Arawa column. Raharuhi, an old native acquainted with the country, agreed to accompany the Arawa. On the 10th Ferris and Preece joined hands, but neither of them had any success to report; the rain had obliterated all tracks. For one day Captain Ferris remained co-operating with Captain Preece and scouting the country. He then left for Ngaputahi, while Preece worked towards Te Putere, south of Waikare-moana. Heavy rain set in, and that day (12th February) he was compelled to allow the men to light fires to warm themselves.

THE LAST SKIRMISH

On the morning of the 13th February Captain Preece sent out parties scouting right and left. One of them returned with news that they had found a trail and a camp seven days old. The heavy and long-continued rains had made the Waiau too high to cross, but Preece marched early the following day and passed three more camps. He then sent Sergeant Bluett along the Mangaone Stream (a tributary of the Waiau), and Sergeant Huta up a small creek where a camp was found with the fires still quite warm. The occupants had only recently left the place, so Huta was despatched to cut them off and Bluett was recalled.

The Maori trail was now followed by a party of about twenty men under Captain Preece for seven miles to the mouth of the Mangaone; the main body was left to come up with the swags. Preece and Bluett and their chase-party, marching very rapidly, at last caught up with the fugitives for whom they had been searching so long. From the top of the high, wooded bank of the Mangaone they caught sight of about twenty Hauhaus scrambling up the steep cliff on the opposite side of the gorge. One of them was Te Kooti. Captain Preece shouted to them calling on them to surrender, but they continued their hurried retreat. The order was given to attack, and sighting for 400 yards the party opened fire, to which the Hauhaus replied with a few shots. About a hundred rounds were fired at the Hauhaus, but to Preece's great annoyance the Terry carbine ammunition was very defective, having been damaged by the heavy rain, and many cartridges were useless. "I got my cartridge jammed," Captain Preece wrote in his diary, "and had to take it out. I could hear curses on each side of me for the same cause." The fugitives safely climbed the cliff and disappeared in the bush.

In the meantime Sergeant Huta and some men had got down through the bush and were climbing the cliff on the other side. After the fruitless firing Preece followed him with the rest of the party. Climbing the cliff they followed the fugitives at their utmost speed, and had a running skirmish for about two miles across wooded ridges, but with no result, and Preece and his score of men had to abandon the chase. This was the last time Te Kooti was seen over a gun-sight, and it was the final engagement in the Maori wars; the date was the 14th February, 1872. The parting shot was fired by Private Nikora te Tuhi, a Ngati-Rangitihi man, at two men going over the last ridge.

The Arawa were becoming exhausted, having had nothing to eat except a mouthful of biscuit and water; a few of the party had apples, and these somewhat allayed their thirst. On returning to the Mangaone the Arawa found the enemy's camp in the bush across the river; they had left all their food there in their haste to escape, and the Government Maoris at last had a satisfying meal. The rest of the party came in with the swags after Preece had established himself in camp about 8 o'clock in the evening.

That night a sentry thought he heard some one moving in the bush. He fired and turned out the guard, but nothing could be found. Captain Preece thought it might have been one of the enemy's dogs, which sometimes got separated from their masters when out pig-hunting. But more than a month later he learned that Anaru Matete, one of Te Kooti's party, related that he hid close to the camp on the night of the skirmish at Mangaone and heard the gun fired, and he remained in concealment until after the Arawa left in the morning. It was afterwards ascertained that, besides Te Kooti and Anaru Matete, the party of Hauhaus included Hirini te Oika, Maaka, Pataromu, Ruru, Maika, and other desperate men, who had stood by their chief through all his misfortunes.

The spot where this encounter took place on the Mangaone is about eight miles south of Lake Waikare-moana.

Had Captain Preece's men been armed with the Snider instead of the Terry carbine—a poor weapon for that kind of fighting—they should have been able to reap the benefit of their long toil; but it was not until the 2nd April that the force was served out with the Snider rifles, for which the commander had repeatedly applied for a long time in vain. It was exasperating for Preece and Mair to know that the Armed Constabulary in camp at Taupo and elsewhere on the plains were armed with

Sniders, then about the most modern weapon obtainable, while the bush expeditionary columns who were doing all the work in pursuit of Te Kooti were handicapped with an inferior arm, the ammunition of which was always liable to be spoiled in rough and wet campaigning.

Captain Preece followed the enemy's trail to Whataroa, near Onepoto, where Captain Ferris took it up. The Arawa remained at the lake a few days to rest after their long and trying marches and then returned to the Rangitaiki Plains. They arrived at Fort Galatea on the 26th February, after having been a month constantly travelling, for the greater part through trackless country.

Te Kooti's movements were marvellously swift; he had a disconcerting trick of appearing in the most unexpected places. Soon after the Mangaone encounter he made a raid on Nuhaka, between Wairoa and the Mahia Peninsula, but did not kill anyone on this occasion. Major Cumming was then officer in command of the Wairoa district, and he sent a force under Captain McLean and Lieutenant J. T. Large to intercept Te Kooti, who made a hurried retreat from Moumoukai Mountain, in rear of Nuhaka. The force from Wairoa went up the Hangaroa River and lay in wait for Te Kooti at a place where it was known he would endeavour to cross the Hangaroa on his way back to the Urewera Country. Lookouts were posted night and day in concealment at short intervals on both flanks for a considerable distance. But one dark night the Hauhaus, unseen and unheard, crept cautiously down the bed of a creek not far from the camp. As they kept to the watercourse no tracks were left. Te Kooti and his men forded or swam the Hangaroa, and with their usual luck got away again into the mountains and made for the rugged country on the southern and western sides of Waikare-moana.

Both Captain Preece and Captain Ferris continued to follow Te Kooti, but they never encountered him again, although Ferris captured Anaru Matete and Maaka (Te Kooti's head executioner) near Te Reinga some weeks later. Maaka was tried at the Supreme Court at Napier and sentenced to death; the sentence was commuted to penal servitude for life, and the prisoner was liberated after serving ten years.

THE LAST BUSH EXPEDITIONS

Working from the Opotiki side, Captain J. R. Rushton had some most arduous bush marching in search of Te Kooti. His last expedition was early in 1872, when he and Wiremu Kingi, chief of the Ngaitai Tribe, with a war-party scoured the wildly broken forest country forming the watershed between the Bay of Plenty and Poverty Bay. Captain Rushton writes: "My friend Wiremu Kingi, of Torere, informed me he had heard that Te Kooti with a few men was hovering about the high country near the Upper Motu and Maunga-tapere Range and Te Wera forest. I knew that some of his best men had left him and were now living with the Ngaitai at Torere. I forthwith informed Sir Donald McLean, Defence Minister, and he at once despatched the Government steamer, commanded by Captain Fairchild, with stores for an expedition to start early in pursuit of the rebel. Wiremu Kingi agreed to raise a party, and with about fifty very good men we marched for the Upper Motu. It was extremely rough work penetrating those trackless forests and ravines. We got on Maori tracks on the Upper Motu, and followed the trail, often finding the last camp-fires still warm. It was most trying work in that broken bush country. We knew the rebels often doubled back on their tracks. However, they had made off through the Urewera Country, and we did not come up with them. The awful marching had its effect on some of our men; Wi Kingi and a number of his Ngaitai got very lame. I think it was on the fourteenth day out that I made up my mind to try and get down to Gisborne. I took two of our best Maoris—Hotene was one—and after hard bush marching got out to the Ormond settlement. There I found two of my old comrades, Majors Pitt and Richardson. Next day I reached Gisborne and sent a message off by mounted orderly to Sir Donald McLean at Napier asking for a steamer to return the force to Torere. Wi Kingi and his men came out, and we were all taken back to the Bay of Plenty by the steamer. So ended my last expedition in search of Te Kooti."*

The chase after Te Kooti was not abandoned while any possibility remained that he was still hiding in the unpeopled parts of the bush country. In another effort to find his trail Captain Preece set out from the Rangitaiki Valley on the 19th April, 1872, with his No. 2 Company of Arawa. This proved to be the final expedition of the war. The route taken was that by way of Ahi-kereru and Maunga-pohatu. The column marched right through the mountains to Puketapu, where Captain Ferris's trail was found on the 27th after very hard

* Letter from Captain Rushton, of Kutarere, Ohiwa, 1st July, 1923. Captain Rushton added: "I saw Te Kooti a few days before he died, at Ohiwa, in 1893. The Native Minister, Mr. Cadman, had granted the request of Te Kooti's relatives for a piece of land on which they could settle; this was at the Wainui, at the head of Ohiwa Harbour. There, I think, the old rebel was buried. Just now most of his followers from all parts are holding the great Hurae (July) meeting in his memory."

travelling in continuous rain. Preece then worked out to Marumaru, and from there went on the Wairoa River to Wairoa for rations and a fresh supply of boots for his men. Having news that Te Kooti had crossed the Maunga-pohatu and Ruatahuna track and was making for Waiau, he marched rapidly for Waikare-moana through Whataroa, and found that Captain Ferris had started from the Marau end of the lake with ten Armed Constabulary and ten natives. It now became evident that Te Kooti was making for the Kaingaroa and Waikato, so Preece communicated with Captain Mair advising him to move up to Heruiwi, and instructed Lieutenant Way to bring ten men from Fort Galatea to watch from that side.

On the 10th May, 1872, Captain Preece left the Waikare-moana and marched southward towards Te Hoe River, a tributary of the Mohaka, over the ground he had travelled in February. Precipitous cliffs about 300 feet high were encountered on the upper part of the proper left bank of Te Hoe Stream, and the men could find no means of descending them, so Preece had to work down towards Ngatapa [not to be confused with the Ngatapa which was the scene of the siege of 1869]. This Ngatapa was an old Maori fortress on the junction of Te Hoe and Mohaka Rivers near Maunga-haruru, where Te Kooti had spent some time in the summer. Finding no trace of him there, Captain Preece determined to work out to the Armed Constabulary post at Te Haroto, on the Napier–Taupo Road, and then make a forced march round by road to co-operate with Captains Ferris and Mair from the Heruiwi side. On his arrival at Te Haroto and Tarawera he sent Sergeant Bluett ahead with a small party to get rations from the Runanga Armed Constabulary station and then work through the edge of the bush towards Ahi-kereru and try and strike the trail there; the captain was unable to push ahead himself owing to a bad leg. However, on the 17th May a telegram arrived from Mr. McLean, the Defence Minister, stating that Te Kooti (who had eluded the Kaingaroa Plains patrols) had got through to Arowhena, in the King Country, a settlement near the Waikato River west of Waotu, on the 15th, and left for Te Kuiti, Tokangamutu, on the 16th. Thus unsuccessfully ended all the expeditions after the outlaw. Captain Ferris had followed the trail through dense bush as far as Heruiwi, but arrived there too late; Lieutenant Way, who met Captain Preece at Tarawera, had seen nothing of the trail.

"Captain Ferris," said Captain Preece, "deserved great credit for the persistent way in which he had followed the trail, from the time we handed it over to him at Whataroa, through to Te Reinga and the bush country at the back of Nuhaka, where

Te Kooti doubled on his own tracks, thence striking his old hiding-place at the head of the Waiau beyond the western end of Lake Waikare-moana, through dense bush in rugged country and up the beds of rivers, and ultimately reaching the open country above the Kaingaroa Plains unfortunately just too late to capture Te Kooti. He never received proper credit for this very arduous service, and it is only proper that, although he has 'gone west' many years, his good work should be recorded."

Captains Mair and Preece worked well together. There was never any question of seniority between them; they consulted one another on every detail, and jointly served their country with zeal and loyalty in a very trying time, giving every assistance and information to other officers who were operating against Te Kooti from different points. Captain Porter and Lieutenant Large, too, gave particularly valuable service in their arduous expeditions with Ngati-Porou, tirelessly scouring the most formidable mountain region in the North Island.

In the safety of the King Country, chiefly at Tokangamutu and Otewa, Te Kooti spent the next eleven years. His pardon in 1883 enabled him to move abroad again, but he was not permitted to return to his old home at Poverty Bay, and he died in 1893 on a reserve at Ohiwa, at peace with the Government he had defied and eluded so long.

* * * * *

So ended, in 1872, the Maori campaigns which began on the Waitara in 1860—a war that at one period necessitated the employment of more than ten thousand troops, and which was brought to a close by native contingents with a few European officers. From war on the grand scale under Imperial generals, with horse, foot, and artillery, and elaborate transport arrangements, the operations had gradually been reduced to a kind of guerrilla warfare in which the men carried all their supplies on their backs and fought the hostile bands in the Maori manner, tracking them through the forests and practising the bush-fighting tactics of surprise and ambuscade.

For eleven years almost continuously the North Island was disturbed by war and alarms, and the expenditure incurred remained a heavy load upon the resources of the young colony. The loss of life was heavy in some of the engagements and sieges—in particular Rangiriri, Orakau, the Gate Pa, Te Ranga, Te Ngaio (Kakaramea), and Ngatapa—yet considering the long period over which the campaigns extended the aggregate of casualties was not great. From the opening of Heke's War in the North in 1845 until the firing of the last shots in the chase after Te Kooti in 1872 the total death roll of the British and colonial troops engaged was 560; the wounded numbered about 1,050. The bodies of friendly natives serving on the Government side lost in the same period about 250 killed. The hostile Maoris lost far more heavily. More than 2,000 were killed, and probably about the same number wounded, but the exact figures could not be ascertained, as it was native policy to minimize their casualties as much as possible.

Chapter 43

FRONTIER PERILS, AND FINAL PEACE

ALTHOUGH THE YEAR 1872 saw the last of the fighting expeditions against the rebel Maoris, it was by no means the last of the anxious times on the borderland of the native territory. In Waikato, in the Taupo country, and in Taranaki there was still material for racial trouble. The Maori King, Tawhiao, and hundreds of his armed followers had their quarters in the Ngati-Maniapoto country, a few miles south of the Puniu River, the frontier of the confiscated lands, and for many years after the war they plotted and planned the reconquest of the Waikato. It was not until 1881 that they finally renounced their hopes and abandoned their policy of sullen self-isolation.

Moreover, for nearly ten years after Te Kooti had taken refuge in the King Country and drawn many of Tawhiao's people to his side there was a feeling of uncertainty on the frontier as to the old rebel's intentions. The King Country was given over to Hauhauism in its various forms, such as the Tariao ritual, and to the Wairua-Tapu faith of Te Kooti, and these fanatic cults were ever-present possible sources of, or incentives to, renewed conflict with the hated *pakeha*. The more thoughtful men among the Kingites had no desire for another war, but there was a large and dangerous element quite ready for raid and plunder had a leader presented himself. Fortunately, the fanatic Mahuki came on the scene some years too late to do much mischief.

Alarms and war-rumours were frequent in Waikato during the period 1870-75. The Kingites strictly enforced their *aukati* —that is, they forbade *pakeha* intrusion on the Maori side of the frontier line. White settlers on friendly terms with the Maoris frequently crossed the Puniu in quest of strayed stock, to traffic with the natives for pigs, and so on, but Government officials and land-seekers were discouraged with *tupara* and tomahawk. In 1870 Mr. Richard Todd, a Government surveyor, was shot on the slopes of Mount Pirongia, not far from the township of Alexandra (now Pirongia). A more alarming tragedy, a murder

Colonel Lyon

(Died at Auckland, 1887)

Colonel William Lyon, an Imperial veteran, commanded the Constabulary and Volunteer forces in the Waikato, with headquarters at Cambridge, during the often critical days of the "seventies," and was in charge of the Auckland Volunteer District, 1884–87. He began his soldiering career as an officer of the Coldstream Guards, and exchanged into the 92nd Highlanders, serving with that regiment for ten months in the Crimea. He lost an arm through a shooting accident in England, and left the Army to settle in New Zealand. When the Waikato War began he was appointed to the New Zealand forces, and served throughout that campaign and afterwards in the wars on the West and East Coasts. He was second in command under Colonel Whitmore in the final campaign against Titokowaru in 1869.

of a particularly savage character, was an affair which occurred in 1873, on the border-line near Roto-o-rangi and Pukekura, at the base of the Maunga-tautari Range, and about midway between the farthest-out farms at Orakau and the township of Cambridge. This was the killing of a farm labourer named Timothy Sullivan, employed by E. B. Walker, of Cambridge, who was breaking in a large area of land he had acquired on the border, in the Pukekura Block. Some of this land was on the Maori side of the frontier, and had been leased from natives of the Ngati-Raukawa Tribe. One of the Maori owners, Mohi Purukutu, who had been absent when the leasing arrangement was made, objected to the occupation of the land by Walker and his men; he received no payment for his share in the block, and he brooded over this until he resolved on desperate measures. On the 25th April, 1873, Purukutu and several other men, armed with guns and tomahawks, came upon three of Mr. Walker's employees engaged in fascining a swamp on the land leased by Walker, on the Maori side of the *aukati* line. The three were David Jones (a stockman), Charles Rodgers, and Timothy Sullivan. When they saw the hostile Maoris, mat-clad and armed, appear from the manuka and fern, they turned and ran for their lives, closely pursued. They ran for more than half a mile, then Sullivan gave in, exhausted, and sat down; his comrades raced on and escaped. Purukutu led the raiders; two of his companions were Pere te Pouturutu and Hori te Tumu. Pere, it is stated, shot Sullivan; then Purukutu and Hori decapitated him and cut out his heart, slashing the body open down to the stomach. They carried the slain man's head to Aotearoa and then to Wharepapa, a Hauhau village three miles south of the Puniu, where it was left. The heart, the Maoris relate, was carried up country, stuck on the end of a *korari* stick (flax-stalk), and was taken to the Kuiti district. "The slayers of Timoti (Timothy)," said the old man Tu Tamua Takerei, of Parawera, "intended to lay the heart before Tepaea, or Tiaho, the Maori Queen, but she disapproved of their actions, so the trophy was not presented to her. The taking of a human heart was an ancient custom of the Maori; it was the practice to offer it up to Tu and Uenuku, the gods of war."*

---

* Mr. Andrew Kay, of Orakau, relates that shortly before Purukutu carried out his raid on Grice and Walker's estate, at Pukekura–Roto-o-rangi, he sent a party of Maoris to Ramsay's farm near Paekuku, opposite Orakau. There an old Maori, who had been taken as a slave in the intertribal wars, was working for Ramsay, pit-sawing timber in the bush which then existed between Rangiaowhia and Puahue. This relic of the old cannibal days they took away with them; it was found afterwards that they wanted him for the work of decapitating a *pakeha* whom they had decided to kill, and to preserve the head by smoke-drying it. The old man did not want to go, but he was compelled to carry out Purukutu's wishes, and when the labourer Timothy Sullivan was killed on the disputed ground his head was removed and carried about the King Country as a Hauhau trophy.

Shortly before Purukutu committed this deed a Maori named Te Wao, who was ditching for Andrew Kay, came to his employer in great alarm and said he was going away because he had heard that a certain man, whom he would not name, had swallowed a *ngarara,* a lizard. The natives usually hold lizards in great dread, and this act of eating a *ngarara* was a prelude to some deed of desperation. The murder on the frontier followed. The Maoris had first killed one or two cattle and driven others off the disputed land—for which Purukutu had never received his rightful share of payment—and as this protest had no effect they decided to kill a man.

About the same time the old *tohunga* Hopa te Rangianini, of Ngati-Matakore, came in across the frontier from Tokanui, and told Mr. Kay that there was going to be great trouble and he did not desire to be concerned in it, so he stayed at Kay's until peace prevailed once more on the border.

Wahanui

Wahanui Huatare, of the Ngati-Maniapoto Tribe, was the leading chief of the King Country tribes in the negotiations with the Government, 1879–85. He was a man of powerful and commanding personality and a great orator, and was regarded as the Kingite "power behind the throne."

This act of savagery—the last instance of decapitation and taking the heart of a foe which occurred in New Zealand—was a revival of barbarous practices that thoroughly shocked and alarmed the European settlers, and indeed, the whole colony, and it was at first regarded at the inevitable prelude to another war.

The Government made arrangements for the better defence of the Upper Waikato border, reinforced the Armed Constabulary, and sent Mr. James Mackay as Commissioner to investigate the murder and strengthen the chain of border posts between Cambridge and the Puniu River. Mr. Mackay had blockhouses erected at Roto-o-rangi and Paekuku, and a redoubt built at the Kihikihi ford on the Puniu; this redoubt was garrisoned by friendly natives of the Ngati-Naho Tribe. The Waikato Cavalry was also called out for service. This corps was a useful and competent body of volunteer frontier horse, consisting of two troops, one at Te Awamutu and the other at Cambridge. Major William Jackson, the veteran Forest Ranger, who had settled at

Drawn from a photo, 1870]

The Orakau Blockhouse

This blockhouse, erected in 1869 on the battlefield of Orakau (see Vol. 1, pages 365-407), was a type of numerous fortified posts established along the frontier. On the ground floor the building, constructed mostly of *kahikatea,* was about 16 feet by 20 feet, with a height of about 9 feet. The upper storey, 12 feet high, overlapped the lower one by about 3 feet all round. The walls were bullet-proof; the space between the outer wall and the lining was filled with gravel. The top storey was loopholed all round; the rifle-apertures, 6 inches by 2 inches, breast-high. There were no rifle-slits in the lower storey, but the palisading was loopholed at intervals of 5 feet. The palisade was 10 to 12 feet high; there was a space of about 6 feet between it and the building. In the front the palisading was double, with a traverse of timber covering the entrance. The front fence was nearly all tall *manuka* stakes, but the main palisading consisted of posts 10 or 12 inches in thickness; *manuka* timber was used to fill the interstices. At the rear of the blockhouse the bank was scarped perpendicularly about 7 feet as an additional protection.

Hairini, commanded the Te Awamutu troop; his lieutenants at this period were Mr. Andrew Kay and Mr. William A. Cowan, the two farthest-out settlers at Orakau. The Cambridge troop was commanded by Captain J. Runciman. These troops of border farmers, well-mounted, and armed with carbine, revolver, and sword, were a highly valuable bulwark for the frontier. Divided into small detachments they patrolled the disturbed country by day and night, watched the fords and tracks, and kept a vigilant eye on all Maori movements. Undoubtedly some of the wilder spirits among the Hauhaus did contemplate a raid on the frontier settlements, but the presence of these resolute settler-soldiers moving about the country and the numerous Armed Constabulary posts deterred them from any forays they might have plotted. The Kingite chiefs disavowed Purukutu's deed, which came to be regarded as an act of protest against unjust treatment. The Maoris concerned only regretted having killed a "*tutua*," a nobody; the object of their wrath was really Mr. Walker. The excitement on the frontier was heightened by an attempt to kill James Mackay when he pluckily went up to Tokangamutu to beard the Kingites in their headquarters and demand the surrender of Purukutu. A man called Ruru entered his tent in the night and attacked him with a native wooden weapon, and would have killed him but for Mackay's superior strength and the assistance of some Maoris who heard his cries. Rewi Maniapoto protected Mackay and set a guard round his tent. Mackay returned safely to Waikato, but without the wanted man. It was many months before the feelings of apprehension in the frontier settlements died away, when it became clear that no invasion of the *pakeha* land was intended.

Several years later another *aukati*-line tragedy excited the Kingites, but did not affect the settlements. This was the killing of Moffatt, a white man who had lived with the Maoris on the Upper Wanganui and who had manufactured a coarse gunpowder for them during the wars. After repeated warnings, he returned to the King Country to prospect for gold, it was said. He was waylaid by a party of Taumarunui natives at Matapuna—close to the present town of Taumarunui—and was shot. This deed was carried out at the behest of Wahanui, in pursuance of the policy to preserve the *aukati* inviolate.

PEACE WITH THE KINGITES

The final assurance of peace in Waikato came in a dramatic manner. On the 11th July, 1881, Tawhiao, escorted by between five hundred and six hundred men, many of them armed, came into Alexandra from his hill settlement at Hikurangi, on the southern shoulder of the Pirongia Range. The settlers assembled to welcome the Maori throng. Tawhiao was accompanied by Wahanui, Manuhiri, and many other chiefs. Major William Mair, the Government Native Officer in the Upper Waikato, went to meet Tawhiao, and there in the main street of the township the Maori King laid down his gun at Mair's feet. Scores of his men followed his example, until seventy-seven guns were lying on the road in front of the Government officer. The herculean Wahanui came forward and said: "Do you know what this means, Mair? This is the outcome of Tawhiao's word to you that there would be no more trouble. This means peace."

"Yes," replied Major Mair, "it is clear to me. I call to mind the words that Tawhiao uttered at Tomotomo-waka (Te Kopua) that there would be no more fighting. This is the day that we all have been waiting for. We know now that there will be no more trouble."

Thereafter Maori and *pakeha* fraternized, and the frontier settlers rejoiced at the final decision for peace. Tawhiao and his followers made a kind of triumphal progress through the Waikato, spending a week at Kihikihi, where the Kingite warriors encamped around Rewi Maniapoto's house, and made the days and nights lively with their hakas and their Hauhau religious chantings. At Ngaruawahia they wept long and loudly over the grave of Potatau, the first Maori King. Tawhiao visited Auckland as a guest of the Government. On his return to Alexandra, Major Mair, with the Native Minister's approval, handed back to him all the surrendered firearms but one, and for this he gave Tawhiao his own gun in exchange.

But the Kingite chiefs, desiring to assure the Government of their earnestness for peace, declined to take back their guns. "No," said Wahanui, "we have given them up; you must keep them. But we will accept your gun in token of the peace between us."

Although peace had formally been made between Tawhiao and the Government, there arose now and again certain elements of disagreement. The principal dispute concerned the opening-up of Kawhia Harbour to *pakeha* shipping and traders. Kawhia had been closed to white enterprise since 1863, and after twenty years of isolation it was decided by the Government in 1883 that the time had come when this fine harbour and the fertile land around it should be made free to the *pakeha*. A small area of land at Pouwewe—the present township of Kawhia—was bought for a village-site, and Captain Fairchild, of the Government steamer "Hinemoa," erected guiding-beacons at the heads and

The Maori King's Flag

This drawing of the flag hoisted on the proclamation of Potatau te Wherowhero as Maori King was made at Ngaruawahia by Lieutenant (afterwards Colonel) H. S. Bates, of the 65th Regiment, in 1863, shortly before the Waikato War began.

buoyed the channel. The Maori King party strongly objected to this; Kawhia was the only harbour now remaining purely Maori, and it was desired to keep it so. In September of 1883 Tawhiao ordered that the beacons should be destroyed, preliminary to sinking the buoys and pulling up the survey pegs at Pouwewe. His intentions were carried out by the Ngati-Mahuta and Ngati-Hikairo, who manned three large war-canoes, paddled down to the heads, and removed and broke up the beacons. The Native Minister, Mr. Bryce, immediately had Kawhia garrisoned with Armed Constabulary. The "Hinemoa" landed 114 of the Armed Constabulary Field Force, under Major Tuke, at Pouwewe; the force had equipage and provisions for two months. A post was established on the hill Te Puru—an olden Maori *pa*—commanding the township-site, and materials for a small blockhouse were landed. This was the last defensible post established against the Maoris. Later the garrison was reduced to seventy-nine men, and these were withdrawn when the Maoris accepted the new order of things. The beacons were re-erected, and the last retreat of Kingism was laid open for the trafficking white man.

From a photo in November, 1881]

Parihaka

THE TARANAKI FRONTIER AND THE EXPEDITION TO PARIHAKA

The story of Parihaka, the one-time famous home of Te Whiti, the Prophet of the Mountain, has an important place in the annals of military enterprise and frontier adventure in New Zealand. Te Whiti was a much-abused, much-misunderstood man. He was execrated as a fanatic and a firebrand by those ignorant of his nobility of character, who made no secret of their desire for the extermination of the Maori. With the calmer judgment that the lapse of forty years has brought, New Zealanders who have studied the tragic history of the west coast have come to admit Te Whiti's sincere patriotism, his disinterestedness in the cause of his people, and, above all, his desire for peace. But for him war would inevitably have been renewed in 1881, when Mr. John Bryce with his army of Constabulary and Volunteers invaded the native town of Parihaka. He preached curious doctrines, he prophesied strange things, but throughout all ran the gospel of peace. He suffered grievously for his people, yet he made no complaint on his own account; his thought was all for his tribesfolk and their welfare.

The history of Parihaka and the Waimate Plains is a sad record of mutual misunderstanding and of Government harshness and blundering. For ten years the Crown had virtually ceased to exercise any right of ownership over the nominally confiscated land beyond the Wai-ngongoro River, and had tacitly acquiesced in the return of the ex-rebels to the land; in fact, an area of 70,000 acres of the confiscated territory had specifically been returned to them. The natives, fortified in the belief that the confiscation had been abandoned, cultivated large areas of these lands. Then, to their dismay, Government surveyors were sent to cut up parts of the land for settlement. The Maoris stopped the surveys in protest, and endeavoured to ascertain the exact intentions of the Government of the day, but this was no easy task. Road-lines were taken through Maori cultivations in spite of protests; one was put through the crops of Titokowaru, at Omuturangi; the old warrior contented himself with a protest, for the days of gun and tomahawk had gone.

The key to the Government's brusque policy in Taranaki is to be found in a minute to Cabinet written on the 22nd May, 1878, by the Hon. Mr. Macandrew. This document made it clear that the survey of the plains was begun because the Government was anxious to market the land. Mr. Macandrew wrote regretting that the Government had been so remiss in putting the land on the market. "My belief," he frankly said, "is that it will place in the Treasury half a million sterling." If the land had been ready it would have placed the Crown in funds to a very large extent, as purchasers were waiting. And so, even before the Maori reserves had been marked out, the Government hurried off advertisements to Australia offering the choice lands of the Waimate Plains to selectors.

By the year 1879 Parihaka had grown into a little republic, with Te Whiti as the temporal and spiritual president. Here gathered the people who were anxious about the future of their race and their lands; here, too, came sundry fugitives, such as Hiroki—who had lately killed one McLean, a member of a survey party, at Moumahaki—and delegations from many tribes who looked to Te Whiti as their counsellor and saviour. Continually the prophet preached passive resistance, but presently he took another step. He sent out parties of natives to plough up European settlers' land at several places between Hawera and the White Cliffs, by way of protest against the white occupation. Six of these localities were on parts of the confiscated territory, but one was a block of land ceded to the Crown in 1848. One

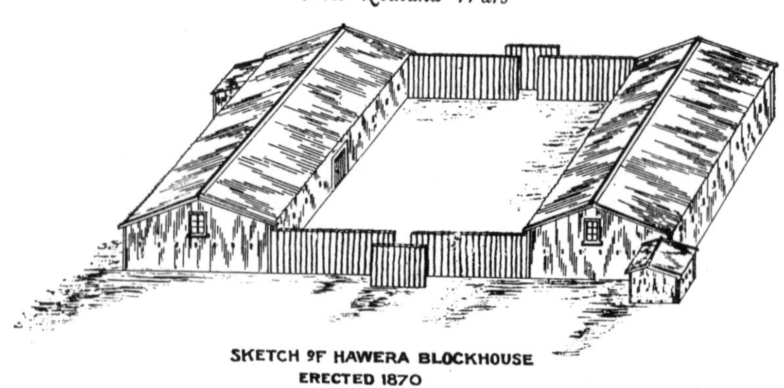

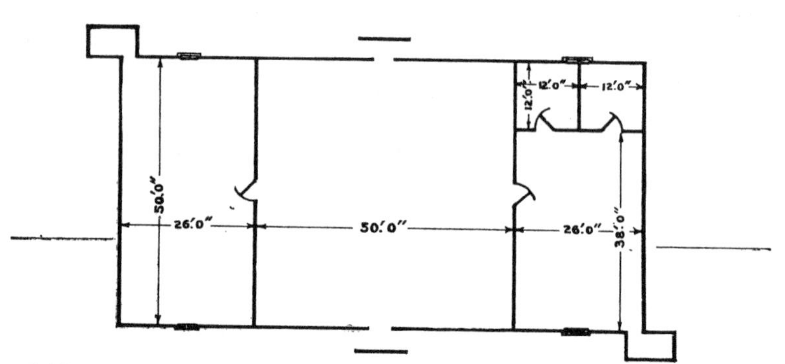

Origin of plans: J. Orchiston, Esq., M.I.E.E. Drawn, C. P., 1920]

The Stockade and Blockhouses at Hawera, Taranaki

This well-designed place of defence was erected in the middle of Hawera Town, facing High Street; the site was about where the town library building now stands. The following details of the fort are supplied by Mr. Orchiston, who was stationed at Hawera in the "seventies":—

Bastions: Four loopholes 5 feet above ground-level and four at ground-level; rifle-pits inside bastions 6 feet below ground-level. Palisades: 8 feet high and 12 inches by 6 inches approximately, of hewn *matai* set close together. Trench was dug 4 feet deep, planks inserted, and earth stamped hard all around them. Walls: Galvanized corrugated iron on outside and 8 inches by 1 inch unplaned boards on inside, 6 inches by 3 inches studs; gravel packed between galvanized iron and internal lining; loopholes 4 feet 8 inches high from floor-level. Roof of galvanized corrugated iron. Floor of 8 inches by 1½ inches dressed *matai*. Courtyard: Loopholes all around inside of courtyard at 4 feet centres and 4 feet 8 inches from floor-level. Entrance through two ledged and braced doors, 4 feet wide.

Colonel J. M. Roberts, N.Z.C.

Colonel John Mackintosh Roberts, who comes of an Inverness family, was born in India, and came to New Zealand with his relatives in 1855. The family settled in the Hunua district, South Auckland. In 1861 Roberts was on the Gabriel's Gully gold-diggings and other fields in Otago. In 1863 he joined the Forest Rangers under Captain W. Jackson, and later was a subaltern in No. 2 Company of the Rangers under von Tempsky. He afterwards served in the West Coast campaigns, and was in the severe actions at Te Ngutu-o-te-manu and Moturoa; his gallantry was recognized by the award of the New Zealand Cross for valour in the field. Colonel Roberts led the right wing of Whitmore's force which invaded the Urewera Country in 1869, and later was on continuous active service until the close of the campaigns. He commanded the Armed Constabulary and Volunteer forces in Taranaki during the Parihaka crisis. For many years Colonel Roberts was Resident Magistrate in the Bay of Plenty district.

after another these ploughing-parties were arrested, until about 180 men had been sent to prison. Te Whiti emphatically stated, in reply to an official's inquiries, that he had authorized the ploughing. His motive for doing so, he said, was to draw a declaration of policy from the Government. Sir George Grey, he recalled, at a meeting with Rewi Maniapoto at Waitara, had said he would "plant a tree of peace whose branches would spread over the land." Instead of this, Sir George Grey—otherwise the Government—had begun, he said, to steal the land of the Maori, the Waimate Plains, and he had therefore ordered the ploughing to probe Grey's heart to prove whether he was a man of peace or not.

One of the farms on which the Maori ploughmen set their teams to work was that of Mr. James Livingston, at Waipapa, near Hawera. Here bloodshed was narrowly averted. The Hawera settlers had armed, and, being unable to obtain a satisfactory reply from the Government as to action against the natives, they solemnly resolved to establish a republic and to maintain the cause of the white settlers on the plains. These adherents of the "Republic of Hawera," under the presidency of Mr. Livingston, garrisoned that stalwart pioneer's house, which was roughly fortified, and determined to put a stop to the Maori ploughmen's operations. When the Parihaka ploughing-parties came once more to continue their work on Livingston's grass fields they were surrounded by about a hundred settlers, armed with loaded rifles, extended in skirmishing order over a rise which commanded the Wai-ngongoro ford where the natives crossed. This demonstration ended the ploughing on the Hawera side of the Wai-ngongoro; the natives came no more that way. Some of the whites were foolish enough to express a wish for an opportunity of exterminating the Maoris; and it was perhaps only the cool restraint of Mr. Livingston and some of the more temperate-minded settlers that averted a conflict. A shot fired at that troubled hour would have started a war likely to set back Taranaki—and, indeed, the whole of the frontier districts of the North Island—for many a year.

Soon after this a Royal Commission, consisting of Sir William Fox and Sir F. Dillon Bell, was appointed to enquire into all questions affecting the confiscated Maori territory on the West Coast. Certain recommendations were made,* and surveyors were put on to define the native reserves, while others were instructed to make a sectional survey of the plains for sale and settlement. The opening of the trunk line of road along the coast was also

* The West Coast Commissioners in their report to the Governor, 15th March, 1880, wrote:—

". . . We believe that if he [Te Whiti] were sure of being let alone at Parihaka he would let us alone upon the Plains. But if we try to occupy the Plains without his having any assurance that he is safe at Parihaka we may find that we can get neither Parihaka nor the Plains except at the price of a struggle which no one can doubt would then be desperate."

The basis of Te Whiti's system was a denial of the reality of the confiscation, and a promise to restore to his people all their land by Divine aid.

The Armed Constabulary Camp at Waikino, Taranaki

This encampment was an historic one, for it was the first Armed Constabulary position taken up after moving camp from Stony River (the Hangatahua), when forming the coast road southward to Opunake, in pursuance of the Government's decision to occupy the confiscated territory between Stony River and the Wai-ngongoro. Colonel Roberts (then Major) commanded the force. A ditch and bank protected the guard-tent on the hillock on the left of the picture. A guard-tent on a mound on the right was similarly entrenched. The Waikino Stream flowed in rear of the camp.

commenced, under the supervision of Mr. C. W. Hursthouse, the parties working simultaneously from the Wai-ngongoro and from Stony River. Te Whiti prophesied that the two sections of road would never meet. As the roadwork approached the front of the Parihaka Block it was deemed necessary to take the line through a Maori cultivation. This created immediate trouble. The Armed Constabulary pulled down the fencing, and a party of natives put it up again. They were arrested and sent to gaol. Others followed their example, and were arrested. This sort of thing went on, the Armed Constabulary demolishing the fence and the Maoris re-erecting it, until 216 natives had been imprisoned. It was uncertain where the farce-tragedy would end, inasmuch as Te Whiti was reported to have said that when all the men had been exhausted he would send the women and children to put up the fence. Probably, had the Government men fenced the road on either side so as to protect the cultivations the native opposition would have subsided, but it was not considered necessary then to consult the Maoris' wishes.

The dispute now assumed a new aspect. A party of forty to fifty men, styled the *morehu,* or "survivors," marched out from Parihaka almost daily, each man carrying a tree-branch, and on arriving at the road where it entered the cultivation on the south side continued to march along the line, reciting an

From a sketch by Mr. James Robson]

The Normanby Redoubt (Taranaki), 1879

This redoubt was built by the settlers at Normanby (Matariki), near Ketemarae, in Taranaki, during the critical times on the Waimate Plains. It was afterwards garrisoned by an Armed Constabulary detachment, and a watch-tower was built as shown below. (See notes in Appendices.)

The Normanby Redoubt in 1880

This illustration shows the drawbridge as constructed in many of the frontier redoubts, also the watch-tower commanding a view over the surrounding country.

A Watchtower of the Plains

This shows the interior of the old redoubt at Manaia, on the Waimate Plains, Taranaki, with the watch-tower built for sentry duty, and one of the loopholed flanking blockhouses at the angle on the right. (See notes in Appendices.)

incantation, until within a short distance of the north boundary of the field, close to the Constabulary camp, and back again to the south boundary, where they planted the branches across the road. Occasionally another party composed of over a hundred small children, in charge of an adult, was sent out from Parihaka to traverse the road through the cultivation warbling an incantation taught them by Tohu.

The Government surveyed a portion of the Parihaka Block, seaward of the new road, for sale and settlement, as recommended by the Royal Commission. The natives were to be given reserves, but they were not informed where these reserves were or exactly what provision was being made for them. The sight of the surveyors at work created an impression among the Maoris that their lands would soon pass from them, and they resolved to make one last protest against the confiscation. They began to fence and make cultivations on parts of the areas surveyed for sale. The Armed Constabulary pulled down the fences. Mr. Hursthouse, engineer in charge of the roadworks, was instructed to make Parihaka his headquarters, and to assist

From a drawing by Mr. G. Sherriff, 1881]

Pungarehu Redoubt and Blockhouse, Taranaki

Rahotu Stockade and Camp, Taranaki, 1881

Taranaki Rifle Volunteers at Parihaka, 1881

Major Roberts in trying to prevent the Maoris taking possession of the confiscated land. The Government now resolved to "extinguish Parihaka," as a speaker of the day phrased it. There were some Ministerial changes, and Mr. John Bryce became Native Minister. A Proclamation was issued, called by some a declaration of war; and action against Te Whiti was left in Mr. Bryce's hands. The Armed Constabulary had been recruited up to a strength of about 1,100 men, and the services of a Volunteer Corps were also called for.

By this time (October, 1881) Taranaki was a great armed camp. Redoubts with tall watch-towers studded the face of the land; loopholed blockhouses stood on commanding hills; Armed Constabulary tents whitened the plains. The devious political history of the hour which led up to the invasion of Parihaka need not be entered into here.

Under Mr. Bryce's personal direction, early on the morning of Saturday, 5th November, 1881, the Volunteers and Armed Constabulary moved off from the Rahotu and Pungarehu camps and marched for Parihaka, under the command of Lieut-Colonel Roberts, N.Z.C. The Volunteers mustered 959 strong and the Constabulary 630. As the Maori town was approached the various units were told off for their positions in surrounding the place. Most of the Volunteers were sent to occupy the small

Photo, November, 1881]

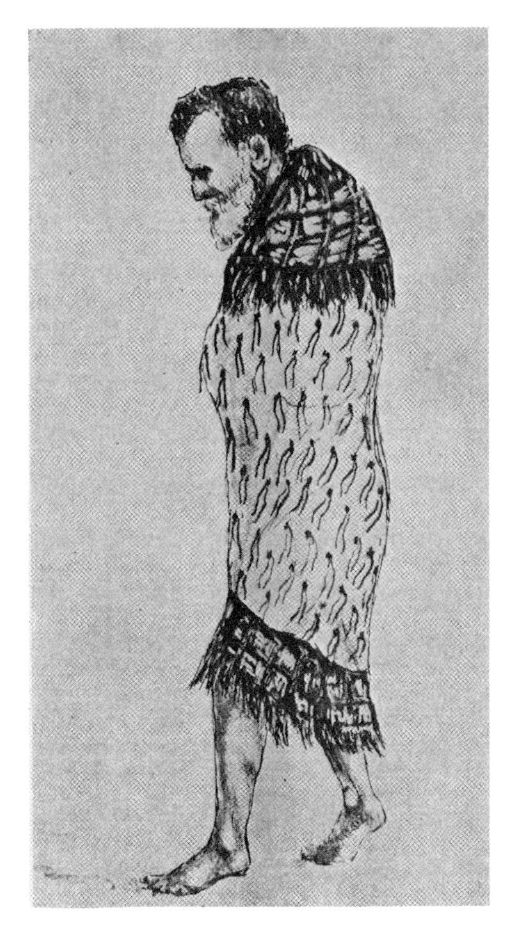

Sketch by Mr. G. Sherriff, at Parihaka, 5th November, 1881]

Te Whiti Surrendering to Mr Bryce

Mr. Sheriff, of Wanganui, accompanied the volunteers to Parihaka in 1881 and made many sketches of the expedition. This drawing of Te Whiti shows the Prophet of Parihaka walking over to the arresting-party of Armed Constabulary. He was attired in a *korowai* cloak of finely dressed and woven flax.

hills overlooking the town on the right, while the Armed Constabulary column, the Thames Scottish corps, and the Mounted Rifles marched for the centre of Parihaka, with an arresting company of about ninety men as advance-guard. The people, to the number of nearly a thousand, were seated in the *marae* unarmed, quietly waiting the coming of the troops. The only demonstration was made by the young children, who held a skipping-rope across the path and chanted a song to the *pakeha* soldiers.

Mr. Butler, the Native Minister's Secretary, advanced and read the Riot Act—which must have seemed a grim kind of joke to any Maoris who understood it—and the Government Proclamation to Te Whiti. Te Whiti, fearing even then that there might be resistance from some of his young men, counselled the people: "Even if the bayonet be put to your breasts do not resist." But nothing could have been more calm and dignified than the attitude of the silent assemblage of natives who listened to the reading of the Riot Act. Presently, in response to Mr. Bryce, Te Whiti offered himself for arrest, and he quietly rose and walked away with the arresting-party, bidding his people in farewell: "Be of good heart and patient. Be steadfast in all things." Tohu, his fellow-prophet, was also arrested. The military encamped around the village, and gradually dispersed all the outside tribes to their homes. They pulled down many houses in the town, including Te Whiti's sacred meeting-house, and destroyed some of the cultivations. The intention was, in short, to demolish Parihaka as a Maori assembly place, and make smooth the way for the white occupation of the plains. Te Whiti was kept in custody, at one place and another, a kind of honourable captivity, for about two years. He was never granted a trial; well the Government of the day knew that no charge could justly lie against him.

History has vindicated the grey old man of Parihaka; we know now how to balance his virtues against his eccentricities and delusions, and to give to him his rightful place in New Zealand's story as the one man who prevented Taranaki becoming a battlefield again in 1881. His patient, strife-hating character stands out in strong contrast to the harsh, overbearing attitude of John Bryce, a man who possessed many of the downright qualities needful in a pioneer, but whose narrow outlook unfitted him for a position involving the handling of delicate inter-racial problems.

An estimate of Te Whiti's policy and of the Maori cause, written by Major R. Parris, of the Native Department in Taranaki, is worth quoting here, inasmuch as it did not come from a philo-Maori: Parris, indeed, was one of those primarily

Sketch by Mr. G. Sherriff, 1881]

Tohu Kakahi After Arrest at Parihaka

Tohu Kakahi was Te Whiti's fellow-prophet and sometime rival, and had many followers at Parihaka. This drawing shows him in the vehicle in which he and Te Whiti were taken from Parihaka to Pungarehu Camp and New Plymouth on the 5th November, 1881. Tohu's form of worship is still followed by some the Taranaki natives, with Ketemarae as the gathering-place.

responsible for the Government's unjust dealings at the Waitara in 1860. His review is a remarkable official admission in Te Whiti's favour. Parris wrote in a report to the Native Minister at the end of 1881:—

" . . . . Those who are capable of taking an impartial view of the whole case and can admit the full right of the Maori to strive by all fair means to retain his old free mode of life and enough of his primeval wilderness of fern and forest to enjoy it in, will find in Te Whiti's conduct as the leader of his people in a trying period much that is worthy of their sympathy and respect. Te Whiti was, in fact, the representative in this part of New Zealand of the love of the Maori people for their ancient customs and ways of living, and of their dread of being hustled off the scene by swarms of strangers, and by the introduction of new conditions of life under which they instinctively feel themselves unable to compete on equal terms with the eager and vigorous newcomers in the struggle for existence. Regarding Te Whiti's position and career from this point of view, all feeling of irritation against the man for his steady opposition to the progress of colonization must disappear, and we can properly estimate the firmness, combined with total absence of any recourse to violent measures, with which he maintained the unequal contest for so many years, and can sympathize with his hopes and understand his prophecies, however quaint their form, that in some mysterious way a higher power would interfere and protect the rights of the weaker race.

" Notwithstanding this rooted preference for the old Maori ways of life and his dread of their disturbance by the intrusion of European settlers, Te Whiti has shown no feeling of dislike or bitterness towards our race. On the contrary, whether at the summit of his prosperity and when he might naturally consider himself to be master of the situation, or when his endurance was tried to the utmost by the near approach of our forces to Parihaka, every one was freely admitted to his settlement and treated there with the greatest courtesy.

" As regards the practical result of Te Whiti's leadership of the Maoris of the West Coast," Parris continued, " it is perhaps hardly too much to say that if he had shaped his course with the special intention of enabling the Government to tide over without bloodshed a period during which there was a constant risk of collision between the races—but during which the Government (from want of funds or other causes) was not in a position to compel submission without involving the country in a ruinous war—he could not have been more successful in accomplishing this difficult task. It would, of course, be absurd to impute to Te Whiti a desire to prepare the way for

Colonel Goring

(Died, 1923)

Colonel F. Y. Goring began his military career in 1863, when he joined the 1st Waikato Regiment of Militia at Auckland. He received a commission as ensign and served throughout the Waikato War. He afterwards served on the West Coast, and for seventeen years was an officer of the Armed Constabulary. He was in many severe actions in the fighting against Titokowaru and Te Kooti, and, after the war, was in charge of important frontier posts. His last command was the Auckland Defence District.

the final bloodless victory of the forces at Parihaka; but it should, I think, always be remembered in his favour that it is mainly in consequence of his strong personal dislike to bloodshed and violence that this happy result has been obtainable."

TE KOOTI'S LAST YEARS

In the King Country lived Te Kooti and his band of warriors and worshippers, who revered him as an *atua* and a worker of miracles. His headquarters were at Tokangamutu, close to the present town of Te Kuiti. The old rebel was anxious for peaceful relations with the Government, and at last, in 1883, Mr. Bryce, Native Minister, met him at Manga-o-rongo, some fifteen miles from Kihikihi, shook hands with him and announced an amnesty for all those who made war on the Government. This arrangement was made possible by the passing of an amnesty Act, the final step in the restoration of friendship between *pakeha* and Maori.

Major F. J. Gascoyne

Major Frederick J. Gascoyne, who was born in India, was given a commission in the Hawke's Bay Squadron of the newly formed Colonial Defence Force Cavalry in 1863, and served in the colonial forces for more than twenty years. He gained great credit in 1868 for gallant rides with despatches, under very perilous conditions, during the early operations against Te Kooti. Major Gascoyne was an officer in the Armed Constabulary until the disbandment of this force in 1885. For some time he was Resident Magistrate and Government officer in charge at Chatham Island.

Te Kooti soon had an opportunity of demonstrating in a practical way his appreciation of the Government clemency, when he assisted in the rescue of Mr. C. W. Hursthouse and a fellow-surveyor from the hands of Mahuki Manukura and his fanatic band, who had imprisoned and chained them up at Te Uira, in the King Country. Hursthouse's mission was to prospect a route for a railway-line through the King Country, and to this the Hauhau irreconcilables strenuously objected. Wahanui and Te Kooti came to the surveyors' help with large bodies of their followers, and Mr. Hursthouse was escorted to Alexandra by armed protectors. A few days later Mahuki and about thirty of his men—the "Tekau-ma-rua," as they styled themselves, in imitation of Titokowaru and his war-parties—had the assurance to ride into Alexandra with the announced intention of looting and burning the township. Fortunately for themselves they were unarmed; they relied—like Te Whiti—on supernatural aid. They were promptly surrounded by Armed Constabulary under Major Gascoyne—who was in charge of the Alexandra Redoubt—and the troopers of the Te Awa-

Tapu

Te Kooti's deserted prayer-house at Te Awahou, Rotorua. The Ngati-Rangiwewehi section of the Arawa people built this meeting-house for Te Kooti on his visit to the Rotorua district some years after the general amnesty to rebels. The large *whare* was regarded as sacred after his departure.

mutu Volunteer Cavalry, and in a few moments were unhorsed and tied up, presently to be lodged in gaol. Mahuki received a term of imprisonment, and a few years later, when he again ran amok—this time in Te Kuiti Township—he was once more imprisoned; he died in gaol. So passed the last of the fanatic prophets of the King Country.

The last years of Te Kooti's stormy life were not without trouble that nearly became tragedy. After his pardon in 1883 he came out of his long retirement in the Rohepotae and visited many Maori tribes, preaching his Wairua-Tapu gospel and practising the art of faith-healing among the credulous natives, even among some of the Arawa who had once been his foes. At Kihikihi, in the mid "eighties," we frequently saw the old cateran passing through the township with his cavalcade of Hauhaus, on his way from his *kainga* at Otewa, on the Upper Waipa, to Tauranga, the Upper Thames, Rotorua, or other native districts. His bodyguard was always armed; his immediate guardians were his two wives, who carried loaded revolvers in their blouses.

In 1889 Te Kooti made an attempt to revisit his old home, Poverty Bay. He went to Auckland, and soon afterwards, in spite of Government warnings, he travelled to the Bay of Plenty with a large body of followers, intending to march overland to the

Turanganui district. The people of the Gisborne district were up in arms at once, and there were many threats that the old rebel would be shot if he ventured to revisit the scenes of his bloody deeds in 1868. The Government took prompt measures to prevent the conflict that would have been inevitable had Te Kooti set foot in the Turanganui country. European and Maori forces were assembled at Gisborne, under Colonel Porter and his old comrade Major Ropata, and marched through the Motu forest to Opotiki. Porter so disposed his command as to block Te Kooti's progress or his flight to the Urewera Country, and arrested him at Waiotahe. He was sent up to Auckland, and released on the understanding that he would not repeat the attempt to visit the East Coast. The Government gave his people a block of land on the shore of Ohiwa Harbour, and there he died in 1893, revered as a demigod by his disciples.

THE ARMED CONSTABULARY

The Armed Constabulary Field Force remained in existence until 1885, and that year saw also the end of the occupation of redoubts on the frontier. Officered by a splendid set of frontier soldiers the Force had been the mainstay of the colony's defences during the dark years of the last war. Its semi-civil foundation did not prevent it carrying through regular campaigns with success in wild, almost impregnable country.

The North-west Mounted Police of Canada is perhaps the frontier body which in organization most nearly resembles our Field Force of 1868–85, but the New Zealand Armed Constabulary had infinitely more fighting. For a long time after the close of our wars the Constabulary were engaged in patrol and garrison duty on the borders of the *pakeha*-settled country. This generation perhaps scarcely realizes the conditions in many farming districts in the North Island up to the beginning of the "eighties." Hauhau incursions were still threatened, and a chain of redoubts and blockhouses, each manned by a detachment of blue-uniformed Armed Constabulary, guarded the pale between settlers and Kingites in the Upper Waikato. These little forts were meant for business, and, though they were never attacked, they frequently sheltered the wives and children of settlers at night up to the year 1873. The blockhouses were modelled on those built by the backwoods settlers in America for defence against the Indians; they were of two storeys, the upper storey projecting about 3 feet over the lower one all round. The redoubts were substantial works, with deep trench and tall earth parapets enclosing the barrack-rooms. Far in the back country the traveller or the land-seeker of those days would see a tall flagstaff flying the British ensign in front of

Drawing by Mr. G. Sherriff, 1881]

The Armed Constabulary Redoubt at Opunake, Taranaki

Photo at Opunake Redoubt]

Armed Constabulary Under Major Goring and Captain Morrison

No. 3 Division, Armed Constabulary, 1881

some little *manuka*-palisaded blockhouse or ditched and ramparted redoubt, the sign that the *pakeha* law kept an armed watch on the still glowering natives. The farthest south blockhouse on the Waikato frontier was that at Orakau, overlooking the farmsteads of one or two pioneer settlers. One of the most important strategic posts of those times, up to the early "eighties," was Taupo, on the shore of the great central lake, and there were stockades and redoubts on the Taupo–Napier Road and on either side of the Urewera Country, garrisoned by men who were none the less smart soldiers because they spent much of their time in cutting roads for the settlers and bridging rivers and helping to lay telegraph-lines.

The palmy days of the Armed Constabulary perhaps were those of the later field operations in Taranaki. The Waimate Plains were alive with war preparations in 1879–81, and many a New Zealander then obtained his first experience of military life under campaigning conditions. A little later came the settled conditions that led to the general disbandment of a force which served New Zealand very well in its time and generation for well-nigh a score of years. Some of the Armed Constabulary were drafted to Auckland, Wellington, and Lyttelton, to help in building the forts for harbour defence under the scheme initiated by Sir William Jervois, and many went into the civilian Police Force.

LATER MILITARY EXPEDITIONS

Minor Maori troubles and a tribal rising necessitated small military expeditions up to about the closing years of the nineteenth century. In April, 1895, the Urewera and Ngati-Whare Tribes turned back two Government survey-parties who had begun a triangulation survey of the so far unmapped Urewera mountain territory, and seized their instruments. One party, Mr. J. Phillip's, was stopped at Te Whaiti by Ngati-Whare; the other, Mr. Foster's, at Waiohau, between Ruatoki and Galatea. The fact was that the Government's intention to survey and road the Urewera Country had not been explained properly to the tribes, who naturally viewed with disfavour and apprehension the arrival of the *kai-ruri* with his theodolite, the forerunner of *pakeha* encroachment and settlement. The Government considered it necessary to make a show of military force, and a detachment of the Permanent Artillery at Auckland, numbering between forty and fifty, armed with carbines and revolvers, was despatched to Whakatane and Ruatoki. Police-Inspector Hickson and Lieutenant (now Colonel) J. E. Hume were in command of the expedition, and Colonel Roberts, Magistrate at Tauranga, accompanied them. It was on Sunday, 21st April, that the force marched into Ruatoki, at the

Sketch by Colonel W. B. Messenger, 1864]

The Urenui Redoubt, North Taranaki

This redoubt at Urenui was built in 1864, and occupied by Captain Good and a party of friendly Maoris. It was a frontier garrison-post for many years. A peculiar feature of the work was a small bastion built in the form of a projecting balcony and carried out on timber brackets, as shown; this was used as a sentry-post.

entrance to the gorge of the Whakatane. We found all the leading men of the Urewera, from Ruatoki to Waikare-moana, assembled there, to the number of about two hundred, seated in half-moon formation on the *marae*. It was an ominous reception. No call of welcome; not a word from the sullen mountain-men squatting there glowering at us. When at last they did speak their speeches were decidedly hostile. They wanted no surveyors in their country; they did not see any necessity for mapping it; they feared some of their land might be taken to pay for the survey. We found, afterwards, that many of the younger men were ready and eager to fight; and practically every man had a gun and ammunition, although they did not parade their arms before us.*

However, patience and diplomacy worked wonders with the "new-caught sullen" Urewera. Mr. James Carroll, always a successful mediator in disputes of this nature, rode through from Gisborne, and after some days' discussion with Numia, Kereru, Te Wakaunua, Rakuraku, and other chiefs the trouble was settled. The Urewera permitted the survey to go on.

---

* The present writer accompanied this expedition as correspondent and also that to Waima, Hokianga, in 1898.

Sketch by Colonel W. B. Messenger, 1871]

Taranaki Bush Rangers' Redoubt at Wai-iti

After the Pukearuhe massacre in 1869 two redoubts were built in the Wai-iti Valley, close to the sea, about two miles south of Pukearuhe. One, shown in this drawing, was garrisoned by a company of Taranaki Bush Rangers; the other, on the edge of the flat overlooking a deep valley near the beach, was occupied by a detachment of Armed Constabulary. These posts and Pukearuhe, with the redoubt at Urenui forming an inner guard, protected the northern part of Taranaki. In 1871 Sub-Inspectors Capel and Crapp were the officers of the Armed Constabulary force at Wai-iti.

Similarly, at Te Whaiti, the Ngati-Whare in the end were won over to the side of progress. A covering-party of the Permanent Force was stationed at Te Whaiti for some weeks, for the protection of the surveyors, but its services were not needed. The survey went on, and there went on also the strategic road through the heart of the Urewera Country, destined to link up with the Waikare-moana side. Suspicious, inimical as these mountain-dwellers were, fearful of the *pakeha's* intrusion, which meant loss of independence, loss of land, they soon came to look with a friendly eye on the new-comers, and even to welcome the new road that slowly pierced the gorges and forests of their rugged country. It was the first stage in the breaking-down of the long isolation which had kept the Urewera people a tribe apart, conservative in the extreme, clinging to the old Maori ways of life.

The Pukearuhe Redoubt, North Taranaki

More serious was an expedition three years later, this time to Rawene and Waima, in the Hokianga district. It was curious that this part of New Zealand, one of the first homes of pioneer white settlement, should be the scene of a determined rising against *pakeha* authority. The chief trouble-maker was Hone Toia, one of the heads of the Mahurehure Tribe, a small clan of the great Ngapuhi; their principal homes were Waima and Taheke. There were various petty grievances, some of them ridiculous to the *pakeha* mind. One was the objection of the natives to the dog-tax levied by the Hokianga County Council; and there was objection, too, to the native-land legislation. Toia excited the tribe by his night seances; he professed to be a spiritualistic medium, and he practised the ancient *tohunga's* trick of *whiowhio*, or whistling, in calling down the spirits of the dead, who were supposed to speak to the assembled people in a ghostly whistling voice. He so worked on the superstitions and the warlike instinct of the Mahurehure that they were soon ready for armed revolt against the *pakeha,* and there were threatening demonstrations against Rawene Township. The result was that the Government despatched a column of the Permanent Force, 120 strong, with two Nordenfeldt field-guns and two Maxims, to the theatre of danger. Lieut.-Colonel Newall, a

Photo at Waima, Hokianga, 6th May, 1898]

The Mahurehure Leaders Under Police Guard After Their Surrender

(From left to right—Romana te Paehangi, Hone Mete, Hone Toia (standing), Wiremu Makara, and Rekini Pehi.)

veteran of the Maori wars, commanded the expedition. A small British warship, the gunboat "Torch," was also sent north, and she anchored off Rawene.

Colonel Newall, on the 5th May, 1898, marched his force in over the hills to the Waima Valley, some twelve miles. The two Maxim machine guns were taken over a rather difficult road. The route ascended the Puke-o-te-Hau Range and wound through a tract of bush, with a deep gully on the right-hand side and wooded hills on the left. Here there was an extremely narrow escape from a disastrous ambuscade. Seventy or eighty men and youths of the Mahurehure were posted in the fern and bush in cunningly selected positions commanding the road; all were armed, some with rifles, most of them with double-barrel guns. Not a sign of a Maori could we see as we entered the bush; nevertheless they were there within a few yards of us. Suddenly, as our rearguard wound into the bush, two shots were fired over our heads—a *tupara* loaded with ball.

"Now we're in for it!" said Mr. John Webster (the veteran settler of Opononi and old-time comrade of Judge Maning), alongside whom I was riding. Every one expected a storm of lead from the bush, and had it come our column marching in close order along the road would have suffered heavily. But not another shot was fired, and soon we learned the reason. A Maori came galloping along the road shouting out to the hidden men in the bush not to fire. When he was stopped he was found to be a messenger from Hone Toia, who had at the eleventh hour decided for peace. This was due to the arrival at Waima of Mr. Hone Heke, member of Parliament for the Northern Maori Electorate, who had ridden hard across country from Whangarei just in time to dissuade his tribesmen from their suicidal folly. A little later and a fight would have begun that would have cost scores of lives. The column marched into the beautiful Waima Valley without further incident, and bivouacked at the native school. The Mahurehure would-be warriors, still in a dangerous mood, gathered that night at their village half a mile lower down the valley. Next morning I went to their *kainga* with one of the friendly chiefs and witnessed a scene of tense excitement when Hone Heke made an appeal to the tribe to surrender. His entreaties carried the people away with emotion, though some of the "die-hards" still talked of battle; and the outcome was that at noon that day Hone Toia and his principal men rode in and surrendered to Lieut-Colonel Newall. They were tried at Auckland for treason in taking up arms against the Government, and terms of imprisonment were imposed. Since that day there has been peace in the North, but very few people realize how much the North owed to the late Hone Heke for his strenuous efforts to preserve that peace and to prevent the Mahurehure firebrands plunging their people into a foolish little war.

* * * * *

So ends the long story of the Maori wars and the final military expeditions that cover the period from 1845 to the closing years of the nineteenth century—a story in which both races may find much matter for pride as well as food for regret, for if the conflicts were born in most instances of mutual misunderstandings and political blundering, the trial of strength developed to the full the virtues of courage and fortitude and self-sacrifice on both sides. *Pakeha* and Maori are now knit in such close bonds of friendship that they can contemplate without a trace of the olden enmities the long-drawn struggles of other years, and find a mutual satisfaction in the thought that the military traditions of the pioneer period have left appreciable lasting impression on the New Zealand national type. One thing only was needed to cement for ever the union of the races, and that opportunity the Great War brought. Maori soldiers fought and died by the side of their *pakeha* fellow-New Zealanders; descendants of Hone Heke's warriors, of Te Kooti's fierce followers, of the gallant Arawa, and the fighting Ngati-Porou suffered and achieved with their white compatriots on the shell-swept slopes of Gallipoli and in the trenches and red fields of France. For the fighting and working capacity of the Native Contingent Imperial and Colonial officers alike had the highest praise. Of some 2,200 Maoris who left New Zealand, 1915–18, 253 met their deaths on active service, and 734 were wounded. So in the greatest of all wars the Maori of the young generation proved his warrior worth, and showed the world that the heroic spirit and the quality of endurance which won the grim defenders of Orakau a deathless fame have not deserted the sons of the ancient fighting-race.

APPENDICES

SUPPLEMENTARY NOTES TO CHAPTERS

VOLUME II

(Chapter 1)

THE PAI-MARIRI RELIGION

Sir William Martin, for many years Chief Justice of New Zealand, wrote to the Native Minister, under date 23rd December, 1865, regarding the Pai-marire fanatic faith:—

"Some accepted it in faith, others in wilfulness and bitterness. Some thought it true; others that it might be useful. Some men separated themselves from their missionaries in perfect calmness and quietness. One of the chiefs of Opotiki informed Bishop Williams of his conversion to the new creed in these words: 'Bishop, many years ago we received the faith from you; now we return it to you, for there has been found a new and precious thing by which we shall keep our land.' (*'Kua kitea tetahi taonga hou a mau ai to matou whenua.'*)

"A common feeling united fanatical believers with cool politicians who believed nothing, but who keep up the fervour of their brethren by false reports of miracles wrought at Taranaki and of great loss sustained by our troops. The new religion combined men of every sort, from the ferocity of Kereopa to perfect inoffensiveness—some of the best as well as some of the worst of the race. It was accepted as the religion of all who were no longer willing to accept religion at the hands of the *pakeha*. As in all times of national ferment the fiercer and more determined natures got the lead."

After discussing the war on the East Coast, Sir William Martin continued:—

"The practical fact with which we have to deal is this: The old feeling of distrust and exasperation towards our Government has been strong enough to lead thoughtful men, incapable of being parties to such acts, to join the Hauhau cause, even after the commission of the great crime at Opotiki. This is our real difficulty, the same in kind as ever, but greater in degree. I believe that this feeling is more wide and deeply spread than at any time. I believe there are now many who are convinced that we are determined, even by fraud and violence, to get possession of their land and force our dominion upon men who have never consented to it. Many, therefore, on their part determine to hold their own as best they may, and are content to sacrifice their lives in the contest. The state of the case is this: We have put too great a pressure upon these people—more than they can bear, more than we can continue to exert; we have driven many of the natives into a state of determined resistance, bordering upon desperation; we have brought upon ourselves the necessity of bearing burdens beyond our strength."

THE SURPRISE AT TE AHUAHU (1864)

Sergeant-Major E. Bezar, ex 57th Regiment, supplies the following account of the discovery of the bodies of Captain Lloyd and the men killed by the Maoris in the ambuscade at Te Ahuahu, Taranaki, which marked the beginning of the Hauhau wars:—

"On the 6th April, 1864, when the news of the slaughter of Captain Lloyd and his men reached us in New Plymouth, my company of the 57th Regiment was immediately ordered to parade and march out to Oakura and Te Ahuahu to the relief, although, of course, relief was then too late. Towards evening, when we reached the place after a hasty and tiring march, I had charge of the advance-guard of six men. When we came up to the party awaiting us near the scene of the surprise I halted the guard. Colonel Warre said, 'Move on, sergeant, but look out.' Hemi, the half-caste guide, was told off to accompany me. Our advance to the spur of the hill where the disaster occurred was from 200 to 300 yards, through high fern. The Maoris, we found, had a very cunningly contrived trench extending up the whole slope, and they were able thus to move up and down the hill quite unseen from the flat and the road. The trench ran out on the level ground a few yards, and the earth thrown out there formed a rise of several feet. On ascending this and looking into the trench I saw the headless body of Captain Lloyd lying there. I waved my arms for the others to come on, and called for a dray to be sent up. The other bodies, all decapitated, were then discovered."

(Chapter 6)

THE CAPTURE OF KETEMARAE (TARANAKI)

Major-General Chute, in a despatch dated 15th January, 1866, reporting his operations in South Taranaki after the storming of Otapawa *pa,* wrote:—

"On the evening of the 14th January I directed the Native Contingent to ascertain the position of Ketemarae, and instructed them to remain near it during the night and to send me information which would enable me to move against it early on the following morning. The force as below [three 6-pounder guns, 510 Imperial troops, 40 Forest Rangers, and 150 Native Contingent] marched at 4.15 a.m. this day and, proceeding over the plains in a northerly direction for two miles, came in front of a line of stockading and earthwork, flanked on either side by bush, and extending across the main track leading into the clearing in which Ketemarae is situated. The position was carried without opposition, though it had evidently been the intention of the rebels to defend it, for we found provisions, and fires still alight within the work. I can only account for their not availing themselves of so formidable a position for opposing our advance by attributing it to the dispiriting effect of their severe loss at Otapawa. The force then advanced on Ketemarae itself, which is about a mile within this entrenchment, and consisted of four palisaded *pas* in echelon, enclosing a large number of *whares;* these were all burnt, and as far as practicable the cultivations destroyed."

The Forest Rangers and Native Contingent then searched the bush about Ketemarae, destroyed some villages, and fought small parties of Maoris; twenty-one Hauhaus were reported killed.

THE 57TH REGIMENT

The 57th Regiment, after its hard campaigning in Taranaki, was transferred to the Waikato in 1866, with headquarters at Te Awamutu. Companies of the Regiment were also stationed at Ngaruawahia and Te Rore for some months, until the corps received orders to return to England.

The famous regiment (the "Diehards") is still in existence as the First Middlesex. It well maintained its ancient reputation in the Great War, when from first to last it recruited forty battalions.

(Chapter 8)

THE FIGHTING AT TE TAPIRI (1865)

A correction is necessary in the narrative of the fighting between the friendlies and Kereopa's Hauhaus at Te Tapiri on the western border of the Urewera Country, 1865 (Chapter 8, pages 84-95). Later information from survivors shows that all the casualties among the Maoris on the Government side during the expedition were sustained in the attack on Te Tuahu-a-te-Atua hill-fort (Te Taumata) and the fighting which followed that morning, as described in the narrative. None of the friendlies was killed in the previous fighting at the stream between Te Tapiri and Hinamoki. The three men decapitated by Kereopa's warriors (page 89) fell in the Tuahu-a-te-Atua battle. The list of those killed is: Eru te Urutaia, Tamehana te Wiremu, Hohepa Matataia, Rorerika, Katu Ririapu Poia, and Hemi Tamehana Anaru. The first four belonged to the Ngati-Manawa Tribe, the other two to the Ngati-Rangitihi clan of the Arawa. The eye-eating by Kereopa at the *niu* and the attacks on the friendlies' redoubts followed this battle.

(Chapter 11)

THE FIGHTING IN THE NGATI-POROU COUNTRY (1865)

At the beginning of the Hauhau troubles in the Ngati-Porou territory, near the East Cape, the chief Mokena Kohere took energetic measures to restore order and loyalty. He asked Mr. Titus White, R.M., to go to Auckland to procure arms for the friendly natives. Mr. White set out in a small schooner, but it foundered with all on board off White Island, in the Bay of Plenty. Mokena then decided to go to Napier and see Mr. Donald McLean. His mission was successful. Captain Deighton, R.M., of Wairoa, was sent up to Waiapu to organize the friendly sections of Ngati-Porou. Lieutenant Biggs (afterwards Major) had lately been sent to Wairoa with some twenty men to build a blockhouse; his men were chiefly disbanded members of the Colonial Defence Force Cavalry. Biggs arrived there from Napier in the schooner "Hero" (Captain John Campbell), a little vessel of about 15 tons, sharp-ended both bow and stern like a whaleboat. The blockhouse was only just finished when the cutter

"Mahia" (Captain W. E. Bendall) arrived with orders for the force to embark for Waiapu, which they did that day. Biggs's Hawke's Bay volunteers were all picked men who had been well trained in the Defence Force Cavalry for two years. These were the first troops to go to the East Cape district. Shortly afterwards Captain Fraser and his Hawke's Bay Military Settlers were sent to Waiapu. Fraser was promoted Brevet-Major and took command of the operations. The friendly Ngati-Porou had by this time had several engagements, and had to retire from one *pa* at Tikitiki and fall back on Te Hatepe, close to the coast.

In the attack on Pa-kairomiromi (early in August) Major Fraser's life was saved by Private Wilford. This man killed a Maori who was aiming a blow at Fraser's head with a long-handled tomahawk. Wilford received a bullet-wound in the wrist.

Captain Deighton, R.M., was in the engagement at Pa-kairomiromi. He returned to Wairoa during August. Mr. G. A. Preece (now Captain Preece) was clerk and interpreter to the Court at Wairoa, and had been in charge of native affairs during the Magistrate's absence. Captain Deighton was ordered back to Waiapu, and Mr. Preece volunteered for service; on arrival at Waiapu he was attached to the force as extra interpreter with relative rank of ensign. Mr. Martin Hamlin was the interpreter with Major Fraser's force; Mr. Preece usually acted with Lieutenant Biggs.

Captain Preece writes: "I think it was about the 20th September, 1865, that Captain Deighton left Napier for Waiapu again (his second trip to Waiapu) in H.M.S. 'Brisk.' The 'Brisk' also took up Captain Westrup and Lieutenant Ross, with fifty or sixty of Von Tempsky's Forest Rangers, and sixty of the Colonial Defence Force. The C.D.F. were landed at Poverty Bay on the following morning (Sunday). A fatigue-party of Rangers was landed and assisted the others to build a redoubt (commenced by Lieutenant Wilson and twenty-five C.D.F.), about where the Farmers' Freezing-works now stand at Gisborne. It was completed with the assistance of friendly natives before we sailed. We landed at Waiapu on the following morning, and attacked Pukemaire *pa* at dawn next day."

Describing the attack on Pukemaire (3rd October, 1865), Captain Preece writes: "Just after we opened fire in front of the *pa* we saw Ropata and Hotene's men crossing the Waiapu River from the Tuparoa side, as had been arranged by Captain Deighton and Lieutenant Biggs the previous day. Biggs and his Hawke's Bay volunteers then worked round under the bank to a flanking angle at the rear of the *pa*. Here they were joined by Ropata and Hotene. A sortie was made from the *pa* by the Hauhaus, holding up their hands to drive the bullets away, but a number of them fell, and the rest got back quickly into the fort. The flanking angle was attacked; we worked up to it with a sap. A man named Hemi Tapeka cut the bush-vines which fastened the palisading of the angle, and killed a man inside the work. We were fighting the enemy from their own works, and should undoubtedly have taken the place had not the heavy rain flooded the streams and prevented Lieutenant Gascoyne reaching the foot of the *pa* with provisions and ammunition. The order to retire was given at 5 p.m. The rebels did not follow us up. The creeks which we crossed the previous night had become mountain torrents. We had difficulty in crossing on our way back to Hatepe, which we reached at 8 p.m. One man died from exhaustion.

"At the second attack on Pukemaire (9th October) it was intended to sap up to the position we had left, put a mine underneath, and blow it up. Supplejack gabions had been prepared for the sap. But the Hauhaus had abandoned the *pa*."

After the capture of Hungahunga-toroa *pa* (near the East Cape) and the surrender of Ngati-Porou, sixteen ringleaders, including Karanama te

Kani and Hiriwetere te Whakamate, were shipped to Napier in the schooner "Surprise," in which Captain Deighton returned to his district. The sixteen were handed over to the police, and were among those exiled to Chatham Island. They escaped in 1868 in the schooner "Rifleman" with Te Kooti. Mr. Preece recognized the man Hiriwetere when he surrenderd. He knew him when he (Preece) was a boy at his father's home at Whakatane. Curious to say, after his second spell of rebellion (1868–70) he surrendered to Captain Preece at Te Teko, having been separated from Te Kooti's party at Taupo.

Captain Hussey and 100 men, Taranaki Military Settlers, arrived from Opotiki just too late to take part in the Hungahunga-toroa expedition. Captain Hussey was killed in the engagement at Omaru-hakeke, Upper Wairoa, on Christmas Day, 1865.

(Chapter 18)

A SCOUTING EPISODE NEAR ROTORUA

Soon after the dispersal of the Hauhaus at Puraku *pa,* Tarukenga (1867), Lieutenant Gilbert Mair was despatched on a scouting expedition into the forest on the ranges above the west and north-west sides of Lake Rotorua. The object was to get into touch with and capture, if possible, a body of about a hundred people of the Ngati-Rangiwewehi who were known to be lurking in the bush. These people, whose homes were at Awahou, Puhirua, and other settlements, were an important clan of the Arawa. They had been in rebellion, and although they had separated themselves from Kereopa's influence and were anxious to return and live in peace, they were ashamed and afraid to do so, and for the present camped warily in the bush hinterland above their olden *kaingas.* Native Commissioner H. T. Clarke, in giving Mair his instructions for the search, told him not to kill any of Ngati-Rangiwewehi if he could help it. It was desired to capture them and induce them to settle down peaceably.

Taking a party of about a hundred Arawa, Mair scouted up to the bush above the Waiteti Stream, to the north-west of Tarukenga. One cold night he came upon the secret camp of the bush people at a place known as Te Ara-piripiri ("The track through the burrs"), about a mile and a half from Tarukenga, near where the present road from Rotorua to Okoroire enters the bush. Close to the edge of the bush, not long before daylight, Mair, in advance of his men, as was his wont, suddenly found traces of habitation and smelt smoke. He passed along the word for half of his men to lie down outside the refugees' camp, and stealthily worked round to the other side of the position with the old chief Aperaniko Parakiri (of Ngati-Manawa) and fifty men, in order to come into the camp by the rear. This operation had almost been completed, just as the faint dawning of day, when a dog barked in the hidden *kainga.* That was enough for the light sleepers of the bush people. The next moment there was a rush like a drove of sheep (said Captain Mair), and off the Ngati-Rangiwewehi dashed for the shelter of the forest, naked just as they sprang from their mat couches in the closely packed *whares.* Mair and Aperaniko ran along a track seeking to stay the rush. A tree-trunk barred the way. Mair, making to pass this tree, heard a metallic snap on the left-hand side of the bole. He leaped round the tree, rifle ready, and in the dim light ran up against the muzzle of a long single-barrel gun just as another snap was heard. He flung himself on the man behind the gun and overpowered him. The prisoner was a young fellow named Te Raho Atua. He had taken two snaps at the *pakeha,* but each time his gun missed fire. This, Mair found, was due to the fact that for want of percussion caps the Maori had used match-heads, cut off and inserted in eyelets, as was the common native fashion when caps ran short, and this bush contrivance failed to detonate.

The expedition was successful in so far that a score or so of prisoners were taken, but the greater number escaped into the bush. However, the desired object was attained, for communication was opened up in order to induce Ngati-Rangiwewehi to come in and make amends for their defection. As for the fighting-men among the prisoners, they were very much relieved at being able to join their kinsmen once more, and they promptly were enlisted in Mair's fighting force.

(Chapter 24)

TE KOOTI'S ESCAPE FROM CHATHAM ISLAND

It appears from official despatches, 1867–68, that the proposed repatriation of the Hauhau prisoners held in exile on Chatham Island was delayed on the representations of Major R. Biggs, who had been entrusted with the duty of arranging with the chiefs of Poverty Bay the areas of land to be confiscated in punishment for the rebellion. Biggs was by no means a suitable man for this difficult task. He wrote to the Government in 1867, urging that it would not be advisable to permit the prisoners to return from the Chathams until the land question was settled, in order to avoid complications. The prisoners were therefore detained indefinitely, and this uncertainty as to the period of their exile hastened the outbreak.

When the Government redoubt at Waitangi (an earthwork 52 feet square) was seized the guard was taken unaware, as the Maoris who went into the post pretended that they were carrying out some fatigue duty. When the alarm was at last given Captain Thomas ran from his house to the redoubt, calling out to some of his men that the prisoners were seizing the place. He was thrown down and bound by five or six Maoris. When the settlers' places were raided twenty-nine males were tied up.

An incident of the search of the European residents' houses was the presence of mind displayed by a quick-witted woman, Mrs. Isabella Alexander, a widow, who kept a small public-house in the Waitangi settlement. When the alarm was given that the Maoris were looting the place she ran for a bag of gold she had, and dropped it into a kettle boiling on the fire. Next moment armed Hauhaus entered and demanded her money. She went into the bar and produced £35, which she gave them, saying it was all the money she had. "They said it was very little," Mrs. Alexander narrated, "and I said the men [the military guard] had not got their pay yet." The widow thus saved her gold, about 300 sovereigns.

The total number of the prisoners who escaped in the "Rifleman," as given by Captain Thomas in his report, was 298, including women and children. This is considerably in excess of the number given by most narrators, but probably the children (seventy-one) had not been taken into account. The official despatches of 1866–68 are not very satisfactory as to statistics of the Maori prisoners, and Captain Thomas's report is the only one which places the number at nearly three hundred all told.

The only prisoners who elected to remain at Waitangi when the "Rifleman" sailed were three men and a woman. One of these men was a negro named Robert Simmonds, who had been one of the rebels taken at Hungahunga-toroa *pa,* East Cape, in 1865.

(Chapter 26)

THE RETREAT FROM MOTUROA (1868)

Colonel Whitmore wrote as follows of the retreat from Moturoa, West Coast, in 1868:—

"The enemy pressed us very hard, dashing in with tomahawks whenever men fell, but recoiling always from the determined front shown and the terrible rapidity with which our breech-loaders enabled the men to fire. On these occasions, which were many along our whole front, the men stood up and fired volley after volley such as I had never before heard in bush fighting. Their resolution may be judged from the fact that the enemy had once seized a man and were tomahawking him, when the men rushed back and rescued him. He is savagely wounded, but he has not one gunshot-wound about him."

(Chapter 29)

THE LAST CAMPAIGN AGAINST TITOKOWARU

Captain G. A. Preece, who served on Colonel Whitmore's staff in the pursuit of Titokowaru on the West Coast, 1869, gives some additional details of operations in February of that year. After the rebels had been driven across the Waitotara River, reconnaissances were made to discover the refuge-place of Titokowaru. The most venturesome of these scouting expeditions was that made by Sergeant Maling and Tom Adamson, of the Corps of Guides, who went out by themselves and spent two days, travelling barefooted, searching the bush for signs of the enemy. On their return they reported to Colonel Whitmore that they had located the enemy, who were making towards Whenuakura. For this enterprise the two scouts were complimented by the Colonel. The whole force then moved out to Moumahaki, and got on the Hauhaus' trail. Heavy rain came on and flooded the Moumahaki flats in the bush, and as conditions for forest operations continued unfavourable Whitmore fell back on Weraroa, Waitotara. When at last the force went forward again it was found that the camp-ground at Moumahaki had been 6 feet under water. This was a very trying time for the Colonel Commanding and for the whole force.

Captain Preece mentions that when the force abandoned the camp at Moumahaki he was sent out with a small party to take a sick man to Wairoa (now the Town of Waverley), where he handed him over to Captain Hawes, in charge of the settlers' redoubt. This man was William Lingard, who had been awarded the New Zealand Cross for his gallantry at Tauranga-ika [see account under heading "The New Zealand Cross," in Appendices].

Finding the Moumahaki bush region in such a state through the floods, Colonel Whitmore decided to move the force northward by the open country and make for the Patea, as Titokowaru was making for the upper part of that district. He had considerable difficulties to surmount; the road had to be made for his transport drays. On the morning of the 12th March he arrived at Patea, and after consulting with Lieut.-Colonel St. John, who was in command of the post, speedy operations against Titokowaru were ordered. The engagement at Otautu (13 March, 1869) followed.

MAJOR NOAKE

Major M. Noake (pages 311-312) was an imperial Cavalry officer before coming to New Zealand. He served in the Scots Greys in the

Crimea, and was severely wounded at Balaclava. He was in command of the Wanganui Military District for some time, and afterwards settled at Onoke, Hokianga.

(Chapter 30)

THE MURDER OF MR. PITCAIRN AT OHIWA

Statements obtained from Maoris by Major Mair, R.M., at Opotiki, showed that Mr. Robert Pitcairn, surveyor, was killed by Te Kooti's raiding-party at Uretara Island, in Ohiwa Harbour, Bay of Plenty, on the 2nd March, 1869. Te Kooti had made Rakuraku's people and the Upokorehe willing prisoners or converts at Whakarae *pa,* and hearing that there was a *pakeha* surveyor camped on Uretara he gave orders that he should be killed, and told off a party of men, four of whom were escapees from Chatham Island, to carry out the deed.

The Maoris went across to the island in a canoe, and one of them, Netana (Nathan) Whakaari, was sent to reconnoitre Pitcairn's camp. He returned with the information that the *kai-ruri* was not at home (he was out shooting *kuaka*). The party waited in ambush until Pitcairn returned.

On the treacherous persuasion of a woman who was Pitcairn's house-keeper, the surveyor gave up his gun to Hemi Kakitu (a Hauhau who afterwards turned to the Government side). Thereupon a Maori—some natives said it was Rangiaho—tomahawked him.

At Waimana in 1921 I questioned the old warrior Netana Whakaari about this murder. His statement was that Wi Piro and Rangi-tahau were the leaders of the party of slayers.

On the expedition to Ohiwa Te Kooti, according to Maori accounts, was armed with four revolvers and a sword, and carried a telescope.

(Chapter 32)

WHITMORE'S EXPEDITION TO THE UREWERA COUNTRY

Captain Preece, who was a Staff officer with Colonel Whitmore in 1869, gives the following details of Whitmore's arrangements for the invasion of the Urewera Country after the close of active operations on the West Coast early in 1869:—

"When we got out of the bush after the Ngaere expedition in Taranaki in March, 1869, Colonel Whitmore decided to move through to Waitara, and thence to Auckland, to begin preparations for the expedition against Te Kooti in the Urewera Country. We had heard when at the Ngaere of Te Kooti's attack on Whakatane. We moved on to Waihi camp, and while there one hundred Ngati-Porou arrived from the East Coast under Acting Sub-Inspector Ferris and Peneamine Tuhaka. Ropata Wahawaha and Hotene Porourangi, with two hundred men, had been sent back from Napier by Mr. Donald McLean, General Government Agent there, as he thought it unwise to denude the East Coast and Poverty Bay of so many men. This caused a rupture between Colonel Whitmore and Mr. McLean; the latter was on the Opposition side of the House. Shortly after this the Government removed Mr. McLean from his position as Government Agent, and appointed Mr. H. R. Russell, M.L.C., in his place at Napier. The Ngati-Porou, under Ferris, were enrolled in the Armed Constabulary, forming No. 9 Division.

"Colonel St. John moved with about half the force by the mountain-track from Ketemarae to Mataitawa (Chute's track of 1866), and thence to Waitara, while Colonel Whitmore with headquarters and the remainder of the Constabulary went round to New Plymouth by the coast route. On the latter route we had to make a road as we went along for the transport drays, so progress was necessarily slow. Early on the fourth day we reached New Plymouth, where Major Stapp was in command. After consultation with him Colonel Whitmore went on to Waitara. Colonel St. John's column joined us there. They had met with no opposition on the bush march, and only found one straggler.

"While we were at Waitara waiting, Colonel Whitmore made a demonstration at Mokau Heads in the steamer 'Sturt,' in order to ascertain whether the Ngati-Maniapoto had a stronghold there. As they did not show fight we left them alone.

"Colonel Whitmore, leaving the West Coast under Colonel Lyon and a sufficient Armed Constabulary force, including No. 9 Division, now moved the rest of the Constabulary to the Bay of Plenty. The 'Sturt' took part of the force from Waitara, under Whitmore's personal command, and landed the men at Onehunga, whence they marched to Auckland, shipping from there to Tauranga by the 'Lord Worsley' the same night. The 'St Kilda' went round the North Cape with part of the force from Waitara, under Lieut.-Colonel St. John. The 'Sturt' returned from Onehunga to Waitara to ship another portion of St. John's force, and took this detachment round via the North Cape and the Bay of Islands to Whakatane, from which place Colonel Whitmore had arranged St. John's column was to march on Ruatahuna when plans were completed for a combined movement. Our force under the Colonel's command camped at The Mount, Tauranga Heads, for a few days to make arrangements for transport services and give the men a rest, and also to allow time for St. John's force to get round the North Cape. We then marched down the coast to Matata. Whitmore would not let the men go to Tauranga Township, as we had had some trouble keeping them in hand when passing through Auckland.

"The Colonel had to make arrangements with Colonel Harrington at Tauranga to provide transport service, and with Civil Commissioner H. T. Clarke to organize the native allies. Mr. Clarke accompanied the force to Maketu and Matata. At the latter place temporary headquarters were established and a base of operations formed.

"The Hon. J. C. Richmond (Defence Minister) visited Matata by steamer, and then went on to Napier to organize Colonel Herrick's force, which was to start from Wairoa for Waikare-moana. It was while getting ready at Matata that we heard of Te Kooti's raid on Mohaka and the massacre at that place. Colonel Whitmore had to arrange a canoe flotilla to take stores up the Rangitaiki River to a post which he established four miles above Te Teko; this station he named Fort Alfred, in honour of the Duke of Edinburgh, who was expected to visit New Zealand.

"The friendly Arawa were organized with the assistance of Mr. Clarke, who accompanied the expedition throughout. All these arrangements took time. Colonel Whitmore also had to visit Whakatane to confer with Colonel St. John, so as to ensure the working of the two columns in concert. Major Mair was in charge of the Whakatane natives and of the Ngaitai under the loyal chief Wiremu Kingi. From Fort Alfred we moved on to Ohuia, on the plain, where Colonel Whitmore established another redoubt, which was named Fort Clarke, after the Civil Commissioner.

"Leaving this post in charge of an officer he moved the force on to Te Karamuramu, where he established Fort Galatea, a redoubt named after the British warship conveying the Duke of Edinburgh to the colonies. From there the Urewera expedition was carried out successfully. The one weak point was the failure of Colonel Herrick's column to fulfil its part of the plan devised so carefully by Colonel Whitmore.

"This summary of the preparations shows the great amount of detail which the colonel had to attend to in organizing the Urewera expedition and co-ordinating the work of the columns. He was a great man in planning a campaign, and personally went into the smallest detail."

Colonel Whitmore in his despatches gave high praise to the Armed Constabulary in the Urewera expedition. "I find it difficult to say," he wrote from Fort Galatea, "without fear of being thought to show partiality, how admirably our men have behaved throughout. Living on potatoes [at Ruatahuna], labouring under heavy packs, with their clothes torn to rags and their boots destroyed, their cheerfulness and ready obedience at all times cannot be too highly praised. Poor fellows who were bleeding in their feet, who had had hardly a days' rest since November last, and, in spite of the quantity of clothes they have purchased since then, can scarcely muster a sound garment amongst them, were yet ready and anxious to face the Huiarau snow-covered heights, and to risk possible starvation or a long retreat, from the moment they heard of my wish to go to Waikare. Toiling up the precipitous hills, or wading in the beds of the slaty rivers, they could always keep up with and continue the march longer than the Maoris. Moreover, during the whole expedition they did not waste a single round of ammunition or throw away one shot when keeping sentry in the bush. If there was anything to be done they were at once ready; and when no duty was required from them they roamed about the country foraging, destroying crops, burning *kaingas,* and seeking the enemy's scouts in their several hiding-places in the vicinity. . . . The officers have all done their duty extremely well, and carried the same loads and fared the same as the men."

Major William G. Mair, reporting on his march out from Ruatahuna to Fort Galatea with the sick and wounded (14th–17th May, 1869) said that the Maoris had stated that the route via the Horomanga was better than that via Ahi-kereru, but he found it "a fearful track." There were five stretchers with wounded men, and there were also twenty sick and lame Armed Constabulary; these men he formed into a rearguard with some of the Maoris. The Urewera pursued the column, and fired on it at long range. The march was over the Tahuaroa Range, and then to the right to the Pukareao village—where the force camped one night, destroying the *kainga* next morning—thence to the Horomanga Gorge and out to Kuhawaea and the Rangitaiki. Mair stated that his Arawa did not do very well in the mountains: they were afraid of the country. However, in later expeditions the Arawa enlisted as a constabulary force under Captains Gilbert Mair and Preece proved excellent soldiers in the numerous marches and skirmishes in the Urewera Country.

THE NGATI-POROU IN TARANAKI

In July, 1869, when Lieutenant Preece was with Colonel Whitmore at Wellington after the return from the Urewera expedition, the steamer "St. Kilda" arrived from the East Coast with one hundred or one hundred and twenty Ngati-Porou men under Hati te Houkamau (a young chief from Hicks Bay), Paratene Ngata (father of the Hon. A. T. Ngata, M.P.), and Peneamine Tuhaka; the last-named had been sent up to recruit the force. Lieutenant Preece was sent in charge of them, with instructions to march them from Wanganui to Patea and hand them over to Major Noake, A.C. On arrival at Patea it was found that Major Noake had just returned from an up-river expedition with about one hundred and fifty prisoners of the Pakakohi Tribe under Taurua, and another very old chief. They were camped at the old Patea Township, about opposite the present railway-station.

After Lieutenant Preece had handed the men over there was a parade, and a curious incident occurred when the parade was dismissed. A man of No. 9 Division, Armed Constabulary (Ngati-Porou), stepped out and advanced with outstretched hands to the spot where the officers were standing; with them was Colonel Thomson, a retired Imperial officer. The Maori cried, "*Aue! Ko Tamihana!*" Surprised at the man's recognition, Colonel Thompson said, addressing Sub-Inspector Ferris, that there must be a mistake. But the Maori said, "You are Tamihana; you were in the 58th at Rua-pekapeka." Then he explained that he had been taken prisoner on the East Coast by the Ngapuhi, as a boy, and carried up to the Bay of Islands. He was with Tamati Waka's friendlies in Heke's War (1845–46), and after many years returned to his tribe. He remembered "Tamihana" at the siege of Rua-pekapeka.

"This is an extraordinary recognition," said Colonel Thomson. "At the Bay of Islands I was a young ensign with black whiskers, and generally in uniform. Now I am an old man with a grey beard, and in mufti, and yet this Maori knows me at first sight."

(Chapter 34)

POSTS ON THE NAPIER–TAUPO ROAD

When Armed Constabulary posts were established in the Taupo district in 1869 a number of fortified stations were erected to protect the line of communication with Napier across the plains and the lofty ranges intervening, a distance of nearly one hundred miles. At Opepe, twelve miles from Taupo, a strong timber stockade was constructed. At Runanga, about thirty-six miles from Taupo, a stockade was built on a hill overlooking the Waipunga and Runanga Streams. There was a sheep-station there. The fort was built in 1869 by No. 2 Division Armed Constabulary, under Sub-Inspector D. Scannell (formerly of the 57th Regiment). The Armed Constabulary hauled timber from the bush and built a stockade after the Maori pattern, as there was no fern handy to bind the loose pumice soil into parapets. The palisade timbers were 10 feet or 11 feet high, with two horizontal rails inside lashed to the uprights with *aka*-vines and *kareao* (supplejack) in the native manner. The main posts were large timbers, and saplings were set between them. Inside the stockade a trench was dug, and the earth and sods were heaped up against the fence, which was loopholed at the ground-level. There were flanking bastions at two diagonally opposite angles of the work. The one weak feature of the post was its distance from water. Its position was on the edge of the bush.

The next post was that at Tarawera (forty-eight miles from Taupo and fifty miles from Napier). The site is near the present hotel. This strong stockade had a one-storey loopholed blockhouse in two of the angles; these blockhouses were constructed of thick logs, roofs as well as walls, for protection from bullets fired from the higher hills.

At Te Haroto (fifty-four miles from Taupo), near the *kainga* of the Ngati-Hineuru Tribe, a blockhouse had been erected earlier than the posts already mentioned. This post was a square building with an upper storey projecting 2 feet or 3 feet over the lower. A deep well was dug inside the blockhouse. The position was a commanding one, with a panorama of the mountainous country for many miles around. A mile away is the highest point on the Taupo–Napier road, Tupurupuru (2,980 feet), on the Turangakumu Range.

At Titiokura, on the Maunga-haruru Range, a stockade was built in a prominent position, about 2,450 feet above sea-level, and about thirty miles from Napier.

(Chapter 38)

CAPTAIN RUSHTON AND THE WHAKATOHEA TRIBE

In July, 1870, Lieutenant (now Captain) J. R. Rushton, acting as scout to the forces at Opotiki, received information through native sources that Te Kooti was in communication with the Whakatohea Tribe (who had shortly before that day taken the oath of allegiance) and that there was danger of the people joining the rebel chieftain. Te Kooti was then making forced marches from the heart of the Urewera Country to get to the rear of Opotiki and the Omarumutu *pa,* expecting the wavering Whakatohea to follow him and attack the Opotiki settlement.

Immediately Rushton heard of the arrival of Lieut.-Colonel McDonnell's Constabulary and native force at Ohiwa (20th July), by the steamer "Luna," he rode through to Ohiwa and suggested to McDonnell that an attempt should be made to get the Whakatohea away before Te Kooti reached Omarumutu. This was approved of, and at great personal risk Rushton went through alone to Omarumutu (on the coast east of Opotiki) the same night. He met the tribe there and urged them to join Lieut.-Colonel McDonnell's force at Ohiwa. An old native scout of Rushton's, who was at the meeting, quietly urged him to leave at once, as there was great danger. Rushton had written a letter to the Whakatohea informing them that he knew all about Te Kooti's movements. His arguments prevailed, with the result that next day about sixty of the pick of the tribe, all armed, and bringing several boxes of ammunition, joined the Government column at Ohiwa. Two days later Te Kooti came down in rear of Opotiki and captured the Omarumutu *pa,* but too late to make the expected addition to his fighting force. For this prompt and skilful foiling of the enemy Rushton was promoted to Captain and received a letter of thanks from the Government.

(Chapter 40)

THE WAIPAOA ENGAGEMENT (1871): TE KOOTI'S GUN

Captain Preece gives the following history of the American repeater which Te Kooti used when he was defeated by Mair and Preece in their surprise attack on the Waipaoa bush camp in the south-eastern part of the Urewera Country, August, 1871:—

"Te Kooti had only one cartridge in his Spencer repeating-rifle and fired this at us as he was escaping into the bush. [See page 439.] The weapon had a curious record. It was originally a present from the Government to the friendly Arawa chief Wiremu Maihi te Rangikaheke, who was stationed at Ohiwa. When Major Mair made peace with Te Whenuanui and his fellow Urewera chiefs at Ruatoki, Wi Maihi sent the gun to be shown to the other Urewera leaders, and Kereru te Pukenui, of the Upper Whakatane, who had not made peace, got hold it. He did not return it, but sent it to Te Kooti, with all the ammunition that was with it. After our defeat of Te Kooti at Waipaoa and his flight towards Maunga-pohatu, he gave back the rifle to Kereru te Pukenui, from whom he had obtained it. [It was useless to him, as he had no more ammunition for it.]"

(Chapter 43)

THE MURDER OF SULLIVAN, UPPER WAIKATO

Mr. George Bailey, of Harwood Street, Hamilton, writes:—

"In the year 1873, in the Waikato, outside the Town of Cambridge, the estates of Monavale and Roto-o-rangi were under the joint management of E. B. Walker and Richard Parker. Timothy Sullivan and another man, Davie Jones, were employed laying *manuka* fascines for making a crossing over a swamp, to facilitate an entrance to a native leasehold property adjoining the Monavale-Roto-o-rangi property on the eastern side, known as the Pukekura Block. One day while this work was in progress the late Richard Parker and a man named Lloyd were carting the *manuka* in a dray, and, nearing the locality where Sullivan and Jones were working, they observed that the tea-billy was upturned on the fire, things were in general disorder, and Sullivan and Jones were missing. As there had been rumours that treacherous natives were about, Parker feared that they might have attacked Sullivan and Jones. After unloading the dray he and Lloyd decided to hasten back up the hill and look round for the missing men. While returning along the track an armed native emerged from the fern on the hillside. He aimed at Parker, but his gun missed fire. Parker and Lloyd, being unarmed, made a hurried retreat to the homestead and reported to Cambridge. In the afternoon of the same day a number of volunteers were called out to make a search, and Sullivan's body, beheaded, was found at the head of a gully, in the *manuka*, where he had apparently run to escape the attacking Maoris. Jones evaded the Maoris and escaped. The Maori credited with killing Sullivan was Purukutu. He claimed interest in the lands in that locality. His sister, Maraea Whakatutu, had a share in the Pukekura lands, and lived there for many years afterwards."

THE CAPTURE OF HIROKI

Hiroki shot McLean, against whom he had a grievance, when the latter was working on the survey of the Moumahaki Block, in the Waitotara district, in 1878. Scouts were sent out from Hawera in pursuit of him, and one of them, William Williams, fired at and wounded him, but Hiroki escaped to Parihaka. When that native town was occupied by the troops on the 5th November, 1881, Hiroki was captured, and was tried, convicted, and hanged.

TARANAKI REDOUBTS, 1879–81

Mr. James Robson, of Wellington (late of "Whitiora," Stratford), who is a pioneer of sawmilling in the Upper Hutt Valley and in Taranaki, thus describes the later critical period on the Taranaki frontier and the building of the redoubt at Normanby settlement:—

"I started the first sawmill at Ketemarae soon after the close of Titokowaru's war. We built the mill about a mile and a half from the present site of Normanby Township, or Matariki, as it was known by the natives; the large Maori *kainga* of Ketemarae was about a mile from the present township. We supplied the timber for many places about Ketemarae and on the Waimate Plains, and amongst them was the Manaia Redoubt. At one time we had seventy bullocks in the teams carting sawn timber around the district. We had some anxious days when the great Maori gatherings at Parihaka in 1879–81 and the increasing feeling of hostility between *pakeha* and Maori created a crisis that threatened to end in a renewal of the war. A redoubt was built at Normanby in 1879 by the men of the district. We were supplied with Enfield rifles by the Government, and Mr. Frank Brett, formerly a sergeant in the Armed Constabulary, a tall athletic frontiersman, was elected captain of the settler volunteers. There were then, I suppose, about fifty men in and around the Ketemarae district. An old Maori friend, Katene Tu-whakaruru, warned Mrs. Robson and me, about the beginning of 1881, that there would be serious trouble, and told me we should go into the redoubt every night. We spent two or three days in the redoubt at the height of the alarms. Captain Brett sent out patrols at night along the road, and we did regular sentry duty. However, at the mill we had six men with rifles, and we could have put up a fight there if attacked. I had a valuable engine at the mill, and, fearing that the place might be burned down by the Maoris if fighting began, we hauled it with bullocks very nearly a mile and a half, to within close range of the redoubt."

The Normanby Redoubt, long since demolished, stood on the spot where the monument to the soldiers in the Maori wars stands to-day in the Domain, close to the railway-station. It was a rectangular work with trench and high parapet, flanked for an enfilading fire along the ditch. At intervals there were regular gaps or embrasures in the top of the sod wall for two or three men who could stand and deliver fire if attacked. The defenders could just see over the parapet at these intervals. The ditch, not very deep, was crossed by a plank; later by a drawbridge. Inside, near the entrance, a timber watch-tower for the sentry by day was built when the Armed Constabulary came to garrison the post. In the middle of the redoubt was a building, a rough shed-like place, of sawn timber, for the shelter of the men and their families at night. The redoubt earthwork was built by volunteer labour, but carpenters were paid for putting up the large shed and the other timber-work. Happily the redoubt was never needed for actual defence, and before the middle "eighties" Taranaki had settled down to permanent peace.

The redoubt at Manaia, on the Waimate Plains, was the best-designed of the later Armed Constabulary posts constructed in Taranaki. It was built on a gentle elevation above the Waiokura Stream; the spot is now the Manaia town park. The earthworks are still standing, with the flanking blockhouses. The redoubt measures, on the outer edge of the trench, 35 paces by 30 paces; the parapet is 6 feet thick and 5 feet above the inside level of the work. On the west side, where the ground falls steeply to the stream, the scarp of the parapet is from 15 to 20 feet in height; on the other side 10 to 12 feet above the bottom of the ditch. At two of the diagonally opposite angles there are flanking bastions, timber blockhouses 12 feet square, iron-roofed, with double walls, originally filled in with gravel to make them bullet-proof. These blockhouses are loopholed and enfilade the ditch. There are four loopholes on each side of the blockhouses, arranged in two tiers, 2 feet and 4 feet 6 inches above the ground. These loopholes were very carefully made by the Armed Constabulary carpenters; they measure on the inside 7 inches by 5 inches, narrowing to about 3 inches by 2½ inches on the outside; the depth (thickness of the double wall) is about 8 inches. The loopholes are closed by sliding wooden shutters. At the seaward flank of the redoubt, surmounting the trench-bridge and entrance, there was a timber watch-tower 35 feet high, ascended by a stair inside the tower. The original structure has disappeared and has been replaced by a concrete tower in the middle of the redoubt.

The small blockhouses, the last remaining in Taranaki, deserve better care; they are in danger of decay and fire, because of the thick fern and other vegetation growing around them and in the trench. The interior of the work has been converted into lawns and flower-plots by the Manaia town authorities, but the earthwork and the well-constructed bastion block-houses are neglected. Manaia is fortunate in possessing so interesting a specimen of the frontier forts, long since razed in most other parts, and the works are worthy of some pains to preserve them as an historical monument.

THE PARIHAKA EXPEDITION (1881)

The principal source of danger in Parihaka, Taranaki, 1879–81, was the chief Te Whetu ("The Star"), who, unlike his superiors Te Whiti and Tohu, was eager for a renewal of war. The old tattooed *tohunga* Tautahi Ariki, or Tu-ahi-pa, went to Captain W. E. Gudgeon at the Pungarehu Armed Constabulary camp one day in 1881 and advised him that Te Whetu was "thirsty for war." "*Kia tupato*," said Tautahi; "beware of him; he is a *toa*, and wishes to fight." Te Whetu was a young man and a firebrand, and Captain Gudgeon, realizing that his counsels were likely to provoke a conflict, in spite of the intense desire of Te Whiti for peace, determined to have him arrested. This was done, and a possible war-raiser was removed from the scene.

The late Colonel W. B. Messenger, narrating (1918) the incidents of the invasion of Parihaka, said:—

"When affairs became critical on the Waimate Plains I was sent for, like Northcroft on the Bench, to leave my farm at Pukearuhe and take charge of 120 Armed Constabulary for Parihaka. Lieut.-Colonel Roberts was in command of the whole force. Although the older Maoris in Parihaka were anxious for peace, there were many young men in the place who wished to fight, and the danger was that one of these would precipitate a battle by firing a shot. When we marched on Parihaka on the 5th November, 1881, their attitude of passive resistance and patient obedience to Te Whiti's orders was extraordinary. There was a line of children across the entrance to the big village, a kind of singing class directed by an old man with a stick. The children sat there unmoving, droning away, and even when a mounted officer galloped up and pulled his horse up so short that the dirt from its forefeet spattered the children they still went on chanting, perfectly oblivious, apparently, to the *pakeha,* and the old man calmly continued his monotonous drone.

"I was the first to enter the Maori town with my company. I found my only obstacle was the youthful feminine element. There were skipping-parties of girls on the road. When I came to the first set of girls I asked them to move, but they took no notice. I took hold of one end of the skipping-rope, and the girl at the other end pulled it away so quickly that it burnt my hands. At last, to make a way for my men, I tackled one of the rope-holders. She was a fat, substantial young woman, and it was all I could do to lift her up and carry her to one side of road. She made not the slightest resistance, but I was glad to drop the buxom wench. My men were all grinning at the spectacle of their captain carrying the big girl off. I marched them in at once through the gap and we were in the village. There were six hundred women and children there, and our reception was perfectly peaceful. We drafted all the women and children out on to a hillside after the arrest of Te Whiti and Tohi. Orders had been given that no Maori property was to be touched, but I know there was a good deal of looting—in fact, robbery. Many of our Government men stole greenstones and other treasures from the native houses; among them were some fine *meres.*"

JOHN WEBSTER, OF OPONONI

Mr. John Webster, of Opononi, Hokianga, who accompanied the troops on the march to Waima (1898), had an uncommonly eventful career. Before coming to New Zealand in 1840 he had fought blacks on the overland trail in New South Wales. After Hone Heke's War, in which he served as a free lance, he went to San Francisco in the days of the "forty-nine" gold rush, and with the celebrated Benjamin Boyd he cruised in the schooner-yacht "Wanderer" through the South Sea islands. This cruise was tragically interrupted by the death of Mr. Boyd at the hands of Solomon Islands cannibals in a bay on Guadalcanar Island in 1851. John Webster helped to serve the schooner's guns against a horde of savages who attacked the vessel in their canoes. "The Cruise of the Wanderer," written and illustrated by himself, gave an account of this Pacific islands voyage. Mr. Webster's beautiful home at Opononi, on Hokianga Harbour, was well known to visitors to the North Auckland country.

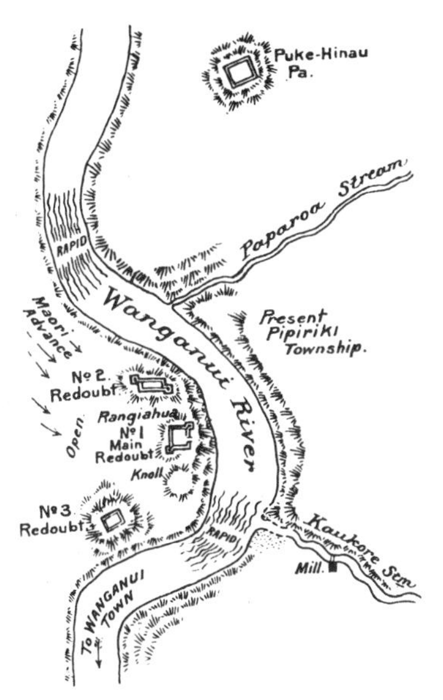

The Redoubts at Pipiriki (Wanganui River), 1865
(See Chapter 4, "The Siege of Pipiriki," pages 37-45.)

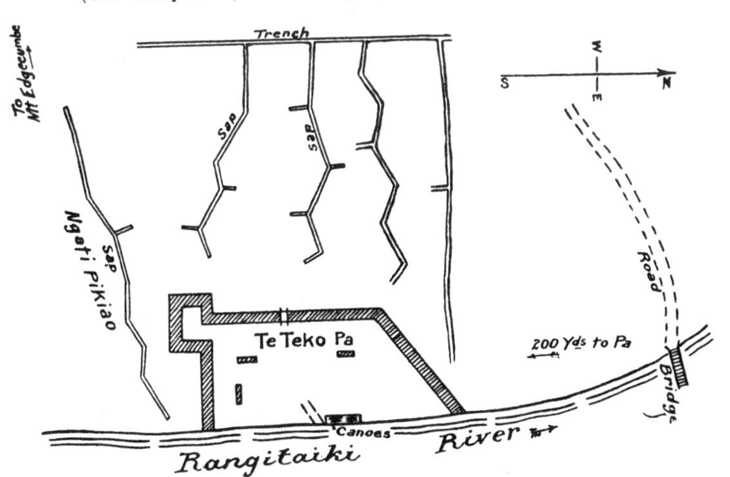

J. C., sketch-map, 1923]

Te Teko *Pa* and Major Mair's Saps, 1865
(See Chapter 9, pages 96-105.)

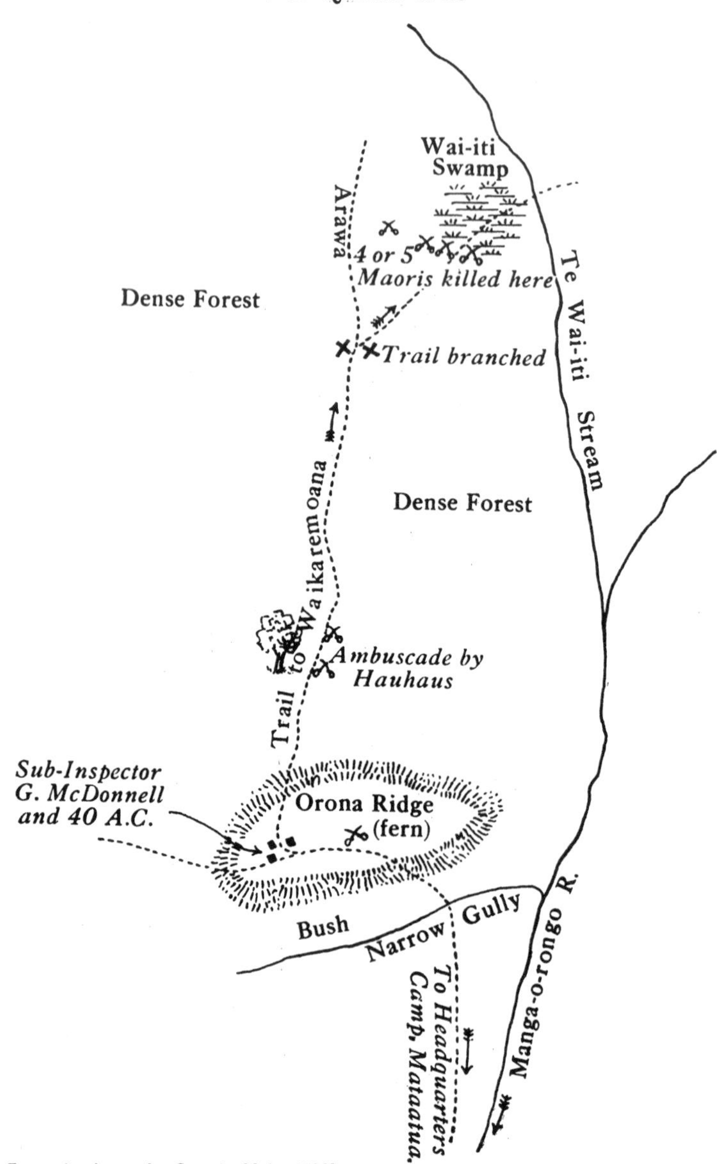

From sketch-map by Captain Mair, 1923]

Scene of Skirmishes at Orona and Te Wai-iti, Urewera Country, 1869

(See pages 354-357.)

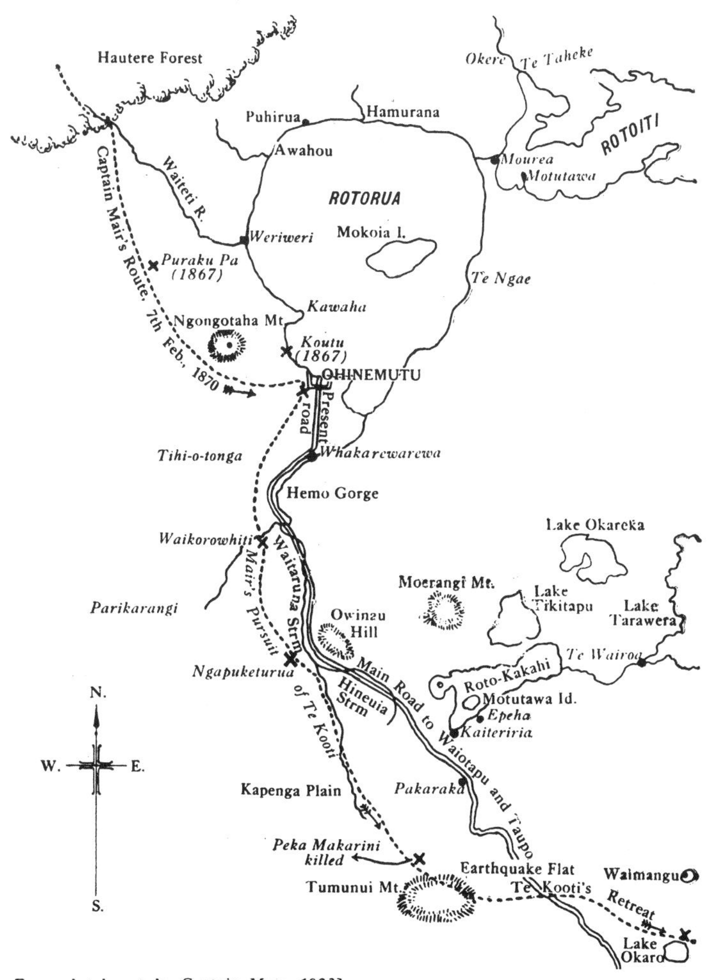

From sketch-map by Captain Mair, 1923]

Scene of Captain Mair's Defeat of Te Kooti, Rotorua, 1870

(See Chapter 35, pages 387-400.)

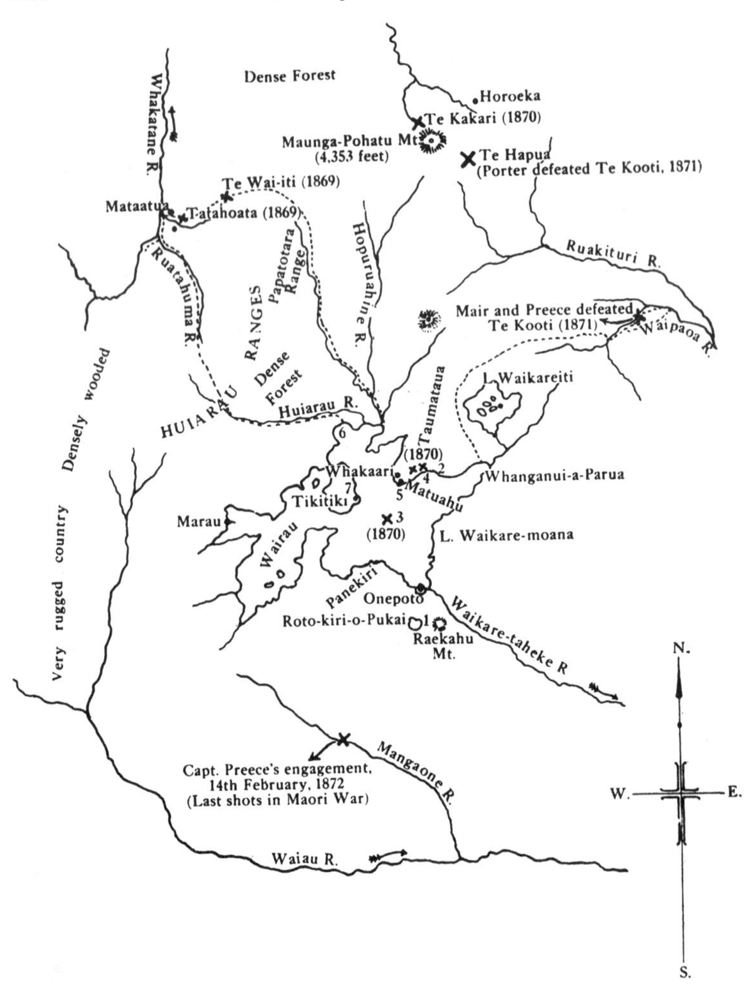

Lake Waikare-moana and the Urewera Country

Showing scenes of the last engagements in the Maori wars.

(See Major Large's notes in Appendices, page 547.)

THE FANATIC FAITH

The following Press cable message is a further illustration of the widespread fanatic faith in supernatural defence against an enemy's bullets, described in Chapter 1:—

"Manila, 21st May, 1923.

"Twenty-four Moro religious fanatics on the Island of Pata (Philippine Islands) were killed by the island Constabulary when the former initiated an attack. It is reported that the Moros were told by a priest that they were immune from the effects of bullets."

MAORI FIELD FORTIFICATIONS

DESCRIPTION OF A PA AT MANUTAHI, TARANAKI

The remarkable skill displayed by the Maoris in the construction of their stockaded entrenchments is particularly well illustrated in a description and plans of a field fortification at Manutahi, in North Taranaki, furnished by Mr. George F. Robinson, of Leinster Road, Christchurch, who was for many years Government Road Engineer in Taranaki. This Manutahi should not be confused with a place of the same name in South Taranaki, where a redoubt (see plan, page 181) was built during the Hauhau wars. Writing under date 21st May, 1923, Mr. Robinson gave the following account of a venturesome expedition by a small party of unarmed settler volunteers which resulted in the discovery of the *pa* described, built during the first Taranaki War:—

"When the Waitara War began I was a young settler on the Bell Block, about four miles from New Plymouth, and the farmers of our settlement built a blockhouse (see pages 165-166, Vol I) on a hill overlooking the open part of the district. Within the boundaries of the block was a native village, Paraiti, and we settlers knew every Maori there. Beyond the block to the northward was another native village, Ninia, and inland from this and near the edge of the bush was the Kaipakopako *kainga*. We knew most of the native inhabitants well. Then came the war. By February, 1861, the Maoris, the Imperial troops, and the settlers were all heartily sick of the fighting. Peace was finally arranged in March of that year. On the Sunday following the making of peace (which was settled on a Thursday or Friday) seven of us young settlers stole away from the Bell Block post—discipline being somewhat relaxed—without arms. Our objective was a peach-orchard which we knew existed at Kaipakopako; the peaches there were especially delicious. We left the blockhouse at about 9 a.m., arrived at the orchard (about three miles away) before 10.30, satisfied our craving, and then decided to make our way to Sentry Hill, about a mile and a half northward. We followed the native track, crossed the Mangaoraka Stream, and climbed the hill; the whole distance was through heavy fern and scrub (excepting at the stream,

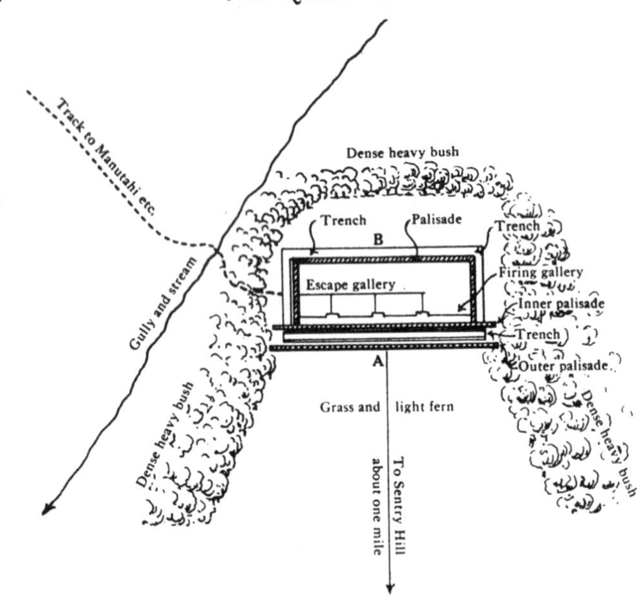

The Manutahi *Pa,* 1861

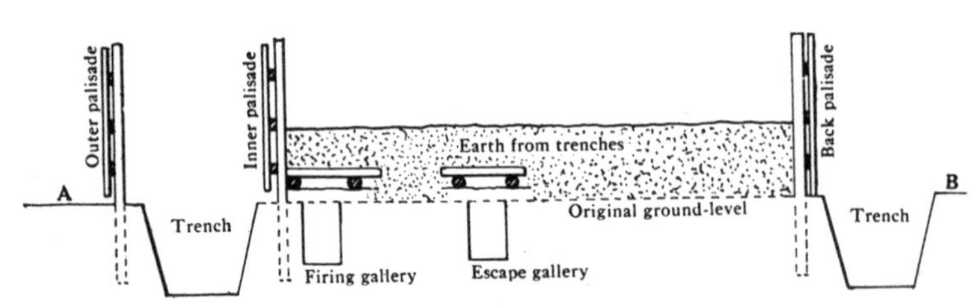

From sketch-plans by Mr. G. F. Robinson]

Cross-section of Manutahi *Pa*

where it was bush). The top of the hill (an old *pa*) was also in fern. This we trod down, and then lay in the sun. About noon one of the party stood up, but at once dropped down again, saying, 'There's a Maori coming along the track from Manutahi.' Peering through the fern we saw a Maori lad walking towards us. When about 200 yards away he saw one of our heads and stopped, but on our showing ourselves and calling to him, telling him who we were, he came on and up the hill. He was a Paraiti Maori, and knew most of us. He told us the Paraiti, Ninia, and Kaipakopako Maoris all lived on the slopes of Mataitawa ridge, three or four miles farther inland, and asked us to go with him and see them. We looked at each other and hesitated; a few days before they would have been glad of the opportunity to tomahawk us, and as we were unarmed we did not like putting too much temptation in their way. The boy, seeing our hesitation, said, 'I was not afraid to come to you; why should you be afraid to go with me?' Of course, it was insufferable to be looked upon by a boy as cowards, so with an air of 'Lead on, Macduff,' we followed him inland.

"About Sentry Hill and for some distance inland the country was covered with fern and *tutu,* 6 to 8 feet high, excepting where the track had been beaten down; we soon, however, came to where the forest commenced. At first it was about 100 yards away on each side, then gradually narrowed like an inverted V, until after travelling about a mile from Sentry Hill we came to the dense bush. On our left was a gully in which ran a small stream, all in the bush, and on our right and front the heavy bush extended for many miles. Across the point of the V (near about where Lepperton Railway-station now stands) was a fighting *pa,* the strongest I have ever seen. The front palisading reached across from bush to bush, perhaps 100 to 120 feet in length, the ends being carried well into the bush and blocked and screened with branches and native briar (*tataramoa*). The supports of the front palisade (as also the others) were of tree-boles about 12 inches in diameter, sunk deeply and firmly into the ground about 10 feet apart and projecting above the ground to a height of 12 to 14 feet. To these were lashed horizontally, with supple-jack and rata-vine, at heights of about 3 feet 6 inches and 10 feet from the ground, heavy split rails (the Maoris before the war possessed axes, saws, wedges, spades, &c.), and to these, vertically and fairly close together, were lashed other split rails, the tops about the height of the posts, and the butts reaching to about 1 foot above the ground. Behind this palisading was a trench 8 feet deep by 10 feet wide at the top and 6 feet wide at the bottom; behind this again was a second palisade similar in design and strength to the front one. Behind this, firing galleries or passages had been dug parallel with the front. The galleries were about 5 feet deep by 3 feet wide—not dug in one straight line, but with blocks or traverses about every 20 feet to provide against the effect of a bursting shell. These galleries were roofed over with logs on which were placed saplings and fern, well trampled down. The whole was covered with the earth from the trenches and galleries; this covering was from 3 to 4 feet deep. The front galleries or firing-trenches extended the full length of the *pa.* Loop-holes were left under the log covering (about on a level with the outer front) through which the Maoris could fire on the advancing foe without themselves being seen or being in danger. From the firing-galleries passages went back to a central passage in the *pa* (covered in the same manner as the others), which in turn led by a covered way to the gully and stream in the bush, by which passage the Maoris could escape in case of defeat, or could be reinforced during the fighting. The sides and rear of the *pa* had single palisading only, inside the trench, as the Maoris did not expect any assault on those sides. In front of the *pa* for a distance of about 300 yards all fern had been broken down or removed; so for that distance no cover was afforded the advancing enemy and the defenders could see them, and fire at them from the loopholes. The twelve months' war experience had taught the Maoris two things: (1) That the military always made frontal attacks; (2) that no soldier would willingly enter the bush, or could make his way through it should he be taken there, being easily entangled amongst the dense scrub and the supplejacks and other vines. The heaviest field-gun used by the troops at that time was the 24 lb. howitzer, throwing solid shot or shell. Either of these striking the vertical palisading would simply cut the piece struck, and, as it was tied in three places, the ends would swing back again, leaving the palisade apparently as before. Should a shot strike a post it might smash it down, but rarely did so. [At Puke-ta-kauere in 1860 I saw the artillery, at 300 yards and under, fire at palisading for over an hour without doing any appreciable damage.] Artillery-fire usually commenced at about 800 yards from a *pa,* and was taken closer. Should a shot strike the palisading, the effect would be as I have described. Should the aim be low, and the ball strike the ground in front of the *pa,* it would ricochet over it. The chances were more than a hundred to one against a ball or shell entering a loophole through which the Maoris fired; they were screened by the two palisades, though the vertical rails, not coming within a foot of the ground, did not obstruct the Maoris' view of the enemy nor interfere with their firing. Assuming the outer palisade was broken down, the assaulting-party would have to face the trench and inner palisade, and were these overcome and the enemy get into the *pa,* they would see nothing but a bare earth surface. The Maoris could not be got at, but would escape by the covered way into the gully and bush, where they would not be followed. The only effective way of dealing with such forts was by the use of heavy Coehorn mortars, which threw a shell at a high angle, descending vertically after describing a parabolic curve. Up to the date of this *pa,* however, such guns were not available.

"The *pa* I have described was built towards the end of 1860. It was never fully occupied, and when we saw it in March, 1861, it had been abandoned and partly dismantled. About three years after the events I have decribed the district we travelled over was occupied by the Hauhaus, and all signs of the *pa* were obliterated. We were curious to know why the fort had been built at such an enormous cost of material and labour and then abandoned, and learned later that the three sections or *hapus* of Maoris I have mentioned (Paraiti, Ninia, and Kaipakopako), having been driven from their homes, had taken refuge near Mataitawa, where they made new *whares* and cultivations, and the *pa* was built across the then only known track leading to their new homes. The tide of war having drifted to other districts, they thought the *pa* was no longer needed, and it was therefore abandoned.

"Having well examined the fortification above and below, under the guidance of the Maori boy, we followed him by the escape track across the gully and stream, then along through the bush to the Waiongona Stream, which we forded, and so on to the foot of Mataitawa Hill (just beyond Manutahi), where we found the Paraiti people's settlement. The Maoris were startled at our appearance, not knowing our numbers or how we came there, but our guide calling out the explanation, they rushed forward to welcome us in the good old Maori way, shouting, laughing, crying, all but embracing us. We stayed with them about half an hour, and then moved on and up the hill to a plateau, where we found the Ninia natives. A messenger having warned them of our approach, we received from them the same riotous welcome. After staying awhile we moved on to the Kaipakopako settlement, accompanied by a bodyguard of excitable chatty friends, and were again cordially welcomed by hundreds of our old friends and recent foes, who anxiously inquired as to who were killed or wounded amongst those they knew at Bell Block, and told us of their own fatalities. They showed no signs of rancour or ill feeling. I was talking to a chief when suddenly he opened the blanket he had around him and showed me his right arm: it had been shot through the elbow, the bone broken, and, being badly set, the arm had withered and was useless. He told me he was shot at Puke-ta-kauere, and on my saying I was present at that engagement he explained how he received his wound. The troops having retired from the battlefield and returned to Waitara, the natives (who were left in possession) hunted about amongst the high fern for wounded soldiers, tomahawking all they found—for the Maoris took no prisoners. The chief was searching with the rest, and, hearing a shot near by, rushed forward to the spot, and saw a sergeant of the 40th Regiment lying wounded. The soldier was unable to get away, but he had his rifle and was shooting all who came near. The chief bounded forward to tomahawk him, but received a bullet through his arm, and shouted for help. A number of Maoris came, and, first disabling the sergeant with gun-fire, they tomahawked him. The chief said the sergeant shot seven of the Maori who attacked him before he was killed.

"As we had about eight miles to travel by the nearest route to get back to the Bell Block post, and as the sun was nearing the horizon, we had to say good-bye to our friends and hurry back, so as to get through the bush before dark. We reached the blockhouse before 9 p.m. in time to answer to our names at roll-call. Our party consisted of the following young men besides myself: Thomas Kelly (afterwards M.H.R. and M.L.C.), his brother John Kelly (afterwards Captain in the New Zealand Militia), William Rundle and his brother Richard Rundle, George Bertrand (afterwards in Von Tempsky's force), Harry Morrison (afterwards Captain in the Armed Constabulary). All of us but young Morrison (who had arrived from England in 1860) had lived and farmed on the Bell Block for several years. Two beside myself are still living—William Rundle (now over ninety-four years of age), of New Plymouth, and G. Bertrand (aged eighty-two), of Urenui."

In September, 1864, Colonel Warre, with a force of Regulars and Militia, advanced on Mataitawa and captured a stockaded *pa* at Manutahi, which blocked the way. (See page 28.) It is uncertain whether this was the original Manutahi *pa* renovated and somewhat altered in design, or whether it was a new field-work constructed on a different site.

SURVEYING UNDER FIRE

PIONEER WORK ON THE TARANAKI FRONTIER

The surveyors engaged in cutting up the South Taranaki confiscated lands for settlement, 1866–68, carried on their work under adventurous and often very perilous conditions. It was remarked of the surveyors that they really performed the duty of outlying pickets to the troops garrisoning the frontier redoubts. The following are extracts from the private journal kept by the late Mr. S. Percy Smith, F.R.G.S., ex-Surveyor General, when he, as a district surveyor in Taranaki, was employed in laying out roads and surveying sections for townships and military settlements between the Wai-ngongoro and the Waitotara. With Mr. Smith at this period were his fellow-surveyors, Messrs. G. W. Williams, C. A. Wray, and F. Wilson, each in charge of a party.

19th April, 1866 (at New Plymouth).—Getting ready for Patea, for the survey. Received from the Militia officer five tents and ten revolvers, &c., for the men. Many people think we are running a great risk by going to such a dangerous place as Patea.

7th June (Camp at Kakaramea).—Upon coming into camp we found that Captain Newland's Company of Patea Rangers had arrived to furnish us with covering-parties.

14th June.—Rode with Mr. Carrington, Major McDonnell, and troopers to choose sites for blockhouses. First went to a hill inland of Kakaramea, where a good site was chosen, as was also the site of the township for military settlers. This is Colonel Haultain's idea of putting the town near the bush. Will it ever be a town? We shall see. We then rode to another hill, near the old settlement of Manutahi, which was also selected. Here we discovered fresh traces of the Hauhaus, and a place where they had been lying in wait. We then returned to camp.

15th June.—Rode with Mr. Carrington and McDonnell to Wai-ngongoro. After passing Manawapou we went over a most beautiful country for ten miles—very level, and a great deal of grass, especially near the sea. We were most hospitably received by Captain Dawson and the other officers of the 18th quartered there.

16th June (Wai-ngongoro).—This is one of the nicest posts in this part of the country. One redoubt is situated on the southern bank of the river, and on top of the cliff overhanging the sea. The other is on the northern side of a rise commanding a beautiful view of the plains around here, dotted with "hostile" cattle and horses and backed by Mount Egmont, which on this clear frosty morning looked superb. At 12 we started back for Kakaramea and got on all well as far as the Waihi Stream, some three miles from the Wai-ngongoro. Here Lieutenant Wirihana, of the Native Contingent, advised us to ride on, in case of the Hauhaus being about. My horse, being very fresh, would insist upon keeping about 40 yards ahead of the rest. As we reached the point where the Ketemarae Road turns off from the General's road along which we were travelling I heard Wirihana call out something to me which I did not catch at first, but tried to pull up my horse; this after a time I succeeded in doing. I then saw that they all had stopped, and I heard them call out "Hauhaus," and they pointed behind me. I turned my head towards a clump of flax-bushes and then saw a lot of Hauhaus about 40 yards from me rising up out of the fern, and at the same instant they poured in a volley at us. Of course we all rode off as fast as possible, with the bullets flying about our ears, as they kept up an incessant fire for a long way. Some of the balls were unpleasantly near, and I could see them and hear them striking the flax as we rode along. We recrossed the Waihi, where we saw another party trying to cut us off, and reached our last night's quarters, Waingongoro, in safety, and very thankful to God I feel for our miraculous escape. None of us was hit, though there were more than forty Hauhaus firing at us as hard as they could. If it had not been for Wirihana, who saw their heads moving in the flax, we should all have just ridden into the ambush and probably all have perished. Captain Dawson gave us some ten troopers and fifty of the 18th Regiment to go back as an escort part of the way. Upon reaching the scene of the ambush we saw some of the wretches in the distance inland, and reached Manawapou in safety. Thence we had another escort as far as Maori Bridge—needless, I think—and I finally reached my camp at Kakaramea at 8, whilst Mr. Carrington and McDonnell and the two troopers went on to Patea.

18th June.—Rode into Patea first thing to see Mr. Carrington. The rebels have written in to say that they are about to commence "slaying the *pakeha*" again. Returned and commenced laying out township. Always take out covering-party now.

7th July.—A Hauhau boy captured the other day was sent back and came in again to-day with letters from Te Ranga-o-te-whenua, one written in English (or rather Irish), telling the commanding officer to put a stop to the surveys or the surveyors will be killed.

9th July.—About 130 more military settlers arrived from Opotiki, on the east coast, to be stationed here. Surely they have enough men to furnish us more covering-parties now.

19th July.—Have been principally in the bush lately cutting out sections, roads, &c., but get on very slowly, as I often have to work three parties in one, as the Militia can only supply one covering-party of twenty men for my three parties. To-day cut one road through the township (Kakaramea) towards Manawapou through the bush—beautiful level country and open bush. The covering-parties come to great grief generally in the bush. Don't think they would be of much use if attacked.

20th July.—Explored across Von Tempsky's Gorge for road, but only discovered a pretty waterfall. Afterwards found a good crossing and carried the road from the township to the top of "Gentle Annie." Find it is a beautiful place; old cultivations surrounded with *ngaio* trees. Covering-parties came to great grief coming home a short-cut across the mouth of the gorge.

21st July.—Traversing the Patea until stopped by an impassable cliff. Left the covering-party on a hill all day. Discovered fresh signs of the rebels having been down here in canoes.

23rd July.—Ross's Rangers left for Manawapou preparatory to the whole force leaving. I understand that Major McDonnell has instructions to "go in" at the Hauhaus.

27th July.—Captain Newland having sent down three carts, we packed up and left for Kakaramea at 12 for Manawapou, and I am not sorry to leave the place either.

28th July.—The men all refused to go out to work as they consider it too dangerous with only a covering-party of twenty men. Several of our men have left and joined the Military Settlers.

1st August.—Have been doing nothing all this time. This evening the Major goes out with some two hundred men to attack the rebels. Most of our men go also.

2nd August.—Expedition returned. They spent a very cold night, and at daylight rushed and took a village called Pokaikai, killing some seven natives and taking four or five prisoners. Aperahama, a man of some note, was killed. Poor Spain, a man who lately left us to join Wilson's Company, was shot by our own men whilst rushing into a *whare* where there were a lot of rebels. Lots of guns brought back.

4th August.—Last night an expedition consisting of two hundred men went out to attack a supposed stronghold at Manutahi. Williams, Wray, and I accompanied them. We marched all night through beautiful country, but found nothing of the rebels except some fresh signs and the cavalry horses which strayed away a few days since.

6th August.—Got to work again after a fortnight's idleness, cutting out sections inland of the redoubt. The force moves on again soon to a place called "The Round Bush" (near Hawera). That will suit us capitally as a camp.

7th August.—Went out with McDonnell and the Native Contingent to meet the Hauhaus of the Pakakohe section, who have after their thrashing at Pokaikai expressed a wish for peace. We met about thirty of them at Ohangai, a beautiful old *pa* between the Tawhiti and the Tangahoe Streams. It is the same place that we spent our Sunday at on our return from the Taupo journey (1858). The Hauhaus appear a miserable lot of dirty-looking wretches. They brought in their arms and took the oath, but, strange to say, McDonnell allowed them to keep their arms. I think he is wrong. However, I suppose he knows best. They had a 70th rifle amongst them, and a Military Train carbine.

14th August.—Some mounted rebels came down to Waihi and fired into the military convoy, but did no damage.

16th August.—Traversing the Tawhiti (near Hawera); very bad cutting. Newland went to-day to swear in some of the rebels at Meremere, but left them their arms. What a farce it is!

28th August.—Cutting on the main road to Ketemarae Road. Here two rebels galloped down and fired at us, but at such a distance that they did no harm.

30th August.—Carried on the main road to the Waihi Stream. Fired into again, but at such a distance as to do no harm. It appears that they keep two videttes there always.

31st August.—Wray, whilst out, suddenly saw two natives ride in to within 80 yards of his party and deliberately fire into him. They returned the fire, when the rebels quietly rode off.

1st September.—Traversing the Tawiti not far from Keteonetea, the Hauhaus came down and fired at us at 500 yards and kept it up for some time. The Native Contingent doubled out to our relief, when the covering-party mistook them for rebels and fired into them, but luckily without effect.

14th September.—Having completed all the work about here (Hawera district)—eighty allotments—we removed camp to Ketemarae, as the new camp is called, though not where the *pa* of that name used to be. Skirmishes going on all day at the edge of the bush between our men out hunting and the natives.

23rd September.—The Hauhaus laid a successful ambush to-day for the bread-cart coming from Hawera. They rushed into it, killed one of the troopers, and got some of the bread. We could see some of the affair from the redoubt. Newland turned out and exchanged shots with them, then sent down and put Captain Smith, commanding at Hawera, under arrest for sending up only three troopers as an escort. The man's name was Haggerty; he was most brutally tomahawked.

25th September.—The Native Contingent had a skirmish with the Hauhaus near the scene of the ambush on Sunday. They killed and cut up one man.

28th September.—Saw some Hauhaus on the north side of the Wai-ngongoro when at work. Wright, who went down to the river to bring up some meat killed yesterday, saw some and fired at them; they ran.

2nd October.—Men off pay yesterday and to-day. Refused to go out without covering-parties. McDonnell returned this morning after attacking a village last night on the north side of the Wai-ngongoro called Pungarehu. They rushed the place at dawn, and had a tough fight of it before the place was burnt and the inhabitants killed. The Hauhaus from a neighbouring village came down, it is said, to the number of a hundred and tried to surround our people, who, after some time, were obliged to retire with the wounded, the Hauhaus following them up to the edge of the bush. Two of our men went out with the expedition—Wright and Allen. The former, while trying to save a wounded man, was shot in the knee, and, poor fellow, died soon after reaching Wai-ngongoro. Another man, Green, who had lately left us to join the Wanganui Rangers, was shot whilst trying to carry Wright, and died soon after. The farrier-major of the cavalry, Duff, a most plucky fellow, was shot at the beginning of the affair. Three were killed; Cornet Hirtzel wounded, and Spencer, volunteer attached to the Native Contingent, and two other men wounded. The Hauhaus lost killed thirty-five, and nine prisoners, several of whom are wounded. Surely this ought to make them give in, although our people had to retreat. This is their most severe loss for a very long time.

3rd October.—All hands went down to the Wai-ngongoro to bury poor Wright. The three dead men were all buried with military honours in the little graveyard [Ohawe] used by the soldiers on the southern side of the river. Our men carried Wright to his last resting-place.

8th October.—Morrison's Company of Taranaki Military Settlers arrived here from New Plymouth to reinforce the Major. Some of them are left at Hawera.

17th October.—Doing nothing all day. The men would not go out to go on with the work. Some Hauhaus came in (to give themselves up); only a few, however. At 8 p.m. McDonnell started with all the men in camp for Keteonetea.

18th October.—The expedition returned which started out last night. It appears they attacked the village of Oraukawa, but owing to the mismanagement of one of the subalterns it was a failure, so far. They succeeded in killing four Hauhaus and in bringing in one wretched old woman a prisoner. She seemed awfully frightened as she came up to the redoubt, no doubt thinking she was going to be killed. The Native Contingent always makes an immense fuss returning from an expedition, with war-dances and songs. Our men succeeded in shooting two bullocks, which will keep us in meat for some time, but our other stores are nearly out, and the difficulty of getting anything up from Patea here is tremendous. We have to trust entirely to the Government convoys, and they have as much as they can do in supplying the forces.

19th October.—Captain Newland went out last night with a considerable force to try Keteonetea again; left at 10.30 and returned this morning. The natives were on the alert, however. Captain McDonnell was leading with the best of the Contingent through a patch of bush where it was as dark as Erebus, when a Hauhau sentry jumped up close to him and fired, sending the ball right through his thigh. Firing also commenced on their right and front, so Newland thought it best to retire, which he did, the Hauhaus following to the edge of the bush. It is said that two or three Hauhaus were killed, but it is not known for certain. Winiata, the celebrated *toa* of the Contingent, killed the man who shot McDonnell, who, it is said, will not be able to take the field for many months.

20th October.—Doing nothing all day, as we could not obtain a covering-party. Sir George Grey has arrived at Manawapou.

21st October (Sunday).—Ten *kupapas,* or allies, arrived in camp to-day from Wanganui. As they came near the three clumps of trees—which, by the way, is a very favourite place for ambushes—we saw from the redoubt about sixty Hauhaus creeping up to intercept them. A party was sent out and drove them back. It is thought they knew of the Governor's arrival in the district and thought to catch him.

23rd October.—His Excellency Sir George Grey arrived in camp; came round by Wai-ngongoro, where he was yesterday digging *moa*-bones. He succeeded, I believe, in getting a good many on the sandy neck of land on the south side of the mouth of the river. Sir George sent for me soon after his arrival, and I had a long talk with him about the surveys. He proposes to raise a corps of Guides, composed of the natives who have given in, to be under the direction and for the protection of surveyors. If the natives will go, it will do very well.

27th October.—McDonnell took out a lot of men and brought in part of the mill in Ketemarae clearing. They exchanged shots with the Hauhaus, but nothing more came of it. Three hundred and twenty men of the 18th Royal Irish marched into camp from Wai-ngongoro and Manawapou, under Major Rocke, who takes command of the post of course. I don't think McDonnell likes it. It looks as if the Governor was going to pitch into the Hauhaus, massing all these men here. The Governor and staff came up also and pitched their tents near the 18th.

29th October.—Sir George Grey has asked me to make him a map of the district. An expedition started at midnight last night and returned this morning, under Major Rocke, consisting mostly of the 18th. They attacked the place where McDonnell was wounded, Popoia, and took it, but only killed one Hauhau, with one of the troopers on our side mortally wounded. The Hauhaus appear to have taken warning from the lessons McDonnell has given them, and it is very difficult to catch them napping now.

28th November (At Ketemarae).—It is reported that the Waikatos have arrived at Pungarehu with the intention of "eating up" the *pakeha.* No Hauhaus have been seen here for some time. It is supposed that they have gone a long way inland to get out of the road of the troops. There are none but colonial troops at this post now, the 18th having retired to their own posts, and have taken up a new one about two miles from here towards Keteonetea. They (the soldiers) are to give us covering-parties now.

30th November.—Moved over to Turuturu-mokai and camped close to the redoubt.

1st December.—Major Noblett (in charge of the redoubt) told me that the natives are coming about again—that the friendly natives of Matangarara have seen their fires in the bush.

9th December.—We have been laying out roads in the country lying inland of the Tawhiti and inland as far as Mangemange. This is a most beautiful country. The bush contains no end of lovely little clearings with quantities of fruit-trees. There are constant reports that the Hauhaus have returned, so that perhaps we may meet some of them. I hope not, however, for some of the soldiers would come to grief. They make most excellent fellows for covering-parties. They are not afraid of getting wet nor of going first through the high fern; and, best of all, they do not grumble as those wretched Rangers do. Besides, it is as good as a play to hear the extraordinary comical tales they are always spinning to each other in the richest brogue. Some of them sometimes take a billhook from the men and go on working for a change. I was through this country in 1858, on my way from Wanganui to Taranaki, but remember very little of it. We were through at Keteonetea the other day. There is nothing left of the fine *pa* there used to be there but a few posts and acres of clover. I saw Hone Pihama on the 7th. He told me that the Waikato are coming down in three weeks' time on their way to Rangitikei, and that it won't be safe for any of us to come across them.

1st January, 1867 (at Camp Turuturu).—Engaged in cutting up sections inland of the Tawhiti Stream. For the last few days we have observed a very large fire away inland, some miles apparently, and the friendly natives tell me that it is the Hauhaus burning some large swamps which exist in that direction and which are called Te Ngaere. In all probability they are the same places that are to be seen from the top of Mount Egmont. The Hauhaus, having been driven from this neighbourhood by the troops, have retired there, where they have some plantations.

7th January.—The Waikato who arrived a short time since at Pungarehu are said to be disgusted at the people here because they won't fight, and are going back.

11th January.—Went out with Wray to the place where the natives stopped him on the 7th. It was just at Taumaha, the place where we all went with McDonnell one night when we recovered the cavalry horses. We had not gone very far when several natives came up and insisted upon our stopping, as we were not on our land—which, by the way, we were. After a great deal of talk we agreed to refer the matter to the Major. We then adjourned with the natives to the village they are building at Taumaha, where we partook of potatoes and pumpkins. This is a most beautiful little spot, a clearing in the high scrub and bush, surrounded by and divided by belts of beautiful *ngaio* trees; under these the natives are building their huts, and they look very pretty indeed. On returning to camp I reported our stoppage to McDonnell, who rode up at once, and we then went on to Paraone's *whare,* and had a long talk with him and other natives. It ended in their promising not to interrupt us again.

11th February.—Could not get a covering-party today, so both survey-parties went out together and cut line back into the bush. At 2 p.m. we got into a pretty little clearing, where our dogs were driven in by some native dogs. It being such an unusual thing for native dogs to show so much pluck, we imagined there might be some Hauhaus about, so left for camp.

14th February.—Went back to Turuturu-mokai. I hear from the friendly natives that it was very lucky for us we did retire on the 11th when we heard the dogs barking, as a Hauhau has since come in who says that they saw us just as we disappeared into the bush. Good job we did not get a volley.

19th February.—Out in the bush. A large covering-party to-day under command of Lieutenant Chapman.

20th February.—Took my party and traversed up the Tawhiti in the forest. Covering-party under Lieutenant Haines, 18th Regiment (Royal Irish). Wilson with covering-party from Ketemarae went up to the mill and traversed down. At about 4 o'clock we were very near each other. Our dogs got hold of a pig a little ahead of the party. The Native Contingent, who were with Wilson's party, immediately they heard the dogs dashed off through the bush in a tremendous fright, fancying the Hauhaus were upon them, and were only prevented from going right home by Lieutenant Gudgeon, after they had got some distance. This shows how much they are to be depended on.

26th February.—In cutting a line a little inland of Keteonetea to-day I came across a strong fortification built right across the path inland, but so that forces coming along the track would never know of its existence until they received a murderous volley. The inside of the redoubt was shaded by a beautiful growth of *karaka* trees. It is along this path that the 18th Regiment (Royal Irish) went when they took Tirotiro-moana. From the account of those who accompanied the expedition it would appear that they had some exceedingly bad country to cross, and in the forest, too; but the soldiers appear to have been able to get along quite as well as the Militia and the Native Contingent. It had always been supposed, until General Chute's march behind Mount Egmont proved the contrary, that British troops could not get along in the bush, but from what I have seen of them—and I have had plenty of opportunities of seeing them in every description of rough country lately—they are every bit as good as the Military Settlers who formed part of the column which took Opotiki under Major Brassey, and who were supposed to be (at least by themselves) very excellent bushmen. I must say that I like the 18th very much, and that my respect for the soldier has considerably increased lately. I have had these men out with me, wet through all day long and forced to push their way through heavy fern and scrub, encumbered by their heavy rifles, bayonets, and cartouche-boxes, and not a grumble to be heard.

20th March (at Manutahi).—All hands are engaged in cutting up the land for Jonas's and Ross's companies [military settlers]. I took two parties and encamped for a few days between Otoki and the Hingahape. One of Williams's men set fire to the country some time during the great gale, and it has made a clean sweep of everything and extended some miles inland. It is a very good thing, as otherwise this country would be almost impenetrable owing to the dense character of the scrub. The Maoris are furious about it. They say it has burnt their houses and cultivations, but I think they are disgusted because it has opened up a road by which their settlements may be reached by troops. There is a nice lot of rascals congregated a little way inland at a place called Whakamara.

23rd March.—Returned to Manutahi. I met a native to-day just as I was leaving off who told me the people would not allow us to go on with the survey. I hope we are not going to have any trouble with them. Colonel Gorton returned to Wanganui yesterday, having been relieved by Colonel Lepper. They are getting up two companies of Militia to protect this district, as the 18th will soon leave and the Military Settlers will soon be off pay. I believe they get men readily at 2s. 6d. per diem.

29th March.—Returned to headquarters camp at Manutahi, having been stopped by the natives several times. They seem determined not to allow the survey to go on. I hardly like going up so near Whakamara when they offer so much opposition, as they could so easily cut us off, and I think there are plenty of men at that place who would be only too glad to do it, but they won't so long as Paraone and the Mokoia people live where they are. Reported the matter to Mr. Richmond.

24th April.—Was stopped again to-day by the natives of Whakamara. I don't know when this part of the survey will be finished. I expect some of us will come to grief yet.

29th April (at Wanganui).—Saw Mr. Parris, who gave me letters of instructions from Mr. Richmond to carry on the survey of the block between the Whenuakura and the Waitotara for Nos. 8 and 10 Taranaki Military Settlers and the Patea Rangers. This is good news for them, as it is a very fine district, and much nearer Wanganui than the north side of the Wai-ngongoro, where they expected to get their lands.

2nd May.—Rode on (from Kakàramea) to Manutahi, and thence accompanied Messrs. Parris and Booth to see Paraone, who informed us that the Hauhaus of Whakàmara would turn us back if we attempt to survey again. The natives are evidently getting cheeky now that the soldiers are leaving. Hear that some Hauhaus who came to visit the friendly natives at Opunake have cut down the flagstaff in the redoubt. There are no troops there now.

11th May.—Hearing that all the Hauhaus were holding a meeting at Putahi relative to the new survey, I determined to take the opportunity to finish a line that was very much needed near Whakamara. Wray and I went out there and luckily finished it without interruption.

15th May (at Kakaramea).—Moved from our tattered tents to a house inside the redoubt, which is a deal more comfortable. Mr. Booth held a meeting of natives at Hukatere (on the Patea River) to-day. They informed him that they would offer every obstacle to the prosecution of the survey. This is a nice state of affairs, truly! The matter has been referred to Wellington, so we may have to wait a month before we can get to work.

THE NEW ZEALAND CROSS

Lieut.-Colonel Thomas McDonnell, writing from Wanganui in 1897, referred to a number of colonial soldiers whom he had recommended for the decoration of the New Zealand Cross, but who had not received it. He said, "I especially recommended the following men: Mr. Northcroft, S.M., of Wanganui, for protecting Economedes (Taranaki Rangers) when mortally wounded in the forest below Tirotiro-moana. Captain Northcroft stuck to his man, defending him till the brave Greek expired, when assistance came up and the body was taken to the Waihi camp and interred. There are numerous other instances where this gallant officer did similar unselfish service. Our fellow-townsman, Mr. McKenna, got the V.C. for exactly similar service in Waikato. Again, Hirtzel: At the fight at Pungarehu, when the order was given to retire, Sergeant Tarrin de Courcey Duff, of the Wanganui Yeomanry Cavalry, fell mortally wounded inside the fence of the fortified *pa* or village. Hirtzel never hesitated, but sprang over the fence, followed by Captain Northcroft, whilst heavy volleys were being fired into our small band by the strong rebel reinforcements, who came from distant villages farther in the forest to assist the belligerent tribes. Thus Duff was rescued, but Hirtzel got severely wounded in the shoulder. I recommended this brave officer for the Cross for his devotion, but no notice was taken for it. Again, at Turuturu-mokai Redoubt, when attacked by Ngati-Ruanui, Connor of the Army Constabulary, now a messenger in the Government Buildings, formerly a 57th man, was recommended by me for the Cross for his bravery in defending his wounded comrades who were lying helpless at the mercy of the foe, who knew none. Connor and one or two others could have got away, as some did, but they elected to risk death at their posts rather than desert the wounded. A Committee of Parliament some two or three years since investigated this case and did its duty by recommending Connor. No notice was taken of this either. Major Scannell I also recommended for his heroic devotion on the retreat from Te Ngutu, to which many owe their lives. This was also ignored. Private James Shanagan, serious wounded in the act of trying to rescue Major Von Tempsky, is also entitled to the Cross; I would recommend him, but it would be useless. And last, but by no means least, Sir George Grey and Sir Walter Buller, for incidents I well remember before the famous Weraroa *pa* in 1865. Sir George should receive the Cross and be made Chancellor of the Order. If exception is taken because Sir Walter Buller was a civilian, why, then, did His Honour the late Dr. Featherston get the decoration recommended by General Sir Trevor Chute?"

Of those mentioned by Lieut.-Colonel McDonnell, Captain Northcroft received the New Zealand Cross many years later—in fact, some forty years after the events in which he earned it.

HOW TROOPER LINGARD WON THE NEW ZEALAND CROSS

The first award of the New Zealand Cross was that made to Trooper William Lingard, of Bryce's Kai-iwi Cavalry, Wanganui, in 1869. Mr. Lingard (died in Wellington, 1922) was born in County Clare, Ireland; he was the son of an Imperial officer who had fought at Waterloo. Lingard was intended for the Army, but he came out to New Zealand in 1863 to try his fortune. He served in the Auckland Militia during the Waikato War, and followed a farmer's life in the Wanganui and Waitotara districts. He was a trooper in the Alexandra Lancers, a troop formed about 1865, and afterwards in the Kai-iwi Cavalry (Captain John Bryce), a corps which did a great deal of patrol and scouting duty. It was while serving in the Cavalry in front of Tauranga-ika *pa,* inland from Nukumaru, in 1869, that he won the decoration of the New Zealand Cross by an act of great gallantry.

Four troopers of the Cavalry rode up to the front of the *pa* one day in order to ascertain whether there were any Maoris in the stockade, as the place seemed unusually silent. These cavalrymen were Troop Sergeant-Major George Maxwell, Troopers Arthur Wright, Henry Wright, and William Lingard. They rode close up to the *pa* and galloped past the palisade. Suddenly a heavy fire was opened on them, and Maxwell was shot. He stuck to his saddle until he had ridden about a hundred yards from the stockade before he fell. Troopers George Small and Allan Campbell galloped forward and recovered his body under heavy fire. At the same time the horses of both the Wright Brothers were shot down about a chain from the palisading. Arthur Wright jumped off his horse before he fell, and, taking his saddle, ran down near the bush and rejoined the troop in the valley below, 400 or 500 yards from the *pa.* Henry Wright's horse did not fall until Arthur Wright was half-way to the troop. When the horse tumbled over he rolled on to his rider's leg and pinned him to the ground. The trooper lay in this position under fire, within a very short distance of the stockade; he kept firing his revolver at the palisade, but was unable to use his carbine. A Maori warrior, the locally celebrated Big Kereopa, came out from under the palisading with a long-handled tomahawk, and Wright would have been killed had it not been for the promptitude of Trooper Lingard, who galloped up and helped him away. He pulled him clear of the horse, and protected him under the heavy fire, while he (Wright) retreated, crouching. Lingard, when he saw Wright was in comparative safety, then turned his horse and galloped round to the far side of the *pa.* A few moment later he returned leading a Maori horse (looted from a settler) which had been tethered to a *tutu* bush; he cut the line with his sword. After assisting Wright to mount this horse the two troopers rode down the hill and safely rejoined their corps. Undoubtedly, had it not been for Lingard's courage and alacrity, combined with good horsemanship, Trooper Wright would have been tomahawked. The rescue was performed under a heavy fire at close quarters, and Lingard well deserved the New Zealand Cross bestowed upon him on the recommendation of Colonel Whitmore.

Lingard was soon afterwards put in charge of a small party of scouts organized by Colonel Whitmore; he was invalided at Patea, and Sergeant (later Captain) C. Maling was then appointed to the command of the scouts, styled the Corps of Guides.

SERGEANT CARKEEK

Sergeant Arthur Wakefield Carkeek received the New Zealand Cross in 1870 on the recommendation of Lieut.-Colonel McDonnell. On the 7th February 1870, while the force under the command of Lieut.-Colonel McDonnell was serving in the Patetere country, Te Kooti, with his men, came out of the bush on the Rotorua side of the ranges and was engaged by Captain Mair. It was of the utmost importance that immediate notice should be sent to McDonnell of the whereabouts of the enemy, and Sergeant Carkeek, who was then at Ohinemutu, used every exertion to get natives to convey a note to him at Tapapa through the bush, but no one could be induced to incur the risk. Sergeant Carkeek then determined to take the information himself, and, having found one native who agreed to accompany him, he started at daylight on the 8th, and arrived at Tapapa about 3 p.m. He travelled over thirty miles, through dense bush known to be haunted by the enemy, and in danger of being surprised by them at any moment, when certain death would have been his fate.

THE POVERTY BAY MASSACRE

Mr. H. Strong, of Christchurch, who was a settler at Matawhero, Poverty Bay, at the time of the massacre in 1868, and who served in the operations against Te Kooti, supplies some notes on the events immediately following the landing of the escapees from Chatham Island, and describes the raid on the Bay settlements. He states that he, with others, was engaged in service in a church at Matawhero, a few miles from the present town of Gisborne, when a messenger arrived with the news of Te Kooti's landing. It was Sunday afternoon, the 12th July, 1868, and all the men in the church, without waiting to change their clothes or obtain supplies, saddled their horses and went south in the direction of Whare-ongaonga. On the track, at the late Mr. Woodbine Johnson's property at Muriwai, orders were received from Major Biggs to continue the march to Whare-ongaonga. The escapees, however, had refused to surrender, and had stated their intention of going into the Urewera Country. Major Biggs ordered a pursuit, and the engagement at Paparatu followed. When the fight began, the men, though cheerful enough, were in a state of exhaustion, and were almost starving. The retirement was a most difficult task, carrying the wounded through mountains, creeks, and over steep hills. After a severe night march they reached Captain Charles Westrup's out-station, where they were met by Colonel Whitmore, with the Napier volunteers and others. He immediately ordered the Poverty Bay settlers to be paraded, and warned them that they must be ready to start back in pursuit in an hour. The settlers considered this impossible, and a spokesman detailed the privations they had undergone, and said that under similar circumstances Colonel Whitmore himself would hardly have been prepared to march in an hour. "The Colonel's language in reply," says Mr. Strong, "was such as to preclude all possibility of the settlers working harmoniously with him on any future occasion. Captain Westrup, by his silence, endorsed our action; had he said the word, I and many others would have followed in hot pursuit, for a better man than Captain Westrup never lived." All the settlers asked was that they should be allowed to return home and obtain proper food and a change of clothing (they had been in the field in bad weather for ten days) before again engaging in the arduous pursuit. The courage and promptitude of the Poverty Bay men, and their cheerful willingness to take up arms, were displayed in their action when they were disturbed in church on the Sunday afternoon, and Colonel Whitmore's criticisms in his book were entirely unjustified. In the course of the next march, Mr. Strong says, the settlers were again subjected to abuse from Colonel Whitmore. The country was rough, and on the Ahimanu Range the force was delayed by heavy snowstorms. When the Waihau lakes were reached the provisions were exhausted, and the men were suffering greatly. "We, the Poverty Bay men, then held a meeting, and decided unanimously that, on account of the way in which Colonel Whitmore had treated us from the day we started, we should go no farther, and I believe that Captain Westrup once more endorsed our action." The settlers then returned to the Bay.

At that time Mr. Strong lived a considerable distance from the Turanganui landing-place; his home was near the Patutahi crossing of the Waipaoa River. On the same side of the river there was another settler, Mr. James Wyllie, who had incurred the special displeasure of Te Kooti. Mrs. Wyllie was well acquainted with the friendly Maoris in the district.

Some time before the massacre occurred she repeatedly expressed fears that, before long, Te Kooti would make a raid on the settlements. It was believed that he would come down the Patutahi Valley, and accordingly Mr. Strong, with the Wyllies and some other settlers in the district, arranged to keep watch, day and night, at the crossing of the Waipaoa, taking turns of duty, and keeping the saddles on their horses. From the crossing there is a good view up the valley. Government scouts (under Lieutenant Gascoyne) had been sent out, but the settlers took their own steps to prevent surprise. One day Mrs. Wyllie informed Mr. Strong that she had been told by an old Maori woman that Te Kooti was coming down the valley. Mr. Strong rode in and informed Major Biggs. His reply was: " Well, you know, I have scouts out, and I will receive twenty-four hours' notice before anything can happen. The story is absurd, and you are all in an unnecessary state of alarm." Mr. Strong returned home, and the settlers' vigilance committee ceased its watch. A few nights later the Hauhaus came down to Patutahi and crossed the very ford that the farmers had been guarding. Had Biggs heeded Strong's warning, the massacre would have been averted.

Te Kooti's men passed by the settlers' homes at Patutahi, intending to raid them on their return from the Matawhero settlement. When the alarm was given the Wyllies hurried off southward in the direction of the Mahia. It was then remembered that Mr. Strong was in his house, which was close to the track of the marauders, and Mr. W. Benson crossed over and warned him of his danger, shouting, " Clear out, the Hauhaus are down !" As, however, Strong had sent a boy to the township at Waerenga-a-Hika and expected him back, he decided to stay and await his return. The Wyllies went on, and Mr. Strong, who had taken his horse into some dense scrub, at about 10 a.m. saw the Hauhaus pass close to him and enter Wyllie's house, and he heard their shouts of disgust when they found that their intended victims had escaped. They did not search Mr. Strong's place, otherwise he would almost certainly have been captured. Shortly afterwards Sergeant Butters arrived with the news of the massacre of settlers. The boy arriving later, Mr. Strong took him on his horse, and they rode into Turanganui safelv.

Had Major Biggs taken the settlers' warning, Mr. Strong declares, the Hauhaus would have been heard and seen when they started to cross the Patutahi at the wide, shingly ford, and all the Europeans would have been warned in time.

Another fatal blunder was the failure to erect a fortification at Matawhero. It was proposed in October, 1868, to construct a redoubt in the middle of that farming area, and the loyal Maoris agreed to supply and erect palisades if the Europeans would assist in the work of construction. However, the authorities did not approve of the erection of a redoubt there, and so nothing was done to provide a place of refuge for the settlers and their families in case of an attack.

THE PUKEARUHE MASSACRE

MAORI STATEMENTS

Several conflicting accounts have been given by the Ngati-Maniapoto natives of Mokau regarding the massacre at the Pukearuhe Redoubt, White Cliffs, North Taranaki, in 1869. The most reliable narrative appears to be the confession of a half-caste named Henare Piripi, which follows. Captain Messenger, who was in command of the Pukearuhe Armed Constabulary station for many years after the raid, made every endeavour to obtain an accurate statement from the Maori side, and reported to Lieut.-Colonel Roberts, then commanding the Armed Constabulary, at Opunake.

Hone Wetere te Rerenga, the leader of the Mokau war-party, made a statement in 1882, but his version of the massacre is not reliable. Captain Messenger, writing from New Plymouth, 14th July, 1882, to Lieut.-Colonel Roberts, said:—

"I have the honour to report for your information that during a recent visit to the Mokau district I gained the following information with regard to the murder of the Rev. John Whiteley in 1869:—

"Te Rerenga (Te Wetere), who was the leader of the war-party on that occasion, stated to Sergeant J. Gilbert, who was with me, that it was his intention shortly to visit Wellington for the purpose of 'turning Queen's evidence' if the Government would hold him harmless. He then stated that Mr. Whiteley's horse was first shot, he (Te Wetere) being at the time in a *whare* near; that he ran out on hearing the shots and saw Mr. Whiteley standing unhurt; that he told him to go back, which Mr. Whiteley refused to do, saying, 'I must first see what bad work you have been doing here.' One of the party then fired a double-barrel gun and missed. Mr. Whiteley then knelt down to pray, when Colburn [David Cockburn], the white man who is now living at Mokau, called out, 'Shoot him! Dead men tell no tales!' A volley was fired, which killed Mr. Whiteley instantly.

"Te Rerenga gave the names of the whole party who fired—Colburn (the white man), Philps (a half-caste), Ben, Titokorangi, and other natives. Te Rerenga stated that when he found he was powerless to prevent the murder he turned away so that he should not see it.

"Whilst at Mokau I heard that Colburn intended shortly moving into the interior."

[Wetere's accusation against the white man David Cockburn was, I believe, false. Cockburn had been a private in a company of Military Settlers stationed at Pukearuhe in 1865, and he deserted to the natives and lived a *pakeha-Maori* life in the Mokau district for many years. When going up the Mokau River by canoe in 1905 I saw the old man at the Wai-ngarongaro coal-mines, twenty miles from the heads, and he told me of his life among the Maoris. He declared that he was inland of the Mokau at the time of the Pukearuhe massacre. He always strenuously denied any share in the expedition to the White Cliffs, and his denial was, I think, the truth.—J.C.]

Captain Messenger, writing from Pukearuhe Station, 11th September, 1882 to Lieut-Colonel Roberts, commanding the district, Opunake, forwarded the following document signed by Henare Piripi (a half-caste), being an account of the murders at Pukearuhe in 1869. Piripi, Messenger said, was evidently uneasy in his mind, hence his confession, which was made to two white residents of Mokau:—

"Mokau, Sept. 7, 1882.

"To whom it may concern:

"Confession of Henry Phillip [or Phillips] taken before John Shore, of Mokau, and Thomas Atkin Poole, of the same place. The undermentioned statement is given voluntarily by me respecting the massacre at Pukearuhe in 1869. I, Henry Phillip, on the day of the massacre came from Urenui with three more natives. Captain Messenger put us across the Mimi River in a canoe or punt. I with the other natives came as far as the Parininihi Hill [White Cliffs]. We met Te Wetere and a party of about fifteen natives. When we met them Titokorangi asked the party where they were going and what they were going to do. Te Wetere announced they were going on to kill the whole of the Europeans at Pukearuhe. Titokorangi said, 'You had better not,' and advised them to go back. Te Wetere said, 'I won't go back, and I will not allow you to go back,' alluding to Titokorangi, myself, and the other two natives, who names are Richmon ——, and Johnny Pihama. They forced us to go back, at the same time asking us how many men there were at the camp. We were compelled to go with them to save our own lives, Wetere compelling me to go back to interpret for him. We all went on to the creek at the foot of the hill. They left their guns there in charge of some of the natives. Te Wetere, Tukerau [Takirau], Te Oro, Torton [or Turton, in Maori Tatana], Manuel and myself went up to the blockhouse. When we got in front of the blockhouse Te Wetere told me to call the men out, that he (Wetere) wanted to see them.

"The two men that were in the blockhouse came out and shook hands with the natives and with me. After shaking hands the men asked what the natives wanted with them. Wetere told me to tell them he wanted them to go on the beach to look at some pigs. The two men were glad when they heard the natives had brought up some pigs, at the same time asking Wetere, through me, if they had any peaches. Wetere told me to say 'Yes.' Then the men went down accompanied by three natives—Tukerau [Takirau], Ben, and Manuel. I watched them to the bend of the road, and as soon as they got to the bend I saw Tukerau strike one of the Europeans with his *taiaha*. He hit him behind the head, and he fell dead on the spot. The other European, seeing his mate fall, turned round, holding up his arms for protection. Manuel struck him with a long-handled tomahawk, striking him on the head or forehead, at the same time breaking the handle of the tomahawk with the blow. Then Ben hit him with the *taiaha*, and the man fell.

"At the same time Wetere sent two men to the Captain's (Lieutenant Gascoigne's) house to see if he was there or not. The men returned telling Wetere Captain Gascoigne and his wife and family were not in. Torton [Tatana] and Te Oro were the two men sent. Then Wetere sent one of them to the beach to tell the whole of the natives to come to the camp and bring their guns with them, and they all came up. Wetere then told them to go and break open the Captain's house, which they did, and took away a rifle and ammunition, and a revolver and ammunition. Wetere told them to leave the rest until their work was done. They then went on to the front to keep a lookout for the Captain. We were not long waiting when he came with his wife and children—I think three children, the Captain carrying one in his arms. He came close up to us and he said to me, 'Hallo, are you back again?' I said, 'Yes.' He shook hands with Ben and Te Ho [? Te Oro], then he went straight on for his house, walking fast. Ben followed him close up with his *taiaha*. When near his house Ben struck him behind the head. He fell forward on his face and never moved after. Te Ho then took up the firewood-axe belonging to the camp and struck him on the head with the sharp side, cutting the head in halves. Manuel then followed the child, and with a short-handled tomahawk cut the top of the child's head clean off. Manuel and Te Oro then went into a parapet where Mrs. Gascoigne and, I think, two children were hiding. When Manuel and Te Oro came back to where Te Wetere and myself were seated Wetere asked them if they had killed the woman. They replied, 'Yes, and the children too.' Wetere then said, '*Ka pai*.' Te Wetere then said, 'We can now take all the things out of the house and divide them amongst us,' which they did, Wetere claiming the revolver, watch, and opera-glass. Te Wetere gave me a clean white shirt, six boxes of matches, and a new pack of playing-cards.

"While dividing the plunder they saw some one coming on horseback at a distance. Wetere then said, 'Whether it is a white man or a native we must kill him.' He sent five men on to watch. Te Oro sang out, 'It is a white man,' Te Wetere answering, saying to let him come. Mr. Whiteley, the minister, then rode up to the natives. I at the time was about 30 yards from them. I was on the bastion. Tanui fired the first shot, the horse falling at once. As soon as the horse fell, Te Oro, Torton, Manuel Hawpoe (?) fired at Mr. Whiteley and he fell dead. As soon as he fell I saw Tanui take the vest and watch from him. Soon after this we left, Manuel taking a horse with him. We left two men behind, named Daniel and Ben. Wetere told them to burn the houses before they left. When we got into the creek after the massacre Torton, having two guns, gave me one, which was a rifle, telling me it was too heavy for him to carry.

(Signed) "HENARE PIRIPI

"Witnesses: John Shore, Thomas A. Poole."

Shore, in a note accompanying this statement, said that he had given Piripi his word of honour that Captain Messenger would not divulge his confession until the necessary time came. "If anything does move the Government," Shore added, "I wish you would give him timely warning, as it would endanger him to the greatest extent here, for I am sure you must know as well as myself that the scoundrel Wetere would just as soon have him put out of the way as not, to save himself. So I entirely depend on you giving us the necessary information. The statement referred to is, I believe, the honest truth, as it was given with a good will, unasked for."

Wetere te Rerenga was in fear of retribution or punishment by the Government until 1883, when a general amnesty was proclaimed for all who had taken part in the wars against the Queen's authority. In 1878 and following years he assisted Mr. Joshua Jones to open up the Mokau River for trade and settlement, and in 1882 he ventured to go to Wellington with Mr. Jones to see the Native Minister in reference to the opening of his lands for lease or sale. While in Wellington he was quietly warned that an information had been laid against him for the murder of Mr. Whiteley in 1869, and he was hurried out of the town at night by his friends, catching the west-coast coach on the Porirua road. In the "eighties" he gained great credit for his plucky rescue of Mr. C. W. Hursthouse, the surveyor, and a companion who were capsized while taking soundings on the Mokau bar, and who would have been drowned but for Wetere's prompt assistance. He put off from the shore in a canoe and rescued the surveyors struggling in the surf at the peril of his own life.

Wetere died at the Mokau in 1889.

TE KOOTI AT ROTORUA (1870)

Captain Gilbert Mair, writing from Tauranga, 8th June, 1923, gave the following account of the principal episodes in his running fight with Te Kooti near Rotorua on the 7th February, 1870; the narrative contains details supplementary to those given in Chapter 35:—

" After engaging Te Kooti's force at Rotorua (on the site of the present town) and driving him off south-eastward, our first close encounter was on the Waikorowhiti. Here the enemy, hidden in a small patch of *manuka* along a low ridge, held up my advance for several minutes. Then they retired, carrying a wounded man; we heard afterwards that his name was Hohepa, and that he died three days later up the Horomanga Gorge, and was buried at Tutaepukepuke, in the Urewera Mountains. The second stand was made by the Maoris at a spot where my brother Major Mair three days later found a man dead, a very tall fellow. Farther on another ambuscade was laid, and we were held up some time. A little later I saw a wounded man being carried off on horseback.

" The principal skirmish occurred on the fern ridge opposite Owhinau Mountain (six miles from Rotorua). About seventy Hauhaus lined the reserve slope of the ridge in almost a semicircle; this ridge sloped abruptly about 100 feet to the stream below (alongside the present Rotorua–Waiotapu Road). My men, with myself and a seventeen-year-old lad, Te Waaka, in the advance, blundered in a straggling manner right into the ambuscade. Suddenly a row of shaggy black heads rose above the fern, just showing from the chin upwards, on practically three sides of us. The nearest was less than 20 yards away. I had a beautiful Westley-Richards breech-loading carbine, a gift from Sir Cosmo Gordon, uncle of my friend Gordon, the first lieutenant of H.M.S. "Rosario." I was the first to fire, killing a big fellow named Henare Rongowhakaaata, who was shot in the month. The enemy fired a volley from end to end of the line, while I and my men lay flat. By practice I had learned to fire twenty-eight to thirty shots per minute, particularly if I stuffed my mouth full of cartridges. I kept firing madly from right to left, which made the Hauhaus keep low and never take proper aim, but fire from the hip. All at once a middle-aged man sprang up, shouting '*Kokiri!*' ('Charge!') He fired both barrels of his double-barrel gun. I fired point-blank, and he fell face forward; his lower jaw was blown away. How long I could have held them I cannot say, when five of my men—Taekata, Tokoihi, Whakatau, Wehi-peihana, and Te Tupara—went round the shoulder of the hill and took the enemy in flank. The rear-guard, having gained 300 or 400 yards start for their main body, rapidly withdrew, dragging off five or six bodies. Some of these they hurled 50 feet or more down the hill into two small quaking morasses [see narrative in Chapter 35], where they lie to this day.

" I was at least 30 yards ahead of my small body of men when I found myself in that ambuscade. Then it was that my plucky lad Te Waaka, with great devotion, rushed up to my side, and was shot down. The bullet first broke the point of his chin, then entered the lower part of the throat, and passed out between the shoulders. It was a mortal wound. There were several others wounded: Hori Kirieke (shot through both thighs), Karanama, and Tame Wikitari, then Taekata, Whakatau, and two others slightly. When I look back and remember the loyalty of my Maori comrades and their generous self-sacrifice in trying to get between me and an enemy's bullet my heart thrills with pride and gratitude, and I regret the many acts of devotion I have left unrecorded.

"My brother found four bodies of Hauhaus on top of the hill where this fight took place. The man who fired his *tupara* at me was Timoti te Kaka; he was found some days later a little farther on, dreadfully wounded.

"A long chase followed across the undulating country (Kapenga and the rear of Pakaraka) and it must have been close on 7 p.m. when I and three men—Rewi Rangiamio, Te Warihi, and Ngahere te Wiremu—ran right into Peka te Makarini and his rear-guard among some rocks at the foot of Tumunui. I was ahead, Te Warihi some 50 yards behind, then Rewi and Ngahere together. There were five or six others out of sight, not within 100 yards. I think Peka had nearly thirty men, but as they were among the rocks I only saw eight or ten. About 100 yards beyond Peka, Te Kooti's main force was bunched up, climbing with difficulty into the forest on Tumunui. A few on horseback (including Te Kooti, his wife, and their guide Ihaia te Waru, of Ngati-Whaoa, at Paeroa Mountain) got round on the plain on the east side of the hill. It was there that I shot Peka Makarini, and the rear-guard took to flight.

"We got back to the camp at Kaiteriria, dead-beat, at about 9 p.m. There I got some food, refilled my ammunition-pouches, and got some fresh men of Ngati-Rangitihi and others—Huta Tangihia, Hohepa, Rakorako, gallant old Te Araki te Pohu, and also my faithful Ngahere te Wiremu—some ten in all, and then took the trail again in the night. On reaching Waikorua (Earthquake Flat) and inspecting the track by match-light we found that Te Kooti, after debouching from the Tumunui forest, had headed for Okaro Lake, in the direction of the Kaingaroa Plain. We went on as fast as we could in the darkness, and found his camp half-way along the east side of Okaro. When we were some 50 yards or more off the camp a dog barked, giving the alarm. A hot fire was exchanged, without inflicting casualties, and the enemy retreated at a great pace, leaving some guns behind them, also some food (fat pork, &c.). Passing south of Rotomahana and Rerewhakaitu lakes, they struck the main old war-trail from Te Ariki, on Lake Tarawera, and followed down the Kaiwhatiwhati Valley (a famous old battlfield, where a hundred years previously Tuhoe had destroyed Ngati-Hinewai and Tuhourangi). Then they reached Te Taupaki crossing on the Rangitaiki River, whence they had a clear course up the Horomanga Gorge into the Tuhoe country. We returned to our camp after the surprise attack at Okaro.

"I am pretty confident my tally in the day's fighting was no fewer than eight men. Out of fifty-eight shots, I don't remember ever pulling trigger without aiming at something, though often they were disappearing targets. It is quite wonderful how a man, fired at point-blank at 40 yards, can avoid being hit by instantaneously dropping to the ground. I had practised what is called the unsportsmanlike but very necessary trick of 'ducking,' and I was an adept at it or I should not be alive now. It would not be much use nowadays with smokeless powder and bullet-velocity more than double, but with slow powder there was always a bright flash and a huge puff of smoke, particularly when Maori powder of inferior quality was being used against one.

"As for the slain desperado Peka Makarini, two or three days after the fight Paurini and Mohi Aterea went out, and, tying their horses' tails to the body, they dragged it a quarter of a mile or more down to my pack-track which ran from Pakaraka across to my Niho-o-te-Kiore camp on the Waikato River. Here on the plain they lashed the body in an erect position to a large *whanake* (cabbage-tree) and left it there. Two years afterwards the Ngati-Pahauwera Tribe, of Mohaka (Hawke's Bay),

From a sketch by Captain Mair]

Te Kooti's War-flag, "Te Wepu"

sent an old *tohunga* to take away the bones of their *ito*, their detested enemy. From the bones were made fish-hooks, *poria-kaka* (leg-rings for pet parrots), charms, and even a flute from the bone of the right arm. [This is now in the Auckland Museum.] Such was the Mohaka tribe's mode of revenge on their arch-foe Peka Makarini, who had earned their hatred by his many murders and his share in the massacre of their people in the raid of 1869.

"Peka Makarini, using the bugle he captured on Chatham Island, often deceived our troops in bush-fighting by blowing the contrary calls to those sounded by our buglers.

"I must make it clear why the Tuhourangi and Ngati-Rangitihi failed to join in the fight on the 7th. I had sent them an urgent mounted messenger telling them to hurry along the straight track from Parikarangi and lie across Te Kooti's line of retreat. Paora te Konui, who dominated them, persuaded them that such action would deflect Te Kooti's strong force to the left, and cause him to make a flying raid through my Kaiteriria camp, where there were some fourteen old men, under Te Araki te Pohu and Hohepa Tauhuroa, armed with Tower muskets and only about five rounds each. The enemy would then destroy the Wairoa village, where there were no men at all, in a few minutes, and then have a short, straight run past Lake Tarawera, wipe Te Ariki village out, and so get clean away. Had Paora with his compact body of a hundred well-armed men joined me we would have been strong enough to cover both Kaiteriria and Te Wairoa and force Te Kooti out into the great open Kaingaroa.

"I was in fear that when the enemy retreated after the main skirmish on the ridge that he would still dash down on Kaiteriria to the left, but he was deterred by seeing old Te Araki and Hohepa appearing right across the track to the village, with their 'old guard' of twelve men. This had the effect of deflecting Te Kooti's march to the right, to Tumunui.

"Some years after the war, when I met Te Kooti at Matata, I twitted him with his failure to wipe out my handful of tired, hungry men, and he replied: 'I was told by the Arawa whom we had made prisoners that all the big force you brought from Tapapa had gone to Parikarangi, and I feared they would get across my line of retreat, hence my haste to get clear.'"

This remarkable flag was taken from Peka Makarini when Captain Gilbert Mair shot that half-caste warrior, the leader of Te Kooti's rear-guard, in the action at Tumunui, near Rotorua, 7th February, 1870. (See Chapter 35, pages 393-396.) It was Te Kooti's custom to unfurl it in his camps before starting out on a fighting expedition. It was called "Te Wepu" ("The Whip"). When "Te Wepu" "to the masthead flew," the rebel chief followers prepared for the war-trail.

Captain Mair gives a description and sketch of this flag. It was a long pennant or streamer of bright-red silk; the emblems were worked on this ground in white silk—the young moon, a cross, a star, a mountain (representing Aotearoa or New Zealand), and a bleeding heart, symbolizing the sufferings of the Maori nation. The flag was 52 feet in length, representing the number of weeks in the year, and was about 4 feet in the hoist, tapering to a fine point. It was made by the Roman Catholic nuns in the mission school at Meeanee, Hawke's Bay, for the friendly chiefs of the Ngati-Kahungunu Tribe, but fell into Te Kooti's hands in 1868. Captain Mair writes: "That celebrated Maori lady Airini Karauria Pupu, who became Mrs. G. P. Donnelly, told me that she used to visit the Catholic school at Meeanee, and was much interested in the beautiful work which the nuns were putting into the flag. She little thought that not long afterwards Te Kooti's force would hoist the flag in triumph when her father, Karauria Pupu, fell mortally wounded in the fighting at Makaretu, inland of Poverty Bay (November, 1868). When I shot Te Kooti's notorious bugler and butcher, Peka Makarini, he was carrying 'Te Wepu' in a leather case. I took great pride in presenting it to my old friend Mr. Hector (later Sir James Hector) for the Dominion Museum in Wellington, giving a full history of it. Judge of my amazement and disgust when on visiting the Museum a few years afterwards the custodian (Captain Beamish) informed me that the silken relic had been cut up into convenient lengths and given to the charwoman to use as floor-cloths and dusters!"

SIKHS AGAINST THE MAORIS

It is curious to recall the fact that there was a time when it was suggested that Sikhs should be used against the Maoris. The resources of the colony were strained to their utmost in the final wars of 1869–70 and in the maintenance of large Armed Constabulary and Maori field forces, and, although the services of Imperial troops had been discontinued for some years, it was proposed to apply for them again if they were available. The Hon. F. D. Bell and Dr. J. E. Featherston, New Zealand Commissioners, went to London and endeavoured to obtain Imperial troops, and they consulted Lord Napier of Magdala, who was Commander-in-Chief in India, on the question of the employment of an Indian force against the Hauhaus.

Lord Napier informed the Commissioners at this interview that they could not hope to induce the Indian authorities to allow of volunteering from the Gurkha regiments (of which there were only four), nor could they succeed themselves in raising a true Gurkha force of trained men, in the face of the obstacles against their leaving India. As regarded a Sikh regiment, they might without difficulty raise a corps of two thousand trained men or even more; for various reasons it would be expedient first to obtain the concurrence of the Home Government in the proposal. Though Lord Napier did not think obstacles would be interposed by the Indian Government, under fair conditions of service, against the enrolment of Sikhs, he expressed great repugnance to the suggestion of employing the Indian race against the Maori, and strongly advised the Commissioners not to resort to enlistment in India at all, but to engage European soldiers, and these only in England, on the ground that an Indian force would be found in every respect inferior to a European, and cost very nearly if not quite as much in the field, besides the ultimate expense of its return to India. The end of it all was that the New Zealand Government carried on the final campaign against Te Kooti with friendly Maori contingents and the Armed Constabulary.

THE WAIKARE-MOANA EXPEDITION (1870)

Major J. T. Large supplied the following notes explanatory of the sketch-map of Lake Waikare-moana, showing scenes in the operations of Hamlin's and Witty's expedition in 1870 described on pages 401-408.—

" Our first main camp (marked 1 on map) in the expedition of 1870 was on the east side of the small lake called Roto-kiri-o-Pukai (near Raekahu Mountain, 2,421 feet). In the bush on the west side of the lake two large *kahikatea* (white-pine) trees were felled, and canoes were made; these hewn-out craft and the dinghy made by Herrick's men the previous year were used in expeditions on the lake. About the first of these expeditions was that across the Whanganui-a-Parua branch of the lake from Motakitaki to Te Mara-o-te-Atua (" The Garden of the Gods ") (2).

" The middle of the lake, as indicated on the map (3), was the scene of the engagement between the Hauhaus in their war-canoes and the whaleboat they had found (one of those built in 1869) and a party of the Government natives, led by me (then Acting-Lieutenant), in the two new *kakikatea* canoes and the dinghy.

" Our shooting was too good for the Hauhaus, whom we chased back under the shelter of their *pa* at Matuahu; casualties unknown. They apparently had intended to land a force at Ohiringa, on the steep shore below the Panekiri Range, and then work round to the rear of our camp at Onepoto, as they did during Herrick's time the previous year, when they shot Trooper Noonan, engaged in despatch duty between Onepoto and Wairoa.

" Soon after our engagement on the lake our picked fighting-men, under Lieutenant Witty, started on a foraging raid which culminated in our defeat of the Hauhaus. We landed at Te Mara-o-te-Atua and fell into an ambush laid by the enemy. In this affair we had a few men wounded but none killed. We drove the Maoris out of their position at Taumataua (marked 4 on map). They returned on the following day and attacked us again, when their fighting-chief Enoka was killed; he was left in our hands when they retreated, having, it was reported, suffered other casualties. At any rate they were so disheartened at our success that when we rushed the Matuahu *pa* (5) on the following day we found it deserted.

" The number 6 near the head of the northern arm, not far from the canoe landing-place at Hereheretau, indicates the scene of our most successful surprise expedition from our new main camp in the captured Matuaha *pa*. Setting out at 3 o'clock one morning in the two canoes and the dinghy, we went high up the northern inlet and captured the Hauhau village on a foreland. We took the inmates prisoners without a fight, and also captured a number of fine canoes and the whaleboat, which we took home in triumph to Matuahu. This enterprise gave us the complete command of the lake.

" Matuahu was a roughly palisaded *pa* on the low headland running into the lake; rather a good position, as it commanded the north inlet. Tikitiki, on the opposite side of the entrance to this arm, was occupied as a Constabulary post for a short time in 1871. There were settlements all the way up the inlet on both sides. At Pukehuia (7) there was a large tribal meeting-house, which we burned down before we left."

Major Large died at Auckland in July, 1923.

TURUTURU-MOKAI REDOUBT, TARANAKI

A close examination of the remains of Turuturu-mokai Redoubt, near Hawera, the scene of the fight of the 12th July, 1868 (Chapter 21), shows that the fieldwork was not exactly equilateral in figure. The two flanks most plainly traceable, the western and southern sides, measure respectively 15 paces and 14 paces, exclusive of the flanking bastion at the north-west angle, which has an exterior measurement, in the ditch, of about 20 paces. The interior measurement on the long face, from the inner end of the bastion to its side facing the present road, is about 25 paces. Compass bearings show that the Tawhiti Road, which intersects the south-east angle of the work, runs north-north-east and south-south-west.

RUA KENANA, THE PROPHET

Long after the wars shots were again fired in the heart of the Urewera Country (1916). This was an unfortunate affray arising out of the arrest of Rua Kenana (Canaan), otherwise Ruatapu, on charges of breaches of the liquor law. Rua posed as a kind of Messiah; he assumed the role of prophet in succession to Te Kooti, and built a curious round timber temple of worship at a *kainga* which he called the "New Jerusalem," at Maunga-pohatu. He had seven wives, a privilege for which he took Biblical sanction, and he wore his hair long in imitation of the Israelites. Rua obtained great influence not only over the Urewera, but over other tribes in the neighbourhood and as far away as Rotorua and Gisborne. His flouting of the law when an attempt was made to arrest him led to an armed police expedition in 1916. Commissioner John Cullen and a force of between fifty and sixty men, twenty of whom were armed with rifles and the rest with revolvers, went in from Rotorua via Te Whaiti and Ruatahuna, and marched into the Maunga-pohatu settlement on Sunday, 2nd April. Rua attempted to evade arrest, and when he was seized some of his people opened fire on the police with rifles and shot-guns. A lively skirmish followed, lasting for about half an hour. One of Rua's sons and another Maori were shot dead, and four constables were wounded. The Maori resistance, however, was not premeditated; otherwise, Rua's men, had they been so minded, could have successfully ambuscaded the force in many places on the bush track between Ruatahuna and Maunga-pohatu. They took to their arms on impulse when they saw their prophet and "Messiah" felled and handcuffed.

Rua was tried in Auckland on the charge of resistance to the police and was sentenced to imprisonment. On his release he behaved admirably by assisting the Government to raise recruits for the Maori Pioneer Battalion in the Great War.

Kenana, Rua's father, was one of Te Kooti's warriors, and was killed in November, 1868, in the fighting at Makaretu, on the Wharekopae River, near Ngatapa.

"LEST WE FORGET"

Mr. John Finlay, of Tokaora, Hawera, has done his district and the Dominion good service by his patriotic appeals for fitting recognition of those who fell in the Maori wars. A number of burial places of soldiers in the South Taranaki district were neglected or unmarked until Mr. Finlay took up the question in his excellent articles in the Hawera *Star* under the heading "Lest We Forget." His appeals in the cause of those who had helped to make the country fit for white settlement were warmly supported by Mr. James Livingston, of Waipapa, and other South Taranaki residents, and the memorials at Ohawe, Waihi, and elsewhere were the result.

John Finlays are needed in other parts of the North Island. The soldiers' graves in most districts have been attended to carefully by the Department of Internal Affairs and its enthusiastic officer Miss Statham, but there are still unmarked places where soldiers were buried on the battlefields.

Equally important is the duty of indicating in some conspicuous way the sites of notable battlefields, and also the graves, where they can be located, of the gallant Maoris in such places as Orakau. The following are the principal battlefields requiring attention, a duty devolving in the first place on the local residents; public roads in every case pass through or alongside the old fortifications:—

Puketapu *pa,* Lake Omapere; Rua-pekapeka; No. 3 Redoubt, Huirangi, Waitara; Rangiriri; Rangiaowhia and Hairini; Gate *Pa;* Sentry Hill, Taranaki; Moturoa (near Waverley, West Coast). At these places and numerous others a wayside cross or other memorial is desirable in order to indicate the sites.

THE SOLDIERS' GRAVES AT OHAEAWAI

In the Ngapuhi country, North Auckland, the Maoris set a chivalrous example to the *pakeha* in the care of their antagonists' graves. At Ohaeawai, near Kaikohe (see Vol. I), a monument to the Imperial soldiers who fell there stands in the Maori church cemetery which occupies the site of the fortification of 1845. Governor Sir George F. Bowen, in a despatch in 1870 to the Secretary of State for the Colonies, mentioned a visit he had recently made to Ohaeawai, North Auckland, and said that the Maoris there had lately erected a pretty church "among the now decayed palisades and rifle-pits," and that they had reserved the whole of this *pa* as a cemetery. The Governor continued: "When the Bishop of Auckland shall have consecrated this new burial ground the Maoris intend to remove into it the remains of our soldiers who now lie in unmarked graves in the neighbouring forest, and to erect a monument over them; so that, as an aged chief, formerly conspicuous among our enemies, said to me, 'The brave warriors of both races, the white skin and the brown, now that all strife between them is forgotten, may sleep side by side until the end of the world.'

"I question," the Governor concluded, "if there be a more touching episode in the annals of the warfare of even civilized nations in either ancient or modern times." (Appendices to Journal of the House of Representatives, 1871.)

LIST OF ENGAGEMENTS AND CASUALTIES (1864-1872)

In the following chronological list of the principal engagements, sieges, and skirmishes in the campaign against the Hauhau Maoris from the early part of 1864 to 1872, the casualty figures in most cases are taken from official returns, checked by reference to survivors of the wars. Over 120 engagements are given here; of some there is no official record, and despatches did not always give the Maori casualties correctly. It was often difficult to estimate the natives' losses owing to their practice of carrying off the dead. It is impossible to state the Maori wounded with any degree of accuracy, hence the figures in that column are given in only a few cases. Numerous petty skirmishes are omitted from this list. (For engagements and casualties from 1845 to 1864 see Appendices to Volume I.)

Date	Engagement	British and Colonial Forces and Friendly Maoris		Hostile Maoris	
		Killed	Wounded	Killed	Wounded
1864					
April 6	Te Ahuahu, Taranaki	7	12	..	..
April 30	Sentry Hill, Taranaki	1	..	50	About 60
May 14	Moutoa Island, Wanganui ..	16	30	50	40
Sept. 8	Manutahi, Taranaki	..	..	..	..
1865					
Jan. 24	Nukumaru, West Coast ..	16	32	23	..
Jan. 25	Nukumaru, West Coast ..	..	..	..	..
Feb. –	Ohoutahi, Wanganui	..	..	..	..
Mar. 15	Te Ngaio (Kakaramea) ..	1	3	80	..
Mar. 31	Waihi River, Taranaki ..	..	..	..	..
June 1	Whatino, Taranaki	1	..	3	..
June 10	Mangaone, East Coast	6	..	..	..
June 13	Villages inland of Warea, Taranaki	..	..	..	..
June –	Te Tapiri (Urewera)	6	..	20	..
July –	Te Horo, East Coast	..	..	5	..
July 18	Te Hatepe, East Coast ..	..	..	..	..
July 21	Weraroa, Waitotara	..	..	..	..
July 28	Warea, Taranaki	2	..	..	..
July 19–30	Pipiriki, Wanganui River ..	..	4	20	..
Aug. 2 and 3	Warea district, Taranaki ..	5	6	16	..
Aug. 3	Pa-kairomiromi, East Coast ..	..	8	25	..
Aug. –	Te Mawhai, East Coast ..	..	2	13	..
Aug. –	Pukepapa, East Coast	..	..	14	..
Aug. 18	Tahutahu-po, East Coast ..	1	..	12	..
Sept. 8	Opotiki, East Coast	..	..	1	..
Sept. 9	Opotiki, East Coast	..	..	6	..
Oct. 3	Pukemaire, East Coast	2	..	9	..
Oct. 4	Te Tarata and Kiorekimo, Opotiki	3	9	35	40

LIST OF ENGAGEMENTS AND CASUALTIES—*continued*

Date	Engagement	British and Colonial Forces and Friendly Maoris		Hostile Maoris	
		Killed	Wounded	Killed	Wounded
1865					
Oct. –	Hungahunga-toroa, East Cape ..	..	..	20	..
Oct. –	Te Teko (siege of), Rangitaiki River	..	..	..	..
Oct. 20	Koingo, Waimana	..	..	3	..
—	Te Kuwini, Waimana	..	..	..	..
Nov. –	Waerenga-a-Hika (seven days' siege), Poverty Bay	11	20	100	..
Dec. –	Omaru-hakeke, Wairoa, Hawke's Bay	3	..	12	..
1866					
Jan. 4	Okotuku, West Coast	1	6	6	..
Jan. 7	Te Putahi, West Coast ..	2	12	15	..
Jan. 13	Te Kopane, Upper Wairoa, Hawke's Bay	14	..	60	..
Jan. 14	Otapawa, Taranaki	11	20	30	..
Jan. 15	Ketemarae, Taranaki	..	..	10	..
Jan. 15	Mawhitiwhiti, Taranaki ..	..	..	7	..
Jan. 17	Near Ketemarae, Taranaki ..	..	..	3	..
Jan. 20	Ahipaipa, etc., Taranaki ..	..	1	5	..
Feb. 1	Waikoko, Taranaki	1	3	4	..
Feb. –	Various skirmishes in Waioeka Gorge, Opotiki	..	..	..	..
Mar. –	Kairakau, Opotiki	..	..	4	..
April –	Otara Gorge, Opotiki	..	..	2	..
Aug. 2	Pokaikai, Taranaki	1	..	3	1
Sept. 2	Ketemarae, Taranaki	1	4	2	..
Sept. 23	Near Hawera, Taranaki ..	1	..	..	..
Sept. –	Near Waihi, Taranaki	..	..	1	..
Oct. 2	Pungarehu, Taranaki	3	4	30	..
Oct. 12	Omarunui, Hawke's Bay ..	2	14	21	30
Oct. 12	Petane, Hawke's Bay	..	1	12	1
Oct. 18	Popoia, Taranaki	..	1	..	..
Oct. 22	Popoia, Taranaki	1	..	2	..
Nov. 5	Tirotiro-moana, Taranaki ..	1	..	..	..
1867					
Jan. 18	Te Irihanga, Tauranga ..	1	..	..	..
Jan. –	Whakamarama, Tauranga ..	1	..	..	..
Feb. 4	Te Akeake, Tauranga	..	..	..	..
Feb. 4	Taumata, Tauranga	..	..	..	..
Feb. 15	Te Irihanga and Whakamarama, Tauranga	1	4	3	..
Mar. 3	Te Kaki, Tauranga	..	1	2	..
Mar. 17	Te Koutu, Rotorua	1	5	11	..
—	Puraku, Rotorua	..	..	11	..
May 21	Waioeka, Opotiki	2	..	..	..
—	Te Pokopoko, Waimana ..	..	1	7	..
Sept. 1	Waioeka	..	..	..	..

LIST OF ENGAGEMENTS AND CASUALTIES—*continued*

Date	Engagement	British and Colonial Forces and Friendly Maoris		Hostile Maoris	
		Killed	Wounded	Killed	Wounded
1868					
Feb. 10	Waimana Gorge	..	2	3	5
Mar. –	Hokianga Island, Ohiwa Harbour	1	..	..	..
Mar. 11	Te Ponga, Waimana Valley ..	1	..	1	..
June 9	Te Rauna, Taranaki	3	..	..	..
June 20	Waihi, Taranaki	..	2	2	..
July 12	Turuturu-mokai, Taranaki ..	10	6	3	..
July 20	Paparatu, East Coast	2	7	..	..
July 24	Te Koneke, East Coast ..	1	1	3	5
Aug. 8	Ruakituri, East Coast	6	5	8	3
Aug. 21	Te Ngutu-o-te-manu, Taranaki ..	4	8	7	..
Sept. 7	Te Ngutu-o-te-manu, Taranaki ..	24	27	28	..
Nov. 7	Moturoa	19	20	1	..
Nov. 10	Poverty Bay	70	..	..	..
Nov. 20	Patutahi	..	..	2	..
Nov. (10 days)	Makaretu	8	20	18	..
Dec. 3	Makaretu	1	2	60	..
Dec. 5	Ngatapa	6	..	10	..
1869					
Jan. 1–5	Ngatapa (siege of)	11	11	136	..
Feb. 2	Tauranga-ika, West Coast ..	..	..	..	..
Feb. 3	Karaka, West Coast	1	4	3	..
Feb. 14	Pukearuhe redoubt, West Coast ..	9	..	..	..
Feb. 18	Papatupu, West Coast	7	1	..	..
Mar. –	Ohiwa, Bay of Plenty	1	..	..	..
Mar. –	Te Poronu, Whakatane ..	5	..	7	..
Mar. –	Rauporoa, Whakatane ..	4	..	10	..
Mar. –	Whakatane, various skirmishes ..	..	..	..	..
Mar. –	Tauaroa, Rangitaiki	1	..	..	..
Mar. 13	Otautu, West Coast	6	12	4	..
Mar. –	Whakamara bush pursuit ..	..	..	11	..
April 10–12	Mohaka, Hawke's Bay	60	..	10	..
May 6	Te Harema, Urewera Country ..	..	..	5	..
May 6	Whataponga, Urewera Country ..	..	1	9	..
May 7	Manawa-hiwi, Urewera Country	1	2	..	..
May 7	Te Paripari, Urewera Country ..	1	..	..	..
May 7	Hukanui, Urewera Country ..	1	..	..	..
May 7	Tahora, Urewera Country ..	..	..	..	..
May 8	Orangikawa (Tatahoata), Urewera Country	5	6	1	..
May 9–14	Orona and Te Wai-iti, Urewera Country	..	1	5	..
June 7	Opepe, Taupo	9	1	..	..
Sept. 9	Tauranga-Taupo	..	..	3	..
Sept. 25	Pononga, South Taupo ..	2	4	10	..
Oct. 3	Te Porere, South Taupo ..	4	4	37	1

LIST OF ENGAGEMENTS AND CASUALTIES—*continued*

Date	Engagement	British and Colonial Forces and Friendly Maoris		Hostile Maoris	
		Killed	Wounded	Killed	Wounded
1870					
Jan. 24	Tapapa	..	..	1	..
Jan. 25	Tapapa	4	4	6	..
—	Paengaroa	4	..	..	..
Feb. 7	Waikorowhiti, Rotorua ..	1	7	20	..
—	Omarumutu, Bay of Plenty ..	2	..	..	..
Mar. 13	Toreatai, Urewera Country ..	1	..	..	..
Mar. 23	Maraetahi, Waioeka Gorge ..	..	..	20	..
—	Tolago Bay skirmishes ..	1	..	..	..
—	Ohiwa	..	..	1	..
May 21	Waikaremoana	..	..	1	..
May –	Waikaremoana	..	..	1	..
1871					
Aug. 15	Waipaoa, Urewera Country ..	..	..	4	..
Sept. 1	Te Hapua, Urewera Country ..	..	..	11	..
Oct. –	Okahu River, Urewera Country	..	..	..	1
1872					
Feb. 14	Mangaone (south of Waikaremoana)	..	..	..	..
	Totals	423	361	1,330	192

APPROXIMATE TOTAL CASUALTIES IN THE NEW ZEALAND WARS FROM 1845 TO 1872

British and Colonial Forces		Friendly Maoris	Hostile Maoris	
Killed	Wounded	Killed	Killed	Wounded
560	1,050	250	2,000	2,000

CORRECTION

Page 64.—Mangamingi Stream, shown in the plan of Otapawa, on the Tangahoe River, should be " Mangemange ".

A comprehensive index has been compiled by the Alexander Turnbull Library, Wellington, and may be consulted there.

Index

Adamson, Steve, 342–344
Adamson, T., N.Z.C., 300, 301, 313, 342, 343, 416
Adamson, W. B., 55
Ahuahu, Te, 16–18, 30
Ahuru, Kepa te, N.Z.C., 421, 437
Amohau, Te, 389
Amopo, Timoti te, 80, 82
Aotearoa, 470
Araki te Pohu, 165, 544, 545
Arama Karaka, 86, 87
Arawa Constabulary (Flying Column), 419–426, 432–446, 458–466
Arawa Tribe, 12, 72, 77, 79, 80–82, 94, 96–105, 153, 155–160, 161, 167–171, 177–178, 277, 281, 282, 292, 298, 300, 303, 327, 338–344, 354, 357, 358, 375, 376, 380, 384, 385, 387–398, 417, 420, 421, 493, 507, 511, 512, 545
Armed Constabulary, N.Z., 177–178, 187–201, 202, 206, 207, 220, 236, 239–242, 248, 251, 259, 260, 275, 276–282, 285, 287–291, 292–293, 294–296, 298, 309, 313, 316, 322, 337–360, 371, 373–376, 398, 462, 465, 471, 475, 476, 481, 483, 485, 486, 488, 494–496, 510–514
Atkinson, Major, 16, 28, 38, 59
Awa-a-te-Atua, 96, 97, 324

Baker, Louis, 72, 76, 88, 388–389
Ballance, John, 260
Bates, Colonel H. S., 30, 475
Bates, H. D., 31
Bay of Plenty Cavalry, 362, 364–370
Beamish, Alexander, 193–199
Beamish, John, 193–200
Bell Block, 523, 526, 527
Benson, W., 268, 539
Bent, Kimble, 7, 14, 15, 66, 72, 145, 151, 183–184, 190, 205, 217, 218–221, 262, 291, 294, 296, 303
Best, Dr., 206, 216
Bezar, Sergeant-Major E., 504
Biddle, Ben, N.Z.C., 278, 294, 333, 386, 415
"Big Jim" the Scout, 342, 344
Biggs, Major R., 118–122, 125, 132, 133, 224, 236, 237, 263–264, 265–266, 267, 505–506, 539
Black, Trooper A., 368–369
Black, Solomon, N.Z.C., 241, 278, 415
Bluett, Sergeant (afterwards Captain), 433, 435, 443, 444, 458, 461, 465
Bower, Captain, 242
Brassey, Major W., 37–39, 42, 44, 45, 106, 110, 534
"Brisk," H.M.S., 106, 107–108, 121, 125, 506
Broughton, C., 61, 313
Brown, Captain, 206, 208, 211, 214, 259, 278
Bryce, John, 260, 287, 311, 475, 476, 485, 488, 491, 536
Buchanan, Captain, 139
Buck, Captain G., 206, 208, 211–212, 214, 215
Burt, F., 105
Butler, Lieutenant-Colonel, 64, 70

Cameron, Lieut.-General Sir D. (in West Coast campaign), 46–60
Cannibalism revived, 176, 182, 218, 219, 257, 258
Canning, D., 239, 240
Capel, Captain, 278, 498

Carkeek, Sergeant A. W., 537
Carr, Captain, 139, 239, 240
Carré, Lieutenant, R.A., 61, 63, 69, 70
Carroll, John, 238
Carroll, Sir James, 401, 206, 497
Casualties, list of, 550–553
Chapman, Lieutenant, 39
Chatham Island, 128, 222–234, 508
Christian, Captain, 229
Chute, Major-General Sir T., 61–71
Clarke, Lieutenant Mansfield, 16
Clarke H. T., 159, 511
Clery, Lieutenant, 391
Close, Captain, 57
Cockburn, D., 540
Coffey, D., 256
Colvile, Lieut.-Colonel, 57
Cooper, Sergeant George, 256, 257
Cowan, W. A., 473
Crapp, Captain A., 158, 498
Crosswell, Trooper George, 363–368
Cumming, Major, 433, 441

Davis, C. O., 82–83
Deighton, Captain, R.M., 122, 236, 237, 505, 506
Deighton, R. J., 135
"Die-Hards" (57th Regiment), 16–17, 21, 45, 56, 64, 65, 70, 71, 504, 505
Dommett, Alfred, 379
Douglas, Sir R., 71
Duff, Sergeant-Major, 112, 148, 149, 536
Dunn, John, 256

"Eclipse," H.M.S., 78
"Eclipse," schooner, 74–77
Emus, Sergeant-Major, 154
Eria Raukura, 451

Featherston, Dr. J. E., 67, 68
Ferris, Captain, 461, 463, 464, 465
Finlay, John, 549
Finnimore, Captain, 260
Firth, J. C., 381, 382
Foreman, George, 40
Forest Rangers, 43, 51, 52, 62, 65, 68, 121
Fort Alfred, 511
Fort Clarke, 511
Fort Galatea, 338, 511
Fougeraud, Pierre de, 289
Fraser, Major J., 125, 130, 131, 132, 133, 135, 139, 141, 236, 237, 240, 386

Gascoigne, Lieutenant, 304–309, 540–542
Gascoyne, Major F. J., 118, 119, 235, 237, 238, 239, 263, 264, 268, 269, 276
Gaynor, W., 192, 200
George, Major F. N., 43, 106, 110
Gibbs, Dr., 359
Gill, Michael, 195, 197, 198
Goldsmith, E., 158
Goring, Lieut.-Colonel F. Y., 206, 254, 491
Grace, Dr., 53, 54
Grace, Rev. T., 74, 77
Grey, Sir George, 46, 49, 51, 52, 53, 60, 315, 532, 536
Gudgeon, Lieut.-Colonel W. E., 51, 62, 180, 253, 259, 359, 517, 523,
Guerren, Jean, 315–319
Guides, Corps of, 287–290, 338, 341–347, 384
Gundry, A., 295
Gundry, Captain W., 277, 295, 347

Haerehuka, 166
Hairini, 549
Hamilton, R. B., 246, 256, 311
Hamlin, E., 401–408
Hamlin, M., 506
Hapua, Te, 447–452
Haroto, Te, 465, 513
Hartnett, Michael, 228
Hauhau, or Pai-marire religion, 1–20
"Hauhau", the term, 5–6
Haultain, Colonel T. M., 156
Hautere, 161
Hawera blockhouses, 478
Hemana, 168, 170
Heni Pore (Te Kiri-karamu), 12–14, 97, 101, 103
Hepanaia Kapewhiti, 18, 21–25
Heretaunga, Wi, 440, 441
Herrick, Lieut-Colonel J. L., 338, 354, 357, 359, 360, 361
Heruiwi, 363, 368, 369
Heuheu, Horonuku, 370, 371, 374, 378
Hewett, Captain J. D., 46
Hill, George, N.Z.C., 331, 332, 334, 335
Hinamoki, 85, 88, 95
Hipango, Hone Wiremu, 36
Hiroki, 384

Hiroti, Haimona, 33–36
Hirst, Lieutenant J., 37
Hirtzel, Lieutenant C. A. M., 148, 213
Hokianga, 499–502
Horne, Lieutenant, 158
Hotene Porourangi, 118, 135
Huaki Matene te, 338, 354–355
Huirangi, 549
Hukanui, 349
Hume, Colonel J. E., 496
Hungahunga-toroa, 121–122, 506, 508
"Huntress", steamer, 106
Hurepo, Te, 317
Hussey, Captain, 129–130, 133, 507

Irihanga, Te, 154, 156–157

Jeffs, Private H., 155
Johnson, Woodbine, 538
Johnston, Cosslett, 188–189, 192–193
Johnston, Lieutenant (Assistant Adjutant-General), 47, 48
Jones, D., 515
Jones, Joshua, 542
Jordan, T., 158–159

Kahu-pukoro, Te, 22–29, 47, 190, 200
Kahuwera, 79, 81
Kai-iwi Cavalry, 260, 287, 289, 536
Kairakau, 174, 175
Kaiteriria, 394, 395
Kaka, Timoti te, 74, 265, 392, 396
Kakaramea, 53, 54, 144, 246
Kakari, Te 411, 414
Kaokaoroa 82
Karaitiana Roto-a-Tara, 238, 241–242
Karaitiana Takamoana, 137
Karaka Flat, 52
Karauria, 137, 269
Kareke, 177
Katene Tu-whakaruru, 180, 181, 218, 251
Kawhia Harbour, 474, 475
Kay, Andrew, 459, 470, 473
Kells, Captain, 311, 313
Kepa (Te Rangihiwinui), Major, 38, 43, 66, 206, 207, 215, 248, 251–253, 292–294, 295, 296, 298–302, 376, 380, 382, 384, 385, 414, 415, 420
Kereopa, "Big," 293, 537
Kereopa te Rau (Kai-whatu), 9, 17, 18, 72–79, 84–95, 114, 123, 415, 454–457
Ketemarae, 66, 68, 146, 504, 515
Kihikihi, 474
Kihitu, 161, 166, 171, 173
Kingi Parengarenga, 25
Kingi, Wiremu (Turanganui), 372, 373
Kingi, Wiremu (Ngaitai), 463–464
Kiorekino, 110–111, 114
Kiri-karamu, Heni te, 12–14, 97, 101
Kiro-o-Tautini, 13, 14
Kohimarama Redoubt, 454
Kohitau Redoubt, 453
Kooti, Te, 127, 128, 179, 222–234 (escape from Chatham Island), 235–243, 263–269 (Poverty Bay massacre), 270–284 (at Ngatapa), 314–325 (at Whakatane), 326–335 (Mohaka massacre), 354, 357, 359, 362, 363, 368, 369, 370, 371–386 (Taupo-Tapapa campaign) 387–399 (Rotorua-Tumunui action), 401–408, 411, 415, 416, 417, 418, 419–467 (in Urewera Country), 468, 491–494 (last years and death), 538–539 (Poverty Bay), 543–546 (Rotorua)
Kopane, Te, 133, 135
Kopu (star), 91
Kopu-parapara, 129, 133, 135
Koutu, Te 163–165
Kuhawaea, 84
Kuiti, Te (Tokangamutu), 15, 451
Kutarere, 41, 147

Lambert, Colonel, 140, 242, 243, 333
Large, Major J. T., 360, 401–408, 427–431, 447–452, 547
Leach, Captain E., 69, 70
Levy, Captain, 74, 106
Lloyd, Captain, 16, 17, 30
Lyon, Colonel William C., 174, 261, 287, 303, 311, 469

MacDonald, Trooper D., 368, 369
Mackay, James, 471
Mackenzie (scout), 289, 290
Maeneene, 52

Mair, Captain Gilbert, 94, 95, 154–156, 157, 158, 161–165 (Te Koutu, Rotorua), 166–173 (Puraku, Rotorua), 233, 234, 322–325, 338, 339, 340, 344, 352, 353, 354–356, 387–408 (defeat of Te Kooti, Rotorua), 419, 422, 423, 424, 425, 426, 442 (Waipaoa), 443, 444, 446, 458, 465, 466, 543–546
Mair, Captain Henry A., 176, 322, 323, 325
Mair, Major William G., 94, 96–105 (Matata and Te Teko campaign), 155–160 (Tauranga), 177, 322, 323, 338, 347, 348, 357, 358, 474, 511, 512
Makaretu, 269, 270, 271
Maling, Captain C., 289, 290, 298, 301, 342–344, 346, 376, 382–383
Manaia Redoubt, 483, 516, 517
Manawapou, 54, 55, 57
Mangaone (East Coast), 118
Mangaone (Waikaremoana district), 461, 462, 463
"Manu-rau" (Major Von Tempsky), 217, 219, 220, 221
Manutahi (North Taranaki), 23, 26, 523–527
Manutahi (South Taranaki), 54, 534
Maraetahi, 415, 416
Mataitawa, 28, 68
Matamata, 381–382
Matata, 96–98, 103, 105, 322–323
Matawhero (Poverty Bay), 263–269
Matene te Rangitauira, 18, 30, 31, 32, 35
Matuahu (Waikare-moana), 400–408, 547
Maunga-pohatu, 409, 410, 411, 414, 425, 427, 437, 442, 446, 447, 451, 453, 464, 548
Maunga-tautari, 469
Mawhai, Te, 120
Maxwell, Sergeant-Major, 260
McCulloch, Alexander, 246
McDonnell, Lieut.-Colonel Thomas, 51, 52, 62, 65, 110, 112, 114, 115, 143–152, 180, 181, 182, 189, 201, 202, 203, 204, 206–216 (Te Ngutu-o-te-manu), 244, 373–386 (Taupo-Tapapa campaign), 387, 388
McDonnell, Captain W., 206, 211, 215
McLean, Sir Donald, 137–139, 224, 242
Messenger, Captain W. B., 304–310
Mete Kingi, 32, 361
Mohaka, Te Kooti's attack on, 327–335
Mokau, 304, 305, 307, 308, 309, 310
Mokena Kohere, 118, 122
Mokomoko, 104, 115
Moorsom, Captain, 362
Morere, Te (Sentry Hill), 21–29
Motu, 464
Moturoa, 244–262, 509
Moumahaki, 248, 292, 509

Nahu, Rewi te, 128
Netana Whakaari, 114, 445, 510
Newland, Captain W., 37, 39–40, 43, 114, 146, 149, 174, 175, 206, 208, 215
New Zealand Cross, 149, 200, 212, 252, 253, 275, 278, 289, 299, 331, 334, 335, 368, 383, 390, 415, 416, 423, 479, 536–537
Ngaere, Te, 302, 304
Ngaio, Te (Kakaramea), 53, 54
Ngatapa, siege of, 270–284
Ngutu-o-te-manu, Te, 182, 183, 184, 190, 200, 201, 202–221
Nihoniho, Henare, 118
Nihoniho, Tuta, 118, 126
Niu (Hauhau pole of worship), 6–15, 23, 28, 31, 32, 35, 38–39, 41, 44, 57, 71, 74, 78, 85, 88, 89, 92, 95, 99, 110, 111, 112, 114, 115, 126, 140, 157, 168, 172, 296, 297
Noake, Major M., 311, 312, 509–510
Normanby Redoubt, Taranaki, 482, 515–517
Northcroft, Captain H. W., 148, 149, 298, 299, 349, 359, 376
Nuhaka, 463
Nukumaru, 47, 48, 49, 52, 259, 260, 292

Oakura, 16, 18, 23
Ohaeawai, 549
Ohaua-te-rangi, 454
Ohawe, 143
Ohinemutu (near Pipiriki), 37, 39, 43

Ohinemutu (Rotorua), 161, 163, 387–391, 537
Ohiwa, 314, 420, 421, 510
Ohoutahi, 36, 37
Okahu, 341, 344, 445, 446
Okautiro, 185
Okehu, 287, 289, 290
Okoheriki, 173
Okotuku, 62, 247, 249, 250, 261
Okupu, 85, 86, 90
Omaru-hakeke, 129–133
Omarunui, 137–142
Onepoto, 358, 359, 360, 401–408, 433, 434, 458, 459, 547
Opepe, 362–370, 513
Opokere, 451
Opotiki, 72–77, 103, 104, 106–116, 174–178, 282, 322, 325, 415, 416, 426
Opunake, 55, 495
Orakau, 469, 470, 472, 473
Orangikawa, 345, 351–354
Oraukawa, 531
Ormond, Hon. J. D., 137, 142
Orona, 354, 355, 356
Otapawa, 63–66
Otara, 282–283
Otautu, 294–296, 347, 509
Otewa, 466, 493
Otoia, 53, 61
Otupuraho (Pye's Pa), 155

Pa-harakeke, 100–103
Pai-marire religion, 1–20, 503–504
Pa-kairomiromi, 119
Pakakohi Tribe, 310–313
Pakura, 120
Panapa, 138, 139, 140
Paparatu, 235–236
Papatupu, 292
Parawai, Te, 96, 97
Parihaka, 476–491, 517–518
Parikino, 51
Paripari, Te, 348–350
Patara Raukatauri, 17, 18, 72, 73, 74, 77
Patea, 49, 53, 54, 55, 63, 70, 244, 246, 247, 261
Patea Rangers, 37–45, 106–116, 143
Patohe, 47, 48, 53
Patua, 16, 17
Peita Kotuku, 138, 141, 230–233, 265, 271, 279, 368, 369, 376, 377
Peka te Makarini, 228, 234, 386, 393, 395, 396, 544, 545
Penetito, 103, 104
Perekama, 36, 46, 52
Petane, 138, 139, 141
Pihama, Hone, 49
Pipiriki, 30–32, 36, 37–45
Piri-Rakau, 153–160
Pitcairn, R., 314, 510
Pokaikai, 145–146
Pokiha, Te (Major Fox), 338
Pokopoko, Te, 177
Pomare, Hon. Sir Maui, 44
Ponga, Te, 178
Ponongá, Te, 374–375
Popoia, Te 150, 151
Porere, Te 376–380
Poronu, Te, 315–319
Porter, Colonel T. W., 127, 277, 279, 282, 283, 292, 293, 298, 300, 410–418, 447–452 (Te Hapua engagement), 452–457, 494
Potae, Henare, 118, 119, 120
Potatau te Wherowhero, 474, 475
Pou-whareumu Toi, 66
Poverty Bay, 122–128, 223, 235, 236, 239, 240, 243, 263–269, 538–539 (Massacre at)
Preece, Captain G. A., 133, 236, 237, 238, 240, 241, 242, 270, 271, 273, 275, 276, 278, 337, 341, 345, 353, 357, 361, 371, 373, 375, 376, 380, 382, 384, 385, 418, 419–426, 432–442 (Waipaoa engagement), 443–446, 458–466, 506–507, 509, 510, 512, 514
Puhirua, 12–14
Puia, Te, 110, 111, 114
Pukearuhe, 55, 304–310, 498, 499, 540–542
Pukemaire, 121
Pukeroa, 162, 389
Puketapu, 239, 263
Puna-a-Tuhoe, Te, 164
Pungarehu Redoubt, 484
Pungarehu, Te 147, 149
Puniu, 468, 471
Puraku *pa*, 161, 166,–173
Purukutu, Mohi, 469–473, 515
Putahi, Te 62

Rahotu, 484, 485
Rangiahua, 38, 39
Rangi-hina-kau, Te, 209, 220
Rangihiroa, 319
Rangihiroa, Te, 138, 139, 140, 141
Rangitahau, Te, 138, 232, 264, 265, 328, 335
Rauporoa, 318, 319–325

Rawene, 499
Reinga, Te, 223, 238, 410
Renata Kawepo, 137, 140, 269
Rewi Maniapoto, 138, 372, 373, 375, 473
Richardson, Captain, 237, 238, 239, 240, 241
"Rifleman," schooner, 226–233
Rikirangi (see Te Kooti)
Ringa-tu, 4, 25, 114, 225, 234, 451
Ringiringi (Kimble Bent), 183–184
Roberts, Colonel J. M., 210–214, 245, 248, 251, 253, 254, 262, 419, 485, 540
Robinson, George F., 523
Roland, Father, 202, 207
Rookes, Major, 43–44, 52
Ropata Wahawaha, Major, 118, 120, 121, 122, 129, 133, 135, 342, 270, 275–281, 409–418, 427, 442, 446, 452–457
Ross, Captain, 186–197
Rotorua, 166, 387–399, 543–544
Rua Kenana (Ruatapu), 548
Ruakituri, 239–241
Ruatahuna, 337–361
Ruatoki, 314, 316, 496, 497
Runanga, 465, 513
Rushton, Captain J. R., 40, 41, 113, 115–116, 147, 149, 178, 420–421, 463–464, 514
Rutherford, Major, 28
Ryan, Major, 28

St. George, Captain, J., 371, 373, 374, 375, 376, 377, 378, 379
St. John, Lieut.-Colonel, 338, 345, 347, 359, 362, 363, 364, 367, 368, 370, 420
Saltmarshe, Major, 28
Scannell, Major D., 256, 360, 513
Scott, Dr. M., 130–133, 328, 332
Sentry Hill Redoubt, 21–29
Sikhs, 546
Smith, Cornet Angus, 362, 367, 368
Smith, S. Percy, 143, 144, 528–535
Stapp, Major, 114
Stephenson, Trooper George, 365, 368
"Stormbird," steamer, 106, 361
Strong, H., 538
Sullivan, Timothy, 469–470, 515

Tahora (Urewera Country), 348
Taiporohenui, 15, 26
Tamaikowha, 174, 175, 176, 177, 178, 420, 421, 427, 444
Tamati Hone, 23, 26
Tangahoe, 63, 64, 65, 66, 250
Tapapa, 382–386, 388, 415, 424
Tapiri, Te, 84–95
Tapuae-haruru (Lake Taupo), 367, 371
Taranaki Bush Rangers, 57, 70, 498
Taranaki Military Settlers, 37, 38, 39, 45, 143
Taranaki Mounted Corps, 57, 58, 70
Taranaki Rifles, 485
Tarata, Te (Opotiki), 111–114
Tatahoata, 351–354
Taumarunui, 38, 381
Tauranga bush campaign (1867), 153–160
Tauranga-ika *pa*, 285–292
Tautahi Ariki, 66, 218
Tawhitinui (Wanganui River), 30, 32, 34, 35
Tekau-ma-rua, 150, 183, 209
Teko, Te, 96–105
Thomas, Captain, 224, 226, 228, 229, 508
Tihirua, 191, 209, 253, 261–262
Titokowaru, 26, 179–185, 190–192, 200, 206–221 (at Te Ngutu-o-te-manu), 244–262 (at Moturoa), 285–293 (at Tauranga-ika), 294–295 (at Otautu), 296–301 (Whakamaru pursuit), 302 (at Te Ngarere), 303 (on the Waitara)
Toia, Hone, 499–502
Tokaanu, 373
Tokangamutu (Te Kuiti), 15, 229, 451
Topia Turoa, 411
Travers, Captain, 349–353
Tu (God of War), 191, 210
Tuahu-a-te-Atu, 166
Tuke, Major, 224, 268, 270, 475
Tumunui, 393, 395, 396
Tupaea, Hori, 77, 79–83
Tu-Patea te Rongo, 47, 48, 53, 249, 253–254, 257–258, 261, 295, 296–297
Turanganui (Gisborne), 117, 122, 125–128, 223, 234, 235, 270, 275, 227, 355–356
Turangarere, 244, 246
Turuturu-mokai, 187–201, 548
Tutange Waionui, 209, 293, 396

Ua, Te, 4–9, 17, 21, 23, 30, 48, 71, 72

Uenuku (God of War), 179, 180, 210, 470
Urenui Redoubt, 497
Uretara Island, 314, 510
Urewera Country, campaigns in, 337–361, 409–418, 419–426, 427–431, 432–446, 447–457, 458–467
Urewera turn back surveyors (1895), 496–498

Von Tempsky, Major, 62, 65, 67, 107, 195, 198, 199, 202, 203, 207–221 (killed at Te Ngutu-o-te-manu)

Waerenga-a-Hika *pa*, 125–128
Wahanui, 474
Waiapu, 117, 118–122
Waihi Redoubt built, 146, 185
Waikare-moana, 359–360 (first expedition), 401–408 (second campaign)
Wai-ngongoro River, 53, 55, 60, 66, 70, 143, 144, 147, 150, 181, 185, 202, 204, 208, 214, 216
Waipao (engagement, 1871), 432–443
Wairoa, Hawke's Bay (1866), 129–142
Wairua-Tapu religion, 4, 225, 451
Waitotara River, 46–51, 62, 260, 285, 287, 291, 292, 293, 310
Wallace, Sergeant W., 111–112, 146, 185, 204–205, 220–221, 244–246, 254–257, 261, 297, 347, 377
Warihi Potini, Te (thrown overboard from "Rifleman"), 226, 230–232
Weld, Sir Frederick, 58–59
Weraroa *pa*, 47, 48, 49, 50, 51, 52, 62
Weraroa Redoubt, 259
Weriweri, 66
Whakaahurangi track, 67
Whakamara 296–297
Whakamarama (Tauranga campaign), 154–160
Whakatane, 73 (Pai-marire at), 77–78 (murder of J. Fulloon), 314–325 (Te Kooti's raid)
Whakatane column of Whitmore's force (1869), 347–351
Whareongaonga 233, 236
Whenuakura River, 62, 294, 311, 313
Whiti, Te, 23, 48, 476–491
Whitmore, Major-General Sir George, 139, 236–240, 244–262 Moturoa operations), 276–282, 285–310, 337–361 (Urewera expedition), 509, 510–512, 538
Wilson, Captain J., 265, 266